A DOCUMENTARY HISTORY OF

The Negro People in the United States

Also by Herbert Aptheker

American Negro Slave Revolts (1943)

Essays in the History of the American Negro (1945)

The Negro People in America:
A Critique of Myrdal's "American Dilemma" (1946)

To Be Free: Studies in Afro-American History (1948)

Laureates of Imperialism: Big Business Re-Writes American History (1954)

History and Reality (1955)

Toward Negro Freedom (1956)

The Truth About Hungary (1957)

The Colonial Era (1959)

The American Revolution (1960)

The World of C. Wright Mills (1960)

Dare We Be Free?
The Meaning of the Attempt to Outlaw the Communist Party (1961)

American Foreign Policy and the Cold War (1962)

Soul of the Republic: The Negro Today (1964)

Mission to Hanoi (1966)

Nat Turner's Slave Rebellion (1966)

The Nature of Democracy, Freedom and Revolution (1967)

The Urgency of Marxist-Christian Dialogue (1970)

Afro-American History: The Modern Era (1971)

Edited

A Documentary History of the Negro People in the United States:
From the Colonial Period to Establishment of the N.A.A.C.P. (1951)

Disarmament and the American Economy (1960)

And Why Not Every Man? A History of the Struggle against Slavery (1961)

Marxism and Democracy (1964)

Marxism and Alienation (1965)

One Continual Cry: Walker's Appeal to Colored Citizens (1965)

Marxism and Christianity (1968)

Autobiography of W. E. B. Du Bois (1968)

The Correspondence of W. E. B. Du Bois (Vol. I, 1879–1934) (1973)

The Published Writings of W. E. B. Du Bois: An Annotated Bibliography (1973)

The Education of Black People, by W. E. B. Du Bois (1973)

A DOCUMENTARY HISTORY

OF

The Negro People in the United States
1910-1932

Edited by
HERBERT APTHEKER

Preface by
DR. CHARLES H. WESLEY

A Citadel Press Book
Published by Carol Publishing Group

First Carol Publishing Group Edition 1990

Copyright © 1973 by Herbert Aptheker

A Citadel Press Book
Published by Carol Publishing Group

Editorial Offices
600 Madison Avenue
New York, NY 10022

Sales & Distribution Offices
120 Enterprise Avenue
Secaucus, NJ 07094

In Canada: Musson Book Company
A division of General Publishing Co. Limited
Don Mills, Ontario

Manufactured in the United States of America
ISBN 0-8065-1006-4

10   9   8   7   6   5   4   3   2   1

*To Angela Y. Davis and Bettina Aptheker
—and to the future their solidarity symbolizes*

Preface

DOCUMENTS ARE the historical sources and traces which have come to us out of the past through the thoughts, words and actions of men and women in their times. Much of the history of years passed is obscured and unknown because of the lack of documents which would furnish the desired information. Truth is often crushed to earth because of this deficiency. "No documents, no history," state C. V. Langlois and Charles Seignobos in their *Introduction aux études historiques* (Paris, 1898). Later, Allen Johnson, Professor of History at Yale University, declared in *The Historian and Historical Evidence* (New York, 1926), "In the absence of records and remains there is no history." In Europe and the United States efforts have continued to collect, collate and edit materials for the historian, reader and teacher. True history requires a body of source materials and a critical method applied to them.

The primary materials assembled in this volume represent the efficient work of the proficient historian, Herbert Aptheker, who has assembled these sources from public and private libraries, archives and museums. He has catalogued and edited these basic historical materials so that they would be available for use. These documents can be known as the starting points, and the facts are the goals as the process of teaching continues.

Numerous efforts have been made to collect and publish the documents of American history, and as usual these dealt with white history. Blacks were left out of these volumes as well as the school textbooks. None presented the documents treating creditably the Black Americans, despite the fact that for many decades Black Americans had written and published their thoughts, ideas, purposes and hopes in pamphlets which were distributed by them and often were soon lost to history. In fact they were not regarded as history.

Sporadic endeavors were made by Blacks in several cities to develop organizations similar to the American Historical Association and the Southern Historical Association. However it was not until 1915 that this purpose was achieved in the Association for the Study of Negro Life and History under the leadership of Carter G. Woodson and four associates. The original purpose was stated as, "the collection of sociological and historical documents and the promotion of studies bearing on the Negro."

This purpose was attained in January, 1916, when the *Journal of*

Negro History published in its first issue a collection of documents, and others in later issues. This may have been the first publication of a group of documents of Negro History in a collected form in a scholarly journal. Since then other quarterly issues have followed with the same inclusion. This action was initiated by Negro-Americans with Carter G. Woodson as Editor, with myth after myth disappearing before its waves of truth.

White and Black historians and readers began to realize that there was some merit in the claim of the Association for the Study of Negro Life and History that theirs was truthful and factual history of Black folk of marked significance. But it was Herbert Aptheker who directed attention to the dissatisfactions which slaves had with slavery, although Coffin, Higginson, Drewry, Cromwell and Joseph C. Carroll had made brief descriptions of several slave revolts interspersed with other materials. In 1937 Aptheker completed his Master of Arts thesis at Columbia University entitled "Nat Turner's Revolt."

He then subjected to criticism the view of Ulrich B. Phillips that "slave revolts and plots very seldom occurred in the United States" and that Black folk were "by racial quality stupid." In combating these views there appeared in 1943 his *American Negro Slave Revolts,* a doctoral thesis first published by the Columbia University Press in its Studies in History, Economics and Public Law. In the meantime he had published *The Negro in the Civil War,* 1938; *The Negro in the American Revolution,* 1940; and *The Negro in the Abolitionist Movement,* 1941.

His relationships and membership in the Association for the Study of Negro Life and History were paralleled by his contributions to the *Journal of Negro History* and his friendship with Du Bois and Woodson. An article published in the *Journal of Negro History,* volume 24, 1939 was "Maroons Within the Present Limits of the United States." This publication showed that Blacks had established at least fifty camps for runaway slaves along the frontiers. There were additional articles and documentaries which were the results of his researches in the *Journal of Negro History,* revealing a productive historian and a scholarly writer.

It was during these results of his researches that I had the opportunity of knowing him; I wanted to know the historian who sought to set the record straight and correct the misconceptions and misrepresentations about the people called "the Negro," and contribute to the truth in history in which Black people were concerned.

The *Documentary History of the Negro People in the United States* volume I was published in 1951 by the Citadel Press in 942 pages. Many of us in school and college had waited with hands folded for a collection of valid documents which could be used in Negro history. We had known the need and wondered who would supply this need so long neglected in American history. Carter G. Woodson had brought out his *The Mind of the Negro as Reflected in Letters Written During the Crisis,* 1926. We had known Helen Catterall, *Judicial Cases Concerning American Slavery and the Negro* in five volumes, 1926–1937; Elizabeth Donnan, *Documents Illustrative of the History of the Slave Trade* in three volumes 1930–1935, and Sterling A. Brown, Arthur P. Davis and Ulysses Lee, *The Negro Caravan; Writings by American Negroes* in 1941. These were documentaries on aspects of the subject. Herbert Aptheker's volume was a comprehensive one which could be used as a source book.

The author announced in his Introduction to this first volume that a second and a third volume would bring this presentation of documents through World War II. The 153 major groups of documents in this volume II have been collected, researched, edited and combined in an effective way by this indefatigable historian so that African-Americans in their struggle for their continued freedom from racism under the Constitution and the courts, and their search for equality as citizens of a great nation are seen and read in their own words. Their words live because they are real. Such people can no longer be regarded as negligible in the study of American history. The literature is here and the introductory narrative paves the way for the understanding of the document.

These documents prove that there is Negro History and that in it there is historical truth, not exaggeration and not falsehood. This volume is an important milestone in the research and historiography of the darker peoples in the United States. It shows diligence and thoroughness in the procural of documents, judgment in their selection, analysis and classification, so that there can be a rightful understanding of our history as a people in a nation of peoples. These documents reveal the life, thought and the actions—positive and negative—of Negro-Americans so long negelected and pigeonholed by most historians. These omissions have made it so easy for readers to form false opinions of Blacks, not knowing them as they were.

It is still true—"No documents, no history."

CHARLES H. WESLEY

Washington, D.C.
October, 1972

Contents

Introduction

IN 1951, the first volume of this work was published; it spanned the years from 1661 to 1910. At that time, I hoped to be able to carry this history forward until the end of the Second World War. In the intervening two decades, while engaged in other endeavors, this purpose never disappeared, and work to realize it went forward. So far as I am able, it has now been done; volume two, dealing with the years from the founding of the National Association for the Advancement of Colored People to the defeat of Herbert Hoover in 1932 and the commencement of the "New Deal" era, is in the reader's hands. Volume three, treating of the years from the New Deal through the conclusion of the Second World War, is finished and its publication is expected some six months after the initial appearance of the present volume.

I believe I will hold to my original plan—conceived in 1946—of documenting the history of the Afro-American people from the beginning and terminating with World War II. No doubt others will carry this forward through the nearer past and into the infinite future; I am the more willing to conclude with the commencement of the post-war world since that period—especially the 1950's and 1960's—has seen a considerable literature pouring forth from the Black people in the United States and bespeaking their plans, differences, visions and hopes.

*   *   *

It is, I think, in the period covered by this volume that what may be called the modern history of the Afro-American people really commences. Booker T. Washington passes on; Du Bois comes to towering dimensions; the Garvey movement and its intense nationalism, the Pan-African movement and its powerful internationalism both mature; questions of resistance, self-determination, separation, so-called integration all come to the fore and are weighed; the impact of the trade union movement, of Marxism, of the Bolshevik Revolution and of the very existence of the Soviet Union all make their mark. The struggles against lynching, peonage, and all forms of racism reach nationwide proportions and attract increasingly worldwide attention, and tactical forms of resistance in the economic and political fields are strikingly like those making current newspaper headlines.

Again, as in the earlier volume, the Afro-American people speak for themselves, and editorial apparatus in the form of introduction and footnotes is kept to a minimum consistent with placing the documents in their context and indicating their sources.

Though in this volume the time range is but one generation, while that of the first volume was two and a half centuries, in both cases one of the major editorial problems was selection. The basis of that selection was historical significance, typicality and vividness, as well as an effort to reflect myriad aspects of the Afro-American experience.

In addition to a rather considerable collection of relevant literature made by the Editor and the treasure represented by the Du Bois Papers placed in his custody by the late Doctor, the New York Public Library, the Library of Congress, and the libraries of Harvard, Columbia, Atlanta, Fisk and Tulane Universities have been helpful. But, as is true of everyone laboring in this field, it is the Schomburg Collection in New York City that has been quite basic, and the devoted personnel of that Collection whose aid has been indispensable.

All documents are reproduced with no substantive change whatsoever; misspellings and grammatical errors have been corrected if they appeared in printed sources and clearly were typographical mistakes. The word Negro has been capitalized throughout.

All who work in Afro-American history stand upon the shoulders of the late Dr. Carter G. Woodson and Dr. W. E. B. Du Bois; both saw fit to assist and befriend the Editor many years ago. He has always striven not to fall too far short of the standards they set. That motivation persists, and, in a professional sense, these two, above all, were his teachers.

In the tradition of Woodson and Du Bois stands Charles H. Wesley; the Editor is most grateful to Dr. Wesley for his generous and probing preface.

For over thirty years, the Editor has had the comradeship, support and guidance of Fay P. Aptheker; words fail to express his indebtedness.

HERBERT APTHEKER

October, 1972

A DOCUMENTARY HISTORY OF

The Negro People in the United States

1

BOOKER T. WASHINGTON: PRO AND CON

In the preceding volume of this work, in section VIII (pp. 827–928), material was presented reflecting, as there stated, "the developing Negro liberation movement, 1901–1910." Illustrative were the mounting protests, led by William Monroe Trotter and W. E. B. Du Bois, against the program associated with Booker T. Washington and—as Du Bois called it—the Tuskegee Machine.

Documents [a] and [b] below further illustrate this momentous confrontation. The first document reproduces a drawing which covered a full page of Trotter's paper, *The Guardian,* of August 27, 1910 (published in Boston, at 21 Cornhill Street, "Garrison's old stand"—as Trotter put it—for from that address *The Liberator* thundered its attack upon slavery from 1831 to 1835). The artist John Henry Adams, Jr., taught at Morris Brown College in Atlanta. He had frequently contributed to the militant *Voice of the Negro,* which was published in that city until forced out by the pogrom of 1906, and was to appear often in Du Bois' *Crisis.*

The second document reproduces in full the second part of the sequel to Washington's *Up From Slavery;* this sequel was published in the influential monthly *World's Work,* issued in Chicago and edited by the Virginian, Walter Hines Page, partner with Frank N. Doubleday in the publishing house of Doubleday & Page and later to be Wilson's ambassador to Great Britain. The document conveys Washington's memories of his historic Atlanta speech of 1895, the momentous Trotter-led attack upon him in Boston in 1903, and his own attitude toward "intellectuals"—by which he meant the position favored by Du Bois.

1

[a]

KEYS TO THE SITUATION
See Who Holds Them, for What and Where the Race Is

[b]

CHAPTERS FROM MY EXPERIENCE
by Booker T. Washington

It makes a great deal of difference in the life of a race, as it does in the life of an individual, whether the world expects much or little of that individual or of that race. I suppose that every boy and every girl in poverty have felt at some time in their lives the weight of the world against them. What the people in the community did not expect them to do it was hard for them to convince themselves that they could do.

After I got so that I could read a little, I used to take a great deal of satisfaction in the lives of men who had risen by their own efforts from poverty to success. It is a great thing for a boy to be able to read books of that kind. It not only inspires him with the desire to do something and make something of his life, but it teaches him that success depends upon his ability to do something useful, to perform some kind of service that the world wants.

The trouble in my case, as in that of other colored boys of my age, was that the stories we read in school were all concerned with the success and achievements of white boys and men. Occasionally I spoke to some of my schoolmates in regard to the characters of whom I had read, but they invariably reminded me that the stories I had been reading had to do with the members of another race. Sometimes I tried to argue the matter with them, saying that what others had done some of us might be able to do, and that the lack of a past in our race was no reason why it should not have a future.

They replied that our case was entirely different. They said, in effect, that because of our color and because we carried in our faces the brand of a race that had been in slavery, white people did not want us to succeed.

In the end I usually wound up the discussion by recalling the life of Frederick Douglass, reminding them of the high position which he had reached and of the great service which he had performed for his own race and for the cause of human freedom in the long anti-slavery struggle.

Even before I had learned to read books or newspapers, I remember hearing my mother and other colored people in our part of the country speak about Frederick Douglass's wonderful life and achievements. I heard so much about Douglass when I was a boy that one of the reasons why I wanted to go to school and learn to read was that I might read for myself what he had written and said. In fact, one of the first books that I remember reading was his own story of his life, which Mr. Douglass published under the title of *My Life and Times.* This book made a deep impression upon me, and I read it many times.

After I became a student at Hampton, under General Samuel C. Armstrong, I heard a great deal more about Frederick Douglass, and I followed all his movements with intense interest. At the same time I began to learn something about other prominent and successful colored men who were at that time the leaders of my race in the United States. These were such men as Congressman John M. Langston, of Virginia; United States Senator Blanche K. Bruce, of Mississippi; Lieutenant-Governor P. B. S. Pinchback, of Louisiana; Congressman John R. Lynch, of Mississippi; and others whose names were household words among the masses of the colored people at that time. I read with the greatest eagerness everything I could get hold of regarding the prominent Negro characters of that period, and was a faithful student of their lives and deeds. Later on I had the privilege of meeting and knowing all of these men, but at that time I had little thought that it would ever be my fortune to meet and know any of them.

On one occasion, when I happened to be in Washington, I heard that Frederick Douglass was going to make a speech in a near-by town. I had never seen him nor heard him speak, so I took advantage of the opportunity. I was profoundly impressed both by the man and by the address, but I did not dare approach even to shake hands with him. Some three or four years after I had organized the Tuskegee Institute, I invited Mr. Douglass to make a visit to the school and to speak at the commencement exercises of the school. He came and spoke to a great audience, many of whom had driven thirty or forty miles to hear the great orator and leader of the race. In the course of time I invited all of the prominent colored men whose names I have mentioned, as well as others, to come to Tuskegee and speak to our students and to the colored people in our community.

As a matter of course, the speeches (as well as the writings) of most of these men were concerned for the most part with the past history, or with the present and future political problems, of the Negro race. Mr. Douglass's great life-work had been in the political agitation that led to the destruction of slavery. He had been the great defender of the race, and in the struggle to win from Congress and from the country at large the recognition of the Negro's rights as a man and a citizen he had played an important part. But the long and bitter struggle in which he had engaged against slavery had not prepared Mr. Douglass to take up the equally difficult task of fitting the Negro for the opportunities and responsibilities of freedom. The same was true to a large extent of other Negro leaders. At the time when I met these men and heard them speak, I was invariably impressed, though young and inexperienced at the time, that there was something lacking in their public utterances. I felt that the millions of Negroes needed something more than to be reminded of their sufferings and of their political rights; that they needed to do something more than merely to defend themselves.

Frederick Douglass died in February, 1895. In September of the same year I delivered an address in Atlanta at the Cotton States Exposition.*

I spoke in Atlanta to an audience composed of leading Southern white people, Northern white people, and members of my own race. This seemed to me to be the time and the place, without condemning what had been done, to emphasize what ought to be done. I felt that we needed a policy, not of destruction, but of construction; not of defense, but of aggression; a policy not of hostility or surrender, but of friendship and advance. I stated, as vigorously as I was able, that usefulness in the community where we resided was our surest and most potent protection.

One other point which I made plain in that speech was that, in my opinion, the Negro should seek constantly in every manly, straightforward manner to make friends of the white man by whose side he lived, rather than to content himself with seeking the good-will of some man a thousand miles away.

While I was fully convinced, in my own mind, that the policy which I had outlined was the correct one, I was not at all prepared for the widespread interest with which my words were received.

I received telegrams and congratulations from all parts of the country and from many persons whose names I did not know or had heard only indirectly through the newspapers or otherwise. Very soon invitations began to come to me in large numbers to speak before all kinds of bodies and on all kinds of subjects. In many cases I was offered for my addresses what appeared to me almost fabulous sums. Some of the lecture bureaus offered me as high as $300 and $400 a night for as long a period as I would speak for them. Among other things which came to me was an offer from a prominent Western newspaper of $1,000

* Published in full in I, 753–57, of this work.

and all expenses for my services if I would describe for it a famous prize-fight.

I was invited, here and there, to take part in political campaigns, especially in states where the Negro vote was important. Lecture bureaus not only urged upon me the acceptance of their offers through letters, but even sent agents to Tuskegee. Newspapers and magazines made generous offers to me to write special articles for them. I decided, however, to wait until I could get my bearings. Apparently the words which I had spoken at Atlanta, simple and almost commonplace as they were, had touched a deep and responsive chord. This gave me much to think about. In the meantime I determined to stick close to my work at Tuskegee.

One of the most surprising results of my Atlanta speech was the number of letters, telegrams, and newspaper editorials that came pouring in upon me from all parts of the country, demanding that I take the place of "leader of the Negro people" left vacant by Frederick Douglass's death, or assuming that I had already taken this place. Until these suggestions began to pour in upon me, I never had the remotest idea that I should be selected or looked upon, in any such sense as Frederick Douglass had been, as a leader of the Negro people. I was at that time merely a Negro school-teacher in a rather obscure industrial school. I had devoted all my time and attention to the work of organizing and bringing into existence the Tuskegee Institute, and I did not know just what the functions and duties of a leader were, or what was expected of him on the part of the colored people or of the rest of the world. It was not long, however, before I began to find out what was expected of me in the new position into which a sudden newspaper-notoriety seemed to have thrust me.

I was not a little embarrassed, when I first began to appear in public, to find myself continually referred to as "the successor of Frederick Douglass." Wherever I spoke—whether in the North or in the South—I found, thanks to the advertising that I had received, that large audiences turned out to hear me.

It has been interesting, and sometimes amusing, to note the amount of variety of disinterested advice received by a man whose name is to any extent before the public. During the time that my Atlanta address was, so to speak, under discussion, and almost every day since, I have received one or more letters advising me and directing my course in regard to matters of public interest.

On day I receive a letter or my attention is called to some newspaper editorial, in which I am advised to stick to my work at Tuskegee and put aside every other interest that I may have in the advancement of my race. A day or two later I may receive a letter or read an editorial in a newspaper saying that I am making a mistake in confining my attention entirely to Tuskegee, to Negro education, or even to the Negro in the United States. It has been frequently urged upon me, for example, that I ought, in some way or other, to extend the work that we are trying to do at Tuskegee to Africa or to the West Indies, where Negroes are a larger part of the population than in this country.

There has been a small number of white people and an equally small number of colored people, who felt, after my Atlanta speech, that I ought to branch out and discuss political questions, putting emphasis upon the importance of political activity and success for the members of my race. Others, who thought it quite natural that while I was in the South, I should not say anything that would be offensive, expected that I would cut loose in the North and denounce the Southern people in a way to keep alive and intensify the sectional differences which had sprung up as a result of slavery and the Civil War. Still others thought that there was something lacking in my style of defending the Negro. I went too much into the facts and did not say enough about the Rights of Man and the Declaration of Independence.

When these people found that I did not change my policy as a result of my Atlanta speech, but stuck to my old line of argument, urging the importance of education of the hand, the head, and the heart, they were thoroughly disappointed. So far as my addresses made it appear that the race troubles in the South could be solved by education rather than by political measures, they felt that I was putting emphasis in the wrong place.

I confess that all these criticisms and suggestions were not without effect upon my mind. But, after thinking the matter all over, I decided that, pleasant as it might be to follow the program that was laid out for me, I should be compelled to stick to my original job and work out my salvation along the lines that I had originally laid down for myself.

My determination to stand by the program which I had worked out during the years that I had been at Tuskegee and which I had expressed in my Atlanta speech, soon brought me into conflict with a small group of colored people who sometimes styled themselves "The Intellectuals," at other times "The Talented Tenth." As most of these men were graduates of Northern colleges and made their homes for the most part in the North,* it was natural enough, I suppose, that they should feel that

---

* Du Bois, of course, did his undergraduate work at Fisk University; at the time Mr. Washington was writing, Du Bois had lived for about fifteen years in Georgia and had made very extensive, on-the-spot studies in Alabama and Virginia as well as Georgia.

leadership in race matters should remain, as heretofore, in the North. At any rate, they were opposed to any change from the policy of un-compromising and relentless antagonism to the South so long as there seemed to them to be anything in Southern conditions wrong or unjust to the Negro.

My life in the South and years of study and effort in connection with actual and concrete problems of Southern life had given me a different notion, and I believed that I had gained some knowledge and some insight which they were not able to obtain in the same degree at a distance and from the study of books.

The first thing to which they objected was my plan for the industrial education of the Negro. It seemed to them that in teaching colored people to work with the hands I was making too great a concession to public opinion in the South. Some of them thought, probably, that I did not really believe in industrial education myself; but in any case they were opposed to any "concession," no matter whether industrial education was good or bad.

According to their way of looking at the matter, the Southern white man was the natural enemy of the Negro, and any attempt, no matter for what purpose, to gain his sympathy or support must be regarded as a kind of treason to the race.

All these matters furnished fruitful subjects for controversy, in all of which the college graduates that I have referred to were naturally the leaders. The first thing that such a young man was tempted to do after leaving college was, it seems, to start out on a lecturing tour, traveling about from one town to another for the purpose of discussing what are known as "race" subjects.

I remember one young man in particular who graduated from Yale University and afterward took a post-graduate course at Harvard, and who began his career by delivering a series of lectures on "The Mistakes of Booker T. Washington." * It was not long, however, before he found that he could not live continuously on my mistakes. Then he discovered that in all his long schooling he had not fitted himself to perform any kind of useful and productive labor. After he had failed in several other directions he appealed to me, and I tried to find something for him to do. It is pretty hard, however, to help a young man who has started wrong. Once he gets the idea that—because he has crammed his head full with mere book knowledge—the world owes him a living, it is hard for him to change. The last I heard of the young man in question, he

* It is probable that this had reference to William Pickens, who will reappear later in this work.

was trying to eke out a miserable existence as a book-agent while he was looking about for a position somewhere with the Government as a janitor or for some other equally humble occupation.

When I meet cases, as I frequently do, of such unfortunate and misguided young men as I have described, I cannot but feel the most profound sympathy for them, because I know that they are not wholly to blame for their condition. I know that, in nine cases out of ten, they have gained the idea at some point in their career that, because they are Negroes, they are entitled to the special sympathy of the world, and they have thus got into the habit of relying on this sympathy rather than on their own efforts to make their way.

In college they gave little thought or attention to preparing for any definite task in the world, but started out with the idea of preparing themselves to solve the race problem. They learned in college a great deal about the history of New England freedom; their minds were filled with the traditions of the anti-slavery struggle; and they came out of college with the idea that the only thing necessary to solve at once every problem in the South was to apply the principles of the Declaration of Independence and the Bill of Rights. They had learned in their studies little of the actual present-day conditions in the South and had not considered the profound difference between the political problem and the educational problem, between the work of destruction and construction as it applies to the task of race-building.

Among the most trying class of people with whom I come in contact are the persons who have been educated in books to the extent that they are able, upon every occasion, to quote a phrase or a sentiment from Shakespeare, Milton, Cicero, or some other great writer. Every time any problem arises they are on the spot with a phrase or a quotation. No problem is so difficult that they are not able, with a definition or abstraction of some kind, to solve it. I like phrases, and I frequently find them useful and convenient in conversation, but I have not found in them a solution for many of the actual problems of life.

In college they studied problems and solved them on paper. But these problems had already been solved by some one else, and all that they had to do was to learn the answers. They had never faced any unsolved problems in college, and all that they had learned had not taught them the patience and persistence which alone solve real problems.

I remember hearing this fact illustrated in a very apt way by a colored minister some years ago. After great sacrifice and effort he had constructed in the South a building to be used for the purpose of sheltering orphans and aged colored women. After this minister had succeeded in getting his building constructed and paid for, a young colored man came to inspect it and at once began pointing out the defects in the building. The minister listened patiently for some time and then, turning to the young man, he said: "My friend, you have an advantage over me." Then he paused and looked at the young man, and the young man looked inquiringly at the minister, who continued: "I am not able to find fault with any building which you have constructed."

Perhaps I ought to add, in order that my statements may not be misleading, that I do not mean to say that the type of college man that I have described is confined to the members of my own race. Every kind of life produces its own peculiar kind of failures, and they are not confined to one race. It would be quite as wrong for me to give the impression that the description which I have given applies to all colored graduates of New England or other colleges and to none others. As a matter of fact, almost from the beginning we have had men from these colleges at Tuskegee; I have come into contact with others at work in various institutions of the South; and I have found that some of the sanest and most useful workers were those who had graduated at Harvard and other New England colleges. Those to whom I have referred are the exception rather than the rule.

There is another class of colored people who make a business of keeping the troubles, the wrongs, and the hardships of the Negro race before the public. Having learned that they are able to make a living out of their troubles, they have grown into the settled habit of advertising their wrongs—partly because they want sympathy and partly because it pays.

Some of these people do not want the Negro to lose his grievances because they do not want to lose their jobs.

A story told me by a colored man in South Carolina will illustrate how people sometimes get into situations where they do not like to part with their grievances. In a certain community there was a colored doctor of the old school, who knew little about modern ideas of medicine but who in some way had gained the confidence of the people and had made considerable money by his own peculiar methods of treatment. In this community there was an old lady who happened to be pretty well provided with this world's goods and who thought that she had a cancer. For twenty years she had enjoyed the luxury of having this old doctor treat her for that cancer. As the old doctor became—thanks to the cancer and to other practice—pretty well-to-do, he decided to send one of his boys to a medical college. After graduating from the medical school, the young man returned home, and his father took a vacation. During this time the old lady who was afflicted with the "cancer" called in the young man, who treated her; within a few weeks the cancer (or what was supposed to be the cancer) disappeared, and the old lady declared herself well.

When the father of the boy returned and found the patient on her feet and perfectly well, he was outraged. He called the young man before him and said: "My son, I find that you have cured that cancer case of mine. Now, son, let me tell you something. I educated you on that cancer. I put you through high school, through college, and finally through the medical school on that cancer. And now you, with your new ideas of practising medicine, have come here and cured that cancer. Let me tell you, son, you have started all wrong. How do you expect to make a living, practising medicine in that way?"

I am afraid that there is a certain class of race-problem solvers who don't want the patient to get well, because as long as the disease holds out they have not only an easy means of making a living, but also an easy medium through which to make themselves prominent before the public.

My experience is that people who call themselves "The Intellectuals" understand theories, but they do not understand things. I have long been convinced that, if these men could have gone into the South and taken up and become interested in some practical work which would have brought them in touch with people and things, the whole world would have looked very different to them. Bad as conditions might have seemed at first, when they saw that actual progress was being made, they would have taken a more hopeful view of the situation.

But the environment in which they were raised had cast them in another world. For them there was nothing to do but insist on the application of the abstract principles of protest. Indignation meetings in Faneuil Hall, Boston, became at one time so frequent as to be a nuisance. It would not have been so bad if the meetings had been confined to the subjects for which they were proposed; but when "The Intellectuals" found that the Southern people rarely, if ever, heard of their protests and, if they did hear of them, paid no attention to them, they began to attack persons nearer home. They began to attack the people of Boston because they said that the people of Boston had lost interest in the cause of the Negro. After attacking the friends of the Negro elsewhere, particularly all those who happened to disagree with them as to the exact method of aiding the Negro, they made me a frequent and favorite object of attack—not merely for the reasons which I have already stated, but because they felt that if they attacked me in some particularly violent way it would surprise people and attract attention. There is no satisfaction in holding meetings and formulating protests unless you can get them into the newspapers. I do not really believe that these people think as badly of the persons whom they have attacked at different times as their words would indicate. They are merely using them as a sort of sounding-board or megaphone to make their own voices carry farther. The persistence and success with which these men sought this kind of advertising has led the general public to believe the number of my opponents among the Negro masses to be much larger than it actually was.

A few years ago when I was in Boston and the subject of those who were opposing me was under discussion, a colored friend of mine, who did not belong to the so-called "Talented Tenth," used an illustration which has stuck in my mind. He was originally from the South, although he had lived in Boston for a number of years. He said that he had once lived in Virginia, near a fashionable hotel. One day a bright idea struck him and he went to the proprietor of the hotel and made a bargain to furnish him regularly with a large number of frogs, which were in great demand as a table delicacy. The proprietor asked him how many he could furnish. My friend replied that he felt quite sure that he could furnish him with a cart-load, if necessary, once a week. The bargain was concluded. The man was to deliver at the hotel the following day as large a number of frogs as possible.

When he appeared, my friend had just six frogs. The proprietor looked at the frogs and then at my friend.

"Where are the others?" he said.

"Well, it is this way," my friend replied; "for months I had heard those bullfrogs in a pond near my house, and they made so much noise that I supposed there were at least a million of them there. When I came to investigate, however, I found that there were only six."

Inspired by their ambition to "make themselves heard" and, as they said, compel the public to pay attention to their grievances, this little group kept up their agitation in various forms and at different places, until their plans culminated one night in Boston in 1903. To convince the public how deep and sincere they were in their peculiar views, and how profoundly opposed they were to every one who held a different opinion, they determined to do something desperate. The colored citizens of Boston had asked me to deliver an address before them in one of their largest churches. The meeting was widely advertised, and there was a large audience present. Unknown to any of my colored friends in Boston, this group who, as I have stated, were mostly graduates of New England colleges, organized a mob to disturb the meeting and to break it up if possible. The presiding officer at the meeting was the Hon. William H. Lewis, a graduate of Amherst College and of the Harvard Law School. Various members of the group were scattered in different parts of the church. In addition to themselves there were present in the audience—and this, better than anything else, shows how far they had been carried in their fanaticism—some of the lowest men and women from vile dens in Boston, whom they had in some way or other induced to come in and help them disturb the meeting.

As soon as I began speaking, the leaders, stationed in various parts of the house, began asking questions. In this and in a number of other ways they tried to make it impossible for me to speak. Naturally the rest of the audience resented this, and eventually it was necessary to call in the police and arrest the disturbers.

Of course, as soon as the disturbance was over, most of those who had participated in it were ashamed of what they had done. Many of those who had classed themselves with "The Intellectuals" before, hastened to disavow any sympathy with the methods of the men who had organized the disturbance. Many who had before been lukewarm in their friendship became my closest friends. Of course the two leaders, who were afterward convicted and compelled to serve a sentence in the Charles Street Jail, remained unrepentant.* They tried to convince themselves that they had been made martyrs in a great cause, but they did not get much encouragement in this notion from other colored people because it was not possible for them to make clear just what the cause was for which they had suffered.

The masses of colored people in Boston and in the United States indorsed me by resolution and condemned the disturbance of the meeting. The Negro newspapers as a whole were scathing in their criticism of them. For weeks afterward my mail was filled with letters from colored people, asking me to visit various sections and speak to the people.

I was intensely interested in observing the results of this disturbance. For one thing I wanted to find out whether a principle in human nature that I had frequently observed elsewhere would prove true in this case.

I have found in my dealings with the Negro race—and I believe that the same is true of all races—that the only way to hold people together is by means of a constructive progressive program. It is not

---

* The two men jailed, for thirty days, were William Monroe Trotter and Granville Martin; Bernard Charles was fined twenty-five dollars. A good account of this important event is in Stephen R. Fox, *The Guardian of Boston: William Monroe Trotter* (New York: Antheneum, 1970), pp. 49–58.

argument, nor criticism, nor hatred, but work in constructive effort, that gets hold of men and binds them together in a way to make them rally to the support of a common cause.

Before many weeks had passed, these leaders began to disagree among themselves. Then they began to quarrel, and one by one they began to drop away. The result is that at the present time the group has been almost completely dispersed and scattered. Many of "The Intellectuals" today do not speak to one another.

The most surprising thing about this disturbance, I confess, is the fact that it was organized by the very people who have been loudest in condemning the Southern white people because they had suppressed the expression of opinion on public questions and denied the Negro the right of free speech.

As a matter of fact, I have talked to audiences in every part of this country; I have talked to colored audiences in the North and to white audiences in the South; I have talked to audiences of both races in all parts of the South; everywhere I have spoken frankly and, I believe, sincerely on everything that I had in my mind and heart to say. When I had something to say about the white people I said it to the white people; when I had something to say about colored people I said it to colored people. In all these years—that is the curious thing about it—no effort has been made, so far as I can remember, to interrupt or to break up a meeting at which I was present until it was attempted by "The Intellectuals" of my own race in Boston.

I have gone to some length to describe this incident because it seems to me to show clearly the defects of that type of mind which the so-called "Intellectuals" of the race represent.

I do not wish to give the impression by what I have said that, behind all the intemperance and extravagance of these men, there is not a vein of genuine feeling and even at times something like real heroism. The trouble is that all this fervor and intensity is wasted on side-issues and trivial matters. It does not connect itself with anything that is helpful and constructive. These crusaders, as nearly as I can see, are fighting windmills.

The truth is, I suspect, as I have already suggested, that "The Intellectuals" live too much in the past. They know books but they do not know men. They know a great deal about the slavery controversy, for example, but they know almost nothing about the Negro. Especially are they ignorant in regard to the actual needs of the masses of the colored people in the South today.

There are some things that one individual can do for another, and there are some things that the race can do for another. But on the whole, every individual and every race must work out its own salvation. Let me add that if one thing more than another has taught me to have confidence in the masses of my own people, it has been their willingness (and even eagerness) to learn and their disposition to help themselves and depend upon themselves as soon as they have learned how to do so.

World's Work (Chicago), November, 1910, pp. 13627–40.

2

"DOOMED TO DESTRUCTION"

by Black Ministers of Washington

In the Summer of 1910 a reign of terror broke out in Anderson County, Texas—in and around the towns of Slocum and Palestine. Sharecroppers were protesting the peonage that prevailed and were attempting to terminate it and were demanding the payment of wages; the result was slaughter which seems to have continued for several days and to have taken the lives of an undetermined number of Afro-American people. Contemporaries wrote of "20 or 30 Collored Peopple Murdered" as of August 1. A white man named John A. Siddon wrote from Volga, Texas, on August 1 to Cecil A. Lyon, also white, of Sherman, Texas, telling of the slaughter and asking if something might not be done by the federal government to halt it and to end the conditions which produced such events. Lyon, who was a member of the Republican National Committee, wrote to Attorney General George W. Wickersham in Washington, praying for action and adding that "it is probable that any investigation of this in the state courts would be a farce."

Early in August a mass meeting of Black people in Washington, D.C., to protest the massacre was held; it appointed a Committee of Colored Ministers which drafted an address to President Taft. That address, together with a covering letter on behalf of the committee (dated Washington, August 13, 1910) to the President, are published below. In response to both documents the attorney general wrote the Reverend Mr. Waldron on August 24 that "the protection of life and property is generally a duty devolving upon the state authorities, and except when the deprivation of life and property involves a violation of some right secured by the Constitution or laws of the United States, the Federal Government can take no action." None was taken by either the federal or the state authorities.

Washington, D.C.
August 13th, 1910

President William H. Taft

Dear Sir:

The undersigned have been appointed a Committee by the Colored Ministers—numbering more than 150—of the city of Washington to convey to you the enclosed address to the President and the American people relative to the murdering of 20 or more innocent and unarmed colored men near Palestine, Texas recently. It is the hope of the colored Ministers of this city, and of the many thousands whom they represent, as well as the hope of the colored people throughout America, that you may use the powers of your great Office to suppress lynching, murder and other forms of lawlessness in this country. According to the most recent and reliable statistics there are eight times more murders committed in the United States of America each year, than are committed in Great Britain, and six times more than in France, and five times more than of the German Empire. Our Nation is already the laughing stock of civilized peoples throughout the world, and unless something is done to make human life more valuable and law more universally respected, we feel that our beloved country is doomed to destruction at no distant date. We believe that you are as much interested in the suppression of lawlessness and crime in this country as we are, and we feel confident that you will do all in your power to help bring about this much to be desired end.

We beg, sir, to remain

Yours very respectfully

(signed)

J. Milton Waldron, J. Anderson Taylor, W. J. Howard
Committee

To President Wm. H. Taft, and to the American People:—

We have come together tonight to make a sane protest to the reason and enlightened conscience of the great American people. We deplore the fact that such a meeting as this should be necessary. An impartial enforcement of law and unprejudiced treatment of citizens, regardless of ancestry, would leave little excuse for a meeting like this. But when so many black men are murdered without indictment, trial or conviction, as so recently happened in Texas and Florida, we feel it our duty to appeal to the American people to aid us in reenthroning law and order in every community of our country. To God, the Executive head of the Nation, and the American people we make this appeal as descendants of citizens who were, even in bondage, warm friends of the Southern white people; and who, until a half-hundred years ago made history for others, but none for themselves. Since then we have striven against race antipathy and the stigma of previous condition, and have rapidly improved in literacy, morals and economic status. In the past we put confidence in Statecraft to save us from exploitation at the behest of the strong, but the best we have ever received from it is not enough to deliver us from the troubles of which we now complain. We sought strength thru education, but the more we advance along this line, the greater the discrimination. We have bought land, built homes and established Churches, but those states as desire to do so go on disfranchising us, lynching our men on frivolous charges and unproved allegations, and widening the chasm which race differentiation has made broad enough. When progress does not promise to save a people, that people is near unto desperation. But let us appeal to the best instincts of men as long as reason has a chance or argument a hearing. While the brotherhood of man is a doctrine of our religion we must believe that this world can be made better, and ultimately set right. There is no wrong that cannot be put away by good men determined to do it. We pledge ourselves to this gigantic task, especially in agitating for the enforcement of law. It is pitiable to note that the white man who makes laws for men of other races to live under has not succeeded in ruling according to the laws he has made, nor has he the courage or fairness or courage to punish himself for the greatest crime against the State, which he has ordained—the crime of lynching. Within a month approximately a hundred citizens have suffered death or persecution in a community of the State of Texas. They have been lynched, murdered, burned and persecuted, the State apparently powerless to help them. This sad condition of racial strife, ever present like a smothering volcano ready to emit the lava of race hatred, makes it imperative for us as Colored Ministers, servants of the public and friends of justice, to make this impassioned protest—this earnest appeal:

(1) This is not intended to be an indignation meeting, but one expressive of our weakened confidence in the custodians of the law in certain sections of our country, and of an avowed sympathy for those of our people who suffer not from wrong doing, but from race hatred.

(2) We believe in democracy; which we interpret to mean government by suffrage and protection by law. The mission of the law is: justice to every man at any price. Now God's arbiter for humanity

is justice; not for any one race or nation above another, but for the human race. Humane treatment, establishing the guilt of evil doers, as a part of justice, is absolutely necessary.

(3) We urge in favor of political and judicial fairness for our people, their historic relations to the progress of our country. Traditions of beautiful sentiments and unparalleled fidelity ought to be enough to give our fathers a wreath of honor and to secure for us, their descendants, a place as men and citizens on equal terms with other men. Negro brawn and adaptability did much to make the South prosperous and beautiful and happy.

(4) We argue that the colored race deserves the appreciation of the American Nation—North and South. Besides his hundreds of years of unrequited toil, at a critical moment in the history of our country, when our brothers were torn by internecine strife from '61–'65, our people fought for liberty in the army of the Union—and worked to feed and protect the women and children of the confederacy. No slave race ever had such a record under such difficulties. No base charge of the present should rob the colored people of this glory of the past; still we are last in the hearts of our countrymen.

(5) We are alarmed that out of the wrong so generally acknowledged—the national sin of lynching and mob rule—no voice rings out sufficiently clear to check the mad career of the lawless who murder innocents whom the law has promised to protect. We ask the sympathetic consideration of the President of the U.S., the Judges of the Supreme Court, the Governors of States, the officials of law, the pulpit and press, and fair-minded people everywhere, to the end that lynching and mob rule and race riots be driven from the American commonwealth.

(6) We earnestly ask that this Government which has shown its sympathy with the weak of foreign nations by sending an army to Cuba, by joining with the powers in settling the Boxer Movement in China, by suggesting that honor had been satisfied to Russia and Japan, that is in sympathy with Russian Jews and Armenians in their suffering, that has often protected an individual abroad in the name of humanity—we insist that this Government shall protect its weak at home as well as abroad.

(7) We commend every brave man who has in the past or present, in the North or South, East or West, spoken out boldly for justice and right.

We make this appeal to the reason of all true Americans. We invoke the good office of blind-folded justice, who has no respect of persons. We appeal to the home-loving instinct of the real American—descendant of Saxons, Teutons and Celts, whose motto is "A man's home is his castle," to espouse the cause of law for all alike. We appeal to the love that gave birth to the Golden Rule that lives in the Declaration of Independence and in the justice of the Constitution of the United States.

COMMITTEE

M. W. D. Norman,	W. D. Jarvis, President
J. M. Waldron,	E. B. Gordon,
W. J. Howard,	J. H. Randolph,
A. Sayles,	J. A. Taylor,
S. L. Corrothers,	J. I. Loving,
N. B. Marshall,	T. L. Jones,
	A. Wilbanks,
	M. W. Gibbs,
	I. N. Ross,
	A. C. Garner,
	J. I. Loving, Sec'y

Legislative, Judicial and Fiscal Branch, Civil Archives Division, National Archives, Washington, D.C., Department of Justice, file 152961–3. The editor's attention was called to this event by the work of Mary Frances Berry, *Black Resistance/ White Law* (New York: Meredith Corp., 1971), p. 134. For contemporary accounts of the slaughter, see *The Literary Digest,* August 13, 1910.

3

THE "UNITED COLORED DEMOCRACY" AND THE NEW YORK ELECTION OF 1910

As part of the breakaway of the Black electorate from nearly unanimous allegiance to the party of Abraham Lincoln, the United Colored Democracy of the State of New York was organized in October, 1898. Its influence grew in the succeeding years; Black men—of whom nearly fifty thousand were voting in New York in 1910—played a role in electing John A. Dix as governor over the Republican, Henry L. Stimson.

Prominent in this organization were Bishop Alexander Walters, of the A.M.E.Z. Church, Edwin F. Horne, and James D. Carr. Two of the leaflets issued by this organization—around October, 1910—are reproduced below.

[a]

"REMEMBER BROWNSVILLE"

The New York *Sun* says that one of the characteristics of colored people is short memories. Is this true? If it is the race cannot permanently progress. We must remember the past in order to insure the future.

Mr. Colored Voter, do you remember Theodore Roosevelt? Do you remember that when white soldiers in Ohio were proven to be murderers they escaped with one fine and one man imprisoned, while of the black soldiers of Brownsville against whom not a single crime was ever proven, 134 were unceremoniously kicked out of the army in disgrace? * Who did this? Theodore Roosevelt.

Mr. Colored Voter, do you remember that when these same black soldiers saved Theodore Roosevelt from being "beaten to a frazzle" at San Juan Hill, he returned to the United States and sneered at them as cowards?

Mr. Colored Voter, have you forgotten that it was Mr. Theodore Roosevelt who stood up in New York but two months ago and told you to stop "whining"? †

Who is it that owns the Republican party in New York today? Theodore Roosevelt. Who is it that is soft-soaping and flattering the white South? Theodore Roosevelt. Why? He wants to be president again to gratify his over-weaning ambition, to make Negroes stop "whining" and crawl to race prejudice.

How does Theodore Roosevelt propose to do this? *By your votes.* He expects you to vote for him. He doesn't think you dare vote for anyone else. He thinks he owns you. He appeals to everybody else with soft phrases and double-faced lies, but when he turns to you, he kicks you and tells you to stop "whining."

Every black vote cast for the Republican party in New York on November 8th is a vote for Theodore Roosevelt. Every vote cast for the amiable H. L. Stimpson [sic] is a vote for Theodore Roosevelt.

* In 1904 about seventy men of the Regular Army liberated a comrade from prison in Athens, Ohio, killing one and wounding two people. One soldier was fined; one was jailed for a year. The Brownsville event occurred in 1906—see I, 869-71 of this work.
† In August, 1910—soon after returning from his African journey—Theodore Roosevelt addressed the Eleventh Annual Meeting of the National Negro Business League, held in New York City. With Booker T. Washington on the platform, he hailed the League because "it teaches you not to whine and cry about privileges you do not have. . . ." The speech was printed in the *New York Age,* August 25, 1910.

THE "UNITED COLORED DEMOCRACY"

Mr. Colored Voter, are you a man? Can you resent insult and injury? Then vote like a man. *Remember Brownsville,* and bury Theodore Roosevelt so deep on Election day that his advice to "stop whining" will be buried with him.

[b]

WHAT DO WE WANT?

Political parties are organizations to do things and to get things. They have no past. It is not a question as to what they did forty years ago. The question is, what are they doing *now?*

It is not a question as to what parties are doing in *Alabama,* but simply what are they doing in *New York.*

What are the parties doing for you in the states? They are doing what you ask them to do.

How does a man, or a city, or a race ask favors of a party? It takes a ballot in its fist and marches up to the polls and says: Mr. Political Party if you want my vote, do the things I want done, appoint the men I want appointed, pass the laws I want passed; and if you don't, *you can't get my vote.* No sentiment, no "grand old party" flap-doodle, just plain business.

Is this the method which the Colored Voters of New York have followed? No. They have tied their votes to their tails and scurried like sheep at the snap of the Republican whip. What have they got for it? Nothing! A man without sense enough to vote intelligently doesn't deserve intelligent treatment and he doesn't get it. What city and state offices has the Republican party given black men? It won't take you over two years to count them. What has the Republican Party done to stop the shameful discrimination in civil rights? Nothing. Why? It doesn't have to.

Some Negroes would vote for the Republican party even if the party put them back into slavery.

I would *not,* would you?

Let's see: What do we want?

We want Colored Policemen.

We want Colored Firemen.

We want garbage removed from our streets before noon.

We want crooks driven out of the tenements.

We want "blind tigers" caught.

We want work for our boys and protection for our girls.

We want our civil rights as citizens in theatres and restaurants.

We want a colored regiment in the National Guard.

How shall we get these? By voting right.

We've tried voting for Republicans for forty years and they spit in our faces. The Democratic Party in this State has done more for us on less votes than any party ever did.

Give them more votes and they'll do more. Let's try them. They *cannot* do less than the Republicans. They will do more.

Vote the Democratic ticket November eighth.

These leaflets are in the possession of the editor.

4

FROM THE FIRST NUMBER OF *THE CRISIS*

Dr. Du Bois edited *The Crisis* from its first number in November, 1910, until he resigned from the N.A.A.C.P. in the summer of 1934. In Volume I, pages 927–28, of this work is printed the editorial appearing in that original issue. Below are published other selections from that number, conveying some idea of developments in 1910; note also Du Bois' reprinting of an item concerning Africa's past, a subject which held his interest for over seventy years.

SEGREGATION

Some people in Chicago, Philadelphia, Atlantic City, Columbus, O., and other Northern cities are quietly trying to establish separate colored schools. This is wrong, and should be resisted by black men and white. Human contact, human acquaintanceship, human sympathy is the great solvent of human problems. Separate school children by wealth and the result is class misunderstanding and hatred. Separate them by race and the result is war. Separate them by color and they grow up without learning the tremendous truth that it is impossible to judge the mind of a man by the color of his face. Is there any truth that America needs to learn more? Back of the demand for the segregation of black folk in public institutions, or the segregation of Italians, or the segregation of any class, is almost always a shirking of responsibility on the part of the public—a desire to put off on somebody else the work of social uplift, while they themselves enjoy its results. Nobody pretends to deny that probably three-fourths of the colored children in the public schools of a great Northern city are below the average of their follow students in some respects. They are, however, capable of improvement, and of rapid improvement. This improvement can be carried on by the community. The community can, however, if it is cowardly and selfish, shirk this responsibility and pile it on the shoulders of the Negroes represented by the one-fourth of Negro children who are above the average, or equal to it; and they can, if they are persistent, succeed in pushing back and possibly overwhelming a deserving and rising class of colored people.

This is the history of color discrimination in general in Philadelphia, New York and Chicago. When the discrimination comes in various lines of life, it does not bear simply on those who are not hurt by it—who do not feel it, and who by their position naturally fall outside the lines of discrimination, but it comes with crushing weight upon those other Negroes to whom the reasons for discrimination do not apply in the slightest respect, and they are thus made to bear a double burden. Further than this, when the discrimination is once established, immediately the public provisions for the segregated portion become worse. If it is discrimination against poor people, then the schools for the poor people become worse than those for the rich—less well equipped and less well supervised. If it is discrimination against colored people, the colored school becomes poor, with less money and less means of efficiency.

The argument, then, for color discrimination in schools and in public institutions is an argument against democracy and an attempt to shift public responsibility from the shoulders of the public to the shoulders of some class who are unable to defend themselves.

BALTIMORE

An inevitable step forward in anti-Negro prejudice is being taken in Baltimore, and threatened elsewhere. The colored folk of that city long ago became dissatisfied with a particularly bad system of alley homes. They saved their money and purchased nearly the whole length of Druid Hill avenue—one of the best colored streets in the world. Then they began to expand into parallel streets, one of which was McCulloh. They had been told that "money talks," and that the surest road to respect in America was financial success. The result was inevitable. The white people of McCulloh street rose in indignation and are importuning the City Council to pass an ordinance prohibiting colored people from "invading" white residential districts, and *vice versa*. Their argument sounds strong: colored residents bring down the price of property, therefore get rid of colored residents.

Is this the real logic of the situation? Why do colored people depress property values? Because of an exaggerated and persistently encouraged racial prejudice. In the encouragement of such prejudice, Baltimore and Maryland have particularly sinned. Would not an attempt to allay prejudice be wiser than laws against thrift?

VOTING

If there is one thing that should be urged upon colored voters throughout the United States this fall it is independence. No intelligent man should vote one way simply from habit. Only through careful scrutiny of candidates and policies can a man put himself in position to help rule one hundred million people. It is because of the suspicion that colored men are not capable of doing this, or are unwilling to do it, that so many American citizens acquiesce in the nullification of democracy known as disfranchisement. Let every colored man who can, vote; and whether he vote the Republican or Democratic or Socialist ticket, let him vote it, not because his father did or because he is afraid, but because after intelligent consideration he thinks the success of that ticket best for his people and his country.

AGITATION*

Some good friends of the cause we represent fear agitation. They say: "Do not agitate—do not make a noise; *work*." They add, "Agitation is destructive or at best negative—what is wanted is positive constructive work."

Such honest critics mistake the function of agitation. A toothache is agitation. Is a toothache a good thing? No. Is it therefore useless? No. It is supremely useful, for it tells the body of decay, dyspepsia and death. Without it the body would suffer unknowingly. It would think: All is well, when lo! danger lurks.

* This is reprinted in Du Bois, ed., *The ABC of Color* (Berlin: Seven Seas Publishers, 1963), pp. 39–40; reissued by International Publishers (New York, 1967), but the final two paragraphs were omitted.

The same is true of the Social Body. Agitation is a necessary evil to tell of the ills of the Suffering. Without it many a nation has been lulled to false security and preened itself with virtues it did not possess.

The function of this Association is to tell this nation the crying evil of race prejudice. It is a hard duty but a necessary one—a divine one. It is Pain; Pain is not good but Pain is necessary. Pain does not aggravate disease—Disease causes Pain. Agitation does not mean Aggravation—Aggravation calls for Agitation in order that Remedy may be found.

Two Italians were lynched in Florida. The Italian Government protested, but it was found that they were naturalized Americans. The inalienable right of every free American citizen to be lynched without tiresome investigation and penalties is one which the families of the lately deceased doubtless deeply appreciate.

That powerful Negro empires of great size and some culture existed in the Sudan before the white races entered Africa is the conviction of a French scientist, M. Zeltner, who reports in *La Nature* on the results of his archaeological investigations in the basins of the rivers Niger and Senegal.

Within a triangle formed by the towns of Timbuctoo, Kayes and Bamako he located fifty-two archaeological deposits consisting of ruins of unknown cities. M. Zeltner's most interesting finds were made in caves on the upper Senegal. Here an abundance of runic signs and drawings were found traced on rocks. They were similar in character to those discovered in South African caverns. The writings have some resemblance to those signs found on ancient ruins further eastward in the Sahara desert, and are believed by M. Zeltner to be related to the present Tuareg alphabet.

The discoveries made have yet to be thoroughly studied. M. Zeltner thinks that the archaeological exploration of the African continent is yet in its infancy and will doubtless yield surprising results in establishing the advanced state of development attained by the black races in early times.

ORGANIZATIONS AND MEETINGS

Clark University has held an interesting conference on the East and Africa.

The subjects discussed were Turkey, Persia, Bulgaria, Arabia, Egypt and Africa. Among the speakers were: Dr. A. T. Chamberlain, on "The Contributions of the Negro to Human Civilization"; G. W. Ellis, F.R.G.S., on Liberia; the Rev. L. P. Clinton, on West Africa; Professor Frederic Starr, on the Congo, and E. A. Forbes, on French Africa. Messrs. Ellis and Clinton are colored.

Colored people in Ohio and Maryland have held celebrations commemorating the issuance of Lincoln's preliminary Emancipation Proclamation in 1863.

At the Appalachian Exposition, which is being held in Knoxville, the Negroes have a special exhibit and are conducting a series of celebrations.

During the summer the following colored organizations have held annual meetings: National Association of Colored Women's Clubs, at Louisville, Ky.; National Association of Colored Physicians and Surgeons, at Washington, D.C.; National Colored Baptist Association, at New Orleans, La.; The Niagara Movement, at Sea Isle City, N.J.; the Independent Political League, at Atlantic City, N.J.; the Negro Business League, in New York City; the Colored Elks, at Washington, D.C., and the Grand United Order of Odd Fellows, at Baltimore. It is estimated that nearly 12,000 people attended these various conventions.

THE N.A.A.C.P

On the one hundreth anniversary of Lincoln's birth a call was issued in New York signed by prominent people all over the country for a conference on the status of the colored people.

The first conference met in New York May 31 and June 1, 1909.

The second conference was held in New York May 12–14, 1910.

The second conference organized a permanent body to be known as the National Association for the Advancement of Colored People. The officers of this association are:

National President: Mr. Moorfield Storey, Boston, Mass.
Chairman of the Executive Committee: Mr. Wm. English Walling, New York.
Treasurer: Mr. John E. Milholland, New York.
Disbursing Treasurer: Mr. Oswald Garrison Villard, New York.
Director of Publicity and Research: Dr. W. E. B. Du Bois, New York.
Executive Secretary: Miss Frances Blascoer, New York.

The work of the N.A.A.C.P. can be summarized as follows up to the present date:

Four mass meetings and ten other meetings have been held to discuss the status of the colored people and efforts for betterment.

One volume of speeches and 6,000 separate pieces of literature are being distributed.

A bureau of information has been maintained which has corresponded with over 500 persons in all parts of the country.

Six articles have been furnished to magazines and eight to newspapers.

Two investigations into educational conditions are in progress.

Effort has been made in three cases to secure legal redress of grievances.

This Association needs $10,000 for its year's work. We ask for donations and we especially want members who pay from $1 to $25 yearly, according to ability. Anybody may join.

The future plans of the organization include:

The publication of *The Crisis*.

Co-operation with all agencies working for the uplift of colored people.

The holding of mass meetings and conferences.

The issuing of pamphlets at the rate of one every other month or oftener.

The publication of articles in magazines and in the daily press.
The discovering and redress of cases of injustice.
The systematic study of the present conditions among colored people.

The General Committee consists of the officers and the following persons:

* Miss Gertrude Barnum, New York.
Prof. John Dewey, New York.
Mrs. Florence Kelley, New York.
* Mrs. F. R. Keyser, New York.
Mr. Jacob W. Mack, New York.
Rev. Horace G. Miller, New York.
Mr. James F. Morton, Jr.,
    New York.
Miss Leonora O'Reilly, New York.
* Mr. Charles Edward Russell,
    New York.
Prof. E. R. A. Seligman, New York.
Mrs. Anna Garlin Spencer,
    New York.
Miss Lillian D. Wald, New York.
Dr. Stephen S. Wise, New York.
* Rev. John Haynes Holmes,
    Brooklyn, New York.
* Miss M. W. Ovington,
    Brooklyn, N.Y.
Mrs. M. H. Talbert, Buffalo, N.Y.
* Mr. W. L. Bulkley, Ridgewood, N.J.
Miss Maria Baldwin, Boston, Mass.
Mr. Archibald H. Grimké,
    Boston, Mass.
Mr. Wm. Monroe Trotter,
    Boston, Mass.
Prest. Chas. T. Thwing,
    Cleveland, O.
Prest. King, Oberlin, O.
* Miss Jane Addams, Chicago, Ill.
* Rev. W. H. Brooks, New York.
Miss Maud R. Ingersoll, New York.
* Mr. Paul Kennaday, New York.
Dr. Chas. Lenz, New York.
* Mrs. M. D. MacLean, New York.
Mrs. Max Morgenthau, Jr.,
    New York.
Mr. Henry Moskowitz, New York.
* Rev. A. Clayton Powell, New York.
Mr. Jacob H. Schiff, New York.

* Rev. Joseph Silverman, New York.
Mrs. Henry Villard, New York.
* Bishop Alexander Walters,
    New York.
Rev. Jas. E. Haynes, D.D.,
    Brooklyn, N.Y.
Miss M. R. Lyons, Brooklyn, N.Y.
* Dr. O. M. Waller, Brooklyn, N.Y.
Hon. Thos. M. Osborne,
    Auburn, N.Y.
Mr. George W. Crawford,
    New Haven, Conn.
Mr. Francis J. Garrison,
    Boston, Mass.
* Mr. Albert E. Pillsbury,
    Boston, Mass.
Miss Elizabeth C. Carter,
    New Bedford, Mass.
Mr. Chas. W. Chesnutt,
    Cleveland, O.
Prest. W. S. Scarborough,
    Wilberforce, O.
* Mrs. Ida B. Wells Barnett,
    Chicago, Ill.
Dr. C. E. Bentley, Chicago, Ill.
Mr. Clarence Darrow, Chicago, Ill.
Miss Sophronisba Breckenridge,
    Chicago, Ill.
* Mrs. Celia Parker Woolley,
    Chicago, Ill.
* Dr. N. F. Mossell, Philadelphia, Pa.
* Dr. Wm. A. Sinclair,
    Philadelphia, Pa.
Miss Susan Wharton,
    Philadelphia, Pa.
Mr. R. R. Wright, Jr.,
    Philadelphia, Pa.
Mr. W. Justin Carter,
    Harrisburg, Pa.
Rev. Harvey Johnson, D.D.,
    Baltimore, Md.

Hon. Wm. S. Bennett,
  Washington, D.C.
Mr. L. M. Hershaw,
  Washington, D.C.
Prof. Kelly Miller,
  Washington, D.C.
Prof. L. B. Moore,
  Washington, D.C.

Justice W. P. Stafford,
  Washington, D.C.
* Mrs. Mary Church Terrell,
  Washington, D.C.
Rev. J. Milton Waldron,
  Washington, D.C.
Prest. John Hope, Atlanta, Ga.
Mr. Leslie P. Hill, Manassas, Va.

* Executive Committee. [Of the sixty-five people listed on the General Committee, thirty-nine were white and twenty-six were Black.]

5

THE OPERA HOUSE LYNCHING

One of the central concerns of the N.A.A.C.P., in the first generation of its existence, was the struggle against lynching. From the mimeographed minutes of a meeting of its Executive Board, May 2, 1911, is taken the following account of a lynching conducted in a rather unusual setting.

Mr. [William A.] Sinclair then presented a strong resolution of condemnation of the horrible lynching in Livermore, Ky., as follows:

Whereas, the Press Dispatches show that one M. Potter, a colored man, charged with killing a white man, was taken from the jail at Livermore, Ky., last week, and taken to the town Opera House, and tied on the stage, and that an admission fee was charged to witness the lynching, the prices ranging from those usually charged for orchestra and gallery seats, and that a feature of the lynching was that the audience was allowed to shoot at the suspended body of the victim, and, as in the words of the Press reports, "Those who bought orchestra seats had the privilege of emptying their six shooters at the swaying form above them, but the gallery occupants were limited to one shot," and

Whereas, the Press Dispatches further show that, "the money taken in at the door went to the family of the white man the Negro had killed," and

Whereas, this culmination of spectacular, revolting, barbarous brutality, defies alike the laws of God and the laws of the Nation, disgraces our country and impeaches our civilization: therefore,

Be it resolved, that this Association appoint a Committee of seven (7) to prepare a Memorial, and that said Committee present identical copies of said Memorial to the President of the United States, the President of the Senate, the Speaker of the House of Representatives, the Chairmen of the Judiciary Committees of the Senate and House of Representatives, to the Associated Press, and to such other persons and newspapers as it deems wise.

And be it further resolved, that the said Committee earnestly implore the President to send a Special Message to both the Senate and House of Representatives, calling attention to the terrible iniquities and intolerable conditions of Lynch Law, and ask Congress to take such action as will save this nation from this foul blot and curse on its civilization, its honor and its Christian religion.*

* President Taft said nothing; Theodore Roosevelt in his Sixth Annual Message (December 3, 1906) had denounced lynching.

6

PEONAGE

In 1867 the federal government outlawed debt slavery, or peonage. Though, nevertheless, the practice was widespread, the first conviction for the practice of peonage did not come until 1901, and the criminal was soon pardoned by President Theodore Roosevelt. The U.S. Attorney-General's Report of 1911 affirmed that peonage was "extensively carried on"; in the preceding year Black people had appealed convictions under various state laws virtually legalizing peonage and the federal government acted to support these appeals. It is to this that document [a], taken from "Along the Color Line," in *The Crisis,* December, 1910 (p. 7), refers. Document [b] is a letter "From the South," dated May 8, 1911, and sent to Dr. Du Bois.

[a]

Several Southern laws, which have reduced Negro farm hands to virtual peonage, are to be tested before the United States Supreme Court. The case is the appeal of an Alabama Negro convicted of violating the contract law, upheld by the State Supreme Court, under which he was sentenced to a fine equivalent to 126 days' hard labor for the county. The Federal Department of Justice believes that the law imposes compulsory service in satisfaction of debt, reducing the Negroes to actual slavery.

The law provides that in contracts of service entered into by a laborer, where money was advanced, and the contract broken without just cause, and the money not refunded, the laborer is guilty, and may be sentenced to hard labor until the fine is worked out. The Federal Department contends that the purpose and effect of the law is not to stop fraudulent practices so much as to impose compulsory service upon the Negroes who constitute the bulk of the farm labor of the State. The point that will be attacked most vigorously is the Alabama rule of evidence in such cases, which, in practice, assumes the Negro accused was guilty of intent to defraud, "contrary to the axiomatic and elementary principle of presumption of innocence in a criminal procedure."

The reports of the abuses existing under this contract system in the South have aroused widespread indignation as they have appeared from time to time when some exceptionally flagrant case was forced into publicity. Now that the Department of Justice has become interested, and the issue is to be placed before the supreme tribunal, a definite pronouncement may be expected.*

[b]

FROM THE SOUTH

Kind Sir:

I am not an educated man. I will give you the peonage system as it is practised here in the name of the law.

If a colored man is arrested here and hasn't any money, whether he is guilty or not, he has to pay just the same. A man of color is never tried in this country. It is simply a farce. Everything is fixed before he enters the courtroom. I will try to give you an illustration of how it is done:

I am brought in a prisoner, go through the farce of being tried. The whole of my fine may amount to fifty dollars. A kindly appearing man will come up and pay my fine and take me to his farm to allow me to work it out. At the end of a month I find that I owe him more than I did when I went there. The debt is increased year in and year out. You would ask, "How is that?" It is simply that he is charging you more for your board, lodging and washing than they allow you for your work, and you can't help yourself either, nor can anyone else help you, be-

* The Supreme Court upheld the constitutionality of the anti-peonage law (219 U.S. 191 [1911]: *Bailey* v. *Alabama*); nevertheless, peonage remained widespread in the South for another thirty years.

cause you are still a prisoner and never get your fine worked out. If you do as they say and be a good Negro, you are allowed to marry, provided you can get someone to have you, and of course the debt still increases. This is in the United States, where it is supposed that every man has equal rights before the law, and we are held in bondage by this same outfit.

Of course we can't prove anything. Our word is nothing. If we state things as they are, the powers that be make a different statement, and that sets ours aside at Washington and, I suppose, in Heaven, too.

Now, I have tried to tell you how we are made servants here according to law. I will tell you in my next letter how the lawmakers keep the colored children out of schools, how that pressure is brought to bear on their parents in such a manner they cannot help themselves. The cheapest way we can borrow money here is at the rate of twenty-five cents on the dollar per year.

Your paper is the best I have read of the kind. I never dreamed there was such a paper in the world. I will subscribe soon. I think there are a great many here that will take your paper. I haven't had the chance to show your paper to any yet, but will as soon as I can. You know we have to be careful with such literature as this in this country.

What I have told you is strictly confidential. If you publish it, don't put my name to it. I would be dead in a short time after the news reached here.

One word more about the peonage. The court and the man you work for are always partners. One makes the fine and the other one works you and holds you, and if you leave you are tracked up with bloodhounds and brought back.

The Crisis, August, 1911, pp. 166–67.

7

THE NATIONAL ASSOCIATION
OF COLORED WOMEN
by Addie W. Hunton

The organization and activity of Black women has been a decisive historical force. An account of the early work of one such organization, by an active participant, is published below. The author, Mrs. Hunton, was born in Norfolk, Virginia, in 1875 and died in Brooklyn, N.Y., in 1943. Mrs. Hunton was a national secretary of the Y.W.C.A. and a leader in the N.A.A.C.P. and very active in Pan-African movements after World War I. She was the mother of the distinguished attorney, Mrs. Eunice Carter, and of the scholar and militant fighter, the late W. Alphaeus Hunton.

While Club work among colored women really antedates the organization of the National Association of Colored Women* at Washington, D.C., in 1896, it is customary now to reckon all progress in this direction from that event. Doing so, we believe that the National Association has not only developed strongly and steadily until it has won the cordial and discriminating approval of the best people, irrespective of color or section, but that the ideals held by our women fifteen years ago relative to the possibilities of the club movement as a social, economic and moral force have been overreached, and we are now exhilarated by the vision of larger possibilities.

There have been three distinct periods in the work of the National Association—organization and expansion, departmental, State federation. It was in the first period that women in every section of the country heard the clarion call of the new movement, awakening them to thought, to action, to life. The response was generous. Women, the most cultured of the race; women, students only of the great school of humanity, but with keen desire and courageous hearts; women from every section came flocking, that through the National Association of Colored Women they might be united into a working force.

This unifying process in the spirit and aim of the intelligent colored woman has been one of her strongest blessings in the past decade. It has not only brought the women of New York and California, of Massachusetts and Texas, to know the needs and realize the advantages and disadvantages each of the other, but it has been their open sesame to modern methods and aims of philanthropy and their favorite resource for sympathetic encouragement and support in their various efforts.

With such a flocking into camp of its forces, the Association soon realized the necessity of working in groups, so various departments were formed, as the occasion demanded, and placed under the direction of women either experienced or peculiarly fitted for the work assigned them. Of the many departments that now constitute the Association may be mentioned Kindergarten, Mothers' Meetings, Day Nurseries, Humane and Rescue, Temperance, Religion, Literature, Domestic Sci-

* On its earlier history, see the present work, I, 889–90.

ence, Music, Art, Forestry and Statistics. Hence the inspiration for kindergartens that overtook New Orleans, Charleston, Atlanta and other cities of the South; the successful efforts for probation officers in Denver, Pittsburgh, Atlanta and a few other cities; the zeal that made nine women of Vicksburg raise $2,000 more and convert into an old folks' home a picturesque old ante-bellum mansion, standing upon a knoll of that historic city and overlooking the dark waters of the Mississippi; that caused still another group to crown one of the many hills of the famous Hot Springs of Arkansas with a similar home, and that lent enthusiasm to the women of New Bedford to persevere until they had won confidence and support for the erection of an old folks' home, at once a joy to their city and the pride of colored women everywhere.

The three homes just mentioned present a fascinating story, but there are many other homes as a result of Association work—for old folk, for orphans, for fallen girls, for business girls, telling stories of just plain, hard sacrifice. Mothers' meetings, notable in results at Tuskegee, Louisville, St. Louis, Jacksonville, and at Jackson and Westside, Mississippi, have proven one of the most helpful and interesting features of the movement, and the results have been far-reaching.

The next period of Association activity was represented by the forming of State Federations. This was not only foreseen to be wise as a means of greater strength, influence and unity of purpose for the club movement in various States, but a resource for harmonious adjustment of representation in the National Association at some future time when the members in individual clubs would become unwieldy. The development in State organization has been very rapid. Already every important State of the country has a State Federation. Every Gulf, South Atlantic and South Central State has been organized. The Northeast is represented by the Northeastern Federation, in itself a powerful organization. The North Central and Northwest are almost solidly organized, while California, Colorado, Utah and other Western States have strong organizations, and are thoroughly liberal in their financial support of the National Association.

Aside from the efforts of its individual clubs, each State Federation has for its object the promotion of some cause that will make for the good of the people of the whole State. The State Federation of Alabama has labored for several years for the erection of a reformatory that should save their youth from the coal mines of that State. Their prayers and work have finally borne themselves upon the Legislature of Alabama, until it has recognized the splendid efforts of these colored women and rewarded them by State appropriation for their reformatory. A similar effort by the Virginia State Federation in the interest of an industrial home for the wayward girls of the State, also promises to meet with like approval by State appropriation.

Conventions of the National Association have been held at Nashville, Chicago, Buffalo, St. Louis, Detroit, Brooklyn and Louisville, and have been thoroughly national in character. Each of these conventions has added something of strength, permanence and influence to the movement, and has brought before the American people, as never before, the colored woman of character and intellect.

A word with reference to the women who have guided this Association will further emphasize the reasons for its admirable construction and policy. Mrs. Mary Church Terrell was the first president, and, standing at the head in the important period of organization, her splendid ability was of inestimable value. She was followed by Mrs. J. Silone Yates, under whose guardianship the National Association reached its second period and made great progress in departmental work. The impetus for State federation was given and was further emphasized during the administration of Mrs. Lucy Thurman. Miss Elizabeth C. Carter, of New Bedford, has, in the three years of her administration, traveled throughout the country, and is known and loved in a personal way by the humblest sister of the ranks. Her administration has been marked by great harmony and increased activity and results all over the country.

Among the women who have worked faithfully for the Association from its beginning, none have been more constant nor more energetic than its first vice-president, Mrs. Booker Washington. The names of Ida Joyce Jackson, of Columbus, O.; Mary E. Stewart and Mary Parrish, of Louisville; Sylvania Williams, of New Orleans; Josephine Bruce, of Washington; Josephine Holmes, of Atlanta, and Hester Jeffries, of Rochester, are among those who have followed the cause from its very beginning till the present.

The National Association of Colored Women became affiliated with the National Council of Women in 1900, and has been regularly represented in its conclaves since that time. Only recently Mrs. Mary Talbert, of Buffalo, and Mrs. Ida Joyce Jackson, of Columbus, were most warmly welcomed and entertained as delegates to the National Council in its sessions at Cleveland, O. A few years ago Mrs. Terrell represented the National Association at the meeting of the International Council of Women, held in Berlin. Mrs. Terrell was most enthusiastically received, and delivered her address in German and French as well as in English.

Such is a very brief outline of the most interesting and helpful work being done by colored women. Every feature of it has a story all its own. There are many individual clubs whose accomplishments are well worth relating. One might tell of the Fresh Air and Empty Stocking Association of Baltimore; of the Women's Era Club, of Boston; the Phyllis Wheatley Clubs, of Chicago and New Orleans; the Kindergarten Associations of Charleston and Atlanta; Loyal Union, of Brooklyn; Lincoln Home Club, of Springfield, Ill.; the Jackson (Miss.) Woman's Club and others—each one doing its work in its own chosen way, and yet each seeking to follow the motto of the Association, "Lifting as We Climb."

No, the Association is not yet perfect; for all of its planting there has not been golden grain, but we have reaped abundantly, and miracles that only unselfish, determined, enthusiastic service can bring to pass have been wrought for us.

Resting upon the unified aim and spirit of 45,000 workers, quick to discern opportunities, what can the National Association of Colored Women not achieve?

The Crisis, May, 1911, II, 17–18.

8

SECOND ANNUAL REPORT, N.A.A.C.P.

From May through December, 1911, the total receipts of the N.A.A.C.P. came to $10,317.43—of which $5,208.53 derived from *The Crisis.* Total expenses, including the production of that magazine and all salaries and so on, came to $9,671.43. Despite these minuscule sums, its work was making an impact as its Second Annual Report, dated January 1, 1912, makes clear. The substance of that report, issued as a small-sized fifteen-page pamphlet, is reprinted below.

ACTIVITIES

The work of the National Association during the past year falls under two heads: Legal Redress and Publicity and Research.

LEGAL REDRESS

The Association aims to furnish legal aid to Negroes in cases where the discrimination is obviously because of color. Its resources have made it possible to handle only a few of the many cases that have come to its notice. Among the more important during the year 1911 were the following:

In New Jersey the Association took up the case of Henry Graham of Lakewood. Graham was arrested because he was found near the scene of a murder. Word of the case came to the Association through the man's wife and we at once sent a lawyer to investigate. He found that the former work of the Association had been noted throughout that part of the State, and that the authorities were eager to tell him that no third degree had been practiced as had been the case with Williams, mentioned in our last report. There was no evidence against Graham, and in a few hours our lawyer secured his release. The man had been ill in prison and he and his wife wrote to the Association in terms of deep gratitude.

In Delaware we were instrumental in securing sentences of life imprisonment in the cases of two colored lads condemned to be hanged.

In Baltimore, where the constitutionality of the city's segregation ordinance is being questioned, we have offered to be of service to the lawyers conducting the cases.

In November a colored resident of Kansas City wrote us:

We desire to place before the legal department of the N.A.A.C.P. the case of a group of Negroes of Kansas City, Mo., who have suffered repeated attempts to destroy their property by an organization of white men who have demanded that they leave the neighborhood. There are nine Negro families in one block and twelve in the next who have purchased or are in progress of buying their homes, ranging in price from $1,500 to $4,000. In the block in which I live five explosions of dynamite have occurred in the past year, causing considerable damage to our homes and much mental uneasiness on the part of our families. The last of these, which happened Saturday, November 11, was by far the most destructive of them all, completely wrecking the home of Mr. Hezekiah Walden. At that time, Mr. Walden was working in Salt Lake City and his wife with two small children were alone in the house.

We have again and again appealed to the mayor and the chief of police to give us protection from these crimes, but the detectives have been of no help either in running the perpetrators to earth or in checking further threats and outrages. We feel that we have a clear case against the city, inasmuch as we have faithfully discharged our duties as citizens, and we are about to retain eminent legal counsel to defend our cause. In addition to this, we beg that we may have the assistance of some member of the legal department of the N.A.A.C.P., who will join us in vigorously prosecuting this case.

Our attorney at once corresponded with white attorneys in Kansas City, from whom no facts could be secured. Investigation, however, is continuing. That the Negro may be segregated by intimidation and lawlessness, ending with black-hand methods, or by city ordinances and State statutes, creating districts that recall the worst conditions of the medieval Ghetto, is an idea far too common in America today. During the coming year we shall strive further to combat it.

The lynchings in the United States, in 1911, have been many and terrible. The number recorded is 71, 8 white and 63 colored; but unquestionably not all are reported. Many entirely innocent persons are among the victims. Thus, in the lynching at Lake City, Fla., six Negroes were strung up as targets to be riddled with bullets in revenge for the killing in self-defense of one white man. In Oklahoma, Georgia and Kentucky innocent men have died deaths of torture at the hands of mobs. Women, too, have been among the victims. As these terrible happenings have occurred, the Association has written to the governors of the various States demanding the punishment of the criminals, and has instigated protests from individuals in nearly every State of the Union. The executives have sent courteous replies, but the end of the year, 1911, sees no lyncher punished.

On November 15 the Association held a meeting in Ethical Culture Hall to protest against lynching. Resolutions were sent to the President, declaring that the reign of lynch law in this country, North and South, constitutes the worst indictment of American democracy that can be drawn. A fund was started to make an investigation of lynching in some chosen centre and $260 was raised. On January 1 the fund stood at $400.67, and the investigation is now under way. Details cannot at present be published, but important material is already in the Association's hands.

Postal cards, printed in Germany, which reproduce in horrible detail lynchings in the South, are circulating in the United States. They are for sale in Southern towns, and are sent about as one sends a souvenir of a cathedral or a landscape. One shows a group of seventy white men and boys, standing in a semi-circle, the dead body of the Negro in the centre of the picture. We have brought this to the attention of the Postmaster-General, and it has been declared unmailable. Another shows a Negro strung to a tree in a lonely pine wood. These pictures, put up for sale at news stands, viewed, as they must be, by women, by boys and girls, stamped to be circulated throughout the world, show, beyond any writing, the small regard in which America holds a Negro's life.

PUBLICITY AND RESEARCH

In the fall of 1910 the Association secured the services of Dr. W. E. B. Du Bois, as Director of Publicity and Research, and in November of that year began the publication of *The Crisis,* the official organ of the National Association. The need of a magazine devoted to the manhood rights of the Negroes was shown by the instant demand for this publication. The November issue of 1,000 copies was at once exhausted, and at the end of the Association's year, January, 1912, the edition is 16,000, with less than 500 returns. The magazine has 4,000 subscribers, and sells from 11,000 to 12,000 copies through its staff of 223 agents. Out of its receipts it pays all printing and postage expenses, buys all stationery and supplies, and pays the salaries of stenographer, advertising agent and office boy. It hopes, by January 1, 1913, to be financially independent.

The Crisis circulates in every State of the Union, except South Dakota. Its sales run from 1,665 in Pennsylvania and 1,015 in Illinois, to 3 in Maine and 2 in Wyoming. It has subscribers in Hawaii and the Philippines, in Liberia and Cape Town. About three-quarters of this circulation is among colored people, who thus show their belief in the Association's ideals and methods of work.

While *The Crisis* is the Association's first and most important medium of publicity, its work is carried on through the publication of newspaper and magazine articles, the holding of meetings and the sending out of speakers. The Director of Publicity, Dr. Du Bois, has spoken at one hundred meetings, in the North, South, East and West of the United States, and in London at the Races Congress.* Others among the officers and members have addressed audiences in many of the large cities. It is part of the work of the Association to furnish speakers for societies that desire to hear of the larger aspects of the Negro problem.

Among the Association's own meetings was the third and very successful annual conference held in Boston in the Park Street Church on March 30 and 31. The centenary of Wendell Phillips was celebrated in Boston, at the Park Street Church, and in Brooklyn, at Plymouth Church. Washington's Birthday saw a gathering in Philadelphia at the

---

* This refers to the Universal Races Congress, held in London in July, 1911. Its papers were edited by Gustav Spiller and published at the time; a new edition, with an introduction by H. Aptheker, was published by Citadel Press in 1970, as *Inter-Racial Problems.*

Friends' Meeting House of 1,500 white and colored people. These were our largest meetings, but others were held in both the East and the West.

Publicity work in the form of newspaper and magazine articles, editorial comment, and the publication of social studies on the Negro, is carried on by the officers of the Association and by many of its members. We are fortunate in having able and influential writers in our membership. . . .

BOSTON BRANCH

The Third Annual Conference of the National Association was held in Boston on March 30 and 31. The meetings took place in the Park Street Church. Among the speakers were Dr. Charles Fleischer, Mr. R. R. Wright, Jr., Miss Adelene Moffat, Mrs. Mary Church Terrell, Mrs. Florence Kelley, Rev. Garnett R. Waller, Mr. Oswald Garrison Villard and Dr. Stephen S. Wise. A reception was given to the members and their friends at the Twentieth Century Club. Mr. Moorfield Storey and Mr. Albert E. Pillsbury were the presiding officers.

After the conference the Boston members appointed a committee to organize a Boston Branch of the Association. The organization was effected on January 8, 1912, with Mr. Francis J. Garrison as president and Mr. Butler R. Wilson as secretary. From the Association's inception Boston has taken a large share in its work. At home it has secured justice for colored persons in cases of discrimination; and it has largely aided the Association in its national undertakings. Its membership equals that of New York.

CHICAGO BRANCH

Chicago formed a Branch of the Association in the fall of 1910. Its work during the past year has been chiefly in aiding the National Association; two of its members are among our most generous subscribers. The Branch is making arrangements to hold the fourth annual conference in Chicago at the end of April.

NEW YORK BRANCH

The Association's New York Branch is known as the Vigilance Committee, with headquarters at 268½ West 135th Street. A stenographer is always at the office during the day, and the officers can be reached by night telephone, so that any colored man suffering injustice before the law may at once receive attention. The President of the Branch is Prof. J. E. Spingarn, and the chairman of the Vigilance Committee, Mr. Gilchrist Stewart.

The New York Vigilance Committee was organized for active prosecution of all infringements of the legal rights of the colored man. It was necessary to have an organized protest against racial discrimination in order to combat the increasing number of outrages against colored men and women, and to make effective the laws of the State which guarantee them equal rights. This organization has attacked the problem of police discrimination against prisoners, their unjust arrest for trivial offenses and their maltreatment often on their way to the station house, and has through the co-operation of the Commissioner of Police of New York City, Rhinelander Waldo, secured the same protection and justice for colored prisoners as are given to all others. No longer are colored prisoners or citizens misused by policemen in the city of New York. The Committee was also instrumental in dispersing the gangs which, in certain neighborhoods, had been in the habit of insulting colored people. Now it is vigorously attacking the custom of discrimination in public places, in restaurants, theatres, hotels, cafés and halls. It has brought a number of successful suits against these places to enforce the civil-rights law. The custom of refusing to colored people seats in the orchestras of the theatres has been growing in New York City. On a test case which was brought by the Committee, Harry A. Levy, assistant treasurer of the Lyric Theatre, was convicted of a misdemeanor for excluding a colored man and a young lady from the orchestra seats of his theatre. His offer to exchange the seats for two in the balcony was refused. It was a hard and long legal fight, conducted by the Hon. Chas. S. Whitman, the District Attorney, through Mr. James A. Smith, as assistant, who had immediate charge of the case, and Charles H. Studin, one of the advisory legal counsel of the Committee. This first criminal conviction under the statute of New York State was given much publicity by the daily press. The Committee believes that it is of the highest importance that an organized effort be made to maintain the civil rights of all citizens regardless of race or color. This can only be accomplished by such vigorous prosecution in every case of discrimination, that the certainty of punishment will deter even prejudiced persons from offending against the law.

"The New York Branch," to quote its president, "finds that the colored people of the city are confronted every day of their lives with the most galling conditions, are subjected to insult, are refused service and courteous treatment, and that, unless the forces opposed to caste and to privilege join together to combat these conditions and to educate public opinion, it will not be long before the conditions in New York are the exact counterpart of those in the Southern cities. It is to this work that the New York Branch has committed itself."

The advisory legal committee consists of the following: Wm. S. Bennet, Edward Lauterbach, Chas. H. Studin, Melville H. Cane, D. Macon Webster, John Wm. Smith and Walter N. Flannagan.

9

THE NEGRO AT WORK IN NEW YORK CITY

by George E. Haynes

A pioneering, full-length study of Black people in New York City with the above title constituted a doctoral dissertation done at Columbia University. George E. Haynes (1880–1960), at the time this work was published, was a professor of sociology at Fisk. He later became director of the Division of Negro Economics in the U.S. Department of Labor, Secretary of the Commission on the Church and Race Relations of the Federal Council of the Churches of Christ in America, and for the decade prior to his death taught at City College of New York. He was a charter member of the N.A.A.C.P. and a founder of the National Urban League.

The urban concentration of the Negro is taking place in about the same way as that of the white population. In proportions, it varies only to a small extent from the movement of the whites, save where the conditions and influences are exceptional. The constant general causes influencing the Negro population have been similar to those moving other parts of the population to cities. The divorce from the soil in the sudden breaking down of the plantation regime just after the Civil War and the growth of industrial centers in the South, and the call of higher wages in the North, have been unusually strong influences to concentrate the Negro in the cities. It is with him largely as with other wage-earners: the desire for higher wages and the thought of larger liberty, especially in the North together with a restlessness under hum-drum, hard rural conditions and a response to the attractions of the city have had considerable force in bringing him to urban centers. Labor legislation in the South has played its part in the movement.

The growth of the industrial and commercial centers of the South, the larger wages in domestic and personal service in the North, and social and individual causes of concentration bid fair to continue for an indefinite period. The Negro responding to their influence will continue to come in comparatively large numbers to town to stay.

But the Negro's residence in the city offers problems of maladjustment. Although these problems are similar to those of other rural populations that become urban dwellers, it is made more acute because he has greater handicaps due to his previous condition of servitude and to the prejudiced opposition of the white world that surrounds him. His health, intelligence and morals respond to treatment similar to that of other denizens of the city, if only impartial treatment can be secured. Doubtless death-rate and crime-rate have been and are greater than the corresponding rates for the white populations of the same localities, but both crime and disease are a reflection of the urban environment and are solvable by methods similar to those used to remedy such conditions among white people, if prejudiced presuppositions, which conclude without experiment or inquiry that Negroes have innately bad tendencies, give place to open-minded trial and unbiased reason. Snapshot opinions should be avoided in such serious questions and statesmen, philanthropists and race leaders should study the facts carefully and act accordingly.

The study of the wage-earners among the Negroes of New York City has disclosed conditions and led to conclusions in line with the foregoing inferences. The Negro population was solidly segregated into a few assembly districts, thereby confining the respectable to the same neighborhoods with the disreputable. This population is made up mainly of young persons and adults of the working period of life, attracted to the city largely from the South and the West Indies, principally by the thought of better industrial and commercial advantages. Single persons predominate and the percentage of the aged is low. High rents and low incomes force lodgers into the families to disturb normal home life.

From the early days of the Dutch Colony the Negro has had a part in the laboring life of this community. While most of the wage-earners have been engaged in domestic and personal service occupations, figures that are available warrant the inference that the Negro is slowly but surely overcoming the handicaps of inefficiency and race prejudice, and is widening the scope of employment year by year. What the individual asks and should have from the white community is a fair chance to work, and wages based upon his efficiency and not upon the social whims and prejudices of fellow-workmen, of employers, or of the community.

In domestic and personal service the Negro is poorly paid compared with the cost of living. And even in skilled occupations, where unions admit him and wages are offered equal to those of white workmen, the Negro must be above the average in speed, in quality of work done, and in reliability to secure and hold places.

In domestic and personal service, the verdict from a large body of evidence is that, judged by the testimony of employers as to the length of time employed, the capability, sobriety and honesty of the workers, Negroes furnish a reliable supply of employees that need only to be properly appraised to be appreciated. What is needed for the workers in this class of occupations and for those in the skilled trades, is that more attention be given to adequate training, that more facilities be offered and that a more sympathetic attitude be shown them in their efforts for better pay and better positions.

In reviewing the Negro's business operations judgment should be tempered by consideration of his past and of the tremendous odds of the present. There are handicaps due to the denial of the chances of getting experience, to inefficiency born of resulting inexperience, to the difficulty of securing capital and building credit and to the low purchasing power of the patronage to which a prejudiced public limits him. He is not only denied experience, sorely limited in capital and curtailed in credit, but his opportunities for securing either are very meagre. In spite of all this, there has been progress which is prophetic of the future.

From the days of slavery Negroes have tried the fortunes of the market place and under freedom their enterprises have increased in number and variety. At the present time Southern-born and West Indian Negroes form the bulk of the business men, the latter far in excess of their proportion in the Negro population. This success of West Indians is partly a result of training and initiative developed in a more favorable environment, as they had the benefit of whatever opportunities their West Indian surroundings offered.

Although they gained the meagre capital chiefly from domestic and personal service occupations, Negroes have entered and maintained a foothold in a number of lines of business unrelated to these previous occupations. One of the most important findings is that Negroes form few partnerships and that those formed are rarely of more than two persons. Co-operative or corporate business enterprises are the exceptions. This fact has its most telling effect in preventing accumulations of capital for large undertakings. But co-operation in business is largely a matter of ability born of experience and where can Negroes get this experience in well-organized firms, under experienced supervision? For it is more than a matter of school instruction in book-keeping and the like. In practically the entire metropolis, they rarely get beyond the position of porter, or some similar job. Some fair-minded white people who wish to help the Negro help himself could do great service for the economic advancement of the Negro by throwing open the doors of business positions to a number of ambitious, capable Negro youths, who would thus enter the avenues of economic independence. The writer knows of three Negroes in New York City who proved themselves so efficient in their respective lines that they were taken in as members of large firms.

Another serious matter is connected with this point. All 309 firms were retail establishments, all of them bought from wholesale suppliers who so far as could be ascertained were white firms. In some lines, there were sufficient retailers to support a wholesale house if their purchases were combined. For example, the group of 50 barber shops or of 36 grocers would each support a jobber if they pooled their patronage. But this would demand an organizing power, a business initiative, a fund of capital and a stretch of credit, which only some men experienced in the method of the modern business world could possess.

The small size and scope of Negro enterprises cannot be attributed to lack of business capacity alone. For the gross receipts of the selected years taken in connection with the valuation of tools and fixtures, and with the stock of merchandise on hand showed considerable diligence and thrift in turning these small resources to active use.

The variety of the many small establishments indicates also the initiative of the Negro in using every available opportunity for economic independence. As we have seen, some of the proprietors had early ambitions for business careers, and others had worked hard and saved carefully from small wages that they might rise from the class of the employed to that of employers. The public to which the Negro business man caters should accept his wares and his services for their face value and not discount them because of the complexion of his face. Then, too, Negroes must learn that the purchasing public desires to be pleased and is larger than the limits of their own people.

Negro wage-earners and business men have great difficulty in scaling the walls of inefficiency and of race prejudice in order to escape the discomforts and dangers of a low standard of living.

George E. Haynes, *The Negro At Work in New York City: A Study in Economic Progress* (New York: Columbia University Press, 1912), pp. 143–48.

10

A SOUTHERN DOMESTIC WORKER SPEAKS

In an important New York weekly early in 1912, there was published—under the title "More Slavery at the South"—the following account by an unnamed Black woman living in Georgia. The editor stated that the story was obtained by its representative "but the facts are those given" by the woman involved.

I am a Negro woman, and I was born and reared in the South. I am now past forty years of age and am the mother of three children. My husband died nearly fifteen years ago, after we had been married about five years. For more than thirty years—or since I was ten years old—I have been a servant in one capacity or another in white families in a thriving Southern city, which has at present a population of more than 50,000. In my early years I was at first what might be called a "house-girl," or, better, a "house-boy." I used to answer the doorbell, sweep the yard, go on errands and do odd jobs. Later on I became a chambermaid and performed the usual duties of such a servant in a home. Still later I was graduated into a cook, in which position I served at different times for nearly eight years in all. During the last ten years I have been a nurse. I have worked for only four different families during all these thirty years. But, belonging to the servant class, which is the majority class among my race at the South, and associating only with servants, I have been able to become intimately acquainted not only with the lives of hundreds of household servants, but also with the lives of their employers. I can, therefore, speak with authority on the so-called servant question; and what I say is said out of an experience which covers many years.

To begin with, then, I should say that more than two-thirds of the Negroes of the town where I live are menial servants of one kind or another, and besides that more than two-thirds of the Negro women here, whether married or single, are compelled to work for a living,—as nurses, cooks, washerwomen, chambermaids, seamstresses, hucksters, janitresses, and the like. I will say, also, that the condition of this vast host of poor colored people is just as bad as, if not worse than, it was during the days of slavery. Tho today we are enjoying nominal freedom, we are literally slaves. And, not to generalize, I will give you a sketch of the work I have to do—and I'm only one of many.

I frequently work from fourteen to sixteen hours a day. I am compelled by my contract, which is oral only, to sleep in the house. I am allowed to go home to my own children, the oldest of whom is a girl of 18 years, only once in two weeks, every other Sunday afternoon—even then I'm not permitted to stay all night. I not only have to nurse a little white child, now eleven months old, but I have to act as playmate or "handy-andy," not to say governess, to three other children in the home, the oldest of whom is only nine years of age. I wash and dress the baby two or three times each day; I give it its meals, mainly from a bottle; I have to put it to bed each night; and, in addition, I have to get up and attend to its every call between midnight and morning. If the baby falls to sleep during the day, as it has been trained to do every day about eleven o'clock, I am not permitted to rest. It's "Mammy, do this," or "Mammy, do that," or "Mammy, do the other," from my mistress, all the time. So it is not strange to see "Mammy" watering the lawn in front with the garden hose, sweeping the sidewalk, mopping the porch and halls, dusting around the house, helping the cook, or darning stockings. Not only so, but I have to put the other three children to bed each night as well as the baby, and I have to wash them and dress them each morning. I don't know what it is to go to church; I don't know what it is to go to a lecture or entertainment or anything of the kind; I live a treadmill life; and I see my own children only when they happen to see me on the streets when I am out with the children, or when my children come to the "yard" to see me, which isn't often, because my white folks don't like to see their servants' children hanging around their premises. You might as well say that I'm on duty all the time—from sunrise to sunrise, every day in the week. I am the slave, body and soul, of this family. And what do I get for this work—this lifetime bondage? The pitiful sum of ten dollars a month! And what am I expected to do with these ten dollars? With this money I'm expected to pay my house rent, which is four dollars per month, for a little house of two rooms, just big enough to turn round in; and I'm expected, also, to feed and clothe myself and three children. For two years my oldest child, it is true, has helped a little toward our support by taking in a little washing at home. She does the washing and ironing of two white families, with a total of five persons; one of these families pays her $1.00 per week, and the other 75 cents per week, and my daughter has to furnish her own soap and starch and wood. For six months my youngest child, a girl about thirteen years old, has been nursing, and she receives $1.50 per week but has no night work. When I think of the low rate of wages we poor colored people receive, and when I hear so much said about our unreliability, our untrustworthiness, and even our vices, I recall the story of the private soldier in a certain army who, once upon a time, being upbraided by the commanding officer because the heels of his shoes were not polished, is said to have replied: "Captain, do you expect all the virtues for $13 per month?"

Of course, nothing is being done to increase our wages, and the way things are going at present it would seem that nothing could be done to cause an increase of wages. We have no labor unions or organizations of any kind that could demand for us a uniform scale of wages for cooks, washerwomen, nurses, and the like; and, for another thing, if some Negroes did here and there refuse to work for seven and eight and ten dollars a month, there would be hundreds of other Negroes right on the spot ready to take their places and do the same work, or more, for the low wages that had been refused. So that, the truth is, we have to work for little or nothing or become vagrants! And that, of course, in this State would mean that we would be arrested, tried, and despatched to the "State Farm," where we would surely have to work for nothing or be beaten with many stripes!

Nor does this low rate of pay tend to make us efficient servants. The most that can be said of us Negro household servants in the South—and I speak as one of them—is that we are to the extent of our ability willing and faithful slaves. We do not cook according to scientific principles because we do not know anything about scientific principles. Most of our cooking is done by guesswork or by memory. We cook well when our "hand" is in, as we say, and when anything about the dinner goes wrong, we simply say, "I lost my hand today!" We don't know anything about scientific food for babies, nor anything about what science says must be done for infants at certain periods of their growth or when certain symptoms of disease appear; but somehow we "raise" more of the children than we kill, and, for the most part, they are lusty chaps—all of them. But the point is, we do not go to cooking-schools nor to nurse-training schools, and so it cannot be expected that we should make as efficient servants without such training as we should make were such training provided. And yet with our cooking and nursing, such as it is, the white folks seem to be satisfied—perfectly satisfied. I sometimes wonder if this satisfaction is the outgrowth of the knowledge that more highly trained servants would be able to demand better pay!

Perhaps some might say, if the poor pay is the only thing about which we have to complain, then the slavery in which we daily toil and struggle is not so bad after all. But the poor pay isn't all—not by any means! I remember very well the first and last place from which I was dismissed. I lost my place because I refused to let the madam's husband kiss me. He must have been accustomed to undue familiarity with his servants, or else he took it as a matter of course, because without any love-making at all, soon after I was installed as cook, he walked up to me, threw his arms around me, and was in the act of kissing me, when I demanded to know what he meant, and shoved him away. I was young then, and newly married, and didn't know then what has been a bur-den to my mind and heart ever since: that a colored woman's virtue in this part of the country has no protection. I at once went home, and told my husband about it. When my husband went to the man who had insulted me, the man cursed him, and slapped him, and—had him arrested! The police judge fined my husband $25. I was present at the hearing, and testified on oath to the insult offered me. The white man, of course, denied the charge. The old judge looked up and said: "This court will never take the word of a nigger against the word of a white man." Many and many a time since I have heard similar stories re-peated again and again by my friends. I believe nearly all white men take, and expect to take, undue liberties with their colored female serv-ants—not only the fathers, but in many cases the sons also. Those servants who rebel against such familiarity must either leave or expect a mighty hard time, if they stay. By comparison, those who tamely submit to these improper relations live in clover. They always have a little "spending change," wear better clothes, and are able to get off from work at least once a week—and sometimes oftener. This moral debasement is not at all times unknown to the white women in these homes. I know of more than one colored woman who was openly impor-tuned by white women to become the mistresses of their white husbands, on the ground that they, the white wives, were afraid that, if their husbands did not associate with colored women, they would certainly do so with outside white women, and the white wives, for reasons which ought to be perfectly obvious, preferred to have their husbands do wrong with colored women in order to keep their husbands *straight!* And again, I know at least fifty places in my small town where white men are positively raising two families—a white family in the "Big House" in front, and a colored family in a "Little House" in the backyard. In most cases, to be sure, the colored women involved are the cooks or chambermaids or seamstresses, but it cannot be true that their real con-nection with the white men of the families is unknown to the white women of the families. The results of this concubinage can be seen in all of our colored churches and in all of our colored public schools in the South, for in most of our churches and schools the majority of the young men and women and boys and girls are light-skinned mulattoes. The real, Simon-pure, blue-gum, thick-lip, coal-black Negro is passing away—certainly in the cities; and the fathers of the new generation of Negroes are white men, while their mothers are unmarried colored women.

Another thing—it's a small indignity, it may be, but an indignity just the same. No white person, not even the little children just learning to talk, no white person at the South ever thinks of addressing any Negro man or woman as *Mr.,* or *Mrs.,* or *Miss.* The women are called, "Cook," or "Nurse," or "Mammy," or "Mary Jane," or "Lou," or "Dilcey," as the case might be, and men are called "Bob," or "Boy," or "Old Man," or "Uncle Bill," or "Pate." In many cases our white employers refer to us, and in our presence, too, as their "niggers." No matter what they call us—no matter what they teach their children to call us—we must tamely submit, and answer when we are called; we must enter no protest; if we did object, we should be driven out without the least ceremony, and, in applying for work at other places, we should find it very hard to procure another situation. In almost every case, when our intending employers would be looking up our record, the information would be given by telephone or otherwise that we were "impudent," "saucy," "dishonest," and "generally unreliable." In our town we have no such thing as an employment agency or intelligence bureau, and, therefore, when we want work, we have to get out on the street and go from place to place, always with hat in hand, hunting for it.

Another thing. Sometimes I have gone on the street cars or the railroad trains with the white children, and, so long as I was in charge of the children, I could sit anywhere I desired, front or back. If a white man happened to ask some other white man, "What is that nigger doing in here?" and was told, "Oh, she's the nurse of those white children in front of her!" immediately there was the hush of peace. Everything was all right, so long as I was in the white man's part of the street car or in the white man's coach as a servant—a slave—but as soon as I did not present myself as a menial, and the relationship of master and servant was abolished by my not having the white children with me, I would be forthwith assigned to the "nigger" seats or the "colored people's coach." Then, too, any day in my city, and I understand that it is so in every town in the South, you can see some "great big black burly" Negro coachman or carriage driver huddled up beside some aristocratic Southern white woman, and nothing is said about it, nothing is done about it, nobody resents the familiar contact. But let that same colored man take off his brass buttons and his high hat, and put on the plain livery of an average American citizen, and drive one block down any thoroughfare in any town in the South with that same white woman, as her equal or companion or friend, and he'd be shot on the spot!

You hear a good deal nowadays about the "service pan." The "service pan" is the general term applied to "left-over" food, which in many a Southern home is freely placed at the disposal of the cook, or, whether so placed or not, it is usually disposed of by the cook. In my town, I know, and I guess in many other towns also, every night when the cook starts for her home she takes with her a pan or a plate or cold victuals. The same thing is true on Sunday afternoons after dinner—and most cooks have nearly every Sunday afternoon off. Well, I'll be frank with you, if it were not for the service pan, I don't know what the majority of our Southern colored families would do. The service pan is the mainstay in many a home. Good cooks in the South receive on an average $8 per month. Porters, butlers, coachmen, janitors, "office boys" and the like receive on an average $16 per month. Few and far between are the colored men in the South who receive $1 or more per day. Some mechanics do; as, for example, carpenters, brick masons, wheelwrights, blacksmiths, and the like. The vast majority of Negroes in my town are serving in menial capacities in homes, stores and offices. Now taking it for granted, for the sake of illustration, that the husband receives, $16 per month and the wife $8. That would be $24 between the two. The chances are that they will have anywhere from five to thirteen children between them. Now, how far will $24 go toward housing and feeding and clothing ten or twelve persons for thirty days? And, I tell you, with all of us poor people the service pan is a great institution; it is a great help to us, as we wag along the weary way of life. And then most of the white folks expect their cooks to avail themselves of these perquisites; they allow it; they expect it. I do not deny that the cooks find opportunity to hide away at times, along with the cold "grub," a little sugar, a little flour, a little meal, or a little piece of soap; but I indignantly deny that we are thieves. We don't steal; we just "take" things—they are a part of the oral contract, expressed or implied. We understand it, and most of the white folks understand it. Others may denounce the service pan, and say that it is used only to support idle Negroes, but many a time, when I was a cook, and had the responsibility of rearing my three children upon my lone shoulders, many a time I have had occasion to bless the Lord for the service pan!

I have already told you that my youngest girl was a nurse. With scores of other colored girls who are nurses, she can be seen almost any afternoon, when the weather is fair, rolling the baby carriage or lolling about on some one of the chief boulevards of our town. The very first week that she started out on her work she was insulted by a white man, and many times since has been improperly approached by other white men. It is a favorite practice of young white sports about town— and they are not always young, either—to stop some colored nurse, inquire the name of the "sweet little baby," talk baby talk to the child, fondle it, kiss it, make love to it, etc., etc., and in nine of ten cases every such white man will wind up by making love to the colored nurse and seeking an appointment with her.

I confess that I believe it to be true that many of our colored girls are as eager as the white men are to encourage and maintain these improper relations; but where the girl is not willing, she has only herself to depend upon for protection. If their fathers, brothers or husbands seek to redress their wrongs, under our peculiar conditions, the guiltless Negroes will be severely punished, if not killed, and the white blackleg will go scot-free!

Ah, we poor colored women wage-earners in the South are fighting a terrible battle, and because of our weakness, our ignorance, our poverty, and our temptations we deserve the sympathies of mankind. Perhaps a million of us are introduced daily to the privacy of a million chambers throughout the South, and hold in our arms a million white children, thousands of whom, as infants, are suckled at our breasts—during my lifetime I myself have served as "wet nurse" to more than a dozen white children. On the one hand, we are assailed by white men, and, on the other hand, we are assailed by black men, who should be our natural protectors; and, whether in the cook kitchen, at the washtub, over the sewing machine, behind the baby carriage, or at the ironing board, we are but little more than pack horses, beasts of burden, slaves! In the distant future, it may be, centuries and centuries hence, a monument of brass or stone will be erected to the Old Black Mammies of the South, but what we need is present help, present sympathy, better wages, better hours, more protection, and a chance to breathe for once while alive as free women. If none others will help us, it would seem that the Southern white women themselves might do so in their own defense, because we are rearing their children—we feed them, we bathe them, we teach them to speak the English language, and in numberless instances we sleep with them—and it is inevitable that the lives of their children will in some measure be pure or impure according as they are affected by contact with their colored nurses.

The Independent, January 25, 1912; LXXII, 196–200.

11

DIVINE RIGHT
by W. E. B. Du Bois

If a more bitter and militant statement has ever come from a Black person than the one published below, the editor has not seen it.

We would like to know what rights the white people of this land are going to be able to retain? Step by step their dearest and most cherished prerogatives are being invaded, and *The Crisis* wants to say right here and now that it does not countenance oppression of the downtrodden whites by arrogant black folk. A few years ago the right to kick a darky off the sidewalk was unquestioned in the most devout circles, and yet to-day they actually complain at being called by their front names.

Everybody knows that for three hundred years the most jealously guarded right of white men in this land of ours has been the right to seduce black women without legal, social or moral penalty. Many white mothers and daughters of the best families have helped to maintain this ancient and honored custom by loading the victims of their fathers' and husbands' lust with every epithet of insult and degradation. Thus has the sweet cleanness of their own race virtue shone holier and higher.

Yet what do we see to-day? The black husbands and brothers are beginning to revolt. In three separate cases, in three consecutive months and in three localities of the southern South have these blind and ignorant fellows actually killed white men who were demanding these ancient rights, and have compelled the chivalry of the land to rise and lynch the black defenders of defenceless virtue; also two strangely illogical black women have been simultaneously killed and a dark and whimpering little girl burned to a quivering crisp.

What does all this mean? Does it portend an unthinkable time when the white man can only get his rights by lynching impudent black husbands and squeamish sweethearts? If so, then, by the Great Jehovah, we can depend on the best friends of the Negro to vindicate the ancient liberties of this land! Anglo-Saxon freedom seems safe at least in the hands of most leaders of Southern society, not to mention the blue blood of Pennsylvania.

Meantime, dear colored brethren, we confess to the error of our ways. We have steadfastly opposed lynching on all occasions, but the South is converting us. We acknowledge our fault. Hereafter we humbly pray that every man, black or white, who is anxious to defend women, will be willing to be lynched for his faith. Let black men especially kill lecherous white invaders of their homes and then take their lynching gladly like men.

It's worth it!

Editorial, *The Crisis*, March, 1912; III, p. 197.

12

A BLACK MAN'S APPEAL TO HIS
WHITE BROTHERS
by R. S. Lovingood

Dr. Lovingood, president of Samuel Houston College in Austin, Texas, wrote the public appeal that follows; it was widely published—including in *The Literary Digest* and in *The Crisis* (March, 1912, p. 196).

I was in a Northern city recently. I was a stranger. I was hungry. There was food, food on every hand. I had money, and finally I was compelled to feast on a box of crackers and a piece of cheese. I did not ask to eat with the white people, but I did ask to eat.

I was traveling. I got off at a station almost starved. I begged the keeper of a restaurant to sell me a lunch in a paper and hand it out of the window. He refused, and I was compelled to ride a hundred miles farther before I could get a sandwich.

I was in a white church on official business. It was a cold, blowing day, raining, sleeting, freezing. Warm lunch was served in the basement to my white brothers. I could not sit in the corner of that church and eat a sandwich. I had to go nearly two miles in the howling winds and sleet to get a lunch.

I have seen in the South white and black workingmen elbowing each

other, eating their lunches at noon and smoking the pipe of peace.
Worldly men give me a welcome in their stores. The Government post
office serves me without discrimination. But not so in that church run
in the name of Jesus.

I could not help but feel that Jesus, too, like me, an unwelcome visitor, was shivering in the cold, and could not find a place in that inn,
and was saying: "I was an hungered and ye gave me no meat. I was
thirsty and you gave me no drink." For Jesus was not an Anglo-Saxon.

I went to a station to purchase my ticket. I was there thirty minutes
before the ticket office was opened. When the ticket office opened I at
once appeared at the window. While the agent served the white
people at the other side I remained there beating the window
until the train pulled out. I was compelled to jump on the train without
my ticket and wire back to have my trunk expressed to me. Considering
the temper of the people, the separate-coach law may be the wisest
plan for the conditions in the South, but the statement of "equal accommodations" is all bosh and twaddle. I pay the same money, but I cannot have a chair car, or lavatory, and rarely a through car. I must
crawl out all through the night in all kinds of weather, and catch another "Jim Crow" coach. This is not a request to ride with white people.
It is a request for justice, for "equal accommodations" for the same
money. I made an attempt to purchase some cheap land in a frontier
section. The agent told me that the settlers, most of whom were North-
erners, would not tolerate a Negro in that section. So I could not purchase it. I protest.

I rode through a small town in Southern Illinois. When the train
stopped I went to the car steps to take a view of the country. This is
what greeted me: "Look here, darkey, don't get off at this station." I
put my head out of the window at a certain small village in Texas,
whose reputation was well known to me. This greeted me: "Take
your head back, nigger, or we will knock it off."

13

VOTES FOR WOMEN
by W. E. B. Du Bois

The enhancement of the rights and status of women was urged from early
in the nineteenth century by various Afro-Americans.* Du Bois was out-
* See, for example, the letter from "Matilda," in my first volume (I, 89).

standing in this regard and a typical illustration is the following *Crisis* editorial published seven years prior to the passage of the nineteenth Amendment.

Why should the colored voter be interested in woman's suffrage? There are three cogent reasons. First, it is a great human question. Nothing human must be foreign, uninteresting or unimportant to colored citizens of the world. Whatever concerns half mankind concerns us. Secondly, any agitation, discussion or reopening of the problem of voting must inevitably be a discussion of the right of black folk to vote in America and Africa. Essentially the arguments for and against are the same in the case of all groups of human beings. The world with its tendencies and temptations to caste must ever be asking itself how far may the governed govern? How far can the responsibility of directing, curbing and encouraging mankind be put upon mankind? When we face this vastest of human problems frankly, most of us, despite ourselves and half unconsciously, find ourselves strangely undemocratic, strangely tempted to exclude from participation in government larger and larger numbers of our neighbors. Only at one point, with disconcerting unanimity, do we pause, and that is with ourselves. That we should vote we cannot for a moment doubt even if we are willing to acknowledge, as most of us are, that we are neither all wise nor infinitely good.

This fact should give us pause; if we in our potent weakness and shortcomings see the vast necessity for the ballot not only for our own selfish ends, but for the larger good of all our neighbors, do not our neighbors see the same necessity? And is not the unanswerable cogency of the argument for universal suffrage regardless of race or sex merely a matter of the point of view? Merely a matter of honestly putting yourself in the position of the disfranchised, and seeing the world through their eyes? The same arguments and facts that are slowly but surely opening the ballot box to women in England and America must open it to black men in America and Africa. It only remains for us to help the movement and spread the argument wherever we may.

Finally, votes for women mean votes for black women. There are in the United States three and a third million adult women of Negro descent. Except in the rural South, these women have larger economic opportunity than their husbands and brothers and are rapidly becoming better educated. One has only to remember the recent biennial convention of colored women's clubs with its 400 delegates to realize how the women are moving quietly but forcibly toward the intellectual leadership of the race. The enfranchisement of these women will not be a mere doubling of our vote and voice in the nation; it will tend to stronger and more normal political life, the rapid dethronement of the "heeler" and "grafter" and the making of politics a method of broadest philanthropic race betterment, rather than a disreputable means of private gain. We sincerely trust that the entire Negro vote will be cast for woman suffrage in the coming elections in Ohio, Kansas, Wisconsin and Michigan.

Editorial, *The Crisis,* September, 1912; IV, 234.

14

WOODROW WILSON: RHETORIC AND REALITY

Some Black people—including Du Bois and Bishop Walters—hoped that Wilson's promises of a "New Freedom" did not mean to exclude them. The reality, therefore, was to be all the more bitter. Illustrating this are four documents. The first, [a], originally was published last but it contains the pre-election promise made in writing to Bishop Walters; document [b], from the Reverend Francis J. Grimké, written just after Wilson's election in November, 1912, conveys a sense of the hope widely felt; document [c], from *The Crisis*—through Du Bois' pen—shows the persistence of this hope and spells out its programmatic content; the final document, [d], is a petition from the N.A.A.C.P. board, already reflecting—less than six months after Wilson's inauguration—the bitter disappointment in the deeply racist nature of Wilson's "New Freedom."

[a]

WILSON TO BISHOP WALTERS

During the campaign of 1912, in response to an invitation to be present at a mass meeting at Carnegie Hall, under the auspices of the National Colored Democratic League, of which I was president, I received the following letter from Hon. Woodrow Wilson, then Democratic candidate for President:

38 W. State St., Trenton, N.J.

My dear Bishop Walters:

It is a matter of genuine disappointment to me that I shall not be able to be present at the meeting on Saturday night, but inasmuch as I am cancelling every possible engagement, in view of the distressing assault upon Mr.

Roosevelt, I do not feel that I can properly add others. I am fulfilling only those to which I have been bound for many weeks.

It would afford me pleasure to be present, because there are certain things I want to say. I hope that it seems superfluous to those who know me, but to those who do not know me perhaps it is not unnecessary for me to assure my colored fellow-citizens of my earnest wish to see justice done them in every matter, and not mere grudging justice, but justice executed with liberality and cordial good feeling. Every guarantee of our law, every principle of our Constitution, commands this, and our sympathies should also make it easy.

The colored people of the United States have made extraordinary progress towards self-support and usefulness, and ought to be encouraged in every possible and proper way. My sympathy with them is of long standing, and I want to assure them through you that should I become President of the United States they may count on me for absolute fair dealing and for everything by which I could assist in advancing the interests of their race in the United States.

Very cordially yours,
Woodrow Wilson

Personally, Mr. Wilson, since becoming President, has been very kind to me, as will be seen by further reference in this chapter. But so far as my race is concerned, I regret to say that he has failed to realize any of the expectations raised by his fair promises and sweet-sounding phrases about justice and equal opportunity uttered in pre-election days. His "New Freedom," it seems, has been all for the white man and little for the Negro. One can hardly reconcile his resentment of the manly presentation of the Negro's cause by Mr. Monroe Trotter, editor of the Boston *Guardian,* with the liberal sentiments toward the colored man quoted in the above letter.

Contrary to the precedent established by former Presidents of either party, Mr. Wilson has up to this writing never visited any colored school, church or gathering of colored people of any nature whatever. It has been the custom of the President of the United States to be present at the commencement exercises of Howard University and the Washington Colored Schools at some time during his administration; the administration of President Wilson, in spite of his assurance of sympathy with the race and the fact that they could "count upon him for everything by which he could assist in advancing the interests of the race," has been a notable exception to this pleasant custom.

Alexander Walters, *My Life and Work* (New York, 1917), pp. 194–96.

[b]

FRANCIS J. GRIMKÉ TO WOODROW WILSON

Washington, D.C., November 20, 1912

Dear Sir:

I am a colored man. I am a graduate of the Princeton Theological Seminary. I am pastor of the Fifteenth Street Presbyterian Church of Washington City where I came immediately after my graduation in 1878.

You may not know it, but the triumph of the Democratic Party has always been attended, more or less, with a sense of uneasiness on the part of the colored people for fear lest their rights might be interfered with. It is unfortunate that the ascendency of any party in this country should seem to any class of citizens to imperil their rights. But such, unquestionably, is the feeling on the part of the great majority of the colored people, induced by what has been the general attitude of the Democratic Party towards their rights as citizens. I have shared, somewhat, this feeling myself. I have just finished reading, however, an address by you, made, I should judge, to a body of Sunday school teachers, on the "Importance of Bible Study," and printed in the November number of the *Expositor,* and cannot tell you how greatly it has relieved my mind as to the treatment which the colored people are likely to receive from you and your Administration. I said to myself, No American citizen, white or black, need have any reasonable grounds of fear from the Administration of a man who feels as he does, who believes as he does in the Word of God, and who accepts as he does, without any reservation, the great, eternal, and immutable principles of righteousness for which that Word stands.

This impression, in the light of that address, was so strongly borne in upon my mind, that I felt that I would like to have you know it. The simple fact is, the only hope which the colored man has of fair treatment in this country, is to be found in men, who like yourself, believe in God and in his Son, Jesus Christ, and who feel that the greatest service they can render to their fellow men is to square their lives with the principles of the Christian religion, and to bear about with them ever the noble and beautiful spirit of the Man of Nazareth.

With a man of your known Christian character at the head of affairs, I am sure that the race with which I am identified will have no just grounds for complaint. It is a comforting thought, especially, to those who are struggling against great odds, to know that the God of Abraham, of Isaac, and of Jacob—the God that the Bible reveals, is on the throne, and that under Him, as His vice-regent, will be a man who has the courage of his convictions, and who will not falter where duty calls.

You have my best wishes, and the earnest prayer that you may be guided by Divine wisdom in the arduous duties and responsibilities that are so soon to devolve upon you as the Chief Executive of this great nation.

I am,
Very truly yours,
Francis J. Grimké

Carter G. Woodson, ed., *The Works of Francis J. Grimké*, 4 vols. (Washington: Associated Publishers, 1942), IV (*Letters*), 129–30 (hereafter cited as *Francis J. Grimké*).

[c]

AN OPEN LETTER TO WOODROW WILSON

Your inauguration to the Presidency of the United States is to the colored people, to the white South and to the nation a momentous occasion. For the first time since the emancipation of slaves the government of this nation—the Presidency, the Senate, the House of Representatives and, practically, the Supreme Court—passes on the 4th of March into the hands of the party which a half century ago fought desperately to keep black men as real estate in the eyes of the law.

Your elevation to the chief magistracy of the nation at this time shows not simply a splendid national faith in the perpetuity of free government in this land, but even more, a personal faith in you.

We black men by our votes helped to put you in your high position. It is true that in your overwhelming triumph at the polls you might have succeeded without our aid, but the fact remains that our votes helped elect you this time, and that the time may easily come in the near future when without our 500,000 ballots neither you nor your party can control the government.

True as this is, we would not be misunderstood. We do not ask or expect special consideration or treatment in return for our franchises. We did not vote for you and your party because you represented our best judgment. It was not because we loved Democrats more, but Republicans less and Roosevelt least, that led to our action.

Calmly reviewing our action we are glad of it. It was a step toward political independence, and it was helping to put into power a man who has to-day the power to become the greatest benefactor of his country since Abraham Lincoln.

We say this to you, sir, advisedly. We believe that the Negro problem is in many respects the greatest problem facing the nation, and we believe that you have the opportunity of beginning a just and righteous solution of this burning human wrong. This opportunity is yours because, while a Southerner in birth and tradition, you have escaped the provincial training of the South and you have not had burned into your soul desperate hatred and despising of your darker fellow men.

You start then where no Northerner could start, and perhaps your only real handicap is peculiar lack of personal acquaintance with individual black men, a lack which is the pitiable cause of much social misery and hurt. A president of Harvard or Columbia would have known a few black men as men. It is sad that this privilege is denied a president of Princeton, sad for him and for his students.

But waiving this, you face no insoluble problem. The only time when the Negro problem is insoluble is when men insist on settling it wrong by asking absolutely contradictory things. You cannot make 10,000,000 people at one and the same time servile and dignified, docile and self-reliant, servants and independent leaders, segregated and yet part of the industrial organism, disfranchised and citizens of a democracy, ignorant and intelligent. This is impossible and the impossibility is not factitious; it is in the very nature of things.

On the other hand, a determination on the part of intelligent and decent Americans to see that no man is denied a reasonable chance for life, liberty and happiness simply because of the color of his skin is a simple, sane and practical solution of the race problem in this land. The education of colored children, the opening of the gates of industrial opportunity to colored workers, absolute equality of all citizens before the law, the civil rights of all decently behaving citizens in places of public accommodation and entertainment, absolute impartiality in the granting of the right of suffrage—these things are the bedrock of a just solution of the rights of man in the American Republic.

Nor does this solution of color, race and class discrimination abate one jot or tittle the just fight of humanity against crime, ignorance, inefficiency and the right to choose one's own wife and dinner companions.

Against this plain straight truth the forces of hell in this country are fighting a terrific and momentarily successful battle. You may not realize this, Mr. Wilson. To the quiet walls of Princeton where no Negro student is admitted the noise of the fight and the reek of its blood may have penetrated but vaguely and dimly.

But the fight is on, and you, sir, are this month stepping into its arena. Its virulence will doubtless surprise you and it may scare you as it scared one William Howard Taft. But we trust not; we think not.

First you will be urged to surrender your conscience and intelligence in these matters to the keeping of your Southern friends. They "know the Negro," as they will continually tell you. And this is true. They do know "the Negro," but the question for you to settle is whether or not the Negro whom they know is the real Negro or the Negro of their vivid imaginations and violent prejudices.

Whatever Negro it is that your Southern friends know, it is your duty to know the real Negro and know him personally. This will be no easy task. The embattled Bourbons, from the distinguished Blease to the gifted Hoke Smith, will evince grim determination to keep you from contact with any colored person. It will take more than general good will on your part to foil the wide conspiracy to make Negroes known to their fellow Americans not as flesh and blood but as beasts of fiction.

You must remember that the ability, sincerity and worth of one-tenth of the population of your country will be absolutely veiled from you unless you make effort to lift the veil. When you make that effort, then more trouble will follow. If you tell your Southern friends that you have discovered that the internal revenue of New York is well collected and administered, they are going to regard you in pained surprise. Can a Negro administer! they will exclaim, ignoring the fact that he does.

But it is not the offices at your disposal, President Woodrow Wilson, that is the burden of our great cry to you. We want to be treated as men. We want to vote. We want our children educated. We want lynching stopped. We want no longer to be herded as cattle on street cars and railroads. We want the right to earn a living, to own our own property and to spend our income unhindered and uncursed. Your power is limited? We know that, but the power of the American people is unlimited. To-day you embody that power, you typify its ideals. In the name then of that common country for which your fathers and ours have bled and toiled, be not untrue, President Wilson, to the highest ideals of American Democracy.

Respectfully yours,
THE CRISIS

Editorial, *The Crisis*, March, 1913; V, 236–37.

[d]

FROM THE BOARD OF THE N.A.A.C.P.

New York, Aug. 15, 1913

To WOODROW WILSON, *President of the United States.*

Dear Mr. President:

The National Association for the Advancement of Colored People, through its Board of Directors, respectfully protests the policy of your Administration in segregating the colored employees in the Departments at Washington. It realizes that this new and radical departure has been recommended, and is now being defended, on the ground that by giving certain bureaus or sections wholly to colored employees they are thereby rendered safer in possession of their offices and are less likely to be ousted or discriminated against. We believe this reasoning to be fallacious. It is based on a failure to appreciate the deeper significance of the new policy; to understand how far reaching the effects of such a drawing of caste lines by the Federal Government may be, and how humiliating it is to the men thus stigmatized.

Never before has the Federal Government discriminated against its civilian employees on the ground of color. Every such act heretofore has been that of an individual State. The very presence of the Capitol and of the Federal flag has drawn colored people to the District of Columbia in the belief that living there under the shadow of the National Government itself they are safe from the persecution and discrimination which follow them elsewhere because of their dark skins. Today they learn that, though their ancestors have fought in every war in behalf of the United States, in the fiftieth year after Gettysburg and Emancipation, this Government, founded on the theory of complete equality and freedom for all citizens, has established two classes among its civilian employees. It has set the colored apart as if mere contact with them were contamination. The efficiency of their labor, the principles of scientific management are disregarded, the possibilities of promotion if not now will soon be severely limited. To them is held out only the prospect of mere subordinate routine service without the stimulus of advancement to high office by merit, a right deemed inviolable for all white natives as for the children of the foreign born, of Italians, French and Russians, Jews and Christians who are now entering the Government service. For to such limitation this segregation will inevitably lead. Who took the trouble to ascertain what our colored clerks thought about this order, to which their consent was never asked? Behind screens and closed doors they now sit apart as though leprous. Men and women alike have the badge of inferiority pressed upon them by Government decree. How long will it be before the hateful epithets of "nigger" and "Jim-Crow" are openly applied to these sections? Let any one experienced in Washington affairs, or any trained newspaper correspondent answer. The colored people themselves will tell you how soon sensitive and high-minded members of their race will refuse to enter the Government service which thus decrees what is to them the most hateful kind of discrimination. Indeed, there is a widespread belief among them that this is the very purpose of these unwarrantable orders. And wherever there are men who rob the Negroes of their votes, who exploit and degrade and insult and lynch those whom they call their inferiors, there this mistaken action of the Federal Government will be cited as the warrant for new racial outrages that cry out to high Heaven for redress. Who shall say where discrimination once begun shall cease? Who can deny that every act of discrimination the world over breeds fresh injustice?

For the lowly of all classes you have lifted up your voice and not in vain. Shall ten millions of our citizens say that their civic liberties and rights are not safe in your hands? To ask the question is to answer it. They desire a "New Freedom," too, Mr. President, yet they include in that term nothing else than the rights guaranteed them by the Constitution under which they believe they should be protected from persecution based upon a physical quality with which Divine Providence has endowed them.

They ask therefore that you, born of a great section which prides itself upon its chivalry towards the humble and the weak, prevent a gross injustice which is an injustice none the less because it was actuated in some quarters by a genuine desire to aid those now discriminated against.

Yours, for justice

THE NATIONAL ASSOCIATION FOR THE ADVANCEMENT
OF COLORED PEOPLE

By Moorfield Storey, *President*

W. E. Burghardt Du Bois, *Director of Publicity*

Oswald Garrison Villard, *Chairman of the Board*

A printed folder from the N.A.A.C.P., containing this heading: "The following may be published in morning papers of Monday, August 18, without further notice of release.

Melville E. Stone,
General Manager, The Associated Press."

The above is in the editor's possession. The text was prominently carried in many papers—as the Cleveland *Plain Dealer*, August 18, 1913.

Earlier in 1913 a "strictly confidential" *Proposal for a National Commission to be appointed by the President of the United States* was presented (in printed folder form) to Wilson by the N.A.A.C.P. leadership, but Wilson rejected the suggestion. There is a revealing essay by Oswald Garrison Villard, "Woodrow Wilson and the Negro," in *The Crisis*, December, 1938 (XLV, 384–85), which tells of Villard's meeting with Wilson in October, 1913, and the failure to dent his racist policies.

15

FOR AN AFRO-AMERICAN LITERATURE
by William H. Ferris

One of the earliest explicit calls for a racially conscious Afro-American literature came from William H. Ferris (1874–1941). Prior to his two-volume work, *The African Abroad,* from which the following selection is taken, Ferris had published *Typical Negro Traits*. He was a member of The Negro Society for Historical Research which preceded Carter G. Woodson's Association for the Study of Negro Life and History, to be founded in 1915. For a time in the nineteen twenties Ferris was prominently associated with Marcus Garvey's movement.

But in adapting itself to the ideals and standards of an Anglo-Saxon civilization the Negro went too far in taking his ideas ready-made from the Anglo-Saxon, and in letting his Caucasian brother do his thinking for him. The result is that Negro writers and speakers only utter commonplaces and platitudes. They efface their individuality and lack originality. The style of these colored writers lacks the color and flavor of individuality. The tropical imagination and ardent temperament of the Negro ought to give richness and warmth to his style, ought to cause the Negro essayists and journalists to excel in the sensational, picturesque and spectacular kind of writing. But in pruning their style and modeling it after the models of English prose, these colored writers not only prune off their flamboyant barbaric extravagances but lose virility and a terse, trenchant and telling way of putting things. What does that quality called magic of style or charm of style consist in? When the writer's style expresses his own personality, and his personality is interesting, there is a flavor to his style that charms us in spite of the fact that he cannot coin those magic phrases that haunt the memory and linger in the mind for days. We get up from reading his easy, natural colloquial ways of putting things, feeling that we have had a heart-to-heart talk with him.

When colored men write as colored men and not as white men, only then will they be interesting. In assimilating the culture and traditions of Anglo-Saxons, they must not lose their rich and luxuriant African heritage, they must not lose the barbaric splendor of the African imagination or the fervid eloquence of the native African. The charm of individuality is the charm of naturalness. This is true of manners, and of writing and speaking, and acting and reading and reciting. The full meaning and significance of Emerson's now hackneyed phrase, "Be yourself," should dawn upon the budding Negro writer. The world will always lend a listening ear to the writer or speaker who has a message for it from out of the heart of the eternal. The man who has a personality and an individuality, who is rooted and grounded upon his own convictions, and whose writings reflect and reveal that personality, will always be listened to.

The Negro race must come to a consciousness of itself before it can produce great literature. The civilization of a people is reflected in its literature. Literature is something that wells up spontaneously from the soul-depths of the race. It is the expression, in artistic form, of the deep-seated thought and feelings, dreams and longings of the race.

W. H. Ferris, *The African Abroad, or, His Evolution in Western Civilization Tracing His Development Under Caucasian Milieu,* 2 vols. (New Haven: Tuttle, Morchirise & Taylor, 1913), I, 267–68.

16

"A GLORIOUS SIGHT TO SEE"—THE I.W.W. IN LOUISIANA IN 1913

The Brotherhood of Timber Workers was established by workers in 1910 in Louisiana, Arkansas, and Texas; it was strongest in the former state. In 1912 the Brotherhood joined the Industrial Workers of the World (I.W.W.); following this, the Brotherhood sought to force the companies to pay monthly wages in money and not in scrip, to curtail company stores, to recognize the union, and to raise wages. The Southern Lumber Operators' Association locked out men at scores of mills and the workers retaliated with strikes. Of some thirty-five thousand workers in the Brotherhood, about half were Black and the unity of these workers in the South was marked. Some concessions were won by the workers, but after three years of violence, intimidation, and racist propaganda, the Brotherhood was terribly weakened for a time. From the Afro-American press of the time comes the following account.

The timber workers are striking at Merryville, La. The strikers in a circular say:

It is a glorious sight to see, this miracle that has happened here in Dixie. This coming true of the "impossible"—this union of the workers regardless of color, creed or nationality. To hear the Americans saying, "You can starve us, but you cannot whip us"; the Negroes crying "You can fence us in, but you cannot make us scab"; the Italians singing the *Marseillaise* and the Mexicans shouting vivas for the Brotherhood. Never did the Sante Fe Railroad, the Southern Lumber Operators' Association and the American Lumber Company expect to see such complete and defiant solidarity, else they would have thought long and hard before the infamous order penalizing men for obeying the summons of a court was issued.

From "Along the Color Line," in *The Crisis,* February, 1913; V, 164.

17

WORK FOR BLACK FOLK IN 1914
by W. E. B. Du Bois

As Dr. Du Bois notes in the postscript to the following essay, it was written at the request of the liberal magazine, the *Survey,* but its editors refused to publish it with item six and Du Bois refused to allow its deletion. It conveys, with characteristic clarity, demands being raised at the time by decisive segments of the Afro-American population.

American citizens of Negro descent and their friends have much to do in 1914, if they are to stem the rising tide of racial proscription.

First—They must meet the new attack on property rights of colored people which, under the name of "segregation" and under the excuse of such equitable adjustment of social relations as to avoid "friction," is really a widespread attempt to prevent colored people from making good investments or living in decent homes. Its latest appearance is directed toward preventing Negroes from buying agricultural land, and against this last and most dangerous propaganda what honest American can withhold his influence and help?

Second—The attack on property is the natural child of the refusal of the right to work to Negroes. The year 1914 should see a determined attempt to break down the rules and customs which bar black men from labor unions and discriminate against them in other ways in their attempt to earn a living. The worst examples of this are in the contract labor laws of the South which virtually legalize peonage in agriculture. All of the advance labor legislation in the South specifically excepts "agriculture and housework"!

Third—We might wait for all-healing time and reason in these economic difficulties if education was all right. But education for Negroes is awry, and our work for 1914 is to begin to right it. Under the guise of introducing "industrial" training the colored city public school has, first, been differentiated from the white system; secondly, shortened in length so as to end at the sixth and seventh grades, while the white schools have usually ten and twelve grades; and, finally, it is now openly proposed to so change the character of grade work that even the lower-grade work will not be concentrated on reading, writing and ciphering, but will teach Negroes to work, which, as Supervisor Guy, of Charleston [S.C.], thinks, is more important than their learning to read. Of course the majority of Negroes in the country districts have no decent school facilities at all and here, surely, is work for 1914.

Fourth—The civil rights of Negroes need defense in 1914. The annoying and illegal race discrimination in the civil service, in hotels, restaurants, theatres, churches and Young Men's Christian Associations must be squarely and frankly investigated and systematically opposed.

Fifth—The robbery of the Negroes' political rights is the cause, and was intended to be the cause, of the invasion of the Negroes' civil, educational and economic rights. Disfranchisement for race or sex must go, and the work of 1914 is flatly and fearlessly to restore democratic government in the South and overthrow the oligarchy which rests on the worst rotten borough system known to the modern world in civilized States.

Sixth—Finally, in 1914, the Negro must demand his social rights: His right to be treated as a gentleman when he acts like one, to marry any sane, grown person who wants to marry him, and to meet and eat with his friends without being accused of undue assumption or unworthy ambition.

This is the black man's program for 1914, and the more difficult it looks the more need for following it courageously and unswervingly. It is not a radical program—it is conservative and reasonable.

P.S.—The above statement was solicited by the *Survey* and accepted; then it was returned because the writer refused to omit number six!

The Crisis, February, 1914; VII, 186–87.

18

"TOO READY TO SACRIFICE OUR RIGHTS"
by Francis J. Grimké

A spirit very similar to that infusing the preceding document from Dr. Du Bois is the following entry from the Reverend Grimké. This was written sometime in September, 1914, in what Carter G. Woodson, editor of Grimké's works, called "Stray Thoughts and Meditations."

Dr. Booker T. Washington told the colored people of Burlington, N.J., Sept. 8, 1914, that instead of fighting segregation they had better give their attention to improving their homes, so that white people would not object to living near them.

The implication here is, that the reason why white people object to living near colored people is because their homes are shabbily kept. Now Dr. Washington knew perfectly well that such was not the case. The objection is not to living near the poorer and lower classes of colored people, but to living near any class of colored people. The more advanced the colored people are the greater is the objection. And, for the reason, they are the ones, they think, who are anxious for social equality. Mr. Washington knows this perfectly well; and the ignoring of this fact which he did in his Burlington speech was purposely done, evidently, with a view of currying favors with the whites upon whom he was dependent for money to carry on his work. In this way the weight of his influence was thrown against the anti-segregation agitation, which he knew the whites were opposed to; but which the better think-ing, self-respecting members of the race all over the country were steadily pushing.

And this is in line with what has been Mr. Washington's policy all along. And, it is because of this cowardly, hypocritical course on his part, that the enemies of the race, even the bitterest, have always been able to quote him in support of their low estimate of the race and of the treatment that ought to be accorded to it. Mr. Washington ought to be heartily ashamed of himself; and, one reason why, the most intelligent, manly, self-respecting elements of the race, have so little regard for him is because he is so lacking in manly self-respect, and in loyalty to those great fundamental principles of human rights, without which life is not worth living. Mr. Washington has been too ready to sacrifice the rights of his race for a temporary material advantage. Out of such a spirit there never can come the highest moral and spiritual development. Men who stress, as he does, success as measured by mere material well-being, are never exponents of a lofty morality, theoretically or practically. They move on the lower plane of the material, and estimate things by material values or standards. The great man, in Mr. Washington's estimation, is the man who owns the most property, carries on the largest business, has the biggest bank account, which is a wretchedly poor way of estimating greatness or worth.

19

THE TROTTER ENCOUNTER
WITH PRESIDENT WILSON

Dr. Du Bois' previously quoted editorial and the Reverend Grimké's "meditations" came to life in the encounter between the redoubtable William Monroe Trotter and President Wilson in November, 1914. This created a sensation in the nation and was front-page news in both the white and Afro-American press. The account that follows is taken from pages one and three of the *Chicago Defender* for November 21, 1914; headlines and subheads are reprinted as in that newspaper.

AFRO-AMERICANS DO NOT
CRINGE; PRESIDENT OF
U.S. BECOMES INCENSED

William Monroe Trotter, Editor of the Boston Guardian, Arouses Ire of Nation's Chief Executive As Spokesman of Committee Protesting Against Segregation of Race Employees in Federal Service

TALKS TO PRESIDENT AS ANY AMERICAN SHOULD

In Fervor of Plea for Justice for His People Speaker Forgets to Assume Servile Attitude Once Characteristic of the Race and President Tells Delegation It Must Get Another Chairman If He Receives Them Again

OTHER RACES DEMAND RIGHTS AND ARE NOT CALLED INSOLENT

Washington, D.C., Nov. 20—Thursday afternoon of last week President Wilson became indignant when William Monroe Trotter, editor of the Boston *Guardian,* as chairman of a committee of protest from the National Independence Equal Rights League against the segregation of Afro-American employes in the government departments in Washington, plainly told the nation's chief executive about it.

Waits Two Years

The committee met the president by appointment after waiting a year for a personal interview with him. Mr. Trotter was the spokesman, and in the fervor of his plea for equal rights for his people he forgot the servile manner and speech once characteristic of the Afro-American and he talked to the president as man to man, addressing the head of the government as any American citizen should especially when discussing a serious matter. But the president did not like Mr. Trotter's attitude and said that if the committee came to him again it would have to get a new chairman. The president added he had not been addressed in such a manner since he entered the White House.

No Discrimination Intended

The delegation charged that Secretary McAdoo and Comptroller Williams in the treasury and Postmaster General Burleson had enforced segregation rules in their offices. The president replied that he had investigated the question and had been assured there had been no discrimination in the comforts and surroundings given to the Afro-American workers. He added he had been informed by officials that the segregation had been started to avoid friction between the races and not with the object of injuring the Afro-American employes.

The president said he was deeply interested in the race and greatly admired its progress. He declared the thing to be sought by the Afro-American people was complete independence of white people, and that he felt the white race was willing to do everything possible to assist them.

Seek Neither Charity Nor Aid

Mr. Trotter and other members at once took issue with the president, declaring the Afro-American people did not seek charity or assistance, but that they took the position that they had equal rights with whites and that those rights should be respected. They denied there had been any friction between the two races before segregation was begun.

The president listened to what they had to say, and then told the delegation that Mr. Trotter was losing control of his temper, and that he (the president) would not discuss the matter further with him.

The president is understood to have told the committee the question was not a political one, and that he would not take it up on political grounds.

The delegation presented a resolution of the Massachusetts legislature and letters from several Massachusetts Democratic members of congress protesting against race segregation in the government departments.

Denies Disadvantage Was Intended

The president said he thought his colleagues in the government departments were not trying to put the employes at a disadvantage, but simply to make arrangements which would prevent friction. He added that the question involved was not a question of intrinsic qualities, because all had human souls and were equal in that respect, but that for the present it was a question of economic policy whether the Afro-American race could do the same things that the white race could do with equal efficiency. He said he thought the Afro-American people were proving that they could, and that everyone wished to help them and that their conditions of labor would be bettered. The entire matter, however, should be treated with a recognition of its difficulties. The president said he was anxious to do what was just, and asked for more memoranda from the committee as to the instances of segregation about which they complained.

Did Not Come as Wards

Mr. Trotter said in his address that the committee did not come "as wards or looking for charity, but as full-fledged American citizens vouchsafed equality of citizenship by the federal constitution.

"Two years ago," said Mr. Trotter, "you were thought to be a second Abraham Lincoln." The president tried to interrupt, asking that personalities be left out of the discussion. Mr. Trotter continued to speak and the president finally told him that if the organization he represented wished to approach him again it must choose another spokesman. The president told Mr. Trotter that he was an American citizen as fully as anybody else, but that he (Trotter) was the only American citizen who had ever come into the White House and addressed the president in such a tone and with such a background of passion.

Denied That He Had Passion

Here Mr. Trotter denied that he had any passion, but the president told him he had spoiled the cause for which he had come, and said he expected those who professed to be Christians to come to him in a Christian spirit.

The spokesman continued to argue that he was merely trying to show how the Afro-American people felt, and asserted that he and others were now being branded as traitors to the race because they advised the people "to support the ticket."

This mention of votes caused the president to say politics must be left out, because it was a form of blackmail. He said he would resent it as quickly from one set of men as from another, and that his auditors could vote as they pleased, it mattered little to him.

WILLIAM MONROE TROTTER'S ADDRESS
TO THE PRESIDENT

Full Text of the Protest Against Segregation—The Speech That Upset the Equilibrium of the Nation's Chief Executive

---

(Special to the *Chicago Defender.*)

Washington, D.C., Nov. 20—William Monroe Trotter's address to President Woodrow Wilson Thursday November 12, is as follows:

One year ago we presented a national petition, signed by Afro-Americans in thirty-eight states, protesting against the segregation of employes of the National government whose ancestry could be traced in whole or in part to Africa, as instituted under your administration in the treasury and postoffice departments. We then appealed to you to undo this race segregation in accord with your duty as president and with your pre-election pledges. We stated that there could be no freedom, no respect from others, and no equality of citizenship under segregation for races, especially when applied to but one of the many racial elements in the government employ. For such placement of employes means a charge by the government of physical indecency or infection, or of being a lower order of beings, or a subjection to the prejudices of other citizens, which constitutes inferiority of status. We protested such segregation as to working conditions, eating tables, dressing rooms, rest rooms, lockers and especially public toilets in government buildings. We stated that such segregation was a public humiliation and degradation, entirely unmerited and far-reaching in its injurious effects, a gratuitous blow against ever-loyal citizens and against those many of whom aided and supported your elevation to the presidency of our common country.

Instances Cited

At that time you stated you would investigate conditions for yourself. Now, after the lapse of a year, we have come back having found that all the forms of segregation of government employes of African extraction are still practiced in the treasury and postoffice department buildings, and to a certain extent have spread into other government buildings.

Under the treasury department, in the bureau of engraving and printing there is segregation not only in dressing rooms, but in working positions, Afro-American employes being herded at separate tables, in eating, and in toilets. In the navy department there is herding at desks and separation in lavatories. In the postoffice department there is separation in work for Afro-American women in the alcove on the eighth floor, of Afro-American men in rooms on the seventh floor, with forbidding even of entrance into an adjoining room occupied by white clerks on the seventh floor, and of Afro-American men in separate rooms just instituted on the sixth floor, with separate lavatories for

Afro-American men on the eighth floor; in the main treasury building in separate lavatories in the basement; in the interior department separate lavatories, which were specifically pointed out to you at our first hearing; in the state and other departments in separate lavatories; in marine hospital service building in separate lavatories, though there is but one Afro-American clerk to use it; in the war department in separate lavatories; in the postoffice department building separate lavatories; in the sewing and bindery divisions of the government printing office on the fifth floor there is herding at working positions of Afro-American women and separation in lavatories, and new segregation instituted by the division chief since our first audience with you. This lavatory segregation is the most degrading, most insulting of all. Afro-American employes who use the regular public lavatories on the floors where they work are cautioned and are then warned by superior officers against insubordination.

We have come by vote of this league to set before you this definite continuance of race segregation and to renew the protest and to ask you to abolish segregation of Afro-American employes in the executive department.

Humiliation Alleged

Because we cannot believe you capable of any disregard of your pledges we have been sent by the alarmed American citizens of color. They realize that if they can be segregated and thus humiliated by the national government at the national capital the beginning is made for the spread of that persecution and prosecution which makes property and life itself insecure in the South, the foundation of the whole fabric of their citizenship is unsettled.

They have made plain enough to you their opposition to segregation last year by a national anti-segregation petition, this year by a protest registered at the polls, voting against every Democratic candidate save those outspoken against segregation. The only Democrat elected governor in the eastern states, was Governor Walsh of Massachusetts, who appealed to you by letter to stop segregation.* Thus have the Afro-Americans shown how they detest segregation.

In fact, so intense is their resentment that the movement to divide

* David I. Walsh, Governor, 1914–1915. He represented Massachusetts in the U.S. Senate for five terms, commencing in 1918. In addition to an anti-segregationist stand, Mr. Walsh spoke out for Tom Mooney, favored trade unions and ardently supported Ireland's struggle for full independence. He died in 1947.

this solid race vote and make peace with the national Democracy, so suspiciously revived when you ran for the presidency, and which some of our families for two generations have been risking all to promote, bids fair to be undone.

Only two years ago you were heralded as perhaps the second Lincoln, and now the Afro-American leaders who supported you are hounded as false leaders and traitors to their race. What a change segregation has wrought!

Ask Executive Order

You said that your "Colored fellow citizens could depend upon you for everything which would assist in advancing the interests of their race in the United States." Consider this pledge in the face of the continued color segregation! Fellow citizenship means congregation. Segregation destroys fellowship and citizenship. Consider that any passerby on the streets of the national capital, whether he be black or white, can enter and use the public lavatories in government buildings while citizens of color who do the work of the government are excluded.

As equal citizens and by virtue of your public promises we are entitled at your hands to freedom from discrimination, restriction, imputation and insult in government employ. Have you a "new freedom" for white Americans and a new slavery for your Afro-American fellow citizens? God forbid!

We have been delegated to ask you to issue an executive order against any and all segregation of government employes because of race and color, and to ask whether you will do so. We await your reply, that we may give it to the waiting citizens of the United States of African extraction.

VAST CROWD ATTENDS DENUNCIATION
MASS MEETING SUNDAY

William Monroe Trotter Receives Great Ovation When He Relates Details of His Interview with President Wilson

---

Washington, D.C., Nov. 20—William Monroe Trotter, editor of the Boston *Guardian,* is the "man of the hour." Sunday night at the Second

Baptist Church at a mass meeting held in protest against the segregation policy of the Wilson administration he was given an ovation by more than 2000 citizens, both white and black. When the name of the president was mentioned the crowd groaned.

Mr. Trotter's manly stand at the now famous White House meeting last Thursday has made him the idol of the people. Members of the delegation which went to the White House last week laid their case before the meeting.

Adopt Formal Protest

The meeting adopted a formal protest to the American people against "the pronounced tendency in American law and public opinion to draw the color line."

"We make this appeal at this time," said the statement, "because it has been ascertained by us from the highest authority in the nation that it is the policy of the federal government to draw the color line, to make what the newspapers of the country denominate and denounce as 'Jim Crow' government."

Speakers Approved

At every opportunity the hundreds of people present signified their approval of the speakers. W. Monroe Trotter who was the chief speaker denied he had used insulting or impertinent language to the president at his interview.

"For the first time in history," declared Mr. Trotter, "a president had pronounced his administration's policy as one of racial discrimination. Our delegation wanted him to stop departmental segregation or say where he stood. Now at last, after two years' silence, he has told."

Recalls New Jersey Visit

Trotter then drew a picture of the different reception which Mr. Wilson had accorded a delegation from the Equal Rights League in July, 1912, when he was governor of New Jersey.

"At that time," said Mr. Trotter, "we were received open-handed, we Afro-Americans, over the heads of a score of 'non-Afro-Americans,' who were waiting in the anteroom. The governor had us draw our chairs right up around him, and shook hands with great cordiality. When we left he gave me a long handclasp and used such a pleased tone that I was walking on air. What a change between then and now!"

Other Speakers Voice Denial

Other speakers voiced similar sentiments, all disclaiming that Trotter had been insulting or impertinent, and declaring against the president's attitude. On the platform were many of those who had composed the delegation on Thursday, besides the following; Thomas Walker, Judge C. M. Hewlett, T. T. Fortune, M. W. Spencer, F. Morris Murray and W. Bishop Johnson. At the conclusion of the mass meeting a resolution was adopted appealing to all Afro-Americans to "stand fast for equal rights."

Mr. Trotter and his companions accomplished one thing. They forced the administration to come out in the open on the segregation question. Heretofore there have been more or less qualified statements on that subject ranging from a denial that there is actual separation of the races in the government offices to assertions that the hands of the administration did not authorize it. At this point it is interesting to hear what Mr. Trotter says. The *Chicago Defender* received the following telegram Tuesday.

BOSTON, MASS., NOV. 16—CHICAGO DEFENDER: YOUR CONGRATULATIONS RECEIVED AND READ AT WASHINGTON MEETING SUNDAY. MANY THANKS. I DID NOT INSULT PRESIDENT WILSON, OR LOSE MY TEMPER. HE, HOWEVER, INSULTED EVERY INTELLIGENT, SELF-RESPECTING MEMBER OF THE RACE.— W. M. TROTTER.

The incident has been the talk of the nation. Despite the president's statement to the contrary, it has become a political issue.

20

THE ULTIMATE EFFECTS OF SEGREGATION AND DISCRIMINATION
by William Pickens

William Pickens was born in South Carolina in 1881 and educated at Talladega, Yale, and Fisk. He began his teaching career at Talladega and then went to Wiley University in Texas, at which time he wrote the selection published below. The occasion for the essay was a request from the National Conference of Charities and Correction in Baltimore in May, 1915. Subsequently, Mr. Pickens was a dean at Morgan State College in Baltimore and for a generation served as field secretary of the N.A.A.C.P., commencing in 1920. His best-known book is his autobiography, *Bursting Bonds,* published in 1923.

From a moral point of view the Negro question is the most important question before the American people. And in the long run the morale of a nation will be prepotent among the factors of its destiny. In none of our problems is there more need of the scientific spirit, which seeks the facts, all of the facts, and faces the full meaning of those facts, regardless of prejudice or preconception.

One of the greatest defects in the reasoning of many who have dealt with this problem is the lack of adequate knowledge of the Negro's real interest, motives and opinions. On this question it is very probable that colored people know the opinions of white people much better than white people know the opinion of colored people: the Negro reads the white man's opinion in the daily, weekly and monthly press; he hears it reiterated in the debates of Congress and in a dozen state legislatures; he hears the white man talk much oftener than the white man hears him talk. The inevitable result is that the Negro knows his own opinion and the white man's too, while the white man as a rule knows only his own opinion. This lack of contemporary knowledge concerning the Negro causes many white speakers to appeal to far-fetched evidence, even to the foreordainments of providence: ever since my childhood I have heard it said that providence ordained the Negro for such and such a destiny, and that God created the Negro to be so-and-so. I learned later that the creation antedates all history and all human experience, so that its facts and motives are inadmissible evidence. My faith has been further shaken by the gradual discovery that those who quote providence are almost without exception the Negro's most active enemies, and the Negro should be very suspicious of a providence that reveals its will concerning him only to his enemies.

In our present discussion we aim to state plainly the ultimate meaning of segregation and discrimination in the life of the American Negro; and we make less appeal to providences, which we understand not, than to the evidences of our senses and to the ordinary everyday arguments of justice and humanity.

Why does the Negro oppose:

Jim Crow Cars,
Residential Segregation,
Civil Service Segregation,
Separate School Laws, in large Northern cities with large Negro population,
And Laws Forbidding the Intermarriage of the Races, in places where such
   prohibition has not heretofore been established?
And finally, what does the Negro want with full, voting citizenship?

How many of the Negro's friends know the motives behind his attitude? I admit that I have great patience with those who are shocked at his position on the intermarriage question, and that is just why I shall state plainly the motives which hold the Negro to this position, so that his sincere friends may judge for themselves whether there be any justice in his contention. I have learned through my acquaintance with some of these friends that the shock which they feel arises not from the Negro's real motives, which they know not, but from motives which their own imaginations postulate in the Negro. I have even seen some shocked in the opposite direction when they first saw the thing from the Negro's standpoint.

But first as to separate railway cars. The Negro opposes them, and the real motive of his opposition is wrongly assumed to be a desire to ride with white people. The fact is ignored that on every separate car system white people are given superior accommodations and black people are given inferior accommodations. Reverse the conditions and black people would prefer to ride with black people—and some white people would too. In Europe there are first, second and third class accommodations on the railroads. In America the difference between white and black accommodations is often as great as the difference between first and third class in Europe—but in Europe the fares are as different as the accommodations, while in America the fares are the same. Now let an American white man imagine that in Europe he is compelled to ride in third class but to pay for first class, while other travelers, even yellow and black, are admitted to first class for the same fares. When he opposed this arrangement as legalized robbery, what a joke it would be for the yellow and black folks to ask, "Why do you want to get away from your own people?" The truth is, he would want to get away from that injustice and carry all of his "own people" away with him.

But suppose the Negro were given absolutely equal accommodations, what then? That would be a decent supposition if human nature and all of the facts were not against it: nowhere in the whole separate car system has there ever been systematic equality of accommodations. In the majority of cases colored men and women are put into one end of a smoker, not always fully screened off from smoking white passengers.

This is just as if the law required white people and black people to pay three dollars for each pair of shoes but allowed the merchant to sell the Negro, for his three dollars, shoes that were worth only one dollar. In that case a merchant with a large Negro trade could afford to sell to a hard-to-please white customer shoes actually worth more than the three dollars which he paid. The Negro would pay the difference. The passenger in the "jim crow car" supplements the luxury of the "parlor car"—and the same principle of indirect robbery pervades the whole system of jim crowism and segregation in public conveniences.

This glaring financial and material injustice makes it hardly necessary to mention the Christian-democratic argument. But if a people were singled out from among all the other peoples of the world for public stigmatization, that people could hardly be expected to accept it cheerfully even on a plane of absolute equality. An insignificant right becomes important when it is assailed: you do not much value your right to walk the streets bareheaded, but you would claim the right if it were denied. If such a right were successfully denied, the more vital rights would be exposed to attack.

Now, as to segregating Negroes into restricted areas of our cities. Why are Negroes not willing to live by themselves? To live themselves would be more comfortable for the Negroes, all other things being equal. But there's the "rub:" all other things are not equal and will not be, wherever segregation opens the door and lays the temptation to inequality. We speak now of segregation by law; segregation *in fact* has existed since the day of the "slave quarters." Since emancipation this segregation has been more or less continued by buying out the Negro, outwitting his ignorance, and even by violently forcing him out. But against this economic and brute-force opposition the Negro had hope based on at least a fighting chance. He could "fight it out on this line," if it took generations. But the opponent, in spite of his overwhelming advantages in the struggle, has appealed for laws that will eliminate the Negro from the contest altogether.

And why does the Negro oppose legal segregation? Because a generation of experience has taught him the meaning of successful segregation: a general absence of improvements in the Negro sections,—sometimes no pavements, no lights, no sewers, and no police protection against brothels and saloons. The Negro section is equally taxed: they must pay taxes on all the city improvements and bonded indebtedness. This injustice is similar to that imposed by the jim crow car, for the Negro is constantly paying to improve other people's property. If he could live on any street anywhere, this discrimination would be impossible; but legal segregation is a devil which drags in its tail a host of petty discriminations.

To ask the Negro to accept this ghetto and do these things for himself, would be a capital joke if it were not so serious a matter. The Negro could only do that if his section were set apart as an independent municipality, with its own mayor and government and the control over its own taxes—and this will not be allowed.—But, says the opponent, the law is just and equal and constitutional, is it not? It does not discriminate; it says that blacks shall not move in where there is a majority of whites, but it also says that whites shall not move in where there is a majority of blacks. That is constitutional in letter and equal in phraseology, but I believe it is unconstitutional in spirit and I know it is unequal in effect. The effect of a law, and not its rhetorically balanced phrases, should be the test of its constitutionality. It may be literally constitutional to make a law that the rich shall not lend to the poor, nor the poor to the rich,—that the intelligent shall not teach the ignorant, nor the ignorant the intelligent. It should not make a law constitutional to thus simply convert its terms in successive phrases. The segregation law *in effect* means that those who have no homes shall not acquire homes of those who have homes; and aspires to constitutionality by adding that those who have homes shall also not acquire homes of those who have them not.

As to civil service segregation. The Negro's opposition to this type of discrimination, which is new, is not based directly on experience; but it is based indirectly on his experience with other forms of segregation. But his reasoning by analogy is being justified: in the Carolinas, as soon as it proved possible to segregate the Negro railway mail clerks, on one line they were given the hardest runs and put on mostly at night; when bathroom segregation appeared in one of the departments at Washington, it proved convenient to assign the colored women a toilet that faced the one assigned to white men.—Nowhere in this country have the results of segregation inspired the Negro with the hope of a "square deal."

The undermining of the democratic foundation principles of a great government may be even more serious than the injury done the Negro, but in this discussion we are taking up only the Negro's independent case against segregating policies.

The separate school and intermarriage questions come up chiefly in Northern communities where there is not yet a rigid opinion on these matters. Let us feel, if we can, as if we have no interest in the whole matter and are now examining the Negro's side of it for the first time—

not what others said about him but what the Negro says for himself.

The Negroes in Northern communities are generally opposed to the separate school idea and face the usual accusation that they "do not want to associate with their own people," which ignores the more positive reason which the Negro himself advances—the universal temptation and tendency of the school authorities to degrade the Negro schools wherever they have been successfully segregated. The separate system prevails in the South, and in many of those states the neglect of the Negro school is a disgrace to civilization. Besides, there is perhaps not a state in the Union, certainly not in the South, with a segregated school system which gives the Negro an absolutely equal chance for public education. The legislature may determine the amount to be appropriated by a per capita reckoning including black and white, but when this appropriation is expended the Negro child may get only one dollar out of eight or ten, on the same per capita basis. By having been counted equal for appropriation purposes he has helped the white child to a per capita expenditure that is higher than the per capita appropriation. I heard a state supervisor of education say to Negroes that whenever retrenchment was necessary the Negro's share was always trimmed down first. He said that the white officers dislike to do this, but he defended it on the plea of "human nature." Perhaps the Northern Negro who opposes the separate school movement, has reckoned on this same *human nature* and has little hope that mere geography will modify it. He knows that where black and white attend the same school this discrimination is forever impossible.—The Negro pays an equal rate of direct school taxes, and where other forms of discriminaton exist, like jim crow cars and exorbitant rents, he pays a higher indirect tax. A man may pay a tax without knowing the tax exists; the buyer pays the seller—the consumer pays the retailer. Besides, a percentage paid out of poverty means more as a sacrifice than the same percentage paid out of wealth. By the law of marginal utilities, ten per cent to the possessor of a few hundred dollars means more than ten per cent to the possessor of thousands.

Cincinnati, Washington and St. Louis have the best separate schools for the Negro in the United States, and it is significant that the percentage of attendance of colored children at these schools is lower than at the mixed schools of Boston, Cleveland and New York. The percentages of attendance of Negro children from ten to fourteen years of age are these—

In the segregated schools: Cincinnati, 93.1; Washington, 90.5; St. Louis, 89.4.

In the mixed schools: Boston, 95; Cleveland, 94; New York City, 93.1.

These figures, made from the United States Census, indicate at least that even the best separate schools are unfavorable to the attendance of colored children. It is not to be supposed that colored children simply enjoy going to school with white children, where in fact they are often woefully ostracized, but it is rather to be supposed that the white school attracts colored people for the same reason why it would attract any people, because of its superior location and equipment. The low public school attendance of colored children in the South is largely due to the inconveniently located and miserably equipped school houses.

And now we come to the most interesting question of all—the one on which more passion is felt, more opinions expressed and less investigation and thought are put than on any of the others. Why under heaven do Negroes oppose laws forbidding white to marry colored and colored to marry white? Is it not simply because the Negro wants to marry a white person? Some say, the Negro may be right on other questions, but surely he is wrong here: this law cannot possibly discriminate, it always concerns both a white and a colored person, and squares absolutely with the 14th and 15th Amendments. Let us see if the Negro has any decent motive to state for himself. The literal constitutionality of such a law must be admitted; it would also be constitutional to make a law to hang children of six years or to grant divorces for poorly prepared meals—but it would not be humane or wise. It would be a mad legislature that considered only the constitutionality of a bill; bare constitutionality is no proof of its wisdom, its morality or its justice. The ultimate test of a law is its effect—and the Negro claims that the effect of a law forbidding intermarriage is to lower the status of colored women, without raising the status of white women, and that it protects and fosters miscegenation and bastardy. Such a law promotes the very thing it intends to defeat, race intermixture, by giving perfect immunity to the men of the stronger race. It is natural and logical to ask—Does it not give like immunity to the men of the minority race? No. For not since the foundation of human society has any serious problem existed between the men of a weaker and the women of a stronger group. The weak are never tempted to impose upon the strong, and a prohibition of marriage simply further protects the strong in its impositions upon the weak, by nullifying the traditional rule of objective morality which compels the man to accept his mate and acknowledge his offspring. The intermarriage law is in effect a discrimination against the women of the weak. And wherever any race is ninety millions and rich and powerful, while another race is ten millions and poor and disadvantaged, the case will be the same.

The constitutionality of a law, I suppose, can be taken care of in its phraseology, but its wisdom and justification must exist in the conditions to which the law is to apply. This is the special nature of laws intending to regulate the relations of a stronger and a weaker group; for here the actual conditions, the laws of human nature and the laws of relative power must be figured into a fair equation. A color line law is not fair simply because it has "black" written into one phrase and "white" written into the homologous part of the next phrase. It may be unconstitutional in spirit and effect. To show the insecurity of mere verbal equality: if the weaker race were put temporarily in charge of Congress it might think out a law on this very question of miscegenation which would be absolutely "constitutional" in a literal sense and yet bear harder upon the stronger race—for example, "Be it enacted that when a white child is born into the colored race, or a black child is born into the white race, the father of such child is to be immediately hanged." Such a law would not hang one Negro in a hundred thousand, but I know communities, *where the Negro does not vote,* and where such a law would be so unpopular as to be overwhelmingly defeated in a *referendum.*

The primary motive of the black man is not a desire for a mixed family but for the protection of his own colored family. He believes that a law to compel fathers to marry the mothers would break up more miscegenation in a week than a law prohibiting marriage will break up in twenty-five years. This motive is proven by the fact that the Negroes who oppose the prohibitive laws are already married, and would not consent for their children to get into the trouble which it costs to marry a white person in America, legally or illegally. Again the Negro's contention is supported by the United States Census. Listen—in forty years the mulatto part of the population has increased:

- In Michigan, where there are no laws against intermarriage, 48 per cent.
- In Arkansas, where there are strict prohibitive laws, 559 per cent.

It is further noticeable that in Indiana, just over the line from the South and where public sentiment if not the law is prohibitive of lawful relations, the increase of mulattoes was still only 107 per cent,—while in South Carolina, where strict law is added to the most violent sentiment, the increase was about 383 per cent. The law seems to help the violator of "race integrity;" for the mulatto is not a theory, he is a fact. What is the difference between Michigan and Arkansas? In Michigan the man of the stronger race is faced by at least the legal threat of compulsory inter-marriage, if he crosses the line, while in Arkansas he is so far protected by law. I ask in the most solemn earnestness, might it not prove more sobering to a white youth to be directly told, "You would have to marry your colored associate,"—than to be indirectly informed that he will have immunity in that case?

We have purposely confined our discussion to the Negro's vital interest in the question, and have avoided its wider phase—the revolutionary, or the *devolutionary,* idea of taking marriage, the most honorable institution of the human species, and putting it on a legal plane with fornication, adultery and all the other most horrible sins catalogued in the Old and New Testaments. Such a subversion of objective morality may have far-reaching consequences, indeed, in which white and black will reap equally.

These are the opinions and the arguments of practically all of the most intelligent Negroes in the United States, many of whom I know personally, and if they do not convince the race's avowed enemies they should at least cause the impartial to believe that the real motives are not what they are popularly said to be. The intelligent Negro, in his arguments against segregation and discrimination, seldom sinks to the level of mere "social equality" considerations.

Finally, is the reason not now apparent why the Negro wants to vote? Is he after "black supremacy" in a country where his ratio is one to ten and growing less all the time? Segregation and discrimination are a sufficient justification of his desire for the ballot; these evils get their greatest support from disfranchisement, and they vary directly as the Negro's unjust exclusion from participation in self-government. A minority group in a democratic-republican form of government needs the ballot more desperately than the majority group needs it.

It is unfair to expect a white administration to protect the Negro when the Negro has been stripped of his only power to support or check that administration. Neither education nor money will settle the question without the ballot; for a ballotless group cannot command the resources of public education, and a subject and helpless class by growing richer only endangers its life by becoming a more tempting prey to any powerful oppressor. The officers of the law could not, if they would, be impartial to a decitizenized people: the elected are obligated to the electors. A disfranchised group could fare much better under hereditary independent rulers than under elective obligated officers. The very advantages of a democracy make disfranchisement therein the worst of tyrannies. This principle will be true as long as human nature is human and not divine. The only way to insure the Negro against injustice in other particulars is to remove the most effective defense of injustice,— discriminatory disfranchisement. The Negro does not object to impartial disfranchisement, incident upon a failure to meet prescribed and attainable qualifications; the white man may prescribe a college education, if he deem it reasonable and make it impartial.— Besides, the white population outnumbers the Negro population ten to one, and according to the census it is outgrowing the Negro population by immigration and natural increase; so that the statesman does not have to look out for "white supremacy"—the history of three hundred years has already looked out for that. What the statesman does need to look out for is justice to the Negro and the avoidance of national moral degeneration because of injustice to the Negro. Impartial suffrage cannot mean "black supremacy" in America, but would mean healthier self-government by giving the Negro here and there a better chance to speak for himself and locally to defend his nearest and dearest interests.

The Ultimate Effects of Segregation and Discrimination: The Seldom Thought in the Negro Problem (n. p., 1915, published by the author), published above in full.

21

PROTESTING *BIRTH OF A NATION*

As part of the legalization of Jim Crow, starting about 1890 and continuing for some twenty years, there appeared an intensive racist propaganda campaign. Prominent in this was the best-selling novel, *The Clansman* (1905), by Thomas Dixon, Jr., glorifying the K.K.K. This was the basis for *Birth of a Nation,* a movie seen by millions throughout the nation commencing in 1915. Dixon arranged a private showing of this vicious film for President Wilson who remarked: "It is like writing history with lightning and my only regret is that it is all so terribly true." The President approved a showing of the film for Edward White, Chief Justice of the U.S. Supreme Court (See David M. Chalmers, *Hooded Americanism* [Doubleday, 1965], pp. 26–27.)

The Afro-American population mounted a vigorous and prolonged campaign against the showing of this film. Characteristic is [a], a report from Boston in May, 1915, and the publication of a critique of the film by the Reverend F. J. Grimké, which resulted in the correspondence between him and Hollis B. Frissell the (white) head of Hampton Institute, which appears as documents [b] below.

[a]

"BIRTH OF NATION"
PROTESTED AGAIN
Opinion Club Sends Resolutions to Mayor from Faneuil Hall

Faneuil Hall was taxed to its capacity yesterday afternoon at a public meeting held under the auspices of the New Public Opinion Club to commemorate the semi-centennial observation of Memorial day and the fiftieth anniversary of Negro freedom.

Dr. W. E. B. Du Bois was the principal speaker, taking as his subject, "The Outlook for the Future." At the conclusion of Du Bois' address it was voted to send to Mayor James F. Curley this resolution, adopted by a rising vote:

Colored Americans assembled under the auspices of the New Public Opinion Club, on Memorial Sunday, to be addressed by Dr. W. E. B. Du Bois, on "Fifty Years of Negro Freedom" in Faneuil Hall, sacred edifice which, as Boston's mayor rightly says, has ever stood against prejudice, contempt, injustice, enslavement of race, petitions the Boston Censor Board to stop the photoplay *Birth of a Nation,* which teaches race prejudice, racial injustice, racial disfranchisement against colored Americans, falsifying reconstruction.

From Faneuil Hall itself, we protest the proposition that the pictured slander and disparagement of a minority race shall make licensed amusement for the rest of the people. This is but a step from that brutal tyranny when men were slaughtered to make a Roman holiday.

The meeting was presided over by President F. B. Washington, and on the platform with Dr. Du Bois were these officers of the club: Vice President Miss Crystal Bird of Boston Normal School; Secretary Nadine Wright, Radcliffe, 1917; Treasurer John Bowen; Rev. Osmond Walker, Harvard Divinity School; Miss Gertrude O'Neil of the Boston Conservatory of Music, Wesley Howard and Louria Jones.

Boston *Journal,* May 31, 1915.

[b]

HOLLIS B. FRISSELL TO FRANCIS J. GRIMKÉ
Hampton, Virginia, November 6, 1915

Dear Dr. Grimké:

Your pamphlet in regard to *The Birth of a Nation* is at hand. I wonder if it occurred to you to give a little more charitable interpretation to my action concerning the Hampton pictures.

The question came to me in New York as to what could be done about the play. I saw the censors and expressed my strong disapprobation of it, and they told me it would be impossible to discontinue it and that no court would take action against it. Mr. Wilcox, one of the Tuskegee trustees, felt that if it could not be suppressed that it ought to be improved, and that the other side could best be shown by giving some idea of the great advance made by the race in education and industry through the Hampton moving pictures. I consulted with some of my trustees and they approved the suggestion.

I wonder if you have not felt that if you can not alter unfortunate conditions it is wise to attempt to improve them. It seemed to me that here was a chance to show to many thousands of people another side of the colored race than that set forth by this play which is so unfair not only to the Negro but to the white man as well, and I embraced this opportunity with the best of motives. I appreciate how strongly you feel but I want you to see the other side of the affair.

Sincerely yours,

H. B. Frissell

FRANCIS J. GRIMKÉ TO HOLLIS B. FRISSELL

Washington, D.C., November 8, 1915

Dear Dr. Frissell:

I am glad to get your letter, and to have your explanation as to why you allowed your name and the name of Hampton Institute to be associated with the Photo-play, *The Birth of a Nation*. I think I fully appreciate your motive, but still think it was a mistake to have allowed your name and the name of the Institution over which you preside to be in any way connected with a play which is so manifestly hostile to the Negro race. The drama occupies nearly three hours, and only after everything has been done to blacken the character of the Negro, to set him forth in the most repulsive light, is this little annex, consisting of the pictures of Hampton, with your permission to present them blazoned in large letters, tagged on, and tagged on in such a way as to make them of no value in counteracting the bad impression already made against the race,— of no value in accomplishing what you hoped— to accomplish by it. The play is bad, and only bad in its aims and purposes. What you say in reference to "unfortunate conditions which can-

not be changed," may be true; but in our attempt to improve such conditions we ought to be very careful that what we do is not construed into
an endorsement of the very conditions which we are seeking to improve.
The great majority of persons who witness this Photo-drama and these
pictures and your permission to present them in connection with it,
will not think of them as indicating a better outlook for the Negro, but
only of them as showing that you do not feel about the drama as others
do; that you see nothing particularly objectionable about it. The pictures
are presented in such a way as not only to destroy their value, from
your standpoint, but as to make them a positive aid in breaking down
the opposition against the drama that is felt by the colored people, and
by some of the whites. It seems to me, under the circumstances, permission to parade your name, and the pictures of Hampton Institute
in connection with it, ought to be withdrawn. If you were a private individual, and if it had been an institution, not identified as Hampton
has been with the best interest of the colored people, it would be different. Your name, as a known friend of the Negro, and Hampton
Institute, ought not to be used to popularize on, to break down the opposition to this deliberate attempt to destroy the good name of a race.
And one of the things that surprised me was that you did not see that
such would be the effect.

Sincerely yours,
Francis J. Grimké

Woodson, ed., *Francis J. Grimké*, IV, 153–54.

22

MR. B. T. WASHINGTON IN LOUISIANA
by V. P. Thomas

The author, a member of the N.A.A.C.P. and a resident of New Orleans,
conveys in the following article a sense of the public functioning of Booker
T. Washington in the South shortly prior to his death.

THE FACTS

Probably you have heard something of the tour Dr. Booker T. Washington made in Louisiana. It was a round of grand receptions for him
everywhere he went. Thousands saw and heard him speak in Burn's

Arena. Thousands saw and heard him speak in the Dauphine Theatre, and as big a crowd as 5,000 saw and heard him speak at Violet, a settlement in St. Bernard Parish, 18 miles from this city. At New Iberia thousands saw and heard him there, as did thousands at Baton Rouge, Lafayette, Crowley, Lake Charles, Alexandria, Shreveport and Gibbsland, and all applauded his addresses on industrial and agricultural training for the Negro, and their accompanying anecdotes.

An account of his first speech will illustrate the general tenor of his remarks in the various places. This speech was made at Violet.

The party was met by a crowd estimated to number about 5,000 people, including colored school children of all the colored schools of the parish, which were closed by order of the parish superintendent for the occasion. In the gathering was the superintendent of schools himself and other officials of the parish, as well as other white citizens.

To this meeting Dr. Washington made the first address of his tour. He expressed gratification at the evidences of the friendly relations existing between the two races living side by side in the parish of St. Bernard. He said he had long wished to see for himself the actual attitude of the white people and the Negro people toward each other in Louisiana, and that what he had seen on his way from New Orleans to Violet of the wealth of opportunities fully persuaded him that the Negro people needed only to be thrifty, industrious and law-abiding in their habits to help the white people make that section one of the most prosperous and happy in the country. He commented on the apparent fertility and productive quality of the land and urged the Negroes to stick to the farms and farm life and away from the bigger cities.

Dr. Washington thanked the white officials for what was being done for the industrial education of the colored children of the parish and admonished the colored people to take advantage of the opportunities given them to benefit by it. He told them that there was nobody that can get what he wants out of white people easier than a Negro, and that it is seldom, indeed, that a Negro goes after something he wants to get from white people that he fails to get it. He said the white man or woman may swear or fuss at the Negro for bothering them, but the Negro usually gets what he wants just the same.

The inimitable way in which Dr. Washington told this part of his knowledge of the traits of the Negro and the white man tickled the risibles of everybody who heard him; laughter was general. Other amusing anecdotes, the butt of which was Negro character were frequently told to illustrate or emphasize an idea by Dr. Washington during the delivery of his advice and admonition.

Dr. Washington confined his advice wholly to the idea of industrial and domestic training for the Negro, on the theory that an education that is not useful is useless to any boy or girl of the race and that the Negro is adapted especially to agricultural and domestic service. He did not once, in the slightest way, suggest the need of preparation of Negroes for the business of banking, the profession of law, medicine, pharmacy, teaching or the ministry. And the characters he held up as deserving the confidence and admiration of the white people were always such as Uncle Tom, Aunt Chloe, old Aunt Mary, or old Uncle Joe. Men of the Negro race like Frederick Douglass, Crispus Attucks, [John M.] Langston, [Hiram] Revels and others, whose worth and characters first opened the eyes of conscience and the world upon the possibilities of the Negro were never mentioned. Nor did he think to choose any of the number of living men and women of the race to set up as examples before the school children he addressed to emulate.

He said, "The Negro is just 50 years old, and his history in this country is yet to be made."

This speech, with local variations, was made throughout the State of Louisiana to thousands of white and colored people.

COMMENT

There is no doubt that agricultural and industrial training is one of the needs of the Negro, just as it is one of the needs of every race; but to hold up this one training as practically all the training the Negro in this nation needs is to close the door of initiative to the Negro and put him in the class of the domestic animal that is broken or trained to perform one useful service alone. The theory that an education that is not useful is useless is true; but to assume that the only education that is useful to the Negro is agricultural and industrial is to deny that the Negro is a human being.

The advocates of the industrial and agricultural system of education for Negroes use the arguments that buying and owning homes, growing crops, saving the earnings, living in the open air of country life, modesty of dress and pretentions, cleanliness of person and home and its surroundings and neighborly disposition, (things which this system of training, like other educational systems include in their teaching), insure respectability, health and standing to individuals in every community. This is true; but there is not a scintilla of evidence to show that the increase in these ventures and in property owning by Negroes is due solely or even mainly to the influence of industrial and agricultural education. As a matter of fact while general industrial training of colored children is hardly begun, the home-loving Negro has been breeding in the race for more than a century, beginning by buying himself, his mother, his father, his wife, and his children, and property on which to live even in slavery times, and since freedom buying not only homes, but every comfort that his earnings could command.

While preaching to Negroes to stay in the country, to buy and occupy homes there, it is a notorious fact that Mr. Washington and others rarely, if ever, point out in their addresses the real reasons why Negroes find it very difficult to live in the country on account of the trying and troublesome conditions for thrifty Negroes out there. They never appeal to the white people of the country in their speeches to afford the Negroes the same protection of the laws against malice, abuse, unjust treatment, overbearing conduct, false accusation, summary punishment, lynching, confiscation or usurpation of property, expulsion from the community for trivial offenses that the white man enjoys.

Mr. Washington forgot to tell his white audience that thirteen Negroes were lynched in Louisiana last year alone and not a single person punished for these mob murders.

Taking advantage of the complacency with which colored people (long in the habit of taking abuse) received denunciation, the advocates of industrial training for Negroes do most of their preaching on the shortcomings of the black people. Every shortcoming of the Negro, whether real or imaginary, is described with great emphasis and every good quality is treated with silence. The Negro that is lazy and good for nothing, is described with minuteness and with indignation. Right by the side of this worthless Negro may be four decent Negroes about whom these industrial preachers never say a word, never describe with the same minuteness or with any applause in their public addresses.

Abuse and denouncing of Negroes for political purposes and to help men into office got fresh impetus after disfranchisement had followed Reconstruction. It became the most popular thing in the South for helping white men to office. Practically all Negroes in the South were driven out of the electorate and politics, as a result of this wholesale denunciation of the race. Practically nobody was brave enough to defend the race and the whole race passed for a lot of vicious, ignorant, barbarous people, fit only for menial service and the laborious work of the plantations.

May we not well fear that, because of the demoralized state into which the race was unmercifully thrown by this denunciation, the beginning of the propaganda of industrial training for Negroes with all of its fault finding of the race was planned by Negroes who saw a chance to become popular with the white people of the South?

The Louisville *Courier-Journal* says:

The workers for Negro welfare in this country are divided into those who believe that the Negro's destiny and salvation lie in manual labor and menial service, and those who claim that his potential capabilities are no more restricted than those of his white neighbor.

Ask any intelligent well balanced Negro to which group of these two he belongs and he will declare himself forever on the side of the group who believes in the capabilities of the Negro. By so declaring himself on this question the Negro but proves that he is human, that he is a man like other men; that he believes that what thousands of the Negro race builders, dead and living, have done for race uplift and advancement can be done, is being done and will continue to be done by the Negro as long as a provident Ruler of all things spares the Negro to live upon the face of the earth. In a word, he but proves his faith in his race and refuses to do what no other race ever has done against itself—preach its own inferiority at the suggestion of its enemies.

The Crisis, July, 1915; X, 144–46.

23

VOTES FOR WOMEN:
A SYMPOSIUM BY LEADING THINKERS
OF COLORED AMERICA

Reflective of the great interest in and, generally, strong support among the Afro-American people for the movement to enhance the rights of women, is the symposium published in *The Crisis,* August, 1915. Individual titles and the identifications of authors are republished as appearing in the original.

THE LOGIC OF WOMAN SUFFRAGE
by Rev. Francis J. Grimké
Pastor 15th St. Presbyterian Church, Washington, D.C.

I am heartily in favor of woman suffrage. I did not use to be, but it was simply because I had not given the subject due consideration. The moment I began to think seriously about it, I became convinced that I was wrong, and swung over on the other side, and have been on that side ever since. I do not see how any one who stops to think, who takes a common sense view of things, can be opposed to the franchise for women. What is this right to vote, after all? Is it not simply the right to form an opinion or judgment as to the character and fitness of those who are to be entrusted with the high and responsible duty of making laws and of administering the laws after they are made, and of having that judgment count in the selection of public officials? The ballot is simply the expression of the individual judgment in regard to such matters. Such being the case three things are perfectly clear in my mind:

(1). The interests of women are just as much involved in the enactment of laws, and in the administration of laws, as are the interests of men. In some respects they are even more so. In many things, such as the liquor traffic, the social evil, and other demoralizing influences, which directly affect the peace and happiness of the home, the kind of laws that are enacted, and the character of the men who are to enforce them, have for women a peculiar, a special interest.

(2). The average woman is just as well qualified to form an opinion as to the character and qualifications of those who are to be entrusted with power as the average man. The average man is in no sense superior to the average woman, either in point of intelligence, or of character. The average woman, in point of character, is superior to the average man; and, in so far as she is, she is better fitted to share in the selection of public officials.

(3). To deprive her of the right to vote is to govern her without her consent, which is contrary to the fundamental principle of democracy. That principle is clearly expressed in the Declaration of Independence, where we read: "Governments are instituted among men, deriving their just powers from the consent of the governed." Under this principle, which is a just principle, women have the same right to vote as men have. Are they not governed? And being governed, can the government imposed upon them be justly imposed upon them without their consent? It is simply to treat them as minors and inferiors, which every self-respecting woman should resent, and continue to resent until this stigma is removed from her sex. The time is certainly coming, and coming soon I believe, when this just claim on the part of women will be fully recognized in all truly civilized countries.

CHICAGO AND WOMAN'S SUFFRAGE
by Hon. Oscar de Priest
Alderman of the City of Chicago

I favor extension of the right of suffrage to women. The experience in Chicago has been that the women cast as intelligent a vote as the men.

In the first campaign in which the women voted in Chicago, a certain degree of timidity attended their advent. In the recent campaign, however, the work of the women was as earnest and the interest as keen as that of the men and in some instances the partisanship was almost bitter. As far as the colored men are concerned, in the aldermanic campaign of 1914 the feeling was so high that it penetrated social, church and other circles and some friendships of long standing were threatened. In the campaign of 1915 when colored men were primary candidates for alderman, the women of the race seemed to realize fully what was expected of them, and, with the men, rolled up a very large and significant vote for the colored candidates; and they were consistent at the election, contributing to a plurality of over 3,000 votes for the successful colored candidate in a field of five. Personally, I am more than thankful for their work and as electors believe they have every necessary qualification that the men possess.

POLITICS AND WOMANLINESS
by Benjamin Brawley
Dean of Morehouse College, Atlanta, Ga.

The argument is all for woman suffrage. More and more one who takes the opposing view finds himself looking to the past rather than to the future. Each woman as well as each man is a child of God, and is entitled to all the privileges of that high heritage. We are reminded of the heroine in *A Doll's House:* "Before all else you are a wife and mother," says the husband in Ibsen's play. "No," replies Nora, "before all else I am a human being."

There is one objection which many honestly find it difficult to overcome. There are thousands of men in this country who are theoretically in favor of woman suffrage, but who would be sorry to see their wives and sisters at the polls. They cannot overcome the feeling that woman loses something of her fineness of character when she takes her place with a crowd of men to fight out a live issue. Her very need of a protector calls forth man's chivalry; take away that need and the basis of woman's strongest appeal to man is gone.

Even this last objection, merely a practical one, can be overcome. The finest and deepest culture is not that which keeps its possessor forever enclosed in a Doll's House. It is rather that which looks at life in the large, with a just appreciation of its problems and sorrow, and that labors in the most intelligent manner to right the wrongs that are in existence. When once everywhere woman has entered the fray and helped to clean up some of the graft in our cities and to improve the tone of our voting places, even this last fear will disappear.

CHRISTIANITY AND WOMAN
by John Hurst, D.D.
Bishop of the African M.E. Church
and Secretary of the Bishops' Council

The earlier civilizations seem to have conspired to limit woman's sphere; her position and functions as member of the community were to extend so far and no further. Intellectual accomplishments and graces could raise her beyond the status of the slave, but not beyond the estimate put upon a toy, a bauble or a common-place ornament. Often she was subjected to systems leading to degradation, stifling her soul and stealing away from her the qualities that make an individual and a woman. The law forbidding her to abstain from the service at the Jewish Synagogue, said she should not be seen. Amidst the civilization of classic antiquity, even down to the enlightened age of Pericles, she was subservient to the caprices and rude passions of the other sex. Her fate was disposed of with little regard to her wishes. She had even no choice as to whom she should marry. The sacred fire of love was not supposed to burn upon the altar of her heart. She was but a commodity, a chattel to be bartered off. Under the Roman law, her status was hardly that of a human being. Whether under the Empire or the Republic, she had not even a first name.

But with the advent of Christianity, the path for a true, honorable and lasting civilization was laid. It discarded and upset the teachings of the past. It gave woman her freedom, and womanhood has been lifted to the place where it justly belongs. Christianity established equality and community of woman with man in the privileges of Grace, as being heir together with all the great gifts of life; receiving one faith, one baptism and partaking of the same holy table. Its thundering message to all is "There is neither Jew nor Greek, there is neither bond nor free, there is neither male nor female, for we are all one in Christ Jesus," and the echo of its teachings the world over is to "Loose her and let her go."

"ABOUT AUNTIES"
by Hon. J. W. Johnson
Formerly U.S. Consul to Nicaragua

There is one thing very annoying about the cause of Woman Suffrage and that is the absurdity of the arguments against it which one is called upon to combat. It is very much more difficult to combat an absurd argument than to combat a sound argument. The holder of a sound argument is generally a person amenable to reason and open to conviction; whereas, the holder of an absurd argument is always a person blinded by prejudice or bound by some such consideration as custom or sentiment; a person, indeed, to whom it is often impossible to prove that 2 and 2 make 4.

The people who oppose votes for women are divided into two classes: —those who boldly declare that women are inferior beings, neither fit nor capable of becoming fit to exercise the right of suffrage, and those who apologetically contend that the ballot will drag woman down from her domestic throne and rob her of all gentleness, charm, goodness,— this list of angelic qualities may be extended to any length desired.

It takes only a glance to see the striking analogy between these two arguments and the old pro-slavery arguments. The very ease with which they can be disproved makes them exasperating.

But, regardless of all arguments, for or against, woman is going to gain universal suffrage. The wonderful progress made by the sex in the last century and a half places this beyond doubt. This progress is nowhere more graphically indicated than by the fact that in the first edition of the *Encyclopedia Britannica* (1771) the article "Woman" consisted of seven words, "Woman,—the female of man—See Homo." In the edition of 1910 the article "Woman" takes up seven pages. Besides there are thirty women among the writers of the Encyclopedia, and the work contains articles on more than five hundred women, distinguished in history, literature and art.

Woman has made her place in the arts, she is making her place in the economic world, and she is sure to make her place in the political world.

OUR DEBT TO SUFFRAGISTS
by Hon. Robert H. Terrell
Justice of the Municipal Court, District of Columbia

Of all the elements in our great cosmopolitan population the Negro should be most ardently in favor of woman suffrage, for above all others, he knows what a denial of the ballot means to a people. He has seen his rights trampled on, he has been humiliated and insulted in public, and he has brooded over his weakness and helplessness in private, all because he did not possess the power given by the vote to protect himself in the same manner as other classes of citizens defend themselves against wrong and injustice. To those who oppose the right of women to vote it may be well to quote the stirring words of Benjamin Wade, of Ohio, uttered on the floor of the United States Senate, when he was advocating Negro Suffrage. He said: "I have a contempt I cannot name for the man who would demand rights for himself that he is not willing to grant to every one else."

Finally, as a matter of sentiment, every man with Negro blood in his veins should favor woman suffrage. Garrison, Phillips, Frederick Douglass and Robert Purvis and the whole host of abolitionists were advocates of the right. I often heard it said when I was a boy in Boston that immediately after the Civil War Susan B. Anthony, Julia Ward Howe, Elizabeth Cady Stanton and other leaders of the women's rights movement at the request of these men devoted all of their efforts towards obtaining the ballot for the Negro, even to the neglect of their own dearly cherished cause, hoping, indeed, that the black man, who would be in some measure the beneficiary of their work and sacrifice, would in turn give them the aid they so sorely needed at that time. Now what our fathers failed to do for these pioneers who did so much for our cause before and after the great war, let us do for those who are now leading the fight for woman suffrage. I believe that in supporting them we will render our country a great and much needed service.

WOMAN IN THE ANCIENT STATE
by W. H. Crogman, Litt. D.,
Professor of Ancient Languages, Clark University, S. Atlanta, Ga.

Slowly but steadily woman has risen from a state of servile dependence to her legitimate position of respect and consideration, and it needs no prophetic vision to see that the full recognition of her civic rights is near at hand. To form a just estimate of her achievements to date one must necessarily take into consideration the point from which she started, that is to say, the condition of her sex in the ancient state.

For light on this we turn naturally to the two most enlightened nations of antiquity. In the Homeric age woman was treated, we should infer, with tender and affectionate regard, and her virtues were sung by the greatest of poets. Even today, after twenty-seven centuries have rolled by, one cannot read without emotion and a thrill of admiration the story of Penelope's conjugal fidelity to her absent husband. Nor are we less affected by the scene of Hector and Andromache with the babe in her arms. Yet it would not be safe to conclude that these instances were fairly representative of the general status of woman in the ancient state, for at the same period there also existed cruelty, brutality, treachery. Beside the fidelity of Penelope may easily be placed the infidelity of Helen and the perfidity of Paris. Women were captured in war and subjected to the unspeakable. The greatest poem of the ages is but a recital of the fatal quarrel of two brutal men over the disposal of a captive maiden. Woman had practically no part in state affairs. Her duties were chiefly confined to the home. Says one writer:

"At no time of her life could a woman be without a guardian. If her husband was not alive, it would be her nearest male relative, and this person remained her guardian even when she was married. After her husband's death her son was her guardian. She could not legally make any contract beyond a shilling or two—there was no occasion for an Athenian to advertise that he would not be responsible for his wife's debts—and she could not bring actions at law."

And all this in Athens, in Athens at the summit of her greatness!

It is needless to say that a somewhat similar state of things existed at Rome where the father had the right of life and death over every member of the family. Verily it is a far cry from the rostrum of today, graced by the presence of a woman earnestly pleading for her civic rights, to that dismal period when she was a negligible factor in human affairs.

WOMEN'S RIGHTS
by Charles W. Chesnutt
Author of The Wife of His Youth, The Marrow of Tradition, *etc.*

I believe that all persons of full age and sound mind should have a voice in the making of the laws by which they are governed, or in the selection of those who make those laws. As long as the family was the social unit, it was perhaps well enough for the householder, representing the family, to monopolize the vote. But with the broadening of woman's sphere the situation has changed, and many women have interests which are not concerned with the family.

Experience has shown that the rights and interests of no class are safe so long as they are entirely in the hands of another class—the rights and interests of the poor in the hands of the rich, of the rich in the hands of the poor, of one race in the hands of another. And while there is no such line of cleavage between the sexes as exists between other social classes, yet so far as women constitute a class as differentiated from men, neither can their rights be left with entire safety solely in the hands of men. In the gradual extension of statutory rights, women are in many countries, the equals of men before the law. They have always been subject to the burdens of citizenship. The burden of taxation, generally speaking, falls more heavily upon them, perhaps because they are more honest in returning their personal property for taxation, or less cunning in concealing it. They are subject, equally with men, to the criminal laws, though there, I suspect, for sentimental reasons, the burden has not fallen so heavily upon them. Their rights need protection, and they should be guarded against oppression, and the ballot is the most effective weapon by which these things can be accomplished.

I am not in favor of woman suffrage because I expect any great improvement in legislation to result from it. The contrary, from woman's lack of experience in government, might not unreasonably be expected. Women are certainly no wiser or more logical than men. But they enjoy equal opportunities for education, and large numbers of them are successfully engaged in business and in the professions and have the requisite experience and knowledge to judge intelligently of proposed legislation. Even should their judgment be at fault—as men's judgment too often is—they have fine intuitions, which are many times a safe guide to action; and their sympathies are apt to be in support of those things which are clean and honest and just and therefore desirable—all of which ought to make them a valuable factor in government.

STATES' RIGHTS AND THE SUFFRAGE
by Hon. John R. Lynch
Major, Retired, U.S. Army; formerly Speaker of the House of Representatives of Mississippi; U.S. Representative, 6th District of Mississippi, 43rd, 44th and 47th Congresses; 4th Auditor of the U.S. Treasury, 1889–93; etc.

What the friends and advocates of equal suffrage have to fear more than anything else, is the dangerous and mischievous doctrine of "States' Rights." Those who are opposed to equal suffrage contend that it is a local and not a National question—one that each State must determine for itself. But what is a state? It seems to be an indefinable abstraction. "The United States," the National Constitution declares, "shall guarantee to every state in this Union a republican form of government," but this is a meaningless declaration. It has remained a dead letter since the adoption of the constitution, because some of the so-called states were and are nothing more nor less than despotic oligarchies. We have seen and now see that what is called the "State," in some parts of the country, is simply a part of the white males who obtained (it matters not how), possession of the local machinery which they call, and the National Government recognizes, as the "State Government." This government never allows any of the inhabitants of the "State" who are not identified with the ruling oligarchy to have any voice in its government. The friends of Equal Rights can hope for no favorable action from such governments as these, for they are not only close corporations, but they are determined to allow none to become members of the corporation that the managers can not absolutely and easily control. With a view of perpetuating themselves in power through the local machinery called "the State," some of them have, during the past twenty-five years, practically nullified the fifteenth amendment of the Federal Constitution. The recent decision of the Supreme Court by which some of the different schemes and devices for this purpose were declared unconstitutional and void is a most hopeful and encouraging indication. Let the friends of equal suffrage take on renewed hope. Victory, and that too on a national basis will ultimately be an accomplished fact.

DISFRANCHISEMENT IN THE DISTRICT OF COLUMBIA
by L. M. Hershaw
Of the United States Land Office

As regards the ballot, men and women are equal in the District of Columbia; both are deprived of it. Citizens of the District of Columbia have not voted since 1874, the year in which the ballot was taken from them by act of Congress. From time to time since then fitful efforts have been made to recover the lost right, but there has been no properly organized sustained movement with that object in view.

The female population of the District of Columbia exceeds the male population in round numbers by 16,000. In intelligence, in public spirit, in moral influence and in support of established institutions and philanthropies the female population is the equal, and in some instances the superior of the male population. If suffrage is ever restored to the citizens of the District it should be made to include the women. The right of the woman to vote rests on the same basis as the right of the man: her humanity. "Homo sum, et humani a mi nil alienum puto;"— I am a human being, and I consider nothing belonging to the human race foreign to me is the maxim constituting the major premise of the logic of human rights. To deny woman the right to vote is so far forth a denial of her humanity.

In the District of Columbia where neither man nor woman votes, the woman is as worthy a member of the community as the man. If Congress should reenact suffrage in the District it is difficult to see how it could except women from its exercise without fixing upon them an undeserved stigma. The example of women voting in the District would go a long way toward educating the backward and unprogressive throughout the country to the necessity of doing justice to the other half of our common humanity.

VOTES AND LITERATURE
by Mrs. Paul Laurence Dunbar

Matthew Arnold defined literature as a "criticism of life." By that he meant life in its entirety, not a part of it. Therefore, if a woman is to produce real literature, not pretty phrasing, she needs to have a firm grasp on all that makes life complete. The completion and perfection of life is love—love of home and family, love of humanity, love of country. No person living a mentally starved existence can do enduring work in any field, and woman without all the possibilities of life is starved, pinched, poverty-stricken. It is difficult to love your home and family if you be outcast and despised by them; perplexing to love humanity, if it gives you nothing but blows; impracticable to love your country, if it denies you all the rights and privileges which as citizens you should enjoy.

George Eliot, George Sand, Harriet Beecher Stowe wrote great novels because they looked at life from the point of view of the masculine mind, with a background of centuries of suffrage. Yet each was peculiarly feminine. It is a significant fact that the American and English women who are now doing the real work in literature—not necessarily fiction—are the women who are most vitally interested in universal suffrage.

WOMEN AND COLORED WOMEN
by Mrs. Mary B. Talbert
Vice-President-at-large, National Association of Colored Women

It should not be necessary to struggle forever against popular prejudice, and with us as colored women, this struggle becomes two-fold, first, because we are women and second, because we are colored women. Although some resistance is experienced in portions of our country against the ballot for women, because colored women will be included, I firmly believe that enlightened men, are now numerous enough everywhere to encourage this just privilege of the ballot for women, ignoring prejudice of all kinds.

The great desire of our nation to produce the most perfect form of government, shows incontestable proofs of advance. Advanced methods in prison reforms are shown by our own state Commissioner, Miss Katherine B. Davis. Advanced methods in school reforms are shown by Mrs. Ella Flagg Young, Superintendent of Education of Chicago. Advanced methods in the treatment of childhood and adolescence, are shown by the bureau of child welfare under Mrs. Julia C. Lathrop. Each of these women have been most kindly toward the colored women. In our own race advanced methods of industrial training are shown by Miss Nannie H. Burroughs, Mrs. Charlotte Hawkins Brown, and Mrs. Mary McLeod Bethune, and numbers of other colored women in various lines have blazed the path of reform.

By her peculiar position the colored woman has gained clear powers of observation and judgment—exactly the sort of powers which are to-day peculiarly necessary to the building of an ideal country.

"VOTES FOR MOTHERS"
by Mrs. Coralie Franklin Cook
Member of the Board of Education, District of Columbia

I wonder if anybody in all this great world ever thought to consider *man's* rights as an individual, by his status as a father? yet you ask me to say something about "Votes for Mothers," as if mothers were a separate and peculiar people. After all, I think you are not so far wrong. Mothers *are* different, or ought to be different, from other folk. The woman who smilingly goes out, willing to meet the Death Angel, that a child may be born, comes back from that journey, not only the mother of her own adored babe, but a near-mother to all other children. As she serves that little one, there grows within her a passion to serve humanity; not race, not class, not sex, but God's creatures as he has sent them to earth.

It is not strange that enlightened womanhood has so far broken its chains as to be able to know that to perform such service, woman should help both to make and to administer the laws under which she lives, should feel responsible for the conduct of educational systems, charitable and correctional institutions, public sanitation and municipal ordinances in general. Who should be more competent to control the presence of bar rooms and "red-light districts" than mothers whose sons they are meant to lure to degradation and death? Who knows better than the girl's mother at what age the girl may legally barter her own body? Surely not the men who have put upon our statute books, 16, 14, 12, aye, be it to their eternal shame, even 10 and 8 years, as "the age of consent!"

If men could choose their own mothers, would they choose free women or bond-women? Disfranchisement because of sex is curiously like disfranchisement because of color. It cripples the individual, it handicaps progress, it sets a limitation upon mental and spiritual development. I grow in breadth, in vision, in the power to do, just in proportion as I use the capacities with which Nature, the All-Mother, has endowed me. I transmit to the child who is bone of my bone, flesh of my flesh and *thought of my thought; somewhat* of my own power or weakness. Is not the voice which is crying out for "Votes for Mothers" the Spirit of the Age crying out for the Rights of Children?

"VOTES FOR CHILDREN"
by Mrs. Carrie W. Clifford
Honorary President of the Federation
of Colored Women's Clubs of Ohio

It is the ballot that opens the schoolhouse and closes the saloon; that keeps the food pure and the cost of living low; that causes a park to grow where a dump-pile grew before. It is the ballot that regulates capital and protects labor; that up-roots disease and plants health. In short, it is by the ballot we hope to develop the wonderful ideal state for which we are all so zealously working.

When the fact is considered that woman is the chosen channel through which the race is to be perpetuated; that she sustains the most sacred and intimate communion with the unborn babe; that later, she understands in a manner truly marvelous (and explained only by that vague term "instinct") its wants and its needs, the wonder grows that her voice is not the *first* heard in planning for the ideal State in which her child, as future citizen, is to play his part.

The family is the miniature State, and here the influence of the mother is felt in teaching, directing and executing, to a degree far greater than that of the father. At his mother's knee the child gets his first impressions of love, justice and mercy; and by obedience to the laws of the home he gets his earliest training in civics.

More and more is it beginning to be understood that the mother's zeal for the ballot is prompted by her solicitude for her family-circle.

That the child's food may be pure, that his environment shall be wholesome and his surrounding sanitary—these are the things which engage her thought. That his mind shall be properly developed and his education wisely directed; that his occupation shall be clean and his ideals high—all these are things of supreme importance to her, who began to plan for the little life before it was even dreamed of by the father.

Kindergartens, vacation-schools, playgrounds; the movement for the City Beautiful; societies for temperance and for the prevention of cruelty to children and animals—these and many other practical reforms she has brought to pass, *in spite of not having the ballot.* But as she wisely argues, why should she be forced to use indirect methods to accomplish a thing that could be done so much more quickly and satisfactorily by the direct method—by casting her own ballot?

The ballot! the sign of power, the means by which things are brought to pass, the talisman that makes our dreams come true! Her dream is of a State where war shall cease, where peace and unity be established and where love shall reign.

Yes, it is the great mother-heart reaching out to save her children from war, famine and pestilence; from death, degradation and destruction, that induces her to demand "Votes for Women," knowing well that fundamentally it is really a campaign for "Votes for Children."

TRAINING AND THE BALLOT
by Mary Fitzbutler Waring, M.D.
Chairman of the Department of Health and Hygiene, N.A.C.W.

In the earlier ages, the thought was common among the nations of the world, that woman was not the equal of man. Socially, religiously and politically she was compelled to take an inferior position and to submit to the will and wiles of man. In some countries she was not even considered as the legal parent of her own child.

The ability to weigh the merits of the persons to fill office and the value of ordinances which govern the people, requires a knowledge of men and affairs. A trained mind, no matter in what profession, is more capable of making logical deductions; therefore the people naturally turn for information to the enlightened. The question of sex is of no importance.

The work of the professional woman just as that of the professional man places her in a position to help the many with whom she necessarily comes in contact, and therefore her influence is a power to be reckoned with. The ethical relations of the professional woman make her, ofttimes, the confidant and advisor of others and for that reason she should be well informed on political issues and aspirants for public office.

Trained judgment is needed everywhere and it should always be armed with the ballot.

DEMOCRACY AND ART
by William Stanley Braithwaite
Author of Anthologies of Magazine Verse, etc.

We find that at almost every stage of its development Democracy has been betrayed by one or another of its idealist professors, except one. Democracy has its source in political ethics, but neither religion nor social justice has performed towards it, in practice, those strict obligations which are defined by the nature of their idealisms. Art alone has kept her covenant with Democracy.

Art is the embodiment of spiritual ideals. There is no human progress without a previsioning of the aspiration through one of the symbolic languages of art. All the great craving desires of humanity have been promised and attained through the message of art. Art cannot flourish in a democracy, is the critical opinion common to a good many. I say, that in the future, art will not flourish without democracy. All that democracy has gained in the last twenty years it has owed to the ideals of art. Was the social conscience of America vitalized by religion or the justice and wisdom of political enactments? No; but by an art, the art of poetry. The undemocratic methods of industrial power, did the Christian church protest against it? No; it was a poet with a passion and a message. Now, art has seen to it that public opinion consider all the rights and demands that democracy makes towards the justification of its ideals. These have not all been accomplished. It has got to eliminate racial prejudice which has governmental sanction, and it has got to win sufferance for all citizens alike. Art is bringing democracy face to face with beauty, and beauty knows neither race, caste nor sex. The social vision of art is complete. And its light is ever shining upon the luminous figure of Democracy, the ideal Mother of human hopes, the hopes of the rejected, of the denied, of the subjected individual.

The voice of art expressing the spirit of democracy is beautifully illustrated in this passage from Mr. Witter Bynner's recently published poem "The New World:" *

To stop the wound and heal the scar
Of time, with sudden glorious aptitude
Woman assumes her part. Her pity in a flood
Flings down the gate.
She has been made to wait
Too long, undreaming and untaught
The touch and beauty of democracy.
But, entering now the strife
In which her saving sense is due,
She watches and she grows aware,
Holding a child more dear than property,
That the many perish to empower the few,
That homeless politics have split apart
The common country of the common heart.

BLACK WOMEN AND REFORM
by Miss N. H. Burroughs
Secretary of the Woman's Auxiliary
to the National Baptist Convention

The Negro Church means the Negro woman. Without her, the race could not properly support five hundred churches in the whole world. Today they have 40,000 churches in the United States. She is not only a great moral and spiritual asset, but she is a great economic asset. I was asked by a southern white woman who is an enthusiastic worker for "votes for (white) women," "What can the Negro woman do with the ballot?" I asked her, "What can she do without it?" When the ballot is put into the hands of the American woman the world is going to get a correct estimate of the Negro woman. It will find her a tower of strength of which poets have never sung, orators have never spoken, and scholars have never written.

Because the black man does not know the value of the ballot, and has bartered and sold his most valuable possession, it is no evidence that the Negro woman will do the same. The Negro woman, therefore, needs

* Published by Mitchell Kennerley (New York, 1915); the greater part of this poem was delivered in June, 1911, before the Harvard Chapter of Phi Beta Kappa.

the ballot to get back, by the wise *use* of it, what the Negro man has lost by the *misuse* of it. She needs it to ransom her race. A fact worthy of note is that in every reform in which the Negro woman has taken part, during the past fifty years, she has been as aggressive, progressive and dependable as those who inspired the reform or led it. The world has yet to learn that the Negro woman is quite superior in bearing moral responsibility. A comparison with the men of her race, in moral issues, is odious. She carries the burdens of the Church, and of the school and bears a great deal more than her economic share in the home.

Another striking fact is that the Negro woman carries the moral destiny of two races in her hand. Had she not been the woman of unusual moral stamina that she is, the black race would have been made a great deal whiter, and the white race a great deal blacker during the past fifty years. She has been left a prey for the men of every race, but in spite of this, she has held the enemies of Negro female chastity at bay. The Negro woman is the white woman's as well as the white race's most needed ally in preserving an unmixed race.

The ballot, wisely used, will bring to her the respect and protection that she needs. It is her weapon of moral defence. Under present conditions, when she appears in court in defence of her virtue, she is looked upon with amused contempt. She needs the ballot to reckon with men who place no value upon her virtue, and to mould healthy public sentiment in favor of her own protection.

THE SELF-SUPPORTING WOMAN AND THE BALLOT
by Miss M. E. Jackson
Of the Civil Service of the State of Rhode Island,
President of the R.I. Association of Colored Women's Clubs

Looked at from a sane point of view, all objections to the ballot for women are but protests against progress, civilization and good sense.

"Woman's place is in the home." Would that the poorly paid toilers in field, work-shop, mill and kitchen, might enjoy the blessed refreshment of their own homes with accompanying assurance that those dependent upon them might be fed, clothed, properly reared and educated.

Each morning's sun beholds a mighty army of 8,000,000 souls marching forth to do battle for daily bread. You inquire who they are? Why, the mothers, wives, sisters and daughters of the men of America. "The weaker vessels," the majority of whom are constrained from necessity.

There is no field of activity in the country where women are not successfully competing with men. In the agricultural pursuits alone, there are over 900,000. In the ministry 7,000 dare preach the gospel with "Heads uncovered." And 1,010 possess the courage to invade the field of the Solons, bravely interpreting the laws, although their brothers in all but twelve of the forty-five States (so far as the ballot is concerned), class them with criminals, insane and feeble-minded.

The self-supporting woman out of her earnings, pays taxes, into the public treasury and through church, club and civic organization gives her moral backing unstintingly to her Country.

Imagine if you can the withdrawal of this marvelous economic force,—the working women of America! It is a fundamental necessity of modern civilization.

The laboring man has discovered beyond peradventure that his most effective weapon of defense is the *ballot in his own hand.* The self-supporting woman asks for and will accept nothing less.

"TRUST THE WOMEN!"
by Mrs. Josephine St. Pierre Ruffin
Pioneer in the Club Movement among Colored Women
of the United States

Many colored men doubt the wisdom of women suffrage because they fear that it will increase the number of our political enemies. I have been in suffrage work in Massachusetts for forty years and more. I have voted 41 times under the school suffrage laws. I was welcomed into the Massachusetts Woman's Suffrage Association by Lucy Stone, Julia Ward Howe, Ednah Cheney, Abby Morton Diaz and those other pioneer workers who were broad enough to include "no distinction because of race" with "no distinctions because of sex." I feel that a movement inaugurated by men and women of such wisdom and vision as that of the early workers, cannot dwindle or be side-tracked, and that today, as in those early days, the big women, the far seeing women, are in the ranks of the suffragists. We can afford to follow those women. We are justified in believing that the success of this movement for equality of the sexes means more progress toward equality of the races. I have worked, along with other colored women with those pioneers in the Abolition movement, in the various movements to open educational opportunities for women, business opportunities for women and to equalize the laws; the longer I have been associated with them, the more deeply I have been impressed by this farsightedness and broadmindedness of the leaders, both early and late, in the Woman Suffrage Movement.

Y.W.C.A.
by Mrs. A. W. Hunton
Formerly Adviser to the National Board of Directors, Y.W.C.A.

A membership of more than a half million, representing some seventeen nationalities, makes the Young Women's Christian Association a world movement.

In the United States three hundred thousand members, distributed in 979 college, city and county associations have as their objective the advancement of the "physical, social, intellectual, moral and spiritual interests of young women."

One of the most unique and wonderful characteristics of the association is the adaptability to meet the needs of all types of women, so that its membership is as diversified as women's lives and interests. This diversified membership, constituting at once the governing and sustaining force of the association, is its strongest barrier to any creed save that upon which the movement is founded.

However difficult it is to express any relation between the association and the suffrage movement, it is not difficult to understand that the association spirit dominating womanhood would count for righteousness in the solution of this important question.

Acutely suffering from the wrongs and humiliations of an unjustly restricted suffrage, it is but natural that the colored woman should feel deeply and keenly wherever the question of suffrage arises. But the colored woman within the association, in common with thousands of her sisters who have been touched by other spiritual forces, is animated by a fine spirit of idealism—an idealism not too far removed from everyday existence to find expression in service. Hence she is giving her energy largely to the development of the highest qualities of mind and soul—for these alone can give to the nation the best there is in citizenship.

VOTES FOR TEACHERS
by Miss Maria L. Baldwin
Principal of the Agassiz Public School, Cambridge, Mass.

Women teachers in those states where school suffrage has already been granted them have found out that even so meagre a share of voting power has given them a definite influence, and has brought about a few notable results. In several cases local schools have been kept, by the women's vote, from the control of persons who threatened all that was best in them. Candidates for election to school boards reckon early with the "teacher vote" and hasten to announce their "rightness" on this or that issue supposedly dear to teachers. It is wholly reasonable to infer that the extension of the suffrage will enable teachers to secure more consideration for themselves, and to have an important influence on the quality of the persons chosen to direct the schools.

At the outset teachers will be confronted by the temptation of power —the temptation to use it for personal or selfish ends. What, as a class, will they do with this temptation! What motives will lie behind their advocacy of men and measures? What tests of fitness will they apply to the candidate for their votes? Will they decline to recognize fine qualities for school service in one who may hold heretical views about increase of salaries, or length of vacations? These questions, which would test any group of workers, I cannot answer. I can only submit what seems an earnest that this group may stand the test.

The profession of teaching has a rich inheritance. These convictions were bequeathed to it, to have and to hold: that the dearest interests of life are in its keeping; that its peculiar service to society is to nourish and perpetuate those noblest aspirations called its ideals; that to do such work one must be devoted and unselfish.

This tradition still inspires the teacher. Some of the unrest, the dissatisfaction with conditions that are everywhere has penetrated her world, but probably no other work is done less in the commercial spirit nor any service more expanded beyond what "is nominated in the bond." Many school rooms are moving pictures of this spirit at work.

One is warranted in thinking that teachers will transfer to their use of the ballot this habit of fidelity to ideals.

WOMAN SUFFRAGE AND SOCIAL REFORM
by Miss Anna H. Jones
Chairman of the Department of Education,
National Association of Colored Women

Of the four great institutions of human uplift—the home, the school, the church, and the State, woman has a direct controlling force in the first three institutions. In the State her influence at present is indirect.

Since her control in the three is unquestioned, should she not have the legal means—the ballot—to widen and deepen her work?

In terms of today, her work is the conservation and improvement of the child; child labor laws, inspection of the health of school children, safeguarding the youth in the home, in the school, in the court, in the street, in the place of amusement. Her work is the prevention of vice with its train of physical and moral evils; the enactment of laws to secure and regulate sanitation, pure food, prohibition, divorce; the care of the aged, the unfortunate, the orphan. All the questions touch in a very direct way the home—woman's kingdom.

When an experiment has been tried for a certain purpose it seems logical to refer to its success or failure. A review of the States in which women have had the ballot will show that their exercise of the franchise has been along the lines of reform mentioned above. Her ballot has not been cast against the forces of right. Is it probable that in the other, the more conservative States, her course will be less judicial?

It may take a little time for woman to learn to make the ballot count for righteousness, but her closer view, and sympathetic touch will be of material assistance in the solution of the social problems that confront her as the homemaker.

The century awaits the "finer issues" of woman's "finely touched spirit."

COLORED WOMEN'S CLUBS
by Mrs. B. K. Bruce
Editor of the Official Organ of the National Association of Colored Women

The national club movement among colored women began definitely in 1895, when a call was sent out from Boston by Mrs. Josephine St. P. Ruffin to a number of prominent colored women to meet in conference.

The special object of that conference was to repel and refute a vicious statement by an evil minded individual who had given currency to his false and misleading statements in book form. A national association called The National Federation of Colored Women, was formed at this conference.

The first convention of the new organization was called to meet a year later in July 1896, in Washington, D.C. In August of 1896 the first convention of the National League of Colored Women was held. The two organizations united under the name, National Association of

Colored Women. In 1916 this organization will hold its tenth biennial session in Baltimore, Maryland. One year ago in Wilberforce, Ohio, the largest and most successful convention in its history was held. Over four hundred delegates, representing 50,000 women organized in clubs throughout the country were present. The delegates came from the East, the West, the North, the South. The burden of the song of the numberless reports and addresses was social service not alone for colored people but for humanity. Miss Zona Gale said of the meeting that she had never attended a convention which so confirmed her belief in the possibilities of the common human race.

One thousand clubs are numbered with The National Association of Colored Women. In 1912–13 these clubs raised $82,424. Over $60,000 was spent in purchasing property for Orphans' Homes, Working Girls' Homes, Christian Association Homes, Social Settlements and so on. In 1914 the valuation of the various properties exceeded $100,000.

VOTES FOR PHILANTHROPY
by Mrs. Elizabeth Lindsay Davis
National Organizer, National Association of Colored Women

The New citizen is no longer a novelty nor an experiment. She is demonstrating at all times her fitness for her duties and responsibilities by study; by insistent investigation of all candidates for public office regardless of party lines; by an intelligent use of the ballot in correcting the evils arising from graft, dishonesty and misappropriation of public funds; by persistent agitation to arouse civic consciousness, until now she is a potent factor in the body politic.

Men recognize her intuitive ability to think and decide for herself, respect her opinions and bid for her vote.

The keynote in the music of the Twentieth Century is Social Service, and in no better way can systematic philanthropy be done than by using the power of the ballot upon the heads of the great corporations and private individuals to direct their attention to the serious consequences of present day industrial and social unrest, the crime, disease, and poverty emanating from bad housing and unwholesome environment, to train their hands to give systematically to the cause of human betterment.

Woman is a pioneer in the forward movement for Social uplift, racial and community development, whether for the abandoned wife, the wage earning girl, the dependent and delinquent child or the countless hordes of the unemployed.

The highest and most successfully developed philanthropical work depends absolutely upon the control of political influence by the best American citizenship, men and women working in unity and cooperation at the polls.

WOMAN SUFFRAGE AND THE FIFTEENTH AMENDMENT
by Mrs. Mary Church Terrell
Honorary President of the National Association of Colored Women

Even if I believed that women should be denied the right of suffrage, wild horses could not drag such an admission from my pen or my lips, for this reason: precisely the same arguments used to prove that the ballot be withheld from women are advanced to prove that colored men should not be allowed to vote. The reasons for repealing the Fifteenth Amendment differ but little from the arguments advanced by those who oppose the enfranchisement of women. Consequently, nothing could be more inconsistent than that colored people should use their influence against granting the ballot to women, if they believe that colored men should enjoy this right which citizenship confers.

What could be more absurd and ridiculous than that one group of individuals who are trying to throw off the yoke of oppression themselves, so as to get relief from conditions which handicap and injure them, should favor laws and customs which impede the progress of another unfortunate group and hinder them in every conceivable way. For the sake of consistency, therefore, if my sense of justice were not developed at all, and I could not reason intelligently, as a colored woman I should not tell my dearest friend that I opposed woman suffrage.

But how can any one who is able to use reason, and who believes in dealing out justice to all God's creatures, think it is right to withhold from one-half the human race rights and privileges freely accorded to the other half, which is neither more deserving nor more capable of exercising them?

For two thousand years mankind has been breaking down the various barriers which interposed themselves between human beings and their perfect freedom to exercise all the faculties with which they were divinely endowed. Even in monarchies old fetters which formerly restricted freedom, dwarfed the intellect and doomed certain individuals to narrow circumscribed spheres, because of the mere accident of birth, are being loosed and broken one by one. In view of such wisdom and experience the political subjection of women in the United States can be likened only to a relic of barbarism, or to a spot upon the sun, or to an octopus holding this republic in its hideous grasp, so that further progress to the best form of government is impossible and that precious ideal its founders promised it would be seems nothing more tangible than a mirage.

VOTES FOR HOUSEWIVES
by Mrs. Lillian A. Turner
Honorary President of the Minnesota Association
of Colored Women's Clubs

That the housewife, that great reasoner, will vote intelligently, is my happy conclusion, after reading the ponderous decision of a wise man, who protests that voters should be "only those who are able to substitute reason for sentiment." It is such a relief to have an impartial definition even though its close analysis might exclude a large portion of present voters. But my concern is with the housewife, the future voter, as tested by the wise man's definition.

Now, Sentiment is the housewife's most cherished possession; to this assertion all agree—the man, the anti-suffragist and the rest of us. Furthermore, lack of excessive use will keep it so, for the housewife early learns to substitute Reason for Sentiment. When Sentiment wails because husband walks two steps ahead instead of beside her; weeps because Boy's curls are shorn; foolishly resents the absence of the old attentions, and more foolishly dwells on an infinite variety of things, Reason comes nobly to the rescue and teaches her that none of these things are necessary to life. Reason is the constant substitute for her cherished Sentiment. But Reason's assertion, that protection from vice for Son of the Shorn Curls, is impracticable for business reasons, is too difficult for mental gymnastics. Sentiment conquers, and the housewife unreasonably demands the ballot to protect Son! However, Reason being already so well developed through "discipline by substitution" (still quoting the wise man) I have ceased to tremble when I hear dire predictions of the ruin that is expected to follow the rapid approach of woman's franchise.

The Crisis, August, 1915; X, 178–92. In the issue of November, 1911, *The Crisis* rejoiced that Black men had supported the effort to enfranchise women in California (III, 7).

24

MY VIEW OF SEGREGATION LAWS

by Booker T. Washington

Booker T. Washington died November 14, 1915. In what must have been nearly his last piece of writing—if not the last—he expressed his views on the legalization of segregation (a movement then very nearly completed). This essay was dated Tuskegee Institute, Alabama, September 13, 1915. It is instructive to compare this with the writing on the same subject that same year by William Pickens—as printed in preceding pages.

In all of my experience I have never yet found a case where the masses of the people of any given city were interested in the matter of the segregation of white and colored people; that is, there has been no spontaneous demand for segregation ordinances. In certain cities politicians have taken the leadership in introducing such segregation ordinances into city councils, and after making an appeal to racial prejudices have succeeded in securing a backing for ordinances which would segregate the Negro people from their white fellow citizens. After such ordinances have been introduced it is always difficult, in the present state of public opinion in the South, to have any considerable body of white people oppose them, because their attitude is likely to be misrepresented as favoring Negroes against white people. They are, in the main, afraid of the stigma, "Negro-lover."

It is probably useless to discuss the legality of segregation; that is a matter which the courts will finally pass upon. It is reasonably certain, however, that the courts in no section of the country would uphold a case where Negroes sought to segregate white citizens. This is the most convincing argument that segregation is regarded as illegal, when viewed on its merits by the whole body of our white citizens.

Personally I have little faith in the doctrine that it is necessary to segregate the whites from the blacks to prevent race mixture. The whites are the dominant race in the South, they control the courts, the industries and the government in all of the cities, counties and states except in those few communities where the Negroes, seeking some form of self-government, have established a number of experimental towns or communities.

I have never viewed except with amusement the sentiment that white people who live next to Negro populations suffer physically, mentally and morally because of their proximity to colored people. Southern white people who have been brought up in this proximity are not inferior to other white people. The President of the United States was born and reared in the South in close contact with black people. Five members of the present Cabinet were born in the South; and many of them, I am sure, had black "mammies." The Speaker of the House of Representatives is a Southern man, the chairmen of leading committees in both the United States Senate and the Lower House of Congress are Southern men. Throughout the country to-day, people occupying the highest positions not only in the government but in education, industry and science, are persons born in the South in close contact with the Negro.

Attempts at legal segregation are unnecessary for the reason that the matter of residence is one which naturally settles itself. Both colored and whites are likely to select a section of the city where they will be surrounded by congenial neighbors. It is unusual to hear of a colored man attempting to live where he is surrounded by white people or where he is not welcome. Where attempts are being made to segregate the races legally, it should be noted that in the matter of business no attempt is made to keep the white man from placing his grocery store, his dry goods store, or other enterprise right in the heart of a Negro district. This is another searching test which challenges the good faith of segregationists.

It is true that the Negro opposes these attempts to restrain him from residing in certain sections of a city or community. He does this not because he wants to mix with the white man socially, but because he feels that such laws are unnecessary. The Negro objects to being segregated because it usually means that he will receive inferior accommodations in return for the taxes he pays. If the Negro is segregated, it will probably mean that the sewerage in his part of the city will be inferior; that the streets and sidewalks will be neglected, that the street lighting will be poor; that his section of the city will not be kept in order by the police and other authorities, and that the "undesirables" of other races will be placed near him, thereby making it difficult for him to rear his family in decency. It should always be kept in mind that while the Negro may not be directly a large taxpayer, he does pay large taxes indirectly. In the last analysis, all will agree that the man who pays house rent pays large taxes, for the price paid for the rent includes payment of the taxes on the property.

Right here in Alabama nobody is thinking or talking about land and home segregation. It is rather remarkable that in the very heart of the Black Belt where the black man is most ignorant the white people should not find him so repulsive as to set him away off to himself. If living side by side is such a menace as some people think, it does seem as if the people who have had the bulk of the race question to handle during the past fifty years would have discovered the danger and adjusted it long ago.

A segregated Negro community is a terrible temptation to many white people. Such a community invariably provides certain types of white men with hiding-places—hiding-places from the law, from decent people of their own race, from their churches and their wives and daughters. In a Negro district in a certain city in the South a house of ill-repute for white men was next door to a Negro denominational school. In another town a similar kind of house is just across the street from the Negro grammar school. In New Orleans the legalized vice section is set in the midst of the Negro section, and near the spot where stood a Negro school and a Negro church, and near the place where the Negro orphanage now operates. Now when a Negro seeks to buy a house in a reputable street he does it not only to get police protection, lights and accommodations, but to remove his children to a locality in which vice is not paraded.

In New Orleans, Atlanta, Birmingham, Memphis—indeed in nearly every large city in the South—I have been in the homes of Negroes who live in white neighborhoods, and I have yet to find any race friction; the Negro goes about his business, the white man about his. Neither the wives nor the children have the slightest trouble.

White people who argue for the segregation of the masses of black people forget the tremendous power of objective teaching. To hedge any set of people off in a corner and sally among them now and then with a lecture or a sermon is merely to add misery to degradation. But put the black man where day by day he sees how the white man keeps his lawns, his windows; how he treats his wife and children, and you will do more real helpful teaching than a whole library of lectures and sermons. Moreover, this will help the white man. If he knows that his life is to be taken as a model, that his hours, dress, manners, are all to be patterns for someone less fortunate, he will deport himself better than he would otherwise. Practically all the real moral uplift the black people have got from the whites—and this has been great indeed—has come from this observation of the white man's conduct. The South to-day is still full of the type of Negro with gentle manners. Where did he get them? From some master or mistress of the same type.

Summarizing the matter in the large, segregation is ill-advised because

1. It is unjust.

2. It invites other unjust measures.

3. It will not be productive of good, because practically every thoughtful Negro resents its injustice and doubts its sincerity. Any race adjustment based on injustice finally defeats itself. The Civil War is the best illustration of what results where it is attempted to make wrong right or seem to be right.

4. It is unnecessary.

5. It is inconsistent. The Negro is segregated from his white neighbor, but white business men are not prevented from doing business in Negro neighborhoods.

6. There has been no case of segregation of Negroes in the United States that has not widened the breach between the two races. Wherever a form of segregation exists it will be found that it has been administered in such a way as to embitter the Negro and harm more or less the moral fibre of the white man. That the Negro does not express this constant sense of wrong is no proof that he does not feel it.

It seems to me that the reasons given above, if carefully considered, should serve to prevent further passage of such segregation ordinances as have been adopted in Norfolk, Richmond, Louisville, Baltimore, and one or two cities in South Carolina.

Finally, as I have said in another place, as white and black learn daily to adjust, in a spirit of justice and fair play, those interests which are individual and racial, and to see and feel the importance of those fundamental interests which are common, so will both races grow and prosper. In the long run no individual and no race can succeed which sets itself at war against the common good; for "in the gain or loss of one race, all the rest have equal claim."

New Republic, December 4, 1915; V, 113–14.

25

ARE WE MAKING GOOD?

by Mrs. Booker T. Washington

In an article written from Tuskegee and published a month prior to the death of her husband, Mrs. Booker T. Washington offered some views on the activities of Afro-American women. Mrs. Washington was a leading force in the organizations and efforts of Black women for a full generation.

A few weeks ago, I was returning from a country school, where I had gone to help the teacher raise money to finish the schoolhouse, which had been begun some two or three years ago. It was a cold, dark afternoon and one would have expected every woman, at least every country woman, to be close up to the fireside. Country people love to stay near their hearthstones, at least my country folks do. But as I drove on slowly, Topsy, my little black horse, who takes me all about among my country friends, pricked up her ears. I listened a moment and in the distance I heard the soft, plaintive tones of a dozen or more women, as they sang, as no other women can sing:

> Don't call the roll till I get there,
> Don't call the roll till I get there.
> Oh Mary, Oh Martha, don't call the roll till I get there.
> I want to answer to my name,
> I want to answer to my name.
> Oh Mary, Oh Martha, I want to answer to my name.

The country woman expresses herself generally in song, whether she is sad or happy. This afternoon these women were—shall I say happy? —well, they were content. Once inside the building, I was not long in finding out that I was in a woman's club, a real club, where subjects of vital interest to a community were being discussed, not something these women had read about, for not a single one of them could read an ordinary book or newspaper, not a subject that some lecturer had discussed in their church, for lecturers do not usually spend their time with this sort of people, in this sort of a community—if they only would! —but these women, some young, more older, had for that meeting the subject: "How to make hard water soft." This is a limestone district. These women work in the fields until Friday night or Saturday noon, when they go down to the creek to do their week's washing, and the hardness of the water is of the greatest interest to them. It had set them to thinking, and where a community of women begin to think there is sure to be action, the result of which will be their general intellectual development.

On a great Southern cotton plantation there lives a family consisting of a mother, father and four children, the oldest a woman nearly thirty and the youngest fourteen or fifteen. The father is a hard taskmaster, unable himself to read and naturally not at all interested in the education of these daughters of his. These young women, who had worked in the fields for years with the promise of going off to school, at last, seeing that the father had no thought of keeping his word, as far as sending them to school, crept out stealthily one night as the old people slept and made their way to the little station, purchased their tickets to a far-famed university and turned their backs for years upon all they had known and held dear. These girls scarcely knew their letters. They did not know even in what direction they were to travel. They belonged to a class which some people call ignorant, but they had begun to think and their thinking made them act. They are now all four at this famous school and are doing their best. They will come out all right. These women represent a large class of colored women everywhere, who are thinking, who are studying, who are interested thoroughly in their own salvation, morally as well as intellectually, and who realize that it must be bought by their own strength and blood.

There are five hundred or more mothers in the little town where I live who hold four meetings a month, at which any one who feels like it sings and any one who is moved by the spirit prays; any one speaks upon the subject given. It is a free speech meeting. At one of the recent meetings the question was thrown out, "How many little babies have been born in my community in the last twelve months and where are they?" Another was "How shall I keep the affection of my husband?" One woman laughed good-naturedly and said: "We women ought to go to all the conventions and things where our husbands go. They travel, they read, they study and we should do this, too, or fall behind them." Another one spoke up and said: "Don't let us be so tired all of the time when he comes home." One of these women has bought a nice four-room cottage, painted it, has a good cow, a good horse and buggy, always makes her own garden, and more than all, has remade her husband from a cobbler into a real respectable carpenter. Others of this organization are following her example. Where will it all end? No one can tell, except to see that the revolution has begun, regeneration has set in and these women who have gone thru trials and tribulations are going to take their stand at no distant day with the great American Womanhood, and share their part of the responsibility in increasing the nation's efficiency.

There are more than two million Negro women in this country, on the plantations, in small towns, and in the cities. We are seldom heard from, and not always considered as a factor in the solution of the great problem in which our husbands and brothers figure so largely. Yet twenty thousand of us are banded together with small material resources, with but one national paper, the monthly called the *National Notes,* for our children, our homes, our people. Today the people of this country are asking, What can we do to solve the Negro problem? Over and over again scholars have told us that no people can rise above their source—the mothers of the land—and there at the fountain head must the work begin. The home and the family is the starting point.

Since the spirit of the age demands that the mother should have a wide knowledge of all matters pertaining to the moral, spiritual and intellectual training of her children, we women must meet the demands by making our organizations avenues of help to the better way.

We club women have made a beginning in laying a foundation as a means to an end. The work of such organizations as I have described influences not only the women directly connected with them, but reaches out to the homes that are not represented in clubs. The incidents given above are typical of the awakening and growing activities of our women all over this country—for our National Association is made up of women from every state in the Union. The women of each state direct their energies toward some particular local need. Indiana women have for some time been maintaining a tuberculosis camp; New York women, an old folks' home. The colored women of Alabama, some years ago, founded at Mt. Meigs a boys' reformatory for which they raised out of their meager stores $2000 each year until, thru the energetic lobbying of the three women's clubs that had worked hardest for it, the state was persuaded to take it over.

We can make no proposition which will hold absolutely good for these and many essentially different groups of colored women. It is a task which I shall not undertake. We can not find the average colored woman any more than we can find the average woman in other races.

But I wonder if there are still those who ask: "Are Negro women making good?"

The Independent, October 4, 1915; LXXXIV, 22.

26

INSTALLATION ADDRESS AT TUSKEGEE
by Robert R. Moton

Robert Russa Moton (1867–1940) was born in Virginia and was educated at Hampton Institute. He was its commandant from 1890 until 1915; upon the death of Mr. Washington, Moton was selected to succeed him. His installation address as Tuskegee's second principal was delivered May 25, 1916; he held this position until his death. In 1932 he was awarded the Spingarn Medal.

At a time when racial misunderstanding and sectional strife, resulting from the Civil War and subsequent reconstruction had reached an acute stage, when well-meaning men were trying to find an adequate method of racial readjustment, a southern white man, one who had strong southern feelings, who saw the great need of the Negro here in Alabama and the South, and who was filled with an honest desire to help him, wrote to a northern white man with equally strong northern feelings inquiring if a colored man could be sent to Tuskegee to begin a work similar in plan and purpose to that which had been started at Hampton —a type of education which was at that time not only woefully misunderstood, but bitterly opposed by many of the leading men of the Negro race.

On that day, in July 1881, when the modest, quiet, unassuming young man, Booker T. Washington, reported with a letter from General Armstrong, his former teacher, and was cordially received and welcomed to this community by Mr. George W. Campbell, then it was that a form of cooperation began, the scope and effectiveness of which was destined to command the respect and admiration, not only of this country, but also of the entire civilized world. Here met the three elements, the North, the South, and the Negro—the three elements that must be taken into account in any genuinely satisfactory adjustment of race relationships. It was natural for white men to be considered as important factors in any and all adjustments and problems, whether civic, business, educational or otherwise. Up to this time, the Negro had usually been the problem and not an element worthy of serious consideration, so far as any first-hand contribution he could make toward the solution of any large social question was concerned.

These two men, representing the two extremes of sectional sentiment, Mr. Campbell, a former slave-owner, the South, and General Armstrong, a former officer in the Federal Army, the North, both broad in sympathy and wise in judgment, and entirely void of any selfish motives, both actuated by a sincere desire to reunite the nation in spirit and purpose, as well as in law and lineage, both patriotic American citizens—these two gentlemen united their forces for the primary object of lifting the burden of ignorance, and all the consequences resulting therefrom, in the South. Mr. Campbell wanted a Negro to undertake the work, and General Armstrong knew of at least one Negro who could do the work.

These three far-sighted men, agreeing on a united purpose, for the common good of humanity, began a cooperation which has been strikingly characteristic of Tuskegee Institute, and a cooperation vitally necessary for the permanent betterment of the Negro race in our country.

MORAL AND MATERIAL RESULTS

The Tuskegee school, from the very beginning, has had a moral and material support and backing from Mr. Campbell and other white people in this community, without which this institution would have been impossible. No one knew and appreciated this fact more than did Dr. Washington, and no one has been more grateful than he. There were also colored men who stood by the Founder of the Tuskegee Institute in those early days. In his autobiography, *Up From Slavery,* Dr. Washington fittingly says:

In the midst of all the difficulties which I encountered in getting the little school started, and since then through a period of nineteen years, there are two men among all the many friends of the school in Tuskegee upon whom I have depended constantly for advice and guidance; and the success of the undertaking is largely due to these men, from whom I have never sought anything in vain. I mention them simply as types. One is a white man and an ex-slave-holder, Mr. George W. Campbell; the other is a black man and an exslave, Mr. Lewis Adams; I do not know two men whose advice and judgment I would feel more like following in anything that concerns the life and development of the school than that of these two men.

Needless to say, Mr. Wright W. Campbell has stood by Dr. Washington and the school with the same devotion and sacrifice as did his noble father. I might mention also such men as Mr. Hare and scores of the other white and colored people in this country and state who were also very kind, sympathetic and generous in those early days of the school, and I am glad to state that they are equally as sympathetic today.

The experimental seed of this new cooperation which was planted in 1881, by Mr. Campbell, and which during thirty-five years was so wisely, patiently and devotedly nurtured by Dr. Washington, has grown into a genuine reality in successful racial cooperation and helpfulness here at Tuskegee. It has far exceeded the most sanguine expectations of fifty years.

This unselfish working together of the white and colored races was truly of very great importance, but it was of equal importance to prove what was at that time very seriously doubted—whether there could be developed within the Negro race any forceful, unemotional, business-like, harmonious working together. This was a moot question, and one about which there was much real, though often kindly, sympathetic skepticism even among our own people. Dr. Washington, believing as he always did in the possibilities of this race, set out to prove that the

Negroes could work together and under Negro leadership, too, in educational as well as in business organizations. The success which those who compose the membership of the National Negro Business League, as well as many others outside the League, have had, was to him a reward of genuine satisfaction for his unfaltering faith in his people.

RESULTS OF COOPERATION

While he always sought the advice, criticism and help of the white race, he drew the "color line" when it came to the actual work of the institution. How well he succeeded is too self-evident for comment. These grounds and buildings, the consecrated lives and work of the men and women whom he gathered about him, are eloquent and convincing evidence of the wisdom of his course. I think now of such workers as Mr. Lewis Adams, Mr. R. R. Hamilton, and Mrs. Adella H. Logan, who like our great leader, "have conquered in the fight." We have with us still such faithful workers as Mr. Warren Logan, Mr. John H. Washington and Mr. C. W. Greene, who were willing with Dr. Washington to bear the burden and heat of those early days—these, my friends, with many others of the pioneer, as well as the present-day workers, because of their service and sacrifice have made possible the Tuskegee Institute of today, not only this splendid body of students, but transcendingly more significant and beautiful, they gave us the "Tuskegee Spirit"—the spirit of cooperation and consecration.

That spirit was not and it could not be confined to the campus. It is equally as manifest in the lives and work of the thousands of graduates and former students, such as William J. Edwards, W. H. Holtzclaw, Edgar A. Long and Cornelia Bowen,* who are but types of hundreds of others. They, like our great teacher, are working earnestly to bring about a clearer and better understanding between the races, "hastening that far-off divine event towards which the whole creation moves."

OVERCOMING OBSTACLES

Dr. Washington's ideas of education appeared so simple, so unconventional, and even unacademic, so vastly different from what had previ-

* William J. Edwards, '93, established the Snow Hill Normal and Industrial School in Wilcox County, Alabama; William H. Holtzclaw, '98, established, in 1903 the Utica Normal and Industrial Institute, in Utica, Mississippi; Cornelia Bowen, '85, established in 1889 the Mt. Meigs Colored Institute at Waugh, Alabama.

ously been expected of an educational institution, that he was often misunderstood. His methods and motives, in some quarters, were candidly questioned by honest people, especially members of his own race. This feeling took such form as would have discouraged and hampered an ordinary man, but with Dr. Washington, who was truly a prophet and a real seer, such opposition served only to spur him to greater and more persistent efforts.

When it was said that he did not approve of higher education for the Negro, he was at that time giving employment here to more Negroes with college training than any other single institution in the land. The fact that he was trustee of Howard and Fisk universities shows that he was in accord with such work.

Education was to him the means only, and not the end. The end was life—the life of the ignorant, poverty-stricken Negro who was earnestly longing for a chance. Dr. Washington cared little about the kind of education the Negro received, but he was exceedingly anxious that it should be thorough and well-suited to his reasonably immediate needs. The truth is, the need of industry and skill, of honesty and efficiency, the lack of land and decent homes, the imperative necessity for better methods of farming, together with the woeful lack of morality which was so prevalent among many of the untrained millions of Negroes—all this made such a strong appeal that any system of education which did not offer immediate relief for these masses made comparatively little impression on him.

TUSKEGEE SPIRIT

Dr. Washington worked out a plan of education which showed that the training of the mind should strengthen and supplement the physical and moral activities, especially of those who were fitting themselves for leadership. This system of all-round education for larger service which was so effectively carried on under his direction, has been so productive of good results, that it has attracted the attention and respect of educators, the world over. He worked out here a system of correlation of work and study, of industrial and academic instruction as complete and as satisfactory as probably could be found anywhere. Important and as satisfactory as this system was, however, the spirit back of it was of infinitely greater importance. It was the spirit of cooperation between the colored workers in the school and the white citizens outside of the school, and a consecration for the relief of mankind everywhere, whether in Macon County, the State of Alabama, or in the nation.

WE CAN DO IT

No greater or more serious responsibility was ever placed upon the Negro than is left us here at Tuskegee. The importance of the work and the gravity of the duty that have been assigned the Principal, the officers and the teachers in the forwarding of this work cannot be over-estimated. But along with the responsibility and difficulties, we have a rare opportunity, one almost to be envied,—an opportunity to help in the solution of a greater problem—the human race problem, not merely changing the modes of life and the ideas of a race, but of almost equal importance, changing the ideas of other races regarding that race.

Let us keep in mind the fact that, while the outlook was never more hopeful, the Negro problem is not yet solved. True, there are many people who thoroughly believe in Negro education, but we must remember that there are also many honest, sincere white people who are still doubtful as to the wisdom of educating the colored man. We can and we must convince that class of people that Negro education from every point of view is worthwhile. While there is great encouragement in the fact that seventy percent of the Negro population can read and write, it is not safe to assume that seventy percent of the Negro race are really and truly educated. Our progress in this country has been wonderful, and we have every reason for rejoicing; but ignorance, shiftlessness, disease, inefficiency and crime are entirely too prevalent among our people. Color and conduct still count in this question, but let us remember, my friends, that conduct counts a great deal more than color.

General Armstrong, Dr. Washington and Dr. Frissell, with the support and influence of such southern men as Mr. Campbell, have shown us the way out, and how these perplexing questions may be met and solved. If we follow the course mapped out here, we shall have the hearty cooperation and support of as distinguished, as wise, as unselfish, and as devoted a body of men as are to be found anywhere in this land. I refer to the Board of Trustees of this Institute. Not only so, but we will have also the cordial help and sympathy of the white and colored people of this state, from His Excellency, Governor Henderson and Superintendent Feagin, who honor this occasion by their presence, down to the humblest citizen. This whole country, too, will stand by us, if we are wise, sincere and unselfish. I again repeat, our responsibility is tremendous, and our opportunity is great. We should measure up to our responsibilities and our opportunities, and we can do it! Not by arrogant self-seeking, not by shrinking at difficulty, or shirking from duty, not by the cherishing of prejudice against white man or black man can the Tuskegee Institute live and prosper and serve.

In order that this institution shall continue to carry forward the ideas and ideals of its great Founder, in order that it shall not cease to render large service to humankind, in order that we shall keep the respect and confidence of the people of this land, we must, first, everyone of us, Principal, officers, teachers, graduates and students, use every opportunity and strive in every reasonable way, to develop and strengthen between the white and black people, North and South, that unselfish cooperation which has characterized the Tuskegee Institute from its beginning. Second, we must patiently and persistently and in the spirit of unselfish devotion, follow the methods of education which, in this school, have been so distinctive, so unique, and so helpful. Third, we must consecrate and reconsecrate our lives to this work as instruments in God's hands for the training of black men and women for service, in whatever capacity, or in whatever locality they may find a human need. Fourth, there must be no cantankerousness here—we must all work absolutely together.

SUCCESS THROUGH TEAM-WORK

In his last talk from this platform, Dr. Washington spoke on the value and importance of team-work. He urged that officers, teachers and students in every department, and in every phase of the work, should practice more than ever before, team-work, emphasizing the necessity of this vital essential of the school's success. If team-work, my friends, was necessary in this school under the leadership of Dr. Washington, how much more imperative the necessity is now, in as much as we have not the help and inspiration of his strong words and visible presence.

If we are to be true to this great and sacred trust, if we are to carry out the aims and purposes of Booker T. Washington, the Founder of this institution, we must each cherish and maintain the spirit which has always permeated the life and work of this place—the spirit of self-forgetfulness—the spirit of service and sacrifice—the "Tuskegee Spirit" —the spirit of cooperation and consecration. It is only in this spirit that the Tuskegee Normal and Industrial Institute can continue to render service to our people, to our state, to our country.

I cannot more fittingly or forcibly close these remarks than with the use of the following words from Dr. Washington's last Sunday evening talk:

"We want to have team-work," he said, "not only in the direction to which I have referred, but most of all, highest of all, we want to have team-work in our spiritual life, in our religious life, in the prayer meetings, in the preaching service, in every devotional exercise. We can get it by each one forgetting his own personal ambitions, forgetting selfishness, forgetting all that stands in the way of perfect team-work."

Published as an appendix in Anson Phelps Stokes, *Tuskegee Institute: The First Fifty Years* (Tuskegee Institute Press, 1931), pp. 80–86; originally published in *Tuskegee Student,* June 3, 1916.

27

THE AMENIA CONFERENCE OF 1916

With the death of Booker T. Washington, the firm establishment of the N.A.A.C.P., and the widening influence of *The Crisis,* it seemed apparent to many Afro-American leaders—and white associates—that the opportunity and the need existed for a fresh collective appraisal of the so-called "Negro Question." An added sense of urgency for such an effort derived from the fact that World War I was raging; actually, it was the entry of the United States into that war some eight months later which made academic the Amenia Conference. Nevertheless, its very convening marked an historic moment.

In addition to fifty Black "conferees"—as they were called—there were three white people: Mary W. Ovington, Joel E. and Arthur B. Spingarn. The Black people were listed as follows, in the original Program of the Conference:

Dr. Charles E. Bentley, Dentist .... Chicago
Rev. Hutchins C. Bishop, Rector of St. Philip's .... New York
Mr. W. L. Bulkley, Principal, Public School 79 .... New York
Mr. Charles Burroughs, Dramatic Reader .... New York
Miss Nannie Burroughs, Pres., School for Women .... Washington
Mr. W. Justin Carter, Lawyer .... Harrisburg
Mr. Charles W. Chesnutt, Author .... Cleveland
Mr. James A. Cobb, Lawyer .... Washington
Bishop L. J. Coppin, of the A.M.E. Church .... Philadelphia
Mr. George W. Crawford, Lawyer .... New Haven
Dr. W. E. B. Du Bois, Editor of *The Crisis* .... New York
Mr. G. W. Ellis, K.C., F.R.G.S., ex-Sec'y of Legation in Liberia .. Chicago
Prof Montgomery Gregory Howard University .... Washington

Rev. Francis J. Grimké, Clergyman .... Washington
Mr. John R. Hawkins, Financial Sec'y, A.M.E. Church ..... Washington
Mr. Mason A. Hawkins, Principal, High School .... Baltimore
Mr. W. Ashbie Hawkins, Lawyer .... Baltimore
Mr. L. M. Hershaw, of the Federal Civil Service .... Washington
President John Hope, Morehouse College .... Atlanta
Mrs. W. A. Hunton, Secretary, Y.W.C.A. .... Brooklyn
Bishop John Hurst, of the A.M.E. Church .... Baltimore
Mr. J. Rosamond Johnson, Composer, and
  Supervisor of the Music School Settlement ....New York
Hon. James W. Johnson, Contributing Editor, the *Age* .... New York
Mr. Robert E. Jones, Editor, *Christian Advocate* .... New Orleans
Dr. Ernest E. Just, Biologist and Spingarn Medallist .... Washington
Miss Lucy C. Laney, Principal, Haines Industrial Institute ...... Augusta
Hon. William H. Lewis, Ex-Asst. Att'y Gen. of U.S. .... Boston
Prof. Kelly Miller, Dean, Howard University .... Washington
Mr. Fred R. Moore, Editor of the *Age* .... New York
Major Robert R. Moton, Principal, Tuskegee Institute .... Alabama
Mr. J. C. Napier, Banker; ex-Register of the U.S. Treasury .... Nashville
Mr. Roy Nash, Secretary, N.A.A.C.P .... New York
Dr. I. G. Penn, Secretary, Freedmen's Aid M.E. Church ..... Cincinnati
Dean William Pickens, Morgan College .... Baltimore
Mr. Emmett J. Scott, Secretary, Tuskegee Institute .... Alabama
Dr. Wm. A. Sinclair, Douglass Memorial Hospital .... Philadelphia
Mr. Brown S. Smith, Lawyer .... Minneapolis
Mrs. M. B. Talbert, President, Nat'l Ass'n of Colored Women .... Buffalo
Mrs. Mary Church Terrell, Lecturer .... Washington
Judge Robert Terrell, Municipal Court, D.C. .... Washington
Mr. Neval H. Thomas, Teacher in the Public Schools .... Washington
Mr. Wm. Monroe Trotter, Editor, the *Guardian* .... Boston
Rev. Garnett R. Waller, Baptist Clergyman .... Springfield
Bishop Alexander Walters, A.M.E. Zion Church .... New York
Mr. Francis H. Warren, Lawyer .... Detroit
Mr. E. C. Williams, Librarian, Howard University .... Washington
Mr. W. T. B. Williams, Field Agent, Slater Fund .... Hampton
Mrs. Butler R. Wilson, Lecturer .... Boston
Dr. C. G. Woodson, Editor, *Journal of Negro History* ...... Washington
Pres. R. R. Wright, Sr., State Industrial College .... Savannah
Dr. R. R. Wright, Jr., Editor, *The Christian Recorder* ...... Philadelphia

Present also were twenty-nine people listed as "Guests for the Day"—
these included Black and white men and women as follows:

Mr. C. W. Anderson, Department of Agriculture .... New York
Mr. Ray Stannard Baker, Magazine Writer .... Amherst
Hon. William S. Bennett, Member of Congress .... New York
Mr. W. Scott Brown, Lawyer .... Oklahoma
Mr. A. G. Dill, Business Manager, *The Crisis* .... New York
Miss Rheta Childe Dorr, Magazine Writer .... New York
Mr. T. J. Elliott, President, State Negro Business League ...... Oklahoma

Miss Martha Gruening, Social Investigator .... New York
Mr. C. T. Hallinan, American Union Against Militarism .... Washington
Col. William Hayward, Public Service Commission .... New York
Mr. Fred C. Howe, Commissioner of Immigration .... Ellis Island
Mr. H. A. Hunt, Principal. Fort Valley Industrial School .... Georgia
Mrs. Paula Jakobi .... New York
Dr. V. Morton Jones, Headworker, Lincoln Settlement .... Brooklyn
Miss Fola LaFollette, Dramatic Reader .... New York
Miss Inez Milholland, Lawyer .... New York
Mr. John E. Nail, Real Estate .... New York
Hon. Herbert Parsons, Republican National Committee ...... New York
Mr. George Foster Peabody, Banker .... New York
Mr. H. T. Pulsifer, Editorial staff of the *Outlook* .... New York
Mr. Gilchrist Stewart, Real Estate .... New York
Miss Leila Stott .... Stottsville
Mr. Charles H. Studin, Lawyer .... New York
Lieut. V. M. Tandy, Architect .... New York
Mr. O. G. Villard, President, the *Evening Post* Company ..... New York
Miss Nell Vincent, Social Worker .... Princeton
Mr. Walter E. Weyl, Editor, *The New Republic* .... New York
Mr. Wm. R. Willcox, Republican National Committee .... New York
His Excellency, Charles A. Whitman, Governor of .... New York

Note that included in the above list were a Republican governor of the state, a Republican congressman from New York, and two members of the Republican Party National Committee—and no Democratic politicians, reflecting the estrangement Wilson's racism had caused.

Published below are [a] the Call for the Conference, from which are omitted only travel directions; and [b] the Program of the Conference.

[a]

THE CALL
Its Purpose

Few today deny the national character of Negro problems. Few leaders of the race will differ as to the wisdom of the colored millions in America acting together as a unit in opposition to the prejudices and discriminations which hamper practically every colored man, woman, and child in the United States, and every force which is working to advance their status. At last the time has come for a frank and free discussion on the part of the leaders of every school of thought, in an endeavor to ascertain the most advanced position that all can agree upon and hold as vantage ground from which to work for new conquests by colored Americans. In this belief the Amenia Conference is called.

Its Personnel

Fifty leaders of the colored race representing every school of thought and every form of activity—business, law, medicine, education, politics, scholarship, literature, art, social work, fraternal organizations, the church, the stage, music—have been invited to be the guests for three days of Dr. J. E. Spingarn, Chairman of the Board of Directors of the National Association for the Advancement of Colored People, at his home, "Troutbeck." Representative white men and women have also been invited to take part in the discussion from day to day.

The Place

The Conference will begin with luncheon on Thursday, August 24, in the village of Amenia, New York; which is eighty-five miles north of New York City, amid the hills and woodlands of Dutchess County.

The Time

The Conference will begin with luncheon on Thursday, August 24, and will be continued until late Saturday afternoon, August 26.

The Camp

The members of the Conference will be the guests of Dr. Spingarn from the time they arrive at Amenia station. A tent colony will be pitched on the shore of a three acre pond, equipped with cots and bedding, a commissariat, and a mess tent where the conferences can be held in case of rain. It will be camp accommodation and fare, but we believe the more enjoyable because made an informal gathering in the open air. Everyone is advised to bring a bathing suit.

Publicity

The Conference will not be open to the public; no reporters will be present; and the name of no one present will be published without his consent.

Patronage

The Conference has the approval and support of the National Association for the Advancement of Colored People, but the Association will
exercise neither authority nor responsibility in connection with any of
the proceedings. No member of the Conference is committed in any
way to the Association's programme or principles.

The Board of Directors of the Association consist of Moorfield Storey,
Oswald Garrison Villard, Archibald H. Grimké, Rev. John Haynes
Holmes, John E. Millholland, Mary White Ovington, Dr. W. E. B.
Du Bois, Rev. G. R. Waller, Jane Addams, Dr. C. E. Bentley, Rev. H. C.
Bishop, Dr. F. N. Cardozo, Rev. W. H Brooks, Prof. George W. Cook,
George W. Crawford, Bishop John Hurst, Dr. V. Morton Jones, Flor-
ence Kelley, Paul Kennaday, Joseph P. Loud, Charles H. Studin, John G.
Underhill, Lillian D. Wald, Dr. O. M. Waller, William English Walling,
Butler R. Wilson, and J. E. Spingarn.

[b]

PROGRAM

First Session, Thursday Afternoon—One to Five Opened with Prayer
by Bishop L. J. Coppin.
Introduction by J. E. Spingarn.
Mr. W. Ashbie Hawkins, presiding.
Subject: "Education and Industry."
Discussion opened by—Dean Kelly Miller,
                Mr. Emmett J. Scott.

Second Session, Thursday Evening at Seven
Mr. J. C. Napier, presiding.
Subject: "Industry and Education."
Discussion opened by—Mr. W. T. B. Williams,
                President John Hope.
Impromptu Entertainment.

Third Session, Friday Morning—Ten to Twelve
Judge Robert Terrell, presiding.
Subject: "The Negro in Politics."
Discussion opened by—Mr. William H. Lewis,
              Bishop Alexander Walters.

Fourth Session, Friday—One to Five
Major Robert R. Moton, presiding.
Subject: "Civil and Legal Discrimination."
Discussion opened by—Mr. George W. Crawford,
              Mr. Fred R. Moore.

Fifth Session, Friday Evening at Seven
Mr. Charles W. Chestnutt, presiding.
Subject: "Social Discrimination."
Discussion opened by—Mrs. Mary Church Terrell,
              Mr. Brown S. Smith.
Impromptu Entertainment.

Sixth Session, Saturday Morning—Ten to Twelve
Pres. R. R. Wright, Sr., presiding.
Subject: "Practical Paths."
Discussion opened by—Dean William Pickens,
              Mr. Robert E. Jones.

Seventh Session, Saturday Afternoon—One to Four-Thirty
Major John R. Lynch, presiding.
Subject: "A Working Programme for the Future."
Discussion opened by—Hon. James W. Johnson,
              Mr. L. M. Hershaw.

Two separate printed folders on "The Amenia Conference," printed privately at the time; in editor's possession.

28

LILY-WHITE LINCOLN

The spirited character of the Reverend Francis J. Grimké has already been manifest in preceding documents. There follows additional evidence, in an exchange between Dean George Johnson at Lincoln University in Pennsylvania and Mr. Grimké, early in 1916, concerning the then lily-white character of Lincoln's administrative trustee, and professional personnel— a condition not to be overcome for a generation.

THE COLLEGE
LINCOLN UNIVERSITY
CHESTER COUNTY, PENNA.

OFFICE OF THE DEAN

March 15, 1916

Reverend Francis J. Grimké, D.D.,
Pastor of 15th St. Presbyterian Church,
Washington, D.C.,
Dear Dr. Grimké:—

I have to make an address shortly on the relation of Lincoln University to the large cities of the country, and I should be very much obliged if you should find time to drop me a letter telling me in detail (1) what Lincoln graduates are doing for the betterment of conditions in Washington, and (2) what suggestions you could make as to what Lincoln could do to meet the conditions in these large cities.

Hoping to hear from you at your earliest convenience, I remain,

Yours very truly,
George Johnson

Washington, D.C. March 18, 1916

Dear Dr. Johnson,

Your note of March 15th has been received. Lincoln University has been so far behind all other Negro institutions in the country in its attitude toward colored people that I have had but very little patience with it for many years. Do you realize the fact that it is the only university in the United States for colored people that has never had a Negro among its professors or on its Trustee Board? When it celebrated its

Fiftieth Anniversary the one thing that it ought to have been proud of, and, doubtless, was, was the fact that during those fifty years, it alone of all Negro institutions had succeeded in shutting colored men out of its professorships and off its Trustee Board! How colored people with any self-respect can continue to feel kindly towards an institution that takes that attitude towards their race, I am unable to understand. I remember years ago a statement made to me by Rev. Mr. Webb, who was then acting as financial agent for the University, when I discussed the matter with him: He said: "Lincoln University has made no progress in that direction; Lincoln University has resolved not to." Is not that an astounding position for a Negro University to take.

You will pardon me if I say, I am unable to respond to your letter. I have no suggestions to make in regard to the University until it changes its attitude in regard to this matter. I am

Yours truly,
Francis J. Grimké

Washington, D.C., March 25, 1916

Dear Dr. Johnson:

Your note, in reply to my letter, has been received. I did not intend, in what I said in my letter, to hold you in any way responsible for conditions at Lincoln. I believe that you feel just as you say you do: "I am not conscious of any race prejudice and could work, as I have done in the past, along side of a man of any race without friction." If all the men at Lincoln felt as you do, this stigma which rests upon the University would long since have been removed. You say also, "Dr. Webb, I never knew, but from what I have been told he had no right to speak for the governing board since he was merely an employee, engaged for a definite time and a stated work. His opinion should not be quoted as expressing the policy of Lincoln University. He had neither voice nor vote in the Trustee Board." But, whether he had a right to speak or not, what he said was true, as attested by the history of the University during its entire existence. And, it is this fact, in its history, which cannot be denied, to which I am calling attention and which puts the University in a very bad light,—a light in which it ought to be ashamed, longer to remain.

Is it possible that the men who have been connected with Lincoln University are so far superior to the white men who have been connected with other Negro institutions of the country, that they alone feel themselves above being associated with colored men as professors and trustees? In all the other institutions,—in Howard, in Hampton, in

Fisk, in Atlanta, in Talladega, in Clark, the two races are represented in the governing boards and on the faculties. Why, I ask, is Lincoln the sole exception? The white men, as far as I know, who are teaching in these other institutions and serving on their governing boards, are not a whit inferior, judged by any test, to the white men who have been connected with Lincoln, or who are now connected with it. If they have not been afraid of being contaminated by contact with the brother in black in the capacity as trustees and professors, why should the men at Lincoln be? Lincoln, in this respect, has isolated itself from all the other Negro institutions of the country; and, it is an isolation that is not to its credit, an isolation that speaks badly for its professed Christianity. Judged, in the light of its history, in this respect, what faith, real, true faith, has Lincoln shown in the Negro as a man and a brother, when, in the election of its trustees and professors, it has said to him, Thus far, and no farther: you may come here as students, but never as professors and trustees. The remarkable thing is, that such a position should be taken by a Negro institution, and a professedly Christian institution!

Is it not strange, passing strange, that at the end of fifty years of freedom, it should be necessary to be discussing the question as to the propriety, the advisability of admitting colored men to the trustee board and to the faculty of a Negro institution, manned by professedly Christian men? The statement of the case alone is enough to show the absurdity of the position taken by the officials of Lincoln and the utterly unchristian spirit of the men who are responsible for it. The time has come, when it ought to end, when Lincoln ought to abandon the unworthy position which it has occupied during these fifty years, and take its place by the side of Howard, Atlanta, Fisk, Talladega and other institutions that are laboring for the uplift of the race. An institution, maintaining the attitude of Lincoln, whatever else may be said of it, is not helpful in developing in the race a manly self-respect; and is a standing argument against the professed friendship and Christian character of the men who have permitted this condition of things to continue as long as it has. There is no good or sufficient reason why Lincoln University should be the only one of all Negro institutions of higher learning to shut colored men out of its trustee board and out of its professorships. In the last analysis, when we get down to the bottom fact, the real reason will be found to be, though there isn't honesty enough, moral courage enough, to own up to it, *race prejudice*. This, I know, will be denied, but no denial can alter the fact. Lincoln, while professing faith in the Negro as a man and a brother, is not willing to accord to him the same rights, the same privileges that it accords to white men. And, when you ask why? the question is evaded, or some flimsy excuse is given, when as a matter of fact, the real reason is this accursed race prejudice, this dread of social equality, which is so widely prevalent in this country, and, which, even Christianity, the Christianity that is current in this country, is powerless to eradicate.

Lincoln ought to be ashamed of its record in this respect, and the men who are on its Trustee Board and in its faculty ought to see that a change is made; or else get out and let others get in who will have the moral courage and the Christian grace to put the University on a par with other Negro institutions in this respect. It is time, I say, that something was done. Let us hope that it will not be much longer delayed.

From what I have said, you will understand why I still cannot comply with your request. I am

Yours truly,
Francis J. Grimké

Woodson, ed., *Francis J. Grimké,* I, 123–26.

29

AN APPEAL TO REJECT WILSON, 1916

As noted earlier, there was a significant turn toward Woodrow Wilson by some Black voters in the 1912 election; but, after four years of his administration, the return to the Republican party was fairly complete. Indicative is the following advertisement which filled three pages of *The Crisis* for November, 1916 (XIII, 4–6).

ADDRESS TO THE COLORED VOTERS
by the
COLORED ADVISORY COMMITTEE
of the
REPUBLICAN NATIONAL COMMITTEE
Adopted in New York on
October 6, 1916

The Committee of Colored Citizens selected from the country at large as Advisory to the Republican National Committee having met this day in New York City and desiring to express to the colored voters of the country the necessity for supporting the Republican Party candidates for President, Vice-President, Senate and House of Representatives addresses this letter to the colored voters of the country whose duty it is to register in order that they may perform their duty to the country in this National crisis.

This is the Presidential year. The time has come to hold the Wilson Administration and the Democratic Party to a *"strict accountability."* Are you ready for the fight? Or do you desire four years more of what the New York World calls the "Jim Crow Government at Washington"? No campaign since that for the second election of Abraham Lincoln has been more vital to the liberty and happiness of the 10,000,000 of colored citizens than is the present campaign for the election of Charles Evans Hughes for President, and a Republican Congress.

Four years ago a considerable number of the race helped to elect a Democratic president. This was done under fair promises of just treatment, "not grudgingly given but in generous fashion." The result has shown the experiment to have been the utmost political folly and race-suicide, and has shown that the Democratic party cannot be trusted to deal fairly with our race in this country. The votes of the men of color for the Democratic candidates for President were obtained by fine phrases and false pretenses. No sooner had the Democratic Administration come into power than Mr. Wilson and his advisors entered upon a policy to eliminate all colored citizens from representation in the Federal Government. The offices of Assistant Attorney General, Recorder of Deeds, Register of the U.S. Treasury, Auditor for the Navy, Minister to Hayti, Collectorships of Internal Revenue in New York, Florida, and Hawaii, were vacated and filled by white Democrats. There were no "deserving Colored Democrats" to be found in the country. Not only did the Administration proceed to demote and eliminate the Negro from the Civil Service of the United States by scores, and to segregate those remaining in the service, but also to make impossible further appointments by requiring the race of the applicant to be shown by his photograph.

The Administration was "too proud to fight" Mexico but did not hesitate to conquer the Black Republic of Hayti and Santo Domingo. There was one policy of International justice for Mexico and another one for the Negro Republics to the south of us. The President has expressed himself as in sympathy with the "enslaved men and women of Mexico," but has found no words of sympathy for the Colored citizens of America. "The New Freedom" does not include the Negro. "Humanity" for which the President has expressed such great love, does not include the Colored Race. The President said in a notable address that "the man who seeks to divide man from man, group from group, and interest from interest is striking at the very heart of America." No man has done so much since Emancipation to separate and divide the Nation into groups, and to eliminate the Colored Race as a representative group of Americans, as has the President himself.

Colored men, we must arise! Those who vote and those entitled to vote must strike for their liberties. This is a campaign for the restoration of the rights, privileges and immunities that we have heretofore enjoyed under a Republican Administration of the National Government. Four years more of President Wilson will mean our complete elimination from American politics. We submit that the man who is ready to die for his country at Carrizal is good enough to serve his country at Washington; and that the man who is fit to be buried in the National Cemetery at Arlington, is fit to serve his country in the Capitol of the Nation.

The Republican candidate for President, Charles Evans Hughes, has shown himself to be a man of highest character and of absolute sincerity in his devotion to the cause of liberty, justice, and humanity, and when he is elected President of the United States, we may confidently expect from him a square deal and complete protection in all our sacred rights as citizens, and the full enjoyment of the opportunities to which we are justly entitled, under the Constitution and Laws of our Country.

SIGNED:

Charles W. Anderson, of N.Y.
William H. Lewis, of Mass.
William Oscar Payne, of N.Y.
Andrew F. Stevens, of Pa.
W. Justin Carter, of Pa.
Charles A. Cottrill, of Ohio.
William P. Dabney, of Ohio.
Harry S. Cummings, of Md.
Charles Colburn, of Del.
Philip Waters, of W. Va.
Whitfield McKinlay, of D.C.
James A. Cobb, of D.C.
Charles Pickett, of D.C.
R. R. Church, Jr., of Tenn.

Fred R. Moore, of N.Y.
W. C. Matthews, of Mass.
Rev. Richard M. Bolden, of N.Y.
Junius M. Green, of N.Y.
Gilchrist Stewart, of N.Y.
Harry G. Tolliver, of Conn.
Rev. Ernest Lyon, of Md.
J. C. Napier, of Tenn.
A. A. Felding, of Tenn.
Henry Lincoln Johnson, of Ga.
Benjamin J. Davis, of Ga.
Perry W. Howard, of Miss.
Joseph E. Lee, of Fla.

30

LYNCHING AND THE N.A.A.C.P.

In 1916, after thousands of white people in Waco, Texas, had made a holiday out of the torture and burning of Jesse Washington, the N.A.A.C.P. issued a four-page folder commencing " 'Life, Liberty and the Pursuit of Happiness' On Our Own Side of the Border"—the latter phrase an ironic reference to U.S. intervention in Mexico, then in progress. Below this appeared a photograph of the lynching of five men—hung together on one tree—in Lee County, Georgia, on January 20, 1916. The text of the two inside pages is reproduced below. The fourth page reproduced a postcard, received by Rev. John H. Holmes, a vice-president of the N.A.A.C.P., postmarked Andalusia, Alabama, with a photograph of perhaps fifty white men (and boys) surrounding the body of a lynched Black man. The postcard bore the legend PRINTED IN GERMANY. Below the reproduction of the card was the following: "The colored voter who votes for a man who acquiesces in, or 'pussy-foots,' on this issue of lynching and lawlessness, is a traitor to his race. FIND OUT WHERE THEY [political candidates for the November, 1916, elections] STAND. THE SOUTH IS IN THE SADDLE!"

RAPE IS NOT THE REASON

A Lee County Farmer named McGuinn, shot by a mob, took refuge in old man Lake's house. The sheriff came for the wounded man while the Lake boys were out of the house, and was shot by McGuinn. Although the mob knew the Lakes had nothing to do with the shooting, they returned the next night and hanged old man Lake, his three sons, and a nephew to "The Dogwood Tree," merely as an expression of White Supremacy.

THIS WOMAN DID NOT COMMIT RAPE

Albany, Ga., October 4, 1916.—A Negro woman, named Connelly, whose son is charged with killing a white farmer after a quarrel in which she took part, was taken from the jail at Leary, Ga., some time Monday night and lynched, according to reports reaching here to-day. Her body, riddled with bullets, was found to-day.

The son is under arrest.—*Associated Press dispatch, New York Times,* Oct. 5.

FIVE HUNG FOR A HOG

On August 18, 1916, the sheriff went from Gainesville, Florida, at two o'clock in the morning to arrest Boisy Long for hog stealing. Boisy shot the sheriff and escaped. In retribution next morning, the mob hanged Boisy's wife, Stella Long; Mary Dennis (pregnant), James Dennis, and Bert Dennis, neighbors; and Josh Baskin, a colored preacher—all to the same "Dogwood Tree," as an expression of White Supremacy.

Here is a typical year—1915

Colored men lynched	74	For Murder	32
Colored women lynched	5	For Stealing	9
Colored children lynched	1	For Rape and attempted rape	9
Colored Citizens	80	For Resisting arrest	6
		For Unknown reasons	6
		For Improper Advances to women	5
		For Assault	3
Hanged	71	For Threats and insults	3
Shot	3	For Poisoning mules	3
Drowned	1	For Concealing fugitives	2
Burned alive	5	Miscellaneous	2
Tortured Citizens	80	American Citizens	80

THREE REGIMENTS, 2850, LYNCHED SINCE 1885
LESS THAN 33 PER CENT, FOR RAPE, ATTEMPTED RAPE, AND ALLEGED RAPE

THE WACO HORROR
THERE ARE CRIMES EVEN WORSE THAN RAPE
HERE IS ONE:
[A Photo of the Lynch Scene Appears]

On May 8, 1916, Jesse Washington, a boy of seventeen, of deficient mentality, raped and murdered the wife of his employer.

On May 15, 1916, he was tried in Waco, Texas, and condemned to hang that same afternoon. With the connivance of Sheriff Fleming and without protest from Judge Munroe, the mob took the prisoner from the courtroom to the square under the Mayor's window, where the camera was set up which took the above photograph. Fifteen thousand

Texans shouted their approval while those near enough unsexed him; cut off his fingers, nose, and ears; and burned him alive; after which the remains were dragged through the streets of a city of 40,000, bouncing at the end of a lariat.

The teeth brought five dollars each, and the links of the chain, twenty-five cents.

This while the gallant Negro Troopers of the Tenth Cavalry were on their way to Carrizal.

HOW LONG ARE SUCH MOBS TO BE ALLOWED TO DRAG THE NATION'S GOOD NAME IN THE DUST?

31

BATTLE REPORTS FROM THE FIELD, 1916

As of December, 1916, the N.A.A.C.P. had a membership of 8,642 men and women; there were, then, only three branches in the South—New Orleans, Shreveport, and Key West—with a total of 348 members, and three college chapters—Howard, Lincoln (Pa.), and Virginia Union—with a total of 243 members.

On that date the N.A.A.C.P. commenced publication of its *Branch Bulletin,* an inner organ to make known to the leadership and membership details, projects, and problems at the local level. The reports in these *Bulletins* constitute a splendid source for grass-roots history. Published below are those made as of November 15, 1916, and the Annual Reports from several branches, as published in the *Bulletin* for January, 1917, pp. 14–15.

[a]

FOR PERIOD OCTOBER 15–NOVEMBER 15, 1916

Providence, R.I.—From October 11 to November 15 we have taken in ten new members. On Sunday, November 19th, we had a "Brotherhood Day" in Providence. As the Providence Branch looks back over its three years effort, not one stands out more conspicuously than that of Brotherhood Day.

In the minds of many of the active workers the ideal of the

N.A.A.C.P. has not been reached, for with few exceptions our membership was almost entirely colored.

The interest of the white people was confined mostly to annual membership fees.

Our committee decided to bring our work before as many white audiences as possible.

At the First Baptist Church, the pastor kindly gave up his morning service to our speaker, President John Hope, of Morehouse College, Atlanta, Ga. The congregation was made up very largely of the most conservative and wealthy people of the city, besides many college men.

At the noon hour President Hope addressed the Brotherhood of the Calvary Baptist Church—audience made up almost entirely of business men.

At the Civic Forum in the afternoon, the speaker, Mr. Butler R. Wilson, of Boston, spoke to a mixed audience, which packed one of the theatres of the city. Mrs. Sarah Algeo, chairman of the Woman Suffrage Party, presided.

At 7:30 P.M. an appreciative audience greeted Mr. Wilson at the Beneficent Congregational Church. The Rev. Asbury Krom, a member of the Providence Branch, very heartily welcomed the speaker.

At 8 o'clock Dr. J. Robinson, president of the local branch, spoke before a packed audience at the Peoples Forum, a gathering made up of the most radical thinkers in the community.

At both the afternoon and evening Forum questions ranging from women's suffrage to intermarriage were hurled at the speakers, and in answering much valuable information was given to people, who know so little of Negro problems.

At a very conservative estimate more than 2,000 persons were reached on Brotherhood Day. National Association literature was freely distributed at both forum meetings.

At the afternoon meeting Mrs. Ethel J. Minton sang several solos.

Monday morning President Hope addressed the students at chapel at Brown University, and also spoke at the quarterly meetings of the Rhode Island Ministers Union.

We are interested in trying to secure a position for one of our trained nurses as a District Nurse in Providence.

So far as we have investigated we are pretty sure it is a matter of color prejudice which is keeping her back. She is a graduate from a hospital of recognized standing, and also has received a certificate of training for a special course in district work.

For the next few months, we are going to bend all our energies

But there is evidence that the present city administration is losing no time in acting to improve the Harlem situation; partly no doubt upon the specific findings and recommendations of the recent investigation, but largely from previous plans, seriously delayed by lack of capital funds or federal subsidies such as are now financing some of the major items of the reform program. Within recent months, in some cases weeks, Harlem's urgent community needs have been recognized in the reconditioning of its sorely inadequate and formerly overcrowded municipal hospital, the completion and equipment of a long delayed women's hospital pavilion approximately doubling the bed capacity of the Harlem Hospital, the remodelling of a temporary out-patient department, and the recommendation by the Commissioner of Hospitals of a new out-patient building and of plans for a new independent hospital plant. Similarly, in the school system's 1937 budget two new school plants for Harlem have been incorporated. On June 20, the Mayor and the Secretary of the Interior spoke at the dedication of the foundations of the new Harlem River housing project, which will afford model housing for 574 low income families with also a nursery school, community playground, model recreation and health clinic facilities—a $4,700,000 P.W.A. project. On June 24, the Mayor drove the last foundation piling for another P.W.A. project, the $240,000 district health clinic for the badly congested Central Harlem section, where the incidence of tuberculosis, social disease and infant mortality is alarmingly high, and announced the appointment of an experienced Negro physician as head officer. It has been announced that a stipulation had been incorporated in the contract specifications for these new public works that Negro skilled labor was to have its fair share of consideration.

All this indicates a new and praiseworthy civic regard for Harlem welfare, contrasting sharply with previous long-standing neglect. The Commission in complaining of present conditions is careful to make plain that the present city administration has inherited most of them and that, therefore, they are not to be laid at its door. Yet they are on its doorstep, waiting immediate attention and all possible relief. The conditions are a reproach not only to previous politically minded municipal administrations but also to the apathy and lack of public-mindedness on the part of Harlem's Negro politicians and many professional leaders who either did not know or care about the conditions of the masses.

Recent improvements will make some sections of the Commission's report contrary to present fact when it appears, but few will care to cavil about that. Yet, both for the record and for the sake of com-

will be in February. We also arranged to have a public meeting in December to raise funds for our treasury, and took up the matter of discrimination against colored people, relative to using public tennis courts in the parks of this city. The matter came up when some time late last summer two of our colored teachers rented a court on what is known here as Penn Common, and, after playing a short while, were handed back their money and told that they could not play any longer because of complaint from white citizens. The Grievance Committee took the matter up with the Park Commissioners, who are City Council men, and they, the Commissioners, decided that we colored folks can use the court in the morning, but not in the afternoon. We have no reply as yet to the following letter:

November 6, 1916

My Dear Mr. Stuffer: The Executive Committee of the local branch of the N.A.A.C.P. has received a report from Miss Ella J. Robertson, chairman of the Grievance Committee, relative to restrictions placed on colored people using tennis courts in this city. Her report states that the Park Committee decided at a meeting at which you presented the matter, that colored people may use the court on Penn Common at certain hours in the morning but not in the afternoon.

We are heartily sorry to see the widespread and growing discrimination in the simplest matter of public accommodation in this community, and especially when it is unjustly sanctioned by officers of the law, whose duty it is to uphold and secure for all the full enjoyment of their rights as citizens.

We respectfully ask that the matter be given further consideration and that the final decision be communicated to us. We are yours very respectfully,

Rev. W. Edward Williams, President
Dr. Wm. W. Gittens, Secretary

Lincoln University, Pa.—Our regular meeting night is Tuesday of every week. However, during the first part of the term it is difficult to do any efficient amount of work because of the fact that football, athletic meetings and class affairs occupy most of the students' spare time. As the school term grows older our work is progressing. At our regular meetings we have discussed various race questions with a great deal of interest and with good results. On every meeting night there are several essays read. Comments in the form of impromptu speeches are then made. We intend in the near future to have a prize essay contest at Lincoln in order to interest the whole student body in the work of the organization.—J. A. Creditt, secretary.

Virginia Union, Richmond, Va.—We have had four public meetings. Literature was distributed and new members taken in. We have had

of its trade was with Negroes, has always discriminated against Negroes in employment. Shortly before the riot it had been the objective of a picketing campaign for the employment of Negro store clerks, had grudgingly made the concession of a few such jobs and then transferred the so-called "clerks" to service at the lunch counter. While the original culprit slept peacefully at home, a community of 200,000 was suddenly in the throes of serious riots through the night, with actual loss of life, many injuries to police and citizens, destruction of property, and a serious aftermath of public grievance and anger. The careful report of the Commission on this occurrence correctly places the blame far beyond the immediate precipitating incidents. It was not the unfortunate rumors, but the state of mind on which they fell; not the inflammatory leaflets issued several hours after the rioting had begun by the Young Liberators, a radical Negro defense organization, or the other broadside distributed a little later by the Young Communist League, but the sense of grievance and injustice that they could depend on touching to the quick by any recital of fresh wrong and injustice.

The report finds that the outbreak was spontaneous and unpremeditated; that it was not a race riot in the sense of physical conflict between white and colored groups; that it was not instigated by Communists, though they sought to profit by it and circulated a false and misleading leaflet after the riots were well underway; that the work of the police was by no means beyond criticism; and that this sudden breach of the public order was the result of a highly emotional situation among the colored people of Harlem, due in part to the nervous strain of years of unemployment and insecurity. ". . . Its distinguishing feature was an attack upon property rather than persons, and resentment against whites who, while exploiting Negroes, denied them an opportunity to work." The report warns of possible future recurrences, offering as the only safe remedy the definite betterment of economic and civic conditions which, until improved, make Harlem a "fertile field for radical and other propaganda."

It is futile, [the report continues] to condemn the propagandists or to denounce them for fishing in troubled waters. The only answer is to eliminate the evils upon which they base their arguments. The blame belongs to a society that tolerates inadequate and often wretched housing, inadequate and inefficient schools and other public facilities, unemployment, unduly high rents, the lack of recreation grounds, discrimination in industry and the public utilities in the employment of colored people, brutality and lack of courtesy by police. As long as these conditions remain, the public order can not and will not be safe.

also the unionization of Negroes in the South before the conference. A review of work of this convention will show the Ohio delegates did introduce such resolutions.

Some method should be discussed to have members pay their dues from year to year and promptly, without undue urging or effort on part of officers, as they are usually busy themselves.—S. P. Keeble, secretary.

Columbus, O.—Several letters from you recently have been unanswered because the vice-president and other executive members thought I should not reply until the branch or Executive Committee had authorized the answer. When the president called the Executive Committee, only three members were present—the president, treasurer and secretary.

The president of our branch was re-elected to the Legislature. Mr. Jones is a member of the Democratic party, yet he has been faithful and earnest, missing only two or three meetings since his election two or three years ago. He has shown more interest in us than many of our own race, to say nothing of white Republicans of our city. He feels very keenly the lack of support given him by the Executive Committee, and will not longer remain at the helm.

The protest filed with the Chief of Police relative to the boys who were ordered from the park, was filed by the president. The chairman of the Legal Redress Committee, Mr. Robert Barcuss, opposed the same, but the president, who is a lawyer also, told the branch he thought some action should be taken and the branch voted to have Mr. Jones take charge of the matter.

The lack of interest on the part of several of the members of the Executive Committee in the branch work, and their untiring effort in behalf of the Y.M.C.A., has called forth some comment and dissatisfaction in the branch. The Y.M.C.A. is tangible results, and many of our people are poor workers where results are not obvious.

The Meetings Committee, of which Mr. J. Foster Lewis is chairman, has rendered splendid service during the past year. The October meeting was a mass meeting, a real free floor meeting, to discuss the question of race discrimination; as a result, letters of protest were sent to Mr. Fred Harvey because of discrimination against one of our citizens in the railroad station restaurant, St. Louis, Mo.; to Mr. Fred Lazarus, Sr., because of discrimination against colored women in sewing class conducted by the F. & R. Lazarus Co., of this city; and resolutions expressing appreciation, gratitude and respect to Mr. Sherman Eley, of Lima, Ohio. A reply from Mr. Harvey stated that he had been unable to find any one familiar with the case cited in our letter; that the instance is one where an employee oversteps authority, as they are opposed to that sort of discrimination.

The November meeting furnished a splendid program—a paper on "The Migration of the Negroes from the South," and other on "Civil Rights of Negroes in Ohio." (Two new members October 1 to November 15, 1916.)

The high schools of Columbus have an arrangement with Indianola Park authorities for space where football games are played. Several high school teams have colored boys on them. All members of teams are admitted by "pass" to see any game being played. In September four colored boys were ordered out of the park by the manager. One of the boys, a member of the playing team, was permitted to remain when the coach declared the game was off if the colored boy could not play. The three other boys were ordered out of the park. They refused to leave and the manager called the police. A sergeant and patrolman arrived, ordered the boys out, calling them "niggers" and threatening arrest. The boys then left the park and witnessed the game from a tree-top on the outside. Our branch has filed a protest with the Chief of Police. (Will advise later of results.)

Many hindrances have confronted us this fall and our election has been unavoidably delayed. We are arranging to have election take place in a few days.—Minnie B. Mosby, secretary.

Dayton, O.—I am pleased to say that I have at last succeeded in getting our members together and have had election of officers. Our work has not been very prosperous; nothing of note. Have had only four meetings during the year. Our president, Mr. Farrow, resigned his work. I trust this coming year will be prosperous, as there is much important work that might be done here.—Mrs. D. Richardson, secretary.

Springfield, O.—To create a deeper interest in the branch and as a means of acquainting the people generally with the work of the association, the new president thinks it would be well to divide the city into districts and establish a neighborhood betterment club in each district. The object of this is to reach the people who are not members and to induce them to join the branch. The work of these clubs will be confined to their immediate district, and any discrimination or grievance is to be presented to the Grievance Committee of the branch, and the matter adjusted through the branch.

A great deal of attention will be given the schools, through the Educational Committee, which will try to organize a High School Club to encourage students to finish the high school course, to help students decide which course to pursue, and to do what they can to secure them situations.

No new members have been received since October 1, but this branch hopes to come to the front after the new organization is effected at the meeting to be held Tuesday, December 5, at which time other plans will be presented and worked out.—M. Sula Butler, secretary.

Toledo, O.—We have about $200 in the local treasury after all bills are paid; have received six new members since October 1, and we had a magnificent public meeting on October 8, with Frank A. Mulholland as the speaker.

Through the work of the branch we have had a member of the race on the Grand Jury and also in the Court of Common Pleas, Judge Byron F. Ritchie sitting. Mr. Albertus Brown, president of the branch, occupied the bench in Police Court two days last month, while Judge Austin was out of the city.

Our branch has made a donation to the Colored Working Girls' Home, also to the Florence Crittendon Home here.

We find frequent meetings are needed to keep alive the interest in the work, and are planning for at least six this year.—Della H. Fields, secretary.

Buffalo, N.Y.—The Buffalo branch held a mass meeting in connection with the meeting for the election of officers.

The Educational Committee is organizing a branch of the Camp Fire Girls.

Plans for a membership campaign are being made, by which the Buffalo branch hopes to increase its membership two or three hundred during the coming year.—Amelia G. Anderson, secretary.

Cincinnati, O.—With reluctance I am compelled to impart to you the true state of affairs here. As you know, no doubt, I have never been elected to office. Yet I have striven to carry on the work of branch secretary since last January. My only purpose has been to help keep the organization going, and I have given my time cheerfully, realizing the overwhelming need for the organization's ideals to become felt. Neither do I feel that I have made any sacrifice, for I am one of those whose interests are centered in the success of the N.A.A.C.P.

To relate to you my experience at the meeting of our branch held August 9 there was no official present, save one member of the Executive Committee. This threw the entire responsibility upon me, and I was not in the best of shape to meet it, having come from a long and exacting day's work.

Since that time I have called a meeting of the Executive Committee to confer upon matters brought to my attention by your office, with the result that I have had one member present. Our president, Mr. Stevenson, is out of the city the great part of his time, and advised me that he could not say when he could be present at a meeting for election of officers. Still, I absolutely cannot muster time or energy at present or in the very near future, on account of the rigorous nature of my work, but shall endeavor to find somebody who will make things go, and will advise you accordingly. A. L. Imes, acting secretary.

Indianapolis, Ind.—I regret to say I see no way of electing officers of our local just now. I wish it was so that some one from the Association could come here.—Sallie B. Henderson, secretary.

St. Paul.—The St. Paul branch held its annual election November 9. After the business of the evening was finished the Rev. J. M. Henderson, of the St. James M. E. Church, gave an address.

This branch has opened a forum, which meets the second and fourth Sundays of each month.—Charlotte Gillard, secretary.

Gary, Ind.—Regarding the question of school segregation, the secretary of the Gary branch, Elizabeth Lytle, writes:

In reply to your inquiry concerning the schools, I think I can best reply by just a statement of facts as I see them.

Over six years ago, when I became connected with these schools, the colored children were in a building by themselves. Later, a large building—Froebel—was completed, and both colored and white children placed in it, the colored classes remaining separate as when in the former building. All the formal work of the colored children in the first five grades was done with colored teachers in separate classes—the special teachers receiving them in the same way as class units.

In September last two classes were removed from the Froebel Building to a small school more convenient to their homes, as it appeared, and the idea became spread abroad that it was done because they were colored.

A committee of this branch of the N.A.A.C.P. visited the superintendent and school board, with but small satisfaction resulting. Then an effort was made to prevent the children from attending the small school above named, but without success.

After some while, it now seems that some white classes are to be placed in other small buildings now being erected in the same yard (temporarily), and I am somewhat of the opinion that the general fear of complete segregation has lessened to a degree.

As to what best to do about the matter, I am unable to say.

The claim is made by the school authorities that a request came eight years ago from a few of the earliest colored citizens for a separate school, on account of many unpleasantnesses between them and the various nationalities found here.

On November 20, the superintendent of schools wrote the national secretary:

The colored children in the public schools in Gary, Indiana, have been segregated from the very beginning. It is a settled policy in this community to continue this segregation.

Sincerely yours,
William A. Wirt
Superintendent of Schools

Gary, Ind., November 22, 1916

I received the copy of your letter to the superintendent of the Gary schools of the 18th. We had planned a meeting for Tuesday to prepare to meet with the school board Thursday, but there were not enough members out to appoint a committee, so we will not meet with the school board this week. Everybody seems to be fatigued or worked down. Some of the members are disgusted at the parents who are still keeping their children in the 21st street school. The parents who still have their children in the 21st street school say that they would like to be assured that their children will be given their lessons before they send them back to the Froebel school, as their children had to go without their lessons for two weeks when they were sent away by the principal September 12. And, to add to our burden, our arch enemy, *The Birth of a Nation,* is reported to be shown here the first part of December. We have not had a day's rest since we have been organized here. I noticed that you speak of the much advertised Wirt system. On account of the discrimination against the colored children in almost every department of the school we can only recommend it for just what it stands for—one of the most discouraging and complicated systems that has ever been instituted into public schools.

I can only speak for myself. Again, I think there ought to be somebody here to revive and help us, as this may be in the future one of the most important branches of the West. There is now a constant influx of colored people from the South, and Gary's population is almost twice what it was two years ago. Among the colored people this movement of the school board may be to discourage the settlement of colored people in Gary, or the superintendent thinks, like the Southern gentlemen, that he knows better what the colored man needs than he does himself.

Louis Campbell, Secretary

At last the terrible thing has happened to Gary. *The Birth of a Nation* has arrived. This is the first time it has been tried here. Every effort is being put forth to stop the production. But the Mayor of Gary says he does not see any harm in the show; so you see what we are up against. May God help us as a race.

John A. Melby

St. Louis, Mo.—In response to your letter regarding segregation in the Postoffice Department here, I found upon investigation conditions as follows:

There are two general sections—paper section and letter section. Paper section is made up almost entirely of colored clerks. When for any reason the necessity arises and an extra clerk or clerks are needed, then a white man is used in this section. The letter section is made up of an almost entirely white force, except when the necessity arises. Then a colored man is used in this section. It is noticeable that the lockers are separate in that the lockers for the paper section clerks are at one end of the locker room and lockers for the letter section clerks are at the other end of the room.

Colored clerks and carriers are not being called any more. In applying for either position it is required of one to send photograph with application, thus giving them the privilege of rejection if the applicant is a person of color..

I think the best method of fighting it would be through the Postoffice Department at Washington. The postmaster (Mr. Selph) is aspiring for an executive position there. He is striving to have the best managed postoffice in the United States. Therefore, any criticism or investigation coming from headquarters, in my opinion would be more effective. Mr. Selph usually resents, and feels most keenly, outside criticism. In order to cater to his prejudices (Southern) he is most anxious to practice color prejudice but at the same time it is my opinion that, since he has the ambition heretofore mentioned, he might not wish to go on record before the country at large as one of the "Tillman" type —Cora F. Wilkerson, secretary.

Quincy, Ill.—On November 23 we had an inaugural meeting at the A.M.E. Church, to create an interest in the organization. The program consisted of general remarks, and an appeal by the president, Dr. H. J. Nichols. Music, Miss Estella Zimmerman and Miss Ida Drake Garnett; address, "Club Woman," Mrs. Julia Dyson; vocal solo, Miss Ida Drake Garnett; address, "A Mere Child Can Whip Us," Mrs. F. E. Cook. Rev. H. W. Trueblood, one of the leading white ministers of the city, installed the officers, and talked on loyalty to each other. He seems to think that is the biggest problem that the colored man has. Several renewed their membership.—Florence E. Cook, secretary.

Topeka, Kan.—The Branch will hold regular monthly meetings on the first Wednesday of each month, and is now planning a campaign for new members.—Julia B. Rountree, secretary.

New Orleans.—The following letter which the New Orleans branch sent to every colored organization in the city, and to business and professional groups, indicates how vigorously they are fighting, and one abuse against which the whole organization should help them protest:

The New Orleans Branch of the National Association for the Advancement of Colored People has taken up the task of removing from the public the most humiliating and disgraceful scene that can be imposed upon a race of people, that is, the use of *Negro Women* prisoners upon all the public works. We presume that during your daily travels over this city in whatever walks of life you may be engaged, you encounter with the prisoners, either in the public parks, markets, building, etc.

We shall not ask from you any financial favors, but we are seeking your moral and unlimited support.

In dealing with a question so vital as that of public servitude by women, it must be remembered that the moral and civic sides of this question are paramount to all others. The very menial aspect of the problem—for problem it is—clearly renders these unfortunate women less culpable than those invested with power to inflict or nullify these means of punishment for female prisoners; for every man in the land with any sense of reason and justice knows that superiority never was made manifest by discourtesy, inconsideration, or oppression, and it is no less clear to the sound thinker that women were never made better when encouraged or forced into degrading position or condition, and their mere inferiority in strength of character warrants for them this consideration.

The standard of every race being measured by that of its women, then, as we have stated above, according to your candid opinion, do you believe that our race is up to the standard of any other race, without exception? It is flagrantly unfair to the law-abiding and conservative element of our race to so advertise for the mere sake of punishment these less fortunate and miserably needy women.

The only advantage derived by the prisoners used on the public works is that they are given one-half time off, but such only encourages their violation of the law more frequently; this should not be considered, as prisoners should not have any wants; further, can prisoners have any wants in preference of 100,000 law-abiding Negroes?

As a peaceful and progressive people, honest in your efforts to better your conditions, we are seeking your approval and hearty co-operation.

It has been said that only a few of our people have been interested in such a move, that the majority are somewhat indifferent, but we believe that the matter has not been thought of seriously by the race, and the thought of any hope of being able to remedy the matter is available. Surely, the good results obtained therefrom are incommensurate with the immense train of evil wrought.

It is absolutely necessary that each and every colored man and woman of the race should take active interest in the propaganda of this irreparable wrong.

A committee from this branch is to call on the Mayor of this city and it is absolutely necessary that they should have the support of your organization. Therefore, you should pledge yourselves by sending resolutions to the as-

27

"THERE GOES GOD!"
THE STORY OF FATHER DIVINE
AND HIS ANGELS

by Claude McKay

There is no adequate study of the Father Divine Movement—one of the remarkable phenomena in U.S. history. George Baker, a Black man from Georgia, attracted some attention as early as 1919 as the leader of an all-Black communal group in Sayville, Long Island, in New York. His followers increased slowly in the nineteen-twenties, though whites had become adherents by 1926. With the depression it grew by leaps and bounds and, while overwhelmingly Afro-American, did contain many whites—especially women. Branches appeared in many cities in the East, Midwest, and Pacific states— these were known as Peace Missions or heavens. Until World War II Father Divine's followers numbered in the tens of thousands; his program was pacifistic and anti-racist and also called for government ownership and operation of all factories lying idle. An essay on his movement by Claude McKay is published below.

The most African characteristic of Harlem, after the color of its people, is the multitude of amazing cults. Native African churches (so-called), groups of Negro-Jews, and a host of straight Christian and revival sects pullulate in Harlem. To say that there is a cult to every block would be no exaggeration.

It is through religion, more than any other channel, that primitive African emotions find expression in our modern civilization. Indoors and along the pulpit pavements of Harlem, black men and women, some singularly robed, ecstatically prance and reel and writhe with a fervor that is tolerated simply because their exhibitions bear the label of religion. No Negro cabaret or Negro theater could permit the display of such very African antics.

Returning to Harlem after three years spent in North Africa, I had a queer, topsy-turvy sensation when I mingled with folk who were so similar physically to those of North Africa (and from the same cause —miscegenation) but in spirit so different, though they have precisely the same strenuous preoccupation with religion. My arrival in Harlem coincided with a big religious parade. The streets were massed with marching people, led by bands of music, shouting, singing, bearing

on these public occasions have been unusually large, and thus the propaganda of the national organization has spread throughout the cities about the bay. The Executive Committee held twelve meetings.

Finances: From the membership contest, the branch sent to the national $50 membership and $19 *Crisis* subscriptions; the Louisville segregation case, $25; Anti-Lynching Fund, $220.12; raised from annual concert, $181.45; net proceeds, $127.10, deposited to assist in carrying on the local work of the branch.

This organization is receiving the desired recognition, and we are working to make it an effective auxiliary to the great national body. The membership is now 205.

The Northern California Branch owes its existence to our national secretary, Mr. Roy Nash, who, when visiting the Coast four years ago, spent much time in presenting the future possibilities of the N.A.A.C.P.

Activities: One case, that of a café hanging a sign displayed, NO COLORED PATRONAGE SOLICITED, has been brought to the attention of the branch. A committee waited on the President of the Board of Commissioners, Mr. F. F. Jackson, and as a result President Butler received a letter stating that the Chief of Police had ordered the sign removed.

The case of a Sacramento woman, claiming the non-payment of a loan because of color discrimination, was referred to the branch and was investigated by Director B. A. Johnson, of Sacramento, to the satisfaction of the branch and the national.

The branch proposes to hold a conference in the spring, such as is held by the Cleveland branch, to be known as the Pacific Coast Conference. —Mrs. H. E. De Hart, secretary.

[b]

ANNUAL REPORTS FOR 1916

Albuquerque, N. M.—Things accomplished this year:

1st. Determined, but unsuccessful fight against the appearance of *The Birth of a Nation.*

2nd. Bringing to time a policeman for brutal treatment of a prisoner.

3rd. Several successful campaigns for funds for the local organization, also the raising of funds to assist the National organization in their Supreme Court cases and anti-lynch propaganda.

existence and had no record of his life. Thereupon the judge committed him to jail, to obtain further information and to have his mental condition determined by a psychiatrist. When the case came up for final trial, the judge sentenced Father Divine to a year in prison and $500 fine. Curiously, three days after the sentence the judge died suddenly. He was very old and had been stricken by heart disease. To the Divine disciples the hand of their Father had struck the judge dead. They even reported that Father Divine had said that he regretted having to make an example of the judge. The news spread through the country.

Father Divine's attorney appealed the sentence. The verdict was reversed by the Brooklyn Supreme Court, which ruled that the presiding judge had injected prejudice into the minds of the jurors. Upon being released, Father Divine entered into his apotheosis. Overnight his following had developed into a vast army. The man who had retired to Sayville emerged as God. He came to New York again and thousands flocked to the Rockland Palace to hear him speak.

"Peace!" he cried to them; "Good health, good appetite, prosperity, and a heart full of merriness. I give you all and everything." And his people responded: "God! It is wonderful! I thank you, Father." Such is the essence of the Divine message and the response it calls forth. And so greatly grew that response that Father Divine alone could not handle it as he had done at Sayville. More and greater "kingdoms" had to be created. Father Divine declares, and his followers believe, that he is in all of them at the same time. "I am here and I am there and I am everywhere," he says. "I am like the radio voice. Dial in and you shall always find me."

Fifteen Divine kingdoms are maintained in New York City alone. In fine buildings all. The finest is the former bath premises in 126th Street, now know as the Faithful Mary Kingdom. Other kingdoms are in Jamaica, Brooklyn, and White Plains, in New Jersey and Connecticut. From Washington, D.C., to Seattle, Washington, centers have been established by Father Divine enthusiasts. Headquarters Kingdom, where Father Divine has office and residence, is in 115th Street. In whichever "kingdom" he eats, Father Divine himself serves his flock. The food goes through his hands before it is served. He pours and passes the coffee and cream in the grand style of a maître d'hôtel. And he has more dignity and naturalness doing that than when he is haranguing an audience.

The kingdoms are sanitary and apparently well managed. They pay their way. The secret of their financing is Father Divine's. Rooms are rented to individuals at a dollar a week, but there is more than one

friends and serve refreshments, and to make a long story short, we had a jolly, good time. Miss Johnson found the branch disorganized, in financial straits, and everything but what it should have been. She organized the branch, then numbering 60 members, into teams of 12 members. Wm. E. Jones was made captain of team No. 1, E. P. Ricard of team No. 2, Miss Leonora Jackson of team No. 3, Rev. W. K. Hopes of team No. 4 and H. Geo. Davenport of team No. 5. Then came the tug-of-war. At the meeting it was decided to banquet the winning team, the losers to pay for same.

Meeting places were the next thing to dispose of, and luckily for New Orleans, she affords, next to colored saloons, an abundance of colored churches. I suppose Miss Johnson spoke in every large church of any consequence in New Orleans and Algiers, and the results were gratifying indeed. In a campaign lasting about 20 days we averaged 10 members a day, and the banquet was given in honor of team No. 5, captained by H. Geo. Davenport, who canvassed and landed 40 of the 80 brought in by his team.

The banquet was indeed a grand affair, being a banquet in name only, for we only served refreshments, but every one went away feeling better for having been present to meet Miss Johnson. Toasts were given by the president, Mr. Casa Calvo, Ricard, Lopez and Davenport. Mr. Holsey, a former attache of the N.Y. Office, was also present on this occasion, being in New Orleans in the interest of the Negro Business League.

We owe the success and work of building this branch to the aggressiveness of Miss Johnson, for without her I doubt whether we would have made such a showing.

We have done nothing much to speak of except protest in letter against *The Birth of a Nation*. This letter appeared in the New Orleans *Item*. A second protest was made after the Chief of the New Orleans Police force gave orders to shoot down all "armed blacks." Miss Johnson was here at the time and urged our president to forward an intelligent protest to the Chief about this order. This Mr. Casa Calvo did. The letter also appeared in the *Item*. A third protest was issued by Prof. Ricard in a letter sent to the *Item* and *State* relative to the segregation in a public square in the rear of our city largely populated by colored people. He also touched upon the preparedness parade, which barred colored people from participating. Our biggest protest is on foot now, relative to the use of colored women prisoners on the public streets of New Orleans. We have written a letter to every colored organization in the city, asking them to endorse this movement, and upon receiving these replies, the committee will present this monster petition to the Mayor of New Orleans and request him to discontinue the use of colored women prisoners in public places.

We have selected the colored Y.M.C.A. as our general headquarters, 2220 Dryades Street, New Orleans, La.

What we need now is some one to come here and push us along just like Miss Johnson did, and the sooner they come the better it will be. If you can arrange to have some one come here, I think the branch can be increased to double or triple its number.

More colored people would join this branch, but it is my candid opinion that most of them are afraid and the rest perfectly indifferent and satisfied to let well enough alone. We are optimistic about the future of our branch and we hope to see it with the leading branches in membership and advancement. H. Geo. Davenport, Secretary.

Springfield, O.—The secretary of the Springfield, Ohio, Branch N.A.A.C.P. begs to leave to submit her report for the year ending Nov. 17th, 1916 as follows:

Meetings: Seven executive meetings have been held and four public meetings, and literature from the National Association has been distributed.

The Grievance committee investigated a report that no mention of the death of Booker T. Washington had been made in the public schools, which resulted in more than thirty minutes being given over to the eulogy of Mr. Washington before the entire student body of the High School in its auditorium.

The High School athletics were also investigated and it was found that some of the discrimination was due to hesitancy on the part of colored students to join the teams and apply for their uniforms.

The Branch approved the application of Dr. R. E. Peteferd as assistant Sanitary Officer, and wrote the City Manager a letter of endorsement.

In reference to the manner in which the pictures of the graduates of Class 1916 of the High School appeared in the *Daily News,* a committee interviewed the managing editor and secured his statement that no offense was intended when the colored students' pictures were not printed with those of the white students but that it was done at the request of a former colored student.

The legal redress committee took up the case of Harry Smey indicted on a charge of murder, and found that the court had appointed able counsel to represent him, and that the charge of murder has been changed to carrying concealed weapons, on which charge Mr. Smey received a fair and impartial trial.

In the division of the territory in which there are Branches of the

N.A.A.C.P. this Branch has been placed in the Great Lakes District, and sent one representative to the first annual conference held in Cleveland, May 30 and 31st, 1916, and has contributed its share for the expenses of the District Delegate to the Annual Meeting in New York City, in January, 1917.

It also contributed $10.00 to help the city of Louisville in its fight against segregation and has raised $34.38 for the Anti-Lynching fund. M. Sula Butler, Secretary.

Des Moines Branch.—The close of the National Association year 1915–16 finds the Des Moines Branch sympathetic and in loyal accord with the Association.

Last year's report showed the membership of this Branch to be 225. During the months of October and November of last year by means of earnest appeals and splendid entertainments of an educational nature the Branch was enabled to reach and interest a great many people— 70 or more becoming members. Our membership during these same months this year has decreased considerably, due not from lack of interest but to the increased and ever-increasing "High Cost of Living." The membership at this time is 127. All officers of Branch were re-elected at the November meeting and plans are a-foot, the details of which are not worked out yet, to re-secure to the Association the support, financial and otherwise, of those delinquent.

The Branch activities of special importance were limited to the effort to suppress *The Birth of a Nation,* and while unsuccessful, still there was revealed to us the possession of earnest and loyal friends of the other race hitherto undreamed of, and they acting in conjunction with the Branch, caused the discontinuance of the engagement in the city earlier than scheduled. The Branch, however, expects to have much of importance to engage them this winter, since the Iowa legislature opens January 1, and rumors are even now afloat as to several proposed laws affecting our people.

A series of high class lectures have been given free during the winter months for the benefit of the public which proved quite popular.

Miss Elizabeth Freeman proved to be a splendid attraction.

This Branch contributed $10.00 to the Louisville fight and $80.00 toward the $10,000 Anti-Lynching fund. In the neighborhood of $330 has been raised by Branch this year and close to $100 has gone into the treasury of the Association.

The Des Moines Branch hopes for the National Association the united, earnest and active support of all of its Branches. Mrs. Jessye E. McClain, Secretary.

Denver, Colo.—The Denver Local of the N.A.A.C.P. begs leave to report that at a regular meeting held in this city on the night of December 15th, the following officers were elected:

President, Geo. W. Gross, 2324 Ogden St.; Vice-President, James T. Smith, 208 E. & C. Bldg.; Treasurer, James Cooper, 2227 Tremont St.; Secretary, Luther H. Walton, 162 Fillmore St.; Ass't Secretary, Mildred Abernathy, 2231 Glenarm; Delegate to National Meeting, Geo. W. Gross.

We beg to further report that our Local has grown from a membership of 36 to 89, thus entitling us, we feel, to the full rank as a Branch. Our treasurer has been instructed to forward to you the 50 per cent due your body on the above membership. I confidently believe in and predict as rapid and healthy growth in the future as in the past.

The most notable duty assigned us during the year was to meet and overcome a segregation movement started here. Our fight has been very successful so far, though, of course, it may break out again any time.

We desire to keep in closest touch with the National body and shall strive to measure up to our fullest responsibilities in the future.— George W. Gross, President.

Columbus, O.—The work of the past year has been less productive of results than we had hoped it might be, but the Branch is awake to the necessity for united and earnest effort.

We have had a number of public meetings and have some interesting and able speakers to address large audiences, which always showed an enthusiastic interest.

In a financial way we have had some success. We have raised and forwarded to the National Office, $151.30 for the Anti-Lynching Fund and $35.00 to be used in supporting the Louisville, Ky., Segregation case pending in Washington, D.C.

The Home and School Association of Columbus, Ohio, in an effort to create a desire in children for better picture shows, arranged with the proprietors of the Majestic Theatre for fine picture exhibitions on Saturdays during the months of January and February, 1916. The management of the Theatre at first refused to admit colored children to these shows. Through the effort of the Columbus Branch the restriction was removed and all children were admitted and treated alike.

In litigation in the Supreme Court of Ohio, it was held by the Court that the State Board of Film Censors had the power to refuse to allow the infamous picture known as *The Birth of a Nation* to be exhibited upon the stage or elsewhere in Ohio. It is, however, understood that the company owning the picture are making further effort in said Court to get a hearing on the question with the purpose of causing the Court to reconsider its former ruling. Nothing, however, has yet resulted from that effort.

It was ascertained by the effort of some of the Committees of the Branch that certain discriminations were being made against the colored people in the city, most notably at sewing classes at the Lazarus Store, in the City of Columbus; also a case at the Harvey Restaurant at St. Louis, Mo. Letters were sent by our Branch to the Lazarus Store but no response was ever received thereto. Mr. Harvey of St. Louis, responded stating he had not been able to ascertain anything definite about the matter but disclaiming any purpose or custom of discrimination in any of his restaurants and apologizing for any wrong done in this case.

A protest was also sent to the Chief of Police of Columbus, regarding certain unlawful discriminations by police officers of the city against certain orderly colored boys at Indianola Park in Columbus in refusing them permission to witness a football game in the park. This matter is now in the hands of said Chief and is being investigated.

A resolution was adopted by the Branch expressing the appreciation of the members of the courage of Mr. Sherman Eley, Sheriff of Allen County, Ohio, at Lima, in protecting a Negro prisoner from violence of a mob which was attempting to lynch the prisoner and would have done so, but for the courageous effort of Sheriff Eley, who came near losing his own life in the struggle.

There being a vacancy in the Board of Education of our city, the Branch put forth a vigorous effort to induce the Board to fill the vacancy by appointing a colored person. The effort, however, was not successful.

We have now an enrollment of 353 members in the Columbus Branch. Geo. D. Jones, President.

32

TUSKEGEE CONFERENCE, 1917

Beginning in 1891, annual conferences were held at Tuskegee Institute where Afro-American people, working the soil, met to discuss problems of economic improvement. The 26th Annual Conference met January 17–18, 1917; much attention was focused upon the migration of Black people out of the South—a movement already well under way and soon to reach flood proportions. From the press service of Tuskegee Institute came the following "Declarations" of this conference.

The Twenty-Sixth Annual Tuskegee Negro Conference takes this opportunity through these declarations, to send a message to the Negro people of the South. To them the Conference would say, we are in the midst of serious times.

In some sections there is much distress and suffering because of the floods and boll-weevil. On the other hand there is everywhere in the South much unrest because of the opportunities which are being offered our people to go North to work in the many industries where there is now a shortage of labor.

The Conference would also say: these are transitory times. We recognize and appreciate the opportunities offered in the North to our people and the necessity which is compelling many of them to go there. Right here in the South, however, are great and permanent opportunities for the masses of our people. This section, we feel, is just entering upon its greatest era of development. There are millions of acres of land yet to be cultivated, cities to be built, railroads to be extended, hundreds of mines to be worked. Here your labor in the future is going to be in still greater demand.

Of still more importance to us, however, is the fact that in the South we have acquired a footing in the soil. It is here that more than 90 per cent of all the farms we own are located. It was here in the decade just past that the value of the farm property we own, increased from less than Two Hundred Million Dollars to Five Hundred Million Dollars. The great bulk of all the property we own is here.

Just now the South is the only place where with little capital, land can be bought. Because of this fact and also on account of the progress we have already made in land ownership, this Tuskegee Negro Conference in the midst of present conditions would again say, stay on the soil. In the language of the great founder of this Conference, "Let down your buckets where you are." Let them down into the ownership of more land, better farming and better homes.

This Conference especially urges upon the farmers of the South not to plant too much cotton another year. Do not be carried away by the high price which it is bringing. Do not depend entirely upon this staple; diversify your crops. Plant corn, oats, velvet beans, peas, peanuts, raise more poultry, hogs and cattle. On the other hand, we would urge those farmers in sections where the boll-weevil is and will be, to learn how to raise cotton under boll-weevil conditions.

This Conference, also begs leave to say to the white people of the South a word on behalf of the Negro. We believe that now and in the near future the South will need his labor as she has never needed it before. The disposition of so many thousands of our people to leave is not because they do not love the Southland, but because they believe that in the North, they will have, not only an opportunity to make more money than they are making here, but also that they will there get better treatment, better protection under the law and better school facilities for their children. In a word, that they will get more of a square deal than they are now getting in the South.

This Conference finds that one of the chief causes of unrest among the colored people is the lack of adequate protection under the law.

This Conference is pleased to note and takes this occasion to express its appreciation for the strong editorials that have appeared in the leading daily newspapers of Alabama, Georgia, South Carolina, Louisiana, Texas and other sections of the South, concerning the importance of giving better treatment to the colored people, affording them better protection under the law and providing better educational facilities.

We believe that now is the greatest opportunity that the South has ever had for white and black people in the various communities to get together and have a thorough understanding with reference to their common interest, and also to co-operate for the general welfare of all.

We believe that the time has come for the best element of the white people and colored people to unite to protect the interest of both races to the end that more effective work may be done in the up-building of a greater South.

33

THE BOSTON BRANCH OF THE N.A.A.C.P.
TO 1917
by Butler R. Wilson

In the early years of the N.A.A.C.P., its leading branch was that of Boston—locale of Moorfield Storey, its national president. At the end of 1916, for example, Boston was first in active members, the number being over seven hundred at a time when New York City's membership equaled 142 and Chicago's 171.

A history of that branch, written by the Afro-American lawyer Butler R. Wilson, its founding secretary, follows.

The Boston Branch was organized February 8, 1912, with 56 members. Its first officers were Mr. Francis J. Garrison, president; Mr. George G. Bradford, treasurer; Mr. Butler R. Wilson, secretary; and Mr. Joseph P. Loud, Dr. Horace Bumstead, Miss Adele Moffat, Mr. Clement G. Morgan, Miss Maria L. Baldwin, and Mrs. Maria Hallowell Loud, executive committee.

The growth has been steady. In 1912 its membership was 198; in 1913 it was 336; in 1914 it was 443; in 1915 it was 615, and in 1916 it was 745. More than two-thirds of the persons who joined in 1912 are still members. The list of members contains a majority of the sons and daughters of the most noted New England Abolition leaders, as well as the names of persons distinguished in Massachusetts civic life, in philanthropy, literature, the professions, and business men and women of twelve different races.

A report of the national body says:

"From the Association's inception, Boston has taken a large share in its work. At home it has secured justice for colored persons in cases of discrimination, and it has largely aided the Association in its national undertakings."

As the work of the Boston Branch has been done almost wholly by volunteers—no officer or member of the executive committee is paid— the bulk of the money raised in Boston is sent to New York for the national work. For instance, in 1915 the Branch contributed $7000, of which only $997 was spent in Boston, much of it in connection with the fight against *The Birth of a Nation*. In 1916 the total was $8700, of which $1322.96 only went to local work. Of this latter amount, $227.37 only was used for office rent and miscellaneous expenses and the remainder for the expenses of the Spingarn Medal meeting and for printing and circulating 11,050 copies of appeals, circulars, cards and for many meetings, including a dinner to the president of the National Association.

These considerable sums contributed by the Boston Branch to the national work include multitudes of small or moderate donations and the efforts of many committees. For instance, in 1915 fifty colored women sent $157.03, the proceeds of a series of musicals and dances; and twelve women, under the direction of Mrs. Francis J. Garrison, sent $278, the proceeds of a concert by the Carolyn Belcher Quartette.

The great accomplishments of the Boston Branch have been through the voluntary efforts of its members and committees in influencing public opinion. An immense amount of permanent constructive work has been done in that direction.

For lack of space but a single accomplishment in each year can be mentioned. In 1912 the attempt was made to exclude colored members from the American Bar Association. The Branch, by means of a circular signed by Hon. Albert E. Pillsbury, Hon. Dana Malone, Hon. Herbert Parker, Mr. J. Mott Hallowell, Hon. Hugh Bancroft and Mr. Robert Homans, secretary of the State Bar Association, made a canvas of the Massachusetts members of the National Association. Of 231 replies to the circular received from the most distinguished lawyers in the state, 227 were flatly opposed to drawing the color line in the Association, and their attitude had great influence in saving the lawyers of America from a lasting disgrace.

In 1913 the Young Men's Christian Associations in Greater Boston, in the language of one of them, "The Board of Directors of this Association, at its meeting held last night, decided to reaffirm the basis of membership privileges, which has been in effect since its organization, namely, that any man of good moral character may be admitted to its privileges"—decided no longer to discriminate against colored men because of race or color.

In 1914 the Branch convinced the Boston School Committee that a book entitled *Forty Best Songs* which contained such words as "darky," "nigger," "massa" and other terms tending to humiliate colored pupils were not proper books to be used in the public schools, and the School Committee after a public hearing promptly unanimously voted to withdraw the book and while doing full justice to colored citizens incidentally taught school book publishers the danger of publishing such books.

In 1915 a memorable campaign was carried on against Tom Dixon's vicious film, *The Birth of a Nation*. Rallying under Mott Hallowell's slogan, "It's not the Birth of a Nation, but the Assassination of a Race," the abolition spirit was aroused, a new censor law was secured, and although the play was not stopped in Boston it was refused in many New England cities and towns and public opinion was aroused against it in many parts of the country. The Branch published a pamphlet, *Fighting a Vicious Film,* which had wide circulation and was used all over the country in the protests made against it.

The best work done in 1916 was causing a hospital, exempt from all taxes because its doors were open to citizens of the State, which had flatly discriminated against a woman because of her color, to see the error of its way and to declare that in future it would open its doors without regard to the race or color of its applicants.

In each year great meetings have been held. One in memory of Wendell Phillips, another in memory of Abraham Lincoln, a third in memory of Maria Hallowell Loud, whose loss to the Branch, like that of Francis J. Garrison, will long be felt. The Spingarn Medal meeting was the event of 1916. Governor McCall in the presence of a notable audience awarded the medal to Major (now Lieutenant-Colonel) Charles Young. Great crowds attended the meetings of protest against segregation and against *The Birth of a Nation*. A list of some of the speakers (not including the officers of the Association) at these meetings will indicate the success of the Boston Branch in bringing the work of the Association great men and powerful influences. Here is a partial list:

Hon. Albert E. Pillsbury, President Emeritus Charles W. Eliot, Rev. Samuel McChord Crothers, D.D., Bishop John Hurst, Rev. Alexander Mann, D.D., Senator Moses E. Clapp, Judge Wendell Phillips Stafford, Bishop John W. Hamilton, Congressman J. B. Madden, Mrs. Edwin D. Mead, Rev. Theodore A. Auten, Dr. Ernest H. Gruening, Dr. Horace Bumstead, Dr. Benjamin W. Swain, Judge Philip Reubenstein, Dr. Francis H. Rowley, Rabbi Eichler, Mr. Rolfe Cobleigh, Miss Maria L. Baldwin, Prof. Albert Bushnell Hart, Mr. Archibald H. Grimké.

Undoubtedly the influence of Mr. Moorfield Storey, and of Hon. Albert E. Pillsbury, never too busy to respond to its call, has most to do with the success of the Branch in meeting and lessening discrimination and in attracting substantial and influential members. And, too, the wisdom, the fairness, the broad vision and painstaking care of the Executive Committee in getting at the facts and then in dealing with them in a common sense way, and in appealing for fair play and a spirit of brotherhood in bringing about right conditions has without question won public confidence and established the Branch upon a sound footing. The Committee has gone upon the principle that reasoning with, persuading and appealing to the sense of Justice in people who discriminate against colored people is far more likely to cure evils than is a policy of attack, of publicity, and of the calling of names. Few men wittingly yield to coercion. Most men are amenable to persuasion.

Branch Bulletin, N.A.A.C.P., March, 1917; I, No. 4, 25–26.

34

ORGANIZING IN THE SOUTH, 1917
by James Weldon Johnson

James Weldon Johnson (1871–1938), one of the most distinguished figures of his time, was born in Jacksonville, Florida, and attended Atlanta University. He served as a teacher and principal in his home city, and then passed the Florida bar. In 1901 he and his brother Rosamond went to New York and began a very successful career in the field of musical comedy. Continuing graduate studies in literature at Columbia, Mr. Johnson then served as U.S. consul in Venezuela and Nicaragua (1906–1913). Meanwhile, in 1912, his novel, *The Autobiography of an Ex-Colored Man*, was published anonymously. His volumes of poetry and anthologies were outstanding. From 1916 to 1920 he served as field secretary for the N.A.A.C.P., and from 1920 to 1930 was its executive secretary. Thereafter he served at Fisk and New York University as a professor of literature; in 1938 he died in an accident.

His first report as field secretary is published below.

I left New York on January 16 [1917] to organize branches in the principal cities of the South. I stopped at Baltimore and spoke at a meeting held by the branch in that city, and then went to Richmond. Up to the present, branches have been organized in Richmond, Norfolk, Raleigh, Durham, Greensboro, N.C., Atlanta, Athens, Augusta Columbia, Charleston, Savannah and Jacksonville.

The response of our people in the South to the call being made to them shows the wisdom of the Association in taking the step to organize south of Washington. In every city that I have visited I have found the thinking men and women of the race alive to the situation and ready to take part in the work that must be done. They also realize that the condition that has been brought about by the movement of colored people from the South to the North gives the greatest opportunity that has come in the last forty years for a demand to be made for those things to which the Negro is rightly entitled.

The Branch of the Association which was formed in Atlanta has already taken action on the public school question in that city. A while ago the Board of Education cut off the eighth grade from all the colored public schools. It now proposes to cut off the seventh grade. This proposal is simultaneous with another to build a Junior High School for white children, so it looks as though the means to provide for this new High School for white children are to be secured by the further cutting down of the colored schools. The new Atlanta Branch intends to make a fight not only to retain the seventh grade for the colored schools but to have the eighth grade restored. The branch formed in Savannah has suggested a united effort of all the newly organized Georgia branches to fight the present "Jim Crow" condition. There is no doubt that the new organizations in all of the southern cities will soon be actively engaged in work to change and better conditions in the communities which they represent.

It is wonderful to note how in the very heart of the South the New Spirit is seizing the race, the Spirit which makes our people feel and know that they must not only strive to perform the duties of citizenship but must also claim and secure the rights of citizenship. The time is now ripe for spreading the ideals of the Association all through the South.

The turning point of my trip will be Tampa, Fla. After visiting Tampa I shall revisit all of the cities in which branches have been formed and do all that I can to further perfect those organizations.

Branch Bulletin, N.A.A.C.P., March, 1917; I, No. 4, 30–31.

35

A MEMORIAL TO THE ATLANTA, GEORGIA, BOARD OF EDUCATION, 1917

In the preceding document, reference was made to the movement to prevent the further eroding of education for the Black children of Atlanta. In the documents that follow, this effort is illuminated: [a] is the text of the memorial presented to the Atlanta Board of Education by several Black men; [b] is commentary on the presentation of the memorial from young Walter F. White, then secretary of the Atlanta branch of the N.A.A.C.P.; and [c] are comments from Atlanta offered by Mrs. Addie W. Hunton, who was there at the time.

[a]

MEMORIAL TO THE ATLANTA BOARD OF EDUCATION

Gentlemen: Believing as we do that the public schools of Atlanta, like the public school system common in every state in the Union, are public institutions, created for the benefit of all the people, we come to you as representatives of 75,000 citizens of Atlanta, to state a grievance, reciting the inadequacy and inefficiency of the Atlanta system as it provides for Negro education.

The public school is a public gift, the burden of which is borne by the taxpayers of the city and state without regard to race, color or conditions; and in like manner all of the citizens and their children should be benefited in common without regard to race, color or previous condition of servitude. And unless the benefits of the public schools are shared alike by every child who is entitled to education in the system, the institution is misused and those charged with responsibility of administration of the system are at fault; and those affected or discriminated against ought to call the attention of those responsible for the defects in the administration of a public duty.

The public schools were instituted to give all of the children of Atlanta an elementary English education, not the white children to the exclusion of the black, nor the black to the exclusion of the white, but the white and black in common, and you, gentlemen, to whom we are appealing, are charged with the just, fair and equitable administration of this public trust. You are charged with a double responsibility —that of citizen and that of public servant. You are servants of all of the people—the white and black in common, and the services that you render each must be equal in adequacy and efficiency. If you discriminate in favor of either, you are recreant to the trust imposed.

Where to Look for the Money

We come to you in the capacity of both citizens and taxpayers, exercising our constitutional right of petition, to pray that your Excellencies will make the same adequate and ample provision for the education of the Negro boys and girls in the city that you have made for the white boys and girls. We do not ask that the white boys and girls be denied any facility that they now enjoy; but if you can increase the facility for their education and enlightenment, we sanction it; and we ask that you discharge your public function honestly and conscientiously to the black boys and girls by providing them with the same adequate ample and efficient facilities in the grades, in industries, in preparation for a high school—and a high school. You may ask, "Where are we to get the money from?" Our answer to this oft repeated statement is that you have been entrusted with the responsibility of providing just and adequate educational facilities for all the people, and this question is a part of that responsibility.

Because of your good judgment, acumen and special fitness, you have been selected to perform these functions, and its does not become us to tell you from where the money must come. But we would respectfully suggest that you can get the money from the same sources you got the money to build creditable and ample school houses for white children; from the same sources from which you got money to build industrial, technical and high schools for white children. You have the ability to find money to provide the white children with every facility necessary for their education and enlightenment, and you have the ability to find it to provide the same facility for the Negro child.

The Philosophy of Taxation

Any service that is a public service, that reaches and benefits a part of the people at the expense of the other part, is only half performed, and the service does not measure up to the standard of the trust imposed in the servant. It has sometimes been claimed that the Negro gets in school facilities more money already than he pays taxes. To such a statement, we quote our Senators Hardwick and Smith, in reply to Senators Smoot and Penrose in discussing the "pork barrel" bill before Congress. Senator Penrose alleged that the state of Pennsylvania paid more internal revenue to the Union than the eleven Southern states and Missouri included, and Georgia received more consideration in the pork barrel appropriation than did the state of Pennsylvania, New York and all New England. Senator Hardwick for the South, ably and correctly replied that when the eleven Southern states and Missouri contributed their mite to the Federal exchequer, they paid in proportion to the protection they received, by reason of property holdings, and that when the Southern states paid their money to the government, it became a public fund—a trust fund—belonging to all of the people, and that the Southern states lost their identity as taxpayers; and in like manner, when Pennsylvania paid her millions into the public trust, she paid in proportion to the protection she received by reason of her property holdings; and that she lost her identity; and her millions, in common with the Southern States' mite, became public funds, trust funds to be administered for the best interest of a common government in the interest of all of the people. That is our answer to the charge that we are receiving more money than we contribute as taxpayers.

The city of Atlanta owes the black child the same opportunity to fit himself for usefulness and helpful citizenship that it owes the white child, and it cannot do less and serve the interest of humanity and good government; and we feel quite certain that you, gentlemen, realizing these principles of humanity, cannot in good conscience spend all the money in the interest of your children and see our children groping in ignorance and neglect not only to the detriment of the Negro immediately, but to the detriment of the white man in common.

50:14

You, with fifty schools, most of them ample, efficient and comfortable, for the education of your children in English, industries and preparation for high schools, and in the high schools, can square neither your conscience with your God nor your conduct with your oaths, and behold Negro children in fourteen unsanitary, dilapidated, unventilated school rooms, with double sessions in half of the grades, no industrial facilities, no preparation for high schools and no high schools for the blacks.

The Seventh Grade, Too!

We are moved to come before you now, for information comes to us that you are preparing to displace the seventh grade in the Negro schools to find money to provide a junior high school for the white children. If our information is correct, then this use of the public funds is unfair and unjust. If the department of whites is in need of a junior high school, they ought to have it, and we ask that you provide it; and as a matter of justice and as a crying need, ask in the same breath that you not only do not take out the seventh grade of the Negro department, but that you provide facilities and teachers that Negro children may be able to do the eight years' work in seven years as the white children are able to do, by eliminating double sessions from the Negro department. Therefore, we ask that the seventh grade be retained and that double sessions be eliminated from the Negro department, and that ample teachers be provided that Negro children may do the eight grades in seven years.

Again, we protest against the displacement of the seventh grade with the vocational idea. We are entitled to the seventh grade and the vocational idea, in common with your children.

Are These Immoderate Demands?

Second, we submit that you provide ample industrial features, including the vocational ideas for the Negro schools, providing them with practical work shops. We mean practical industries. We do not mean simply making baskets, toys, paper boxes and needle work. We mean the allied trades that our boys may become shoemakers, carpenters, brick layers, tinsmiths, etc., and that our girls may become stenographers, bookkeepers, trained cooks and laundresses and that they may have opportunity to acquire such other industrial training as is fitted to their sex.

Third, we submit that there should be some provision to prepare our children to enter high schools. If our children are to be cut off at the sixth grade, what is to cover the gap between the sixth grade and the high schools? Where will they prepare themselves to enter private high schools or colleges? We submit that the system is deficient in this respect, as it affects Negro children.

Fourth, we submit that you provide a high school to prepare our boys and girls to enter the colleges of the city, state and country, in like manner as you provide high schools for your boys and girls to enter the colleges of the country.

Harken, Atlanta!

These betterments we ask, because they are justly ours; because they are right. They are fully ours, because we are citizens and taxpayers, and because the State instituted this system for our benefit in common with yours. Now gentlemen, we have come to you after serious reflection on the wretched condition of our children traceable directly to the poor public school facilities for them. *We are interested in our children just as you are interested in yours. We are interested in our race, just as you are in yours. We are here and here to stay. It is our city and country, in common with yours. We have lived for it, bled and died for it, and we have lives yet to live and give for its supremacy as a world power. We are a part of the thought, conscience and tradition of the Southland. This is our home and our country; we are not going to leave it, but we are going to stay here and help build it up. The blood of our fathers was shed for its independence. The bones of our dead ones are buried in the clay hills of our State. We are law-abiding tax payers and it is your duty to encourage us, to uplift and help us.*

We come to you as men talking to men, as citizens talking to public officials, to respectfully remind them of their duty and insisting that they perform it without fear or favor, in the interest of all the citizens. We make no plea for ourselves that we do not make for you, and we ask you to be as liberal, as patriotic and as manly as we are. Much of the unrest in the South to-day which prompts migration North, grows not only out of mob law, which prevails so largely in our State, but because public officials charged with the responsibility of public trust, fail to make ample and adequate protection for the education of Negro children. When you fail to provide a Negro with a place to educate his children, and an atmosphere in which he can serve his God, and when you fail to protect him in the enjoyment of life, property and happiness, he has a tendency to hunt a country where he can serve God, educate his children and enjoy life and property in common with all men. Migration to the North can be stopped; unrest among the working blacks can be dispelled if you will give us ample educational facilities and make safe our lives.

In conclusion, we come to you as public servants, owing us a duty that you have not discharged, and ask in the interest of our children and the welfare of the city as a whole, that you replace the insufficient schoolhouses you provide for Negro children with respectable and modern school rooms. You admit that they are a disgrace, not only to our city, but to civilization. The physical condition of these schools is intolerable. The closets and sanitary conditions are a menace to the health of the children and therefore to the entire city. Summing it all up, we present in concrete form four propositions, and ask that they all be granted, *and serve notice on you, gentlemen,* for whom we have the highest respect and whom we love in common with all the good folk, *that we are going to dwell on your tracks and continue to pursue you until these betterments are realized.* We are not asking for anything unreasonable. We are asking for no more than every Southern city in Atlanta's class, and some beneath her class, have already provided for the Negro department in their public school system. Will Atlanta do less for her colored folk?

1—Relief in all of the grades where there are double sessions.
2—Industrial features along practical lines.
3—Facilities for thorough preparation for high school entrance.
4—A high school for Negro boys and girls.

Respectfully submitted,

> John Hope
> Harry H. Pace
> T. K. Gibson
> Wm. F. Penn
> B. J. Davis
> W. S. Cannon
>
> Committee, N.A.A.C.P. Atlanta *

* John Hope was president of Morehouse College; William F. Penn was a physician; Benjamin J. Davis edited the Atlanta *Independent;* the others were officers of the Standard Life Insurance Company.

[b]

In regard to the presentation of the memorial, Secretary Walter F. White* writes:

Although there are approximately 75,000 Negroes in Atlanta, there are no high schools for Negroes, no commercial or industrial schools, and the teachers in the public schools are compelled to teach double sessions in some of the lower grades. This means that some teachers have to teach from fifty to sixty children from eight-thirty in the morning to twelve o'clock, and another group of equal numbers from twelve-thirty to four in the afternoon. The condition holds, although colored people in this city pay taxes on more than a million and a half dollars worth of property. Two years ago the eighth grade was taken away with hardly a word of protest from the colored people, and now the seventh grade was slated to go. The committee, however, got word of the move and learned the time of the meeting. They went before the board and presented their views in a frank, straightforward manner and told the board that they, as representatives of the best element of the colored people, did not propose to allow such a step to be taken. Dr. Penn acted as spokesman; Mr. Davis and President Pace also spoke.

In answer to our petition, one member of the board claimed that the city did not have the money. Our spokesman told them that he was not there to tell them how or where to get the money, but to tell them that they could obtain it from the same sources that they had gotten money to build fifty fine schools for whites. The board then claimed that the members of the committee should get the schools in Atlanta [their own privately supported schools] to modify their curricula so as to meet the cutting off of the seventh grade. In answer to this it was stated that they were private schools and that the men on the committee had no authority to dictate to these schools, and that it was not for the board to offer substitutes, but to grant what they as citizens and taxpayers were justly entitled to. Mr. James L. Key then arose and said:

"Gentlemen, I want to plead guilty to every word that these men have spoken. We have the government in our hands, we control the finances, and

* At this time, Walter White was cashier of the Standard Life Insurance Company.

we should be derelict to our duty if we did not grant their demands."

Mayor Candler interrupted Mr. Key at this point, saying, "I do not agree with the gentleman who has just spoken. I did not wish to plead guilty. Let us not give way to hysteria but look at this matter in a sane manner." To which Mr. Key replied:

"The seat of all hysteria in this city is the Mayor's office and the chief professor of that science is the Mayor himself. I do plead guilty, and as long as I am a member of this board I pledge my word here to-day that I shall fight for the rights of these men. Every move that is for the giving of justice to them has my hearty support and I shall cast my vote against every move that tries to take away from them what is theirs."

It was finally voted that the seventh grade should not be taken from us. This is our first fight and our first victory and we feel that we have only begun. Our energies are now turned towards the mass meeting to be held on Sunday afternoon. The people are just beginning to realize just what organized effort will do.

[c]

As the spirit of that gathering, we quote from Mrs. Addie W. Hunton:

It was a pleasant surprise to reach here in time for the first big meeting of the Association. Mr. Hunton had his southern headquarters here for eight years and we made our home here most of that time. I thought I knew the spirit of Atlanta folk pretty well, but that meeting yesterday made my heart rejoice for it seemed an indication of a new era. Mr. Johnson's brave and eloquent address carried with it the soul of that great audience. It responded to his impassioned plea for protest against existing wrongs in a way that was really inspiring.

This is no small thing that Mr. Johnson has undertaken. I have been talking to people here and in Macon about the Association. At first glance it seems an almost impossible work for a section where sleeping furies are so easily awakened, but after hearing Mr. Johnson on southern soil and seeing his audience conquered by the truths he boldly proclaimed, I believe that he will be able to establish thoroughly the Association spirit here in the South. Some will suffer in the evolution but it is the only way to justice.

Branch Bulletin, N.A.A.C.P., April, 1917; I, No. 5, 35–36.

36

THE RED LIGHT AND THE BLACK GHETTO: SAVANNAH, GEORGIA, 1917

For many years, it was a very common practice to locate houses of prostitution—with white women servicing white customers—in the Black ghetto, and often near schools or churches. The story of the battle against one such move—in 1917, in Savannah—is told in the report made that summer by J. G. Lemon, secretary of the N.A.A.C.P.'s branch in that city.

Many have doubtless followed the spirited and bitter fight which has been made by the colored citizens of Savannah on the proposal of the Mayor and Chief of Police to move the segregated or Tenderloin District to Negro neighborhoods west of West Broad Street. The business men and ministers mobilized and chose to fight through our Association —in fact, Messrs. J. C. Lindsay, William Johnson, and the Branch Secretary began the fight and directed it. Our plans involved many details and required unusual tact and some courage at times. We meant to bring every white citizen of Savannah, every Christian, every avowed friend of our people, to meet the issue squarely and in the open, and to declare himself in this matter as for it or against it. We wrote one of those letters that a courageous man cannot refrain from answering; we wrote others when we found the individual growing faint, weak, or mis-informed in the premises; we bombarded them, through carefully prepared newspaper articles, with statistical information, showing the unfairness and inconsistency of the thing; we sent hundreds and hundreds of marked copies of these each week; we made formal protests to the City Council. We put landlords, tenants, the city authorities and all on notice that we would avail ourselves of every resource at law to prevent the carrying out of this proposal; we cited law; we published letters of leading citizens. We had things stirred up. We raised a great fund.

The climax came at a meeting before the Council, at which our resolution was read, followed by a great speech by Judge Samuel B. Adams, Savannah's leading citizen. On that day the Mayor was in New York and his "good man Friday," the Chief of Police was out of town, while their hides were literally riddled in Council.

By unanimous vote the Council commanded the Chief "to cease moving the people to Negro neighborhoods, and to take immediate steps to remove those white women who now reside there," a sweeping order and almost in the very language of our protest. Stock of the N.A.A.C.P. soared.

Branch Bulletin, N.A.A.C.P., August, 1917; I, No. 9, 59–60.

37

ON PAN-AFRICA AND LIBERATION, 1917
by Alexander Walters

Alexander Walters, Bishop of the A.M.E.Z. Church, was active in an early civil rights organization—the National Afro-American Council—and presided, in 1900, over the first Pan-African Congress, held in London. The secretary of that 1900 Congress was the young Dr. Du Bois. That congress established a Pan-African Association, and Bishop Walters referred to it in his autobiography, published in 1917; the concept it embodied was to be revitalized and expanded by Dr. Du Bois, starting at the end of 1918. In what follows, Bishop Walters rather startlingly anticipates not only Dr. Du Bois' efforts but also some of the ideas of Marcus Garvey.

I am of the opinion that our Church should give all the encouragement possible to the material development of Africa, and especially of Liberia. I believe that America is to furnish the Negro Cecil Rhodes to Liberia, the man who is to develop the resources of Africa and to start a line of steamships between that country and ours. Untold wealth and glory await such a financial genius.

I am of the opinion that the Negroes of America should lend their influence to help in the political development of Liberia. The men who compose this historic Republic are our brothers, bone of our bone and flesh of our flesh. Therefore, they have a right to expect encouragement from us. . . .

If political parties, capital and labor see the need of organization, surely, as a race, oppressed and moneyless, we ought to see the necessity of a great National and International organization. It is the aim and hope of the Pan-African Association, which is neither circumscribed by religious, social or political tests as a condition to the membership therein, to incorporate in its membership the ablest and most aggressive representatives of African descent in all lands.

We are not unmindful of the fact that it will require considerable time and labor to accomplish our object, but we have resolved to do all in our power to bring about the desired results.

The numerous letters I have received from different parts of the world commending the work of the Pan-African Association and the National Afro-American Council, the many local organizations which are being formed in various countries for the betterment of persons of African descent, the host of newspaper and magazine articles published by colored men in defense of the race, and the encouragement that is being given to our educational and financial development, are all evidences of a great awakening on the part of the Negroes to their own interests, and an abundant proof that the time is ripe for the inauguration of a great international as well as national organization.

Since these organizations have for their objects the encouragement of a feeling of unity and of friendly intercourse among all persons of African descent, the securing to them their civil and political rights, and the fostering of business enterprises among us, their growth in order to be permanent must necessarily be slow. But since great bodies move slowly, we need not be discouraged. As a race we have learned to laugh at opposition and to bravely overcome difficulties. Let us not be deterred by them in the future, but march steadily forward to the goal.

Walters, *My Life and Work,* pp. 173, 263–64.

38

"IT IS NOT MY PURPOSE TO SPEAK"
by Francis J. Grimké

Under date of July 1, 1917, the Reverend F. J. Grimké delivered himself of the following sentiments—characteristic of him and of the vast majority of his people.

A gentleman said to my brother last week: "A prominent member of your brother's church said to me, 'It is strange that our pastor has never said a word in any of his sermons about loyalty to the Government, or about the Red Cross.' "

That there might be no misunderstanding in regard to the matter, I want to say: I have not, and it is not my purpose to say anything. When the United States Government shows a proper appreciation of the services of the Negro who has never failed it in every crisis of its history to do his whole duty, to shed his blood freely in its behalf; and when the Red Cross ceases to discriminate against colored nurses and physicians, out of deference to the Negro-hating sentiment of the South, then, and not till then, will I be heard on either subject. I hope I have some little self-respect left, enough, at least, not to allow myself to be insulted and to acquiesce in it. No! I have not spoken, and it is not my purpose to speak.

Woodson, ed., *Francis J. Grimké*, III, 25–26.

39

THE SILENT ANTI-LYNCHING PARADE

Commencing at noon on Saturday, July 28, 1917, the first of thousands of Afro-American men and women and children assembled on 55th and 56th streets, west of Fifth Avenue in New York City and soon thereafter these thousands marched with appropriate anti-lynching banners—but without a sound—down the avenue to 23rd Street and Madison Square. A leaflet issued by the Parade Committee on July 24 said: "We march because we want to make impossible a repetition of Waco, Memphis and East St. Louis, by rousing the conscience of the country and to bring the murderers of our brothers, sisters and innocent children to justice."

At the end of June, 1917, the following statement was widely distributed, especially in the Black churches of New York City.

To the People of New York:

The frequency of lynching in this country, culminating in the recent horror at Memphis, Tennessee, caused a committee of ministers to call a mass meeting at St. Philip's Church on June 20, to formulate plans whereby the colored citizens of New York might effectively voice their protest against the unfair, undemocratic and uncivilized treatment to which their fellows are subjected throughout this country, and especially in the South.

An organization was effected with the following officers:

President, Rev. H. C. Bishop
Vice-President, Rev. F. A. Cullen
2nd Vice-President, James W. Johnson
Secretary, Rev. Charles D. Martin
Assistant Secretary, Fitz W. Mottley
Treasurer, John E. Nail

The sense of the organization at first was to hold a meeting of protest at Carnegie Hall, but upon second thought it was decided to hold a silent parade of protest and for the following reasons:

Any plan which would have the desired result must be one which could command the widest possible publicity.

Meetings of protest, with speeches and adopted resolutions, have been so overdone that they now fail to possess any news value. The knowledge of the proceedings of a meeting even at Carnegie Hall would be restricted to the capacity of the hall.

A silent parade of protest, participated in by 10,000 colored school children, men and women, marching on Fifth Avenue in broad daylight, carrying properly inscribed banners and mottoes setting forth our services and loyalty through our whole history in this country and calling attention to the acts of discrimination, "Jim Crowism," segregation, disfranchisement, and of brutal and heathenish lynchings and burnings which have been practiced in return, would be so striking and unusual a demonstration that it would attract and command the attention not only of the whole city of New York, but through the great Metropolitan dailies and the Associated Press the news would be flashed over this country and to the remotest parts of the civilized world. There would be no limits to the publicity gained by such a demonstration, and nothing could better convince America of the new spirit of the New Negro.

We therefore call upon you as one interested in the highest welfare of the race, to lend your fullest assistance to the success of this movement.

We ask that you attend the public meetings in furtherance of these plans, to be held at St. Philip's Church in the evening, at 8 o'clock, on the following dates:

Thursday, July 5
Wednesday, July 11th
Wednesday, July 18th
Wednesday, July 25th

We ask that you take an active part in these meetings and offer any suggestions you may have, and that you interest as many others as possible to attend.

We ask that you show your courage by taking your place, either as an individual or as a member of some organization, in the line of march on Thursday, July 26th.

Funds are needed to carry out the plan for this silent parade, and we appeal to you for your financial aid. Contributions are asked for in sums of from $1.00 to $10.00.

Very respectfully,

Officers and *Executive Committee*	Hutchens C. Bishop Fred A. Cullen J. Weldon Johnson Charles D. Martin Fitz W. Mottley John E. Nail Everard W. Daniel

From the original two-page printed leaflet; in editor's possession.

40

FORCED LABOR AND THE "WAR FOR DEMOCRACY"

Many schemes—ranging from anti-loitering and anti-vagabondage to rather naked efforts at forced labor—were common measures employed against Black people, especially in the South, during World War I. A report of a typical form of such oppression appears in the following front-page story in the New York *Age,* August 23, 1917.

TO DRAFT NEGROES FOR FARM WORK

It is reported that Negroes through the South who are anxious to fight in the United States Army in the present world war are greatly exercised over the talk of Negro conscripts being drafted to work on the farm.

That the officials at Washington are seriously considering the feasibility of such a step was made known recently in dispatches to southern newspapers, which told of the War Department approving the suggestion of Major General Wood that an area of from 120 to 150 acres be set aside at each cantonment for the intensive cultivation of vegetables by troops "especially fitted" for that work.

The dispatch further stated that such a scheme, it was believed, would help solve the race problem at the various camps, inferring that putting Negro conscripts to growing vegetables would please rabid southerners who oppose the bringing together of white and colored soldiers in the same cantonment.

Some profess to see the reason the government singled out its colorec citizens by making reference on the registration card to those of "African descent."

41

THE HOUSTON, TEXAS, UPRISING, AUGUST, 1917

The 24th Colored Infantry Regiment, part of the Regular Army, was transferred to a post in Houston, Texas, in 1917. It was disarmed there, jim-crowed, and members occasionally beaten by local police. Forty-four lynchings were reported in 1917; one—as previously documented—in Waco, Texas, when Jesse Washington was burned alive. A pogrom early in July in East St. Louis resulted in the killing of 125 Black men, women, and children. In August another member of the 24th was beaten by a policeman. When a rumor reached the Black troops that a lynch mob was forming, they armed themselves and on August 23 marched into the city and fought back. Two Black men and seventeen whites, including five policemen, were killed. Ninety-nine of the Black soldiers were sentenced to prison for terms ranging from a few years to life (the last were pardoned in 1938); and thirteen of the Black soldiers were hanged.

An early reaction to the August 23 outbreak follows.

Aroused by the drastic editorials in the white press condemning the members of the 24th Infantry for shooting up Houston, Texas, Bishop A. C. Smith of the A.M.E. Church in Detroit, Michigan has published an open letter on the subject. The Bishop says:

There are so many currents and counter-currents of a disturbing nature in evidence that this is no time for hasty utterances. Public judgment should be suspended until all material facts in the unfortunate and regrettable occurrence have been fully investigated and the result made known by the War Department.

The stories emanating from Houston are one-sided and reflect the prejudices of the dominant element in Houston instead of the facts in the case. A Negro in military uniform is as exasperating to the average Texan as is the flaunting of a red flag in the face of an enraged bull.

When the *Titanic* disaster was reported, it is said, Mr. Andrew Carnegie laconically inquired: "What was she doing up there anyway?" It is equally pertinent to inquire, why were the Negro troops sent to Texas anyway, particularly those of the regular army? Has the remembrance of the Brownsville affair entirely faded from the public memory? Is it so soon forgotten that but a few days ago publicity was given to the report that Negro troops were in a clash with the authorities of Waco, Texas?

Two distinct incidents that occurred during the Spanish-American War are still fresh in my memory—the threat to dynamite a train load of Negro regulars by the dominant element of Texarkana, Arkansas, and the merciless assault made on a train load of Negro volunteers at Nashville, Tennessee while en route from Chattanooga to Cincinnati.

Hon. Joe H. Eagle, M.C. for the Houston district in a dispatch to the Secretary of War said: "Without stating who to blame, it is clearly a race riot and is a tragedy sufficient to compel the statement that it is a tragic blunder to send the Negro troops to southern camps."

Who is to blame for this tragic blunder? The Negro troops went to Houston in obedience to the orders of their superiors whose right it is to direct their movements. A race riot? Yes, and that statement coming from a congressman on the ground, and a chosen representative of the dominant of Houston, ought to be sufficient to induce the public to suspend judgment for the time being.

President Wilson made a trenchant statement in a speech in Philadelphia to the effect that "A man may be too proud to fight." With equal force it may be said that man may be too manly to continually submit to extreme brutal treatment. Even the patient ox may be goaded to desperation.

The fact is the white race by precipitating a world-war has turned man's earthly abode into a veritable hell, and there is no telling when the fires of damnation will be extinguished or what elements will be consummated while they are waging. If plain speaking is in order, let both sides be heard.

Baltimore Afro-American, September 1, 1917, p. 1.

42

THE MIGRATION OF NEGROES
by W. E. B. Du Bois

With the repressions and terror against Black people accompanying the war, tens of thousands migrated from the South in 1916 and 1917; hundreds of thousands were to follow in the years immediately following. An early appraisal of this decisively important development came from Dr. Du Bois in June, 1917.

Much has been written of the recent migration of colored people from the South to the North, but there have been very few attempts to give a definite, coherent picture of the whole movement. Aided by the funds of the National Association for the Advancement of Colored People, *The Crisis* has attempted to put into concrete form such knowledge as we have of this movement.

The data at hand are vague and have been collected from a hundred different sources. While the margin of error is large, the actual information which we have gathered is most valuable.

First, as to the number who have migrated to the North, there is wide difference of opinion. Our own conclusion is that about 250,000 colored workmen have come northward. This figure has been builded up from reports like the following which we take from various personal sources and local newspaper accounts:

From Alabama, 60,000 able-bodied workers; from Savannah, Ga., 3,000; Montgomery, Ala., 2,000; West Point, Ala., 1,000; Americus, Ga., 3,000; Jefferson County, Ala., 10,000; West Point, Miss., 1,000; South Carolina, 27,000; West Point, Ga., 800; Macon, Ga., 3,000; Florida, 15,000; Notasulga, Ala., 3,000. From Abbeville, S.C., "by the hundreds all through the fall and winter." From Muskogee, Okla., "5,000 from the city and vicinity." One day "1,022 Negroes from the South came into Cincinnati." An estimate of the Boston, Mass., *Transcript* gives 200,000 immigrants. From Southwest Georgia, 5,000. *Bradstreet's* estimate: "An immense migration." From Birmingham, Ala., 10,000; Arlington, Ga., 500; Waycross, Ga., 900; Bessemer, Ala., 3,000; Columbus, Ga., 500; Tuscaloosa, Ala., 2,500; Dawson, Ga., 1,500. Immigrants to Springfield, Mass., 500; to Chicago, Ill., 50,000, and "coming in at the rate of 10,000 in two weeks," (estimate of the Chicago *American*).

As to the reasons of the migration, undoubtedly, the immediate cause was economic, and the movement began because of floods in middle Alabama and Mississippi and because the latest devastation of the boll weevil came in these same districts.

A second economic cause was the cutting off of immigration from Europe to the North and the consequently wide-spread demand for common labor. The U.S. Department of Labor writes:

A representative of this department has made an investigation in regard thereto, but a report has not been printed for general distribution. It may be stated, however, that most of the help imported from the South has been employed by railroad companies, packing houses, foundries, factories, automobile plants, in the northern States as far west as Nebraska. At the present time the U.S. Employment Service is not co-operating in the direction of Negro help to the north.

The third reason has been outbreaks of mob violence in northern and southwestern Georgia and in western South Carolina.

These have been the three immediate causes, but back of them is, undoubtedly, the general dissatisfaction with the conditions in the South. Individuals have given us the following reasons for migration from certain points:

Montgomery, Ala., better wages, lack of employment, bad treatment; West Point, Ala., boll weevil; Americus and Cartersville, Ga., lynching, schools, bad treatment, low wages; Birmingham, Ala., right to vote, discontent, bad treatment, low wages; Fairburn, Ga., low wages, bad treatment; Sanford, Fla., low wages, bad treatment; Anniston, Ala., low wages, bad treatment; Jefferson County, Ala., low wages, bad treatment; West Point, Miss., low wages; La Grange, Ga., low wages, bad treatment; Washington, Ga., low wages, schools; Newnan, Ga., low wages; Jackson, Ga., protection, schools; Covington, Ga., low wages; Montezuma, Ga., low wages, oppression; Tallahassee, Fla., unrest, conditions, low wages; Honeapath, S.C., low wages; Douglassville, Ga., bad treatment, poor schools; Raleigh, N.C., protection and the right to vote; West Point, Ga., boll weevil; Franklin, Ga., bad treatment and fear of lynching; Lithonia, Ga., low wages, bad treatment; Rome, Ga., injustice in the courts, low wages, lack of privileges, schools; Live Oak, Fla., low wages, bad treatment; Columbus, Ga., low wages, bad treatment; Atlanta, Ga., low wages; Jackson, Miss., low wages, bad treatment; Augusta, Ga., low wages, bad treatment; Nashville, Tenn., low wages; Meridian, Miss., low wages, discrimination; New Orleans, La., low wages; Mobile, Ala., low wages; South Atlanta, Ga., schools, freedom; Macon, Ga., low wages; Valdosta, Ga., unemployment, bad treatment; Cuthbert, Ga., bad treatment; Wadley, Ga., schools, civil rights; Gainesville, Ga., low wages, bad treatment.

To this we may add certain general statements from colored leaders thoroughly conversant with conditions in their communities and in some cases with large parts of the South.

A colored man of Sumter, S.C., says: "The immediate occasion of the migration is, of course, the opportunity in the North, now at last open to us, for industrial betterment. The real causes are the conditions which we have had to bear because there was no escape."

These conditions he sums up as the destruction of the Negroes' political rights, the curtailment of his civil rights, the lack of protection of life, liberty and property, low wages, the Jim Crow car, residential and labor segregation laws, poor educational facilities.

From Oklahoma we learn that Negroes are migrating because of threatened segregation laws and mob violence.

A colored man from Georgia states: "In my opinion the strongest factor in this migration is a desire to escape harsh and unfair treatment, to secure a larger degree of personal liberty, better advantages for children, and a living wage."

The A.M.E. Ministers' Alliance of Birmingham, Ala., names seven causes for the migration: "Prejudice, disfranchisement, Jim Crow cars, lynching, bad treatment on the farms, the boll weevil, the floods of 1916."

A colored business man of North Carolina believes: "There is a silent influence operating in the hearts of the growing class of intelligent Negroes that the insurmountable barriers of caste unnecessarily fetter the opportunities to which every living soul is entitled, namely, a fair chance to earn an honest living and educate his children and be protected by the laws."

In many sections of Mississippi the boll weevil destroyed the cotton crop; rains and high waters in the spring destroyed other crops.

A well-known investigator reports: "Nothing else seemed left for hundreds of the colored tenants to do but to go into the cities or to the North to earn even their food. Nothing was left on the farms and the landowners could not or would not make any further advances. From the country and even from the cities in these unfortunate sections colored people have in many cases streamed northward."

The centres of this migration have been at Jackson, Hattiesburg, and Meridian, Miss., and many have sacrificed property in order to get away.

A widely-traveled and intelligent colored man writes:

I recently made a trip through the South as far down as New Orleans, La., and I saw hundreds who were making their way northward. When in New Orleans, I learned that there were about 800 in the city from the inland district waiting to go, and who expected to leave during the next week. I went with a friend down where I could meet some of the leaders and talk with them. I met them, and they informed me that they were willing to go anywhere rather than continue to live like they had been. These were heading toward Chicago. I was shocked at the statement made by some of them as to how they lived on those big inland farms, and how badly they were treated by the whites. Many of these men were in overalls. I told them that they were unprepared for the climate; but they were willing to run any risk to get where they might breathe freer. Who blames them?

Many of the southern whites, through their newspapers, are confirming this general unrest. A white woman says:

That which a regard for common justice, fair play, human rights could not accomplish, a fear for our bank account is doing, and we are asking:

Why is the Negro dissatisfied? What can we do to keep him in the South? We can't afford to let him go; he means too much for us—financially. He works for little; his upkeep costs us little, for we can house him in any kind of shack, and make him pay us well for that; we do not have to be careful of his living conditions; he is good-natured, long-suffering, and if he should happen to give us trouble we can cope with that and the law will uphold us in anything we do.

The Columbia, S.C., *State* asks: "If you thought you might be lynched by mistake, would you remain in South Carolina? Ask yourself that question if you dare."

The Greenville, S.C., *Piedmont* feels that,

"The truth might as well be faced, and the truth is that the treatment of the Negro in the South must change or the South will lose the Negro."

The Greenville, S.C., *News* says:

The Abbeville outrage may yet prove more of an economic crime than an offense against the peace and dignity of the state. Where is our labor to come from if not from these people who have lived here beside us for so many generations? Immigration has been a distinct failure in the South; it is expressly declared to be against the policy of South Carolina by our laws.

It is interesting to note that this migration is apparently a mass movement and not a movement of the leaders. The wave of economic distress and social unrest has pushed past the conservative advice of the Negro preacher, teacher and professional man, and the colored laborers and artisans have determined to find a way for themselves. For instance, a colored Mississippi preacher says:

The leaders of the race are powerless to prevent his going. They had nothing to do with it, and, indeed, all of them, for obvious reasons, are opposed to the exodus. The movement started without any head from the masses, and such movements are always significant.

The character of the people who are going varies, of course, but as the Birmingham, Ala., *Age-Herald* remarks:

It is not the riff-raff of the race, the worthless Negroes, who are leaving in such large numbers. There are, to be sure, many poor Negroes among them who have little more than the clothes on their backs, but others have property and good positions which they are sacrificing in order to get away at the first opportunity.

Various reasons are assigned for the migration of Negroes from the South to the North. It was believed for a while that they were lured away by the glowing reports of labor agents who promised high wages, easy work, and better living conditions. But there is something more behind their going, something that lies deeper than a temporary discontent and the wish to try a new environment merely for the sake of a free trip on the railroads. . . .

The entire Negro population of the South seems to be deeply affected. The fact that many Negroes who went North without sufficient funds and without clothing to keep them warm have suffered severely and have died in large numbers, has not checked the tide leaving the South. It was expected that the Negroes would come back, sorry that they ever left, but comparatively few have returned. With the approach of warmer weather the number going North will increase.

How great this migration will eventually prove depends upon a number of things. The entrance of the United States into the war will undoubtedly have some effect. When the war ends it is doubtful if the labor shortage in Europe will allow a very large migration to the United States for a generation or more. This will mean increased demand for colored laborers in the North. A writer in the New York *Evening Globe* predicts that 1917 will see 400,000 of the better class of Negro workers come to the North.

At any rate, we face here a social change among American Negroes of great moment, and one which needs to be watched with intelligent interest.

The Crisis, June, 1917; XV, 63–66.

43

FIGHTING AGAINST RACISM, 1917

Resistance to indignity sometimes burst forth explosively—as at Houston; but everywhere resistance in some form or other was present. Below are characteristic illustrations, coming from [a] the District of Columbia and [b] from Georgia, in 1917.

[a]

District of Columbia.—The District of Columbia Branch has had no meetings during the summer, but an account of the following case is believed to be worthy of report, both on its own account and as an illustration of the effectiveness of the methods of the N.A.A.C.P.

The local postal authorities of a Southern City had brought about the dismissal of a mail carrier on the charge of "pernicious political activity." The charge against him was based upon a personal letter which he had written to a candidate in a local political contest, thanking him for his fair attitude towards colored people. The various candidates in the race were all white; it was a "white man's primary," in which colored men could not participate; political activity, "pernicious" or otherwise, on the part of a colored man was altogether impossible under the circumstances. The letter to the candidate was not intended to have had any political significance or bearing.

The candidate, however, published the letter as an indication of appreciation, and the dismissal of the writer thereof followed. On his way north to obtain work in the early part of the summer, he stopped over in Washington, and was advised by someone who heard his story to lay the facts before Mr. Grimké, President of the Branch. The latter, upon receipt of sufficient evidence that the facts were as stated, took the matter up in person with the first assistant postmaster general, detailing and emphasizing the obvious inconsistency of the charge. After several conferences, the latter offered to send the case to the Civil Service Commission for an opinion. By the time the papers reached the Commission Mr. Grimké had already been there and made an appointment to be heard when the case was considered. The Commissioner to whom the papers were referred, after examining them and hearing Mr. Grimké, promised to give due consideration to all the facts in the case and to render a decision later. Shortly afterwards, Mr. Grimké received the following letter from the young man:

July 28, 1917

Hon. A. H. Grimké,
Washington, D.C.
Dear Sir:

I cannot find words to express my gratitude to you for securing for me my reinstatement as letter carrier in the post office. The Post Office Department has directed the Postmaster to reinstate me at once on my former salary. I shall therefore go to work on the first of August.

You cannot know what this means to me. My vindication, the saving of my home, and the chance to earn a respectable livelihood. I shall remember this as the most crucial period in the history of my life. I shall be glad to be of any service you may wish, if it is in my power.

Wishing you every success, I am

Yours very truly,
(Signed)

Regarding the discrimination now practiced in the restaurants of the

Capitol and in the Ladies' Gallery of the Senate Chamber, the Washington Branch presented the following petition:

To the Honorable,
The Senate of the United States of America:

We, the Washington Branch of the National Association for the Advancement of Colored People, beg to represent to your Honorable Body that we are American citizens under the constitution of our country, entitled to all the rights and privileges, equally with other citizens, pertaining to such citizenship—among which are freedom of access on exactly the same terms as other American citizens to the galleries of the Senate chamber to listen to the discussion of your Honorable Body of subjects for legislative action, and while in the Capitol to visit your restaurant to obtain refreshments. We claim no more than what other American citizens claim and obtain, namely, access to your galleries and service in your restaurant—a privilege or a right which is denied to no class of citizens, to no race of men—not even to aliens or alien enemies.

Your Honorable Body has made, we protest, an exception in the case of but one class of your fellow citizens, namely the Colored people, who are excluded from your Ladies' Gallery and denied service in your restaurant.

Colored women whose fathers, husbands, sons, and brothers have been conscripted into the army of the United States are not allowed access to your Ladies' Gallery, and Colored men, wearing the uniform of American soldiers are denied accommodation in your restaurant for no other and better reason than that they belong to that part of your fellow citizens known as Negroes.

Honorable Senators, is our country at war to make this world safe for democracy, irrespective of the race or color of its multitudinous peoples, or has our country declared war against Germany merely to make the world safe for white peoples? Are its colored citizens not included in this glorious object, for which they are taxed and for which also they are expected to die?

For this our petition, we pray for your Honorable Body favorable consideration, and shall ever pray.

The Washington Branch of the National Association for Advancement of Colored People, by its President,

> Archibald H. Grimké,
> S. M. Kendrick, Secretary

[b]

Atlanta, Ga.—We are at the present time in the midst of a bitter fight to abolish double seesions from the Colored schools of Atlanta. Recently, due to the overcrowded conditions of the north portion of the city it was proposed by the City Board of Education to put double sessions in the Tenth Street School for one year, and it was agreed that this was to be done until the city could build another building in that section of the city. However, as soon as this was mentioned in the papers every civic organization in the city, every person of prominence, and every newspaper editor, immediately began to protest in the very strongest sort of language against such a step being taken. In the face of such united opposition on the part of the white citizens, the Board very soon found out that it could rent a building and thus avoid placing double sessions in the Tenth Street School. The Atlanta newspapers then appeared with an article headed, DOUBLE SESSIONS END TODAY, giving the outside world the impression that the Negro schools as well as the white did not have this barbaric handicap on their activity.

Our community immediately went before the council and there was a prolonged session of two hours discussing this problem of providing better schools for Negro children. One member of the council, a Mr. Terrell, openly stated that he was opposed "to giving one nickel more for the education of the Negro children as they were already getting more than they deserved."

The Branch Secretary wrote a personal letter to Mr. Clark Howell, editor of the Atlanta *Constitution,* calling his attention to the fact that he had stated in his paper that under no circumstances could double schools be tolerated in any of the schools of Atlanta. I asked him in the light of two statements often made by the Southern white man namely, that the Southern white man was the Negro's best friend, and also that the Negro race was an inferior race, how could the white man give the Negro child half the education that he gives his own child and yet hope to make him a decent law-abiding citizen and at the same time be the Negro's best friend. Mr. Howell has seen fit to use this letter, reproducing it almost as written, leaving out, of course, some paragraphs which did not exactly conform to his Southern white ideas, and he also made very favorable comment on it in the editorial column. It aroused a great deal of interest among both the white and colored people of Atlanta, and I think it will do a great deal of good. Mr. [Benjamin] Davis, editor of the Atlanta *Independent,* wrote a very strong editorial on the very same subject.

Mr. Davis has been one of our strongest and most consistent workers in forwarding the work of the Atlanta Branch, and he has been of inestimable aid to us through his articles which have appeared from time to time in his paper.

We are now planning a monster silent protest parade similar to the one held in New York, in order to make some tangible move toward the abolishing of double sessions.—Walter F. White, Secretary.

Branch Bulletin, N.A.A.C.P., October, 1917; I, No. 11, 67, 68.

44

THE NEGRO AND THE WAR DEPARTMENT
by Emmett Jay Scott

Late in 1917, as a result of warnings of mounting disaffection among Black people, President Wilson appointed Emmett J. Scott as Special Assistant to the Secretary of War. Mr. Scott—born in Houston, Texas, in 1873— became Booker T. Washington's secretary in 1897. He wrote a kind of authorized biography of Mr. Washington (with Lyman Beecher Stowe) and served for many years as secretary of Tuskegee Institute and of the National Negro Business League. The purposes of Mr. Scott's appointment are rather clearly, if somewhat delicately, put forth in his following essay.

The Secretary of War recognizes that in the unqualified support of this group of Americans, whom I have the honor to represent, he, in Our Country's Defense, has behind him an asset of appreciable value in the prosecution of the present war. On the other hand, he is equally desirous that we, as American citizens, shall have full and free opportunity to participate, as officers, as soldiers, and as loyal, self-sacrificing citizens, in this, the greatest conflict of all the ages, and that now and hereafter we shall receive the rewards which justly follow upon services well rendered.

The reason which actuated the Secretary of War in this matter is, perhaps, most clearly stated by the *Mobile News-Item,* a southern white newspaper, in an editorial which appeared in its issue of October 5, 1917, under the caption: THE NEGRO RECOGNIZED. With due apology for citing this article, because of the personal reference therein made, I venture to quote the following extract:

The appointment is a wise move and a wise selection. While the Government is coordinating all the interests of the country in the movement to win the war with Germany, it should not overlook the colored people. Thousands of them have been drafted and are being trained for duty in the trenches.

They are to wear their country's uniform and represent their country in the greatest conflict of all times. Millions will stay at home tilling the fields and working in the country's industries. They have their problems no less than others, and it is well that one who knows them so intimately is to advise the Government how to meet those problems.

All who are conversant with the history of our race in this country know that there are and likely will be problems arising out of the presence of white and colored soldiers in National Army cantonments and in National Guard camps, aside from many other delicate matters which have, and will, come up during the progress of the war, involving relationships between the races. It is highly desirable that all these matters shall be equitably adjusted with the minimum of friction in order to produce the maximum of efficiency, to the end that all groups of Americans may work together in harmony and present a solid front to a dangerous and united foreign foe.

I am not unmindful of the fact that the Secretary of War has not sought to honor an individual but to recognize the just claims of a race. Therefore, acting in this representative capacity, it is highly essential and earnestly desired that I have behind me the loyal support of the thoughtful men and women of our race, and I shall value and appreciate at all times their counsel and suggestions.

The Crisis, December, 1917; XV, 76.

45

EDITORIALS FROM *THE MESSENGER,* 1918

From 1917 to 1922 there appeared in New York City a monthly magazine, *The Messenger,* with the subhead: THE ONLY RADICAL NEGRO MAGAZINE IN AMERICA. Its editors were A. Philip Randolph and Chandler Owen, both of militant socialist persuasion. Randolph, born in Florida in 1889, had worked as an elevator operator, porter, and waiter in New York City. He lost the latter job because he tried to form a union. Evenings he took courses in economics at C.C.N.Y. He was arrested in Cleveland in June, 1917, for opposing the war but was held only briefly. The editorials printed below offer [a] comment on the execution of thirteen members of the 24th Infantry in connection with the Houston outbreak, already mentioned and [b] reaction to the Bolshevik Revolution in Russia. Both were published in *The Messenger* for January, 1918.

[a]

THE HANGING OF THE NEGRO SOLDIERS

The hanging of thirteen Negro soldiers for the shooting up in Houston, Texas, a few months ago marks the acme of national indiscretion, on the one hand, and the triumph of Southern race prejudice, on the other. *The Messenger* is not prepared to pass upon the guilt or innocence of the colored men, but, for the sake of argument, we shall assume their guilt. We shall next proceed to compare the punishment of the Negro soldiers with other soldiers guilty of similar or greater offenses. And if we find that the punishment of the black soldiers has been harsher, sterner and more merciless than that meted out to the other races, we shall seek to find out what the cause of the difference was.

Briefly, to compare. On the 1st, 2nd, and 3rd of July in East St. Louis, white troops from Illinois, in broad daylight, under the eyes of tens of thousands of people, shot, wounded and killed over one hundred Negroes without any reasonable or apparent provocation from the Negroes of East St. Louis. It was the most disgraceful and unabashed exhibition of mob violence ever known in the United States. Evidence against the soldiers was not circumstantial, but direct. It was also overwhelming and abundant. Yet in spite of the brazen, unmitigated contempt for the law, no white soldier was even apprehended or tried.

Shortly after that Negro troops taunted by abuses, insults and provoked by the worst race prejudice in the world—Southern race prejudice—were alleged to have shot up the town of Houston, Texas, killing a few people. The Negro soldiers were tried; the verdict was withheld from the public; they were denied the right of appeal, and in medieval fashion, were hustled to the scaffold.

What, we ask, is there to account for this difference between justice to white troops from Illinois and justice to Negro troops from Illinois? Both mutinied in time of war. Both killed citizens. The only answer would seem to be that there is one law for the white man in this country and another for the black man; that the Negro is called upon invariably to defend rights for others, but which he cannot enjoy; that bald, barefaced race prejudice was the moving spirit of the execution of some of the bravest, most patriotic soldiers which the United States has ever had.

This execution, one of the worst in history, of men—most of them some of the bravest soldiers in history—is not calculated to stimulate the very low smoldering patriotism which is still left in Negroes.

We wish also to call the attention of this country to the bold misrepresentation of Negro leaders about the Negro's patriotism. Every ninety out of a hundred Negroes felt before the execution that it was very questionable whether they had any country to fight for. Since that execution, with large and extensive contact, we have not found a Negro man or woman whose position is not either entirely passively against the country, or certainly indifferent to its appeals.

Be not deceived. The law itself is unimportant. The administration is what counts. Especially objectionable is all dark-lantern administration. To deny men the right of appeal, to execute before giving the public a chance to appeal for them—merely because it was known that every self-respecting Negro and large numbers of just, fair and truly patriotic whites would have flooded the White House with telegrams—is a piece of Star Chamber proceedings and Inquisition reaction toward which no harking back can ever be tolerated. The men were denied a right of appeal granted to the vilest criminal.

The Messenger wonders whether the (Mr. X) Colonel House, who publishes the "Harpoon," a slanderously Negro baiting, race hating magazine in Houston, Texas, used his personal friendship with President Wilson to prevent his considering the appeal. And we wonder how the "me and justice" Teddy is thinking on the question. After all Negroes will do well to remember that Theodore Roosevelt started this thing and the South's desire to "go him one better" is the logical consequence of the Brownsville starter.

[b]

THE BOLSHEVIKI

The Bolsheviki are in control of Russia at present. They represent the extreme radicals—not in the sense of being unreasonably extreme in their demands, but in the sense of being unwilling to take a half loaf when they are entitled to a whole loaf. They have sounded the tocsin of farewell, the death knell of half pay to the workers of Russia. They demand that the land which the workers till and mine with their toil shall be owned and operated by the workers for the welfare of the workers. They are uncompromising proponents of peace, too. They see that the common people not only give their lives in war but that it is they who pay the taxes for carrying on the war while their children must pay the burden of extensive pensions after the war. And all for what? the Bolsheviki ask. Simply to help certain capitalists maintain and perpetuate their hold upon the world's goods or to satisfy the imperial whims of kings crowned or uncrowned.

The leaders of the Bolsheviki are Lenin and Trotsky, misrepresented here by the metropolitan press as German agents. This, of course, is simply a malicious libel uttered to discredit these rulers of Russia, lest their teaching should awaken the proletariat of the world to his power and his right to a fair share of the world's goods. Lenin and Trotsky, however, are sagacious, statemanlike and courageous leaders. They have a thorough understanding of the international situation. The ridiculousness of the charge that they are German agents can be shown by the Kaiser's prohibition upon the Russian aeroplanes dropping their literature among the German armies. Even Lloyd George, with a keener mind and a better grasp upon the international situation than President Wilson, observes: "A revolutionary Russia can never be anything but a menace to autocratic Germany."

The Russian people want a general, and not a separate peace. Lenin and Trotsky are working for this result. The Bolsheviki do not want to lose their own revolution for 180 million people in order to try to force revolution upon 66 million Germans. They are calling, nevertheless, upon the people of every country to follow the lead of Russia; to throw off their exploiting rulers, to administer public utilities for the public welfare, to disgorge the exploiters and the profiteers.

46

DENOUNCING LYNCHING AND RACISM, 1918

Imperialist wars abroad intensify repression in general at home and especially that form of repression called racism. As World War I staggered on in blood and especially after the Bolshevik Revolution of November, 1917, domestic repression intensified; hence, fierce discrimination aimed against Black people and lynchings and pogroms multiplied. Protest from the offended never ceased. Two examples, from the month of March, 1918, follow: [a] is the text of a petition adopted at a mass meeting of Black people in Atlanta on March 5. The meeting was chaired by P. J. Bryant and its secretary was L. H. King; the petition—carrying the signatures of 114 of the leading Black men of the city—was addressed to the President, his cabinet, the Congress, and the governors and legislatures of the states; [b]

is the newspaper account, in the Savannah, Ga., *Tribune* of March 23, 1918 (p. 1), of the petition presented in person to President Wilson on March 14. This account speaks for itself and is reprinted in full below, including the paper's headlines. Finally, on July 23, 1918, *The New York Times* reported from Washington that "President Wilson has become concerned over . . . the rise in the mob spirit"; and on July 26 he issued a formal statement, summarized in the headlines of *The New York Times* the next day, in these words: PRESIDENT DEMANDS THAT LYNCHING END. DENOUNCES MOB SPIRIT AND MOB ACTION AS EMULATING GERMAN LAWLESSNESS. Despite these words, lynching of Black people (and some white radicals and labor organizers) and wholesale attacks in ghettoes continued thereafter.

[a]

THE ATLANTA APPEAL

During the past three decades nearly three thousand American colored men, women and children have suffered butchery and death in almost every conceivable form at the hands of the lynchers of America. Last year alone the number thus murdered was *two hundred twenty-two*. The reported causes for such appalling brutality ran the gamut from alleged violation of the honor of white women to disputing the word of white men. The fact however that only about five per cent of these murders are reputed to have been inflicted upon accused violators of womanhood argues almost conclusively that the desire to protect womanhood is almost negligible among the so-called causes of lynchings.

We accordingly regard lynching as worse than Prussianism, which we are at war to destroy. Lynching is not a cure for crime, either imaginary or real. It decreases faith in the boasted justice of our so-called democratic institutions. It widens the frightful chasm of unfriendly and suspicious feeling between the races and positively foments the spirit of antipathy and resentment. We are accused of concealing criminals. Who has concealed the many criminals that have mercilessly murdered these three thousand defenseless men, women and children of our race? That these murderers frequently ply their trade in broad day light and in plain view of the entire citizenry even, does not facilitate their punishment or detection. Within less than one year one state alone has tortured and burned at the stake three colored men without even the semblance of a trial or an effort to apprehend and punish the murderers. In the last instance an entire helpless colored population was marched around the fire amid fumes of a burning human being and put on notice that as that black man was suffering they too should fear to suffer. Thus the defiant lynching giant strides on apace. While we are sacrificing the best blood of our sons upon our Nation's altar to help destroy Prussianism beyond the seas, we call upon you to use your high offices to destroy the lynching institution at our doors.

We are the one group of American people, than whom there is none more loyal, which is marked out for discrimination, humiliation and abuse. In the great patriotic and humanitarian movements, in public carriers, in federal service, the treatment accorded us is humiliating, dehumanizing and reprehensible in the extreme. This persistent and unreasonable practice is but a thrust at the colored man's self-respect—the object being not merely to separate the races but to impress us with the idea of supposed natural inferiority. Such demoralizing discrimination is not only a violation of the fundamental rights of citizens of the United States, but the persistent segregation of any element of our country's population into a separate and distinct group on the sole basis of color is creating a condition under which this nation cannot long endure.

When we reflect upon these brutalities and indignities we remember they are due to the fact that in almost every Southern State we have systematically, by law or chicanery, been deprived of the right of that very manhood suffrage which genuine democracy would guarantee to every citizen in the republic. This propaganda of filching from colored Americans the ballot is but a supreme effort to re-enslave us and to force our assent to, and our impotence against, any legislation of our opponents. To this policy the black man does not, cannot and will not agree. Of it, our intolerance is cumulative. Against it, we shall exert our righteous efforts until not only every eligible black man but every eligible black woman shall be wielding the ballot proudly in defense of our liberties and our homes.

We are appealing to you neither as vassals nor as inferiors. Bull Run and Appomattox fixed our status in this nation. We are free men. We are sovereign American citizens—freemen who purchased with our own blood on every battle field from Bunker Hill to Carrizal full rights and immunities such as are freely granted to others but systematically refused us.

We are writing to you, gentlemen, that you may give us the assurance and guarantee which every American citizen ought to have without reference to color. We are loyal and will remain so, but we are not blind. We cannot help seeing that white soldiers who massacred our black brothers and sisters in East St. Louis have gone scot free. We cannot help seeing that our black brothers who massacred white citizens in Houston have paid the most ignominious penalty that can come in this country to a man in uniform. Do not these undemocratic conditions, these inhumanities, these brutalities and savageries provoke the Rulers of the nation to speak out of their sphinx-like silence and utter a voice of hope, a word of promise for the black man? Do the rulers of the nation also hate us, and will they, Pilate-like, forever give their assent to the crucifixion of the bodies, minds and souls of those in whom there has been found nothing worthy of the death we are dying, save that we are black? May not your silence be construed as tacit approval or active tolerance of these things? The effect on the morale of black men in the trenches, when they reflect that they are fighting on foreign fields in behalf of their nation for those very rights and privileges which are denied at home, might be discouraging.

We appeal to you in the name of Democracy!

We appeal to you in the name of our American citizenship!

We appeal to you in the name of God, and,

We would be heard!

From mimeographed copy of original, in editor's possession

[b]

ASK LYNCHING BE MADE FEDERAL CRIME
PRESIDENT WILSON RECEIVES A.M.E. REPRESENTATIVES
STRONG PROTEST AGAINST LYNCHING AND
JIM CROWISM IS PRESENTED

Washington, D.C., March 14—"Words urging patriotic duties upon the Negroes while they are lynched and jim crowed has the appearance of insincerity" was a sentiment expressed to President Woodrow Wilson by a commission appointed by the Bishops' Council of the African Methodist Episcopal Church to make representations against discrimination against the Negroes of this country.

The appointment with the President was arranged by Prof. John R. Hawkins, financial secretary of the A.M.E. church. The Commission was headed by Bishop W. D. Chapelle of South Carolina. The other members of the committee were Prof. John R. Hawkins of Washington; Dr. W. T. Vernon of Tennessee; Dr. W. H. H. Butler of Pennsylvania; Dr. J. G. Robinson of Tennessee; Dr. A. H. Hill of Arkansas and Dr. A. L. Gaines of Baltimore.

Bishop Chappelle made the representations to the President and left with him a written document setting forth the views of the commission. The response of the President, though guarded, was very gratifying.

The sentiment of the commission follows:

Washington, D.C., March 14, 1918

Hon Woodrow Wilson,
President of the United States.
Mr. President, Sir:

We, the undersigned citizens of the United States, and representatives of the African Methodist Episcopal church appointed by the Bishops' Council of said church, which met at Louisville, Ky., Feb. 14, 1918, beg to submit to you the following memorial or prayer.

With a due sense of appreciation of the great struggle in which we are now engaged, and the arduous task laid upon you as Chief Magistrate of our country we pledge to you our fidelity as loyal citizens of our Republic.

These are trying times, and we are passing through ordeals that try men's souls, and now more than ever before, our people need hope and encouragement.

We believe you have read with deep regret of the inhuman and unlawful treatment of our people in many sections of the country; and we come praying you for relief from mob-violence and other discriminations which are so prevalent.

We do not condone crime committed by our people; nor are we asking that you wink at crime committed by any people; we ask that each and every individual be given a fair and impartial trial by a jury of twelve men of their fellow citizens.

Since Congress has given you, as President, power to conscript citizens from and within all the states of the Union, to fight for the common cause of human liberty, and for protection of this country; we believe that it is equally within the power of Congress to authorize you to enter any state in this union with said power, to protect the life and liberty of the citizens therein.

Believing this as we do, we ask: First, that lynching be made a federal offense. Second, we ask that in all cases of lynching and mob-violence where citizens are guilty of participating in the same, they shall be punished by law and declared ineligible to hold office in our government either federal or state.

Third: We ask that any sheriff allowing his prisoner to be lynched or maimed while in his custody, be declared unfit for that high office and at once removed by the governor.

Mr. President, we make this appeal to you because our people have always been loyal to this government and are still loyal and faithful in this the most trying time of its history.

We are in the midst of a great world-wide war which will take as we see it, the united efforts of all the people to gain victory, and to secure this, we must find a way to suppress mob-violence and lynching.

To tell us that we are fighting for world democracy and that this is a form of that democracy for which we are to fight and for which many of our boys are already on the field of battle, is not to say the least very encouraging.

The Negroes of this country have rallied to your call in this crisis and are doing their bit according to their ability from every view point.

No people have followed so uncomplainingly as have our people, and we are beginning to realize now that we are a part of this government which we have served so faithfully both in war and in peace. Thus we come asking our government through its executive to protect us in the pursuits of life, liberty and happiness.

Mr. President, our treatment upon the railroads of this country is unfair, unjust, degrading and unchristian and we ask that something be done to change such conditions and make them such as will guarantee to us peace and comfort while traveling in the discharge of our several duties.

In the face of such treatment we are being told now that we are fighting for a common cause—freedom.

We compare what is told us with what is being done to us, it must of necessity create a suspicion as to the sincerity of some of those who speak to us. If these difficulties are removed, then you make it easier for the leaders of our people to control them as patriots; and too, to advise and direct their activities in such movements as the purchase of Liberty Bonds, Thrift Stamps and the cheerful enlistment in the United States Army and Navy.

Mr. President, we can ask no less and be men. So in the interest of all that is righteous, of all that is just and of all that is in keeping with true democracy of which you are the exponent, we beg you to act.

Respectfully yours,

W. D. Chappelle, chairman, Bishop 7th Epis. Dist., Columbia, S.C.
John R. Hawkins, Financial Secretary, A.M.E. Church, Washington, D.C.
J. G. Robinson, Sec., P. E., Knoxville Dist., Knoxville, Tenn.
W. T. Vernon, Pastor A.M.E. Church, Memphis, Tenn.
A. H. Hill, Pastor A.M.E. church, Pine Bluff, Ark.
A. L. Gaines, Pastor A.M.E church, Baltimore, Md.
W. H. H. Butler, P.E., Washington District, Washington, Pa.

47

HARASSMENT OF AFRO-AMERICAN SOLDIERS IN THE UNITED STATES

Repeatedly, Black soldiers were subjected to indignities and assaults during the war years. An instance that made some headlines involved a Lt. Charles A. Tribbett; the headlines probably resulted from the fact that a commissioned officer, traveling under military orders, was involved and that this particular one was an electrical engineer and a Yale graduate. An account of this incident, as appearing in a Black newspaper, follows.

NEGRO LIEUTENANT EJECTED FROM PULLMAN
WAS ARRESTED IN OKLAHOMA AND LODGED IN PRISON
INFORMED COURT THAT HE PROPOSED TO SEEK REPARATION

First Lieut. Charles A. Tribbett, 367th, was ejected from the train at Chickasha, Okla., March 1, on train 411 of the Frisco, J. W. Barlow, conductor. He was placed under arrest by Chief Phillips and placed in the county jail. An information sworn to by the county attorney charged him with violating the separate coach laws of the state.

Lieut. Tribbett was riding on transportation furnished by the government of the United States and the cause of the difficulty developed out of the fact that "he was a Negro riding in a Pullman in Oklahoma." His checks showed his reservation to be Car 17 Lower 8. E. R. Biggs, 211 Papen street, St. Louis was the porter in charge. The Pullman reservation had been purchased straight through from Camp Upton to Fort Sill.

When the train reached Chickasha, Chief of Police Mitchell proceeded to the coach and informed the army officer that it was against the law of the State of Oklahoma for him to ride where he was.

Tribbett stood silent for a moment and very diplomatically said, "Sir, I have fully decided not to enter your separate coach, but I want you to know that I am entirely at your service." Conductor Barlow then said, "Well, you see, he refuses to go." The Chief said, "Yes," and placed his hand on Lieut. Tribbett's arm; without offering any semblance of resistance Lieutenant Tribbett submitted to arrest and walked down out of the coach.

Editor Roscoe Dunjee and Staff Correspondent J. M. Anderson, of the *Black Dispatch,* who were riding in the separate coach had hurried to the Pullman when the train stopped, now offered their services. They informed the lieutenant that they would secure the immediate services of an attorney and come to the police station, and so it was that when the Chief reached the station, Attorney Robert L. Fortune was waiting.

Chief Mitchell seemed up in the air as to his jurisdiction and visibly showed signs of not knowing what to do. Leaving his prisoner at the office with his race friends he went off to get his bearing. At last after almost an hour he returned and said that his instructions were to deliver Lieut. Tribbett to the sheriff. From the police station the party proceeded across several blocks to the county jail, where a large crowd of curiosity seekers stood with Sheriff Hodge F. Bailey to actually see an arrested black officer.

"Well this old boy is who you are looking for," said the Chief. "What was the trouble?" said Bailey, whom no one would ever have taken for a sheriff unless told.

"Well, as near as I could understand it," said the Chief, "this fellow was riding in the Pullman and refused to get out, the conductor turned him over to me." "Waal," said the sheriff, as he stood and looked a Yale graduate in the face for the first time, "Wa'al, I'd liked to have been conductor myself fer about 20 minutes," and the crowd laughed. The army officer was silent and paid no attention to this vicious attempt on the part of the sheriff to intimidate.

On the inside, Editor Dunjee secured telegraph blanks and a message was sent to the Commanding Officer at Fort Sill. As Editor Dunjee was inquiring, over the phone what the charge would be on 60 words to Fort Sill, some of the curiosity seekers behind him said, "He will smell brimstone before he reaches Fort Sill," and some young man who evidently was clothed with authority about the jail, for he had a large gun sticking out from under his coat, proceeded in a loud voice to tell the auditors that the conductor would have lost his job had he "permitted a nigger to ride in a Pullman."

Finally Sheriff Bailey returned and read the information, charging Chas. A. Tribbett with violating the separate coach law of the state and commanding him to appear at once before Justice T. P. Moore, for trial.

There wasn't much formality in Justice Moore's establishment. He read the complaint and said: "Guilty or not guilty." Editor Dunjee protested on the ground that a reasonable amount of time should be given to defendant to secure counsel before he pleaded. Lawyer Fortune was away at the time preparing a writ of habeas corpus. Finally over the protest of the assistant county attorney the justice agreed to wait until the lawyer returned. A plea of not guilty was entered on his return and bond fixed at $50 cash or $200 surety. On agreement, Tribbett went to jail for about an hour so that Grady County might go their limit in their humiliation of an officer of the United States. He was plentifully supplied with funds for such an emergency but preferred letting the record show just what democracy means to a patriotic soldier who has volunteered to fight for his country.

Sheriff Bailey entered and searched Lieut. Tribbett's officer's equipment and when the black officer demanded to know why this was done, the sheriff said he was searching for whiskey. He found none.

In about an hour Lieut. Tribbett put up a cash bond of $50 and spent the night as guest of the Colored Red Cross ladies of Chickasha.

The following morning, on advice of his attorney he pleaded guilty and paid a fine of $5 and cost, totaling $24.00.

According to Lieut. Tribbett's statement, he was kangarooed in the jail and forced to pay the prisoners, who were all white.

Lieut. Tribbett is a native of New Haven, Conn. His family is one of the oldest and most respected of the race in the New England states. He is an electrical engineer. On graduation from the New Haven High school he entered Yale, graduating from the Scientific Research Department. Was never in jail before in his life and through all of the trying ordeal conducted himself as a polished and cultured gentleman. He informed the court that he proposed to seek reparation.

Savannah, Ga., *Tribune,* March 30, 1918, p. 1; citing the *Black Dispatch,* Oklahoma City—edited by Roscoe Dunjee. Occasionally, similar stories appeared in the white press, as *The New York Times,* June 24, 1918, p. 9.

48

"EXHIBITIONS OF SAVAGERY"
by F. J. Grimké

Again, the "meditations" of the Rev. Francis J. Grimké offer a characteristic commentary on the fantastic degree of ignorance and callousness that racism induces. These thoughts were dated April 16, 1918.

I saw, a few days ago, on Pennsylvania Avenue over one of the moving picture theaters this inscription: SHALL HUMANITY RULE OR THE SAVAGE? The white people in this country seem to be greatly concerned as to whether humanity or the savage is to rule in other lands, but utterly indifferent as to which rules in this. The exhibitions of savagery that are constantly taking place in this country they are perfectly willing to have go on, since the victims are colored people; are perfectly willing to have the savage rule as long as he doesn't rule over white people. A white savage, showing his savagery to darker races, is not objectionable. It is only when shown to whites that it is to be condemned. That shows, as clearly as anything can, that the whites are nothing but savages themselves; that they are still on a very low plane in point of moral development.

Humanity ruling, in any proper understanding of the term, means ruling in the interest of all races, classes, conditions on the broad basis of justice, righteousness, brotherhood; and the savage ruling means ruling in the interest of some particular race or class, regardless of what is right, of what is required by the simple principle of justice, of righteousness. That is not what is meant by humanity ruling in this inscription, however. There is no thought of darker and weaker races, but only of the whites and of their interests.

Woodson, ed., *Francis J. Grimké*, III, 44.

49

WHAT THE N.A.A.C.P. HAS DONE FOR THE COLORED SOLDIER [1918]

In mid-1918 the N.A.A.C.P. and its District of Columbia Branch—chaired by Archibald H. Grimké—issued a four-page leaflet to answer the question in its above-quoted title.

One hundred thousand colored men now serving in the U.S. National and Regular Armies (April 1918).

WHAT ASSOCIATION DID

March, 1916: Appeal to the Chairman of the House Committee on Military Affairs urging the creation of more colored regiments and the establishment of two artillery regiments.

April, 1917: The same appeal to the Executive chiefs in Washington by the National Secretary in person.

May, 1917: After repeated unsuccessful efforts to get colored men into the regular training camps for officers, the Association works for a separate training camp and secures one at Des Moines, Ia.

September, 1917: Commissions held up at Des Moines Camp. Telegram sent to the men at Des Moines urging them to stay until commissions are granted. Personal work at Washington to press the matter of commissions.

September, 1917: Efforts through personal interviews with Secretary Baker to secure reversal of the decision regarding Colonel [Charles] Young's retirement. Unsuccessful.

October, 1917: 678 colored men secure commissions at Des Moines. Des Moines Camp sends contribution of $272 to N.A.A.C.P.

November, 1917: Action against forcing colored men at Camp Meade to act as stevedores and common laborers. Successful. Men transferred to heavy artillery.

February, 1918: Association takes steps to find out status of the five colored soldiers sentenced to death by Houston court martial. Deputation goes to Washington, headed by James W. Johnson, Field Secretary, asking for clemency for these men and for forty-one soldiers of the same regiment sentenced to life imprisonment. Secures a stay of sentence in the case of the five men.

February, 1918: Representative of Association again confers with War Department on Colonel Young case, and on status of colored soldier. Injustice of "Jim-Crow" railroad discrimination against colored soldiers urged. Assurances received that due proportion of colored men would be mobilized for fighting (combatant) service and no undue proportion organized into "service" battalions.

March, 1918: Takes up with Secretary of War case of Lieutenant Tribbett who was taken from a Pullman coach in Oklahoma.

April, 1918: Open letter of protest to the War Department against General [Adin] Ballou's order, Bulletin 35. Publicity secured throughout the country.

From leaflet in editor's possession. Col. Charles Young, a West Point graduate and the highest-ranking Black officer at commencement of the war, was retired—"for reasons of health"—rather than be assigned fitting duty by the army. The case of Lt. Tribbett is elucidated in an earlier document. General Ballou, the white Commanding General of the Black 92nd Infantry Division, had ordered his men not to go where their presence was resented!

50

THE AMERICAN NEGRO AND THE WORLD WAR
by Robert R. Moton

Mr. Moton—now Major Moton—serving as a special emissary for President Wilson performed his duties with articles such as the following.

There have been so many marvelous and unexpected changes in the mental attitude of stronger groups toward weaker ones, and so many efforts to bring about universal democracy, that the Negro himself has experienced much more of a genuinely friendly attitude toward himself from the white race. He has also found so many more doors open to him than hitherto, until he sometimes wonders what it all means. Many sincere people had, just prior to, as well as at the beginning of the war, wondered whether the Negro, because of the many limitations which, as a race, he experienced in this country and the protests which he frequently uttered, would allow himself to become identified with the disloyal elements of this country and fall an easy prey to German propagandists. Others wondered whether Negro leaders would unconsciously or willfully encourage their people to assume an indifferent if not wholly hostile attitude toward the country. But educated and patriotic Negroes knew that these anxious qualms were due rather to lack of knowledge and understanding of Negroes. As a matter of fact, without advice or counsel from any organized body, official or otherwise, the educated Negroes, professional and business men and educators generally, showed themselves as loyal and patriotic as any other Americans, and not only counseled their people to be loyal, but urged them to avoid loose expressions even in jest which might lead others to misunderstand. Not only so, but they urged their people to raise food, to buy Liberty Bonds, to respond to every other demand of the Government, and to serve along any lines that would help in the struggle that was being waged for humanity. Negroes, as other citizens, responded with enthusiasm that is now proverbial. One Negro fraternal organization, the Mosaic Templars of Arkansas, purchased $80,000, worth of Liberty Bonds, and throughout the South more food stuffs were raised by Negroes than ever before in their history. In the appeal from the Food Administration for conservation or saving of these food products for man and beast there was a response such as has never before been witnessed. It is reported by families who employ Negro domestic servants that they have never known their cooks to be more thoughtful and economical than at present. Chancellor D. C. Barrow of the University of Georgia, reported that the Negro cook who had been in his family for a great many years, and who was inclined at first to take the matter of saving as a joke, had come to the point where she was preparing and serving the family dainty, appetizing, nutritious meals from the leftovers and took great delight in so doing. This is the opinion of scores of other people with whom I have talked regarding this matter. Negroes in their own homes, from the lowliest cabin to the best Negro residence, are vying with their white neighbors and their country in helping our government in this struggle, by saving food, and practising every economy.

PERCENTAGE OF NEGRO VOLUNTEERS

It is notorious that when President Wilson asked for 70,000 volunteers, in many cities the Negro volunteers were out of proportion to their percentage of the population. Investigation in three cities has shown that these Negro volunteers were not doing so in a thoughtless, adventurous way, for many of them had jobs and reasonably comfortable homes, but they felt it their patriotic duty to offer their services to their country. In several cities where Negroes volunteered for the Navy, they were frankly and abruptly told that Negroes were only wanted for the mess departments. Many of these same men went from the navy recruiting station to the army and volunteered their services where they could be assigned to direct combative service. When the War Department, as a result of the earnest and persistent efforts on the part of colored people and their white friends, opened a camp for the training of Negro Officers at Des Moines, Iowa, and asked for 1,200 Negroes to offer their services for training, notwithstanding the fact that it was less than 30 days, the required number reported for three months' training. Out of the number that took the training, 625 received commissions. Some people have ventured the suggestions that this present crisis is an opportune time for the Negro to demand "his rights," but subsequent developments have shown that the Negro, while clearly conscious of what he considers his rights, has been most earnest and persistent in his efforts to be granted the chance to do his duty by his country. The leaders have felt that that was sufficient for the present. Just now the important thing is the opportunity to serve in the great struggle for democracy.

A NEGRO DIVISION

Major Thomas B. Spencer, who is on the staff of Gen. A. C. Ballou, of the 92nd Division, a division to be composed of Negroes, has been making a tour of Negro schools and colleges of the country with a view to selecting four or five hundred men for a particular branch in this division. At every school visited he has been asking for men who were below the draft age. He has received a most hearty response in volunteers from practically every school to which he has gone. At Tuskegee Institute thirty of the upper class men with whom he talked offered their services and left within 48 hours for Chillicothe, Ohio, where they are now being trained. About one hundred thousand Negro soldiers are under arms at the present time, as follows:

These troops are divided among many states and many regiments. They are in the infantry, the cavalry, and in considerable numbers in the National Guard, not only in Southern States but also in Northern and Western States. In many instances their officers are men of their own race, but white officers assigned to Negro regiments are almost invariably pleased with their men, and convinced that they are excellent material of which to make soldiers. The Negro is ordinarily proud of his uniform, falls readily into the discipline so necessary to military proficiency, and when occasion demands, he is faithful to his trust even against overwhelming odds. He is of the stuff from which good soldiers are made, and properly officered he becomes a soldier in the best meaning of the word. About 75,000 Negro men were called in the first draft, making as stated, a total of about one hundred thousand men. This, however, is not the largest number of Negro soldiers who have been under arms, for in the Civil War, 178,000 black men bore arms on the Union side. [Actually, about 200,000 Black men so served—H.A.]

Including those who were commissioned at the officers' training camp at Ft. Des Moines, those who were already officers in the four regiments and companies, there are now about one thousand Negro officers in the United States Army.

THE ATTITUDE OF THE NEGRO SOLDIER

But all of the foregoing is wholly physical. One naturally asks what is the inner feeling of these men? How do they feel about the whole thing? I have talked with many of the rank and file of Negro draftees and volunteers as well as of state guards. I talked to one group of a half dozen Negro soldiers in Atlanta, who were at Camp Gordon, I put the question something like this:

"I suppose you feel proud to wear the uniform of your country?"

"Yes," said one.

"Do you like the army life?"

"Not very well. We have not been fitted out yet with all of our equipment. I reckon we'll like it better when we git *more* used to it."

"Would you rather be home?"

"In some ways, yes, We would like to be home with the old folks and with our friends, but I don't b'lieve we colored folks will ever git a chance again like this to serve our country, so for our own race and our country, we feel it's our duty to go."

I talked with men also at Camp Meade, in Petersburg, Virginia, and from the two camps at Newport News—Stuart and Hill. These gave similar answers, the language sometimes crude, but all expressing the same loyal spirit. A colored man who was made a captain at Des Moines leaves an aged mother to care for four children, his wife having died a few years ago. "I could probably resign in view of home conditions but my country is first. I have made ample provisions by insurance, etc., for my mother and children so far as I am able. I feel my country needs me, and I must help my government in the training of these untrained colored soldiers as well as leading them in battle for the protection of our own flag," this man told me. I got a similar expression from a very prominent Negro lawyer and physician, now an officer in the Ohio National Guard. Thousands of black mothers and wives and sisters, to say nothing of fathers, have wept as these men have left home, and very few, if any, have raised a voice in protest on account of the past unfairness which the Negro has had to undergo.

MR. GOMPERS'S OPINION

Mr. Samuel Gompers, of the American Federation of Labor, expresses what in my opinion is not only the Negro's sentiment throughout the country but what is becoming the true American sentiment, when he says:

"What will come out of the war for labor? In a word, emancipation from every vestige of wrong and injustice. Out of this war the men of labor of the democracies of the world will come, standing upright; no longer like the men with the hoe. There is a new concept among mankind—the question 'Am I my brother's keeper?' this war and the democracies of the world are going to answer in the affirmative. If I have read history right there has never been any great struggle in the history of the world that has not had its baptism in blood. And the great cause of human liberty and justice is being baptized in human blood; and the spirit of freedom, of human justice, of human brotherhood, will triumph here, as in Europe. I ask you to believe in the loyalty of the great mass of the people who toil."

And Secretary Daniels, a Southerner, expresses the same democratic idea with equal force, when he says:

"We have done more for democracy in six months of war than in six years of peace. Our soldiers who come back from France aren't going to be anything but men. For in this war we are establishing a new spirit of universal equality and brotherhood. Too long has America been enslaved, too long has caste been enthroned. Kings will be relics, thrones will be in museums, here and abroad."

No finer tribute has been paid the Negro soldier than by Colonel James A. Moss, who recently said:

"Understanding the Negro as I do, and knowing his responsibilities as a soldier, I consider myself fortunate in having been assigned to the command of a colored regiment. Of my twenty-three years' experience as an officer, I have spent eighteen with colored troops, having commanded Negro troops in the Cuban campaign, and in the Philippine campaign, so that what I say about the Negro soldier—my faith, my confidence in him—is based on long experience with him in garrison and in the field; in peace and in war. I do not hesitate to make the assertion that if properly trained and instructed, the Negro will make as good a soldier as the world has ever seen. The proper training and instruction of the Negro soldier is a simple problem—it merely consists in treating him like a man, in a fair and square way, and in developing the valuable military assets he naturally possesses in the form of a happy disposition, pride in the uniform, tractability, and faithfulness. Any one who says that the Negro will not fight, does not of course, know what he is talking about.

"The first fight I was ever in, the battle of El Caney, Cuba, July 1, 1898, I had Negroes killed and wounded all around me, 20 per cent of my company having been killed and wounded in about ten minutes' time, and the behavior of the men was splendid. At no time during that, and in subsequent fights, did my men hesitate at the command to advance or falter at the order to charge. I expect my colored regiment to be fully as well drilled, as well instructed, as well behaved, and as good fighters, as any other regiment in the National Army. Lest some might think that what I have to say about the Negro soldier is only the fulsome words of a "Yankee" Negro-phile, let me say that I am a native Louisianian who did not leave the confines of the State until I went to West Point at the age of eighteen."

THE POINT OF VIEW OF PUBLIC MEN

We have had no finer interpretation of the fundamentals of democracy than from our own President Wilson, and the appointment of Mr. Emmett J. Scott, Secretary of Tuskegee Institute, as Special Assistant to the Secretary of War, is evidence of a growing faith in the Negro race and in its capacity for citizenship. Secretary Baker, in his telegram to the Chicago Colored Branch of the National Security League, said of democracy:

"After all, what is this thing we call 'democracy' and about which we hear so much nowadays? Surely it is no catch phrase or abstraction. It is demonstrating too much vitality for that. It is no social distinction or privilege of the few, for were it that, it could not win the hearts of peoples and make them willing to die for its establishment. But it is, it seems to me, a hope as wide as the human race, involving men everywhere—a hope which permits each of us to look forward to a time when not only we, but others, will have respective rights, founded in the generosity of Nature, and protected by a system of justice which will adjust its apparent conflicts. Under such a hope nations will do justice to nations, and men to men."

NEGRO TROOPS IN THE FRENCH ARMY

When one talks face to face with such a man as Colonel E. M. House as well as other men, newspaper editors, Southern and Northern, as well as certain French officials, as has been my honor and pleasure to do during the past few months; when one remembers that France called to her aid her black troops from Senegal as well as her thousands of black Arabian troops, and when we remember how France has treated these men, not as black men, but as soldiers and patriots who gladly placed their lives at the service of their country, permitting them to have equal share in the blessings and privileges of French democracy in proportion as they have measured up to democracy's requirements, the Negroes of America feel that the world is going to be made safe for democracy. When through the discipline which it is now undergoing, it is stripped of arrogance, selfishness, and greed, and when those who arrogate to themselves the making and execution of the laws, feel, as they ultimately must, that it is their patriotic duty and sacred obligation to see that the humblest citizen is given every privilege to live and to serve that is granted every other citizen within the limits of the law, then we shall have a real democracy in America. We cannot believe these sincere exponents of world democracy mean that the Negroes, 12 million now perhaps in this country, should not be given an equal chance to live, to work, to secure any education, and to ride on public conveyances, without embarrassment and under conditions equal in comfort and safety to that enjoyed by any citizen.

EQUALITY OF OPPORTUNITY

War is teaching us that we are inseparably linked together here in America. Races, creeds, colors, and classes all have their interests interrelated and interdependent. The test of our greatness as a nation is not in the accumulation of wealth, nor in the development of culture merely. The great test is for the fortunate to reach down and help the less highly favored, the poor, the humble—yes, even the black. My race asks no special favors and deserves no special favors. It simply asks an equal chance on equal terms with other Americans, and nothing in the Negro's past record indicates other than that he will give a strict account of his stewardship. Give the Negro race responsibility, and in proportion as he has these race responsibilities placed upon him, in like proportion will his experience broaden and his service in all lines reach a higher level of satisfaction. The social problems of America will never be solved by mobbing or segregating black men in the North, nor by burning or lynching in the South. Injustice and unfairness will never do it. The great Nazarene said: "Inasmuch as ye did it unto one of the least of these ye have done it unto me."

World's Work, May, 1918; XXXVI, 74–77.

51

"HEAR OUR GRIEVANCES"

In June, 1918, there met in Washington, D.C., under the leadership of William Monroe Trotter, a National Liberty Congress. It adopted a petition to be submitted to the House of Representatives of the U.S. Congress; this was signed by eighty-one Afro-American people—all of them well known behind the Veil and some known even on the other side of the Veil, as J. Milton Waldron, J. Finley Wilson, and the Black socialist orator of New York City, Hubert Harrison. Presiding at the Congress was Trotter; the secretary was J. W. Bell of Kentucky. The signers came from twenty-one states (including ten southern) as well as the District of Columbia; among them were five women. The text of the petition follows.

To the House of Representatives of the United States of America:

Honorable Speaker and Representatives, hear and receive, we pray, the petition of the National Liberty Congress, composed of delegates from all sections of this country in behalf of all colored Americans, those of African extraction, 12,000,000 strong, loyal citizens desiring liberty and the rights of democracy, we petition you to hear our grievances, to wit, that—

First. We are the victims of civil proscription, solely because of race and color, in three-fourths of the States and in the National Capital

(Federal territory), barred from places and public accommodation, recreation, and resort; yes, from such places within Government buildings.

Second. We are the victims of class distinction, based solely on our race and color, in public carriers in one-third of the States, segregated even when passengers in interstate travel and with the railroads under the control of the Federal Government.

Third. We are the victims of caste and race prejudice in Government military and naval schools and in officer schools with other citizens solely on the basis of race and color, and in the Navy itself, except as to the service below deck.

Fourth. We are the victims of prospective discrimination, based on our race and color, in the executive departments of the Federal Government, refused employment in many after appointment through the civil service, segregated at work, in the appointments of health and comfort.

Fifth. We are the victims of political proscription in one-third of the States, even in the election of Federal officials, in violation of the Federal Constitution, both indirectly by congressional representation based on disfranchisement and directly through intimidation, trickery, or State statutes and constitutions.

Sixth. We are the victims in many States, as a consequence of the foregoing civil and political proscriptions, of imposition, robbery, ravishing, mob violence, murder, and massacre, because of our race and color, denied protection of police, of sheriffs; denied trial by court or jury, rendered impotent to protect our daughters, wives, or mothers from violation by white men or murder by the mob.

Inasmuch as our country is now engaged in the most gigantic war in recorded history, going to Europe to fight, our President, Woodrow Wilson, now the moral leader and spokesman of the allied nations which are resisting Germanic aggression, having officially declared that our country has entered the fight for the purpose of democratizing the nations of the world and liberating the free people everywhere, that we are embarked upon "an enterprise which is to release the spirits of the world from bondage," that we are "fighting for the rights of those who submit to authority to have a voice in their own government," to "make the world at last free" for "security for life and liberty," to "make the world safe for democracy," which, meaning rule of all people, necessarily carries the presumption of the same public rights for all without differences or distinction because of the accidents of race or creed, thereby not creating class privilege, which means autocracy.

Inasmuch as American citizens irrespective of race or color are subject to draft, or are drafted into fighting, while all citizens regardless of race are expected to aid the Government by moral support, by propaganda, by sacrifice at home to help the Government, all of which our racial element is now doing with a loyalty unsurpassed by citizens of any race or color in every war, and, even now, under present treatment, morally greater than that of others because of the only vicarious loyalty;

In order that our country may not be weakened in moral position, prestige, and power by violations here of the noble pronouncements of its President;

In order that the morale and esprit de corps in this war, both of the soldier and of the civilian part of an element of the American nearly one-eighth, may not be weakened by the consciousness of the present denials to it at home of those conditions and ideals which they are sacrificing or are risking life to secure for others, with their soldiers witnessing the continuance of indignities, oppressions, and killing of their kin ere they leave for the battle front abroad, and without assurance of protection of their family, their sisters, wives, mothers from the lynching mob;

In order that, when this awful world war is over the victory comes to the entente allies, the condition of life of 12,000,000 human beings in the United States of America may not prevent the awful sacrifice from accomplishing the war's moral purpose—democratizing of the nations of the world—and that our own Republic may not be a part of the world not safe for democracy;

We do now petition you, the Congress of the United States of America, as an act of justice, of moral consistency, and to help win the war for world democracy:

First. To abolish and forbid all distinctions, segregations, and discriminations based upon race or color in places of public accommodations, recreation, and resort in Federal buildings and in Federal territory.

Second. To abolish and forbid all distinctions, segregations, and discriminations based upon our race and color or upon prejudice of race or color in the emoluments, the rating, the promotions, the placement of employees in the facilities provided by the Government for eating, rest, recreating, health for Government employees, or for others in Federal Government buildings or in Federal hospitals.

Third. To abolish and forbid any distinction, separation, or discrimination based on race or color in any coach of any public carrier operated by the Federal Government.

Fourth. To open the doors of all schools of the Federal Government and all branches of the Army and Navy to citizens on the same basis, without distinction or discrimination based on race or color.

Fifth. To exercise the mandatory powers of the thirteenth, fourteenth, and fifteenth articles of the Federal Constitution, to the end that there shall be no involuntary servitude, no denial of the equal protection of law, no denial of the exercise of suffrage because of race, color, or previous condition.

Sixth. To pass legislation extending the protection of the Federal Government to all citizens of the United States of America at home by enacting that mob murders shall be a crime against the Federal Government, subject to the jurisdiction of the Federal courts, for, in the words of President Wilson, "Democracy means, first of all, that we can govern ourselves."

Herewith endeth the petition of the colored Americans asking that the words of the President of the United States of America be applied to all at home:

"As July 4, 1776, was the dawn of democracy for this Nation, let us on July 4, 1918, celebrate the birth of a new and greater spirit of democracy, by whose influence we hope and believe that what the signers of the Declaration of Independence dreamed of for themselves and their fellow countrymen shall be fulfilled for all mankind."

Extension of Remarks of F. H. Gillet (R., Mass.) in *Congressional Record*, Appendix, June 28, 1918, 65th Cong., 2nd sess., LVI, 502.

52

ADDRESS TO THE COMMITTEE ON PUBLIC INFORMATION, 1918

In June, 1918, thirty-one representatives of the Afro-American press met in Washington. One of their actions was to adopt the following address; it was drafted by Dr. Du Bois, and approved first by a committee consisting of Dr. R. E. Jones, Fred R. Moore, Benjamin J. Davis, John Mitchell, Jr., W. T. Andrews, and Robert R. Moton. It was unanimously adopted by the conferees, who numbered not only the thirty-one representatives of periodicals but also sixteen additional figures of distinction in the Black community. Their names and positions are also published below.

In *The Crisis* for September, 1918 (XVI, 232), it is stated that in a letter responding to this petition President Wilson wrote: "It is cheering to see that the fine philosophy of democracy, which is at this time the inspiration of the great effort of our country, was felt and expressed by these conferees as the dominant thought which ought to control all Americans in the present crisis."

We, the thirty-one representatives of the Negro press which has a circulation of more than a million copies principally among the colored people of America, and representatives of other racial activities, wish to affirm, first of all, our unalterable belief that the defeat of the German government and what it today represents is of paramount importance to the welfare of the world in general and to our people in particular.

We deem it hardly necessary, in view of the untarnished record of Negro Americans, to reaffirm our loyalty to Our Country and our readiness to make every sacrifice to win this war. We wish, however, as students and guides of public opinion among our people, to use our every endeavor to keep these 12,000,000 people at the highest pitch, not simply of passive loyalty, but of active, enthusiastic and self-sacrificing participation in the war.

We are not unmindful of the recognition of our American citizenship in the draft, of the appointment of colored officers, of the designation of colored advisors to the Government departments, and of other indications of a broadened public opinion, nevertheless we believe today that justifiable grievances of the colored people are producing not disloyalty, but an amount of unrest and bitterness which even the best efforts of their leaders may not be able always to guide unless they can have the active and sympathetic cooperation of the National and State governments. German propaganda among us is powerless, but the apparent indifference of our own Government may be dangerous.

First and foremost among these grievances is *lynching*. Since the entrance of the United States in this war, 71 Negroes have been lynched, including four women, and over 178 have been victims of mob violence. The atrocities committed by American mobs during this time have been among the worst known to civilized life, and yet not a single person has been punished for lynching a Negro, nor have white mob leaders anywhere been brought to adequate justice.

The effect of these facts upon the Negro people has been indescribably depressing, and we earnestly believe, (and growing white and southern opinion is coming to believe,) that Federal intervention to suppress lynching is imperative. We urge a strong, clear word on lynching from the President of the United States, and then such legislation by Congress as will enable the Federal Government to go to the limit of the Constitution, under its war powers and under its other powers, to stamp out this custom which is not only holding our Nation up to just criticism, but is seriously affecting the morale of 12,000,000 Americans.

Secondly,—when American Negroes patriotically offer their services to help win the war, these services are too often refused, or accepted with reluctance, or with disconcerting discrimination. The Nation, for instance, has asked for Physicians and Red Cross nurses, but still refuses to employ any of the three thousand colored nurses, and has accepted only a few colored physicians; the Civil Service officials are advertising for skilled workers and for stenographers and clerks, but successful colored applicants are repeatedly refused appointment on the ground that they are colored; no colored man today can serve in the Navy as able seamen, while in the Army no colored volunteers are received outside of four regiments, and difficulties are put before colored men and officers who seek training and promotion.

If the Nation wants our help, our help has been and will be offered, but what shall we say or think when needed aid is refused?

Finally, attention is called to conditions of travel among colored people. The railroads are now under United States control. Colored people, just as their white fellows, are moving here and there, as soldiers and workers. They feel, therefore, with special keenness the injustice of first-class fares and third-class accommodation and frequent other embarrassing discriminations.

These are the pressing grievances which today are stirring our people; the American Negro does not expect to have the whole Negro problem settled immediately; he is not seeking to hold-up a striving country and a distracted world by pushing irrelevant personal grievances as a price of loyalty; he is not disposed to catalogue, in this tremendous crisis, all his complaints and disabilities; he is more than willing to do his full share in helping to win the war for democracy and he expects his full share of the fruits thereof;—but he is today compelled to ask for that minimum of consideration which will enable him to be an efficient fighter for victory, namely:

(1) Better conditions of public travel
(2) The acceptance of help where help is needed regardless of the color of the helper
(3) The immediate suppression of lynching

All these things are matters not simply of justice, but of National and group efficiency; they are actions designed to still the natural unrest and apprehension among one-eighth of our citizens so as to enable them wholeheartedly and unselfishly to throw their every ounce of effort into this mighty and righteous war.

A BILL OF PARTICULARS ON WHICH, IT IS SUGGESTED, ACTION MIGHT BE TAKEN

(1) National legislation on lynching
(2) Colored Red Cross Nurses
(3) Colored able seamen
(4) Colored volunteer soldiers to the extent of their volunteering
(5) Colored physicians for colored troops
(6) Training of larger number of colored officers
(7) Unlimited promotion of colored officers according to proven efficiency
(8) Utilizing the services of Colonel Charles Young (Retired)
(9) An attempt to equalize among black and white troops the proportion of draftees assigned to stevedore regiments, service battalions, etc.
(10) Systematic getting and dissemination of news of Negro troops at home and abroad
(11) Systematic attempt to correct ridiculous misrepresentation of the Negro and omissions of his achievement in the white press
(12) The consideration of a Government loan to the Negro Republic of Liberia, now actively aligned with the Allies
(13) Executive clemency for the Negro soldiers recently tried and sentenced at Fort Sam Houston, Texas
(14) Condition of travel among colored people

LIST OF CONFEREES

Dr. Robert E. Jones, Editor *Southwestern Christian Advocate*, New Orleans, La.

John H. Murphy, Editor the *Afro-American*, Baltimore, Md.

W. T. Andrews, Editor *Daily Herald*, Baltimore, Md.

Chris J. Perry, Editor the *Tribune*, Philadelphia, Pa.

John Mitchell, Jr. Editor *The Planet*, Richmond, Va.

Charles W. Anderson, Former Collector Internal Revenue for 2nd District of New York City, now Assistant Commissioner of Agriculture for the State of New York; at present serving on Exemption Board, New York City.

Robert L. Vann, Editor the *Courier* and Assistant City Solicitor, Pittsburgh, Pa.

William H. Lewis, Former Assistant U.S. Attorney-General, now Attorney at Law, Boston, Mass.

R. S. Abbott, Editor the *Defender*, Chicago, Ill.

George L. Knox, Proprietor and Publisher *The Freeman*, Indianapolis, Ind.

A. E. Manning, Editor *The World*, Indianapolis, Ind.

John D. Howard, Editor *The Ledger*, Indianapolis, Ind.

Dr. H. M. Minton, 1130 S. 18 St., Philadelphia, Pa.

Rev. Ernest Lyon, Chairman Colored branch of Maryland Council of Defense and Consul-General of the Republic of Liberia to the United States, Baltimore, Md.

C. E. Bush, Publisher *The Mosaic Guide*, Little Rock, Ark.

Ralph W. Tyler, Former Auditor for the Navy Department, contributing editor *The Cleveland Advocate*.

W. E. King, Editor *Dallas Express*, Dallas, Texas.

George W. Harris, Editor the *News*, New York City.

Edward A. Warren, Editor the *Amsterdam News*, New York City.

William Monroe Trotter, Editor the *Guardian*, Boston, Mass.

P. B. Young, Editor Lodge *Journal and Guide*, Norfolk, Va.

W. E. B. Du Bois, Editor *The Crisis*, New York City.

Fred R. Moore, Editor the New York *Age*, New York City.

Kelly Miller, Dean of Department of Arts and Sciences, Howard University, Washington, D.C.

H. C. Smith, Editor *The Gazette*, Cleveland, Ohio.

J. E. Mitchell, Editor the *Argus*, St. Louis, Mo.

C. K. Robinson, Editor the *Clarion*, St. Louis, Mo.

Nelson C. Crews, Editor the *Sun*, Kansas City, Mo.

Benj. Davis, Editor *The Independent*, Atlanta, Ga.

J. Finley Wilson, Editor *The Eagle*, Washington, D.C.

William H. Steward, Editor *American Baptist*, Louisville, Ky.

Robert R. Moton, Principal Tuskegee N. & I. Inst., Tuskegee Institute, Ala.

Major Allen W. Washington, President Virginia Organization Society and representing the *Southern Workman*, Hampton Institute, Hampton, Va.

Henry Allen Boyd, Editor and Proprietor of the *Nashville Globe*, Nashville, Tenn.

Dr. A. M. Curtis, Former President National Medical Association, Washington, D.C.

A. H. Grimké, President Washington branch National Association for the Advancement of Colored People, Washington, D.C.

John R. Hawkins, Financial Secretary A.M.E. Church, Washington, D.C.

Dr. Walter H. Brooks, Pastor 19th St., Baptist Church, Washington, D.C.

James A. Cobb, Former Assistant U.S. District Attorney, Washington, D.C.

George W. Cook, Secretary of Howard University, Washington, D.C.

Roscoe Conklin Bruce, Asst. Supt. Public Schools, Washington, D.C.

John C. Dancy, Secretary Church Extension Board, A.M.E. Zion Church, Washington, D.C.

P. B. S. Pinchback, Former Governor of the State of Louisiana, Washington, D.C.

W. Calvin Chase, Editor of the *Bee*, Washington, D.C.

Chas. N. Love, Editor *Texas Freeman*, Houston, Texas.

Dr. Sumner A. Furniss, Member of City Council, representing the *Ledger*, Indianapolis, Ind.

Robert H. Terrell, Judge, Municipal Court, Washington, D.C.

From a carbon of the original, in editor's possession. The petition was published, in part, in *The Crisis*, August 18, 1918; XVI, 163-64.

53

REASONS WHY WHITE AND BLACK WORKERS SHOULD COMBINE IN LABOR UNIONS

An Editorial from The Messenger

The absence of representatives from *The Messenger* among those attending the June, 1918, conference—referred to in the previous document—should be noticed. Previous editorials from that paper, already published, suggest the reason; another is the following editorial, appearing in its July, 1918, issue (on p. 14).

First, as workers, black and white, we all have one common interest, viz., the getting of more wages, shorter hours and better working conditions.

Black and white workers should combine for no other reason than that for which individual workers should combine, viz., to increase their bargaining power, which will enable them to get their demands.

Second, the history of the labor movement in America proves that the employing class recognize no race lines. They will exploit a white man as readily as a black man. They will exploit women as readily as men. They will even go to the extent of coining the labor, blood and suffering of children into dollars. The introduction of women and children into the factories proves that capitalists are only concerned with profits and that they will exploit any race or class in order to make profits, whether they be black or white men, black or white women, or black or white children.

Third, it is apparent that every Negro worker or non-union man is a potential scab upon white union men and black union men.

Fourth, self-interest is the only principle upon which individuals or groups will act if they are sane. Thus, it is idle and vain to hope or expect Negro workers out of work and who receive less wages when at work than white workers, to refuse to scab upon white workers when an opportunity presents itself.

Men will always seek to improve their conditions. When colored workers, as scabs, accept the wages against which white workers strike, they (the Negro workers) have definitely improved their conditions.

That is the only reason why colored workers scab upon white workers or why non-union men scab upon white union men.

A scab who is ignorant of his class interests does not realize that it is necessary to sacrifice a temporary gain in order to secure a greater future gain which can only be secured through collective action.

Every member which is a part of the industrial machinery, must be organized, if labor would win its demands. Organized labor cannot afford to ignore any labor factor of production which organized capital does not ignore.

Fifth, if the employers can keep the white and black dogs, on account of race prejudice, fighting over a bone; the yellow capitalist dog will get away with the bone—the bone, to which we refer, is profits. No union man's standard of living is safe as long as there is one man or woman who may be used as a scab.

54

SHOOTING BLACK SOLDIERS AT CAMP MERRITT, N.J.

A fairly characteristic outbreak of racist violence directed at Black troops occurred on August 17, 1918. It is commented upon in [a] the private thoughts of the Reverend F. J. Grimké and described at some length in [b] a dispatch published at the time in a leading Black newspaper. *The New York Times,* in its issue of August 19, 1918, placed the onus upon the Black troops—it was when they "entered the fight that the real trouble began." This was as false as its typically demagogic and pious editorial (August 20, 1918) devoted to the incident, which included this sentence: "There is no real prejudice in this country against Negro soldiers." No action seems to have been taken against the white soldiers involved, although those actually wounded and killed were all Black men.

[a]

F. J. GRIMKÉ'S COMMENTS

On August 17, 1918, at Camp Merritt, N.J., there was some trouble between white and colored soldiers, resulting in the death of one colored soldier, a young man from Louisville, Ky. The Negro soldier might just as well lay down his life here in defense of the principles of democracy as to go abroad to do so. The thirteen colored soldiers who were executed at Houston, Tex., died in defense of the principles of democracy just as truly as though they had fallen on the soil of France under the fire of the enemy. They were executed because they resented the manner in which they were treated by southern Negro haters in violation of every principle of democracy: and the fact that they resented it, fully conscious of what the result might be to themselves, showed that their minds were made up to take the consequences; that their minds were made up to begin the fight here which they were going abroad to wage. Dying here in defense of democratic principles is just as honorable as dying on a foreign soil. Every colored soldier who meets his death here before sailing for France because he resents the insults of southern white bullies, or rather, I should say, cowards, belongs on the honor roll of the noble dead who die in the laudable effort to make the world safe for democracy as well as those who die on the other side of the water.

The greatest enemies to true democracy are not in Germany or Austria, but here in these United States of America: and the sooner that fact is recognized the better it will be, not only for this country but for the whole world. The most pressing, present need in this country today is the safe-guarding of democracy here. If it were safe-guarded here, our forces would be worth ten fold more abroad. The democracy that we glory in at home, to our shame, is a democracy in which black men have no rights which white men are bound to respect.

Woodson, ed., *Francis J. Grimké*, III, 50–51 (written sometime after August 17, 1918, and prior to August 29, 1918).

[b]

FROM THE BLACK PRESS

The facts regarding the race riot at Camp Merritt, New Jersey of August 17, in which it was reported that several men were killed and wounded, were ascertained today in an interview with Col. J. A. Marmon, commanding officer of the camp, by Walter F. White, assistant secretary of the N.A.A.C.P. The morning papers of August 20 stated that the camp was closed to newspaper reporters and others seeking information regarding the disturbance, but the Association in keeping with its policy of aiding the government in allaying suspicion and preventing friction between the races, sent Mr. White to obtain the facts in the cases. They were given to him freely by Col.

Marmon and shown that the incident was not as serious as was at first supposed.

On the night when the trouble occurred, two colored soldiers were ejected from Y.M.C.A. (No. 2) by two southern white men, when their presence was resented by the southern white men, although there is no discrimination allowed in any of the Y.M.C.A. buildings and the colored soldiers had a perfect right to be there. As they left the building a chair was thrown at them. Previous to this incident there had been one or two minor clashes between soldiers of both races who were quartered in adjacent sections of the camp, which necessitated both using the same general street. The soldiers involved were from Mississippi while the colored were from Camps Dodge, Taylor, Grant and Sherman. About half an hour after the ejection of the two soldiers from Y.M.C.A. 2, a white soldier was cut by a colored soldier. Contrary to press accounts, he was not badly cut, nor did he die. Col. Marmon stated that his wounds were so trivial that it has been unnecessary for the wounded man to apply at a hospital for treatment. For this reason they have been unable to learn who the wounded man is, nor has it been possible to learn who the assailant is.

Shortly after this occurrence, groups of soldiers of both races gathered in one of the camp's streets and threats were passed. Fearing trouble, the guard was called and orders were given to the men to disperse. The guard consisted of between thirty and forty men in charge of a sergeant. Standing at a short distance from the guard, officers of both the white and colored troops conferred as to the best method of preventing further trouble. A group of the colored troops were moving away in obedience to the command of the guard when suddenly, without a command being given shots rang out and five of the colored men fell. The sergeant in command of the guard rushed in at once and knocked up the guns to prevent further firing. One colored soldier was killed, four wounded, none of them seriously, and all will recover. The most seriously wounded of the four has a bullet wound in his groin and one of his fingers of his left hand is shot off, evidently by the same bullet. The man killed was shot in the back.

The guns of the guard were immediately examined after the shooting and 13 of them were found to have been fired. The 13 men to whom these guns belonged were immediately arrested and placed in the guard house. Col. Marmon stated that these men would be tried for firing without orders and punished if found guilty.

Baltimore Afro-American, August 30, 1918.

55

THE WORK OF A MOB
by Walter F. White

Walter White, whose activity in the Atlanta branch of the N.A.A.C.P. has already been observed, came up to New York in 1918 as assistant secretary of the organization. With great courage—and aided by the fact that in complexion he easily could "pass"—Mr. White effectively contributed to the struggle against lynching by his careful and remarkable reportage of actual incidents. One of his best-known accounts was the following of the several lynchings in Brooks and Lowndes counties, Georgia, in May, 1918.

The recent strong letter of President Wilson on lynching * was undoubtedly called forth by representations from colored people following the lynchings in Brooks and Lowndes Counties, Ga., May 17–24.

Hampton Smith, a white farmer, was killed, and newspaper dispatches report six persons as having been lynched for complicity. Investigation shows that at least eleven persons were killed.

Brooks and Lowndes Counties are situated in the southernmost part of the state of Georgia, near the Florida line. They are in the heart of the richest section of the state.

Hampton Smith, whose murder was the immediate cause of the holocaust of lynchings, was the owner of a large plantation in Brooks County. He bore a very poor reputation in the community because of ill treatment of his Negro employees.

Smith's reputation in this respect had become so wide-spread that he had the greatest difficulty in securing any help whatever. He, therefore, adopted the expedient of going into the courts and whenever a Negro was convicted and was unable to pay his fine was sentenced to serve a period in the chain-gang, Smith would secure his release and put him to work out his fine on his (Smith's) plantation. Sidney Johnson, the Negro who admitted before his death that he killed Smith, had been fined thirty dollars for gaming. Smith paid his fine and Johnson was put at work on the former's plantation until the thirty dollars had been worked out. Johnson had worked out the period and had put in considerable more time and had asked Smith to pay him for the addi-

* As noted earlier, President Wilson issued this letter on July 26, 1918.

228

THE WORK OF A MOB

tional time that he had served. Smith refused and a quarrel resulted. A few days later Johnson did not show up for work in the fields and Smith went to Johnson's cabin to discover the reason. Johnson told Smith that he was sick and unable to work. Smith thereupon began to beat him, in spite of the protestations of the victim. Johnson is said then to have threatened Smith and a few nights later, while sitting in his home, Smith was shot twice through the window near which he was sitting, dying instantly. His wife was also shot, the bullet passing through the center of her breast, miraculously missing both her heart and lungs. Her wound is not believed to be serious. The attending physician, Dr. McMichael, is said to have stated that she would recover.

There seems to be no evidence that Mrs. Smith was raped in addition to being shot.

As soon as news of the murder reached the community, great crowds of men and boys from the two counties hurried to the spot. Excitement ran high and posses were immediately formed to search for Johnson, as suspicion was immediately fastened on him because of the threats he had made against Smith's life. There was also talk of a conspiracy among a number of Negroes to kill Smith, and reports were circulated that the group involved had met at the home of Hayes Turner, another Negro who had suffered at the hands of Smith, and his wife, Mary Turner, whom Smith had beaten on several occasions. Hayes Turner, it is said, had previously served a term in the chain-gang for threatening Smith, following Smith's beating of Turner's wife. Nevertheless, after his release, Turner had gone back to work for Smith again.

The first of the mob's victims to be captured was Will Head, a Negro of the community, who was caught on Friday morning, May 17, at 8:30, near Barney, Georgia; the second was Will Thompson, seized later on the same day. That night both were lynched near Troupeville, about five miles from Valdosta. Members of the mob stated to the investigator that over seven hundred bullets were fired into the bodies of the two men. The investigator learned from a man who admitted being in the mob, but who stated that he had no part in the lynching, the names of the two leaders of the Friday night mob and of fifteen of the other members of the mob. These names were given to the investigator on his promise that he would not divulge the name of the informant, as to do so would mean that he would undoubtedly be subjected to bodily violence and perhaps death, for having given the information. These names were furnished to Governor Hugh M. Dorsey, of Georgia, on July 10, by the investigator in person.

In addition to those named to the Governor there were many more from Quitman and a large number from Valdosta and the surrounding country whose names were not learned.

On Saturday morning Hayes Turner was captured and lynched near the fork of the Morven and Barney roads. On being captured he was placed in the Quitman jail and for some reason unknown to the investigator was taken later in the day by Sheriff Wade and Roland Knight, the clerk of the county court, ostensibly to be carried to Moultrie for safekeeping. Turner was taken from these men *en route* to Moultrie, at the fork of the roads about three and a half miles from town. He was lynched with his hands fastened behind him with handcuffs and was allowed to hang there until Monday when he was cut down by county convicts and buried about half a hundred feet from the foot of the tree on which he was lynched. During Sunday following the lynching, hundreds of automobiles, buggies and wagons bore sightseers to the spot while many more tramped there on foot.

Another Negro was lynched on Saturday afternoon near Morven at a spot known as the Old Camp Ground. This person may have been Eugene Rice whose name appeared in the Georgia press among the identified and acknowledged victims, but who was never even remotely connected with Hampton Smith's killing.

About a week after the tragedy, or tragedies, started, the bodies of three unidentified Negroes were taken from the Little River, below Barney. It is not known whether these bodies were those of some already accounted for or whether these were additional victims of the mob. At the last accounts the bodies themselves had disappeared and could not be located.

The murder of the Negro men was deplorable enough in itself, but the method by which Mrs. Mary Turner was put to death was so revolting and the details are so horrible that it is with reluctance that the account is given. It might be mentioned that each detail given is not the statement of a single person but each phase is related only after careful investigation and corroboration. Mrs. Turner made the remark that the killing of her husband on Saturday was unjust and that if she knew the names of the persons who were in the mob that lynched her husband, she would have warrants sworn out against them and have them punished in the courts.

The news determined the mob to "teach her a lesson," and although she attempted to flee when she heard that they were after her, she was captured at noon on Sunday. The grief-stricken and terrified woman was taken to a lonely and secluded spot, down a narrow road over which the trees touch at their tops, which, with the thick undergrowth on either side of the road, made a gloomy and appropriate spot for the lynching. Near Folsom's Bridge over the Little River a tree was selected for her execution—a small oak tree extending over the road.

At the time she was lynched, Mary Turner was in her eighth month of pregnancy. The delicate state of her health, one month or less previous to delivery, may be imagined, but this fact had no effect on the tender feelings of the mob. Her ankles were tied together and she was hung to the tree, head downward. Gasoline and oil from the automobiles were thrown on her clothing and while she writhed in agony and the mob howled in glee, a match was applied and her clothes burned from her person. When this had been done and while she was yet alive, a knife, evidently one such as is used in splitting hogs, was taken and the woman's abdomen was cut open, the unborn babe falling from her womb to the ground. The infant, prematurely born, gave two feeble cries and then its head was crushed by a member of the mob with his heel. Hundreds of bullets were then fired into the body of the woman, now mercifully dead, and the work was over.

Chime Riley, another Negro who was supposed to have left the community, was found by the investigator to have been lynched instead. By the time that he was killed, the mob evidently had begun to become fearful of too many outrages and determined to conceal his body. Although no one seems to have even remotely connected him with the murder of Smith, he was lynched, his hands and feet tied together and turpentine cups, made of clay and used to catch the gum from the pine trees when "chipped," thus becoming very heavy, were tied to his body and he was thrown into the Little River near Barney. The informant in this case, seen on the spot where Mary Turner was lynched, stated that when the river was low he had gone down to see if the body had come up. Finding no trace of the body, he assumed that it had become lodged in a sand bar. He stated that he found one of the cups, however, which he was keeping as a "souvenir."

During the outbreak, another Negro by the name of Simon Schuman, who lived on the Moultrie Road near Berlin, was called to the door of his home one night between eight and nine o'clock. He was seized and had not been seen since up to the time (seven weeks later) that the investigator was in the section. The interior of his house was demolished, his family being driven out, and the furniture was hacked to pieces. His family, at the time of the investigator's visit, was living on the Bryce Plantation, near Berlin. The offense alleged against Schuman is unknown.

Contrary to press reports, Sidney Johnson was not hiding in the swamps near Valdosta, but was in Valdosta from the time of the murder of Smith to the time that he was killed. During this time, he is said to have made the statement to several persons that he alone, was implicated in the killing of Smith and that he alone killed him. There was no suspicion of Johnson's presence in Valdosta until Johnson went to another Negro, John Henry Bryant by name, and asked for food and aid in making good his escape. Apparently it was Johnson's intention to wait until the vigilance of the mobs was relaxed and the roads no longer watched and then flee from the country. Bryant gave Johnson the food and then hastened to town to tell where Johnson was. The house immediately surrounded by a posse headed by Chief of Police Dampier. This was done with caution as Johnson was known to be armed and had sworn that he would never be taken alive. Johnson had only a shot-gun and a revolver, while the posse was armed with high-powered rifles. The firing began and the Chief was wounded in the hand and one of his men in the neck.

After the firing had gone on for a few minutes, Johnson's firing ceased. A few more bullets were fired into the house for good measure as it was thought that the cessation of firing might be a ruse on Johnson's part. When it did not resume, still acting cautiously, the house was rushed and Johnson's body was found, dead. Cheated out of its prey, the crowd took the body, unsexed it with a sharp knife, threw the amputated parts into the street in front of the house, and then tied an end of a rope around Johnson's neck. The other end was tied to the back of an automobile and the body dragged in open daylight down Patterson Street, one of Valdosta's business thoroughfares, and out to a place near Barney and near the scene of the crime. There the dead body was fastened to a tree and burned to a crisp.

Very careful attention was given by the investigator to the accounts given at the outbreak of the affair that it was caused by the circulation of pro-German propaganda in the section prior to the outbreak in the hope of stirring up racial disturbances. Absolutely no evidence was found.

Since the lynchings, more than five hundred Negroes have left the immediate vicinity of Valdosta alone and many more have expressed the determination that they too were going to leave as soon as they could dispose of their lands and gather their crops. This wholesale migration occurred in spite of threats made that any Negro who attempted to leave the section would thus show that he was implicated in the murder of Smith and would be dealt with accordingly. Hundreds of acres of untilled land flourishing with weeds and dozens of deserted farm-houses give their own mute testimony to the Negroes' attitude toward a community in which lynching mobs are allowed to visit vengeance upon members of their race.

All of the facts outlined above, including the names of mob leaders and participants, were given in a memorandum presented by the investigator on July 10 to Governor Hugh M. Dorsey. Governor Dorsey received the information gladly and has promised to take action on the evidence submitted. In a message addressed to the Georgia legislature on July 3, 1918, Governor Dorsey denounced mob violence in strong terms, saying:

"Mob violence should be suppressed, and by State authorities.

"If this is not done, it is very probable that Federal intervention will not be long delayed."

The Crisis, September, 1918; XVI, 221–23.

56

LIBERTY AND "LIBERTY"

by F. J. Grimké

Once again the "meditations" of the Reverend Mr. Grimké of Washington are marvelously apt; coming after the account of the mob's work in Brooks and Lowndes counties, Georgia, they are especially appropriate.

October 16, 1918

It has never occurred to me before today to ask the question, Why the several loans that have been solicited by the United States Government, are called Liberty Loans, or Bonds. The alleged reason is because the money raised is to be used in defense of Liberty. Liberty is certainly worth fighting for, worth dying for, worth defending with the last drop of blood, and with the last dollar; but it must be liberty—liberty which has to do with the rights of all men regardless of race or color. Liberty in that sense, is not the liberty, however, for which these loans are solicited, but liberty for white men only. It cannot mean resistance to injustice, oppression, wrong wherever found, and against whomsoever practiced. For right here in this boasted land of the free, the very men who are calling for a loan to defend liberty are the oppressors, are the ones who are trampling upon the rights of ten millions of colored people. I have never subscribed a dollar to any of these Liberty Loans: and never will. To do so would be to endorse the American Idea of liberty. How can any colored man, with a particle of self-respect, endorse such an idea? And yet that is just what he does when he subscribes to these liberty bonds. He does it, knowing full well that it is not his liberty that is being thought of, or about which there is any concern. Until liberty means liberty for all, for the black man as well as for the white man, not one cent of my money shall go to help make such a fund. One of the surprising things is that men are being called upon to lay down their lives and to give of their means to safeguard Liberty as the most precious of all possessions, and yet nothing so excites the ire of the white man in this country as an attempt on the part of a colored man to stand up for his rights as an American citizen and as a man. Liberty is a precious thing in the estimation of these white hypocrites, when it has to do with the rights of white men, but counts for nothing when it has to do with the rights of colored men. And they know it: and yet they have the audacity, the brazen effrontery to proclaim themselves the champions of liberty: Liberty long since would have perished from the earth if her fate depended upon such defenders.

Woodson, ed., *Francis J. Grimké*, III, 72–73.

57

THE "MORAL ADVANTAGE"
OF BLACK PEOPLE
by Kelly Miller

In the midst of the war, Dean Kelly Miller of Howard University—whose position in the spectrum of the Afro-American people was centrist (between that of Tuskegee and Du Bois)—published *An Appeal to Conscience* that made something of an impact upon the "Big White Fog." Some paragraphs from the work, conveying its mood and content, follow.

It is not contended that the Negro is inherently better than the white race. If he represented nine-tenths of the population and had the advantage of culture and opportunity and control of the machinery of public and practical power, it is not declared, although it is devoutly hoped, that he would be better in his treatment of the white race than the white race is at present in its treatment of him. But circumstances not only alter cases; they alter character. The Negro has the character and quality of his circumstances, which at present put him in the position of moral advantage whereby he makes appeal to the conscience of the nation in behalf of personal and public rectitude.

An individual or a nation is justly adjudged cowardly which will not exercise the full measure of its power to enforce its just and righteous demands. It is unjust to the wrongdoer to permit him to continue unrestrained in the perpetration of evil deeds. But where power is lacking, resort must be had to the higher ethical principles.

It may be said without blasphemy that the Negro is the only American who, as a class, can conscientiously utter the petition of Our Lord's Prayer: "Forgive us our trespasses as we forgive those who trespass against us." His long-suffering and non-resentful nature would readily forgive the white race all of its historical and contemporary trespasses, enormous as they are, if it would now accord him the consideration and human treatment which the law of human charity demands.

Some one has said: "No man is great unless he is great to his valet." No American statesman can attain transcendent greatness unless it rests upon the broad principles of Righteousness which meet the approval of all of the people, even the despised and rejected Negro.

Negroes all over this nation are aroused as they have never been before. It is not the wild hysterics of the hour, but a determined purpose that this country shall be made a safe place for American citizens of whatever color in which to live and work and enjoy the fruits of happiness. Ten thousand speechless men and women marched in silent array down Fifth Avenue in New York City as a spectral demonstration against the wrongs and cruelties heaped upon the race. Negro women all over the nation have appointed a day of prayer in order that Righteousness may be done to this people. The weaker sex of the weaker race are praying that God may invoke the great American conscience as the instrument of His will to promote the cause of human freedom at home and abroad.

At one of the six o'clock prayer meetings in the city of Washington, two thousand humble women snatched the early hours of the morning before going to their daily tasks to resort to the house of prayer. They literally performed unto the Lord the burden of their prayer and song, "Steal Away to Jesus." There was not a note of bitterness or denunciation throughout the session of prayer. They prayed as their mothers prayed in the darker days gone by, that God would deliver the race. May it not be that these despised and rejected daughters of a despised and rejected race shall yet lead the world to its knees in acknowledgment of some controlling power outside of the machinations of man? To one sitting there, listening in reverent silence to these two thousand voices as they sang,—

On Christ, the Solid Rock, I stand,
All other ground is sinking sand—

there could not but come the thought of this ungodly war which is now convulsing the world—a war in which Christian hands are dyed in Christian blood. It must cause the Prince of Peace to groan as in His dying agony when He gave up the Ghost on the Cross. The professed followers of the Meek and Lowly One, with heathen heart, are putting their trust in reeking tube and iron shard. As God uses the humbler things of life to confound the mighty, it may be that these helpless victims of cruelty and outrage shall bring an apostate world back to God. The Negro's helpless position may yet bring America to a realizing sense that Righteousness exalteth a nation, but sin is a reproach to any people.

Kelly Miller, *An Appeal to Conscience: America's Code of Caste A Disgrace to Democracy* (New York, 1918, reprinted Mnemosyne Pub. Co., Miami, Fla., 1969), pp. 103–4.

58

WHAT WILL THE NEGRO GET OUT OF WAR?
by District of Columbia Branch, N.A.A.C.P.

At a public meeting sponsored by the District of Columbia branch, N.A.A.C.P., and held on December 11, 1918—marking the birthday of William Lloyd Garrison—the above question was put in a challenging sense, in order to affirm the minimum results held to be proper if the blood shed in a "war for democracy" was not to be in vain.

In celebrating the one hundred and thirteenth anniversary of the birth of William Lloyd Garrison, we express a deep and lasting sense of gratitude for a life consecrated to the freedom of a race and to the progress of mankind. It is especially appropriate that the things which he cherished and achieved should be recalled at the close of a war into which the United States entered for the declared purpose of making "the world safe for Democracy." It is true that no civilized nation practices that particular form of slavery based upon the property of man in man; but the declaration upon which the United States entered the world war is an implied admission that all peoples are not yet free, that injustice, inequality and oppression still subsist in forms of government, and in customs and practices of peoples. Therefore, we set forth the following statement for the consideration of all people having the same allegiance as we do.

As the result of the life and labors of William Lloyd Garrison our nation has incorporated into its Constitution, "the supreme law of the land," these principles of the Declaration of Independence: that all men are created equal; that governments derive their just powers from the consent of the governed, and that the right of life, liberty and the pursuit of happiness is inherent in all human beings.

As human beings having these rights by nature, and also by legal sanction, the Colored People of the United States, although loyal to the government without variableness or shadow of turning, suffer wrong in no less than four fundamental particulars: they are not accorded the equal protection of the law, in that it has become practice almost deepened into custom to permit mobs to torture and kill them; in a part of the nation where they most largely reside, they do not receive equal educational advantages with other citizens out of the funds raised by taxation of all the people; they are in the same part of the country, deprived of the ballot, the means whereby the citizen indicates that he consents to be governed; and they are denied the comforts and conveniences of public travel, entertainment and refreshment at hotels and inns, and recreation at places of public amusement. The denial of rights in these basic particulars is absolutely inconsistent with any proper conception of Democracy, and a violation of legal status, and grounds for complaint and remonstrance.

At this time and on this anniversary occasion, we seek redress of these grievances and correction of these wrongs.

And we do especially protest against a practice, existing in some of the Departments of the Federal Government, of segregating employees on account of race, and of denying appointments to persons selected from the Civil Service Eligible Lists, on the same account. Segregation, whether in travel or in working relations is equally unjust with residential segregation, which the Supreme Court of the United States has but recently declared to be unlawful.*

* This refers to *Buchanan v. Warley*, 245 U.S. 60 (1917), striking down a particularly vicious ordinance of Louisville, Kentucky. The device of "restrictive covenants" was then widely used.

We call attention to these things, not only because they are unjust and oppressive to us as a group, but because as long as they exist, they will be a reproach to our Nation, and to its professions of free and democratic ideals.

To those who will look with disfavor upon assertion of right by Colored People, we would say that reason and experience teach that no people who have attained to any stature of self-respect can be contented with a social order and system which in practice denies them any opportunity open to other groups.

As long as unequal conditions exist, there will be protest and remonstrance. It can not be expected to be otherwise, for no group can be rated as intelligently loyal, that is not at the same time conscious of its equal citizenship rights.

From a printed one-page leaflet in editor's possession.

59

"WORK OR FIGHT" IN THE SOUTH

by Walter F. White

Some sense of the realities inside the South during the war—so far as the mass of Black people was concerned—was conveyed in the following essay published in *The New Republic* early in 1919.

In a small town in Alabama, sixteen miles from Montgomery, the state capital, the mayor of the town had a colored cook. This cook one Saturday night asked her employer for a higher wage. The mayor refused, stating that he had never paid any more for a cook and wasn't going to do so now. The woman thereupon quit, and, as the law provided, the mayor took up her employment card which he himself had issued to her. The following morning a deputy sheriff appeared at her door and demanded that she show her work card. Despite her explanation of the reason why she had no card, she was arrested and on Monday morning was brought up for trial *in the Mayor's Court,* before the *mayor* himself. She was found guilty, and fined $14.00, which fine was paid by the mayor, who then said to her, "Go on up to my house, work out the fine and stop yonr foolishness."

This is a striking example of the method by which certain sections of the South have been able to improve on the "Work or Fight Order" of Provost Marshal General Crowder. This order provided that every able-bodied male person between the draft ages, must be engaged in some necessary employment. At first this only included males of a maximum of thirty-one years of age. Later the selective service act was amended to include males up to forty-five years of age. But it was not sufficient for the many employers who found that the war took from them workers they had used in civilian forms of labor, and, North and South, compulsory work laws were passed by various states. Southern states whose legislatures were in session, Louisiana and Kentucky, made a maximum working age for males of fifty-five, and Georgia a maximum of sixty years. The Mississippi legislature was also in session but passed no compulsory work legislation.

These federal and state laws, however, referred only to men. But women's labor was also greatly in demand. The shortage of domestic servants has been felt throughout the whole of the United States, but it remained for the South to meet it in the extraordinary manner exemplified by the mayor in Alabama. Cities and towns and rural communities passed compulsory labor ordinances and by this means met with partial success in keeping the population at its former work and sometimes at pre-war low wages. An effort to include women's labor within the provisions of the Georgia state law was given up when determined opposition was voiced by leading Atlanta Negroes.

An example of the sort of local ordinance referred to is the one passed in the little Georgia town of Wrightsville. This provided that "it shall be unlawful for *any person* from the ages of sixteen to fifty inclusive to reside in or be upon the streets of Wrightsville" unless this person can show that he "is actively and assiduously engaged in useful employment fifty hours or more per week." The law further provided that each person must carry an employment card signed by his or her employer showing that he or she had worked as the law provided. It can easily be seen what a powerful weapon such a law would be in the hands of those who would be unscrupulous enough to use it. In Macon, Georgia, a colored woman was arrested for not working. She told the court at her trial that she was married, that her husband earned enough to enable her to stay at home and take care of the home and her children, and these duties kept her too busy to do any other work. Despite this statement, she was fined $25.75 and told by the court that if she remained in Macon she "would either work in service or on the public works" as being married did not exempt her from the provisions of the law.

In Birmingham, due to the shortage of domestic labor, an article appeared on June 19th in local papers stating that all women must work. The white women immediately protested and on the 21st another article appeared headed NEGRO WOMEN HERE ORDERED TO WORK. About the same time the Municipal Employment Agency issued an order stating that "all *Negro* women . . . must either go to work or to jail." Twenty women were arrested, all colored, on the first day the order went into effect. The following morning the *Birmingham News* carried an ironical article headed: UNITED STATES EMPLOY-MENT BUREAU CALLS BLUFF OF EBONY HUED WORKERS.

Some days later, the wife of a respectable colored man was sitting on her porch one afternoon paring potatoes for supper, waiting for her husband to come home from his work. An officer saw her, asked her if she was working, and on being told that her duties at home required all of her time and that her husband earned enough to allow her to stay at home, he arrested her for "vagrancy," taking her to the county jail. When her husband came home and was told of the arrest, he immediately went to the jail to provide bail for his wife. This he could not do as all of the officials had gone home. His wife was forced to remain in jail all night, and was released on bail the following morning. This case was dismissed when brought to trial.

In Bainbridge, Decatur County, Georgia, in July, the city council passed an ordinance forcing all women (which meant all *colored* women), whether married or not, whose duties were only those of their homes, to work at some particular job. An officer was sent to the homes of colored people who summoned the wives of a number of colored men to appear in court. There they were charged with vagrancy and fined $15.00 each and told that taking care of their homes was not enough work for them to be doing. On the following night an indignation meeting of the colored citizens was held and the city authorities were told that unless this unjust and discriminatory law were repealed, the colored people would resist "to the last drop of blood in their bodies." No further arrests were made.

No record could be found of any able-bodied white woman being molested.

These are some of the cases among colored women. The impulse to secure colored male labor and to hold it for such purposes as the white man felt most important to his own welfare was also in evidence. Among a number of instances the following are worthy of note:

In Pelham, Georgia, Rufus G. McCrary, colored, Agency Director for the Standard Life Insurance Company (Negro), a man who had under his direction twenty-five agents, the group having produced during 1917 over $900,000 worth of paid-for business, was informed by the town marshal that he must get a job as he (the town marshal) did not consider the selling of life insurance an essential occupation for a Negro. This was done in spite of the fact that Provost Marshal General Crowder had expressly stated that the selling of life insurance was essential. McCrary received a monthly salary of $225 and personally cleared over $3,000 annually through the bank at Pelham. The town marshal delivered this ultimatum to McCrary as he was lying in bed dangerously ill with influenza. McCrary died the following night. The marshal stated that he was acting under the orders of the county sheriff.

In the same town, Frank McCoy, a laborer at the Pelham Fertilizer Works, becoming dissatisfied with this work because of the lack of opportunity for advancement, and feeling that he had some ability in salesmanship, applied for and secured a part time contract with the insurance company. He made an unusual success in this effort, producing between $15,000 and $20,000 of paid-for business each month, on which his commissions amounted to between $150 and $175 per month. This work was done on a part time basis, the balance of his time being spent at the fertilizer works. The same town marshal ordered him to stop selling life insurance and to put in all of his time at the plant.

In Columbia County, in the western part of the state, no Negro can work for another Negro. If he wishes to work for an employer, he must work for a white employer.

In Lake County, Florida, eight colored men who were working as pickers in an orange grove where the scale of wages was much below the standard of $3.50 per day set by the Florida Citrus Exchange, like the mayor's cook, quit in order to go to work at another grove where the wages were higher. Their employer notified the sheriff, upon finding that he could not secure other laborers to take their places, and the officer of the law called the men together and told them that they would either have "to go back to work at the former price, to war or to jail." This case, however, was so flagrant that it came to the attention of the State Labor Bureau. An adjuster was sent to the place and he settled the matter by allowing the men to continue at that grove where the wages were highest.

Enough has been said to show that many employers of Negro labor in the South utilized the national emergency to force Negroes into a condition which bordered virtually on peonage. No one can tell how far the system extended, as most of the offenses occurred in the smaller towns and communities where Negroes dare not reveal the true conditions for fear of punishment, a fear which is well founded, as the lynching record of 1918 will testify. In the larger cities the opposition of the Negroes themselves checked too great abuses. The complaint of many reputable colored citizens in the cities is that the police authorities did not molest the criminal type of Negroes, the "blind tigers," gamblers, runners for immoral houses and the inmates of these houses, but only those who did work, even though they were of the casual labor group. If the campaign had been devoted solely to the former class, there would have been no opposition on the part of the better element of colored people, but in many cities there seems to be a reciprocal arrangement between the police and this class of community parasites.

The crux of the whole situation is found in the fact that domestic and farm labor has been affected by the new war-time conditions and the South, in large measure, was unable to adjust itself to a condition where its former plethora of cheap labor was wiped out. It has the opportunity now to clean house and prevent further migration by wiping out the abuses which exist. If it is attempted through the courts to hammer down wages and persecute laborers, the South may expect increasingly to lose its Negro labor. Since 1914, it is variously estimated that between 500,000 and 1,500,000 Negroes have gone North. Without Negro labor, the South will be bankrupt. With it and its great natural resources, it can become one of the richest sections of the country. It remains to be seen whether the better element among the whites can (and will) gain the ascendancy over the larger element of those who practice the policy laid down by the Dred Scott decision of regarding the Negro as "having no rights which a white man is bound to respect."

New Republic, March 1, 1919; XVIII, 144–46.

60

ADDRESS OF WELCOME TO THE MEN WHO HAVE RETURNED FROM THE BATTLEFRONT
by F. J. Grimké

Struggle and resistance are basic constituents of Afro-American history; moments of special consciousness and militancy appear, of course, and one such was the first year after the Great War. It was in 1919 that Claude McKay's poem first is published (in *The Liberator,* antecedent of *The*

Masses) with its immortal opening, *"If we must die, let it not be like hogs/ Hunted and penned in an inglorious spot";* the same year saw the appearance of Du Bois' editorial "Returning Soldiers" in *The Crisis* (May, 1919; XVIII, 14), ending, ". . . we are cowards and jackasses if, now that the war is over, we do not marshall every ounce of our brain and brawn to fight a sterner, longer, more unbending battle against the forces of hell in our own land."

Less well known—and with a calm that intensifies its impact—was an address of welcome to returning Black soldiers delivered in Washington on April 24, 1919, by the Reverend F. J. Grimké. It is published in full below.

Young gentlemen, I am glad to welcome you home again after months of absence in a foreign land in obedience to the call of your country— glad that you have returned to us without any serious casualties.

I am sure you have acquitted yourself well; that in the record that you have made for yourselves, during your absence from home, there is nothing to be ashamed of, nothing that will reflect any discredit upon the race with which you are identified. The colored soldier has always commanded respect, even from his enemies; the colored soldier has always played a man's part in every struggle in which he was engaged; he has never turned his back upon the enemy; has never shown himself a coward. It is generally admitted that there is no better soldier, in all the world, than the colored soldier.

While you were away you had the opportunity of coming in contact with another than the American type of white man; and through that contact you have learned what it is to be treated as a man, regardless of the color of your skin or race identity. Unfortunately you had to go away from home to receive a man's treatment, to breathe the pure, bracing air of liberty, equality, fraternity. And, while it was with no intention of bringing to you that knowledge, of putting you where you could get that kind of experience, but simply because they couldn't very well get along without you, I am glad, nevertheless, that you were sent. You know now that the mean, contemptible spirit of race prejudice that curses this land is not the spirit of other lands: you know now what it is to be treated as a man. And, one of the things that I am particularly hoping for, now that you have had this experience, is that you have come back determined, as never before, to keep up the struggle for our rights until, here in these United States, in this boasted land of the free and home of the brave, every man, regardless of the color of his skin, shall be accorded a man's treatment.

Your trip will be of very little value to the race in this country unless you have come back with the love of liberty, equality, fraternity burning in your souls, and the determination to set other souls on fire with the same spirit. In the struggle that is before us, you can do a great deal in helping to better conditions. You, who gave up everything—home, friends, relatives—you who took your lives in your hands and went forth to lay them, a willing sacrifice upon the altar of your country and in the interest of democracy throughout the world, have a right to speak—to speak with authority; and that right you must exercise.

We, who remained at home, followed you while you were away, with the deepest interest; and, our hearts burned with indignation when tidings came to us, as it did from time to time, of the manner in which you were treated by those over you, from whom you had every reason, in view of the circumstances that took you abroad and what it was costing you, to expect decent, humane treatment, instead of the treatment that was accorded you. The physical hardships, incident to a soldier's life in times of war, are trying enough, are hard enough to bear —and, during this world war, on the other side of the water, I understand they were unusually hard. To add to these the insults, the studied insults that were heaped upon you, and for no reason except that you were colored, is so shocking that were it not for positive evidence, it would be almost unbelievable.

That shameful record is going to be written up, and published, so that the whole world may read it, and learn how black men, who went out from these shores to die at their country's call, were treated simply because of the color of their skin. The world ought to know it; and will know it; and it is your duty to help those who will make the record to make it as complete as possible. The facts as you know them, let them come out; write out your personal experience and put it where it can be available for the historian, in order that the facts may be preserved as one of the most shameful and detestable exhibitions of race prejudice that can be found in all the world. I know of nothing that sets forth this cursed American race prejudice in a more odious, execrable light than the treatment of our colored soldiers in this great world struggle that has been going on, by the very government that ought to have shielded them from the brutes that were over them.

Again, most gladly do I welcome you back home; and most earnestly do we express the hope that every man of you will play a man's part in the longer and more arduous struggle that is before us in battling for our rights at home. If it was worth going abroad to make the world safe for democracy, it is equally worth laboring no less earnestly to make it safe at home. We shall be greatly disappointed if you do not do this— if you fail to do your part.

Woodson, ed., *Francis J. Grimké,* I (*Addresses Mainly Personal and Religious*), 589–91.

61

RESOLUTIONS OF THE N.A.A.C.P., 1919

The Tenth Anniversary Conference of the N.A.A.C.P. met in Cleveland, Ohio, June 21–29, 1919. The resolutions adopted on that occasion reflect mounting impatience with the divergence between rhetoric and reality. The urging of trade union affiliation in accordance with denunciation of the color line at the 1919 meeting of the A.F.L., and the expression of sympathy with Jews suffering from anti-Semitic practices, are new.

The National Association for the Advancement of Colored People, assembled in its Tenth Annual Conference at Cleveland, Ohio, sends greetings to the American people in general and to Colored Americans in particular.

It views with gratification the many achievements of the past year along the line of the important work that it has undertaken to perform for the strengthening of the nation's institutions and the eradication of the evils that have permeated it in past years. Public opinion has been enlightened as never before, with regard to the many evils perpetrated against the colored race. The publicity given through the National Office in New York to the special investigations made by competent agents, of lynching occurring in various parts of the country; pleading for the industrial equality of the colored race before the industrial corporations of the country; scrupulously safeguarding the interests of the colored soldier and obtaining for him better treatment in whole or in part; the organizing of 228 branches in various sections of the country, thereby perfecting more and more the working machinery; the holding of many large anti-lynching meetings in which have appeared leading statesmen of both the North and the South, and many other notable accomplishments which we need not here mention, constitute the program that the Association has carried thru for the year.

While expressing our gratification over these results, we are mindful that much remains to be accomplished which requires sagacity and courage and sacrifice on the part of the members of the Association and on the part of the American public in general who believe in justice and fair play to all Americans. We beg leave to call attention to the following:

All true Americans view with concern the efforts of discontented people to disrupt our government, and we warn the American people that the patience of even colored people can find its limit; that with poor schools, Jim Crow methods of travel, little or no justice in courts or in things economic staring him in the face, while the colored man is called on to bear his part of the burden in taxation, in government, loans, in civic gifts and in fighting the common foes of our government, we are inviting him to grasp the hands which the Bolsheviks, the I.W.W., and other kindred organizations held out to him. It cannot be expected that Negro leaders can forever hold out empty hope to a people deluded in toto.

We are deeply sensible of the campaign of lies that have been subtly and persistently directed against colored officers and men, particularly colored *officers* of the United States army. We have facts to prove that in many instances the least trained among these men were put forward at all; then the Negro's enemies worked zealously to prove that the colored officer was a failure when they ought to "fail" him at the start.

We are aware of the instances in which both officers and men were thrown into prison on the merest pretenses, or on charges which rightfully fell on the shoulders of white officers. We are also cognizant of the fact that the American colored soldiers brigaded with the French did not suffer for recognition through citations, won crosses and even advancement in rank, while the colored soldier's own white countrymen not only stole all possible opportunity for distinctions from him, but actively sought to poison European and American public opinion against their brothers in black.

We demand Congressional investigation of the treatment of colored soldiers at home and abroad. The shameless and cunning manner in which these officers and men have been treated was not only discriminatory, but violative of the spirit of the American people towards men who were offering their lives for a great cause. We make this demand because the facts so evident to us cannot be hidden from all others, and to allow this to go unchallenged is to weaken national and military morale.

We are opposed to race segregation in the army and navy of the United States of America since it cheats our government of that which is best in discipline and spirit; but if that separation is provided by law, then we demand a full division in the new army to be provided for by the present Congress, officered from top to bottom by colored men.

We demand that a larger number of colored men be appointed to West Point and the Naval Academy at Annapolis for training in military and naval service.

We urge an increase in national financial aid to the education of colored people. To keep the colored citizen in the south in ignorance is to chain to this nation a body of death in ignorant colored and white men, from which it can be delivered by no other means than by a square acceptance of the facts and direct application of financial assistance.

Federal aid to a common school training is indispensable and imperative, but wherever separate schools for colored are compulsory all federal appropriations must by law be conditioned on the strict division of the funds between the races according to population and on colored people having representation on the boards that control colored schools.

We regret that much of the advertised improvement of colored public schools of the South finds expression chiefly in promises; that the threadbare illogical argument concerning the proportioning to the education of colored people of taxes paid by colored people is still working overtime. People of other nationalities, even Germans in our American cities, are educated according to the recognized standards and not according to the taxes they pay.

We recognize the problem of the social diseases as serious and we urge all our people to learn the facts and to aid the nation wide movement for control and betterment. We pledge our cooperation with the United States Public Health Service in securing its literature and information for use in building better Americans.

We earnestly appeal to all organizations interested in social and economic welfare to urge all colored laborers not only to know the advantages of organization as offered by the American Federation of Labor in its recent decision to organize colored workers, but to take advantage of them either by application for membership or by forming an organization as the occasion may demand.

We demand such federal legislation as shall give the government at Washington absolute control of the investigation of and punishment for lynching. This hideous barbarism is murder, and when supposedly civilized democratic states, with laws on their books to prevent or punish murder, openly declare that they are powerless to stop lynching, as declared several southern governors to our Association, they thereby confess that they are to that extent incapable of self-government and subject to this only remedy at hand.

We denounce the *Jim Crow* laws of the *South,* as being illegal and unconstitutional, in that such laws interfere with interstate traffic, and deny to a large part of its loyal citizens equal rights guaranteed under the Constitution; and we call upon the *Congress* of the *United States,* to exercise its powers under the *Commerce* clause of the *Constitution* to the end that all such laws be abolished.

We *demand* that the *Congress* take such action as will insure to all citizens, regardless of Race, Color, or Creed *equal* and *unsegregated* service and accommodation on Railroad and Pullman cars.

We demand the enforcement of all constitutional amendments without discrimination. The patience of the colored American is sorely tried by the country's complacent acceptance of these curtailments of his rights. The country has recently called on us to perform unusual duties; we demand that we have the usual rights of American citizens.

We *demand* that the Thirteenth, Fourteenth and Fifteenth Amendments of the Constitution of the United States which guarantee the Citizenship of the Colored American and his enjoyment of all the rights inherent therein and flowing therefrom, be recognized and enforced by the Government, in good faith. To this end we call on all our colored voters in the better civilized parts of the country to see that their representatives in Congress live up to the demands made herein or report the reasons why.

We desire to extend to the members of the Hebrew race our profound sympathy for the cruel and barbarous treatment accorded them in general, and especially in Poland.

Looking to the achievement of the foregoing ends, we declare the platform of the National Association for the Advancement of Colored People to be the following:

1. A vote for every colored man and woman on the same terms as for white men and women.
2. An equal chance to acquire the kind of education that will enable the colored citizen everywhere wisely to use this vote.
3. A fair trial in the courts for all crimes of which he is accused by judges in whose election he has participated without discrimination because of race.
4. A right to sit upon the jury which passes judgement upon him.
5. Defense against lynching and burning at the hands of mobs.
6. Equal service on railroad and other public carriers. This to mean sleeping car service, dining car service, Pullman service, at the same cost and upon the same terms as other passengers.
7. Equal right to the use of public parks, libraries and other community services for which he is taxed.
8. An equal chance for a livelihood in public and private employment.
9. The abolition of color-hyphenation and the substitution of "straight Americanism."

62

ON THE PAN-AFRICAN CONGRESS, 1919

In 1900, as noted earlier, the First Pan-African Conference was held in London; in it Du Bois played a leading part. As the world war was drawing to a close, the idea reappeared of reviving an organizational expression of the common needs of African and African-derived people. Du Bois received the support of the Executive Board of the N.A.A.C.P. for a trip to France in December, 1918, in order to organize such an effort. Published below are [a] Du Bois' memorandum, dated Paris, January 1, 1919, setting forth suggestions for such an organization—from this developed the Pan-African movement of the present century; and [b] the text of the resolutions adopted by the Pan-African Congress, which met at the Grand Hotel in Paris February 19–21, 1919.

[a]

DU BOIS' MEMORANDUM

Gentlemen: *

I beg hereby to lay before you certain tentative suggestions as to a Pan African Congress to be held in Paris in February, 1919.

1. The appointment of a small Committee of arrangements.

2. The sending of personal invitations to representatives of the Negro race who can attend such a Congress and who represent the Governments of Abyssinia, Liberia and Haiti; the French, English, Spanish, Italian, Belgian, Dutch and former German colonies; and the descendants of Negroes inhabiting North and South America and the Islands of the Sea.

3. Invitations to all Governments having Negro citizens and subjects to send representatives to address the Congress; and similar invitations to China, Japan and India.

4. Invitations to join in our open conferences to representatives of organizations devoted to the advancement of the Darker Races.

5. The chief work of the Congress shall be:

---

* Du Bois directed this to "M. Diagne and others." Diagne, a Deputy from Senegal to the French Parliament, was Commissioner-General of Colonial Affairs in Clemenceau's government.

(a) The hearing of statements on the condition of Negroes through the world.

(b) The obtaining of authoritative statements of policy toward the Negro race from the Great Powers.

(c) The making of strong representations to the Peace Conference sitting in Paris in behalf of both voice in and protection for 250,000,000 Negroes and Negroids in the League of Nations.

(d) The laying down of principles upon which the future development of the Negro race must take place, including:

Political rights for the civilized.

Modern education for all children.

Native rights to the land and natural resources.

Industrial development primarily for the benefit of the native and his country.

Development of autonomous government along lines of native custom, with the object of inaugurating gradually an Africa for the Africans.

Full recognition of the independent Governments of Abyssinia, Liberia and Haiti, with their full natural boundaries, and the development of the former German Colonies under the guarantee and oversight of the League of Nations.

The cordial and sympathetic co-operation of the Black, Yellow and White Races on terms of mutual respect and equality in the future development of the world.

6. The program of the Congress might be something as follows: Sunday afternoon: Mass-meeting, addressed by representatives of the Colonial Powers and of the Negro nations.

Night: Reception to delegates.

Monday morning: Closed conference of Negro delegates; appointment of Committees; reports of conditions.

Afternoon: Open conference; reports from Governments.

Tuesday morning: Committees and resolutions.

Afternoon: Closed conference.

Night: Mass-meeting and speeches.

7. The Conference should form a permanent Secretariat with Headquarters in Paris, charged with the duty of:

Collating the history of the Negro race.

Studying the present condition of the race.

Publishing articles, pamphlets and a report of this Congress

Encouraging Negro art and literature.

Arranging for a second Pan-African Congress in 1920.

The Crisis, March, 1919; XVII, 224–25.

[b]

RESOLUTIONS OF THE PAN-AFRICAN CONGRESS

The Negroes of the world in Pan-African Congress assembled at Paris February 19, 20, 21, 1919, demand, in the interest of justice and humanity and for strengthening the forces of civilisation, that immediate steps be taken to develop the 200,000,000 of Negroes and Negroids; to this end, they propose:

A.—That the allied and associated Powers establish a code of laws for the international protection of the natives of Africa similar to the proposed international code for Labor.

B.—That the League of Nations establish a permanent Bureau charged with the special duty of overseeing the application of these laws to the political, social and economic welfare of the natives.

The Negroes of the world demand that hereafter the native of Africa and the Peoples of African descent be governed according to the following principles.

1.—*The land:* The land and its natural resources shall be held in trust for the natives and at all times they shall have effective ownership of as much land as they can profitably develop.

2.—*Capital:* The investment of capital and granting of concessions shall be so regulated as to prevent the exploitation of the natives and the exhaustion of the natural wealth of the country. Concessions shall always be limited in time and subject to State control. The growing social needs of the natives must be regarded and the profits taxed for the social and material benefit of the natives.

3.—*Labor:* Slavery and corporal punishment shall be abolished and forced labor except in punishment for crime; and the general conditions of labor shall be prescribed and regulated by the State.

4.—*Education*: It shall be the right of every native child to learn to read and write his own language, and the language of the trustee nation, at public expense, and to be given technical instruction in some branch of industry. The State shall also educate as large a number of natives as possible in higher technical and cultural training and maintain a corps of native teachers.

5.—*Medicine and Hygiene*: It shall be recognized that human existence in the tropics calls for special safeguards and a scientific system of public hygiene. The State shall be responsible for medical care and sanitary conditions without discouraging collective and individual initiative. A service created by the State shall provide physicians and hospitals, and shall spread the rules of hygiene by written and spoken word. As fast as possible the State will establish a native medical staff.

6.—*The State:* The natives of Africa must have the right to participate in the government as fast as their development permits in conformity with the principle that the government exists for the natives, and not the natives for the government. They shall at once be allowed to participate in local and tribal government according to ancient usage, and this participation shall gradually extend, as education and experience proceeds, to the higher offices of State, to the end that, in time, Africa be ruled by consent of the Africans.

7.—*Culture and Religion:* No particular religion shall be imposed and no particular form of human culture. There shall be liberty of conscience. The uplift of the natives shall take into consideration their present condition and shall allow the utmost scope to racial genius, social inheritance and individual bent so long as these are not contrary to the best established principles of civilisation.

8.—*Civilized Negroes:* Wherever persons of African descent are civilized and able to meet the tests of surrounding culture, they shall be accorded the same rights as their fellow citizens; they shall not be denied on account of race or color a voice in their own government, justice before the courts and economic and social equality according to ability and desert.

9.—*The League of Nations:* Greater security of life and property shall be guaranteed the natives; international labor legislation shall cover the native workers as well as whites; they shall have equitable representation in all the international institutions of the League of Nations, and the participation of the blacks themselves in every domain of endeavour shall be encouraged in accordance with the declared object of article 19 of the League of Nations, to wit: "The well being and the development of these people constitute a sacred mission of civilisation and it is proper in establishing the League of Nations to incorporate therein pledges for the accomplishment of this mission."

Whenever it is proven that African natives are not receiving just treatment at the hands of any state or that any State deliberately excludes its civilized citizens or subjects of Negro descent from its body politic and cultural, it shall be the duty of the League of Nations to bring the matter to the attention of the civilized World.

For The Pan-African Congress, composed of 57 members from 15 countries, inhabited by 85,000,000 Negroes and persons of African descent—to wit:

États-Unis	16	Colonies espagnoles	2	Afrique Anglaise	1
Antilles et Guyane		Colonies		Afrique	
Françaises	13	portugaises	1	Française	1
Haiti	7	Abyssinie	1	Algérie	1
France	7	Saint-Dominique	1	Egypt	1
Liberia	3	Angleterre	1	Congo Belge	1
	46		6		5

TOTAL 57

W. E. Burghardt Du Bois,
Directeur National,
Association for the Advancement
of Colored People, U.S.A.,
Secrétaire

Blaise Diagne,
Député du Sénégal,
Commissaire Général chargé du
Contröle des effectifs coloniaux
français,
Président du Congrès

From a two-page folder, printed in French and English, and issued in Paris in 1919; in editor's possession.

63

BEN FLETCHER AND THE I.W.W.

Of the approximately one million membership cards distributed by the Industrial Workers of the World (I.W.W.) during its most powerful period—the ten years prior to World War I—about one hundred thousand belonged to Black workers. Such workers were especially numerous in the lumber industry in Louisiana, Texas, and Arkansas and among port workers in New Orleans, Charleston, Norfolk, and—in particular—Philadelphia. The Philadelphia local was especially powerful and militant; a leader was the Black man, Benjamin F. Fletcher. Finally, in 1919, Mr. Fletcher was sentenced to ten years in jail under the wartime Sedition Act. Commentary on the latter event came from *The Messenger*.

Negro newspapers seldom publish anything about men who are useful to the race. Some parasite, ecclesiastical poltroon, sacerdotal taxgatherer, political faker or business exploiter will have his name in the papers, weekly or daily. But when it comes to one of those who fight for the great masses to lessen their hours of work, to increase their wages, to decrease their high cost of living, to make life more livable for the toiling black workers—that man is not respectable for the average Negro sheet.

Such a man is Ben Fletcher. He is one of the leading organizers of the Industrial Workers of the World, commonly known as the I.W.W. He is in Leavenworth Penitentiary, Kansas, where he was sent for trying to secure better working conditions for colored men and women in the United States. He has a vision far beyond that of almost any Negro leader whom we know. He threw in his lot with his fellow white workers, who work side by side with black men and black women to raise their standard of living. It is not uncommon to see Negro papers have headlines concerning a Negro who had committed murder, cut some woman's throat, stolen a chicken or a loaf of bread, but those same papers never record happenings concerning the few Negro manly men who go to prison for principle. Ben Fletcher is in Leavenworth for principle—a principle which when adopted, will put all the Negro leaders out of their parasitical jobs.

That principle is that to the workers belongs the world, but useful work is not done by Negro leaders.

We want to advocate and urge that Negro societies, judges, churches, N.A.A.C.P. branches and, of course, their labor organizations begin to protest against the imprisonment of Ben Fletcher and to demand for his release. He has been of more service to the masses of the plain Negro people than all the wind jamming Negro leaders in the United States.

The Messenger, August, 1919; II, 28–29; in the July, 1919, *Messenger* appeared an editorial (p. 8), "Why Negroes Should Join the I.W.W."

64

BLACK AND WHITE PSYCHOLOGY

by Jean Toomer

The Nation, in the issue of June 14, 1919, published an article by the N.A.A.C.P.'s Herbert J. Seligmann, "Protecting Southern Womanhood," which blasted the monstrous lynching besmirching the country and warned that a general explosion from the Afro-American people might well follow. In the same issue, the editors, under the title, "The Negro at Bay," explained that they published the Seligmann article not to justify violent reaction by Black people—indeed, the editors attacked Dr. Du Bois by name for his "most dangerous and mistaken" advocacy of forcible resistance as a basic right of a people daily suffering forcible repression—but to suggest the need for reforms in the South. The editorial was permeated with racist notions and was careful to insist "that the right is not all on one side."

Jean Toomer (1894–1967), grandson of P. B. S. Pinchback—lieutenant governor of Louisiana during Reconstruction—was educated at the University of Wisconsin and C.C.N.Y. He taught for a time in rural Georgia and in 1918 turned to writing, the climax of which was his *Cane* (1923). He published little thereafter and soon "passed." A letter from Toomer attacking the views of Du Bois and supporting *The Nation* editorial follows.

To The Editor of *The Nation*:

Sir: Your editorial, "The Negro at Bay," in *The Nation* of June 14, is significant not so much because it advocates the extension of constitutional rights to the Negro, but for the reason that it indicates and justly condemns the apparent "fighting" psychology of the Negro.

Led for the most part by "leaders" whose vision is circumscribed by the color line, and embittered by opposition and disillusionment, the Negroes, if their "fighting" psychology of today be translated into action, would be likely to direct the conflict not so much against the iniquities of the white race, as against the white race itself. Such an eventuality would inevitably spell disaster to the Negro; nor is it less certain that at this time the condition of one-tenth of a country's population must necessarily be reflected on the other nine-tenths of the people.

Washington, June 29

Jean Toomer

The Nation, July 12, 1919; CIX, 44.

65

HOW TO STOP LYNCHING
by the Editors of The Messenger

The Nation and Jean Toomer to the contrary, the view of *The Messenger* was that physical resistance combined with widespread strikes would be effective in wiping out lynching. The expression of that argument follows. The reference therein to *The Nation* is to the Seligmann article noted earlier. In it (CVIII:938–39), Seligmann reported that when officials of Memphis learned in May, 1919, that Afro-Americans were armed and intended to resist a threatened mob attack they managed to avert the launching of that attack. Armed resistance by Black men also marked the pogrom in Longview, Texas, in June, 1919 (see on this *The Crisis,* October, 1919, p. 297), to which the following also makes reference.

Lynching is our chiefest problem in America today. All Negroes are agreed, and some white people also, that it is the arch crime of America and that it ought to be stopped. The only difference is that of method. The question of How?

We are also pretty well agreed that the methods adopted by Negroes at the behest of Negro leaders, in the past, are futile and valueless.

For instance, we have sent telegrams to Southern Governors only to be told in reply, that they have no power and oftentimes no inclination to stop what they are pleased to characterize as "an orderly lynching." Experience has taught us that appeal to "Big White Politicians" is simply ineffective. For even the President, Woodrow Wilson, made a pronouncement against lynching (Of course he was only interested in Robert Prager, a German who had been lynched, and especially in view of the fact that Germany had threatened to take revenge upon American citizens residing in Germany) with no visible effect upon the Southern mob.

The Messenger proposes an immediate program for Negroes. This program includes two methods. First, physical force and secondly, economic force.

PHYSICAL FORCE

Anglo Saxon jurisprudence recognizes the law of self-defense. Our information also records that the right of self-defense is recognized in the laws of all countries. Not only is the right of self-defense recognized with respect to the person about to be injured, but it is recognized that the person about to be injured may summon others to assist him in repelling an attack. We are consequently urging Negroes and other oppressed groups confronted with lynching or mob violence to act upon the recognized and accepted law of self-defense. Always regard your own life as more important than the life of the person about to take yours, and if a choice has to be made between the sacrifice of your life and the loss of the lyncher's life, choose to preserve your own and to destroy that of the lynching mob. Recently we have had a few instances of the effect of organized self-assertion on the part of Negroes in the South. The Nation points out that on the 25th and 26th of May a mob in Memphis, Tenn., where Eli Persons was lynched a year ago, had settled upon a race riot. It was found out, however, that Negroes were well armed and organized to meet the attack with resistance. This having been learned, the Mayor of Memphis immediately called the Chief of Police, and both together promptly called off the riot. Just a few days ago, the Negroes of Long View, Texas, held up a mob which started to lynch a Negro school teacher who had reported a lynching through the *Chicago Defender*. Instead of leaving the Negro school teacher to himself, to make his own defense, a group of Negroes, well armed and well organized, fired upon the advancing mob, shooting down four members of the mob, whereupon its steps were taken backward rather than forward. The Governor of Texas, as a rule, has always claimed that he had no troops and no power to stop the action of the mob but when the Negroes at Long View protected their lives with shot and shell and fire, the Governor of Texas sent militia and rangers and army planes to restore law and order in Long View. *The Messenger* wants to explain the reason why Negroes can stop lynching in the South with shot and shell and fire. All mobs act on the principle of pessimism. One hundred to fifteen thousand men usually take part in lynching one Negro, with the Negro handcuffed and arrested, unable to defend himself. The very numbers who engage in it are evidence of the cowardice of the mob. But when the mob knows that somebody is going to have to give his life, each man thinks that *he* may have to give *his* life. No one desires to make this sacrifice, and although it is perfectly certain that twenty millions of people can beat down eight millions, if the sacrifice to accomplish this is so great, it will deter the twenty million from its aim: and so with the mob. A mob of a thousand men knows it can beat down fifty Negroes, but when those fifty Negroes rain fire and shot and shell over the thousand, the whole group of cowards will be put to flight.

This may sound rather strange talk for the pacific editors of *The Messenger,* but we are pacific only on matters that can be settled peacefully. The appeal to the conscience of the South has been long and futile. Its soul has been petrified and permeated with wickedness, injustice and lawlessness. The black man has no rights which will be respected unless the black man enforces that respect. It is his business to decide that just as he went three thousand miles away to fight for alleged democracy in Europe and for others, that he can lay down his life, honorably and peacefully, for himself in the United States. In so doing, we do not assume any role of anarchy, nor any shadow of lawlessness. We are acting strictly within the pale of the law and in a manner recognized as law abiding by every civilized nation. We are trying to enforce the laws which American Huns are trampling in the dust, connived in and winked at by nearly all of the American officials, from the President of the United States down.

ECONOMIC FORCE

Physical force is not the only weapon of the Negro. He has tremendous economic power. He constitutes one-seventh of the industrial population of the United States. In the South, his economic power is even greater. According to Professor Albert Bushnell Hart of Harvard, the Negroes in the South produce three-fifths of the wealth, that is, one-third of the population produces over one-half of the wealth. Now one of the best ways to strike a man is to strike him in the pocket-book. Cotton is the staple crop of the South. The Negroes are the chief producers of cotton. They also constitute a big factor in the South in the production of turpentine, tar, lumber, coal and iron, transportation facilities and all agricultural produce. They should be thoroughly organized into unions, whereupon they could make demands and withhold their labor from the transportation industry and also from personal and domestic service and the South will be paralyzed industrially and in commercial consternation. That state of affairs will attract the attention and interest of the whole world. Lynching will immediately be made a national and an international problem.

The problem will become *national* because the textile industries of the North and West are dependent upon the products of Negro labor. When Massachusetts, New Jersey and New York can no longer get cotton for the mills, the mills must close. Machinery stands idle. Men are unemployed. Discontent grows. Social unrest spreads. Revolution stares the government in the face. The building and lumber trades will also be at a standstill. Mechanics will be thrown out of work. Carpenters, masons, moulders, painters, plumbers, electricians, machinists, contractors and architects will have their work cut down. Something will then have to be done. Both capitalists and workers will become interested in abolition of lynching—the capitalists because their profits will be cut off, from the cessation of business, and the workers because their wages will be cut off, from the cessation of work. At this time, the whole of the United States will for the first time, be interested in abolition of lynching, not because they will love the Negro any more, but because it is necessary for their own interests to stamp out this typical American injustice.

Lynching will then become an *international problem,* also. During the Civil War, when the Southern Blockade was on, and cotton could not be shipped to Europe, industrial paralysis was thrown into Great

Britain. In Manchester, Leeds, Liverpool and London, the textile industries had to be closed. Work stopped in those great industrial centers and every Englishman began to inquire about American slavery. The Englishmen wanted slavery abolished, because the fight over the institution was striking them in the pocketbook. Slavery became an international problem because cotton could not be supplied. At that time, however, only a few million bales of cotton were produced. Today over a hundred million bales are being produced each year, largely by Negroes. Now, if the hold up of a few million bales made slavery an international problem, the hold up of hundreds of millions of bales of cotton will make lynching an international problem of prime importance. If Negroes withdraw their hands from the cotton fields, the cotton will rot on the farms. The South will get on its knees, just as it was almost on its knees over the migration during the war. It did not want Negroes to leave there, not because they were hankering for Negro company but because they wanted the Negro's work—his labor power.

At the present time, these two forms of attack will suffice for Negroes to enter upon. Whenever you hear talk of a lynching, a few hundred of you must assemble rapidly and let the authorities know that you propose to have them abide by the law and not violate it. Offer your services to the Mayor or the Governor, pledging him that you can protect the life of any prisoner if the State militia has no such power. Ask the Governor or the authorities to supply you with additional arms and under no circumstances should you Southern Negroes surrender your arms for lynching mobs to come in and have sway. To organize your work a little more effectively, get in touch with all of the Negroes who were in the draft. Form little voluntary companies which may quickly be assembled. Find Negro officers who will look after their direction. Be perfectly calm, poised, cool and self-contained. Do not get excited but face your work with cold resolution, determined to uphold the law and to protect the lives of your fellows at any cost. When this is done, nobody will have to sacrifice his life or that of anybody else, because nobody is going to be found who will try to overcome that force.

Industrially, let the farmers organize farmers' protective unions. Let the lumber workers, moulders, masons, plasterers and other Negro workers on railroads and in mines organize into unions, quietly and unostentatiously. Be prepared to walk out in concert, every man and woman who does any form of work. Let it be known that we are down to plain business, free from any foolishness or play.

Let every Negro in the South, begin to work on this program by agitating for it in the lodges, churches, schools, parlor and home conversation and while at work in factory or field. Write also to us about any detail in entering upon this work. If this program is pressed, a year from now, we can call out of the fields, the factories and the mines between a million and two million Negroes, who will initiate the true work of making America a real "land of the free and home of the brave."

Editorial, *The Messenger,* August, 1919; II, 8–10.

66

A WARNING TO THE PRESIDENT
from Robert R. Moton

On August 8, 1919, after fierce pogroms in Chicago and Washington—where, again, resistance by the Black population was noteworthy—Dr. Moton of Tuskegee wrote as follows to President Wilson.

I want especially to call your attention to the intense feeling on the part of the colored people throughout the country towards white people, and the apparent revolutionary attitude of many Negroes which shows itself in a desire to have justice at any cost. The riots in Washington and Chicago and near-riots in many other cities have not surprised me in the least. I predicted in an address several months ago at the fiftieth anniversary of the Hampton Institute, on the second of May—ex-President Taft and Mr. George Foster Peabody were present at the time—that this would happen if the matter was not taken hold of vigorously by the thoughtful elements of both races.

I think the time is at hand, and I think of nothing that would have a more salutary effect on the whole situation now than if you should in your own wise way, as you did a year ago, make a statement regarding mob law; laying especial stress on lynching and every form of injustice and unfairness. You would lose nothing by specifically referring to the lynching record in the past six months; many of them have been attended with unusual horrors, and it would be easy to do it now because of the two most recent riots in the North, notably Washington and Chicago. The South was never more ready to listen than at present to that kind of advice, and it would have a tremendously stabilizing effect, as I have said, on the members of my race.

You very probably saw the account of the lynching in Georgia, of an old colored man seventy years of age who shot one of two intoxicated white men in his attempt to protect two colored girls, who had been commanded to come out of their home in the night by these two men. The colored man killed the white man after he had been shot by one of the white men because he had simply protested.

I am enclosing the lynching record for the past six months and an editorial from the *Atlanta Constitution,* which strongly denounces mob violence.

With all kind wishes, and assuring you of no desire to add to your burdens, but simply to call attention to what seems to me vital not only for the interest of the twelve millions of black people, but equally as important for the welfare of the millions of whites whom they touch, I am, very sincerely and gratefully,

R. R. Moton

Stephen Graham, *Children of the Slaves* (London: Macmillan, 1920), pp. 263–64.

67

SOCIALISM: THE NEGROES' HOPE

by W. A. Domingo

Mr. Domingo, a leader of the West Indian community in New York City—and at this time a prominent supporter of the Universal Negro Improvement Association, led by Marcus Garvey—offered the following essay in favor of socialism for the magazine edited by A. Philip Randolph.

It is a regrettable and disconcerting anomaly that, despite their situation as the economic, political and social door mat of the world, Negroes do not embrace the philosophy of socialism, and in greater numbers than they now do. It is an anomaly because it is reasonable to expect those who are lowest down to be the ones who would most quickly comprehend the need for a change in their status and welcome any doctrine which holds forth any hope of human elevation. In matters of religion they respond and react logically and naturally enough, for to them, the religion of Christ, the lowly Nazarene, brings definite assurance of surcease from earthly pains and the hope of celestial readjustment of mundane equalities. Their acceptance of the Christian religion with its present day emphasis upon an after-life enjoyment of the good things denied them on the earth is conclusive proof of their dissatisfaction with their present lot, and is an earnest of their susceptibility to Socialism, which intends to do for human beings what Christianity promises to do for them in less material regions.

That they and all oppressed dark peoples will be the greatest beneficiaries in a socialist world has not been sufficiently emphasized by Socialist propaganda among Negroes.

Perhaps this is not clearly understood, but a little examination of the facts will prove this to be the case.

Throughout the world Negroes occupy a position of absolute inferiority to the white race. This is true whether they are black Frenchmen, black Englishmen, black Belgians or black Americans.

As between themselves and the masses of white proletarians their lives are more circumscribed, their ambitions more limited and their opportunities for the enjoyment of liberty and happiness more restricted. White workingmen of England who are Socialists are immeasurably the political and social superiors of the average Negro in the West Indies or Africa; white workingmen of France, who are Socialists are unquestionably the political and social superiors of Senegalese and Madagascan Negroes; white workingmen of the United States who are Socialists are indisputably the social and political superiors of the millions of Negroes below the Mason and Dixon line; yet despite their relative and absolute superiority these white workers are fighting for a world freed from oppression and exploitation, whilst Negroes who are oppressed cling to past and present economic ideals with the desperation of a drowning man.

Socialism as an economic doctrine is merely the pure Christianity preached by Jesus, and practiced by the early Christians adapted to the more complex conditions of modern life. It makes no distinction as to race, nationality or creed, but like Jesus it says "Come unto me all ye who are weary and heavy laden and I will give you rest." It is to procure that rest that millions of oppressed peoples are flocking to the scarlet banner of international Socialism.

So far, although having greater need for its equalizing principles than white workingmen, Negroes have been slow to realize what has already dawned upon nearly every other oppressed people: That Socialism is their only hope.

The 384,000,000 natives of India groaning under the exploitation of the handful of English manufacturers, merchants and officials who profit out of their labor are turning from Lloyd George and the capitalistic Liberal Party to Robert Smillie,* the Socialist and the Independent Labor Party. The 4,000,000 Irish who suffer national strangulation at the hands of British industrialists and militarists have turned to the Socialists of England for relief besides becoming Socialists themselves. The Egyptians who are of Negro admixture being convinced that their only hope for freedom from British exploitation is in international Socialism are uniting forces with British Socialists and organized labor. In fact, every oppressed group of the world is today turning from Clemenceau, Lloyd George and Wilson to the citadel of Socialism, Moscow. In this they are all in advance of Western Negroes with the exception of little groups in the United States and a relatively well-organized group in the Island of Trinidad, British West Indies.

Because of ignorant and unscrupulous leadership, Negroes are influenced to give their support to those institutions which oppress them, but if they would only do a little independent thinking without the aid of preacher, politician or press they would quickly realize that the very men like Thomas Dixon, author of "The Clansman," Senators Hoke Smith of Georgia and Lee S. Overman of North Carolina, who are fighting Socialism or as they maliciously call it Bolshevism, are the same men who exhaust every unfair means to vilify, oppress and oppose Negroes. If anything should commend Socialism to Negroes, nothing can do so more eloquently than the attitude and opinions of its most influential opponents toward people who are not white.

On the other hand, the foremost exponents of Socialism in Europe and America are characterized by the broadness of their vision towards all oppressed humanity. It was the Socialist Vendervelde of Belgium, who protested against the Congo atrocities practiced upon Negroes; it was the late Keir Hardie and Philip Snowdon of England, who condemned British rule in Egypt; and in the United States it was the Socialist, Eugene V. Debs, who refused to speak in Southern halls from which Negroes were excluded. Today, it is the revolutionary Socialist, Lenin, who analyzed the infamous League of Nations and exposed its true character; it is he as leader of the Communist Congress at Moscow, who sent out the proclamation: "Slaves of the colonies in Africa and Asia! The hour of proletarian dictatorship in Europe will be the hour of your release!"

The Messenger, July, 1919; II, 22.

* Robert Smillie was president of the Miners' Federation of Great Britain at this time; he was a Labor M.P. from 1923 to 1929.

68

FOR PROMOTING LABOR UNIONISM AMONG BLACK WORKERS

Early in 1919, Black socialists like the Reverend George Frazier Miller of Brooklyn and Chandler Owen and A. Philip Randolph—with the participation of white Socialists, such as Morris Hillquit, Joseph Schlossberg (of the Amalgamated Clothing Workers), and Charles W. Ervin (editor of the *New York Call*, the Socialist organ)—organized the National Association for the Promotion of Labor Unionism Among Workers. Its seal showed black and white hands clasping each other, surrounded by the words: "Black and White Workers Unite."

Taking off from denunciations of this effort in the commercial press, *The Messenger* published the following essay, repeating, in part, its editorial of July, 1918 (see p. 223).

OUR REASON FOR BEING

First, as workers, black and white, we all have one common interest, viz., the getting of more wages, shorter hours, and better working conditions.

Black and white workers should combine for no other reason than that for which individual workers should combine, viz., to increase their bargaining power, which will enable them to get their demands.

Second, the history of the labor movement in America proves that the employing class recognize no race lines. They will exploit a white man as readily as a black man. They will exploit women as readily as men. They will even go to the extent of coining the labor, blood and suffering of children into dollars. The introduction of women and children into the factories proves that capitalists are only concerned with profits and that they will exploit any race or class in order to make profits, whether they be black or white men, black or white women or black or white children.

Third, it is apparent that every Negro worker or non-union man is a potential scab upon white union men and black union men.

Fourth, self-interest is the only principle upon which individuals or groups will act if they are sane. Thus, it is idle and vain to hope or expect Negro workers, out of work and who receive less wages when at work than white workers, to refuse to scab upon white workers when an opportunity presents itself.

Men will always seek to improve their conditions. When colored workers, as scabs, accept the wages against which white workers strike, they (the Negro workers) have definitely improved their conditions.

That is the only reason why colored workers scab upon white workers or why non-union white men scab upon white union men.

Every member, which is a part of the industrial machinery, must be organized, if labor would win its demands. Organized labor cannot afford to ignore any labor factor of production which organized capital does not ignore.

Fifth, if the employers can keep the white and black dogs, on account of race prejudice, fighting over a bone; the yellow capitalist dog will get away with the bone—the bone of profits. No union man's standard of living is safe so long as there is a group of men or women who may be used as scabs and whose standard of living is lower.

The combination of black and white workers will be a powerful lesson to the capitalists of the solidarity of labor. It will show that labor, black and white, is conscious of its interests and power. This will prove that unions are not based upon race lines, but upon class lines. This will serve to convert a class of workers, which has been used by the capitalist class to defeat organized labor, into an ardent, class conscious, intelligent, militant group.

This statement of the Negro's labor problem, together with the presentation of the radical whites, who recognize no race or color line, brought to the attention of the Union League Club's billionaires, and the Washington Chamber of Commerce, what the new Negro is thinking and Mr. Samuel Gompers, who is a member of the Chamber of Commerce himself, was no doubt promptly informed that the Negroes were getting unruly and from under control of the reactionaries and that some sop would have to be handed out or else the more radical unions would get control of them.

Sixth: The Industrial Workers of the World commonly termed the I.W.W., draw no race, creed, color or sex line in their organization. They are making a desperate effort to get the colored men into the One Big Union. The Negroes are at least giving them an ear, and the prospects point to their soon giving them a hand. With the Industrial Workers Organization already numbering 800,000, to augment it with a million and a half or two million Negroes, would make it fairly rival the American Federation of Labor. This may still be done anyhow and the reactionaries of this country, together with Samuel Gompers, the reactionary President of the American Federation of Labor, desire to hold back this trend of Negro labor radicalism.

Seventh: The Providence *Sunday Journal* of June 1st, 1919, one of the chief plutocratic mouth pieces of the country, carries a whole half page on *The Messenger* and its labor agitation, entitled "Enrolling American Negroes Under Banners of Bolshevism." In speaking of *The Messenger* it says: "What is advocated by *The Messenger,* is a policy of evolution—one that will bring the Negro workers of this country into closer relationship with the white unionists—one that will make a great combination of the white and black laboring vote of this country, and, therefore, one which if brought to a successful culmination would dominate the politics and policies of the entire country."

The Providence *Journal* continues, "The publication in the U.S., spreading this insidious propaganda among Negroes, is *The Messenger.* It is published at 2305 Seventh Avenue, New York City, by *two as well read, well educated and competent Negroes as there are in the United States.* They are A. Philip Randolph and Chandler Owen, and as a contributing editor, they have Dr. George Frazier Miller, one of the best known Negro Divines in New York City. The publication is well gotten up, well printed and in every way put together in a manner which would appeal to the people that it is intended to reach."

After writing a whole half page on the propaganda being carried on by *The Messenger* magazine and the National Association for the Promotion of Labor Unionism Among Negroes, the Providence *Journal* also quoted the preamble of the National Association for the Promotion of Labor Unionism among Negroes.

Eighth: The New York *World,* the mouth-piece of the present administration, and also a plutocratic mouth-piece, says in its issue of June 4, 1919, "The radical forces in New York City have recently embarked on a great new field of revolutionary endeavor, the education through agitation of the southern Negro into the mysteries and desirability of revolutionary Bolshevism. There are several different powerful forces in N. Y. City behind this move. The chief established propaganda is being distributed through *The Messenger,* which styles itself—'The only magazine of scientific radicalism in the world, published by Negroes.' Its editors are A. Philip Randolph and Chandler Owen, with George Frazier Miller, contributing editor. This radical journal is published at 2305 Seventh Ave., New York City. With the exception of *The Liberator,* it is the most radical journal printed in the U.S."

In the issue of the New York *World,* June 8th, Sunday edition, a special article, almost a page long on "Methods Used by Radicals to Destroy the influence of The American Federation of Labor," the following quotation was taken from *The Messenger:* "The dissolution of the American Federation of Labor would inure to the benefit of the Labor Movement in this country in particular, and to the International Labor Movement in general. Why? In the first place it is organized upon unsound principles. It holds that there can be a partnership between capital and labor. Think of it! A partnership between the exploiter and the exploited! Between the spider and the fly! Between the lion and the lamb! Between the cat and the mouse!"

The foregoing comments from such powerful organs as The Providence *Sunday Journal,* the New York *Sunday World,* the National Civic Federation Review and the Union League Club of New York, followed by action of the Legislature of the State of New York *— demonstrates how powerful is the influence of a well written, logical publication, fighting for the interests of twelve million Negroes in particular and the working masses in general. These are the real reasons why the American Federation of Labor decided to lay aside its infamous color line. There is no change of heart on the part of the Federation, but it is acting under the influence of fear. There is a new leadership for Negro workers. It is a leadership of uncompromising manhood. It is not asking for a half loaf but for the whole loaf. It is insistent upon the Negro workers exacting justice, both from the white labor unions and from the capitalists or employers.

The Negroes who will benefit from this decision are indebted first to themselves and their organized power, which made them dangerous. Second, to the radical agitation carried on by *The Messenger;* and third, to the fine spirt of welcome shown by the Industrial Workers of the World, whose rapid growth and increasing power the American Federation of Labor fears. These old line Negro political fossils know nothing of the Labor Movement, do not believe in labor unions at all, and have never taken any active steps to encourage such organizations. We make this statement calmly, coolly and with a reasonable reserve. The very thing which they are fighting is one of the chief factors in securing for Negroes their rights. That is Bolshevism. The capitalists of this country are so afraid that Negroes will become Bolshevists that they are willing to offer them almost anything to hold them away from the radical movement. Nobody buys pebbles which may be picked up

* This refers to the appointment of the Lusk Committee, a forerunner of the activities of Martin Dies in the 1930s and Joseph McCarthy in the 1950's.

on the beach, but diamonds sell high. The old line Negro leaders have no power to bargain, because it is known that they are Republicans politically and job-hunting, me-too-boss-hat-in-hand-Negroes, industrially. Booker Washington and all of them have simply advocated that Negroes get more work. The editors of *The Messenger* are not interested in Negroes getting more work. Negroes have too much work already. What we want Negroes to get is less work and more wages, with more leisure for study and recreation.

Our type of agitation has really won for Negroes such concessions as were granted by the American Federation of Labor and we are by no means too sanguine over the possibilities of the sop which was granted. It may be like the Constitution of the United States—good in parts, but badly executed. We shall have to await the logic of events. In the meantime, we urge the Negro labor unions to increase their radicalism, to speed up their organization, to steer clear of the Negro leaders and to thank nobody but themselves for what they have gained. In organization there is strength, and whenever Negroes or anybody else make organized demands, their call will be heeded.

The Messenger, August, 1919; II, 11–12.

69

THE NEGRO AND THE LABOR UNION: AN N.A.A.C.P. REPORT

As the activities reflected in the preceding document went forward, so too did parallel efforts go forth from organizations such as the N.A.A.C.P. and from within the A.F.L. itself. The following official statement from the N.A.A.C.P. illustrates these developments.

In his study of the "Negro Artisan," Atlanta University, 1902, Dr. Du Bois sums up the matter of the relation of the Negro to the labor union in the following statement.

The rule of admission of Negroes to unions throughout the country is the sheer necessity of guarding work and wages. In those trades where large numbers of Negroes are skilled they find easy admittance in the parts of the country where their competition is felt. In all other trades they are barred from the unions save in exceptional cases, either by open or silent color discrimination. There are exceptions to this rule. There are cases where the whites have shown a real feeling of brotherhood; there are cases where the blacks, through incompetence and carelessness, have forfeited their right to the advantages of organization. But on the whole, a careful, unprejudiced survey of the facts leads one to believe that the above statement is true approximately all over the land.

This view is as correct in 1919 as it was in 1902, but the position of the Negro artisan has, in the meantime, greatly changed. With the European War and its shortage of immigrant labor, the colored man has entered into the industry of the United States. North and South he no longer stands at the foot of the ladder, doing only the heaviest unskilled work; he still performs many of these tasks, but thousands have moved up the rungs and are competing with the white man in well-paid skilled labor. This makes his organization necessary to the labor movement of the United States, and it explains the extraordinary interest and even enthusiasm manifested for him at the recent annual conference of the American Federation of Labor.

The conference met in Atlantic City in June and on the thirteenth of that month the Negro members made themselves heard. They spoke in no uncertain terms. There were twenty-three of them, where the preceding year there had been only six. Among the group were the representatives from the Freight Handlers and Helpers, Memphis; the Shipbuilders' Helpers, Tampa; the Janitors, Charleston; the Stationary Firemen and Oilers, Denver. Men came from the Texas oil fields, from the railroads of Mississippi, and from the shipyards of Norfolk.

John A. Lacey, Secretary of the Labor Council of Norfolk, declared that a serious condition existed in many cities where the labor organizations refused to take Negro laborers—that the Negro in the United States had received dirty treatment. "We don't ask any favors," he said, "we ask for a chance to live like men, with equal rights and democratic rule. The Negro can read now, and the man who can read can think."

Complaints came from the Negro Freight Handlers and the International Longshoremen of discrimination on the part of the Brotherhood of Railway Clerks throughout the South. The Chief Executive of the Brotherhood, aroused by this, admitted that his organization did not give full rights to the Negroes, but hoped that at their next executive board meeting full rights would be allowed them.

The Committee on Resolutions then introduced a resolution that 'the Executive Council give particular attention to the organization of colored workers everywhere and assign colored organizers wherever possible; and that in cases where International Unions affiliated with the A. F. of L. refuse admittance to colored workers, the A. F. of L., organize the workers under charters from the Federation."

This resolution was followed by a demonstration such as made the onlooker believe that the Negro had at length come into his own in a labor world. Forty heads of International Unions arose and welcomed black men into their ranks.

Mollie Freedman, of the International Ladies' Garment Workers, was the first to speak, declaring that her union had six thousand colored girls in its membership and was proud of them; Seymour Hastings, of the Motion Picture Players' Union of Los Angeles, declared, "We draw no distinction as to race or color"; and the Meat Cutters and Butchers Workmen's Union announced large membership of Negroes employed in the packing plants and five Negro organizers on the road. Among others who arose to testify their hearty welcome to the Negro were the Carpenters, Plasterers, Bricklayers, Brick and Clay Workers; Hod-Carriers, Steel and Iron Workers of the Building Trades; the United Mine Workers; Mill, Mine and Smelter Workers; Textile Workers; Laundry Workers; Upholsterers, Leather Workers; Boot and Shoe Workers; Fur Workers; Tailors, Garment Workers; Brewery Workers and Cigar-makers; Teamsters; Firemen and Pilers, Street Railway Employees, Seaman and Maintenance-of-Way Men; Federal Employees, Postal Employees, Letter Carriers; Stage Employees; Motion Picture Operators; Car Builders; Molders, Quarry Workers; Printers, Stereotypers, Barbers; and the Professions of Music and Civil Engineering.

This was the demonstration. And since the American Federation of Labor always desires more power, more money and more men, it is likely to use pressure when necessary upon its local units to bring in the thousands of colored workers, whose dues will help swell its treasury and theirs. It knows, too, that the colored men have learned to organize and constitute a danger outside the Federation. It is not difficult to forget racial prejudice when a high wage is at stake.

What has the N.A.A.C.P. done on this matter?

In January, 1918, at the call of the Urban League, representatives from that body, the N.A.A.C.P., the Slater Fund, the Jeanes Fund, and Tuskegee presented the following memorandum to the A. F. of L.:

• We wish especially to address ourselves to the American Federation of Labor which at its recent convention in Buffalo, N.Y., voiced sound democratic principles in its attitude toward Negro labor.

• We would ask the American Federation of Labor, in organizing Negroes in the various trades, to include: (1) skilled as well as unskilled workmen; (2) northern as well as southern workmen; (3) government as well as civilian employees; (4) women as well as men workers.

• We would have Negro labor handled by the American Federation of Labor in the same manner as white labor: (1) when workmen are returning to work after a successful strike; (2) when shops are declared "open" or "closed"; (3) when Union workers apply for jobs.

• We would have these assurances pledged not with words only, but by deeds pledged by an increasing number of examples of groups of Negro workmen given a "square deal."

• With these things accomplished, we pledge ourselves to urge Negro workingmen to seek the advantages of sympathetic cooperation and understanding between men who work.

This has been the stand of the N.A.A.C.P. for a year and a half. Mr. Shillady has appeared in committee before Mr. Gompers and his executives and now at last, through pressure from without and within, the A. F. of L., has made a good beginning at the "square deal."

From the correspondence with our branches we realize that the choice between organization and non-organization is not always so simple as it seems. At Birmingham we learn that the employers treat their colored workmen fairly, but through agents urge them not to join the union. The President of the Branch adds: "Thus far the Negroes have found it profitable to stay out of the unions, for they have given him a cold deal." A letter from Austin, Tex., says, "There seems to be general unrest between the races and it is thought that labor agitation, the admission of Negroes into the American Federation of Labor, is the cause."

Especially interesting has been a long correspondence with a member at Balboa in the Canal Zone who is strongly in favor of union organization, but who has been telling us of the efforts of white union men in the Zone to prevent the organization of colored men. The A. F. of L. sent two men to Panama especially to organize colored labor. These men, shortly after their arrival, were informed that the white workers were against them, that they did not wish Negro laborers to have the permanent status organization would give them, and white union officials even went so far later as to ask the Governor to have the organizers deported. This was not done, and next an unsuccessful attempt was made to have them recalled from United States Headquarters. The organization of black men continued, however, and will continue, though at Atlantic City a white representative sent up from the Zone offered a resolution against the unionizing of Negro labor at Panama. The resolution was received and referred to the Executive

Committee for investigation, where, it is believed, it will remain indefinitely. The A. F. of L., seems earnest in its desire to bring to American colored labor in the tropics a decent wage.

A press report from Chicago says that a committee of prominent Negroes, speaking on the riots, urged the colored men whenever possible to join the labor unions. We believe this is wise advice. When colored labor enters into competition with white labor, as it is doing increasingly today, it must demand the hours and wages of the white worker, or be counted a scab. To underbid for any length of time is to pull down the standard of living of the working class. The opposition of the white worker on racial lines becomes insignificant when the real issue, the issue "to live like men," as John A. Lacey put it, is before him. For his selfish purposes he must admit America's hundreds of thousands of black workers into his International brotherhood.

The Labor Union is no panacea, but it has proved and is proving a force that in the end diminishes race prejudice. A democracy prospers when laborers of all races work together. Where a despotism is at its height, as in the old days of southern slavery, cracker and black are kept apart, hating one another, ignorant and ragged workers going about their unskilled, wasteful tasks.

It was an immense advance toward harmony between the races when for a half-hour at Atlantic City the Negro was invited into the full and equal privileges of organized labor. It is now his business to accept this invitation to see that given in the heat of enthusiasm it is not withdrawn, to follow it up and to go hundreds strong to the next meeting of the Federation.

The Crisis, September, 1919; XVIII, 239–41.

70

THE RED YEAR OF 1919

The year 1919 was called "red" by many who lived through it: it was the year of the Palmer Raids against "reds" in which young J. Edgar Hoover commenced his illustrious career; * the year of the witch-hunting Lusk Com-

* After Du Bois' May, 1919, editorial on "Returning Soldiers" appeared—to which attention has been called—the Post Office threatened to bar *The Crisis* from the mails, and F.B.I. agents visited Du Bois' office, asking him "what he was up to." Du Bois replied that he was trying to get the Constitution of the United States enforced; he added to the men from the Justice Department: "What are you up to?" Du Bois was attacked in Congress, especially by James F. Byrnes of South Carolina—later Secretary of State and Justice of the U.S. Supreme Court.

mittee in New York State; the year of the founding of the Communist Party of the United States; and the year when red blood flowed freely in a dozen areas as racist mobs broke loose—and often met the resistance of determined Black men and women. The latter are illustrated in three documents: [a] Walter White's account of the outbreak in Chicago in July; [b] a letter from a southern Black woman; and [c] an account of the effort at sharecropper organization in Arkansas and the terror used to crush it.

[a]

CHICAGO AND ITS EIGHT REASONS
by Walter F. White

Many causes have been assigned for the three days of race rioting, from July 27 to 30 in Chicago, each touching some particular phase of the general condition that led up to the outbreak. Labor union officials attribute it to the action of the packers, while the packers are equally sure that the unions themselves are directly responsible. The city administration feels that the riots were brought on to discredit the Thompson forces, while leaders of the anti-Thompson forces, prominent among them being State's Attorney Maclay Hoyne, are sure that the administration is directly responsible. In this manner charges and counter-charges are made, but, as is usually the case, the Negro is made to bear the brunt of it all—to be "the scapegoat." A background of strained race relations brought to a head more rapidly through political corruption, economic competition and clashes due to the overflow of the greatly increased colored population into sections outside of the so-called "Black Belt," embracing the Second and Third Wards, all of these contributed, aided by magnifying of Negro crime by newspapers, to the formation of a situation where only a spark was needed to ignite the flames of racial antagonism. That spark was contributed by a white youth when he knocked a colored lad off a raft at the 29th Street bathing beach and the colored boy was drowned.

Four weeks spent in studying the situation in Chicago, immediately following the outbreaks, seem to show at least eight general causes for the riots, and the same conditions, to a greater or less degree, can be found in almost every large city with an appreciable Negro population. These causes, taken after a careful study in order of their prominence, are:

1. Race Prejudice.
2. Economic Competition.
3. Political Corruption and Exploitation of Negro Voters.

4. Police Inefficiency.
5. Newspaper Lies about Negro Crime.
6. Unpunished Crimes Against Negroes.
7. Housing.
8. Reaction of Whites and Negroes from War.

Some of these can be grouped under the same headings, but due to the prominence of each they are listed as separate causes.

Prior to 1915, Chicago had been famous for its remarkably fair attitude toward colored citizens. Since that time, when the migratory movement from the South assumed large proportions, the situation has steadily grown more and more tense. This was due in part to the introduction of many Negroes who were unfamiliar with city ways and could not, naturally, adapt themselves immediately to their new environment. Outside of a few sporadic attempts, little was done to teach them the rudimentary principles of sanitation, of conduct or of their new status as citizens under a system different from that in the South. During their period of absorption into the new life, their care-free, at times irresponsible and sometimes even boisterous, conduct caused complications difficult to adjust. But equally important, though seldom considered, is the fact that many Southern whites have also come into the North, many of them to Chicago, drawn by the same economic advantages that attracted the colored workman. The exact figure is unknown, but it is estimated by men who should know that fully 20,000 of them are in Chicago. These have spread the virus of race hatred and evidences of it can be seen in Chicago on every hand. This same cause underlies each of the other seven causes.

With regard to economic competition, the age-long dispute between capital and labor enters. Large numbers of Negroes were brought from the South by the packers and there is little doubt that this was done in part so that the Negro might be used as a club over the heads of the unions. John Fitzpatrick and Ed Nockels, president and secretary, respectively, of the Chicago Federation of Labor, and William Buck, editor of the *New Majority,* a labor organ, openly charge that the packers subsidized colored ministers, politicians and Y.M.C.A. secretaries to prevent the colored workmen at the stockyards from entering the unions. On the other hand, the Negro workman is not at all sure as to the sincerity of the unions themselves. The Negro in Chicago yet remembers the waiters' strike some years ago, when colored union workers walked out at the command of the unions and when the strike was settled, the unions did not insist that Negro waiters be given their jobs back along with whites, and, as a result, colored men have never been able to get back into some of the hotels even to the present day. The Negro is between "the devil and the deep blue sea." He feels that if he goes into the unions, he will lose the friendship of the employers. He knows that if he does not, he is going to be met with the bitter antagonism of the unions. With the exception of statements made by organizers, who cannot be held to accountability because of their minor official connection, no statements have been made by the local union leaders, outside of high sounding, but meaningless, protestations of friendship for the Negro worker. He feels that he has been given promises too long already. In fact, he is "fed up" on them. What he wants are binding statements and guarantees that cannot be broken at will.

With the possible exception of Philadelphia, there is probably no city in America with more of political trickery, chicanery and exploitation than Chicago. Against the united and bitter opposition of every daily newspaper in Chicago, William Hale Thompson was elected again as mayor, due, as was claimed, to the Negro and German vote. While it is not possible to state that the anti-Thompson element deliberately brought on the riots, yet it is safe to say that they were not averse to its coming. The possibility of such a clash was seen many months before it actually occurred, yet no steps were taken to prevent it. The purpose of this was to secure a two-fold result. First, it would alienate the Negro set from Thompson through a belief that was expected to grow among the colored vote when it was seen that the police force under the direction of the mayor was unable or unwilling to protect the colored people from assault by mobs. Secondly, it would discourage the Negroes from registering and voting and thus eliminate the powerful Negro vote in Chicago. Whether or not this results remains to be seen. In talking with a prominent colored citizen of Chicago, asking why the Negroes supported Thompson so unitedly, his very significant reply was:

"The Negro in Chicago, as in every other part of America, is fighting for the fundamental rights of citizenship. If a candidate for office is wrong on every other public question except this, the Negroes are going to vote for that man, for that is their only way of securing the things they want and that are denied them."

The value of the Negro vote to Thompson can be seen in a glance at the recent election figures. His plurality was 28,000 votes. In the second ward it was 14,000 and in the third, 10,000. The second and third wards constitute most of what is known as the "Black Belt."

The fourth contributing cause was the woeful inefficiency and criminal negligence of the police authorities of Chicago, both prior to and during the riots. Prostitution, gambling and the illicit sale of whisky flourish openly and apparently without any fear whatever of police interference. In a most dangerous statement, State's Attorney Maclay Hoyne, on August 25, declared that the riots were due solely to vice in the second ward. He seemed either to forget or to ignore the flagrant disregard of law and order and even of the common principles of decency in city management existing in many other sections of the city.

All of this tended to contribute to open disregard for law and almost contempt for it. Due either to political "pull" or to reciprocal arrangements, many notorious dives run and policemen are afraid to arrest the proprietors.

During the riots the conduct of the police force as a whole was equally open to criticism. State's Attorney Hoyne openly charged the police with arresting colored rioters and with an unwillingness to arrest white rioters. Those who were arrested were at once released. In one case a colored man who was fair enough to appear to be white was arrested for carrying concealed weapons, together with five white men and a number of colored men. All were taken to a police station; the light colored man and the five whites being put into one cell and the other colored men in another. In a few minutes the light colored man and the five whites were released and their ammunition given back to them with the remark, "You'll probably need this before the night is over."

Fifth on the list is the effect of newspaper publicity concerning Negro crime. With the exception of the *Daily News,* all of the papers of Chicago have played up in prominent style with glaring, prejudice-breeding headlines every crime or suspected crime committed by Negroes. Headlines such as NEGRO BRUTALLY MURDERS PROMINENT CITIZEN, NEGRO ROBS HOUSE and the like have appeared with alarming frequency and the news articles beneath such headlines have been of the same sort. During the rioting such headlines as NEGRO BANDITS TERRORIZE TOWN, RIOTERS BURN 100 HOMES—NEGROES SUSPECTED OF HAVING PLOTTED BLAZE appeared. In the latter case a story was told of witnesses seeing Negroes in automobiles applying torches and fleeing. This was the story given to the press by Fire Attorney John R. McCabe after a casual and hasty survey. Later the office of State Fire Marshal Gamber proved conclusively that the fires were *not* caused by Negroes, but by whites. As can easily be seen such newspaper accounts did not tend to lessen the bitterness of feeling between the conflicting groups. Further, many wild and unfounded rumors were published in the press—incendiary and inflammatory to the highest degree, a few of them being given below in order to show their nature. Some are:

Over 1,000 Negroes had been slain and their bodies thrown in "Bubbly Creek" and the Chicago River.
A Negro had been lynched and hanged from a "Loop" building overlooking Madison Street.
A white woman had been attacked and mutilated by a Negro on State Street.
A Negro woman had been slain, her breasts cut off and her infant had been killed by having its brains dashed out against a wall.
A white child had been outraged by a colored man.
A white child had been kidnapped by a band of colored men and its body later found, badly mutilated and dismembered.

Immediately following the riots, a white woman was murdered in Evanston, Ill. Immediately the crime was laid at the door of a colored man with whom the woman had been intimate a number of years. Pitiful stories were told of the woman waiting for hours on street corners for "just one look at her Billiken-like, mulatto lover," played up under headlines such as CONFESSION EXPECTED TODAY FROM NEGRO SUSPECT, NEGRO SUSPECT RAPIDLY WEAKENING and the like which clearly led one to believe that the colored man was guilty. A few days later, in an obscure item on an inside page, a short account was given of the release of the colored suspect "because insufficient evidence to hold him" existed. A long period of such publicity had inflamed the minds of many people against Negroes who otherwise would have been unprejudiced. Much of the blame for the riots can be laid to such sources.

For a long period prior to the riots, organized gangs of white hoodlums had been perpetrating crimes against Negroes for which no arrests had been made. These gangs in many instances masqueraded under the name of "Athletic and Social Clubs" and later direct connection was shown between them and incendiary fires started during the riots. Colored men, women and children had been beaten in the parks, most of them in Jackson and Lincoln Parks. In one case a young colored girl was beaten and thrown into a lagoon. In other cases Negroes were beaten so severely that they had to be taken to hospitals. All of these cases had caused many colored people to wonder if they could expect any protection whatever from the authorities.

Particularly vicious in their attacks was an organization known locally as "Regan's Colts."

Much has been written and said concerning the housing situation in Chicago and its effect on the racial situation. The problem is a simple one. Since 1915 the colored population of Chicago has more than doubled, increasing in four years from a little over 50,000 to what is now estimated to be between 125,000 and 150,000. Most of them lived in the area bounded by the railroad on the west, 30th Street on the north, 40th Street on the south and Ellis Avenue on east. Already overcrowded this so called "Black Belt" could not possibly hold the doubled colored population. One cannot put ten gallons of water in a five-gallon pail. Although many Negroes had been living in "white" neighborhoods, the increased exodus from the old areas created an hysterical group of persons who formed "Property Owners' Associations" for the purpose of keeping intact white neighborhoods. Prominent among these was the Kenwood-Hyde Park Property Owners' Improvement Association. Early in June the writer, while in Chicago, attended a private meeting of the first named at the Kenwood Club House, at Lake Park Avenue and 47th Street. Various plans were discussed for keeping the Negroes in "their part of the town" such as securing the discharge of colored persons from positions they held when they attempted to move into "white" neighborhoods, purchasing mortgages of Negroes buying homes and ejecting them when mortgage notes fell due and were unpaid, and many more of the same calibre. The language of many speakers was vicious and strongly prejudicial and had the distinct effect of creating race bitterness.

In a number of cases during the period from January, 1918, to August, 1919, there were bombings of colored homes and houses occupied by Negroes outside of the "Black Belt." During this period no less than twenty bombings took place, yet only two persons have been arrested and neither of the two has been convicted, both cases being continued.

Finally, the new spirit aroused in Negroes by their war experiences enters into the problem. From Local Board No. 4, embracing the neighborhood in the vicinity of State and 35th Streets, containing over 30,000 inhabitants of which fully ninety per cent are colored, over 9,000 men registered and 1,850 went to camp. These men, with their new outlook on life, injected the same spirit of independence into their companions, a thing that is true of many other sections of America. One of the greatest surprises to many of those who came down to "clean out the niggers" is that the same "niggers" fought back. Colored men saw their own kind being killed, heard of many more and believed that their lives and liberty were at stake. In such a spirit most of the fighting was done.

The Crisis, October, 1919; XVIII, 293–97. For a recent full-length treatment of this event, see W. M. Tuttle, Jr., *Race Riot: Chicago in the Red Summer of 1919* (N.Y., 1970).

[b]

A LETTER

A week ago an old friend of mine whom I had not seen for twenty years came to see me.

After talking of old school days and friends, both of us asking and answering many questions, my friend asked, "And what did you think of the Washington and Chicago riots?"

When I answered that question she said, "I wish you would send that answer to *The Crisis,* just as you have told it to me, so that our men can know how we women have felt and how we feel now."

And so I am sending this, regardless of the fact that I am unused to writing for publication.

I said this:

The Washington riot gave me the thrill that comes once in a life time. I was alone when I read between the lines of the morning paper that at last our men had stood like men, struck back, were no longer dumb, driven cattle. When I could no longer read for my streaming tears, I stood up, alone in my room, held both hands high over my head and exclaimed aloud: "Oh, I thank God, thank God!" When I remember anything after this, I was prone on my bed, beating the pillow with both fists, laughing and crying, whimpering like a whipped child, for sheer gladness and madness. The pent-up humiliation, grief and horror of a life time—half a century—was being stripped from me. Only colored women of the south know the extreme in suffering and humiliation.

We know how many insults we have borne silently, for we have hidden many of them from our men because we did not want them to die needlessly in our defense; we know the sorrow of seeing our boys and girls grow up, the swift stab of the heart at night to the sound of a strange footstep, the feel of a tigress to spring and claw the white man with his lustful look at our comely daughters, the deep humiliation of sitting in the Jim Crow part of a street car and hear the white men laugh and discuss us, point out the good and bad points of our bodies. God alone knows the many things colored women have borne here in the South in silence.

And, too, a woman loves a strong man, she delights to feel that her man can protect her, fight for her, if necessary, save her.

No woman loves a weakling, a coward, be she white or black, and some of us have been near to thinking our men cowards, but thank God for Washington colored men! All honor to them, for they first blazed the way and right swiftly did Chicago men follow. They put new hope, a new vision in their almost despairing women.

God grant that our men everywhere refrain from strife, provoke no quarrel, but that they protect their women and homes at any cost.

A Southern Colored Woman

I'm sure the editor will understand why I cannot sign my name.

The Crisis, November, 1919; XIX, 339.

[c]

THE RACE CONFLICT IN ARKANSAS
by *Walter F. White*

Associated Press dispatches of early October informed the country in detail of a plot, by a fortuitous circumstance checked, of Negro assassins conspiring to stage a massacre and to murder, without reason or warrant, twenty-one white citizens of Phillips county, Arkansas. Following closely upon the widespread publicity given this account, an investigation was made by the National Association for the Advancement of Colored People who sent me as their representative into the county. The facts thus secured are totally at variance with the published accounts sent out from the community.

The trouble began on October 1, when W. D. Adkins, special agent for the Missouri Pacific Railway, Charles Pratt, deputy sheriff, and a Negro trusty were driving past a Negro church at Hoopspur in Phillips county, Arkansas, where a meeting of a branch of the Progressive Farmers and Household Union of America was being held. According to Pratt's story, Negroes without cause fired at the party from the church, killing Adkins and wounding Pratt. Negroes in the church at the time, however, declare that Pratt and Adkins fired into the church apparently to frighten the Negroes gathered there, and that the Negroes returned the fire. This started the conflict which spread to all parts of Phillips county.

About the same time that the meeting was being held at Hoopspur, sixty-eight Negro farmers at Ratio, another small town in the county, had met for conference with the son of a white lawyer of Little Rock, to pay retainers' fees for the prosecution, in court, of their landlord who they alleged had seized their cotton and was about to ship it away. During 1918 these same share-croppers charged that their cotton had been taken from them and a settlement had not been made until July, 1919. Fearing that this action would be repeated with this year's crop, the Negroes were taking legal means to prevent it. The lawyer's son and all of the Negroes in the conference were arrested. The white man was kept in jail thirty-one days without a hearing, charged with "barratry"—fomenting legal action. He was finally released on his own recognizance.

When the news of the killing of Adkins spread—vague rumors of the farmers' organization having meanwhile come to the ears of the whites—the entire community was at once thrown into a state of antagonism. White men poured into Helena, the county seat of Phillips county, from all parts of Arkansas, Mississippi, and Tennessee; Negroes were disarmed and arrested; their arms were given to the whites who rapidly thronged the little town of Helena. Those Negroes who escaped arrest took refuge in the canebrakes near the town where they were hunted down like animals. According to the final death list, five whites and twenty-five Negroes were killed. Several white men in Helena told me that more than one hundred Negroes were killed, and that in their opinion the total death list would never be known. The Negroes arrested were herded together in a stockade and were refused communication with relatives, friends, or attorneys. Though a Negro might have been able to prove his innocence, he was released only when a white man vouched for him; a thing which was not done until the Negro agreed to work for the white man for a period of time and for wages determined upon by the employer.

Five times as many Negroes as white persons were killed, according to statements given out in the community, and many more times as many according to unofficial statements. According to the census of 1910, there were 7,176 white people and 26,354 Negroes in the county.

When the alleged conspirators were brought up for trial they were assigned counsel by the court; witnesses for the defense were not allowed to testify; no change of venue was asked, although the trials were held in Phillips county one month after the alleged massacre took place while the feeling was still intense. The first six defendants were jointly indicted, tried and found guilty in exactly seven minutes by a jury from which Negroes were excluded. The six were sentenced to electrocution on December 27, for murder in the first degree. In all, twelve Negroes have been sentenced to death and eighty have been sentenced to terms ranging from one to twenty years—all of these convictions taking place within five days.

These Arkansas Negroes like others in certain parts of the South, have been living under a state of subjection for more than fifty years. The system, known as "share-cropping" or "tenant farming," had become so abusive that these farmers felt its continuance meant nothing except peonage.

The basis of the system in theory is this: Land together with implements, seed, and supplies, is furnished by a landlord; labor is furnished by the share-croppers; and at the end of the year the crop is divided share and share alike. The system, however, rarely works out in actual practice according to this theory. When the season is ended the cotton is taken by the owners, ginned at the plantation gin, and sold. The Negro share-cropper is not allowed to know the weight of the cotton which he raised nor the price at which it is sold. Instead of an itemized statement of the goods received during the year from the plantation commissary (where in most cases he is compelled to purchase his supplies), the Negro is given a lump statement generally marked "to balance due." By always having the charge for goods received larger than the value of the Negro's share of the crop the owner can keep him perpetually in debt. There is an unwritten law which is rigidly observed in this Arkansas district that no Negro can leave a plantation while he is in debt. Thus the owner not only takes the Negro's crop out but is assured of his workers for the following year.

Attempts had been made by individuals to protest against their failure to secure from landlords itemized statements of their accounts and equitable settlements; these resulted not only in failure but in many cases in further persecution of the worker. The organization of the Progressive Farmers and Household Union of America was the Negro's answer—a legitimate alliance of colored farmers in Phillips county to end a vicious system of economic exploitation.

A few of the actual cases taken from court records and from personal interviews with share-croppers, owners, and their agents, will show how the system has worked there and the condition which the farmers' union attempted to remedy.

A Negro raised during the season of 1918, 40 bales of cotton. An average bale of cotton weighs 500 pounds, and at the time that this crop was sold cotton was selling at $.28 a pound. To every bale of cotton there is approximately one-half ton of seed which sells at $70 a ton. The total value of the Negro's crop was, therefore, $7,000, and when this Negro asked for a settlement he was told that he had not only "taken up" goods worth over $7,000 but that his "balance due" amounted to over $1,000.

During the same year in Keo, Lonoke county, Arkansas, a Negro by the name of George Conway, raised 20 bales of cotton, the value of which was $3,500. His landlord refused to furnish him shoes or clothing, so that he was forced to work his crop bare-footed and often hungry. The worker's family consisted of himself, a wife, and two children. Although the value of goods he "took up" did not amount to more than $300, when he asked for an itemized statement at the end of the year he was told that his purchases amounted to $40 more than the value of his crop. When he demanded a settlement and an itemized statement his landlord beat him severely and threatened to kill him if he persisted in his demand. For the $40, balance due, the landlord seized the Negro's household goods and drove him off the plantation, penniless.

A Negro who lived at Watson, Arkansas, produced, during the year 1919, a crop of which his share was 14 bales. The price of cotton when his crop was sold was $.43 a pound, so that the value of the 14 bales with the seed was $3,500. The man "took up" during the year goods valued at $23.50, yet in the statement he received the value of the goods received exactly equaled the value of his crop. This man, though paralyzed in his right leg, walked 122 miles to Little Rock, hoping to secure a lawyer to bring suit against the landlord. But being without funds he was unable to secure one.

Phillips county, in October, is relatively unimportant as an isolated case. As an example of the underlying corruption and injustice that will lead to further and more disastrous conflicts, it is of grave import. Unless there is immediate interference on the part of federal or state officials—and there is little hope of the latter—twelve Negroes will be legally lynched and eighty will continue to serve prison sentences in Arkansas, victims of America's negligence and denial of common justice to men.

The Survey, December 13, 1919; LXIII, 233–34; a somewhat similar account by White appears in *The Nation,* December 6, 1919.

71

BOGALUSA, LOUISIANA, 1919

An event quite different from Chicago or Washington or Elaine, Arkansas, occurred in November, 1919, in Bogalusa, Louisiana. There Black and white workers in lumber, under I.W.W. leadership, organized and struck against conditions of industrial feudalism—complete with company stores and payment of wages in company scrip. Bosses made some concessions, but the strike movement was broken by sheer murder. The headlines in *The New York Times* told the essence of the story: LOYALTY LEAGUERS KILL 3 UNION MEN. BOGALUSA, LA. IS SCENE OF PITCHED BATTLE OVER A NEGRO AGITATOR. UNIONISTS SHIELDED NEGRO, ARE BESIEGED AND SHOT DOWN BY A CROWD REPRESENTING LOCAL BUSINESS INTERESTS (November 23, 1919, p. 1). The "Negro agitator" was a worker and I.W.W. organizer named Sol Dakus; four (not three) white comrades were murdered because they insisted on defending him from a mob. In December thirteen police were actually arrested for these murders, but they were released on bail and a Grand Jury refused to return indictments. It is these events which form the background for the editorial in a Black newspaper that follows.

TWO ADVERTISEMENTS—TWO VIEWS—WHICH WILL WIN?

We have received in the past week two full page advertisements printed in two Southern newspapers. One of these advertisements appears in the Bogalusa *Enterprise,* and was inserted by The Self Preservation and Loyalty League of Bogalusa. The other advertisement appears in the Memphis *Commercial-Appeal,* and was inserted by the Chamber of Commerce of Greenville, Mississippi.

These two advertisements represent the two views of Southern whites on the race question, the two views which are now struggling for ascendancy. One of these views regards the Negro as without any rights that the white man is bound to respect. The other view is the view of that minority in the South which, relatively, may be called liberal. Its main purpose is the establishment of "better relations between the two races."

As an indication of the sentiments expressed in the Bogalusa Loyalty League advertisement, we quote:

Our constitution clearly sets forth the following:
WHITE SUPREMACY
We do not intend to sit supinely by and allow any encroachment on the heritage left us by our fathers, who made the tremendous sacrifices in Reconstruction Days. The Negro in this section will fare well if agitators will allow him to live in peace and contentment, and such publications as *The Crisis, Menace, Crusader, Wichita Herald* and other notorious social equality Negro papers are barred from mails in the Southland.

In another paragraph the Bogalusa advertisement sets forth as one of the causes that led to the organization of the Loyalty League the following:

"The meeting of whites and Blacks together in halls and in private homes on absolute equality."

We turn now to the Greenville [Miss.] Chamber of Commerce advertisement. The difference between the two advertisements which at once strikes the eye is that the Bogalusa statement is not vouched for by any individuals, while the Greenville statement is signed by ninety-one business and professional men and office holders. We quote from the Greenville statement as follows:

[There follows a lengthy quotation which denounces the I.W.W. and affirms that the "Industrial Welfare Committee of the Greenville Chamber of Commerce" will offer "patient and considerate" concern toward reasonable demands. It ends with this paragraph.]

"With confidence between the races there will be mutual benefit which suspicion and distrust or dislike would destroy. We wish to preserve the race relations among the present and coming generations which we see exemplified in the older citizens of the South."

The Greenville statement, despite its reservations, is a step far in advance of the statement coming out of Bogalusa. . . .

Yet, both of these statements are based upon one common error. It is the desire and plan in both of these statements to fix a place for the Negro, to perpetuate a status for him. . . .

In the conquest [misprint for "contest"] for ascendancy between the Southern sentiments expressed by Bogalusa and those expressed by Greenville, we want to see Greenville win. At present, Bogalusa is a long way in the lead. It sometimes seems a hopeless task to get even the sentiment of Greenville accepted as the majority sentiment of the South. And after that is done there is still a long, long way to go.

Both Greenville and Bogalusa have yet to learn that no adjustment of the race situation can be successful or permanent which attempts to place limitations on how far and how high the Negro progresses. The only adjustment that can stand will be one based on the right of every individual to go as far and as high as his powers and ability enable him to go. . . .

We may all of us show due appreciation for what the Greenvilles say and do, but we must not forget that it is our business just now to have the police on the Bogalusas.

Editorial, *New York Age,* January 10, 1920, p. 4.

72

WHAT DOES THE NEGRO WANT
IN OUR DEMOCRACY?
by Richard R. Wright, Jr.

A significant figure in Afro-American life for many years was Richard R. Wright, Jr. (1878–1967). He was born in Cuthbert, Georgia, worked as a farmhand, janitor, and dishwasher, managed a very full education (as his own remarks in the ensuing document show), became senior bishop in the A.M.E. Church and for twenty-five years (1909–1934) edited its organ *The Christian Recorder;* he was president of Wilberforce University in Ohio from 1932 to 1936.

The address that follows was delivered at the 46th Annual Session of the National Conference of Social Work, held in Atlantic City, N.J., in June, 1919.

The invitation to speak at the National Conference of Social Work on this subject, came to me as a great surprise. The subject is not of my choosing. As it came with the ear marks of sincerity, I shall answer as frankly and as clearly as possible.

THE QUESTION

I take it that "Our Democracy" refers to our country, as it is now an ideal, and as it is hoped it will be as a result of the labors of such good people as make up this conference. As we all strive for that ideal, we should all know what each expects to realize. As the Negro has helped in war and peace, in slavery and freedom with labor and life, to make our country what it now is, and what it shall be, a very proper question to ask is "What Does the Negro Want in Our Democracy?" The answer to the question is as applicable to the local as well as to the national community.

It is not at all improper that I should answer this question on behalf of my people, for I have been elected by the secret ballot of 600 representatives who were themselves elected to represent more than a million Negroes in every state in the Union and in Africa, South America and the West Indies, as a spokesman of the Negroes. I am editor of the *Christian Recorder,* the official organ of the African Methodist Episcopal church, the oldest and largest organization of Negroes in America. I keep in weekly touch with its leaders all over the world, I travel constantly throughout the country and make it my business to know Negro thoughts. I am president of the largest local civic organization among Negroes in America—The Colored Protective Association of Philadelphia, and I entered social work among Negroes only after a thorough course in History, Economics and Sociology, taking A.B. degree in a southern Negro college (Georgia State), the A.M. degree in a western university (The University of Chicago), and the Ph.D. degree in an eastern university (The University of Pennsylvania).

As research fellow in Sociology in the University of Pennsylvania, and under a grant from the Carnegie Institution, and as an investigator for the United States government, I traveled during my student days in various parts of the North and South, and upon my responsibility I compared results by study and observations for more than a year in Europe. Since my student days I have had my heart close to the Negro, for upon them and them alone I depend for my livelihood. I was born in Georgia, and have spent over half my life in the South, and I have been in every state in the South from three times to a dozen times within the past ten years. I make these personal statements that you may see that I have some reason for answering this question on behalf of my people "What Does the Negro Want in Our Democracy?" I shall answer the question in a few paragraphs as succinctly as possible.

The Negroes' wants in our democracy are simple and fundamental.

The Negro wants a *democracy* not a "whiteocracy." At present the United States of America is more a "whiteocracy" than a democracy. The Negro wants the sign FOR WHITES ONLY erased from the banner and spirit of "Our Democracy." In other words all the Negro wants is *democracy* in the fundamental sense of the term as explained by the immortal Lincoln in *"A government of the people for the people and by the people"* (not white people only). All the Negro wants in our democracy, is for the spirit of the Declaration of Independence and of the Constitution of the United States to be applied to all citizens without fear or favor. That is not done in the United States today and in so far as it is not, we fall short of anything like a democracy in America. Some of the fundamental things which "Our Democracy" should hold out to all able-bodied, sound-minded men (and women also) should be the right to help make, interpret and execute the laws of democracy, directly or through the representatives they elect; that is, there should be political equality. There should be the equal opportunity of all children to become educated so as to preserve the democracy; there should be equitable conditions of living, including a just division of the products of capital and labor so that there may be progress in democracy. But these things are so fundamental and elemental that the whole nation accepts them in theory at least—but for whites only.

Let me be more specific. What does the Negro want in "Our Democracy"? I answer specifically as follows:

1. *A chance to vote.* The right to express opinion as to what laws shall govern the democracy and who shall execute them is fundamental. It is notorious that where nine-tenths of the Negroes live they are denied the right to vote, and in defiance of the spirit of our democracy. When the draft law was applied in the South, there was no distinction on account of color (except in the cases where Negroes were sent to fill the quotas for which whites should have been sent). Why should there be distinction when it comes to applying the election law? The Negro who enrolled over one million strong and went to France over two hundred and fifty thousand strong—the Negro who presented himself in the defense of his country *in larger proportion than the white man of the South—wants to know why he should work and fight for democracy and cannot vote for it?*

And this Negro will not be satisfied until he gets a fair chance to vote. And until that chance is given, "Our Democracy" is merely a sham and a farce. For the Negro is the acid test of our democracy.

2. *Justice in the courts.* Next to the right to vote, "Our Democracy" should give to all equal justice before the courts. But justice in a large part of America is labeled "for whites only." In cases of Negroes versus Negroes, there is fair enough justice; when a Negro is on one side and a white man is on the other, it is rare, except in trivial cases, for the Negro to get justice. Justice is usually on the side of the voters—in "Our Democracy." Practically every intelligent Negro knows (whether he thinks it politic to state it publicly or not is another matter) that the courts of the South make mockery of justice, so far as the protection of the rights of Negroes against the aggression of lawless whites is concerned. And they forfeit millions of dollars every year because they know the courts are against them. ("What's the use?" is the question of despair so often heard when a Negro knows he is right, but also knows the courts are against him.) So the Negro wants justice in the courts.

3. *Representation on jury.* The right of trial by one's peers is a cornerstone in "Our Democracy," but the Negro does not have it. Every year in "Our Democracy" hundreds of thousands of Negroes are tried, but no Negro who knows Negro life, social conditions, Negro psychology, etc., is ever called to sit on their cases; but men who never enter a Negro home, who never sit in a Negro church, who have nothing but contempt for Negroes and at the very best are ignorant of Negro soul-life, are their jurors. Do you wonder that so many are condemned? Do you wonder that justice is so often miscarried? Do you wonder that there is growing mistrust of the courts? Do you wonder that a leading and powerful Negro paper refers often to the "Department of Justice" as the "Department of *Injustice*"?

So the Negro wants to be and ought to be on the juries of "Our Democracy" to preserve justice.

4. *Representation in the government.* There are twelve million Negroes in this country. They are about 10.5 per cent of the nation's population. In the states south of the Ohio river there are nearly 10,000,000 who are about thirty per cent of the population. Yet, there is not a single Negro in Congress, there is no representation in any Southern state legislature or city council. In sections where a large majority of the vote is Negro, there is no representation. This not only hurts the Negro, but it hurts "Our Democracy." No government, however powerful it may be, can endure upon a basis of insincerity, subterfuge and fraud. And only upon this basis is the Negro kept out of the law-making bodies of the South. Understand, the Negro does not want to "dominate," he only wants to be heard. If he is to obey the law, he wants the right to express himself about it. And not only in the making of law, but in the administering of law, the Negro wants a share. A great deal of friction of race in the local community is due to the fact that the Negro has no chance to help administer the law—not even to do police duty in Negro neighborhoods. More than one race riot would have been averted if the community had been democratic enough to give the Negro a part in administering the law instead of having people do that duty who feel they should cower the Negro. So I repeat, the Negro wants representation in the legislative and executive branches of our local, state and national governments, which their labor and their valor have helped to create. They want it for themselves; they want it that our democracy, as a democracy, shall not perish from the earth.

5. *Better living conditions.* In every community in the South, notwithstanding Negroes pay comparatively higher rents than whites, and

notwithstanding their property is often assessed higher in proportion than the whites, they are shamefully discriminated against in the sharing of public utilities. They are forced to live upon the undrained and unpaved and unlighted streets. They rarely have garbage collection. It is impossible to put sanitary toilets, bath tubs and other improvements their taxes pay for in their homes. They pay higher insurance because the city will not give them water and fire protection. I know the terrible strain many Southern communities are under, but that strain is no excuse for such unfairness which amounts to even robbery in "Our Democracy." Of course, if the Negro had a ballot, he could not be robbed of his proportion of city improvements as he now is. But when the fundamental right to vote is denied in "Our Democracy" you may expect any other injustice.

6. *Fairer wages.* In a democracy there should be an equitable distribution of the combined products of labor and capital. To the laborer this is usually wages. The Negro does not get fair wages. He pays more for rent, more for food, and more for clothes, comparatively, than the white man, but as in the case of the white woman, as compared with the white man, the Negro does not get for the same work the same wages that the whites get.

7. *Better educational advantages.* Wherever separate schools exist, they exist to the detriment of the Negroes—in the length of term, equipment, preparation and pay of teachers. Notwithstanding the Negroes are largely engaged in agriculture, and agriculture is one of the chief supports, states like Mississippi, Georgia, South Carolina, Alabama, Arkansas and others of the South make almost no provision for the training of Negroes as compared with whites. Not only do they neglect to do their duty from the funds of their own treasury, some of them actually steal from the Negro the share which the government appropriates for education.

In "Our Democracy" there is not a single state which has a separate system of schools which does anything like half-way justice (not ideal justice, but in comparison with what is done for other children) to Negro education. The foreigner who has never done a thing for the country gets for his children opportunities for education which the Negro whose ancestors have given ten generations to help the country is denied. Think of it! For ten millions of Negroes there is not a single full-fledged college or technical school of a higher order, supported by public funds, in the whole Southland, and in all of these states Negroes are denied entrance into those technical schools which the states support. Think of it; there are not ten high schools of equal grade with the whites of the Southern states, and one million five hundred thousand Negro children are out of school today in "Our Democracy." The Negro wants a chance to educate his children.

8. *Protection of colored women.* The Negro wants his women protected. If a Negro commits rape upon a white woman, he is lynched, if a mob can get him. "Our Democracy" has a just horror of the rape of white women, and some have gone so far as to justify lynching for that cause. But the most prevalent form of rape in this country is the rape of Negro women by white men—but as yet the conscience of "Our Democracy" is asleep to the rape of Negro women; one rarely hears of a white man being brought to trial for that crime.

The Negro wants fornication and bastardy laws which will make white men support their bastard children and will give a colored woman who is betrayed by a white man some standing in court. Negroes object to anti-intermarriage laws, not because they want to marry white women, but because they know such laws are made purely for the degradation of Negro women and protect white men in their attacks upon our womanhood. I believe every Negro of intelligence would welcome an anti-miscegenation law, which would keep down inter-breeding. Because Negroes have no vote, the white voters permit whorehouses and low dives to thrive in Negro neighborhoods. Indeed, the city council has designated such a district where a Negro school was. In many cities the brothels for white men are in Negro neighborhoods—not by invitation, however, but because a voteless people cannot protect themselves and a democracy which disfranchises any part of its citizens makes them the logical prey of the vicious ones of the enfranchised group.

9. *Abolition of lynching.* There have been over 3,500 in our country; many of them have been for causes more or less trivial; such as "talking back to a white person," disputing about money, theft, resisting arrest, etc., for which the offender would have received a light sentence if convicted in a court by trial. But a democracy which disfranchises a part of its citizens may expect lynching. Sheriffs are slow to protect those who do not vote for them.

10. *Abolition of special laws.* Practically all of the older states, at one time, saw fit to have special laws for the control of Negroes. These laws existed in Ohio, New York and Pennsylvania, as well as Georgia, South Carolina and Virginia. But fortunately, most of them have been abolished. The Negro wants them all abolished, for they do not help the Negro and only harm and degrade the white man. They are instruments to legalize community robbery and oppression. At present

the separate car law is not an instrument of justice, but a mere subterfuge to tax Negroes for comforts for whites. Negroes pay the same as whites for their tickets, but do not get the same accommodation as whites, which is mere robbery. This injustice the Negro wants abolished.

11. *The use of public privileges for which they pay.* Negroes pay taxes, often special assessments for public parks, public libraries, public schools and other public conveniences, even public toilets, from which they are excluded and no provision is made for them. This is not the ideal of democracy and yet there are millions of people today who not only contend against it but think it right.

12. *Negroes want the fruits of victory as well as the burdens of war.* On every hand we have heard the Negro applauded for his loyalty in the war. Only a few days ago a governor of a great Southern state complimented a Negro audience on its loyalty. Said he: "You did everything we asked; you were every bit as loyal as the white people. You showed you are American to the core. When we called for the boys to go to the war, you answered with 26,000; when we called for the Liberty Loan, you gave your hundreds of thousands. You gave to the Red Cross, for the Y.M.C.A., for the Armenian and Syrian Christians. You bought thrift stamps and war savings certificates; your women organized; your churches rallied, and at home you held your own as workers in the home trenches. I say we are proud of your patriotism. And of the 250 boys of this state who gave their lives for our nation, in camp or hospital or transport or in trenches, of those 250 brave boys whom this state and nation must forever honor, you, my splendid colored friends, gave more than one hundred of your boys, your sons, your fathers and brothers to pay the last and greatest price of liberty."

I asked myself as I heard this eloquent governor: "Is this sacrifice not worth the ballot and the privilege of a citizen?" Now that the Negro has helped win the war he wants some of its fruits.

13. *Negroes want the church to be democratic; particularly do they want the Christianity of Jesus as applied to social questions.* Even though the mass of Negroes are untrained in social science or theology, next to the denial of the right to vote, the greatest resentment is felt toward the organized church, which is regarded as either weak or hypocritical in its attitude towards the social welfare of the Negroes. Somehow, the Negro feels that the church ought to be concerned with the things of earth such as legal justice, protection of womanhood, education and conservation of child life, prevention of crime and disease, training and adequate returns for labor, and equal ballot,

fair administration of the law as applied to the Negro. But the church seems to have assumed the position of the priest and the Levite in its relation to the Negro who has fallen among political and economic thieves in "Our Democracy."

14. *The Negro wants recognition of real Negro leadership.* In our democracy we shall not be safe if employers or those whom employers pay are the only spokesmen for labor; or if men or those whom men pay represent women; if English or those dependent upon the philanthropy or the politics of the English, represent the Irish. So if white men or those dependent upon the philanthropy of white men are to be the sole spokesmen to the white world for the Negro race, the Negro will not be fairly represented and will distrust our democracy. The democracy needs the Negro as represented by the Negro Leadership. The Negro churches, newspapers, business and fraternal organizations are developing Negro leaders. The day of the handpicked leaders is over. The men and women who sit at the council table for the Negro, who are to represent the Negro point of view, must be a genuine Negro leader, who is put up by Negroes, supported by Negroes and may be taken down by Negroes when he fails to represent them. Our real leaders are not those gentlemen whose hands are held out for the alms of white people and who live on their "philanthropy."

15. *Negroes want democracy and mutual self-respect among the races which make up our great country.* Negroes do not want to dominate anybody; they merely want representation; they do not want to hate white people. They do not want bolshevism. They do not want anarchy. They want to be American citizens in the greatest democracy of the world. They are not aliens—they were born here. Do you think the Negro wants too much?

In 1619, three hundred years ago this year, twenty Negroes were brought to Virginia, and from that day to this the Negro has done his part to develop the country. And it does seem strange that where the Negro has worked most, he gets less. For two hundred and fifty years he was the unpaid labor of the South. At the bottom of the aristocracy of the South was Negro labor. Negro labor cleared the forest, built the roads, made the cotton, laid the railroad tracks, built the houses, cooked the meals, washed the clothes and nursed the children. It was at the bottom of the grace of dignity of the South (be it remembered that the Southerner who did not rest his welfare on the shoulders of Negroes, i.e., who had no slaves, did not have wealth or culture or power); and what did the Negro get out of these 250 years of unrequited toil—building the great Southland? He got 100 percent illiteracy, 100 per cent poverty, a system of law and government in which he was 100 per cent chattel and no per cent citizen when it came to the act of governing.

Now, for fifty years the Negro has aided in improving the South he helped to build. There is no social student who will say he has not put into it more than he has gotten out of it. Still, notwithstanding what the Negro has put into the building of the South, he must come to the North if he wants to vote or to get reasonably fair trial or to get first-class education or to live on paved streets with electric lights and police protection and civic treatment every citizen of a democracy ought to have.

The Negro wants a fair application of the suffrage laws, the school appropriation, etc., because he got a pretty fair application of the draft law; he sent his boys to the camp to more than 100 per cent of its quota. He got a fair application when it came to sending men to France to help win the war. And as in the last, so has it been in every war since the Negro Crispus Attucks shed his first blood of the Revolutionary War, on Boston Common, 150 years ago, to help free this country from the tyranny of England. And when it comes to having their property assessed and to be taxed, the Negro is 100 per cent of the demand of our country for service. The Negroes are not discriminated against. Then should they be discriminated against when it comes to the privilege of the government? What we want is not only responsibilities, but privileges.

Again I repeat, what the Negro wants in "Our Democracy" is to simply be an American citizen bearing the burdens and sharing the advantages of American citizenship.

Proceedings of the National Conference of Social Work, 1919, 46th Session (Chicago: Rogers & Hall, 1920), pp. 539–44.

73

MOTON ON BLACK TROOPS IN EUROPE

In 1920, Doubleday, Page published Robert R. Moton's autobiography; reproduced below is the section wherein Mr. Moton discusses his mission to investigate the status of Afro-American men fighting in the world war.

On the 2nd of December, 1918, at the request of President Wilson and Secretary of War Newton D. Baker, I went to France to look into conditions affecting Negro soldiers, many of whom were undergoing hardships of one kind and another. Secretary Baker said that he and President Wilson felt that my going to France would be encouraging to the men, and that the presence and words of a member of their own race would be particularly helpful, in view of all the circumstances under which they were serving the nation, at the same time inviting me to make any suggestions that might in my judgment help the situation. In spite of pressing matters in connection with the Institute, I felt that it was the school's duty to do anything possible to help our Negro soldiers, and decided to make the trip.

While in France, I visited nearly every point where Negro soldiers were stationed. At most of them I spoke to the men, and at each place I was most cordially welcomed by the officers and men. I also had the privilege of conferring with Col. E. M. House; Bishop Brent, senior chaplain of the American Expeditionary Forces; General Pershing, and many other high officials of the American and French governments, all of whom I consulted with reference to the record which had been made by Negro troops, and received only words of very highest praise and commendation on their character and conduct in all branches of the service.

During the late summer and early fall of 1918 there were a great many rumours, in and outside of official circles in this country, to the effect that, morally, the Negro soldier in France had failed and that the statement sometimes made that "the Negro is controlled by brutal instincts" was justified. The report was current in France that the "unmentionable crime" was very common; and according to the rumours, Negro officers, as well as privates, in all branches and grades of the service, were guilty of this crime.

A letter I saw that had been written by a lady overseas to another lady in the United States stated that the writer had been told by the colonel of a certain unit, whose guest she was, that he would not feel it safe for her to walk, even with him, through his camp of Negro soldiers. Another letter from a high official in a very important position with the Negro troops overseas, written unofficially to a prominent official on this side, stated that in the 92nd Division alone there had recently been at least thirty cases of the "unmentionable crime."

Another rumour, equally prevalent and damaging, was to the effect that the fighting units which were commanded by Negro officers had been a failure. In other words, "the whispering gallery," which was very active in France on most phases of life overseas, said that the 92nd Division, in which the Negroes of America took special pride, had failed utterly; that, wherever they had been engaged, the Negro officers had gone to pieces; that in some cases the men had to pull themselves together after their officers had shown "the white feather"; and other statements of similar import.

I went to France with authority to go anywhere and get any information from any source, so far as the American Expeditionary Force was concerned. It so happened that I went on the steamer assigned to the newspaper correspondents, a steamer which was one of the convoy ships for the President's party, on which Dr. W. E. B. Du Bois, editor of *The Crisis,* was also a passenger. Mr. Lester A. Walton, of the *New York Age;* Mr. Nathan Hunt, of Tuskegee, together with Doctor Du Bois and myself, occupied the same very comfortable stateroom. We had many frank and pleasant talks, both on the ship and in Paris, where we occupied opposite rooms in the same hotel. The subject that we discussed most often was, of course, some phase of the Negro question, always with a view to helping the situation.

I was accompanied on the trips out from Paris, as well as at many interviews in Paris, by two coloured and two white men—one white newspaper man, Mr. Clyde R. Miller, of the Cleveland *Plaindealer,* and Mr. Lester A. Walton, of the *New York Age.* I also asked to go with me, Dr. Thomas Jesse Jones, of the United States Bureau of Education and the Phelps-Stokes Foundation, and Mr. Nathan Hunt, of Tuskegee Institute.

I realized that the mission was a delicate one, and that questions which I might ask and the things which I would say might probably be misunderstood or misinterpreted. My purpose, however, was to get at the facts and to stop untruthful rumours. In order to ascertain the facts, I made extended inquiries of all those with whom I came in contact. I asked many questions with relation to the conduct and character of the coloured soldiers as compared with other soldiers.

When I reached General Headquarters of the American Expeditionary Force I found that, a few days before my arrival, a young white soldier had been sentenced to be hanged for the "unmentionable crime," but because of his previous good record in every other way the sentence was finally commuted to life imprisonment. The opinion at General Headquarters was that the crime to which I have referred was no more prevalent among coloured than among white, or any other soldiers.

From Chaumont we went immediately to Marbache, the Headquarters of the 92nd Division. I asked the general then in command of this division about the prevalence of the crime in question. He said that it was very prevalent, and that there had been a great many cases over which he was very much disturbed. This statement was corroborated by conversation with two of his white staff officers, who were present. I courteously asked if he would mind having one of his aides get the records. I said that I thought general statements were often very damaging, and that, inasmuch as the reputation of a race was at stake, I was very anxious to get the facts in order to make an accurate report, and, if possible, to stop the damaging rumours which were becoming more and more prevalent in America and were already prevalent in France, especially among Americans, including military circles, the Young Men's Christian Association, the Red Cross, and other organizations.

When the records were brought in and examined, seven cases where this crime had been charged were found in the entire division of more than twelve thousand. *Of these charged, only two had been found guilty and convicted, and one of the two convictions had been "turned down" at General Headquarters.*

In other fighting units, as well as the units of the Service of Supply at Bordeaux, Saint Nazaire, and Brest, and other places, I made the same investigations. I interviewed American and French commanding officers; I talked, as well, with scores of American and French officials of lower rank. When the records were taken, as with the 92nd Division, the number of cases charged was very few and the number of convictions fewer still. I likewise took much time with certain members of the Peace Conference, and with Americans engaged in various branches of war activity, in an effort to disprove and set at rest this awful slander upon the Negro race. I spared no pains or effort to do this, and it would appear, from subsequent investigations on this side of the water and from reports which have come to me from overseas, that the momentum of these damaging rumours perceptibly lessened.

There was apparently no doubt in anybody's mind in France, so far as I was able to find out among the French or the Americans, as to the excellent qualities of the American Negro as a soldier, when led by white officers. There was also little question about the fighting record of four Negro regiments—the 369th, 370th, 371st, and 372nd —which had been brigaded with French divisions; but when it came to the 92nd Division, there was a subtle and persistent rumour in Paris and in other places in France, apparently substantiating the rumour which was prevalent in America—only in France it was much more generally accepted as true; namely, that Negro officers "had been practically a failure," and that it was a mistake ever to have attempted to form a division with Negroes as officers.

I took a great deal of pains and care, as did also the gentlemen with me, to run down every rumour. We spent much time in and out of Paris ferreting out every statement that came from the "whispering gallery." We finally found that, so far as the 92nd Division was concerned, only a very small detachment of a single battalion of one regiment had failed.

Later, in talking with General Pershing in France, regarding this story of the failure of Negro officers, he said that the probabilities were that any officers, white or black, under the same adverse circumstances that these men faced, would have failed. A few officers of the battalion were sent before a court martial for trial for having shown cowardice. Not all of them, however, were found guilty. And since then, these cases have been reviewed by the War Department, and the President, on the recommendation of the Secretary of War, has disapproved the proceedings involving the four officers of the 368th Infantry convicted by court martial abroad. After thorough investigation the War Department issued the following statement with regard to this one battalion of the 368th Regiment:

The 368th Regiment had not had battle experience prior to its assignment to the French brigade. It was expected to operate as a liaison organization, maintaining contact with combat forces on either side, but not itself as an attacking force. In the development of the battle it became necessary to use the regiment in attack.

The ground over which the 368th Regiment advanced was extremely difficult. It had been fought over and fortified for four years, and consisted of a dense belt of intricate barbed wire, through which in four years underbrush had grown, concealing the wire and making any advance most difficult. The section in which the regiment was engaged developed at times intense shell, machine-gun, and rifle fire and subjected those troops to a severe test.

The regiment was not fully supplied with wire cutters, maps, and signalling devices. This was in part due to the fact that the troops were serving at the time with the French, from whom the supply was finally received, the delay being caused doubtless by the hurried movement of the regiment and the assumption on the part of the French that it would be supplied from American depots, and on the part of the Americans that it would be supplied by the French, with whom it was serving—a misunderstanding explained only by the confusion and emergencies of battle.

It was gratifying even then to find that the commanding general, who knew all phases of the affair, did not take this failure nearly so seriously as the rumour about it seemed to suggest. The facts in the case in no sense justified the common report.

In talking with the commanding general at Le Mans, I referred to the fact that something like fifteen Negro officers had been sent back as "inefficient." He said to me: "If it is of any comfort to you, I will tell you this: we sent back through Blois to America, in six months, an average of one thousand white officers a month, who failed in one way or another in this awful struggle. I hope, Doctor Moton," he added, "that you won't lose your faith in my race because of this, and certainly I am not going to lose my faith in your race because of the record of a few coloured officers who failed."

We talked with Colonel House, Mr. Ray Stannard Baker, Captain Walter Lippmann, leading Y.M.C.A. workers, and many others. All assured me that they were glad to get the facts, and that, so far as they were able, they would stop the slanderous rumours concerning our Negro soldiers. I spoke to white officers in a number of places —at one place to two hundred of them—and candidly stated the facts in the case. I raised the question, if they did not think it was a good and fair thing to stop this rumour of the "whispering gallery," which was defaming a race, which threatened to cut down the efficiency of Negro troops, and was, of course, putting America in a bad light before the world.

Robert R. Moton, *Finding A Way Out: An Autobiography* (Garden City, N.Y.: Doubleday, Page, 1920), pp. 250–60.

74

<h1 style="text-align:center">"INJUSTICE MAKES BOLSHEVIKS"</h1>
A Speech by William Pickens

One of the rather early foreign "tourists" visiting Harlem was the British author, Stephen Graham. This occurred shortly after World War I when Graham was one of two thousand people—overwhelmingly Black—who attended a meeting addressed by William Pickens, then a dean at Morgan State College in Baltimore and shortly to become a field secretary of the N.A.A.C.P. Graham wrote: "Just before the turn of Pickens to speak a white lady-journalist had rushed on to the platform and rushed off between two pressing engagements, and had given the audience a 'heart-to-heart' talk on Bolsheviks and agitators, and had told them how thankful the Negroes ought to be that they were in America and not in the Congo still." Then follows Graham's report of William Pickens' remarks.

"Brothers, they're always telling us what we ought to be," said the orator with an engaging smile. "But there are many different opinions about what ought to be; it's what we are that matters. As a coloured pastor said to his flock one day "Brothers and sisters, it's not the *ought*-ness of this problem that we have to consider, but the *is*ness!' I am going to speak about the *is*ness. Sister S——, who has just spoken, has had to go to make a hurry call elsewhere, but I am sorry she could not stay. I think she might perhaps have heard something worth while this afternoon. Sister S—— warned us against agitators and radicals. Now, I am not against or for agitators. The question is, 'What are they agitating about?' Show me the agitator, I say. President Wilson is a great agitator: he is agitating a League of Nations. Jesus Christ was a great agitator: He agitated Christianity. The Pharisees and Sadducees didn't like His agitating, and they fixed Him. But He was a good agitator, and we're not against Him. Then, again the Irish are great agitators; the Jews are great agitators; there are good and bad agitators. But, brothers, I'll tell you who is the greatest agitator in this country . . . the greatest agitator is injustice. When injustice disappears I'll be against agitators, or I'll be ready to see them put in a lunatic asylum.

"Sister S—— was very hard on the radicals. There again, show me the radical, I say. A man may be radically wrong, yes, but he may also be radically *right*.

"As for the Bolsheviks, it's injustice is making Bolshevism. It's injustice that changes quiet inoffensive school-teachers and working-men into Bolsheviks, just as it is injustice is stirring up the coloured people. Not that we are Bolsheviks. I am not going to say anything against Bolsheviks either. Show me the Bolshevik first, I say, and then I'll know whether I'm against him. People are alarmed because the number of Bolsheviks is increasing. But what is making them increase? If America is such a blessed country, why is she making all these Bolsheviks? You know a tree by its fruits, and so you may know a country by what it produces. These Bolsheviks that we read of being deported in the Soviet Ark* weren't Bolshevik when they came to this country. It comes to this: that we've raised a crop of Bolshevism in this country and are exporting it to Europe, and now we're busy sowing another crop. Stop sowing injustice, and Bolshevism will cease growing.

"But there is less Bolshevism among the coloured people than among the white, because the coloured are more humble, more subservient, more used to inequalities. We are always being told that we are backward, and we believe it; bad, and we believe it; untrustworthy,

---

* Nickname of the *Buford*, a ship employed by the U.S. government to deport Emma Goldman and other "reds" to Soviet Russia.

and we believe it; immoral; and we believe it. We are always being told what we ought to be. But I'll come back to what we are.

"We may be immoral; we may be a danger to the white women. But has any one ever honestly compared the morality of Whites and Blacks? They will tell you there is not sufficient evidence to make a comparison, or they will bring you pamphlets and paragraphs out of newspapers, records of disgusting crimes; and we know very well that in twelve million Negroes there are bound to be some half-wits and criminals capable of terrible breaches of morality. But at best it is a paper evidence against the Negro, whilst there is flesh and blood evidence against the White. The moral standard of the Whites is written in the flesh and blood of three million of our race. Brothers, there's one standard for the white man, and another for the coloured man. A coloured man's actions are not judged in the same light as those of a white man.

"Well, I'm not against that. It is giving us a higher ideal. A coloured man has got to be much more careful in this country than a white man. He'll be more heavily punished for the same crime. If he gets into a dispute with a white man he's bound to lose his case. So he won't get into the dispute. Where a white man gets five years' imprisonment the Negro gets put in the electric chair. Where the white man gets six days he gets two years. If a white man seduces a coloured girl she never gets redress. If the other thing occurs the Negro is legally executed, or lynched. What is the result of all that inequality? Why, it is making us a more moral, less criminal, less violent people than the Whites. Once at a mixed school they were teaching the black and white boys to jump. The white boys jumped and the black boys jumped. But when it was the black boy's turn the teacher always lifted the jumping-stick a few inches. What was the consequence? Why, after a while, every coloured boy in that school could jump at least a foot higher than any white boy.

"That is what is happening to the Negro race in America. We are being taught to jump a foot higher than the Whites. We will jump it, or we will break our necks.

"Of course a great difference separates the black from the white still. And I don't say that the white man hasn't given us a chance. If our positions had been transposed, and we had been masters and the white folk had been the slaves, I'm not sure that we wouldn't have treated them worse than they have treated us. But the white folk make a mistake when they think we're not taking the chances they give us. We *are* taking them. We are covering the ground that separates black from white. The white man is not outstripping us in the race. We are nearer to him than we were—not farther away. We haven't caught up, but we're touching. We are always doing things we never did before.

"We shall not have cause to regret the time of persecution and injustice and the higher standard of morality that has been set up. Brothers, it's all worth while. Our boys here have been to France and bled and suffered for white civilisation and white justice. We didn't want to go. We didn't know anything about it. But it's been good for us. We've made the cause of universal justice our cause. We have taken a share in world-sufferings and world-politics. It's going to help raise us out of our obscurity. We have discovered the French, and shall always be grateful to them. We didn't know France before, but every coloured soldier is glad now that he fought for France. If there is to be a League of Nations we know France will stand by us. And we shall have a share in the councils of Humanity—with our coloured brethren in all parts of the world."

[The author added the following]:

The orator spoke for two hours, and the above is only a personal remembrance put down afterwards. His actual speech is therefore much shortened. But that was the sense and the flavour of it. It was given in a voice of humour and challenge, resonant, and yet everlasting whimsical. Laughter rippled the whole time. I shook hands with him afterwards. For he was warm and eloquent and moving, as few speakers I have heard. He was utterly exhausted, for he had drawn his words from his audience, and two thousand people had been pulling at his spirit for two hours.

Graham, *Children of the Slaves,* pp. 64–70.

75

FOR A BLACK GOD

As so much else that is mistakenly thought of as "new," the concept of a Black God or Black Christ is quite ancient. Here is a conversation recorded by the British visitor whose account of William Pickens' speech has just appeared. This is sometime in 1919 and Graham is visiting the Reverend W———, when, as he writes, the following "singular conversation" ensued.

"Now, isn't it absurd for us to have white angels?"

"You surely would not like them black?"

"We give Sunday-school cards to our children with white angels on them. It's *wrong.*"

"Black angels would be ugly."

"No more ugly than white."

I thought the whiteness of the angels was as the whiteness of white light which contained all colour. That, however, was lost on the Reverend, who happened to be a realist.

"Christ himself was not white. He would have had to travel in a Jim Crow car," said he.

"But put it to yourself: isn't it absurd for us to be taught that the good are all white, and that sin itself is black?"

"It does seem to leave you in the shade," said I.

"Expressions such as 'black as sin' ought to be deleted from the language. One might as well say 'white as sin.' "

I ransacked my brain rapidly.

"We say 'pale as envy,' " said I.

" 'Black spite,' " he retorted. "Why should it be black?"

I could not say.

"Then Adam and Eve in the Garden," he went on, "are always shown as beautifully white creatures, whereas, considering the climate, they may well have been as dark-skinned as any Negro couple in Alabama. Babylon itself was built by Negroes."

"Would you have Adam and Eve painted black?"

"Why, yes, I would."

This struck me as rather diverting, but it was quite serious. Later, in New York one night at Liberty Hall, before I was driven out as a white interloper, I heard an orator say to an admiring host of Negroes: "Why, I ask you, is God always shown as white? It is because He is the white man's God. It is the God of our masters. (Yes, brother, that's it.) It's the God of those who persecute and despise the coloured people. Brothers, we've got to knock that white God down and put up a black God—we've got to rewrite the Old Testament and the New from a black man's point of view. Our theologians must get busy on a black God."

Graham, *Children of the Slaves,* pp. 183–85. The Liberty Hall to which Mr. Graham refers was the name of the headquarters of the Garvey Movement in Harlem.

76

HARDING AND THE BLACK VOTER

The racist character of Wilson's administration and the fact that the Cox-Roosevelt ticket of the Democratic party was mute concerning the Afro-

American, led to major efforts by Black people to influence the Republican candidate, Senator Harding—whose own ancestry might well have caused hopes to rise. In his July 22, 1920, acceptance speech, Harding did say more than usual, affirming that "Negro citizens . . . should be guaranteed the enjoyment of all their rights," and so on. Delegations of Afro-American men and women visited the candidate several times that summer. From one such came the following demands upon the future President.

Memorandum to Dr. Du Bois:

The following were the points presented to Senator Harding and upon which he was urged to make statements:

1. The untrammelled right of the Negro to vote under the identical qualifications required for other citizens, with federal action, if need be, to enforce that right.
2. The abolition of segregation in governmental departments at Washington.
3. Promise of a Congressional enactment making lynching a federal offense.
4. The appointment of a commission of members of both races to investigate conditions in Haiti.*
5. The granting of federal aid to education so distributed as to insure to every child, black and white, free common school training.
6. Apportionment of Negro officers and privates in the national guard of the United States in proportion to the number of Negroes in the population, not solely as pioneer troops or as labor battalions in either the national army or the national guard.
7. Investigation by the Interstate Commerce Commission of Jim Crow car conditions in southern states, in interstate traffic, and the correction of this evil.

Typed, unsigned paper in Du Bois Papers. The Cleveland *Gazette* in August, 1920, carried stories on pressures being brought upon Harding. There is a helpful account in R. C. Downes, *The Rise of Warren G. Harding* (Columbus: Ohio State University Press, 1970), pp. 536–44.

77

SERGEANT CALDWELL EXECUTED

One of the innumerable cases illustrating the resistance of Afro-Americans and the process of white supremacist injustice that masquerades as "law and order" was that involving Edgar C. Caldwell. The following account tells the story.

* This had reference to the intervention by U.S. Marines in Haiti, which commenced in 1915 and did not end until 1934.

On July 30 the closing chapter in the life of Sergeant Edgar C. Caldwell was written when he was executed at Anniston, Ala., for the killing of Cecil Linton, a street car conductor in that city on October 1, 1919. Few cases have attracted such nation-wide attention as did this one. The whole story of the alleged crime, together with the long legal fight made to save the life of this colored man who fought in a southern town to save his own life has been told in previous issues of *The Crisis.* Following a dispute with the conductor of a street car in Anniston, Caldwell was kicked from the car. As he was about to rise from the ground, the conductor and motorman of the car advanced on him with weapons in their hands to attack him further. Caldwell drew his revolver and firing from his hip, killed the conductor and wounded the motorman. Caldwell was arrested by civil authorities, although he was a soldier and subject to military trial and punishment if found guilty by a court-martial. He was found guilty of murder in the first degree and sentenced to be hanged.

Through the splendid work of the Anniston-Hobson City Branch of the N.A.A.C.P. in which the Rev. R. R. Williams of Anniston was conspicuously active, the case was fought through the various state courts of Alabama, in which fight the branch was aided by the other Alabama branches and the National Office. The long fight was told of in detail in the January issue of *The Crisis.* After reversals there, the case was carried to the United States Supreme Court where again Caldwell lost. Final appeals to the governor of Alabama to commute the sentence of death to life imprisonment were unavailing.

The National Office wishes especially to commend the Alabama lawyers who fought so determinedly to save Caldwell's life,—Messrs. Charles D. Kline and B. M. Allen, and to Messrs. James A. Cobb and Henry E. Davis of Washington who did the same in the United States Supreme Court. It also wishes to express its sincere appreciation to the large number of its friends, who are too numerous to mention individually, who aided in such wholehearted and loyal fashion in the defense.

Sergeant Caldwell is dead, but the efforts to save him are not lost. No person who is conversant with the facts in his case feels that he was guilty of a crime when he fought to save his own life. No red-blooded person would have done otherwise. Caldwell has been sacrificed on the altar of prejudice. His death means but one more addition to the long list of crimes which have been done in the name of color prejudice. His end means but one more reason for a more unbending and relentless fight on the part of every Negro and every right-minded person of every race to end this farce which allows color prejudice to blind justice and judge a man not on his deeds but on the color of his skin. Caldwell's last words, spoken just before the noose was placed around his neck, express his feeling toward the country that had accepted his services in battle and repaid him by a legal lynching. They close Caldwell's life history but who knows what part his death may play in the ending of the régime that caused his death?

"I am being sacrificed today upon the altar of passion and racial hatred that appears to be the bulwark of America's civilization. If it would alleviate the pain and sufferings of my race, I would count myself fortunate in dying, but I am but one of the many victims among my people who are paying the price of America's mockery of law and dishonesty in her profession of a world democracy."

The Crisis, October, 1920; XX, 282.

78

THE WOMAN VOTER HITS THE COLOR LINE
by William Pickens

The federal enfranchisement of women—achieved after long effort and intense sacrifice—involved, as is characteristic in U.S. history, the special nature of Afro-American oppression. In the following essay, William Pickens illustrates this with specific examples taken from the weeks prior to the 1920 election.

The Pickens article was sent to each of the 160 members of the National Advisory Committee of the National Woman's party and comment was requested. Over one hundred did not reply at all; but most of those who did reply, as Florence Kelley, Jean L. Milholland, and Mary Winsor, stated their opposition to disenfranchisement on the basis of color as well as sex. Mary Winsor, a pacifistic Socialist from Pennsylvania, added a relevant remark in concluding her letter: "I don't know why *The Nation* has arrogated to itself the right to catechize the National Woman's Party. *The Nation* was *utterly indifferent* when the members of the N.W.P. were illegally thrown into jail for asking for the vote."—*The Nation,* February 16, 1921; CXII, 257–58.

The Nineteenth Amendment has become the law of the land and it is constitutionally possible for twenty-five million women to vote. How many of these will actually vote? Three million are colored, and more than three-fourths of them live below Mason and Dixon's Line. There the colored man has been cheated out of nine-tenths of his votes, and only a small proportion of the white men vote because of the indirect reaction of this political dishonesty. Will the colored women of the South be similarly shut out?

The recent registration of voters in South Carolina may be taken as a fair example, as this State has been ever representative of the South. In common with other Southern States, it has, by administration and manipulation of suffrage laws, practically nullified the Fourteenth and Fifteenth amendments, which enfranchised colored men. The black race slightly outnumbers the white in South Carolina, and colored women outnumber colored men. The colored woman is accordingly the largest class in the State, and her right to vote gives a new concern to the maintainers of "white supremacy."

What of the colored women? They have shown themselves in every sense and in every emergency good citizens. In the war their auxiliaries were second to none in efficient service. As the State Federation of Colored Women's Clubs in Alabama founded a reform school for colored boys long before the State would adopt the work, so now the colored women of South Carolina are supporting an Industrial School for Wayward Colored Girls to which they gave $9,000 last year. A colored woman owns and operates the best hospital for her race anywhere in the State, and it is patronized by white physicians.

While colored people predominate in numbers in the whole State, in the city of Columbia, with 37,500 inhabitants, they number about one-third. Let us observe the attempt of colored women to register in this capital city. The registrars are white men, sometimes but half-educated. One can register either as tax-payer on a stated minimum value of taxable property or under the "educational qualification." On the first day of the registration in September the colored women who presented themselves evidently took the registrars by surprise, as the latter seemed to have no concerted plan for dealing with colored women except to register them like the white women; and this they were doing without any test or question whatsoever, save such necessary inquiries as to name, age and residence. The registrars had evidently believed that few colored women would have the nerve to attempt to register, and there was visible disappointment when many colored women, bright and intelligent, in some cases armed with the necessary tax receipt, appeared the first day. While there was apparently no pre-concerted plan not to register them, one ready-made discrimination of the South was freely used, that of "white people first." The registrars would keep numbers of colored women standing for hours while they registered every white person in sight, man or woman, even the late-comers. A registrar was sometimes observed to break off right in the middle of registering a colored woman, and turn to some white new-comer. To the credit of the instinctive fairness of white women it should be said that they at first manifested a disposition merely to fall in line and await their turn until interfered with by the white officers who would call them arbitrarily from behind a group of colored applicants. Yet many of these colored women bravely stayed and patiently stood from 11:30 in the morning till 8:00 at night in order to register to vote! The attitude and the disappointed calculation of the white men can be best expressed by quoting one of them: "Who stirred up all these colored women to come up here and register?" Such persistent courage, however, was too ominous to the white registrars, the guardians of racial supremacy and party success; for although they seemed to have no plan of repulse for the first day, they evidently held a council of war at night—and things looked different on the morrow.

Consider how the law itself is made the vehicle of injustice and oppression in its administration. One can register if one pays taxes on at least three hundred dollars' worth of property, or can read from the State or the Federal Constitution some passage selected by the registrar. It would seem the purpose of such a law merely to determine the general fitness and intelligence of the candidate, or to make a bona fide test of his literacy. But although all women were registered without tests the first day, and white women without test or question throughout the registration, colored women after the first day, in addition to being tortured by long standing, were greeted with scowls, rough voices and insulting demeanor. They were made to read and even to explain long passages from the constitutions and from various civil and criminal codes, although there is no law requiring such an inquisition. On the second day the registrars were assisted by a lawyer, apparently for the special business of quizzing, cross-questioning and harassing the col-ored women, in the manner of opposing counsel in court. He asked questions about all sorts of things from all sorts of documents—ques-tions which he could not himself answer and about which lawyers wrangle every day in court. It was the evident purpose to send back to the colored population so discouraging a report that others would not even try to register. Indeed the Columbia *State,* the morning paper, had suggested that the colored women were manifesting "very little interest," and that "very few" were expected to register.

Well educated colored women were denied the right to register.

Some of the questions actually put to the inexperienced colored applicant were: "Explain a *mandamus*." "Define civil code." "How would you appeal a case?" "If presidential votes are tied, how would you break the tie?" "How much revenue did the State hospital pay the State last year?" "How much revenue does the Baptist Church pay the State?"

South Carolina law requires only that one shall *read,* and not the passing of any examination in law or civil government. If a colored woman mispronounced a word in the *opinion* of the half-educated registrar, she was disqualified. In one of the county registration places a colored man was threatened with disfranchisement because he accented the word "municipal" on the antepenult, where the accent belongs, and not "municipal" as the registrar insisted it should be.

There was not only injustice but rank insult. A colored man was thrown out of the room for speaking with one of the waiting colored women, for fear that he was coaching or prompting her in the manner of primary school discipline. As one colored woman was reading with ease the passage set before her, the registrar blurted out: "Heah, girl, yo' misponounced two words. Yo' git out o' here! Yo' cain't vote—yo' ain't got sense enough to vote!" A graduate of the State College for Negroes was rejected because she "mispronounced a word"—always in the mere opinion of the registrar, with never an appeal to Webster. Some of the colored teachers of Columbia, licensed by the State to teach colored children, were denied the right to register, as being insufficiently educated to read a ballot!

There was not only insult but threatened and actual violence. On the second day when the number of colored people in the room had grown large because the registrars had compelled them to wait while they registered white people out of turn, the "high sheriff" came in and shouted: "Yo' niggahs git out o' de way, git out an' let de whahte people register—an' stay out! An' if yo' don' stay out, dey'll be some buckshot to keep yo' out."—And still the colored people came. The women especially defied all opposition.

By Friday of the registration week more than twenty of the better educated colored women who had been rejected, had signed an affidavit against the registrars. Contrary to calculations, some colored women were even stimulated to go and assert their right to register because they heard that others of their race had been unjustly turned away. They decided either to register or to put the responsibility on the officers of the law. No discouragement, no "test," no petty insult stopped them. Nothing availed against them save the arbitrary will of the tyrants who sat as registrars. The women's suit will be based on the Nineteenth Amendment, to open the way for appeal to federal courts. The colored women of South Carolina may thus play a leading role in the judicial establishment of the enfranchisement of her race and her sex.

According to the press many colored women in Richmond have been denied the right of registration in the same manner and there are similar reports from other localities. Does this mean that the South will resort to the methods to keep Negro women from voting that have been employed to keep the men from the polls? The methods have included every means of trickery and brutality from vague statutes to shot guns. The "white primary" of the dominant and majority party of the South practically ousts the whole colored race from any share in government. There is no trouble in keeping ignorant and shiftless black men from voting—most of them do not want to vote. But the "educational qualification" clauses are chiefly employed to keep industrious and intelligent colored men from the polls, nad some have been disfranchised who were graduates of European universities, in addition to Yale or Harvard. A Norfolk daily paper recently said in an editorial that a law should be enacted by the legislature of Virginia against the passage of the woman suffrage amendment which could be so manipulated as to allow any white man to vote "unless he were an idiot" and to prevent any Negro from voting even if he were "a graduate of Harvard." Every method has been employed against the colored man, up to "red shirt," "Ku Klux" campaigns and less picturesque but equally forceful terrorism. In some districts a colored man seals his death warrant by even attempting to register. Nothing in the code of "Southern chivalry" will prevent similar treatment of colored women. Will the women of the United States who know something at least of disfranchisement tolerate such methods to prevent intelligent colored women from voting?

The Nation, October 6, 1920; CXI, 272–73.

79

TRYING TO VOTE

The three documents that follow bring to life what it meant for Black men and women in the South to seek to vote in the 1920 election. The first document [a] is by Walter White and details experiences in Florida; the second [b] is a letter from Georgia; the third [c] is another letter from a Black woman in Virginia.

[a]

ELECTION DAY IN FLORIDA
by Walter F. White

An unknown number of dead, men of property and standing forced to leave their homes and families under threat of death, thousands of qualified voters debarred from casting their ballots—these constitute a portion of the results of the elections of 1920 in the state of Florida. To that list might be well added an increased bitterness on the part of both white and colored people towards each other.

It is not possible to write of race relations in the South today without giving due prominence to the revival of that sinister organization, the Ku Klux Klan. There is hardly a town or community to be found which does not have its branch. Certain it is that wherever one goes in the South one hears of the "Klucks" and what that order is going to do to maintain "white supremacy."

A new generation of Negroes has arisen with thousands of university, college, high school and grammar school graduates among them; possessing property and the respect for self that accompanies such possessions. In regard to the Klan, even the uneducated Negro looks upon it with amused contempt.

In Jacksonville, a parade of the local Klan was held on Saturday night, October 30. Large numbers of colored people turned out to view the parade. One old colored woman of the ante-bellum type that is fast disappearing, called out derisively to the marching Klucks:

"White folks, you ain't done nothin.' Them German guns didn't scare us and I know them white faces ain't goin' to do it now."

The situation in the smaller towns and isolated rural communities where the Negro population is widely scattered is of a more serious nature. There the Klans can wreak their vengeance on any Negro who dares offend them by being too prosperous or being suspected of some crime, great or small, or by incurring the displeasure of any white man of the community. This vengeance extends to white men who offend some loyal member of a Klan or who dare show too great friendliness for Negroes—whether for selfish or other motives. The following Klan warning was sent to a prominent white lawyer of a Florida town who advised Negroes to qualify, register and vote in the recent election. It reads:

We have been informed that you have been telling Negroes to register, explaining to them how to become citizens and how to assert their rights.

If you know the history of reconstruction days following the Civil War, you know how the "scalawags" of the North and the black republicans of the South did much as you are doing to instill into the Negro the idea of social equality. You will remember that these things forced the loyal citizens of the South to form clans of determined men to maintain white supremacy and to safeguard our women and children.

And now you know that history repeats itself and that he who resorts to your kind of a game is handling edged tools. We shall always enjoy *white supremacy* in this country and he who interferes must face the consequences.

Grand Master Florida Ku Klucks

Copy
Local Ku Klucks.
Watch this man.

An example of what can be done and what has been done in a small town is the election riot at Ococee, Orange County, Florida. For weeks before November 2, word had been sent to the Negroes that no colored man would be allowed to vote. The statement was emphasized with the threat that any Negro attempting to cast his ballot would be severely punished. One colored man disregarded the warning. He was the most prominent man in the community, owned a large orange grove worth more than ten thousand dollars, his own home and an automobile. He had always borne the reputation of being a sane leader among his people and had never been involved in trouble of any kind. Therein lay his unpopularity. He was too prosperous—"for a nigger." He, Mose Norman, attempted to vote. He was beaten severely and ordered to go home. The press reports stated later that he had not paid his poll tax nor had he registered. On this point and the succeeding events, may I quote the statement of a white man of the town who said:

". . . he was denied upon the ground that he had not paid his poll tax, when as a matter of fact, the records of this county (if they have not been doctored since) will show that he had paid his tax. The press claimed that he made a threat that he was going home to get his gun, and see that he did vote. I do not believe that anyone, situated as he was, would have been foolhardy enough to make such a threat. After the polls closed, a number of armed men went to his house, without a warrant and without authority of law as is claimed by those approving their action, to arrest this Negro. Two white men were shot in the Negro's backyard. From that time on for three days the community ran riot. I do not believe it will ever be known how many Negroes were killed. Every Negro home, schoolhouse, church and lodge-room in that community was burned, in some instances with women and children occupying the houses, and thus burned to death. . . . The foregoing is a fair sample of conditions which exist in most parts of the state."

The story is essentially as told above. When Norman left the polls he went to the home of July Perry, another colored man, who likewise was unpopular with the whites in that he was foreman of a large orange grove owned by a white man living in New England—a job which the community felt was too good for a Negro. When the mob attacked the colored community the colored people fought in self-defense, killing two white men and wounding two, according to news accounts. Citizens of the town told me that eight or ten whites were killed but that they could not allow the information to become known, fearing the effect on the colored population. However, the mob surrounded the settlement, set fire to it, shot down or forced back into the flames colored men, women and children who attempted to flee. The number murdered will probably never be known. The figures generally given varied from thirty-two to thirty-five. One lean, lanky and vicious-looking white citizen in Ococee of whom I asked the number of dead, replied:

"I don't know exactly but *I know fifty-six niggers were killed. I killed seventeen myself.*"

Whatever the number, two of those known to have died, *were a colored mother and her two-weeks' old infant.* Before the ashes of the burned houses had cooled, eager members of the mob rushed in and sought gleefully the charred bones of the victims as souvenirs. As I stood on the spot approximately seventy-two hours following the slaughter, the remains looked as though some one had gone over them with a fine-toothed comb.

An amazing aftermath of the occurrence was the attitude of the white inhabitants of Orange County. Talking with numbers of them, the opinion of the majority seemed to be that nothing unusual had taken place—that the white people had acquitted themselves rather meritoriously in checking unholy and presumptuous ambitions of Negroes in attempting to vote. Even the white children of Ococee felt that an event similar in enjoyment to a circus had taken place. One bright-faced and alert girl of eleven when asked what had occurred, told happily of how "we had some fun burning up some niggers."

There was no thought of horror at the deed—it was accepted as a matter of course.

Some of the methods used in the smaller towns in eliminating the Negro vote and particularly the colored woman vote were unique. In Orange and Osceola counties, a colored woman would attempt to register; on being asked her age, for example, she would say twenty-four. She would then be asked the year in which she was born. Many of them being illiterate, would not know. The registrar would then probably say, "If you are twenty-four, you were born in 1892, weren't you?" The applicant, seeking to get the ordeal over, would reply in the affirmative. Before she had been away from the place very long a warrant for perjury had been sworn out against her and she had been arrested. I found many cases equally flagrant where Negro women had been imprisoned for such "offenses" as these.

In the same manner men would be intimidated and threatened. A white lawyer told me laughingly of how a Negro would approach a registration booth in his county, Orange, and ask if he could register. The officials there, in most cases of the poorer order of whites, would reply, "Oh yes, you can register, but I want to tell you something. Some God damn black—— —— —— is going to get killed about this voting business yet."

In Quincy, Gadsden County, the leading colored man of the town, a physician, owner of a drug store and other property including an excellent home, on election day was surrounded as he approached the polling booth to cast his ballot, by a crowd who spat in his face and dared him to wipe his face. His "crime" was that of advising colored men and women to register and vote. He has since been ordered to get out of the town but remains—determined to die rather than submit. He has always been a good citizen and highly respected by both white and colored people.

Two brothers of Lake City, Columbia County, who also were good citizens, prosperous and the owners of a large merchandise business, were called from their homes two weeks before election day, beaten almost to death and ordered to leave town immediately for the same offense of urging Negroes to vote. One has gone; the other lies at the point of death from a stroke of paralysis brought on by the beating.

Nor are these isolated cases but rather are they typical of what took place in many parts of the state. The West Palm Beach *Post* of October 30 carried an article with the significant statement: "Sheriff R. C. Baker will have several deputy sheriffs at the polls to arrest *black* violators of the election laws as fast as they appear and ask for ballots." The inference is that only Negroes violated the election laws while it is generally known that white Democratic voters openly carried memo-

randa into the booths, which is directly contrary to law. Only Negro
Republicans were arrested for this violation.

In Jacksonville, where Negroes form slightly more than half of the
population of 90,000, the situation was different. In spite of parades
of the Ku Klux Klan, vicious newspaper propaganda designed to intimidate Negro voters, and the announcement two days before election
that 4,000 warrants had been sworn out in blank form for the arrest
of Negroes, the colored voter turned out *en masse*. Most of the colored
people live in the second, sixth, seventh and eighth wards. An active
campaign was carried on after the passage of the suffrage amendment
which resulted in the registration of more colored than white women in
all four of the wards. Frantic stories threatening domination by "Negro
washerwomen and cooks" failed to bring out the white women to
register. To the number of women was added the large registration of
men, white and colored, in the spring of 1920. Yet, in the second,
seventh and eighth wards the total vote did not equal the registration
of colored women alone, while in the sixth ward the total number of
votes cast was only a few more than the number of women, white and
colored, registered. Every possible effort was made to hamper the voting of Negroes. The polling places were arranged with four entrances
—one each for white women, white men, colored women and colored men. No delay was caused to white voters. More than four thousand colored men and women, whose names, addresses and registration
certificate numbers are in the hands of responsible colored citizens of
Jacksonville, stood in line from 8:00 A.M., the hour of opening, to
5:40 P.M., the hour of closing the polls, and were not allowed to vote.

Unless the problem of the ballot is solved, either through reduction
of Southern representation, a force bill or by some other means, and the
entire problem of race relations submitted to clear thinking and just
dealing, our race riots and similar disturbances are just beginning.

[b]

LETTER DATED AMERICUS, GA., NOVEMBER 9, 1920

It is a burning shame just how the colored people are treated, *i.e.,*
the mass of them. The register would hide the book or himself, he
would tell the people the registration book was in another precinct or
he'd leave his office and put a lady in there who would know nothing
about registration. All this would happen only to nine-tenths of the
colored people. More than 250 colored women went to the polls to vote

but were turned down or their ballots refused to be taken by the election manager, I mean in the City of Americus, Ga.

[c]

LETTER FROM HAMPTON, VA., OCTOBER 28, 1920

In regard to colored women registering, we all had trouble and no colored women were allowed to register until the last day, which was on Saturday (even though a great many of us had tried to register several times), and because we were allowed only one day there was not time enough for many to register.

It took only a minute or two to register white women, while we were kept anywhere from fifteen to thirty minutes. I am told white women were asked age, residence and etc., while we were given a blank paper and told to write our application and if we left out one of the six points we were told we had failed.

Then we were asked six other questions and in many cases an experienced lawyer could not have answered them.

According to the *Daily Press* fifty colored women were allowed to register and eighty-five paid taxes.

The night Mrs. —— and I went over to register and our applications had been made out and correct, we were told to come back on Saturday at 2:30 o'clock and they would register us, but he said "To tell you the truth we are not going to be bothered with a lot of colored women." He told one of the teachers afterwards he asked us to come late so we would not be able to spread the news to other colored women that we had registered.

It was very humiliating and embarrassing to say the least but we were determined to keep going until we found out exactly their attitude towards us.

From a pamphlet, *Disfranchisement of Colored Americans in the Presidential Election of 1920* (New York: N.A.A.C.P., 1920), pp. 9–12, 16–17. Walter White published an article substantially similar to that above in *The New Republic*, January 12, 1921; XXV, 195–97.

80

A LETTER FROM A LYNCH VICTIM

On Christmas Day, 1920, Henry Lowry, a Black sharecropper working on the plantation owned by O. C. Craig—described by the press of the day as a "wealthy planter residing near Wilson, Arkansas"—had an argument over conditions and income.* The result was that Lowry shot and killed Craig and his daughter, a Mrs. Williamson, and wounded two of his sons.

Lowry fled to Texas, planning to make it to Mexico, but his capture resulted from the following letter he wrote to a friend. The friend together with J. T. Williams, who had helped Lowry and is mentioned in the letter, barely escaped being lynched and were imprisoned. The text below comes from the story as printed in the Memphis *Press,* January 26, 1921.

Lowry was taken from deputies on a train at Sardis, Mississippi, to Memphis, Tenn. He was paraded through the main street of that city, taken across the Arkansas border, and burned alive in a slow fire before a mob of about five hundred men and women. The local press reported: "Not once did he whimper or beg for mercy."

ANXIETY TO HEAR FROM HOME
CAUSE OF NEGRO'S DEATH

Safe in El Paso, Murderer Writes Friend

INTERCEPT LETTER

Could Have Crossed Border to Mexico

Nodena, Ark., Jan. 27—The death of Henry Lowry can be attributed directly to his anxiety to hear from home. A letter written to a lodge member at Turrell, Ark., resulted in his capture at El Paso, Tex., as he was preparing to cross the border town into Mexico.

Lowry directed the letter to Morris Jenkins with the request that he go to the home of J. T. Williams, another Negro, living near Wilson, Ark., and learn the whereabouts of his (Lowry's) wife. The Jenkins Negro instead of doing as requested, wrote a letter to Williams. The letter was intercepted, and El Paso officials were asked to arrest the slayer.

The letter to Jenkins follows:

Mr. Morris Jenkins, Turrell, Ark.:
Dear Friend and Brother—It affords me no small pleasure to write you a few lines to let you hear from me. This leaves me very well in health, and I truly hope these few lines will find you and family well and doing well.

Listen, I have made it to the border line, but I have not crossed yet. I have

* For some details see the essay by William Pickens which follows.

run out of money and am trying to get me a job to work some. Soon as I get money enough I am going over in Mexico. It costs me $10 to cross over.

Have you heard from my wife and girl or [J. T.] Williams? Write now and tell me all you know about the matter. Now I can't see nothing in the paper here where I am at. I am over a thousand miles from you now, and as soon as I get some money, I am going on further. I am now in El Paso, Tex., right on the border, so you write me at once and let me hear how is everything.

Back your letter to S. M. Thompson, 1201 East Third St., El Paso, Tex. If you have not heard from J. T. Williams I would be glad for you to go down there and see him for me. I don't want to put you to so much trouble, but you know how it is with me. I can't take no risk. I want to hear from my wife. I don't know how she is fairing. I left her with a plenty, but you know how it is with the white people in a case like this.

Now listen, you go up there for me. I will draw you the road so you can't miss it without asking anyone the way to Williams' house. You go to his house and get him to carry you where my wife is and tell her to write just how is everything and what she is going to do and what can she do and see if she got her money out of them war stamps.

Tell her I want her to get where I can write her. I want her to come to me later. I will tell her how to come when she gets so she can come. By the time she gets so she can come I will try to send her some money. It takes $41 on the Dallas train for to bring her here.

I am got a job that pays me $40 a month and board, so I guess in a few months I can send her some money. So I will lay out the road to Williams' house from Wilson on the next sheet.

The Negro then drew a crude plan of the road from Wilson, Ark., to the home of Williams.

The letter was signed, "S. M. Thompson."

A postscript read: "My mail comes to my home, 1201 E. Third St. Be sure to tell my wife any time she writes me from there mail it to you and you mail it to me."

The letter was written in pencil, but the El Paso address had been written in with ink. The letter was posted Jan. 11.*

81

LYNCHING AND POGROM

One of the earliest publications of the newly founded American Civil Liberties Union was a pamphlet by William Pickens (document [a]). In

* In 1921 the N.A.A.C.P. issued an eight-page pamphlet entitled *An American Lynching Being the Burning at the Stake of Henry Lowry at Nodena, Arkansas, January 26, 1921, as Told in American Newspapers.* The pamphlet consists entirely of photographic reproductions from newspapers in Tennessee and Arkansas.

terms of the essential commitment of the A.C.L.U., a foreword to the pamphlet affirmed that the solution to lynching was "obviously bound up with the cause of exploited labor—white and black alike." Therefore, the foreword concluded: "And that solution will become possible only as the black and white workers of the South both achieve the right to meet, speak freely, organize and strike."

No sooner was this pamphlet published—in May, 1921—than there broke out in Tulsa, Oklahoma, what began as a pogrom and concluded as a veritable racial war. The latter event is recorded from the scene by Walter White in document [b].

[a]

LYNCHING AND DEBT—SLAVERY
by William Pickens

The race problem in the United States is only an intensification of the wrongs of our economic system. It is fundamentally one with the difference between labor and capital, employee and employer, wages and unearned income.

Lynching and mob violence are only methods of economic repression. Lynching is most prevalent where Negro labor is most exploited; and the spread of mob violence against colored people has followed the spread of this exploitation. It is either due directly to efforts of the exploiting class to repress the Negro, or it is the indirect resentment of the laborers of other racial groups against the exploitation of Negro labor to their disadvantage. This is the difference between Georgia and East St. Louis. The chain of causes which leads from the economic wrong to the lynching may take different directions. It may be that the Negro is the chief labor element, as on the farms of Arkansas, and that the landed employer class will resort to lynching to keep Negroes down, even by a great massacre, as at Elaine, Ark., in 1919. Or it may be that the Negro is a newcomer in need of a job, used by the employers as a tool with which to beat down all labor, and we may therefore see the spectacle of white laborers, making an indirect attack upon the system by killing black laborers, as in East St. Louis, in 1917.

Where Lynchings Occur

It is instructive to note where most lynchings take place. In thirty years the seven states which led in lynching, are in the order of their evil eminence: Georgia, Mississippi, Texas, Louisiana, Alabama, Arkansas and Tennessee. Along with Alabama, Georgia and Texas, therefore, we have the great southern Mississippi Valley, a region which might be termed "the American Congo."

Debt Slavery

The quest of this Congo is not for rubber and ivory, but for cotton and sugar. Here labor is forced, and the laborer is a slave. The slavery is a cunningly contrived debt slavery to give the appearance of civilization and the sanction of law. A debt of a few hundred dollars may tie a black man and his family of ten as securely in bondage to a great white planter as if he had purchased their bodies. If the Thirteenth Amendment, which has never been enforced in this region, means anything, it is that a man's body cannot be held for an honestly contracted debt; that only his property can be held; and that if a contracting debtor has no property, the creditor takes the risk in advancing credit. Otherwise a law abolishing slavery could be easily evaded, for the wealthy enslaver could get the poor victim into debt and then hold his body in default in payment. Wages could then be so adjusted to expenses and the cost of "keep" that the slavery would be unending.

And that is precisely the system of debt-slavery. The only way for this debt-slave to get free from such a master is to get someone else to pay this debt; that is, to sell himself to another, with added charges, expenses of moving and bonuses. By this method the enslaver gets his bondmen cheaper than in a regular slave system, for in the debt system he does not have to pay the full market price of a man.

The effect is to allow the ignorant and the poor unwittingly and unwillingly to sell themselves for much less than an old slaveholder would have sold them. The debtmaster has other advantages. He is free from liabilities on account of the debtor's ill-health or the failure of his crops. The debtor takes all risk. In case of misfortune or crop failure, he gets deeper into debt, more securely tied in bondage.

This is the system that obtains in the great Mississippi Valley, and it has not been modified for thirty years or more. The evil of this system, is responsible for all of the massacres of colored people and for nearly all of the horrible lynchings and burnings of individual Negroes that have lately taken place in this region.

As long as this system lasts there will be lynching and burning and occasional great outbreaks against the colored populations of these states. And of course, under the influence of suggestion, there will be sporadic attacks upon colored people in other parts of the nation. To attack lynching without attacking this system, is like trying to be rid of the phenomena of smoke and heat without disturbing the basic fire. If we examine any, even the most complicated, of these "race" troubles, we will find some economic wrong at the bottom, some trouble about wages or work or property. The existence side by side of two races, one powerful and the other weak, simply lends greater opportunity and freer play to human greed and social injustice.

The Massacre at Elaine, Arkansas

For example, there was the alleged "Negro insurrection" at Elaine, near Helena, Ark., on the last day of September and the first days of October, 1919. In this case the planters and landlords overreached credulity by charging too much. They charged that the black peons and tenants had plotted to murder all the whites, to take possession of all the land and seize the government of Arkansas! Such a wild charge discredited itself with all fair-minded people who know Arkansas or any other part of the South. If all the Negroes from all the insane asylums of all the South were gathered together in one state, they would not attempt such a thing.

It is instructive to review the cause of all this trouble which resulted in the immediate slaughter of at least twenty-five helpless colored people (nobody knows exactly how many), the condemning of twelve to the electric chair by mere travesties of trials, the imprisonment of more than three score in the state penitentiary for life or long terms, and in the terrorizing of the colored population of the whole state. The cause of all this was the attempt of the Negro tenants and share croppers to sell their cotton in the open market for a price between 30 and 40 cents a pound, instead of selling it to their respective landlords for prices ranging around 15 cents. The landlord wanted to be middle man with 100 per cent profit.

The colored tenants organized a farmers' union, a labor union if you will, for the purpose of mutual support in getting the best price for their cotton and to raise funds to sue the landlords for their right to such prices, when necessary. It is pathetic to think that these colored tenants would have had to sue these planters in the planters' own courts, where planters would sit as judge and jurors, where even their own lawyers would be white men. And yet this feeble attack upon their debt-slave system made the landlords so nervous that they seized the first opportunity to accuse the Negroes of a general plot of treason and murder, and they shouted for troops ostensibly to put down "rebellion," but in reality to smash this union of Negro farm laborers.

If it had not led to so great a tragedy, it would now be amusing to review the evidence on which the landlords based their charge of a general conspiracy to "murder all whites." While the planters were in a state of nervous tension over this union movement, the colored organization was holding a public meeting in a church; and two white men passing by, proceeded to "shoot up" the church and the congregation. It may be that the white men intended merely to frighten the colored folk and discourage union meetings, but those in the church could not guess that secret and so fired back, killing one of the whites. This one homicide in self-defense convinced the landlords and Governor Brough that the colored farmers' union was organized to kill off the entire white population, and he immediately seized all the state troops he could lay hands on, borrowed all the Federal troops they would lend him at Camp Pike and hurried down to Phillips County to join the landlords and the great white mobs that poured in from the nearby counties of Tennessee and Mississippi to clear out the Negroes.

No War Profits For Debt Slaves

Why were these landlords so desperately opposed to war profits in cotton going to their tenants? Not simply because they themselves wanted to profit as middle men, but also because they knew that if those Negroes ever got hold of so much money, it would spell the doom of debt slavery. This slavery is based on debt, to avoid the technicalities involved in the 13th Amendment and if the tenants ever got free from debt the system would fall. It is a religious dogma in the South that you cannot keep the free (?) Negro working unless you keep him hopelessly in debt. It is indeed the only way to keep him working for such starvation wages. In 1914, cotton could hardly be sold for seven cents a pound, and it took only a small debt of a few hundred dollars or less to hold a colored man and his family bound to the landlord. But these share-croppers and renters and those who were attempting to buy a small farm from the landlord by paying installments on an endless mortgage, could have become independent in 1918–19 if they had been allowed to get the huge war price for their cotton.

Most of these debts and mortgages had been contracted and made when money was dear and scarce, and they might have been paid in full while money was cheap and plentiful. Millions and millions of other Americans reaped the benefits of this economic change, of this war stimulation of the market, but if Negro tenants in Arkansas had been permitted to get their share, it would have injured debt slavery. One Arkansan said to Walter F. White, of the National Association for the Advancement of Colored People, whom he mistook for a white person also: "Why, if we settled with these niggers accord' to law, they would soon own half of Arkansas!"

Just as unusual prosperity of the working class anywhere threatens the security of wage slavery, so would any real prosperity among the farm-tenants undermine the system of debt-bondage which obtains in the Mississippi Valley states of the South. Therefore, the landlord generally "furnishes rations" and supplies to the tenants at his own figure, endeavored to prevent "war prices" of farm products from increasing the prosperity of his tenants, by raising rations and supplies to a price-level which made war prices look tame. Mr. White found that the tenant had been charged $58.00 for cotton seed worth $4.20; $25.00 for a second-hand plow worth $16.00 when new; and $3.50 for a piece of rope that cost 30 cents.

Why Henry Lowry Was Burned

Is it any wonder that such a monstrous economic system should be the hotbed of the most terrible social crimes? The burning of Henry Lowry at Nodena, Ark., on January 26, 1921, was *occasioned* by the fact that Lowry had killed two white people in a fight, but the cause of the fight was Lowry's persistence in demanding a settlement for two years' work on the farms of a big planter. The debt-slave system could not survive regular and actual accounting on the part of the debt-master to the debt-bondsmen, even if such accounts were rendered only once in two years. And so Lowry was beaten when he first insisted upon a settlement for his work, and when he dared to come three weeks later and renew his insistence, he was murderously assaulted with a gun. Shooting back, he killed two from the group of his assailants. For this he was made the victim in what is perhaps the most barbarous burning of a human being in the history of man.

All the other big planters in Mississippi County, Ark., naturally sympathized with the burning of Lowry, and many of them helped to burn him. According to the sheriff, "every (white) man, woman and child in the county" wanted the Negro burned. This indicates some deeper and more primal feeling than mere aversion to color or even anger at homicide in self-defense. Lowry's act awakened in the landed class a feeling akin to horror at insurrection. It was like a threat of rebellion on the part of the submerged class to overthrow the system on which the power of the landlord rests.

Convict Slavery

The temptation of the large plantation owner to exploit the brawn of the defenseless Negro avails itself of another unfair advantage in which the state becomes a party to the wrong. It is the custom of farming out prisoners—state prisoners and even county and city prisoners. A Negro who has been jailed for some misdemeanor or fined for vagrancy, may be "sold" to some landlord who needs farm hands, for the price of the Negro's fine. The farmer pays the fine and is supposed to work it out of the Negro in a specified time. The colored man is still a prisoner of the state and is kept in chains and stockades, maybe on the landlord's private estate, under guards who may shoot him down if he attempts to escape, or whip his naked back if he does not work to suit them. Thus the state, under the technical right of law, does a slave business.

It can be readily understood why this system is so much more vicious than was the old slave system. In a regular slave system, the owner might have such selfish interest in the slave as any man may have in the preservation of his valuable property. But in the convict lease system of Georgia, it is to the landlord's advantage to put the least into the Negro and get the most out of him whom he owns for a limited time only.

This farming out of convicts also leads to great lynching debauches. In May of 1918, in Georgia, at least eleven colored people were killed in consequence of trouble between a Negro convict-slave named Johnson, and his temporary slaveholder, Smith, who, it appears, had worked the colored man for a longer time than the period for which he had bought him from the state. And when Johnson demanded pay for the considerable overtime, a quarrel ensued and the white man was killed. This white man could not afford to pay Johnson, for then the other overworked convicts might make similar demands.

Even in April, 1921, we read in the daily news that a white man in Georgia who was using such farmed-out Negro convict labor, delib-

erately murdered a dozen or so of the victims because he feared that
if they were ever released at all, they might "squeal" on his system
and his crimes. It is one of the greatest horrors of our history that
colored women have been thus farmed out to work and live in stockades
under the absolute control of brutal men. The multiple lynchings in
Brooks and Lowndes Counties, Georgia, which were caused by this
system in May, 1918, are among the most savage of such occurrences.
The unspeakable vivisection of Mary Turner, a colored woman whose
baby was to be born about four weeks later, was one in this carnival.

There is seldom an effort to avenge anything; there is seldom anything to avenge which the constituted authorities and the law could not
avenge. It is a passion, allied with the deepest instincts of greed, to
keep a submerged group submerged and to keep a downed group
down. It is an appeal to the extra legal, because no law—even the
most defective law of the most backward state—could keep a race
wholly and forever down. The deepest and ugliest human passions
are based on greed.

The Ban on Negro Prosperity

It is therefore intelligible that when race riots break out, especially
in the South, the prosperous and well-to-do colored men who own
business and property, the really most worth-while members of their
race, are the ones most likely to be forced to leave the community.
They may be compelled to abandon all their property post-haste to
get away with their lives, and not being allowed to return, they must
sell out at a great loss. Sometimes when these colored families are in
a position to offer some defiance to the mob, the officers of the law
will take a hand, because as "the law" they can dare more than the
mob. A "committee of prominent citizens," sometimes including the
mayor or the chief of police or the sheriff, will call on the colored man
and *warn* him to leave, either openly espousing the cause of the mob or
declaring their inability to restrain the mob. In a crisis, prosperous and
well-to-do Negroes are treated as "bad examples" to the others; and if
they are so *treated* in a crisis, they are so *regarded* all the time. When
a colored family is thus driven out or exterminated, prominent mention
is always made of their "prosperity" as an indirect emphasis on their
general offensiveness. Jim McIlherron, who was horribly burned to
death at Estill Springs, Tenn., in 1918, was said to be "too prosperous
for a nigger."

Rape in Relation to Negro Lynching

One of the most successful illusions in the history of human relations is the opinion that the extraordinary disposition to lynch Negroes in the United States is due to some extraordinary tendency of the men of that race to commit rape. We call this illusion *successful* because it is actually believed by many, if not by most white people. But facts and evidence point in the opposite direction—that Africans and their descendants are exceptionally uninclined to this particular violence. They are certainly far less addicted than the American white group. At the Anti-Lynching Conference of 1919 in New York City, James Weldon Johnson reported that more cases of rape committed by white men were found in the court records of one borough of that city for one year, than all the cases known to have been charged against colored men in the whole United States for several years together.

But the contrast is much greater than this, for the cases against the white men were matters of court records, while most of the cases charged against colored men were *alleged* merely and never exposed to the light of court. It is well known that any kind of unseemly or illegitimate or uncustomary relationship between a colored man and a white woman in the South is charged against the man as rape. White women missionaries in Africa say that the crime of rape is practically unknown there. One woman said emphatically that she never felt as safe in the streets of New York as alone among black men in Africa. And our lynching statistics show that of the 2,522 colored men lynched in 30 years, less than 19 per cent were even so much as *charged* with this offense. The sex motive is appealed to, because it is an appeal that all men understand, even the most uncultured and the most brainless; and by appeal to this universal passion it is sought to justify the repression and the economic exploitation of a whole people.

The appeal has been wonderfully successful. It is an old ruse of the oppressor. He must find a motive that will justify him in the moral sentiments of his people. In the Russia of the Romanoffs they said that the Jews cooked and ate Christian babies; so that the deep anguish over every lost or kidnapped child became a mighty wrath against the Hebrew. But it should be noted that in the United States the most awful slaughter and lynchings of colored persons in the last few years have not been occasioned by any matter of sex; the massacre at East St. Louis (Ill.) in 1917; the multiple lynchings of Brooks and Lowndes Counties (Ga.) in 1918; the Chicago riots in 1919; the Elaine (Ark.)

massacre in 1919; and the burning of Henry Lowry at Nodena (Ark.) in 1921.

The Washington *Post* and other papers tried to show that the Washington, D.C., riots were occasioned by "assaults on white women," but it has been clearly proven that most of the alleged assaults were pure propaganda, and that the real cause was more likely the new spirit, claims and self-respect of the colored ex-service men and others at the Capital, consequent upon their splendid participation in the World War.

But of course if lynching becomes the fixed habit of one group toward another, it can happen for no crime at all or even for the virtues of the victim, as is proved in five or six percent of the cases for thirty years past. Colored men have been lynched for protecting their own wives and daughters against the ravishment of white men, and in 1919, Governor [Hugh M.] Dorsey, of Georgia, and the *Atlanta Constitution* were aroused over the lynching of an aged and well-reputed colored man for trying to prevent two white men from assaulting two young colored girls.

Class Rule the Cause

But most of the lynching evil is traceable to economic wrong. There is a conviction that the Negro as a class is to be kept under in human society; that when a black man works and sweats, it is not primarily for his own good but for the good of the dominant race in America. This is class-feeling. It is the offspring of the slave system. If the Negro attempts to rise above this condition, he is sinning against God and must be repressed sternly and religiously. Indeed it is remarkable how all of those who wish to keep the Negro down, appeal to God and His foreordinations. Thus they justified slavery and would justify peonage and bastardy against a weaker race. The Negro, who by thrift and hard work rises above this preconceived status, becomes an offender like one who is seeking to violate the sanctions of a religion. An educated, well-to-do Negro is not entirely acceptable to such a civilization.

There must be a change in this attitude toward colored Americans before we can be free from lynching. And we must dispel the old illusion that lynching is a form of opposition to crime. Lynching is itself the greatest crime, a mother of crime. It breeds and fosters crime, even in the victim class.

What Remedy?

Government and law can do much but they cannot do everything as a remedy. The *idea* that one people can exist as legitimate prey for another people must be eradicated by better education and culture. The notion that God made the Negro for the benefit of anybody else must be wiped out. A higher social justice must be inculcated to counteract the persistent poison of the old slavery ideal. In a generation 3,000 colored men and women have been burned and otherwise lynched, not because Negroes are more criminal than other races, nor because Americans are more criminal than other people, but because black and white in America are victims of a medieval conception of the "classes" of man.

Then, how do we explain the lynching of a few white men every year? That is the force of habit, the power of an evil public consciousness. The lynching of the whites is consequential upon the lynching of the blacks. To cheapen the lives of any group of men, cheapens the lives of all men, even our own. This is the law of human psychology, of human nature. And it will not be repealed by our wishes nor will it be merciful to our blindness.

From the original pamphlet, given in full.

[b]

THE ERUPTION OF TULSA
by Walter F. White

A hysterical white girl related that a nineteen-year-old colored boy attempted to assault her in the public elevator of a public office building of a thriving town of 100,000 in open daylight. Without pausing to find whether or not the story was true, without bothering with the slight detail of investigating the character of the woman who made the outcry (as a matter of fact, she was of exceedingly doubtful reputation), a mob of 100-per-cent Americans set forth on a wild rampage that cost the lives of fifty white men; of between 150 and 200 colored men, women and children; the destruction by fire of $1,500,000 worth of property; the looting of many homes; and everlasting damage to the reputation of the city of Tulsa and the State of Oklahoma.

This, in brief, is the story of the eruption of Tulsa on the night of

May 31 and the morning of June 1. One could travel far and find few cities where the likelihood of trouble between the races was as little thought of as in Tulsa. Her reign of terror stands as a grim reminder of the grip mob violence has on the throat of America, and the ever-present possibility of devastating race conflicts where least expected.

Tulsa is a thriving, bustling, enormously wealthy town of between 90,000 and 100,000. In 1910 it was the home of 18,182 souls, a dead and hopeless outlook ahead. Then oil was discovered. The town grew amazingly. On December 29, 1920, it had bank deposits totaling $65,449,985.90; almost $1,000 per capita when compared with the Federal Census figures of 1920, which gave Tulsa 72,075. The town lies in the center of the oil region and many are the stories told of the making of fabulous fortunes by men who were operating on a shoe-string. Some of the stories rival those of the "forty-niners" in California. The town has a number of modern office buildings, many beautiful homes, miles of clean, well-paved streets, and aggressive and progressive business men who well exemplify Tulsa's motto of "The City with a Personality."

So much for the setting. What are the causes of the race riot that occurred in such a place?

First, the Negro in Oklahoma has shared in the sudden prosperity that has come to many of his white brothers, and there are some colored men there who are wealthy. This fact has caused a bitter resentment on the part of the lower order of whites, who feel that these colored men, members of an "inferior race," are exceedingly presumptuous in achieving greater economic prosperity than they who are members of a divinely ordered superior race. There are at least three colored persons in Oklahoma who are worth a million dollars each; J. W. Thompson of Clearview is worth $500,000; there are a number of men and women worth $100,000; and many whose possessions are valued at $25,000 and $50,000 each. This was particularly true of Tulsa, where there were two colored men worth $150,000 each; two worth $100,000; three $50,000; and four who were assessed at $25,000. In one case where a colored man owned and operated a printing plant with $25,000 worth of printing machinery in it, the leader of the mob that set fire to and destroyed the plant was a linotype operator employed for years by the colored owner at $48 per week. The white man was killed while attacking the plant. Oklahoma is largely populated by pioneers from other States. Some of the white pioneers are former residents of Mississippi, Georgia, Tennessee, Texas, and other States more typically southern than Oklahoma. These have brought with them their anti-Negro prejudices. Lethargic and unprogressive by nature, it sorely irks them to see Negroes making greater progress than they themselves are achieving.

One of the charges made against the colored men in Tulsa is that they were "radical." Questioning the whites more closely regarding the nature of this radicalism, I found it means that Negroes were uncompromisingly denouncing "Jim-Crow" cars, lynching, peonage; in short, were asking that the Federal constitutional guaranties of "life, liberty, and the pursuit of happiness" be given regardless of color. The Negroes of Tulsa and other Oklahoma cities are pioneers; men and women who have dared, men and women who have had the initiative and the courage to pull up stakes in other less-favored States and face hardship in a newer one for the sake of greater eventual progress. That type is ever less ready to submit to insult. Those of the whites who seek to maintain the old white group control naturally do not relish seeing Negroes emancipating themselves from the old system.

A third cause was the rotten political conditions in Tulsa. A vice ring was in control of the city, allowing open operation of houses of ill fame, of gambling joints, the illegal sale of whiskey, the robbing of banks and stores, with hardly a slight possibility of the arrest of the criminals, and even less of their conviction. For fourteen years Tulsa has been in the absolute control of this element. Most of the better element, and there is a large percentage of Tulsans who can properly be classed as such, are interested solely in making money and getting away. They have taken little or no interest in the election of city or county officials, leaving it to those whose interest it was to secure officials who would protect them in their vice operations. About two months ago the State legislature assigned two additional judges to Tulsa County to aid the present two in clearing the badly clogged dockets. These judges found more than six thousand cases awaiting trial. Thus in a county of approximately 100,000 population, six out of every one hundred citizens were under indictment for some sort of crime, with little likelihood of trial in any of them.

Last July a white man by the name of Roy Belton, accused of murdering a taxicab driver, was taken from the county jail and lynched. According to the statements of many prominent Tulsans, *local police officers directed traffic at the scene of the lynching,* trying to afford every person present an equal chance to view the event. Insurance companies refuse to give Tulsa merchants insurance on their stocks; the risk is too great. There have been so many automobile thefts that a number of companies have canceled all policies on cars in Tulsa. The net result of these conditions was that practically none of the citizens of the town, white or colored, had very much respect for the law.

So much for the general causes. What was the spark that set off the blaze? On Monday, May 30, a white girl by the name of Sarah Page, operating an elevator in the Drexel Building, stated that Dick Rowland, a nineteen-year-old colored boy, had attempted criminally to assault her. Her second story was that the boy had seized her arm as he entered the elevator. She screamed. He ran. It was found afterwards that the boy had stepped by accident on her foot. It seems never to have occurred to the citizens of Tulsa that any sane person attempting criminally to assault a woman would have picked any place in the world rather than an open elevator in a public building with scores of people within calling distance. The story of the alleged assault was published Tuesday afternoon by the Tulsa *Tribune,* one of the two local newspapers. At four o'clock Commissioner of Police J. M. Adkison reported to Sheriff McCullough that there was talk of lynching Rowland that night. Chief of Police John A. Gustafson, Captain Wilkerson of the Police Department, Edwin F. Barnett, managing editor of the Tulsa *Tribune* and numerous other citizens all stated that there was talk Tuesday of lynching the boy.

In the meantime the news of the threatened lynching reached the colored settlement where Tulsa's 15,000 colored citizens lived. Remembering how a white man had been lynched after being taken from the same jail where the colored boy was now confined, they feared that Rowland was in danger. A group of colored men telephoned the sheriff and proffered their services in protecting the jail from attack. The sheriff told them that they would be called upon if needed. About nine o'clock that night a crowd of white men gathered around the jail, numbering about 400 according to Sheriff McCullough. At 9:15 the report reached "Little Africa" that the mob had stormed the jail. A crowd of twenty-five armed Negroes set out immediately, but on reaching the jail found the report untrue. The sheriff talked with them, assured them that the boy would not be harmed, and urged them to return to their homes. They left, later returning, 75 strong. The sheriff persuaded them to leave. As they complied, a white man attempted to disarm one of the colored men. A shot was fired, and then—in the words of the sheriff—"all hell broke loose." There was a fusillade of shots from both sides and twelve men fell dead—two of them colored, ten white. The fighting continued until midnight when the colored men, greatly outnumbered, were forced back to their section of the town.

Around five o'clock Wednesday morning the mob, now numbering more than 10,000, made a mass attack on Little Africa. Machine-guns were brought into use; eight aeroplanes were employed to spy on the movements of the Negroes and according to some were used in bombing the colored section. All that was lacking to make the scene a replica of modern "Christian" warfare was poison gas. The colored men and women fought gamely in defense of their homes, but the odds were too great. According to the statements of onlookers, men in uniform, either home guards or ex-service men or both, carried cans of oil into Little Africa, and, after looting the homes, set fire to them. Many are the stories of horror told to me—not by colored people—but by white residents. One was that of an aged colored couple, saying their evening prayers before retiring in their little home on Greenwood Avenue. A mob broke into the house, shot both the old people in the backs of their heads, blowing their brains out and spattering them over the bed, pillaged the home, and then set fire to it.

Another was that of the death of Dr. A. C. Jackson, a colored physician. Dr. Jackson was worth $100,000; had been described by the Mayo brothers as "the most able Negro surgeon in America"; was respected by white and colored people alike, and was in every sense a good citizen. A mob attacked Dr. Jackson's home. He fought in defense of it, his wife and children and himself. An officer of the home guards who knew Dr. Jackson came up at that time and assured him that if he would surrender he would be protected. This Dr. Jackson did. The officer sent him under guard to Convention Hall, where colored people were being placed for protection. En route to the hall, disarmed, Dr. Jackson was shot and killed in cold blood. The officer who had assured Dr. Jackson of protection stated to me, "Dr. Jackson was an able, clean-cut man. He did only what any red-blooded man would have done under similar circumstances in defending his home. Dr. Jackson was murdered by white ruffians."

It is highly doubtful if the exact number of casualties will ever be known. The figures originally given in the press estimate the number at 100. The number buried by local undertakers and given out by city officials is ten white and twenty-one colored. For obvious reasons these officials wish to keep the number published as low as possible, but the figures obtained in Tulsa are far higher. Fifty whites and between 150 and 200 Negroes is much nearer the actual number of deaths. Ten whites were killed during the first hour of fighting on Tuesday night. Six white men drove into the colored section in a car on Wednesday morning and never came out. Thirteen whites were killed between 5:30 A.M. and 6:30 A.M. Wednesday. O. T. Johnson, commandant of the Tulsa Citadel of the Salvation Army, stated that on Wednesday and Thursday the Salvation Army fed thirty-seven Negroes employed as grave diggers and twenty on Friday and Saturday. During the first two days these men dug 120 graves in each of which a dead Negro was buried. No coffins were used. The bodies were dumped into the holes and covered over with dirt. Added to the number accounted for were numbers of others—men, women, and children—who were incinerated in the burning houses in the Negro settlement. One story was told me by an eye-witness of five colored men trapped in a burning house. Four burned to death. A fifth attempted to flee, was shot to death as he emerged from the burning structure, and his body was thrown back into the flames. There was an unconfirmed rumor afloat in Tulsa of two truck loads of dead Negroes being dumped into the Arkansas River, but that story could not be confirmed.

What is America going to do after such a horrible carnage—one that for sheer brutality and murderous anarchy cannot be surpassed by any of the crimes now being charged to the Bolsheviki in Russia? How much longer will America allow these pogroms to continue unchecked? There is a lesson in the Tulsa affair for every American who fatuously believes that Negroes will always be the meek and submissive creatures that circumstances have forced them to be during the past three hundred years. Dick Rowland was only an ordinary bootblack with no standing in the community. But when his life was threatened by a mob of whites, every one of the 15,000 Negroes of Tulsa, rich and poor, educated and illiterate, was willing to die to protect Dick Rowland. Perhaps America is waiting for a nationwide Tulsa to wake her. Who knows?

The Nation, June 29, 1921; CXII, 909–10.

82

THE 24TH INFANTRY PRISONERS

The effort to obtain the release of the men of the 24th Infantry, jailed as a result of the Houston outbreak of 1917, continued without letup until the last of them was released in 1938. One of the major efforts in the fall of 1921 is described in the following account.

On Wednesday, September 28, a delegation of 30 leading colored men and women, headed by James Weldon Johnson, Secretary of the N.A.A.C.P., had an audience with President Harding and presented a petition, signed by 50,000 persons, asking for the pardon of the 61 soldiers of the 24th Infantry who are confined in Leavenworth as a result of rioting in Houston, Texas, in August, 1917.

In the delegation with Mr. Johnson, or lending their names to it, were the Hon. Mr. Archibald Grimké, president of the Washington Branch; Major R. R. Moton, principal of Tuskegee Institute; R. S. Abbott, editor of the Chicago *Defender;* Emmett J. Scott, special assistant to the Secretary of War during the World War; Prof. George W. Cook and Kelly Miller, of Howard University; Robert R. Church, colored Republican leader in Tennessee; Dr. Charles E. Bentley, of Chicago; Miss Nannie H. Burroughs; Mrs. Mary B. Talbert, honorary president of the National Association of Colored Women's Clubs; Mrs. Mary Church Terrell; Mrs. Alice Dunbar Nelson, Harry H. Pace, John Hope, the Hon. Mr. J. C. Asbury, member Pennsylvania Legislature; Harry E. Davis, member of the Ohio Legislature; Drs. William H. Washington and W. W. Wolfe, of Newark, N.J.; the Rev. Mr. R. H. Singleton, of Atlanta, Ga.; James A. Cobb, counsel for the N.A.A.C.P., and John R. Hawkins, financial secretary of the A.M.E. Church.

Mr. Johnson in presenting the petition said:

"As Secretary of the National Association for the Advancement of Colored People, and spokesman for this delegation, composed of persons and representatives of bodies deeply concerned for America's good name, I have the honor to present a petition signed by 50,000 American citizens, white and black, praying that you exercise executive clemency, and pardon the 61 members of the 24th U. S. Infantry now in the Federal Prison at Leavenworth, Kansas, convicted on charges of rioting at Houston, Texas, in August, 1917.

"We are a delegation representing the 50,000 signers of this petition which we have the honor to lay before you, and we come not only as a representative of those who signed the petition, but we are spokesmen of the sentiments of the ten millions or more of Negro citizens of the United States.

"The petition, you will note, asks for their pardon on three grounds: first, the previous record for discipline, service and soldierly conduct of the 24th Infantry; second, the provocation of local animosity which manifested itself in insults, threats and acts of violence against colored soldiers; third, the heavy punishment meted out to members of the 24th Infantry of whom 19 were hanged, 13 of them summarily and without right of appeal to the Secretary of War or to the President, their Commander-in-Chief. This wholesale, unprecedented and almost clandestine execution shocked the entire country and appeared to the colored people to savor of vengeance rather than justice. Sixty-one members of the 24th Infantry are still in prison serving life and long time sentences.

"Contrary to all precedent, the provost guard of this colored regiment had been disarmed in a state and in a city where insult was the colored United States soldier's daily experience. Following a long series of humiliating and harassing incidents, one soldier was brutally beaten and a well beloved non-commissioned officer of the regiment was fired upon because they had intervened in the mistreatment of a colored woman by local policemen. The report spread among the regiment that their noncommissioned officer, Corporal Baltimore, had been killed. Whatever acts may have been committed by these men were not the result of any premeditated design. The men were goaded to sudden and frenzied action. This is borne out by the long record of orderly and soldierly conduct on the part of this regiment throughout its whole history up to that time.

"Moreover, although white citizens of Houston were involved in these riots and the regiment to which these men belonged was officered entirely by white men, none but Negroes, so far as we have been able to learn, have ever been prosecuted or punished. In consequence, the wholesale punishment meted out to these colored soldiers of their country bore the aspect of a visitation upon their color rather than upon their crime. The attention of colored people throughout the United States will be focussed upon the action which it may please you to take.

"In consideration, therefore, of the almost five years already served in prison by the 61 men and of the foregoing facts, and because of the long record for bravery, discipline and soldierly conduct of this particular regiment, and in the name of the steadfast loyalty of the American Negro in every crisis of the nation, we bespeak your attention to the petition which we beg herewith to present to you."

The President promised to review the testimony in the cases of the soldiers and to take the request made in this important petition under advisement. Mr. Johnson also made reference to the gratification of the colored people that the government through two channels was investigating the nefarious Ku Klux Klan.

The Crisis, November, 1921; XXIII, 21–22.

83

THE PAN-AFRICAN CONGRESS OF 1921

The Second Pan-African Congress met in London, Brussels, and Paris from August 28 to September 6, 1921. Present were 113 accredited delegates, with 39 from Africa, 35 from the United States, and the remainder from the West Indies and Europe. The press of the United States and, especially, Western Europe gave this meeting great attention; some papers accused it of having been at least inspired—if not financed—by the Bolsheviki. Representatives from this congress presented petitions urging greater autonomy for colonial peoples to the League of Nations.

Three documents illustrate features of this Second Congress: [a] is the first preparatory bulletin announcing the Congress; [b] is the text of the Manifesto of the Congress (written by Dr. Du Bois); [c] is the text of the "Statutes," or Constitution, of what it was hoped would become a permanent organized bureau of the movement—a hope not realized. These Statutes were printed in a four-page folder in a translation from the French, made by Rayford W. Logan, then in Paris and actively associated with the congress.

[a]

THE SECOND PAN-AFRICAN CONGRESS
Bulletin I, March 1921

The first Pan-African Congress met February 19, 20, 21, 1919, at the Grand Hotel, Paris, and was attended by 57 delegates representing 16 different countries. This Congress appointed a permanent committee and ordered a Second Pan-African Congress to meet in Paris in 1921.

In accordance with this decision the Second Pan-African Congress will meet during the first week of September, 1921. There will probably be three successive sessions—one in London, one in Brussels and one in Paris. All the details of time and place have naturally not yet been settled.

Membership in the Second Pan-African Congress will be restricted to regularly chosen delegates. Guests with all privileges, (except that of voting) will be welcome. Any organization of persons of Negro descent or of persons whose chief work is with and for the Negro races, will be entitled to send delegates according to the following tentative plan, which is subject to criticism and change in succeeding bulletins: organizations with a membership under 1000, one delegate; 1000 and under 5000, 2 delegates; 5000 and under 10,000, 3 delegates; 10,000 and under 50,000, 4 delegates; 50,000 and under 100,000, 5 delegates; 100,000 or more, seven or more delegates according to special agreement.

The expenses of each delegate will be borne by the organization which sends him or by the delegate himself. Each organization will be taxed a small sum for each delegate sent. This sum will be used to defray the general expenses of the meeting, and will probably be Ten Dollars per delegate.

The expenses of attendance from New York and return will be between $300 and $750 per delegate, depending upon the class of accommodation on the boat and in hotels, the length of stay, etc.

This bulletin is being sent to as many persons of prominence, and organizations as we can reach in the United States, the West Indies, South America, Africa and Europe.

It is requested that persons receiving it or reading it should write us immediately suggesting other persons to whom invitations might be sent and stating the likelihood of they themselves being able to attend and the organization which they would probably represent.

> Blaise Diagne, *President,*
> W. E. B. Du Bois, *Secretary,*
> 70 Fifth Avenue, New York, U.S.A.

INTERNATIONAL COMMITTEE

J. R. Archer, England
René Boisneuf, Guadeloupe
Gratien Candace, Guadeloupe
Blaise Diagne, France
W. E. B. Du Bois, U.S.A.
John Hope, U.S.A.
Mrs. I. G. Hunt, U.S.A.
Mrs. A. W. Hunton, U.S.A.
G. W. Jackson, France
W. H. Jernigan, U.S.A.
Anne Marie, France
R. C. Simmons, U.S.A.
      (To be enlarged)

[b]

TO THE WORLD
(Manifesto of the Second Pan-African Congress)

The absolute equality of races,—physical, political and social—is the founding stone of world peace and human advancement. No one denies great differences of gift, capacity and attainment among individuals of all races, but the voice of science, religion and practical politics is one in denying the God-appointed existence of super-races, or of races naturally and inevitably and eternally inferior.

That in the vast range of time, one group should in its industrial technique, or social organization, or spiritual vision, lag a few hundred years behind another, or forge fitfully ahead, or come to differ decidedly in thought, deed and ideal, is proof of the essential richness and variety of human nature, rather than proof of the co-existence of demi-gods and apes in human form. The doctrine of racial equality does not interfere with individual liberty, rather, it fulfils it. And of all the various criteria by which masses of men have in the past been prejudged and classified, that of the color of the skin and texture of the hair, is surely the most adventitious and idiotic.

It is the duty of the world to assist in every way the advance of the backward and suppressed groups of mankind. The rise of all men is a menace to no one and is the highest human ideal; it is not an altruistic benevolence, but the one road to world salvation.

For the purpose of raising such peoples to intelligence, self-knowledge and self-control, their intelligentsia of right ought to be recognized as the natural leaders of their groups.

The insidious and dishonorable propaganda, which, for selfish ends, so distorts and denies facts as to represent the advancement and development of certain races of men as impossible and undesirable, should be met with widespread dissemination of the truth. The experiment of making the Negro slave a free citizen in the United States is not a failure; the attempts at autonomous government in Haiti and Liberia are not proofs of the impossibility of self-government among black men; the experience of Spanish America does not prove that mulatto democracy will not eventually succeed there; the aspirations of Egypt and India are not successfully to be met by sneers at the capacity of darker races.

We who resent the attempt to treat civilized men as uncivilized, and who bring in our hearts grievance upon grievance against those who lynch the untried, disfranchise the intelligent, deny self-government to educated men, and insult the helpless, we complain; but not simply or primarily for ourselves—more especially for the millions of our fellows, blood of our blood, and flesh of our flesh, who have not even what we have—the power to complain against monstrous wrong, the power to see and to know the source of our oppression.

How far the future advance of mankind will depend upon the social contact and physical intermixture of the various strains of human blood is unknown, but the demand for the interpenetration of countries and intermingling of blood has come, in modern days, from the white race alone, and has been imposed upon brown and black folks mainly by brute force and fraud. On top of this, the resulting people of mixed race have had to endure innuendo, persecution, and insult, and the penetrated countries have been forced into semi-slavery.

If it be proven that absolute world segregation by group, color or historic affinity is best for the future, let the white race leave the dark world and the darker races will gladly leave the white. But the proposition is absurd. This is a world of men, of men whose likenesses far outweigh their differences; who mutually need each other in labor and thought and dream, but who can successfully have each other only on terms of equality, justice and mutual respect. They are the real and only peacemakers who work sincerely and peacefully to this end.

The beginning of wisdom in inter-racial contact is the establishment of political institutions among suppressed peoples. The habit of democracy must be made to encircle the earth. Despite the attempt to prove that its practice is the secret and divine gift of the few, no habit is more natural or more widely spread among primitive people, or more easily capable of development among masses. Local self-government with a minimum of help and oversight can be established tomorrow in Asia, in Africa, in America and in the Isles of the Sea. It will in many instances need general control and guidance, but it will fail only when that guidance seeks ignorantly and consciously its own selfish ends and not the people's liberty and good.

Surely in the 20th century of the Prince of Peace, in the millennium of Buddha and Mahmoud, and in the mightiest Age of Human Reason, there can be found in the civilized world enough of altruism, learning and benevolence to develop native institutions for the native's good, rather than continue to allow the majority of mankind to be brutalized and enslaved by ignorant and selfish agents of commercial institutions, whose one aim is profit and power for the few.

And this brings us to the crux of the matter: It is the shame of the world that today the relation between the main groups of mankind and their mutual estimate and respect is determined chiefly by the degree in which one can subject the other to its service, enslaving labor, making ignorance compulsory, uprooting ruthlessly religion and customs, and destroying government, so that the favored Few may luxuriate in the toil of the tortured Many. Science, Religion and Philanthropy have thus been made the slaves of world commerce and industry, and bodies, minds, souls of Fiji and Congo, are judged almost solely by the quotations on the Bourse.

The day of such world organization is past and whatever excuse be made for it in other ages, the 20th century must come to judge men as men and not as material and labor.

The great industrial problem which has hitherto been regarded as the domestic problem of culture lands, must be viewed far more broadly, if it is ever to reach just settlement. Labor and capital in England, France and America can never solve their problem as long as a similar and vastly greater problem of poverty and injustice marks the relations of the whiter and darker peoples. It is shameful, unreligious, unscientific and undemocratic that the estimate, which half the peoples of earth put on the other half, depends mainly on their ability to squeeze profit out of them.

If we are coming to recognize that the great modern problem is to correct maladjustment in the distribution of wealth, it must be remembered that the basic maladjustment is in the outrageously unjust distribution of world income between the dominant and suppressed peoples; in the rape of land and raw material, and monopoly of technique and culture. And in this crime white labor is *particeps criminis* with white capital. Unconsciously and consciously, carelessly and deliberately, the vast power of the white labor vote in modern democracies has been cajoled and flattered into imperialistic schemes to enslave and debauch black, brown and yellow labor, until with fatal retribution, they are themselves today bound and gagged and rendered impotent by the resulting monopoly of the world's raw material in the hands of a dominant, cruel and irresponsible few.

And, too, just as curiously, the educated and cultured of the world, the well-born and well-bred, and even the deeply pious and philanthropic, receive their training and comfort and luxury, the ministrations of delicate beauty and sensibility, on condition that they neither inquire into the real source of their income and the methods of distribution nor interfere with the legal props which rest on a pitiful human foundation of writhing white and yellow and brown and black bodies.

We claim no perfectness of our own nor do we seek to escape the blame which of right falls on the backward for failure to advance, but *noblesse oblige,* and we arraign civilization and more especially the colonial powers for deliberate transgressions of our just demands and their own better conscience.

England, with her Pax Britannica, her courts of justice, established commerce and a certain apparent recognition of native law and customs, has nevertheless systematically fostered ignorance among the natives, has enslaved them and is still enslaving some of them, has usually declined even to try to train black and brown men in real self-government, to recognize civilized black folks as civilized, or to grant to colored colonies those rights of self-government which it freely gives to white men.

Belgium is a nation which has but recently assumed responsibility for her colonies, and has taken some steps to lift them from the worst abuses of the autocratic regime; but she has not confirmed to the people the possession of their land and labor, and she shows no disposition to allow the natives any voice in their own government, or to provide for their political future. Her colonial policy is still mainly dominated by the banks and great corporations. But we are glad to learn that the present government is considering a liberal program of reform for the future.

Portugal and Spain have never drawn a legal caste line against persons of culture who happen to be of Negro descent. Portugal has a humane code for the natives and has begun their education in some regions. But, unfortunately, the industrial concessions of Portuguese Africa are almost wholly in the hands of foreigners whom Portugal cannot or will not control, and who are exploiting land and re-establishing the African slave trade.

The United States of America after brutally enslaving millions of black folks suddenly emancipated them and began their education; but it acted without system or forethought, throwing the freed men upon the world penniless and landless, educating them without thoroughness and system, and subjecting them the while to lynching, lawlessness, discrimination, insult and slander, such as human beings have seldom endured and survived. To save their own government, they enfranchised the Negro and then when danger passed, allowed hundreds of thousands of educated and civilized black folk to be lawlessly disfranchised and subjected to a caste system; and, at the same time, in 1776, 1812, 1861, 1897, and 1917, they asked and allowed thousands of black men to offer up their lives as a sacrifice to the country which despised and despises them.

France alone of the great colonial powers has sought to place her cultured black citizens on a plane of absolute legal and social equality with her white and given them representation in her highest legislature. In her colonies she has a widespread but still imperfect system of state education. This splendid beginning must be completed by widening the political basis of her native government, by restoring to the indigenes the ownership of the soil, by protecting native labor against the aggression of established capital, and by asking no man, black or white, to be a soldier unless the country gives him a voice in his own government.

The independence of Abyssinia, Liberia, Haiti and San Domingo, is absolutely necessary to any sustained belief of the black folk in the sincerity and honesty of the white. These nations have earned the right to be free, they deserve the recognition of the world; notwithstanding all their faults and mistakes, and the fact that they are behind the most advanced civilizations of the day, nevertheless they compare favorably with the past, and even more recent, history of most European nations, and it shames civilization that the treaty of London practically invited Italy to aggression in Abyssinia, and that free America has unjustly and cruelly seized Haiti, murdered and for a time enslaved her workmen, overthrown her free institutions by force, and has so far failed in return to give her a single bit of help, aid or sympathy.

What do those wish who see these evils of the color line and racial discrimination and who believe in the divine right of suppressed and backward peoples to learn and aspire and be free?

The Negro race through its thinking intelligentsia is demanding:

I—The recognition of civilized men as civilized despite their race or color

II—Local self government for backward groups, deliberately rising as experience and knowledge grow to complete self government under the limitations of a self governed world

III—Education in self knowledge, in scientific truth and in industrial technique, undivorced from the art of beauty

IV—Freedom in their own religion and social customs, and with the right to be different and non-conformist

V—Co-operation with the rest of the world in government, industry and art on the basis of Justice, Freedom and Peace

VI—The ancient common ownership of the land and its natural fruits and defence against the unrestrained greed of invested capital

VII—The establishment under the League of Nations of an international institution for the study of Negro problems

VIII—The establishment of an international section in the Labor Bureau of the League of Nations, charged with the protection of native labor.

The world must face two eventualities: either the complete assimilation of Africa with two or three of the great world states, with political, civil and social power and privileges absolutely equal for its black and white citizens, or the rise of a great black African state founded in Peace and Good Will, based on popular education, natural art and industry and freedom of trade; autonomous and sovereign in its internal policy, but from its beginning a part of a great society of peoples in which it takes its place with others as co-rulers of the world.

In some such words and thoughts as these we seek to express our will and ideal, and the end of our untiring effort. To our aid we call all men of the Earth who love Justice and Mercy. Out of the depths we have cried unto the deaf and dumb masters of the world. Out of the depths we cry to our own sleeping souls.

The answer is written in the stars.

[c]

THE PAN-AFRICAN ASSOCIATION
DECLARED THE 8 DECEMBER 1921
STATUTES

Seat

Sect. 1.—A Society is hereby formed of all such organized bodies and individuals as adhere to the following Statutes. This Society shall be Known as: The Pan-African Association.

Its Seat of government shall be in Paris.*

* 8, Avenue du Maine, Paris (15c).

Object

Sect. 2.—The Pan-African Association has for its object the study and realisation of all that can be instrumental in improving the conditions of the Black Race all over the world.

In order to attain to this end, the Association proposes to increase the economic, political, intellectual and moral capacities of the race.

Politically, it shall strive to call the attention of the competent authorities of the various Powers entrusted with destiny of the Race, to the need of maintaining friendly relations with it, and of allowing and granting to it the same rights as those accorded to their other citizens or subjects.

From the economic standpoint, it aims to increase the productive faculties of the Race through a sound organisation of its economic power, to teach the individuals of the Race the virtue of cooperation and association, and to lead them to concerted action in both the economic and the political struggle.

From the intellectual and moral standpoints, it being evident that the spiritual forces of a country influence its economic forces and form its most undoubted assets, the Association favors the spread of culture, the creation of an elite in large numbers and the development of leaders with high ideals.

Method

Sect. 3.—The Pan-African Association is an organ of research and action uniting without in the least impairing their autonomy Societies and persons belonging to, connected or associated with the Black Race, so as to unite their efforts and coordinate their labors within the limits set by these rules.

It collects information and receives propositions which it studies with the object of employing them to practical ends.

It works by common and united action in the common interest without interfering in the political affairs of any state.

To this end it makes investigations where needful, encourages the creation of local branches, promotes new organizations which tend to facilitate the progress of the Race and concludes such arrangements as may be favorable to the cause.

It appeals to public opinion and may seek the aid of the press and of all societies of a nature kindred to itself.

Finally it counts on that international fellowship and sympathy which prevails among all members of the Negro Race.

Relations with Responsible Authorities and the League of Nations

Sect. 4.—The Pan-African Association assumes the sole right of negotiating on its own behalf and that of its members with the various competent authorities and the League of Nations; the same applies to all grievances.

A Committee consisting of the President and two members shall be constituted for this purpose.

Members and Subscriptions

Sect. 5.—The national sections created in each country for the pursuit of the ends of the Pan-African Association as defined in these statutes form by right part of the Pan-African Association.

The Pan-African Association accepts for its members:

1. Any person of African origin.
2. Any association, union, or society of people of the colored race.
3. Any individual or Society taking an interest in the progress of the Race.

Individuals admitted into the Association must enjoy full civil rights.

Admission is decided by the Permanent Committee on which the duty particularly devolves of judging whether such associations, societies, and individuals whose candidacy is offered can efficiently co-operate to the result in view.

Such admissions as have been decided by the Committee shall be ratified by the next Congress. Societies adhering to the Pan-African Association pay a tax based upon the number of their members.

The admission of a member in the course of the fiscal year, which begins on the first of January, involves the payment of a full year's subscription.

Any member who shall not have by registered letter made known before the 31st. of December in each year his intention to resign his membership shall pay his membership dues for the following year.

Sect. 6.—The action of the Pan-African Association, as defined in the present statutes, is carried out by a Congress, an Executive Council and a Permanent Committee.

Biennial Congress

The Pan-African Association holds a Congress every two years.

This Congress consists of delegates from the Associations which shall have adhered to these statutes, of honorary members and of members of the Pan-African Association.

Delegates from the Associations shall alone have the right to vote.
Such Associations can be represented in the Congress only if they
are composed of at least 250 paying members.

Each Association is entitled to 2 delegates for a membership of
5,000 and to one additional delegate for each additional 5,000.

Permanent Committee

The Congress appoints one President, one vice-President, one Secretary, one Assistant Secretary and one Treasurer. These five members
form the Permanent Committee of the International Pan-African
Association.

Executive Council

The Congress appoints an Executive Council consisting of 15 titular and
15 substitute members, who shall assist the Permanent Committee.

The Permanent Committee and the Executive Council shall hold a
meeting in December or at any other time, should circumstances require
it, at the seat of the Association, or at any other place.

In the intervals between the General Meetings the Permanent Committee shall administrate for and represent the International Association under all circumstances.

Votes in the Congress

Sect. 7.—Only the delegates of the Association shall have the right to
vote.

All questions shall be decided by a majority vote of the delegates,
except questions pertaining exclusively to a certain country. These
questions, upon the request of the delegates of this country, may be
stricken off the Agenda.

The Congress shall begin work under the presidency of the then
existing Permanent Committee and from the first session after the reading of the report on the activities of the Association and of the financial
report, shall proceed to the election of the new Permanent Committee
and of the new Executive Council which shall be inducted into office
immediately after the end of this first session.

Debates

No question can be debated unless the Permanent Committee has been advised before the session.

No motion can be presented if it has not been communicated to the Permanent Committee before the session.

Budget

Sect. 8.—The annual receipts of the Pan-African Association shall be composed of:

1. Fees of individual members.
2. The tax collected from adhering association.
3. Grants made by national sections.

In view of the application of paragraph 1 of the present section, the individual members shall pay an annual fee of 25 francs in the value of the local money of the country of their residence.

Reserve Fund

Sect. 9.—The Reserve Fund shall be used for the requisition of such offices as are necessary for the realization of the end pursued by the Association.

General Disposition

Sect. 10.—The right of membership in the Association is forfeited by any member whose conduct is dishonorable, who does not observe the present statutes or the discipline of the Association, or who by any act, voluntarily or involuntarily brings reproach upon the Association or the end pursued.

Expulsion is pronounced by the Executive Council, the interested member is heard or duly summoned by a vote of a two-thirds majority of the members present, and the vote of the Council is submitted to the Congress at the next session for ratification.

Expulsion of a member involves forfeiture of all his rights in the

Association. The member concerned is advised by registered letter from the President.

Internal Administration

Sect. 11.—Rules regulating the internal administration of the Association shall be formulated by the Permanent Committee.

Modifications of Statutes

Sect. 12.—The present statutes cannot be modified except by a Congress.

Dissolution

Sect. 13.—The dissolution of the Association cannot be pronounced except by a Congress. The motion to dissolve must proceed from the Permanent Committee.

The dissolution of the Association having been voted by the Congress, the Permanent Committee shall take charge of the liquidation of the Association. Any existing funds shall be assigned to similar associations.

Documents [a] and [c] are in editor's possession; [b] was published in *The Crisis*, November, 1921; XXIII, 6–10.

84

ANALYSES AND PROPOSALS, 1922

With the war ended, the League of Nations functioning, the Bolsheviks not overthrown, "business as usual" in the United States (epitomized in Coollidge), the Klan flourishing and lynchings and pogroms recurring, the early 1920s saw a regrouping and rethinking and experimenting within the Afro-American community—from Pan-Africanism to Garveyism, from A. Philip Randolph's trade union efforts to the African Blood Brotherhood of Cyril Briggs, with much of the ferment eventuating in what became known as the Harlem Renaissance.

There follows a series of documents reflecting much of this thinking as expressed in 1922. Documents [a] and [b] illustrate the thinking of Dr. Carter

G. Woodson, the great pioneer in Afro-American history, and the work for one year of his Association for the Study of Negro Life and History (founded in 1915). Document [c] reflects the feelings of Jessie Fauset, a distinguished novelist and at this time Du Bois' assistant in editing *The Crisis*. Document [d] is from the Reverend F. J. Grimké and again his "meditations" seem to touch the heart of feelings. The final document in this group, [e], consists of two selections from a widely read book by George Edmund Haynes, the publication of which was sponsored by the Council of Women for Home Missions and the Missionary Education Movement of the United States and Canada.

[a]

SOME THINGS NEGROES NEED TO DO
by Carter G. Woodson

There are certain things the Negroes in this country must do if they hope to enjoy the blessings of real democracy, if it ever comes.

In the first place, we need to attain economic independence. You may talk about rights and all that sort of thing. The people who own this country will rule this country. They always have done so and they always will. The people who control the coal and iron, the banks, the stock markets, and all that sort of thing, those are the people who will dictate exactly what shall be done for every group in this land. More than that, liberty is to come to the Negro, not as a bequest, but as a conquest. When I speak of it as a conquest, I mean that the Negro must contribute something to the good of his race, something to the good of his country, and something to the honor and glory of God. Economic independence is the first step in that direction.

I was in Washington the other day and a man told me that the colored people were about to have a new bank there—"and they have two already," he said. I answered, "They should have had ten banks forty years ago." Two banks among a hundred thousand Negroes! We must learn to take these things more seriously.

I was speaking to a gentleman the other day about the organization of an insurance company, and he was telling of the wonderful things we have done in the way of insurance. After he had summarized the receipts of the various companies now organized among Negroes it was just a little modicum, so to speak, compared with the great achievements in insurance on the part of members of the white race. Here we are, rejoicing over these little things, and we have hardly begun to make a beginning.

Then we must have educational independence. If the Negro is not going to become an educational factor among his own people, then education is not the leverage to lift him, in the sense it has lifted other people; for a man is educated when he can do without a teacher, when he can and will develop and grow without the stimulus of instruction. So it must be with a race. If we are not going to reach that point some day in our lives when we shall be able to go out and establish schools and become persons well rounded in philosophy and science and history and what-not, and be able to help one another; if we are not going to prepare ourselves here, three generations from slavery, to do that work for ourselves, then we cannot say that education has done for our group what it has done for others.

Then the Negro needs to develop a press. Some of us never read a Negro newspaper—and some are not worth reading. A few, however, tell the story of the Negro in a cool, calm way. They tell of the strivings of the Negro in such a way as to be an inspiration to youth. Every Negro ought to read the publications of his own race.

I was impressed in California to find that, although there are only ten thousand Japanese in San Francisco, they have two daily papers —only ten thousand, but they have two daily papers of eight pages each. We have over ten million in the United States and we have not yet developed a real daily newspaper. We should not complain if the white papers do not tell our own story. We complain because they publish our crimes and tell of the evils that we do but do not say anything of our achievements in those lines that tend to stamp us as people of the world. We must learn to tell the story ourselves. It is our duty to develop a press.

We should also develop a literature. Negroes should read some things written by their own people that they may be inspired thereby. You will never be a George Washington or a Thomas Jefferson—you will never be a white man—but you will be a Negro, and we must realize that there are certain things in the Negro race worth developing. Those things may be worth as much to the world as the things of the white race when they are properly developed. We must cease trying to straighten our hair and bleach our faces, and be Negroes—and be good ones.

In this literature you will get the inspiration you need to be like Frederick Douglass, Booker Washington, S. Coleridge-Taylor, or Paul Laurence Dunbar. If you can contribute to the world what those men have you will have no reason to regret that you cannot be a George Washington or a Thomas Jefferson, because you will still be identified with some of the greatest men who have ever appeared in the history of the world.

The Negro must learn to preserve his own records. He must learn the value of tradition. I was speaking to a teacher the other day. I wanted to get some information as to his people. I asked him who his grandfather was. "I am not sure," he said, "what my grandfather's name was." It may be that some of you do not know your grandfathers. You have not thought they were worth while. Although they perhaps could not read and write, they contributed much to the making of the race. They made it possible for you to be where you are to-day. They bore the burden and heat of the day. Some of them achieved a great deal more than some of us could have achieved.

If you should go to Cincinnati and speak with some of the old citizens—those who lived there before the Civil War—they would tell you that the Negroes of Cincinnati achieved more prior to the Civil War than they have since. There was a man who had patented a cord-bed which became popular throughout the United States, just as the spring-bed is popular to-day. In the exploitation of that patent he built up a large business and employed scores of white men and Negroes. He was worth thousands of dollars.

There was a Negro who went from this State—a Negro from Richmond, Va., who had worked in a blacksmith shop. His master permitted him to sell the slack of the coal. He accumulated a large sum of money, about $15,000, and he went to his master and purchased himself. He then went North and settled finally in Cincinnati. He knew the coal business and entered that business there. The people thought they would run him out of business and they said, "We coal dealers will get together and lower the price of coal to such an extent that he will be ruined." This Negro was wise. He sent mulattoes around to fill all his orders at the white coal yard, so that his supply would be kept on hand. The white coal dealers exhausted their supply and there came a great freezing. No coal could get through up the river and the railroads had not been constructed. This Negro had all his coal on hand. Nobody else could get any, and he sold out at a handsome profit. He then had so much money to enlarge his business that they never thought of combining against him again. That was in 1869. That Negro was worth something like $60,000. There isn't a Negro in Cincinnati today worth $60,000.*

We have a wonderful history behind us. We of the *Journal of*

* The two men Woodson refers to were Henry Boyd and Robert Gordon; he gives details in "The Negroes of Cincinnati Prior to the Civil War," *Journal of Negro History,* January, 1916; I, 1–22, especially p. 21.

Negro History shall have going the rounds soon a lecture on the ante-bellum period, setting forth the stories of Negroes who did so much to inspire us. It reads like the history of people in an heroic age. We expect to send out from time to time books written for the express purpose of showing you that you have a history, a record, behind you. If you are unable to demonstrate to the world that you have this record, the world will say to you, "You are not worthy to enjoy the blessings of democracy or anything else." They will say to you, "Who are you, anyway? Your ancestors have never controlled empires or kingdoms and most of your race have contributed little or nothing to science and philosophy and mathematics." So far as you know, they have not; but if you will read the history of Africa, the history of your ancestors—people of whom you should feel proud—you will realize that they have a history that is worth while. They have traditions that have value of which you can boast and upon which you can base a claim for a right to a share in the blessings of democracy.

Let us, then, study this history, and study it with the understanding that we are not, after all, an inferior people, but simply a people who have been set back, a people whose progress has been impeded. We are going back to that beautiful history and it is going to inspire us to greater achievements. It is not going to be long before we can so sing the story to the outside world as to convince it of the value of our history and our traditions, and then we are going to be recognized as men.

Souther. Workman, January, 1922; LI, 33–36.

[b]

FROM THE REPORT OF THE DIRECTOR

With respect to the most difficult task of the Director, that of raising money, the work of the Association has been eminently successful. Encouraged by the appropriation of $25,000 from the Carnegie Corporation last year, the Director appealed to several boards for the same consideration. Last February one of these, the Laura Spelman Rockefeller Memorial, appropriated $25,000 to this work, payable in annual installments of $5,000 as in the case of that obtained from the Carnegie Corporation. It is to be regretted however, that smaller contributions, heretofore yielding most of the income of the Association prior to obtaining the two appropriations, have diminished in number and amount. Appealed to repeatedly, many of these persons give the heavy income tax as an excuse, while not a few make the mistake of thinking that the other funds received by the Association are sufficient to take care of the general expenses. During the fiscal year 1921–1922, thirty-seven persons, most of whom were Negroes, contributed $25.00 each, whereas during the previous fiscal year the number was larger.

The following report of the Secretary-Treasurer shows how these funds have been used:

FINANCIAL STATEMENT OF THE SECRETARY-TREASURER
THE ASSOCIATION FOR THE STUDY OF NEGRO LIFE AND HISTORY, INC.
WASHINGTON, D.C.

Washington, D.C., July 1, 1922

Gentlemen:

I hereby submit to you a statement of the amount of money received and expended by the Association for the Study of Negro Life and History, Incorporated, from July 1, 1921 to June 30, 1922, inclusive:

Receipts		Expenditures	
Subscriptions	$ 1,772.63	Printing and Stationery	$ 4,929.97
Memberships	241.00	Petty Cash	670.00
Contributions	9,113.75	Stenographic service	990.23
Advertising	195.45	Rent and Light	714.67
Rent and Light	180.14	Salaries	3,450.00
Books	1.70	Traveling Expenses	468.09
Refunds	50.42	Miscellaneous	286.46
Total receipts	$11,555.09	Total expenditures	$11,509.42
Balance on hand		Balance on hand	
July 1, 1921	43.09	June 30, 1922	88.76
	$11,598.18		$11,598.18

This report does not cover the $5,000 annually received for research into the Free Negro Prior to 1861 and Negro Reconstruction History. This fund was made available on the first of July, the beginning of the fiscal year, and has been apportioned so as to pay three investigators and a copyist employed to do this work.

Respectfully submitted,
(Signed) S. W. Rutherford
Secretary-Treasurer

The appropriation of $25,000 obtained from the Laura Spelman Rockefeller Memorial requires the employment of investigators to develop the studies of the Free Negro Prior to 1861 and of Negro Reconstruction History. The annual allowance of $5,000 is devoted altogether to this work, inasmuch as special instructions received from the Trustees of the Laura Spelman Rockefeller Memorial prohibit the use of this money for any other purpose. The Association has, therefore, employed Dr. George Francis Dow to read the eighteenth century colonial newspapers of New England, C. G. Woodson to make a study of the Free Negro Prior to 1861, A. A. Taylor to study the Social and Economic Conditions of the Negro during Reconstruction, and a clerk serving the investigators in the capacity of a copyist.

At present Mr. A. A. Taylor is spending only one-half of his time at this work, but after the first of next June he will have the opportunity to direct his attention altogether to this task. During this year it is expected that he will complete his studies of the Social and Economic Conditions in Virginia and South Carolina.

In the study of the Free Negro the Director has spent the year compiling a statistical report giving the names of free Negroes who were heads of families in the South in 1830 showing the number in each family and the number of slaves owned. Within a few months that part of the report dealing with Louisiana, South Carolina and North Carolina will be completed.

The Association is also directing attention to the work of training men for research in this field. The program agreed upon is to educate in the best graduate schools with libraries containing works bearing on Negro life and history at least three young men a year, supported by fellowships of $500 from the Association and such additional stipend as the schools themselves may grant for the support of the undertaking. One of these students will take up the study of Negro History, one will direct his attention to Anthropometric and Psychological Measurements of Negroes, and one to African Anthropology and Archaeology. In this undertaking the Director has not only the cooperation of Prof. Carl Russell Fish, of the University of Wisconsin, and Prof. William E. Dodd, of the University of Chicago, who with him constitute the Committee on Fellowships, but also the assistance of Professors Franz Boas and E. L. Thorndike of Columbia University and of Professor E. A. Hooton of Harvard University.

Closely connected with these plans, moreover, are certain other projects to preserve Negro folklore and the fragments of Negro music. In this effort the Association has the cooperation of Mrs. Elsie Clews Parsons, the moving spirit of the American Folklore Society. She is now desirous of making a more systematic effort to embody this part of the Negro civilization and she believes that the work can be more successfully done by cooperation with the Association. As soon as the

Director can obtain a special fund for this particular work, an investigator will be employed to undertake it.

The interest manifested in the study of Negro History in clubs and schools has been very encouraging. Most of the advanced institutions of learning of both North and South make use of *The Journal of Negro History* in teaching social sciences. The Director's two recent works, *The History of the Negro Church* and *The Negro in Our History* are being extensively used as textbooks in classes studying Sociology and History. The enthusiasm of some of these groups has developed to the extent that they now request authority to organize under the direction of the Association local bodies to be known as State Associations for the Study of Negro Life and History.

Respectfully submitted,
C. G. Woodson,
Director

From a four-page folder published by the Association; undated, but probably printed in 1923.

[c]

SOME NOTES ON COLOR
by Jessie Fauset

A distinguished novelist said to me not long ago: "I think you colored people make a great mistake in dragging the race problem into your books and novels. It isn't art."

"But good heavens," I told him, "it's life, it's colored life. Being colored is being a problem."

That attitude and the sort of attitude instanced by a journalist the other day who thought colored people ought to be willing to permit the term "nigger" because it carries with it so much picturesqueness defines pretty well, I think, our position in the eyes of the white world. Either we are inartistic or we are picturesque and always the inference is implied that we live objectively with one eye on the attitude of the white world as though it were the audience and we the players whose hope and design is to please.

Of course we do think about the white world, we have to. But not at all in the sense in which that white world thinks it. For the curious thing about white people is that they expect us to judge them by their statute-books and not by their actions. But we colored people have learned better, so much so that when we prepare for a journey, when we enter on a new undertaking, when we decide on where to go to school, if we want to shop, to move, to go to the theatre, to eat (outside of our own houses) we think quite consciously, "If we can pull it through without some white person interfering."

I have hesitated more than once about writing this article because my life has been spent in the localities which are considered favorable to colored people and in the class which least meets the grossest forms of prejudice. And yet—I do not say I would if I could—but I must say I cannot if I will forget the fact of color in almost everything I do or say in the sense in which I forget the shape of my face or the size of my hands and feet.

Being colored in America at any rate means: Facing the ordinary difficulties of life, getting education, work, in fine getting a living plus fighting every day against some inhibition of natural liberties.

Let me see if I can give you some idea. I am a colored woman, neither white nor black, neither pretty nor ugly, neither specially graceful nor at all deformed. I am fairly well educated, of fair manners and deportment. In brief, the average American done over in brown. In the morning I go to work by means of the subway, which is crowded. Presently somebody gets up. The man standing in front of the vacant place looks around meaning to point it out to a woman. I am the nearest one, "But oh," says his glance, "you're colored. I'm not expected to give it to you." And down he plumps. According to my reflexes that morning, I think to myself "hypocrite" or "pig." And make a conscious effort to shake the unpleasantness of it off, for I don't want my day spoiled.

At noon I go for lunch. But I always go to the same place because I am not sure of my reception in other places. If I go to another place I must fight it through. But usually I am hungry. I want food, not a lawsuit. And, too, how long am I to wait before I am sure of the slight? Shall I march up to the proprietor and say "Do you serve colored people?" or shall I sit and drum on the table for 15 or 20 minutes, feel my anger rising, prepare to explode only to have the attendant come at that moment and nonchalantly arrange the table? I eat but I go out still not knowing whether the delay was intentional or not. The white patron would be annoyed at the delay. I am, too, but ought I to be annoyed at something in addition to that? I can't tell. The uncertainty beclouds my afternoon.

An acquaintance—a white woman—phones me that she can accept a long-standing invitation of mine for luncheon. We meet and I suggest my old standbye. "Let's go somewhere else," she urges. "I don't like that place."

Ruefully but frankly I stammer, "Well you see—I'm not quite sure—that is—"

"Oh, yes," she rejoins in quick pity. "I forgot that. I'm so sorry."

But I hate to be pitied even so sincerely. I hate to have this position thrust upon me.

All of us are passionately interested in the education of our children, our younger brothers and sisters. And just as deliberately, as earnestly as white people discuss tuition, relative ability of professors, expenses, etc., so we in addition discuss the question of prejudice. "Of course he'll meet some. But would *they* let it interfere with his deserts? I don't know. I guess I'd better send him to A. instead of B. They don't cater as much to the South as at B."

I think the thing that irks us most is the teasing uncertainty of it all. Did the man at the box-office give us the seat behind the post on purpose? Is the shop-girl impudent or merely nervous? Had the position really been filled before we applied for it? What actuates the teacher who tells Alice—oh, so kindly—that the college preparatory course is really very difficult. Even remarkably clever pupils have been known to fail. Now if she were Alice—

Other things cut deeper, undermine the very roots of our belief in mankind. In school we sing "America," we learn the Declaration of Independence, we read and even memorize some of the passages in the Constitution. Chivalry, kindness, consideration are the ideals held up before us—

> Honor and faith and good intent,
> But it wasn't at all what the lady meant.

the lady in this case being the white world. The good things of life, the true, the beautiful, the just, these are not meant for us.

So much is this difference impressed on us, "this for you but that quite other thing for me," that finally we come to take all expressions of a white man's justice with a cynical disbelief, our standard of measure being a provident "How does he stand on the color question?"

I am constantly amazed as I grow older at the network of misunderstanding—to speak mildly—at the misrepresentation of things as they really are which is so persistently cast around us. Sometimes it is by implication, sometimes by open statement. Thus we grow up think-

ing that there are no colored heroes. The foreign student does hear of
Garibaldi, of Cromwell, of Napoleon, of Marco Bozzaris. But neither
he nor we hear of Crispus Attucks. There are no pictures of colored
fairies in the story-books or even of colored boys and girls. "Sweetness
and light" are of the white world.

Native Africans are "savages" owing their little knowledge of civilization to the kindly European traveler who is represented as half phi-
lanthropist, half savant. How much do we learn of indigenous African
art, culture, morals? We are told of the horrors of polygamy without a
word of the accompanying fact that prostitution in Africa was comparatively unknown—until the whites introduced it.

We are given the impression that we are the last in the scale of all
races, that even other dark peoples will have none of us. I shall never
forget how astonished I was to see in London at the second Pan-African
Congress the very real willingness of Hindu leaders to cast in their
lot with ours.

More serious still, we are constantly being confronted with a choice
between expediency and an intellectual dishonesty, intangible, indefinable and yet sometimes I think the greatest danger of all. If per-
sisted in it is bound to touch the very core of our racial naturalness.
And that is the tendency of the white world to judge us always at
our worst and our own realization of that fact. The result is a
stilted art and a lack of frank expression on our part. We find *The
Emperor Jones* wonderful, but why couldn't O'Neill have portrayed a
colored gentleman? We wish he had. "Batouala" [a prize-winning
novel by the African, Rene Maran] is a marvellous piece of artistry,
but we are half glad it is written in French so that the average white
American won't insist that here is the true African prototype.

Some one will say: "These are trifles." What have I to complain of
as compared with the condition of Negroes in South Africa, in
Georgia, in the Portuguese possessions? I do not have to fear lynching,
or burning, or dispossession.

No, only the reflex of those things. Perhaps it is mere nervousness,
perhaps it is something more justifiable. Often when I am sitting in a
crowded assembly I think, "I wish I had taken a seat near the door.
If there should be an accident, a fire, none of these men around here
would help me." *Place aux dames* was not meant for colored women.

I have not been dispossessed, but I have had to leave Philadelphia—
the city of my birth and preference, because I was educated to do high
school work and it was impossible for a colored woman to get that
kind of work in that town. So I, too, have assisted in the Negro

Exodus which the student of Sociology considers in class-room and seminary.

And so the puzzling, tangling, nerve-wracking consciousness of color envelops and swathes us. Some of us, it smothers.

The World Tomorrow (New York), March, 1922, pp. 76–77.

[d]

"THE NATION IS DOOMED—"
by F. J. Grimké

May 31, 1922

Yesterday afternoon in our city the Lincoln Monument was formally dedicated. The ceremonies were attended by the President, the Senate and the House of Representatives, the Judiciary, the Diplomatic Corps, and high officials of the Army and Navy. To these exercises a number of prominent colored people,—lawyers, doctors, ministers, professors, bankers, real estate dealers, were invited. And, although it was the dedication of the monument to the great Emancipator, and although the principal address was delivered by Dr. R. R. Moton, when these colored ladies and gentlemen representing the finest culture among the colored people arrived, they found that they were segregated, put off by themselves. Some, as soon as they discovered that they were Jim Crowed, rose and indignantly left before the exercises began, as a protest against being thus discriminated against, and as evidence of their self-respect. Others remained, be it said to their shame.

The whole thing was a studied and deliberate insult to the colored people; it was intended to show their contempt for the Negro race,— The best specimen, the most intelligent, the best to do, the most highly respectable, were invited, and then shoved aside, as if to say, The best of you are not fit even to sit beside white persons.

And this has taken place under a Republican Administration, and under the Administration of a man (President Harding) who when he was to be inaugurated was so awfully pious that he selected the noted passage in Micah 6:8, "He hath showed thee, O man, what is good; and what doth Jehovah require of thee, but to do justly, to love kindness, and to walk humbly with thy God," to be sworn in on, showing that he is nothing but a canting hypocrite. Any one would have supposed that with such lofty sentiments, as are contained in that verse, for his guide,—with the thought of justice and of kindness, and of God, who is no respecter of persons, before him, that he would have set himself like a flint against discriminating against any American citizen on account of his race or color. And, if those had been the real sentiments of his heart, as we know now that they were not, he would have: and what occurred yesterday would not have been possible under his administration.

The colored people all over the country ought to be made acquainted with the treatment that is being accorded to us by this man and should see to it that never again should he receive the vote of a single colored person. Dr. Moton, I am sorry to say, allowed a great opportunity like this to pass by without properly improving it. It was the time, of all others, to call the attention of the nation, in connection with the dedication of this monument to Lincoln, to the fact, that the millions which Lincoln's Emancipation Proclamation set free, were still suffering from evils, which, if possible, were even harder to bear than physical slavery,—the insults, the discriminations which grow out of a debasing race prejudice, and which as a race we meet everywhere. It was the time, and, if Dr. Moton had had the instinct of a true race leader, he would have seen it, and would have used the occasion to call upon the nation to arise and throw off this debasing race prejudice, and to set itself earnestly to work to bring about this greater emancipation,—the emancipation of itself from race hatred and the development of the nobler spirit of justice, of humanity, of brotherhood. The awful things that are going on in this nation,—the wanton disregard of law, the exhibitions of brutality, of savagery—all show, and show with a clearness which none can fail to see, that unless there comes to the Nation a greater emancipation than Lincoln's Proclamation effected, it is doomed, it is bound to go down. This Dr. Moton had the opportunity of saying, at the capital of the nation in the presence of the President of the U.S. and the Senate and the House of Representatives, the Judiciary, the Army and Navy, and in the presence of the representatives of the Press of the country; but he failed to say it, to make use of this great opportunity to do his race a service and to impress a most important lesson upon the Nation. I can't conceive of Frederick Douglass allowing an opportunity like that to pass without making the most of it. But, unfortunately, he is no longer among us. And even if he were here, it is doubtful, whether with his past record as the fearless and uncompromising defender of his race, he would have been invited to speak on that occasion. Our white friends are not anxious just now, when the whole tendency is to cover up, to condone, or palliate the unjust and brutal manner in which colored people are treated, to bring to the front men of the type of Frederick Douglass. They know that he cannot be muzzled, that his lips cannot be padlocked.

Woodson, ed., *Francis J. Grimké,* III, 104–6.

[e]

THE TREND OF THE RACES
by George Edmund Haynes

Public opinion of the Negro world [1] during the present generation has crystallized a belief among Negroes that the race has something to be proud of; that Negro culture and achievement are substantial and worth while. There is a growing Negro race pride. They have tried to make this known to the world. Probably another significant manifestation of this opinion is its interpretation of expressions from white newspapers. For example, the reports in white newspapers of racial clashes are regarded by Negroes as prepared to excuse the white participation and to blame the black ones.

There may be discerned three shades or schools of opinion among Negroes with reference to their relations to their white neighbors. In European terms they may be called "the left wing," "the center," and "the right wing." The left wing is of recent development. It has two divisions. There is first a socialist group which is just beginning, since the World War, to secure recruits among Negroes.[2] There is considerable evidence that it is being fostered by white socialists. The chief organ of propaganda is *The Messenger,* a monthly magazine published in New York and ably edited by two young, college-bred Negro men. They have utilized the dissatisfaction which Negroes have felt because of the evils of lynching, mob violence, disfranchisement, and other things about which the race has been restless. Probably from a fourth to a third of their magazine has been given to reports and

[1] The use of *Negro* as a race designation is to take both terms in their conventional, popular meaning. The terms are not used in an ethnological sense based upon complexions, hair forms, or head forms or upon cultural types, because all forms are found in the group and because in language, literature, art, religion, industry, and other items, Negroes have very largely appropriated and assimilated the culture around them. They have, however, developed a solidarity and race consciousness which make a group life and a Negro world of feeling, thought, and attitude.

[2] Since this was written, an attack upon the Negro Church and upon other Negro leaders, has seemed to weaken greatly the influence of their published organ and their speakers.

editorials on such ills. Their propaganda has served to draw strength from such publicity about ills more than from the intellectual or emotional interest any considerable number of Negroes have in the more general matters of social and economic reconstruction.

Furthermore, a new division has sprung up in the "left wing." It is popularly known as the "Garvey Movement," from the name of Marcus Garvey, its West Indian founder. This is an organized movement, claiming in 1921 from two to three millions of dues-paying members in divisions, branches, and chapters of a "Universal Negro Improvement Association and African Communities League." Such divisions are advertised in the United States, Canada, Central America, South America, the West Indies, and in Africa. The "Garveyites" have a newspaper, *The Negro World,* with substantial circulation in all these parts of the world. A traveler just returned from a year's extensive tour of Africa reported that Garvey and his propaganda were known to the natives wherever he went.

The two ideas this movement is propagating are "Africa for Africans" and the securing of recognition and fair treatment of black people everywhere by organizing the economic, political, intellectual, and moral force of Negroes the world over into a sort of provisional African empire to force recognition from the white world. Business enterprises, a "Black Star Line" to run steamships to regions populated by Negroes, and industrial corporations, are parts of the plans that have drawn during a four-year development about a million dollars from trusting Negroes, to be wasted by visionary and impractical ones.[3] The leaders raised in one year over $200,000 for a Liberian Construction Loan and launched in August, 1921, an additional "African Redemption Fund." The "Garvey Movement" may fail because of bad management, but the ideas which it is propagating have profoundly influenced the thinking and feeling of Negroes in all parts of the United States, to say nothing of other parts of the world.

The second school of Negro public opinion, "the center," is composed of those who might be designated as the spiritual descendants of the aggressive abolitionists of a previous generation. They are actively and hotly protesting and agitating against all forms of color discriminations and injustices. Their slogan for years has been to fight and continue to fight for citizenship rights and full democratic privileges of American life. This school comprises several more or less independent

[3] It is reported that Garvey and some of his associates have been indicted recently by a Federal Grand Jury in New York on charges of using the mails to defraud investors in the Black Star Line enterprise.

groups. The principal one is the National Association for the Advancement of Colored People. Its official organ, *The Crisis,* is the leading and best edited Negro magazine in the world. The Association undoubtedly has the hearty endorsement of the largest number of intelligent Negroes of America that know about it. Its 80,000 members are scattered throughout forty-six states. The Association includes in its membership many white people of prominence. Its annual conventions have presented upon their programs many of America's foremost speakers, publicists, and humanitarians. They have fostered the Pan-African Congress which is agitating for self-determination of African natives.

The third school, "the right wing," believes in full justice, manhood rights, and opportunities for Negroes, but still clings to methods of conciliation and the preaching of cooperation and turns a deaf ear to militant methods of agitation. There is apparently no organization representing this school, but many informal groups and Negro agencies have such an attitude. The ablest advocates of this school have centered at Tuskegee and Hampton Institutes. As a matter of fact, the objectives of "the center" and "the right wing" do not differ. The difference comes only in method and strategy. The two schools are seeking the same city of American opportunity, but each is undertaking to reach it by somewhat divergent roads.

Those of the third school are having difficulty, however, to hold their influence with the masses of Negroes, not only because of the pressure from the other two wings, but more especially because of the tardy response of the white world in removing some of the outstanding ills and allowing Negroes to share in those advantages which make the name of America a synonym for opportunity.

A close observation of opinion among all classes of Negroes discloses a slowly increasing spirit of resistance to injustice and mistreatment. The following are some concrete illustrations from statements of Negroes: In 1919, at the time of the Washington (D.C.) riot, a most reliable Negro, a man of the rank and file of workers, said: "During the riot I went home when through with my work and stayed there, but I prepared to protect my home. If a Negro had nothing but a fire poker when set upon, he should use it to protect his home. I believe all the men in my block felt the same way. I know they stayed 'round home more than usual." Another Negro, a porter, said: "We are tired of bein' picked on and bein' beat up. We have been through the War and given everything, even our lives, and now we are going to stop bein' beat up." A third, commenting on the Chicago riot, said: "These things (meaning riots) will keep on until we peaceable, law-abiding fellows will have nothing to do but to prepare to defend our lives and familes." A Negro teacher said, "The accumulated sentiment against injustice to colored people is such that they will not be abused any longer." [4] Even Negro graduate students are beginning academic analysis of these new currents of thought. . . .[5]

The development of racial self-respect. Another shortcoming has frequently been placed at the door of the Negro. Enemies and some friends complain that Negroes show a lack of belief in their own race; that apparently their highest ambition is to be white. These criticisms apparently have basis in fact. They overlook, however, three cardinal conditions which Negroes confront. First, Negroes are surrounded by white people, ten to one, whose idea of physical beauty is a white skin, sharp features, and straight hair. By a well known principle of group psychology the individuals in the minority tend to conform to the ideas and habits of the majority. David Livingstone, Dan Crawford, in his book, *Thinking Black,* and many other missionaries have testified that Africans regard Europeans as sickly, unnatural, and ugly, and in some tribes the devil is represented by white images. Black skin and native features are to them beautiful. Stanley said he blushed at his repulsion to the pale color of Europeans when he came out of the African forests where he had seen only dark skins and the "richer bronze color." [6] It is significant that with the growing color consciousness among American Negroes, they are even buying Negro dolls for their children and are setting up race ideas of beauty in America.

In the second place, whoever has observed and reflected upon facts open to everyday inspection knows that, on the one hand, to have a white skin or to be known as a white man or woman is to have an open door to whatever ability and effort can achieve. On the other hand, to be dark-skinned or to be known as a Negro, is to be looked down upon and to be discounted by those who hold the key to the American kingdom of achievement. This was a barrier to advancement of Negroes which even such superior achievements as those of Booker Washington did not remove. It does not take a Negro philosopher to conclude that the world of advantage in America is on the side of him who ap-

---

[4] "What Negroes Think of the Race Riots," George E. Haynes, *The Public,* August 9, 1919.
[5] Edward Franklin Frazier, a graduate of Howard University and a former teacher at Tuskegee Institute, submitted as his M.A. thesis at Clark University an unpublished manuscript on "New Currents of Thought Among the Colored People of America." It gives an appreciation of what is termed in this text the "left wing" of Negro opinion. He concludes that "America faces a new race that has awakened."
[6] Henry M. Stanley, *Through the Dark Continent,* II, 462–65.

proaches the appearance of the accepted white type. Negroes have had many of their attempts to set up their own standards blown to the winds by derision. The wonder is not that a few of them want to be white, but rather, that the race has so persistently clung to racial ideas and excellencies through so many generations.

Finally, much of the white man's notion of what the Negro aspires to be is either an imaginative white man's construction of what he conjectures he would strive for, were he a Negro, or it is what some Negro has let the white gather in response to leading questions. The human mind is habitually seeing the thoughts and feelings of others in terms of its own. The Negro is a master in responding to the white man according to the latter's wishes. The Negro already has a feeling for his own kind which draws the thousands together and holds them, just as similar feeling does Italians, Jews, Greeks, and others. What will give the Negro most impetus to a racial "self-sufficiency" is no longer to make a white skin the passport to free American opportunity, but to accord merit in a dark skin its just rewards.

What the Negro wants. There have been among the Negro people those men of intelligence and vision, if not always of learning, who have not bowed the knee to Baal, to the popular superstitions and whims, personal lust of wealth, or the conflicting currents of interracial confusion. Often they have gathered up and expressed the desires of their people for some of the substantial things of American life. These expressions of desire come from Negroes of all occupations and walks of life—workers in mines and factories, porters in stores and hotels, drivers, hackmen, and trucksters, farmers, tenants, and farm hands, tradesmen, business men, doctors, lawyers, teachers, housewives, and ministers.

First, Negroes have a yearning for education, a desire profound in its reach, appealing in its sacrifices, and tragic in its blighted opportunities. The story of their struggles to get an equitable share of public school funds, their willingness to contribute out of their poverty to their private educational institutions and to supplement what they get from the public treasury for school buildings and the lengthening of school terms is an epic awaiting its Homer. They feel keenly when blamed for not having what they have never had a chance to secure. Day-schools, night-schools, vacation schools, summer schools, and their limited colleges are always overcrowded. There is a perennial cry, "To know, to know: to do, to do: to achieve, to achieve."

Second, Negroes have demonstrated, especially when changes like the World War have pushed ajar the doors of equal opportunity to work at just wages and under fair conditions, that they desire a chance to get work and to hold it upon the same terms as other workers. They ask to be freed from the system of debt peonage in its differing forms, both that by which the courts are accustomed to farm out prisoners to private employers who pay their fines, and that by which workers cannot leave one plantation for another so long as any debt remains unpaid. They ask for an armistice in the tacit arrangement of lower wages for the same work, restriction to advancement in occupation, etc., by means, of which they are denied the legitimate fruit which other men are given for their labor.

Third, they want a chance to play, too, when the day's work is done; to play unmolested by law officers seeking by "framed up" gaming bouts to fatten upon fees and fines, "arrestin' fifty fer what one of us done." They want play places where, in recreation and amusement, they and their children may stretch their legs as well as their spirits in wholesome mirth and music. Like other workers they want sufficient wages, reasonable hours and a standard of living which will leave mind and body in vigor. They want good houses in which to live, good roads, well-paved streets, sanitation, fire and police protection, and other facilities which every modern neighborhood now considers necessary to wholesome living.

Fourth, another Negro want has probably been well expressed by an unlettered Southern Negro farmer. Speaking before a large audience of Negroes who were in conference with some of their representative white neighbors, he said, in answer to a question from a prominent white business man who was the presiding officer: "And, sir, we wants to help say who governs us." The officer replied that the liberal-minded white men of his state proposed that their desire should be satisfied. In an open letter to the Constitutional Convention of Louisiana in 1898, Booker T. Washington said: "Any law controlling the ballot, that is not absolutely just and fair to both races, will work more permanent injury to the whites than to the blacks. The Negro does not object to an education or property test, but let the law be so clear that no one clothed with state authority will be tempted to perjure and degrade himself by putting one interpretation upon it for the white man and another for the black man."

Fifth, through painful years of experience Negroes have come to feel as one man that they want to be more secure in their persons and their property and be free from the discriminations and restrictions that seem to them so unnecessary and to have no foundation in right or reason. Burnings and lynchings of innocent persons leave the average Negro with an uneasy feeling that a mob may perchance take him during any excitement. Experience has taught many that in a legal controversy with a white man he and his property are at great disadvantage.

Sixth, Negroes are beginning to ask for the removal of the habitual thought and action which regards and treats them as something less than men and women. They do not phrase it in just those words, but their actions speak louder than words. Experience with and observation of thousands of domestic workers, unskilled and semiskilled laborers in employment placement work has heightened the author's estimation of these people's belief in their own personality: their belief that they are ends in themselves and, along with other people, should have a chance to eat, dress, and live and enjoy some of the happiness which they work to furnish to others. In the upper grades of intelligence these feelings and attitudes express themselves in demands for schools, libraries, newspapers, art, music, and many other means of self-development.

Finally, the Negro wishes to be at peace with all men. He is a man of peace. He has learned war only when taught or when forced to defend himself. He sooner submits to oppressive force than he inflicts it. And he asks, as a citizen, to be left free to laugh and to sing, to play and to pray, to work and to talk, to love and to live with other Americans.

George E. Haynes, *The Trend of the Races* (New York, 1922; reprinted by Mneniosyne Pub. Co., Miami, 1969), pp. 13–17, 91–96.

85

ON MARCUS GARVEY

Several earlier documents have referred to Marcus Garvey—and others will deal with him and his movement. Two that follow present [a] an account of him by Claude McKay, a fellow West Indian and [b] a symposium on his movement published in Randolph's *Messenger,* which strongly opposed Garveyism.

[a]

GARVEY AS A NEGRO MOSES
by Claude McKay

Garveyism is a well-worn word in Negro New York.

And it is known among all the Negroes of America, all throughout the world, wherever there are race-conscious Negro groups. But while Garvey is a sort of magic name to the ignorant black masses, the Negro intelligentsia thinks that by his spectacular antics—words big with bombast, colorful robes, Anglo-Saxon titles of nobility (Sir William Ferris, K.C.O.N., for instance, his editor and Lady Henrietta Vinton Davis, his international organizer), his steam-roller-like mass meetings and parades and lamentable business ventures—Garvey has muddied the waters of the Negro movement for freedom and put the race back for many years. But the followers of Marcus Garvey, who are legion and noisy as a tambourine yard party, give him the crown of Negro leadership. Garvey, they assert, with his Universal Negro Improvement Association and the Black Star Line, has given the Negro problem a universal advertisement and made it as popular as Negro minstrelsy. Where men like Booker T. Washington, Dr. Du Bois of the National Association for the Advancement of Colored People, and William Monroe Trotter of the Equal Rights League had but little success, Garvey succeeded in bringing the Associated Press to his knees every time he bellowed. And his words were trumpeted round the degenerate pale-face world trembling with fear of the new Negro.

To those who know Jamaica, the homeland of Marcus Garvey, Garveyism inevitably suggests the name of Bedwardism. Bedwardism is the name of a religious sect there, purely native in its emotional and external features and patterned after the Baptists. It is the true religion of thousands of natives, calling themselves Bedwardites. It was founded by an illiterate black giant named Bedward about 25 years ago, who claimed medicinal and healing properties for a sandy little hole beside a quiet river that flowed calmly to the sea through the eastern part of Jamaica. In the beginning prophet Bedward was a stock newspaper joke; but when thousands began flocking to hear the gigantic white-robed servant of God at his quarterly baptism, and the police were hard put to handle the crowds, the British Government in Jamaica became irritated. Bedward was warned and threatened and even persecuted a little, but his thousands of followers stood more firmly by him and made him rich with great presents of food, clothing, jewelry and money. So Bedward waxed fat in body and spirit. He began a great building of stone to the God of Bedwardism which he declared could not be finished until the Second Coming of Christ. And in the plenitude of his powers he sat in his large yard under an orange tree, his wife and grown children, all good Bedwardites, around him, and gave out words of wisdom on his religion and upon topical questions to the pilgrims who went daily to worship and to obtain a bottle of water from the holy hole. The most recent news of the prophet was his arrest by the government for causing hundreds of his followers to sell all their possessions and come together at his home in August Town to witness his annunciation; for on a certain day at noon, he had said, he would ascend into heaven upon a crescent moon. The devout sold and gave away all their property and flocked to August Town, and the hour of the certain day came and passed with Bedward waiting in his robes, and days followed and weeks after. Then his flock of sheep, now turned into a hungry, destitute, despairing mob, howled like hyenas and fought each other until the Government interfered.

It may be that the notorious career of Bedward, the prophet, worked unconsciously upon Marcus Garvey's mind and made him work out his plans along similar spectacular lines. But between the mentality of both men there is no comparison. While Bedward was a huge inflated bag of bombast loaded with ignorance and superstition, Garvey's is beyond doubt a very energetic and quick-witted mind, barb-wired by the imperial traditions of nineteenth-century England. His spirit is revolutionary, but his intellect does not understand the significance of modern revolutionary developments. Maybe he chose not to understand, he may have realized that a resolute facing of facts would make puerile his beautiful schemes for the redemption of the continent of Africa.

It is rather strange that Garvey's political ideas should be so curiously bourgeois-obsolete and fantastically utopian. For he is not of the school of Negro leader that has existed solely on the pecuniary crumbs of Republican politics and democratic philanthropy, and who is absolutely incapable of understanding the Negro-proletarian point of view and the philosophy of the working class movement. On the contrary, Garvey's background is very industrial, for in the West Indies the Negro problem is peculiarly economic, and prejudice is, English-wise, more of class than of race. The flame of revolt must have stirred in Garvey in his early youth when he found the doors to higher education barred against him through economic pressure. For when he became a printer by trade in Kingston he was active in organizing the compositors, and he was the leader of the printers' strike there, 10 years ago, during which time he brought out a special propaganda sheet for the strikers. The strike failed and Garvey went to Europe, returning to Jamaica after a few months' stay abroad, to start his Universal Negro Society. He failed at this in Jamaica, where a tropical laziness settles like a warm fog over the island. Coming to New York in 1916, he struck the black belt like a cyclone, and there lay the foundation of the Universal Negro Improvement Association and the Black Star Line.

At that time the World War had opened up a new field for colored workers. There was less race discrimination in the ranks of labor and the factory gates swung open to the Negro worker. There was plenty of money to spare. Garvey began his "Back to Africa" propaganda in the streets of Harlem, and in a few months he had made his organ *The Negro World,* the best edited colored weekly in New York. The launching of the Black Star Line project was the grand event of the movement among all Garveyites, and it had an electrifying effect upon all the Negro peoples of the world—even the black intelligentsia. It landed on the front page of the white press and made good copy for the liberal weeklies and the incorruptible monthlies. *The Negro World* circulated 60,000 copies, and a perusal of its correspondence page showed letters breathing an intense love for Africa from the farthest ends of the world. The movement for African redemption had taken definite form in the minds of Western Negroes, and the respectable Negro uplift organizations were shaken up to realize the significance of "Back to Africa." The money for shares of the Black Star Line poured in in hundreds and thousands of dollars, some brilliant Negro leaders were drawn to the organization, and the little Negro press barked at Garvey from every part of the country, questioning his integrity and impugning his motives. And Garvey, Hearst-like, thundered back his threats at the critics through *The Negro World* and was soon involved in a net of law suits.

The most puzzling thing about the "Back to Africa" propaganda is the leader's repudiation of all the fundamentals of the black worker's economic struggle. No intelligent Negro dare deny the almost miraculous effect and the world-wide breadth and sweep of Garvey's propaganda methods. But all those who think broadly on social conditions are amazed at Garvey's ignorance and his intolerance of modern social ideas. To him Queen Victoria and Lincoln are the greatest figures in history because they both freed the slaves, and the Negro race will never reach the heights of greatness until it has produced such types. He talks of Africa as if it were a little island in the Caribbean Sea. Ignoring all geographical and political divisions, he gives his followers the idea that that vast continent of diverse tribes consists of a large homogeneous nation of natives struggling for freedom and waiting for the Western Negroes to come and help them drive out the European exploiters. He has never urged Negroes to organize in industrial unions.

He only exhorted them to get money, buy shares in his African steamship line, and join his Universal Association. And thousands of American and West Indian Negroes responded with eagerness.

He denounced the Socialists and Bolshevists for plotting to demoralize the Negro workers and bring them under the control of white labor. And in the same breath he attacked the National Association for the Advancement of Colored People, and its founder, Dr. Du Bois, for including white leaders and members. In the face of his very capable mulatto and octoroon colleagues, he advocated an all-sable nation of Negroes to be governed strictly after the English plan with Marcus Garvey as supreme head.

He organized a Negro Legion and a Negro Red Cross in the heart of Harlem. The Black Star line consisted of two unseaworthy boats and the Negro Factories Corporation was mainly existent on paper. But it seems that Garvey's sole satisfaction in his business venture was the presenting of grandiose visions to his crowd.

Garvey's arrest by the Federal authorities after five years of stupendous vaudeville is a fitting climax. He should feel now an ultimate satisfaction in the fact that he was a universal advertising manager. He was the biggest popularizer of the Negro problem, especially among Negroes, since *Uncle Tom's Cabin*. He attained the sublime. During the last days he waxed more falsely eloquent in his tall talks on the Negro Conquest of Africa, and when the clansmen yelled their approval and clamored for more, in his gorgeous robes, he lifted his hands to the low ceiling in a weird pose, his huge ugly bulk cowing the crowd, and told how the mysteries of African magic had been revealed to him, and how he would use them to put the white man to confusion and drive him out of Africa.

Claude McKay, "Garvey as a Negro Moses," *Liberator*, April, 1922; V, 8–9.

[b]

A SYMPOSIUM ON GARVEY
by Negro Leaders

In late September Chandler Owen, Executive Secretary of The Friends of Negro Freedom, sent a questionnaire to twenty-five prominent Negroes of America to see what they thought of Marcus Garvey. Accompanying the questionnaire was a personal letter and a set of facts, which, it was hoped, would assist those who were not so well posted on Garvey's antics, in framing their reply.

The letter sent was as follows:

Dear Sir:
No doubt the sending of the human hand by the Ku Klux Klan to A. Philip Randolph, leader in the fight against Marcus Garvey, directing him to cease his attacks in his *Messenger* Magazine and immediately become a paid-up member in the Garvey machine, has brought forcibly to your attention the fight the Friends of Negro Freedom has been waging against the Garvey menace since last July. Associated in this campaign are Chandler Owen, co-editor of *The Messenger,* Robert W. Bagnall, director of branches of the National Association for the Advancement of Colored People, and Prof. William Pickens, field secretary of the N.A.A.C.P.

The Friends are fighting Garvey because of his non-resistant policy toward the Ku Klux Klan, and because of his flagrant squandering of funds in his Black Star Line and other fantastic schemes.

Garvey denies that he is allied with the Klan, but does not condemn it. He says let it alone. He says do not blame white people for mistreating us. He says this is "a white man's country" and the Negro has nothing and should get out—"and go to Africa."

We believe this policy to be suicidal. We believe the future of the American Negro is here in America. We believe it only takes time to work out this future. We want to know what YOU think. Kindly use the enclosed blank for that purpose.

Very truly yours,
(Signed) Chandler Owen, Ex. Sec.
The Friends of Negro Freedom

P.S.—This letter is being sent to other prominent Negroes for the purpose of a symposium to be published in *The Messenger* Magazine.

* * *

The accompanying set of facts was as follows:
1. Last June Marcus Garvey held a secret conference with Acting Imperial Wizard Edward Young Clarke of the Ku Klux Klan at Atlanta,

Ga. He has never made public that interview although he promised to do so.

2. Shortly after the interview Garvey made a speech at New Orleans in which was this statement:

"This is a white man's country. He found it, he conquered it, and we can't blame him if he wants to keep it. I am not vexed with the white man of the South for Jim-Crowing me, because I am black.

"I never built any street cars or railroads. The white man built them for his own convenience. And if I don't want to ride where he's willing to let me ride, then I'd better walk."

3. On September 5 A. Philip Randolph received through the mails a human hand, accompanied by a letter signed by the Klan saying he had better be a paid up member in the Garvey organization ("your nigger improvement association") "within a week." A second letter came September 12, postmarked New Orleans, from which the first was postmarked.

*   *   *

The questionnaire was as follows:

1. Do you think Garvey's policy correct for the American Negro?

2. Do you think Garvey should be deported as an alien creating unnecessary mischief?

3. Remarks:

*   *   *

Of the twenty-five persons to whom the letter was sent, fourteen replied. The replies are as follows:

HARRY H. PACE
President, The Pace Phonograph Corporation
New York City

Replying to your inquiry concerning Marcus Garvey I beg to advise that I do not think the Garvey policy is the correct one for either the American Negro or any other kind of Negro. Mr. Garvey took advantage of the unrest among Negroes immediately following the world war when they like every other people were clamoring for new ideas and new things. He had enough semblance of substance in his doctrine to make them appeal to the unthinking, but everybody knows how foolish it is to think of any back to Africa movement. The whole scheme of an African Empire is absurd and is merely a romantic ideal with which to separate the fools from their money. Garvey has linked idealism with commercialism and has failed in both things. He had a fine chance to be a huge commercial success had he continued his business as a business proposition instead of as a financial scheme.

With the organization and with the start that he had he ought to have been a tremendous factor for good in the race.

It seems to me that it ought to be suggested very forcibly to him that he adjourn to Africa himself, taking with him the faithful who want to go and it would be much better for both him and those of us who desire to remain behind. He has already done untold damages to the race and has destroyed friends for us whom we never thought could be reached.

* * *

CARTER G. WOODSON
Editor, *The Journal of Negro History*
Washington, D.C.

Replying to your communication of September 21, I beg leave to say that I had given such little attention to the work of Marcus Garvey that I am not in a position to make an estimate of his career.

* * *

CARL MURPHY
Editor, *The Afro-American*
Baltimore, Md.

To question No. 1: No.

To question No. 2: No.

To Remarks: I think the authorities of New York should see to it that Mr. Garvey's stock schemes are kept within bounds of the law.

* * *

O. A. FULLER
Dean, Bishop College
Marshall, Texas

To question No. 1: It is absolutely incorrect, and too wide of the mark to be called really a policy, if what I have seen in print is the thing he is advocating.

To question No. 2: I really do think that he is an undesirable citizen, if he can be called a citizen, and if not a citizen he should be handled for disturbing what may be termed peaceful relations that we are striving to establish between the races.

To Remarks: I have answered the above questions in the light of the information brought me through your recent letter. I have been too busy during the summer months to read anything about Mr. Garvey. I have read a few unfavorable comments in *The Richmond Planet.* I have not the information at hand that I desire. But taking facts as I have been able to see and get hold of them I am of the opinion that Marcus Garvey is a dangerous character. I think the American people can and will be able to settle all of their differences without any interference from abroad, such as Marcus Garvey is advocating.

* * *

W. E. B. Du Bois
Editor, *The Crisis*
New York City

I have published from time to time my opinion of Mr. Garvey in *The Crisis* and shall add to that in the future.

* * *

R. R. Church
Politician, Real Estate
Memphis, Tenn.

In reply to your questions of September 27 I beg to advise that my answer is "no" to both of them.

* * *

Archibald H. Grimké
President, District of Columbia Branch, N.A.A.C.P.
Washington, D.C.

To question No. 1: I do not. It is colossal in its folly.

To question No. 2: I think not. The State and Federal laws ought to be sufficient to take care of him without resort to deportation.

* * *

Robert S. Abbott
Editor, *The Chicago Defender*
Chicago, Ill.

Mr. Abbott desires to acknowledge receipt of your favor of September 20th.

You will note from news articles carried in the columns of *The Defender,* that we have kept pace with most of the information contained in your letter.

I think Mr. Abbott believes that Mr. Garvey's policy is not correct for the American Negro, and I am sure that he feels that any individual who desires to assume a position of leadership for American Negroes, ought to show his sincerity by becoming a citizen of these United States. The question of deportation, is one which I do not believe he cares to give an expression on.

The Robert S. Abbott Pub. Co.
(Signed) A. L. Jackson, Asst. to Pres.

* * *

J. B. Bass
Editor, *The California Eagle*
Los Angeles, Cal.

To question No. 1: I should say not.

To question No. 2: Yes!

To Remarks: I must heartily approve of the gallant fight which you are making against the pernicious propaganda of Garvey. The straw that broke the camel's back was his assimilation of the Ku Klux Klan. He has become a menace to the future progress of the Negro race.

* * *

EMMETT J. SCOTT
Secretary-Treasurer, Howard University
Washington, D.C.

I hold the definite and positive opinion that a too intensive *intra-racial* struggle is most destructive. It opens wider the opportunity for the *inter-racial* struggle which we all agree is the greatest menace from which we colored Americans suffer. Naturally our race must be and is divided into several schools, or groups of thought, each urging a policy which it believes strikes at a common wrong. What we need therefore is a more charitable understanding within and among our race groups. It is just possible and highly probable that there is much right and much wrong in all of us, which if treated with the alchemy of *intra-racial* tolerance and mutual respect will yield a product most serviceable to the race as a whole.

The following are my thoughts with reference to the questions submitted by you:

1. In re Marcus Garvey's policy for the American Negro: I do not for one moment believe that any benefit is to come to Colored Americans in the matter of seriously considering the Garvey suggestion of undertaking to set up a government on African soil. The international questions involved are too great and require no statement from me. There is not a foot of African soil not already claimed by European or other governments. I regard even the suggestion as a fantastic dream.

2. In re Marcus Garvey's deportation: Our government was founded upon the principle of free speech and tolerance of individual opinion. However much I may discredit Marcus Garvey's preachings, I am disposed to be tolerant, feeling that the acid test of truth and time will prove what is right and what is wrong therein. We cannot wander far from the teachings of Gamaliel in such matters. Garvey has set men thinking, and nothing helps a race and a nation so much as serious thought.

* * *

THOMAS W. TALLEY
Professor of Chemistry and Biology, Fisk University
Nashville, Tenn.

I am in receipt of your communication of September 21. I am enclosing the data-sheet sent me. On its face will be found my estimate of all men of the Garvey type.

To question No. 1: No.

To question No. 2: Yes.

To Remarks: Thomas Jefferson, in penning the Declaration of Independence, wrote: "We hold these truths to be self-evident: That all men are created equal; that they are endowed by their Creator with certain unalienable rights; that among these are life, liberty, and the pursuit of happiness."

This is pure unadulterated Americanism. It is the standard set up for and by our government at its very beginning. The loyal American white man and the loyal American Negro have joined hands in an earnest endeavor to bring the masses into harmony with this their rich heritage. There is therefore no place in the American thought and plan for men of the Garvey type who freely pour their oil of vitriol on men of one color while they pat the men of another color on the back until they can empty their pockets; and then, when they have emptied the pockets of these, wantonly appeal to the worst in those whom they have once abused with the hope of somehow reaping a new rich harvest through their chicanery.

* * *

JOHN E. NAIL
Nail & Parker, Real Estate
New York City

To question No. 1: No.

To question No. 2: No.

To Remarks: I believe Mr. Garvey's first program for economic organization of colored peoples in America was sound, but he has deviated considerably from that program and developed a visionary one without substance.

* * *

KELLY MILLER
Dean, Junior College, Howard University
Washington, D.C.

To question No. 1: The redemption of Africa through Negro initiative and genius is worth the strivings of the race for the next half thousand years. While Garvey did not originate this idea, he has given it expression and emphasis beyond all others. It is difficult to disentangle the good from the evil of the Garvey propaganda. In so far as it stimulates Negro initiative and self-realization, good; in so far as impossible hopes may mislead the simple, bad. The movement lacks the practicality and freedom from the taint of suspicion to warrant adoption in its present form as a race policy.

To question No. 2: I do not think that Garvey should be deported and am surprised that the suggestion should come from any Negro. I do not believe that any individual should be banished from America or put in the penitentiary because of his belief or the expression of it. I do not believe in the imprisonment, expulsion or supression of ideas. Freedom of speech is the bulwark of the weak; suppression is the weapon of the strong. If Garvey's doctrines are false, combat them with the truth; if his dealings are devious, correct them with the law; if he misleads the simple, show them the more excellent way. But by no means should the oppressed become oppressor, nor the persecuted turn persecutor.

* * *

ROBERT W. BAGNALL
Director of Branches, N.A.A.C.P.
New York City

To question No. 1: Garvey's policy is, in my opinion, a great menace to the progress of the Negro here and elsewhere.

To question No. 2: Most decidedly he should be deported. He has already increased the friction between the races and race antipathy. He has also essayed to introduce the West Indian problem of color within the race. He has robbed many Negroes of patriotism by developing a cult which believes Africa their country, and America, "the white man's country." He has, beyond doubt, made an alliance with the Ku Klux Klan, an organization hostile to all Negro advancement here.

To Remarks: Not only is Garvey a menace, but so is Garveyism. It fundamentally stands for segregation, the root of all our evils. It is undermining a quality which must be preserved in the American Negro.

The Messenger, December, 1922; IV, 550–52.

86

MARCUS GARVEY AND GARVEYISM

In 1914, in his Jamaica homeland, Marcus Garvey commenced a movement seeking industrial education by and for Black people; the concept at first was not unlike that of Booker T. Washington. Correspondence between Washington and Garvey ensued, and the former invited the latter to visit him. Garvey was not able to make the trip until after Washington's death in November, 1915. When he did arrive in the United States early in 1916, one of the first people he visited was Dr. Du Bois.

In the first years—until around 1920—the relationships between Du Bois and Garvey and the radical Black Left and Garvey were sympathetic. When, however, Garvey took an increasingly nationalistic position—in an exclusionary sense—and especially when his language tended to play off gradations of color among Black people and also to insist that the United States was and would be and *should be* a white people's country— wherefore Blacks should leave the Western Hemisphere and migrate to Africa—suspicion of him and finally antagonism toward him grew in the N.A.A.C.P. and Left groups.

Garvey's increasingly reactionary position vis-à-vis labor unions and domestic U.S. politics and his serious flirtation with the K.K.K.—just when it was at its highest point of power and most intense ruthlessness—sealed this opposition.

Garvey, however, drew a significant mass following exactly because of his nationalistic fervor—characteristic on a world scale after World War I—and for this reason undoubtedly was viewed with alarm by significant components of the ruling class. Financial carelessness helped provide the excuse for his trial and imprisonment—on charges of fraudulent use of the mail. He was convicted in 1923 and in 1925 entered Atlanta Federal Penitentiary on a five-year term. From jail he managed to continue his movement and in fact was basically a political prisoner. He was pardoned by President Coolidge and ordered deported in 1927. He returned to Jamaica and then went to London trying to revive the movement. In London, in the nineteen-thirties, he became increasingly reactionary, deeply anti-Semitic, and openly affirmed his fascist and nazi sympathies. He died in London in 1940; his insistence upon pride in being Black and the future liberation and glory of Africa were permanent contributions which have assured the continuance of Garveyism.

There follow five documents illustrative of the content and nature of Garveyism at its high point in the nineteen-twenties. Document [a] is by William Pickens, one of the intense and effective Black opponents of Marcus Garvey; document [b] is an account of Garveyism by Eric D. Walrond, an influential Black author of the period who was rather sympathetic to the Garvey effort. Walrond was from British Guiana originally, lived for years as a young man in the Canal Zone, Panama, and then studied at City College in New York. He served as a newspaperman in Panama and for a time was associate editor of Garvey's *The Negro World*. Walrond exaggerated Du Bois' opposition to Garvey and was inaccurate when he wrote that Du Bois favored his deportation. Documents [c] and [d] are essays written in 1923 by Marcus Garvey and were published by his Universal Negro Improvement Association; document [e] is the text of a full-page advertisement placed by the U.N.I.A. in the New York City daily newspaper, the *World*, in 1924.

[a]

THE EMPEROR OF AFRICA
The Psychology of Garveyism
by William Pickens

On June 18th, 1923, Marcus Garvey, "Provisional President of Africa," after five weeks of serious trial interspersed with little comedies, was found guilty by a federal court in New York City of using the mails to defraud investors in the "Black Star Line" of dilapidated and mythical ships. This man Garvey was a fast worker: when he arrived from Jamaica just six years ago his friends in New York had to supply him with clothes and food, but when Judge [Julian] Mack pronounced sentence against him he was paying one hundred and fifty dollars a month for a New York apartment furnished in the bizarre south-sea fashion, was drawing ten thousand dollars a year as "President General of the Universal Negro Improvement Association," an additional eleven thousand dollars as "Provisional President of Africa," and boasted a longer string of magniloquent titles than the King of England.

When Marcus Garvey was sentenced to the penitentiary, we wonder if the judge realized how many different personages were to be locked up in that one cell: "The Provisional President of Africa," "The President General of the Universal Negro Improvement Association," "The President of the Black Star Line" of ships, "The Commander in Chief of the African Legion," head of the "Distinguished Service Order of Ethiopia," "The President of the Negro Factories Corporation" and of the "African Communities League," the head of the "Booker Washington University," and the managing editor of *The Negro World* (a weekly), *The Black Man* (a monthly of odd months), and *The Negro Times* (an occasional "daily").

In a brief six years he had not only made a place, and perhaps laid away a fortune, for himself,* but he had also wasted at the very lowest figure one million dollars for Negro washerwomen and workingmen. When the business of his "Black Star Line," for example, wound up, it owed about three-quarters of a million and had on hand just thirty-one dollars and seventy-five cents!

He probably received, managed, and disbursed, or rather disposed

---

* There is no evidence at all of Garvey having "laid away a fortune."

of, a greater variety of unaccounted-for "funds" than any other man of his decade. At frequent intervals *The Negro World* announced the opening of some new "fund" drive, without accounting adequately for the closing of the preceding one. There were "The African Redemption Fund," but Africa is still unredeemed; "The Liberian Loan Fund," and Liberia is still in need of the loan; the perennial "Convention Fund"; funds for factories, stores, and laundries, all of brief duration; "Black Star" funds; "Marcus Garvey Defense" funds, whenever somebody sued him for back salary or other debts; *Negro World* funds, daily paper funds, monthly magazine funds; funds to send emissaries to Liberia, who were allowed to become stranded there, to be a burden on Liberian charity, and to get back however they could; funds for "delegates to the League of Nations," to sit in the galleries and look on, when possible; and each time he married a new wife, his devoted people were inspired to raise an "appreciation" fund which however did not keep him from raiding the "Black Star" funds to the tune of nine hundred dollars for one of his honeymoons to Canada. He claimed Napoleon Bonaparte as his "ideal hero," and he even had his Josephine.

He is himself a Jamaican Negro and his organization began among West Indians in Harlem. Among his American Negro followers the "dues-paying" portion are below the average of intelligence for blacks of the continent, while most of the intelligent United States Negroes who joined the movement were in it for the sake of salaries, titles, and honors.

In the western hemisphere Negroes may be divided into three divisions, according to their relationships to the whites among whom they live: the Latin-American group, where amalgamation is the rule; the British-American group, where subjection with benevolent paternalism is customary; and United States Negroes, where constitutional equality with "racial integrity," supported by varying degrees of segregation, is at present essayed. These differences account for the differing attitudes of these respective groups toward world problems and such schemes as Garvey's Black Republic of Africa.

A comparison of British-American Negroes with those of the United States shows that the phenomena of Garveyism are rather British. British West Indian Negroes are free from spectacular horrors, such as lynchings and mob massacres, yet a settled and fixed policy of caste makes their future outlook more hopeless than that of the Negroes in the Southern United States. The United States Negro, on the other hand, is constitutionally a part of the general citizenship, and although sentiment, maladministration, and unconstitutional procedure may deprive him temporarily of the full exercise of his rights, the *basis* of his claim is broader and better.

The Negro of the States is physically a part of his nation, while the West Indian Negro is a colonial, separated by an ocean from the power which rules over him. And like British colonials of many races he has an idea, tinged with hope, that some time he may become entirely independent. The West Indian blacks whom Garvey found in New York were therefore the first to be moved by the idea of entire racial separateness, even to the absurd extent of having a continent assigned to a color,—a condition which commercial interdependence and scientific intercommunication make impossible.

There are other differences in these group complexes that help to explain Garveyism: the American Negro is used to the theory, and more or less to the actuality, of democracy and equality. If American Negroes had planned the "Republic of Africa," we should have heard nothing of "Knights and Ladies of Ethiopia," "Knights Commander of the Nile," and "Dukes of Uganda." Those are reactions of the British substratum. When Garvey was traveling through the States, advertising "Black Star" stock and "Back to Africa" schemes, he required the men and women of his retinue to address him as "Your Highness," and what was the amused astonishment of a colored American housewife in Ohio, who had rented rooms to Garvey and his followers, when one of Garvey's female attendants descended the stairway and announced: "His Highness would like ham and eggs, or pork chops and gravy, for his supper."

Other British earmarks can be seen in Garvey's "court receptions" and ceremonies, and in the self-awarded title, "Provisional President of Africa," following the example of De Valera, another British subject, who called himself "Provisional President of Ireland." And as soon as the President of Africa was ordered to jail he threatened the United States with a "hunger strike,"—which his healthy appetite has so far successfully opposed.

Another insular complex led Garvey astray when he appealed to the color-prejudice of "black" colored Americans. Being a black man himself, Garvey tried to draw the black Negroes of America away from those of lighter skin. But the color line of the whites against the whole Negro group in this country gives that many-colored group a consciousness of common interests. The British in the islands have three castes: white, colored, and black (or dark brown),—because that makes the matter easier for the whites. A united colored group in the West Indies would be an overwhelming majority, while in the

States all the colored blood of every shade and degree added together constitutes only a one-tenth minority.

The American white, therefore, did not feel it necessary to make the triple distinction. Individual Negroes may have color sentiment, like any other "taste," and it is a vanishing tradition in a few localities where it orignated in the pre-Civil War status of free mulattoes, as in Charleston, S.C., and New Orleans, La. But the color question has never made a group division of the colored people of the United States. With the consciousness of a black West Indian, Garvey had a chip on his shoulder for the lighter skins of the continent, and even after he was put in jail, he voiced the opinion that the whites and light skins were his worst enemies, although these colors had not been distinguished in the trial against him, and in spite of a fact which he knew well: that the four men who during the previous twelve months had done most to expose his frauds and destroy his influence in America, were dark Negroes of the average American type, one of them very dark, none of them a mulatto, and all of them Southern in origin: Chandler Owen and A. P. Randolph, editors, Robert W. Bagnall, and the present writer, citizens of Harlem.

He seemed not to realize that he would have to rule over every race and color under the sun, if he was to be Emperor of Africa,— from yellow Hottentots in the south to white Frenchmen and brunette Spaniards in the north; from the western Liberians, descended from American Negroes to the eastern Abyssinians, claiming descent from ancient Jews; stalwart Zulus and pigmy Bushmen, black Bantus, brown Moors, copper Egyptians; white South Africans, white settlers everywhere, and even Asiatics on the south and east. Nor did he realize how varied his subjects would be in national traditions; he ignored all problems of religious conflict, such as the inroads of Mohammedanism in unexpected corners of Africa; he was not aware that the Liberians are as different from the people of Abyssinia, as Mexicans are different from Russians; that there is no more in common between South Africa and North Africa than between Texas and Turkey. He did not know that the worst enemy a foreign usurper would find in Africa would be the Africans themselves. He had not a grammar grade understanding of Africa.

His government was to be a cross between an empire and a republic; it was to have "dukes" and he was to be the "president." The democratic end of the hybrid may have been the contribution of his salaried American Negroes, and may be due to the "psychology of opposition," which the oppressed exhibit. If England, for example, had been Catholic, south Ireland might have been devotedly Protestant; if George the Third had been president of a republic, George Washington might have been made king. And inasmuch as man makes God in man's own image, he was to have a new religion with a black God and black angels. In short, wherever he had seen a white face and straight hair in his past experience, he would place a black face and kinky hair in his future empire.

We will not be so hard upon the British as to charge also to their training or example the colossal conceit of Marcus Garvey. His megalomania and love of exaggeration are individual freaks, rather than either national or racial traits. During the period of his empire building, perhaps to boost the imaginary grandeur of his sway, he always spoke of "the 400,000,000 Negroes of the world," when there are only about 150,000,000. Two years ago he claimed to have four million members; to-day he claims six million; while most analyses of his other figures and data indicate that he has never had more than twenty or thirty thousand dues-paying members. He loudly announced that his 1922 convention would have "one hundred and fifty thousand delegates," but when his convention had been in session for a month, the most hotly contested issues, like those for offices and salaries, registered a vote of less than two hundred yeas and nays.

Yet his naïve-minded followers accept the myth of "the greatest Negro organization in the world," and look forward confidently to an early conquest of Africa against all the powers of Europe. Indeed Garvey announced, amid thunderous applause, at the opening of his 1922 convention: "If England wants peace, if France wants peace, if Italy wants peace, I advise them to pack up bag and baggage and get out of Africa!" And to substantiate the threat he marched through the streets of Harlem with an "army" assembled from "all over the world" and numbering less than six thousand men, women, little children, "Black Cross Nurses," local sympathizers, and unorganized camp followers. The "President" headed the procession, uniformed and plumed like a German field marshal, and pursued by various kinds of nobles in bright-colored robes and tassels.

Garvey understands mass psychology, with perhaps little formal knowledge of the subject, and the post-war spirit of the world was his ally, as exemplified in "Zionism," the Irish struggle, "self-determination" of peoples, and the great Negro migrations from South to North in this country. Some of these migrants had greatly improved their condition by one move, and, as simple minds run, a longer and more daring move, to Africa, or somewhere, would make their happiness complete. He declared for a "Black House" in Washington, to match the White House. He organized a ten million dollar ship corporation, without any money, and called it the "Black Star Line," to match the "White Star Line."

Each year he held a thirty-one days' convention to dispose of the affairs of the non-existent state of Africa. Before the opening of each big meeting in "Liberty Hall" on West 138th Street, he marched up and down the aisles and finally to the platform, surrounded by a bodyguard and followed by a chorus, carrying the red, black and green tricolor of the African Republic and singing: "God bless our President!" Garvey made these people at least *feel* important. There were the "Black Cross Nurses," for the most part uneducated working women who did not know the first principles of first aid, and there were the soldiers, with uniforms and arms, feeling as heroic tramping through the aisles of "Liberty Hall" as if treading the highways of an empire.

The human mind may dwell so long on an illusion that it will conceive that illusion as a reality. From the Tombs Prison in New York, Garvey proclaims to his subjects that he is "the victim of an international frame-up." He compares himself with O'Connell, MacSwiney, Gandhi, and Jesus. He regarded the judge and the United States district attorney as international and interracial tools. Petulant and suspicious, he dismissed his attorney and took charge of his own case, greatly delaying the progress of the court by his ignorance of the law, and creating a sort of "comedy of errors" by presenting the attorney Marcus Garvey, for the defendant Marcus Garvey, examining the witness Marcus Garvey. In summing up his case to the jury he talked for three hours, in true "Liberty Hall" propaganda style, expecting to overcome the evidence by the sheer multitudinousness and vehemency of his words. If sincere, he did not realize that he was *not* being tried for being the "President of Africa," for attempting to build a ship line, for rating himself as the only saviour of "the 400,000,000 Negroes of the world," nor for meeting the arrogant claim of Caucasian superiority with the equally absurd claim of black superiority,—but that he was being tried for the ordinary private crime of using the United States mail to defraud investors in a mythical ship. For stealing from his own subjects and supporters he was condemned on *their* testimony.

Some of his followers, believing that he was being persecuted for his doctrines, intimidated witnesses, wrote threats to the prosecutor and the court, and when on the last day he was being led away to prison, some of these dropped to their knees on the crowded pavement and asked God to intervene, informing Him that Garvey was being punished for the same reason that Jesus was crucified, ignoring the fact that the Man of Nazareth was never connected with financial fraud and debacle.

Intelligent American Negroes had only laughed at Garveyism, but became almost solid against him when in 1922 he launched the African Republic into the treaty-making business by apparently concluding the first pact with the Ku Klux Klan,—the Klan getting all the advantage in the diplomatic exchanges. When the invisible "government of Africa" came to an understanding with the "invisible empire of America," naturally the terms of agreement had to be a secret but they are easily inferred from Garvey's voluminous speeches immediately following his visit to Atlanta, where he had conferred with the "Imperial Wizard." The Ku Klux Klan were to be given America, so far as Garvey was concerned, and in return for his preaching that "this is a white man's country" he and his followers were to be allowed to take Africa,—so far as the "Imperial Wizard" was concerned.

Then it was that the greater number of intelligent American Negroes decided that Garveyism had passed from the stage of amusing parade into a phase of actual menace to interracial tranquility. Nobody had ever feared that he would lead all Negroes back to Africa,—England and France would see to that,—nor that he could lead as many as one out of every ten thousand American Negroes anywhere. But there was the real danger of robbing the ignorant blacks of the South, thus rousing interracial suspicion and antagonism. It was decided that "Garvey must go!" And the four colored Americans whom we have named, issued a circular bearing that title and arranged a series of meetings to expose Garveyism in Harlem. Some of his uniformed legionaries and fanatics came to break up the meeting with knives and clubs. Police protection was secured and the exposé went on, every meeting drawing a bigger and bigger crowd of determined colored Americans, and the menace and folly of the "back to Africa" program was made plainer than it had ever before been made.

And there is a moral to the tale: it must be considered that Garveyism could never happen simply because there was a Marcus Garvey. There was an opportunity for him and a response to him. This opportunity consists in the general repression of the Negro and Negroid peoples of parts of North America and parts of Africa. Like all humans the Negro is striving for self-expression and self-realization. And if these normal instincts are abnormally repressed, it will make him a prey to sharks and a menace to society. The very nature of this "black world" organization attracted into it sharks who would rend it to pieces, but the instinct for self-realization will still persist and must be invited and guided into useful channels or it will break out again in some new direction of waste and folly.

Life must somehow be made more normal for the colored minorities who live among white populations or who are in the power of governments dominated by whites. Movements for the advancement of the interests of such colored people must involve the co-operation of white and black. A movement of White against Black, like the Klan, or a movement of Black in contradistinction to White, like Garveyism, must do more harm than good.

Human science and intercommunication have made it improbable that the earth will ever again be divided geographically among monochromatic populations. The idea that one race should be set, geographically or otherwise, over against another is a reversion in civilization. Twelve million colored people of the United States can only consider plans for progress *in America,* but no fantastic schemes for egress from America. Any movement pivoted on any outside world is doomed to failure among this people.

The Forum, August, 1923; LXXX, 1790–99.

[b]

IMPERATOR AFRICANUS
MARCUS GARVEY: MENACE OR PROMISE?
by Eric D. Walrond

One of the effects of the World War was the quickening of racial consciousness among the Negroes of the Western Hemisphere, the group to which, because of its industrial, economic, and intellectual solidarity, the bulk of the blacks of the world look for leadership and guidance. Fresh from the war, from the bloodstained fields of France and Mesopotamia, the black troops, bitter, broken, disillusioned, stormed at the gates of the whites—pleaded for a share of that liberty and democracy which they were led to believe were the things for which they had fought. And it was of course a futile knocking. Hardened by the experience of the conflict, the Negroes, drunk, stung, poisoned by the narcotics of white imperialism, rose in all their might to create for themselves those spoils of war and peace which they knew they could not hope for from the ruling whites.

In Egypt and Palestine and other parts of the war area the black troops of the Western Hemisphere met other blacks—native Africans. It was the first mass contact of the Negro from the Old and the New Worlds. Here something which the white war lords had not bargained on resulted. The Negroes met and exchanged and compounded their views on the whites, their civilization, and their masters. Here the policies of France and Britain and Belgium and the United States with regard to their black wards were put in the scales. And when the blacks rose from the resulting pyre of disillusionment a new light shone in their eyes—a new spirit, a burning ideal, to be men, to fight and conquer and actually wrest their heritage, their destiny from those who controlled it.

It was upon this ideal that the gospel of Marcus Garvey came into being. Garvey is a black native of one of a cluster of tropical isles ruled by Great Britain in the Caribbean. He is the head of an international movement of, he says, some 4,000,000 Negroes. Known far and wide as the Garvey movement, its real name is the Universal Negro Improvement Association and African Communities League at 56 West 135th Street, New York. Its history is so inextricably bound up with the affairs of Marcus Garvey that to properly comprehend it and its racial significance one must need study the man's life and the forces that have governed it.

First, Garvey is of unmixed Negro blood. On its surface this may not appear significant, but it is indispensable to any consideration of the man. Goaded on by the memory that the first slaves stolen from Africa were full-blooded Negroes, Garvey and the gospel he preaches appeal particularly and not unexpectedly to the very black Negro element. In the island of his birth Jamaica, a land with as many color distinctions as there are eggs in a shad's roe, and all through his life, the fact that he was black was unerringly borne in upon him. Wherever he went, whether to Wolmer's, the college patronized by the upper-class mulattoes in Jamaica, or to Europe or Central America as student and journalist, he was continuously reminded that he was black and that it was futile for him to rise above the "hewer of wood and drawer of water."

In Jamaica as elsewhere in the United Kingdom, England differentiates between the full bloods and the half bloods. In Garvey's Jamaica, the mulattoes are next in power to the whites. The blacks, who outnumber them three to one, have actually no voice politically or economically.

With such a background, no wonder Garvey, the "Moses of the Negroes,"—applying the law of compensation,—idealizes black.

Coming into the emancipation of his spirit, it was inevitable. No wonder he talks glibly of a black state, a black empire, a black emperor. No wonder he is creating a black religion, a black deity, a black "Man of Sorrows." Who knows, he says, but that Jesus the Christ was not a black man? And, naturally, the hordes of black peasant folk flock to Garvey. They worship him. They feel that he is saying the things which they would utter were they articulate. They swarm to hear his fiery rhetoric. They pour their money into his coffers. They stand by him through thick and thin. They idolize him as if he were a black Demosthenes.

In turn, quite in keeping again with the law of compensation, but undoubtedly overdoing it, Garvey creates a fairy dream world for them which spiritedly makes up for the beauty and grandeur that are lacking in their drab, unorderly lives. Aping the English royalty, he manufactures out of black peasants of the lower domestic class dukes and duchesses, princes and princesses. Shall not, he quotes from the Bible, princes come out of Egypt, and Ethiopia stretch forth her hands unto God? An old white-haired Negro, a veteran agitator, is made Duke of Uganda. A faithful ambassador just returned from a mission to the black Republic of Liberia is made Knight Commander of the Distinguished Order of the Nile. Out of the multitude of black stable-boys, cooks and bottle washers, scullions and jim-swingers, is fashioned the timber of the crack African Legionnaires. Out of sombre-faced maidens from the French and Dutch and English colonies along the Spanish Main he creates "Black Cross Nurses." A black singer with the sacred eyes of a madonna becomes the "African Virgin Mary."

All the glamour, all the technique of delusion, is employed to satisfy the craving for this other thing which is missing in the lives of these long-repressed peasant folk. Essentially a movement of the black proletariat, Garveyism owes its strength largely to jangling swords and flaming helmets, titles and congeries of gold braid.

Arriving in the United States on March 23, 1916, Garvey, with a nucleus of thirteen, started in a Harlem hall bedroom the New York branch of the U.N.I.A. Briefly, the goal of the U.N.I.A. is the redemption of Africa—a black application of the Zionist principles. Afraid, according to its founder, that "if the Negro is not careful he will drink in all the poison of modern civilization and die from the effects of it" and hearing the great cry of "Jerusalem for the Jews—Ireland for the Irish—India for the Indians"—the U.N.I.A. believes that it is about time for the Negroes to raise the cry of "Africa for the Africans," at home and abroad.

In the United States Garveyism runs counter to the ideals governing most of the Negro uplift movements. Garvey's reluctance, for example, to declare himself on the Ku-Klux Klan, with whose whole program he is said to be in perfect accord; his opposition to the Negro middle and professional classes (in August, 1922, he issued a manifesto advising his followers not to invest their money in Negro corporate enterprises other than his own) are indicative of two things: Garvey's slant on the black *bourgeoisie* and the pessimism with which he views the outlook for the Negro in a hostile white world.

To get his ideas abroad Garvey started a weekly newspaper, *The Negro World*. Doubtless, it is the most bitterly racial newspaper published by Negroes. Leading off with a full-page "message" weekly by Garvey, the journal is published in three sections—in Spanish, French, and English. It goes to every part of the world where there are black people. Numberless have been the times when it has been suppressed or otherwise debarred by the British and French authorities from entering the native Negroid possessions. As it is, the *bourgeois* colored people of the United States are ashamed to be seen with it. They do not care for it. It is too upstandingly, too sensationally, racial.

Yet it is through this medium of violence that Garvey hopes to unite the black people of the world. How successful he is in doing this is reflected again and again in the unswerving allegiance to the ideals set up by him no matter what the machinations of the enemy may do to throw him into disrepute.

Soon after he got his organization going Garvey conceived the idea of founding a steamship line to ply between North, Central, and South America, the West Indies, and Africa. And the name with which he christened it is illustrative of the spirit of the whole Garvey movement. He called it the "Black Star Line." Why not? Did not the whites have their "White Star Line"? And from all parts of the world the blacks bought stock in it. It found fertile soil in their repressed consciousness.

Now Garvey, a bewitching orator, a roof-raising propagandist, when it comes to actual comprehension of the forces governing the world of trade and commerce, is a hopeless nincompoop. He said it was not necessary for him to be an experienced seaman nor need he have a technical knowledge of shipping to direct a steamship line. Unwilling to relinquish the actual control of it, he said he'd get people, black people with the brains and experience, to run it. And here again, undoubtedly, Garvey was unconsciously drawing on his Jamaica experience. For back in his Jamaica days there were black pilots and engineers and captains of merchant vessels which traded along the Main. Garvey, his imagination leaping to the contemplation of boundless continents, staked all, some two or three million subscribed by the black folk, on the fulfillment of this exotic dream.

As the world knows, the "Black Star Line" failed, and for a moment Garvey's star took a downward plunge. Incompetency, dishonesty, mismanagement, fraud—these contributed to it. In his eagerness to put the project over, Garvey was a promiscuous chooser of men. He was bombarded on all sides by charlatans. Bogus engineers, unskilled experts, sloop masters all clamored for position and opportunity, and Garvey, blind to the things of the earth, fell prey to them—saw in them spirits hungry to show to the whites the oceanic genius of the blacks.

It was at this point that the opposition to Garvey assumed menacing shape. To understand it one must go into the situation of the Negro in the United States proper and the efforts that are being made to improve it. Constituting one tenth of the 100,000,000 people in our country, the Negro is burned, lynched, segregated, and disfranchised, all on account of his color and abject condition. Ever since the Civil War there have been, of course, efforts by liberal-minded white people, principally from the North, to correct this unseemly treatment of the blacks. It was not until about twenty-five years ago, however, that the blacks began to develop leaders of their own. Of these, Booker T. Washington, the renowned seer of Tuskegee, was by far the greatest. Born a slave, Washington believed that the solution of the Negro problem lay in educating the black masses along industrial and commercial lines. Tuskegee Institute, situated in the heart of the Bourbon South, and erected at a cost of $5,000,000, is a living testimonial to the wisdom of this ideal, where thousands of Negro peasant boys and girls go annually for training in domestic and industrial arts.

Booker Washington prospered and soon had all the large philanthropic interests in the country behind him. That was up to 1906. Along about this time there appeared in the United States a book called *The Souls of Black Folk,* whose author was a colored man.* In that book, which up to this day is read as a sort of *Magna Charta* of the American Negro, there is a scathing denunciation of Booker Washington's theory of industrial education. Discarding it as old-fashioned, out of date, the author pleaded for the higher education of the Negro, for a

* Du Bois' *The Souls of Black Folk* appeared in 1903

share for the black man not only in the industrial and commercial life of the land, but in the social and political and governmental as well.

This, of course, fell on the national ears with the crash of a bombshell. It meant that there had risen out of the bosom of the Black Belt a voice, daring, challenging, disturbing in its ring, and for a time (and ever since) the eyes of the nation were focused on the man uttering it. And that man was W. E. Burghardt Du Bois, at the time an obscure professor of economics at Atlanta University, a Negro school in Georgia, one of the most bitter of the anti-Negro States in the American Union. Ph.D. of Harvard, Du Bois is undoubtedly the most brilliant Negro in the United States today. Poet, scholar, editor, and author, he is the man to whom the country turns with any question bearing on the intellectual life and progress of the Negroes. Proud, haughty, an incurable snob, he is probably the most unfit man temperamentally for the craft of leadership.

Of French and Dutch descent, Du Bois' reaction to the color problem is angrily emotional, baldly personal, amazingly hyperbolical. He has no sympathy for the black masses. He is incapable of comprehending their dreams and aspirations. He himself in his autobiography says that when he was a boy in Massachusetts he despised the poor mill workers from South Germany and annexed as his natural companions the rich and well to do. In short, Du Bois, the aristocrat, the snob, is a poet, an intellectual. He sees things through the eyes of the spirit. Garvey and Booker Washington did not. Naturally, his racial experience is colored by the psychosis of the poet in rebellion with his environment. The accident of birth which made him a mulatto is the only thing that lends significance to what he says or does. Had he been born in a country like France he would still be the same violent sensitive individual.

Ultimately, the attack by Du Bois on Washington, the only Negro of more than sectional stature who could at one and the same time be on terms of comparative placidity with both the North and the South, served to show up Du Bois as good "timber" for leadership. A group of white and colored leaders then got together and founded what is now known as the National Association for the Advancement of Colored People, with a white woman, Mary White Ovington, chairman of the board, and Moorfield Storey, a distinguished white barrister of Massachusetts, president. Nominally and theoretically, Miss Ovington and Mr. Storey are at the head of it, but the brains, the guiding genius is Du Bois.

Having as its *raison d'être* the granting to the United States Negro of equal social, political, and economic rights, the National Association is essentially an American movement concerned with the affairs of the 12,000,000 American Negroes. One of the things it is championing is a national anti-lynching law. It advises the Negroes at election time how to vote. It seeks to put down glaring instances of racial injustice. It seeks to awaken the Christian conscience of the white man. It believes that the destiny of the Negro is in America, and that the solution of the race problem lies in amalgamation.

When Garvey fell into disfavor through the sensational failure of the "Black Star Line," the dogs of the opposition took the opportunity to nip at his heels. Du Bois, the best blood in the native kennel, was set on him. Through *The Crisis,* the monthly magazine published by the National Association, Du Bois started a campaign against Garvey. After bewailing the riot of waste and corruption (Du Bois' association is supported by funds contributed by both white and colored people, whereas Garvey has refused financial aid from the whites, relying solely on the Negro masses) incident to the collapse of the steamship company, Du Bois agreed that the idea of African colonization was not new, and not impracticable, but that Garvey, an "illiterate foreigner," was not the man for it. Going further, Du Bois said, however, that it was madness to try to persuade the American Negro, practical and unimaginative as he is, to settle in Africa. Which, so far, is the only fundamental fallacy of Garveyism.

Numerous others, following Du Bois' footsteps, have duplicated this stand, and for the last two years Garvey has been defending himself against attacks. Eventually, through the efforts of his enemies, he was haled before the United States District Court in New York for using the mails to defraud and sentenced to five years in a Federal penitentiary.

Out on bail, Garvey, while Du Bois asked for his repatriation, held his Fourth International Convention of Negroes in New York from August 1 to 31 to which came over 3,000 Negroes from various parts of the globe. Undaunted, unswerved by the enemy's fire, by an uncanny turn of fate, Garvey, so far as the black masses are concerned, is still at the helm—steering the Negro ship of state and doing it with the old characteristic fire and spirit. Forever hitting at the high spots of the old international Negro problem, it is natural that he should excite the wrath of nationalist Negroes like Du Bois in

America and Herbert George DeLisser in Jamaica *—men who put national above racial consciousness. Yet through some divine mystery, Garvey is the "Moses" of the black masses. Instead of diminishing, his power is growing daily. It is one of the anomalies of the complex racial problem of the age.

The Independent, January 3, 1925; CXIV, 8–11.

[c]

THE NEGRO'S GREATEST ENEMY
by Marcus Garvey

I was born in the Island of Jamaica, British West Indies, on August 17, 1887. My parents were black Negroes. My father was a man of brilliant intellect and dashing courage. He was unafraid of consequences. He took human chances in the course of life, as most bold men do, and he failed at the close of his career. He once had a fortune; he died poor. My mother was a sober and conscientious Christian, too soft and good for the time in which she lived. She was the direct opposite of my father. He was severe, firm, determined, bold and strong, refusing to yield even to superior forces if he believed he was right. My mother, on the other hand, was always willing to return a smile for a blow, and ever ready to bestow charity upon her enemy. Of this strange combination I was born thirty-six years ago, and ushered into a world of sin, the flesh and the devil.

I grew up with other black and white boys. I was never whipped by any, but made them all respect the strength of my arms. I got my education from many sources—through private tutors, two public schools, two grammar or high schools and two colleges. My teachers were men and women of varied experience and abilities; four of them were eminent preachers. They studied me and I studied them. With some I became friendly in after years, others and I drifted apart, because as a boy they wanted to whip me, and I simply refused to be whipped. I was not made to be whipped. It annoys me to be defeated; hence to me, to be once defeated is to find cause for an everlasting struggle to reach the top.

* Herbert George DeLisser (1878–1944) was a writer and novelist and editor of *The Gleaner,* Jamaica's only daily newspaper. Politically, he was quite reactionary—coupling him with Du Bois is absurd, see W. Adolphe Robert, *Six Great Jamaicans* (Kingston, Jamaica, 1952), pp. 104–22.

I became a printer's apprentice at an early age, while still attending school. My apprentice master was a highly educated and alert man. In the affairs of business and the world he had no peer. He taught me many things before I reached twelve, and at fourteen I had enough intelligence and experience to manage men. I was strong and manly, and I made them respect me. I developed a strong and forceful character, and have maintained it still.

To me, at home in my early days, there was no difference between white and black. One of my father's properties, the place where I lived most of the time, was adjoining that of a white man. He had three girls and two boys; the Wesleyan minister, another white man whose church my parents attended, also had property adjoining ours. He had three girls and one boy. All of us were playmates. We romped and were happy children playmates together. The little white girl whom I liked most knew no better than I did myself. We were two innocent fools who never dreamed of a race feeling and problem. As a child, I went to school with white boys and girls, like all other Negroes. We were not called Negroes then. I never heard the term Negro used once until I was fourteen.

At fourteen my little white playmate and I parted. Her parents thought the time had come to separate us and draw the color line. They sent her and another sister to Edinburgh, Scotland, and told her that she was never to write or try to get in touch with me, for I was a "nigger." It was then that I found for the first time that there was some difference in humanity, and that there were different races, each having its own separate and distinct social life. I did not care about the separation after I was told about it, because I never thought all during our childhood association that the girl and the rest of the children of her race were better than I was; in fact, they used to look up to me. So I simply had no regrets.

After my first lesson in race distinction, I never thought of playing with white girls any more, even if they might be next door neighbors. At home my sister's company was good enough for me, and at school I made friends with the colored girls next to me. White boys and I used to frolic together. We played cricket and baseball, ran races and rode bicycles together, took each other to the river and to the sea beach to learn to swim, and made boyish efforts while out in deep water to drown each other, making a sprint for shore crying out "shark, shark, shark." In all our experience, however, only one black boy was drowned. He went under on a Friday afternoon after school hours, and his parents found him afloat half eaten by sharks on the following Sunday afternoon. Since then we boys never went back to sea.

At maturity the black and white boys separated, and took different courses in life. I grew up then to see the difference between the races more and more. My schoolmates as young men did not know or remember me any more. Then I realized that I had to make a fight for a place in the world, that it was not so easy to pass on to office and position. Personally, however, I had not much difficulty in finding and holding a place for myself, for I was aggressive. At eighteen I had an excellent position as manager of a large printing establishment, having under my control several men old enough to be my grandfathers. But I got mixed up with public life. I started to take an interest in the politics of my country, and then I saw the injustice done to my race because it was black, and I became dissatisfied on that account. I went traveling to South and Central America and parts of the West Indies to find out if it was so elsewhere, and I found the same situation. I set sail for Europe to find out if it was different there, and again I found the stumbling-block—"You are black." I read of the conditions in America. I read *Up From Slavery,* by Booker T. Washington, and then my doom—if I may so call it—of being a race leader dawned upon me in London after I had traveled through almost half of Europe.

I asked, "Where is the black man's Government?" "Where is his King and his kingdom?" "Where is his President, his country, and his ambassador, his army, his navy, his men of big affairs?" I could not find them, and then I declared, "I will help to make them."

Becoming naturally restless for the opportunity of doing something for the advancement of my race, I was determined that the black man would not continue to be kicked about by all the other races and nations of the world, as I saw it in the West Indies, South and Central America and Europe, and as I read of it in America. My young and ambitious mind led me into flights of great imagination. I saw before me then, even as I do now, a new world of black men, not peons, serfs, dogs and slaves, but a nation of sturdy men making their impress upon civilization and causing a new light to dawn upon the human race. I could not remain in London any more. My brain was afire. There was a world of thought to conquer. I had to start ere it became too late and the work be not done. Immediately I boarded a ship at Southampton for Jamaica, where I arrived on July 15, 1914. The Universal Negro Improvement Association and African Communities (Imperial) League was founded and organized five days after my arrival, with the program of uniting all the Negro peoples of the world into one great body to establish a country and Government absolutely their own.

Where did the name of the organization come from? It was while speaking to a West Indian Negro who was a passenger on the ship with me from Southampton, who was returning home to the West Indies from Basutoland with his Basuto wife, that I further learned of the horrors of native life in Africa. He related to me in conversation such horrible and pitiable tales that my heart bled within me. Retiring from the conversation to my cabin, all day and the following night I pondered over the subject matter of that conversation, and at midnight, lying flat on my back, the vision and thought came to me that I should name the organization the Universal Negro Improvement Association and African Communities (Imperial) League. Such a name I thought would embrace the purpose of all black humanity. Thus to the world a name was born, a movement created, and a man became known.

I really never knew there was so much color prejudice in Jamaica, my own native home, until I started the work of the Universal Negro Improvement Association. We started immediately before the war. I had just returned from a successful trip to Europe, which was an exceptional achievement for a black man. The daily papers wrote me up with big headlines and told of my movement. But nobody wanted to be a Negro. "Garvey is crazy; he has lost his head." "Is that the use he is going to make of his experience and intelligence?"—such were the criticisms passed upon me. Men and women as black as I, and even more so, had believed themselves white under the West Indian order of society. I was simply an impossible man to use openly the term "Negro"; yet every one beneath his breath was calling the black man a Negro.

I had to decide whether to please my friends and be one of the "black-whites" of Jamaica, and be reasonably prosperous, or come out openly and defend and help improve and protect the integrity of the black millions and suffer. I decided to do the latter, hence my offence against "colored-black-white" society in the colonies and America. I was openly hated and persecuted by some of these colored men of the island who did not want to be classified as Negroes, but as white. They hated me worse than poison. They opposed me at every step, but I had a large number of white friends, who encouraged and helped me. Notable among them were the then Governor of the Colony, the Colonial Secretary and several other prominent men. But they were afraid of offending the "colored gentry" that were passed for white. Hence my fight had to be made alone. I spent hundreds of pounds (sterling) helping the organization to gain a footing. I also gave up all my time to the promulgation of its ideals. I became a marked man, but I was determined that the work should be done.

The war helped a great deal in arousing the consciousness of the colored people to the reasonableness of our program, especially after the British at home had rejected a large number of West Indian colored men who wanted to be officers in the British army. When they were told that Negroes could not be officers in the British army they started their own propaganda, which supplemented the program of the Universal Negro Improvement Association. With this and other contributing agencies a few of the stiff-necked colored people began to see the reasonableness of my program, but they were firm in refusing to be known as Negroes. Furthermore, I was a black man and therefore had absolutely no right to lead; in the opinion of the "colored" element, leadership should have been in the hands of a yellow or a very light man. On such flimsy prejudices our race has been retarded. There is more bitterness among us Negroes because of the caste of color than there is between any other peoples, not excluding the people of India.

I succeeded to a great extent in establishing the association in Jamaica with the assistance of a Catholic Bishop, the Governor, Sir John Pringle, the Rev. William Graham, a Scottish clergyman, and several other white friends. I got in touch with Booker Washington and told him what I wanted to do. He invited me to America and promised to speak with me in the Southern and other States to help my work. Although he died in the Fall of 1915, I made my arrangements and arrived in the United States on March 23, 1916.

Here I found a new and different problem. I immediately visited some of the then so-called Negro leaders, only to discover, after a close study of them, that they had no program, but were mere opportunists who were living off their so-called leadership while the poor people were groping in the dark. I traveled through thirty-eight States and everywhere found the same condition. I visited Tuskegee and paid my respects to the dead hero, Booker Washington, and then returned to New York, where I organized the New York division of the Universal Negro Improvement Association. After instructing the people in the aims and objects of the association, I intended returning to Jamaica to perfect the Jamaica organization, but when we had enrolled about 800 or 1,000 members in the Harlem district and had elected the officers, a few Negro politicians began trying to turn the movement into a political club.

Seeing that these politicians were about to destroy my ideals, I had to fight to get them out of the organization. There it was that I made my first political enemies in Harlem. They fought me until they smashed the first organization and reduced its membership to about fifty. I started again, and in two months built up a new organization of about 1,500 members. Again the politicians came and divided us into two factions. They took away all the books of the organization, its treasury and all its belongings. At that time I was only an organizer, for it was not then my intention to remain in America, but to return to Jamaica. The organization had its proper officers elected, and I was not an officer of the New York division, but President of the Jamaica branch.

On the second split in Harlem thirteen of the members conferred with me and requested me to become President for a time of the New York organization so as to save them from the politicians. I consented and was elected President. There then sprung up two factions, one led by the politicians with the books and the money, and the other led by me. My faction had no money. I placed at their disposal what money I had, opened an office for them, rented a meeting place, employed two women secretaries, went on the street of Harlem at night to speak for the movement. In three weeks more than 2,000 new members joined. By this time I had the association incorporated so as to prevent the other faction using the name, but in two weeks the politicians had stolen all the people's money and had smashed up their faction.

The organization under my Presidency grew by leaps and bounds. I started *The Negro World*. Being a journalist, I edited this paper free of cost for the association, and worked for them without pay until November, 1920. I traveled all over the country for the association at my own expense, and established branches until in 1919 we had about thirty branches in different cities. By my writings and speeches we were able to build up a large organization of over 2,000,000 by June, 1919, at which time we launched the program of the Black Star Line.

To have built up a new organization, which was not purely political, among Negroes in America was a wonderful feat, for the Negro politician does not allow any other kind of organization within his race to thrive. We succeeded, however, in making the Universal Negro Improvement Association so formidable in 1919 that we encountered more trouble from our political brethern. They sought the influence of the District Attorney's office of the County of New York to put us out of business. Edwin P. Kilroe, at that time an Assistant District

Attorney, on the complaint of the Negro politicians, started to investigate us and the association. Mr. Kilroe would constantly and continuously call me to his office for investigation on extraneous matters
without coming to the point. The result was that after the eighth or
ninth time I wrote an article in our newspaper, *The Negro World,*
against him. This was interpreted as criminal libel, for which I was indicted and arrested, but subsequently dismissed on retracting what I had
written.

During my many tilts with Mr. Kilroe, the question of the Black Star
Line was discussed. He did not want us to have a line of ships. I told
him that even as there was a White Star Line, we would have, irrespective of his wishes, a Black Star Line. On June 27, 1919, we incorporated the Black Star Line of Delaware, and in September we
obtained a ship.

The following month (October) a man by the name of Tyler came
to my office at 56 West 135th Street, New York City, and told me
that Mr. Kilroe had sent him to "get me," and at once fired four shots
at me from a .38-calibre revolver. He wounded me in the right leg
and the right side of my scalp. I was taken to the Harlem Hospital,
and he was arrested. The next day it was reported that he committed
suicide in jail just before he was to be taken before a City Magistrate.

The first year of our activities for the Black Star Line added prestige
to the Universal Negro Improvement Association. Several hundred
thousand dollars worth of shares were sold. Our first ship, the steamship *Yarmouth,* had made two voyages to the West Indies and Central
America. The white press had flashed the news all over the world. I,
a young Negro, as President of the corporation, had become famous.
My name was discussed on five continents. The Universal Negro Improvement Association gained millions of followers all over the world.
By August, 1920, over 4,000,000 persons had joined the movement.
A convention of all the Negro peoples of the world was called to meet
in New York that month. Delegates came from all parts of the known
world. Over 25,000 persons packed the Madison Square Garden on
Aug. 1 to hear me speak to the first International Convention of
Negroes. It was a record-breaking meeting, the first and the biggest of
its kind. The name of Garvey had become known as a leader of his
race.

Such fame among Negroes was too much for other race leaders and
politicians to tolerate. My downfall was planned by my enemies.
They laid all kinds of traps for me. They scattered their spies among

the employes of the Black Star Line and the Universal Negro Improvement Association. Our office records were stolen. Employes started to be openly dishonest; we could get no convictions against them; even if on complaint they were held by a Magistrate, they were dismissed by the Grand Jury. The ships' officers started to pile up thousands of dollars of debts against the company without the knowledge of the officers of the corporation. Our ships were damaged at sea, and there was a general riot of wreck and ruin. Officers of the Universal Negro Improvement Association also began to steal and be openly dishonest. I had to dismiss them. They joined my enemies, and thus I had an endless fight on my hands to save the ideals of the association and carry out our program for the race. My Negro enemies, finding that they alone could not destroy me, resorted to misrepresenting me to the leaders of the white race, several of whom, without proper investigation, also opposed me.

With robberies from within and from without, the Black Star Line was forced to suspend active business in December, 1921. While I was on a business trip to the West Indies in the Spring of 1921, the Black Star Line received the blow from which it was unable to recover. A sum of $25,000 was paid by one of the officers of the corporation to a man to purchase a ship, but the ship was never obtained and the money was never returned. The company was defrauded of a further sum of $11,000. Through such actions on the part of dishonest men in the shipping business, the Black Star Line received its first setback. This resulted in my being indicted for using the United States mails to defraud investors in the company. I was subsequently convicted and sentenced to five years in a Federal penitentiary. My trial is a matter of history. I know I was not given a square deal, because my indictment was the result of a "frame-up" among my political and business enemies. I had to conduct my own case in court because of the peculiar position in which I found myself. I had millions of friends and a large number of enemies. I wanted a colored attorney to handle my case, but there was none I could trust. I feel that I have been denied justice because of prejudice. Yet I have an abundance of faith in the courts of America, and I hope yet to obtain justice on my appeal.

The temporary ruin of the Black Star Line has in no way affected the larger work of the Universal Negro Improvement Association, which now has 900 branches with an approximate membership of 6,000,000. This organization has succeeded in organizing the Negroes all over the world and we now look forward to a renaissance that will create a new people and bring about the restoration of Ethiopia's ancient glory.

Being black, I have committed an unpardonable offense against the very light colored Negroes in America and the West Indies by making myself famous as a Negro leader of millions. In their view, no black man must rise above them, but I still forge ahead determined to give to the world the truth about the new Negro who is determined to make and hold for himself a place in the affairs of men. The Universal Negro Improvement Association has been misrepresented by my enemies. They have tried to make it appear that we are hostile to other races. This is absolutely false. We love all humanity. We are working for the peace of the world which we believe can only come about when all races are given their due.

We feel that there is absolutely no reason why there should be any differences between the black and white races, if each stops to adjust and steady itself. We believe in the purity of both races. We do not believe the black man should be encouraged in the idea that his highest purpose in life is to marry a white woman, but we do believe that the white man should be taught to respect the black woman in the same way as he wants the black man to respect the white woman. It is a vicious and dangerous doctrine of social equality to urge, as certain colored leaders do, that black and white should get together, for that would destroy the racial purity of both.

We believe that the black people should have a country of their own where they should be given the fullest opportunity to develop politically, socially and industrially. The black people should not be encouraged to remain in white people's countries and expect to be Presidents, Governors, Mayors, Senators, Congressmen, Judges and social and industrial leaders. We believe that with the rising ambition of the Negro, if a country is not provided for him in another 50 or 100 years, there will be a terrible clash that will end disastrously to him and disgrace our civilization. We desire to prevent such a clash by pointing the Negro to a home of his own. We feel that all well disposed and broad minded white men will aid in this direction. It is because of this belief no doubt that my Negro enemies, so as to prejudice me further in the opinion of the public, wickedly state that I am a member of the Ku Klux Klan, even though I am a black man.

I have been deprived of the opportunity of properly explaining my work to the white people of America through the prejudice worked up against me by jealous and wicked members of my own race. My success as an organizer was much more than rival Negro leaders could tolerate. They, regardless of consequences, either to me or to the race, had to destroy me by fair means or foul. The thousands of anonymous and other hostile letters written to the editors and publishers of the white press by Negro rivals to prejudice me in the eyes of public opinion are sufficient evidence of the wicked and vicious opposition I have had to meet from among my own people, especially among the very light colored. But they went further than the press in their attempts to discredit me. They organized clubs all over the United States and the West Indies, and wrote both open and anonymous letters to city, State and Federal officials of this and other Governments to induce them to use their influence to hamper and destroy me. No wonder, therefore, that several Judges, District Attorneys and other high officials have been against me without knowing me. No wonder, therefore, that the great white population of this country and of the world has a wrong impression of the aims and objects of the Universal Negro Improvement Association and of the work of Marcus Garvey.

Having had the wrong education as a start in his racial career, the Negro has become his own greatest enemy. Most of the trouble I have had in advancing the cause of the race has come from Negroes. Booker Washington aptly described the race in one of his lectures by stating that we were like crabs in a barrel, that none would allow the other to climb over, but on any such attempt all would continue to pull back into the barrel the one crab that would make the effort to climb out. Yet, those of us with vision cannot desert the race, leaving it to suffer and die.

Looking forward a century or two, we can see an economic and political death struggle for the survival of the different race groups. Many of our present-day national centres will have become overcrowded with vast surplus populations. The fight for bread and position will be keen and severe. The weaker and unprepared group is bound to go under. That is why, visionaries as we are in the Universal Negro Improvement Association, we are fighting for the founding of a Negro nation in Africa, so that there will be no clash between black and white and that each race will have a separate existence and civilization all its own without courting suspicion and hatred or eyeing each other with jealousy and rivalry within the borders of the same country.

White men who have struggled for and built up their countries and their own civilizations are not disposed to hand them over to the Negro or any other race without let or hindrance. It would be unreasonable to expect this. Hence any vain assumption on the part of the Negro to imagine that he will one day become President of the Nation, Governor of the State, or Mayor of the City in the countries of white men, is like waiting on the devil and his angels to take up their residence in the Realm on High and direct there the affairs of Paradise.

Originally in *Current History*, September, 1923; republished as one of three essays, from same source, by the press of the Universal Negro Improvement Association, New York City, in 1924, as a twenty-nine-page pamphlet entitled *Three Articles on the Negro Problem*. The other two were by Robert W. Winston, Judge of the Superior Court of North Carolina, 1889–1895, and a planter, and by Eric D. Walrond. Winston's essay "Should the Color Line Go?" argued "no"; Walrond wrote on "The Negro Exodus from the South."

[d]

AN APPEAL TO THE SOUL OF WHITE AMERICA BY MARCUS GARVEY

Surely the soul of liberal, philanthropic, liberty-loving white America is not dead.

It is true that the glamour of materialism has to a great degree, destroyed the innocence and purity of the national conscience, but, still, beyond our politics, beyond our soulless industrialism, there is a deep feeling of human sympathy that touches the soul of white America upon which the unfortunate and sorrowful can always depend for sympathy, help, and action.

It is to that feeling that I appeal at this time for four hundred million Negroes of the world, and fifteen million of America in particular.

There is no real white man in America, who does not desire a solution of the Negro problem. Each thoughtful citizen has probably his own idea of how the vexed question of races should be settled. To some the Negro could be gotten rid of by wholesale butchery, by lynching, economic starvation, by a return to slavery and legalized oppression; while others would have the problem solved by seeing the race all herded together and kept somewhere among themselves, but a few—those in whom they have an interest should be allowed to live around as the wards of a mistaken philanthropy; yet, none so generous as to desire to see the Negro elevated to a standard of real progress, and prosperity, welded into a homogeneous whole, creating of themselves a mighty nation with proper systems of government, civilization, and culture, to mark them admissible to the fraternities of nations and races without any disadvantage.

I do not desire to offend the finer feelings and sensibilities of those white friends of the race who really believe that they are kind and considerate to us as a people; but I feel it my duty to make a real appeal to conscience and not belief. Conscience is solid, convicting and permanently demonstrative; belief, is only a matter of opinion, changeable by superior reasoning. Once the belief was that it was fit and proper to hold the Negro as a slave, and in this the Bishop, Priest and layman agreed. Later on they changed their belief or opinion, but at all times the conscience of certain people dictated to them that it was wrong and inhuman to hold human beings as slaves. It is to such a conscience in white America that I am addressing myself.

Negroes are human beings—the peculiar and strange opinions of writers, ethnologists, philosophers, scientists and anthropologists, notwithstanding—they have feelings, souls, passions, ambitions, desires, just as other men, hence they should be considered.

Has white American really considered the Negro in the light of permanent human progress? The answer is *No*.

Men and women of the white race, do you know what is going to happen if you do not think and act now? One of two things. You are either going to deceive and keep the Negro in your midst until you have perfectly completed your wonderful American civilization with its progress of art, science, industry, and politics, and then, jealous of your own success and achievements in those directions, and with the greater jealousy of seeing your race pure and unmixed, cast him off to die in the whirlpool of economic starvation, thus, getting rid of another race that was not intelligent enough to live, or, you simply mean by the largeness of your hearts to assimilate fifteen million Negroes into the social fraternity of an American race, that will neither be white nor black. Don't be alarmed! We must prevent both consequences. No real race loving white man wants to destroy the purity of his race, and no real Negro conscious of himself, wants to die, hence there is room for an understanding, and an adjustment, and that is just what we seek.

Let white and black stop deceiving themselves. Let the white race stop thinking that all black men are dogs and not to be considered as human beings. Let foolish Negro agitators and so-called reformers, encouraged by deceptive and unthinking white associates, stop preaching and advocating the doctrine of "social equality," meaning thereby the social intermingling of both races, intermarriages, and general social co-relationship. The two extremes will get us nowhere, other than breeding hate and encouraging discord, which will eventually end disastrously to the weaker race.

Some Negroes in the quest of position, and honor, have been admitted to the full enjoyment of their constitutional rights, thus we have some of our men filling high and responsible Government positions, others on their own account, have established themselves in the professions, commerce and industry. This the casual onlooker and even the men themselves, will say carries a guarantee and hope of social equality, and permanent racial progress. But this is the mistake. There is no progress of the Negro in America that is permanent, so long as we have with us the monster civil prejudice.

Prejudice we shall always have between black and white, so long as the latter believes that the former is intruding upon their rights. So long as white laborers believe that black laborers are taking and holding their jobs, so long as white artisans believe that black artisans are performing the work that they should do; so long as white men and women believe that black men and women are filling the positions that they covet; so long as white political leaders and statesmen believe that black politicians and statesmen are seeking the same positions in the Nation's Government; so long as white men believe that black men want to associate with and marry white women, then we will have prejudice and not only prejudice, but riots, lynchings, burnings, and God to tell what next and to follow!

It is this danger that drives me mad. It must be prevented. We cannot allow white and black to drift along unthinkingly toward this great gulf and danger, that is nationally ahead of us. It is because of this, that I speak, and now call upon the soul of great white America to help.

It is no use putting off, the work must be done, and it must be started now.

Some people have misunderstood me. Some don't want to understand me. But I must explain myself for the good of America and for the good of the world and humanity.

Those of the Negro race who preach social equality, and who are working for an American race that will in complexion be neither white nor black, have tried to misinterpret me to the white public, and create prejudice against my work. The white public, not stopping to analyze and question the motive behind criticism and attacks, aimed against new leaders and their movements, condemn without even giving a chance to the criticized to be heard. Those who oppose me in my own race, because I refuse to endorse their program of social arrogance and social equality, gloat over the fact that by their misrepresentation and underhand methods, they were able to have me convicted for a frame up crime which they calculate will so discredit me as to destroy the movement that I represent, in opposition to their program of a new American race; but we will not now consider the opposition to a program or a movement, but state the facts as they are, and let deep souled white America pass its own judgment.

In another one hundred years white America will have doubled its population, in another one hundred years it will have trebled itself. The keen student must realize that the centuries ahead will bring us an overcrowded and over populated country; opportunities, as the population grows larger will be fewer; the competition for bread between the people of their own class will become keener, and so much more so will there be no room for two competitive races, the one strong and the other weak. To imagine Negroes as District Attorneys, Judges, Senators, Congressmen, Assemblymen, Aldermen, Government Clerks, and Officials, Artisans and laborers at work while millions of white men starve, is to have before you the bloody picture of wholesale mob violence, that I fear, and against which I am working. No preaching, no praying, no presidential edict, will control the passion of hungry unreasoning men of prejudice when the hour comes. It will not come I pray in our generation, but it is of the future that I think and for which I work.

A generation of ambitious Negro men and women, out from the best Colleges, Universities, Institutions, capable of filling the highest and best positions in the nation, in industry, commerce, society and politics! Can you keep them back? If you do so they will agitate and throw your constitution in your faces. Can you stand before civilization and deny the truth of your constitution? What are you going to do then? You who are just will open up the door of opportunity and say to all and sundry "Enter in." But ladies and gentlemen, what about the mob, that starving crowd of your own race? Will they stand by, suffer and starve, and allow an opposite and competitive race to prosper in the midst of their distress? If you can conjure these things up in your mind, then you have the vision of the race problem of the future in America.

There is but one solution, and that is to provide an outlet for Negro energy, ambition, and passion, away from the attraction of white opportunity and surround the race with opportunities of its own. If this is not done, and if the foundation for same is not laid now, then the consequences will be sorrowful for the weaker race, and be disgraceful to white ideals of justice, and shocking to white civilization.

The Negro must have a country, and a nation of his own. If you laugh at the idea, then you are selfish and wicked, for you and your children do not intend that the Negro shall discommode you in yours. If you do not want him to have a country and a nation of his own; if you do not intend to give him equal opportunities in yours; then it is plain to see that you mean that he must die even as the Indian to make room for another race.

Why should the Negro die? Has he not served America and the world? Has he not borne the burden of civilization in this Western world for three hundred years? Has he not contributed of his best to America? Surely all this stands to his credit, but there will not be enough room and the one answer is "find a place." We have found a place, it is Africa and as black men for three centuries have helped white men build America, surely generous and grateful white men and women will help black men build Africa.

And why shouldn't Africa and America travel down the ages as protectors of human rights and guardians of democracy? Why shouldn't black men help white men secure and establish universal peace? We can only have peace when we are just to all mankind; and for that peace, and for the reign of universal love I now appeal to the soul of white America. Let the Negroes have a Government of their own. Don't encourage them to believe that they will become social equals and leaders of the whites in America, without first on their own account proving to the world that they are capable of evolving a civilization of their own. The white race can best help the Negro by telling him the truth, and not by flattering him into believing that he is as good as any white man without first proving the racial, national constructive metal of which he is made.

Stop flattering the Negro about social equality, and tell him to go to work and build for himself. Help him in the direction of doing for himself, and let him know that self progress brings its own reward.

I appeal to the considerate and thoughtful conscience of white America not to condemn the cry of the Universal Negro Improvement Association for a nation in Africa for Negroes, but to give us a chance to explain ourselves to the world. White America is too

big and when informed and touched, too liberal to turn down the
cry of the awakened Negro for "a place in the sun."

An Appeal to the Soul of White America: The Solution to the Problem of Com-
petition Between Two Opposite Races: Negro Leader Appeals to the Conscience
of White Race to Save His Own. By Marcus Garvey, President General of the
Universal Negro Improvement Association (New York: press of the U.N.I.A.,
1924)—a six-page pamphlet, printed above in full.

[e]

ADVERTISEMENT IN *NEW YORK WORLD*

Colonization of Africa by Negroes as Solution of Race Problem

---

Universal Negro Improvement Association working to
develop colonies in Liberia as peaceful homes for Negroes—
similar to Homeland in Palestine for Jews

Over a hundred years ago the white friends of the Negro in America,
known as the American Colonization Society, helped establish the
Black Republic of Liberia with the hope that it might become the
home of those Negroes who wanted a home among themselves. After
great sacrifice and with much difficulty the early settlers of the
republic have perpetuated the government until it stands out to-day
as the most serious attempt of the race to help itself.

The Universal Negro Improvement Association, organized under
the laws of the State of New York, aims at assuming the responsibility
of helping to develop Liberia as a natural home for Negroes. Toward
this end several missions have been sent to Liberia for the purpose
of arranging for the repatriation of as many Negroes as desire to
go to that country to settle and to help in her industrial, agricultural
and cultural development.

The following plans have been decided on by the Universal Negro
Improvement Association: That the Association is to build four
colonies in the Republic, the first on the Cavalla River, for which
a group of civil and mechanical engineers have been sent to start
preparatory work for the accommodation of the first batch of colonists
who will sail from New York during the Fall of the present year and
following years.

The Association is raising a fund of $2,000,000 to bear the cost of constructing and establishing the first colony. The building plan for each colony is as follows (all Government buildings to be under the control of the Liberian Government):

BUILDING PLANS

GOVERNMENT

1. Court House and Post Office
2. Town Hall
   a. Public Safety
      1. Police Station
      2. Fire Protection
      3. Hospital

COMMUNITY INTEREST AND ENTERTAINMENT

1. National Theatre
2. Churches (2)
3. Large Public Hall
4. Public Park

PUBLIC EDUCATION

1. Public Library
2. Public Schools (2)
3. Public High School (1)
4. College of Arts and Sciences
5. Trade School and Engineering Works

PUBLIC UTILITIES

1. Electric Light and Power Plant
2. Water Filtration Plant

3. Sewerage System and Sewage Disposal Plant
   a. Transportation Facilities
      1. Roads, Streets and Pavements
      2. Wharf and Dock and Water Front Improvement
      3. Railroad, 4-15 miles
   b. Commissaries (2)
   c. Dormitories (2)

THIS IS THE BEST SOLUTION OF THE NEGRO PROBLEM

All those who desire to help the Negro under the auspices of the Universal Negro Improvement Association in developing himself, are asked to subscribe to the fund of two million ($2,000,000) dollars now being raised for the promotion of the Cavalla Colony.

Address your donation to the "Treasurer, Colonization Fund, Universal Negro Improvement Association, 56 West 135th Street, New York, U.S.A." Bankers: Chelsea Exchange Bank, Harlem Branch, 135th Street and Seventh Avenue.

THE FUND

Marcus Garvey	$ 100.00
Mrs. Marcus Garvey	50.00
William C. Ritter	25.00
New York Division, U.N.I.A.	250.00
Mrs. Leola Warden, Columbus, Ohio	5.00
G. E. Barnes and others, Victoria de Lastunas, Oriente, Cuba	25.65
Mrs. P. S. Watterhouse, New Orleans, La.	15.00
Mrs. Peter Jackson and others of the Milwaukee Division Universal Negro Improvement Association	93.10

Friend of U.N.I.A. Francisco, Province Camaguey, Cuba	100.00
Mrs. Lucy Johnson, Cincinnati, Ohio	4.00
Other donations	2,734.87
Motor Corps, Unia, Pittsburgh, Pa.	11.00
Mrs. Malinda Hopkins, Chicago, Ill.	5.00
Laura Lee Div., No. 450, Lumberport, W. Va.	15.00
New Orleans Div., New Orleans, La.	15.00
Richmond Div., No. 193, Richmond, Va.	7.50
Mrs. Mary Belgrave, Boston, Mass.	8.00
Blue Island Division, Blue Island, Ill.	15.00
Holdenville Div., Holdenville, Okla.	51.00
Mrs. Annie Darden, Columbus, Ohio	5.00
J. W. Green, Seattle, Wash.	5.00
E. A. Nibbs, Seattle, Wash.	2.50
N. W. Hudgins, Seattle, Wash.	1.00
A. M. Brown, Seattle, Wash.	1.20
C. D. Cristman, Seattle, Wash.	1.00
J. B. Martin, Seattle, Wash.	1.00
Nellie E. Brown, Seattle, Wash.	1.00
Mr. Rufus A. Reid, Seattle, Wash.	1.00
H. Maitland, Seattle, Wash.	1.00
Mattle L. Maitland, Seattle, Wash.	1.00
W. A. McLine, Seattle, Wash.	1.00
S. P. Moore, Seattle, Wash.	1.00
Joseph Lynch, Seattle, Wash.	1.00
Sarah Lynch, Seattle, Wash.	.50
A friend, Seattle, Wash.	.20
Marie Jones, Seattle, Wash.	.25
Wilford Edwards, Seattle, Wash.	.50
Frank C. Williams	.50
James Moore, Seattle, Wash.	.50
J. D. Nelson, Seattle, Wash.	1.50
E. Chambers, Seattle, Wash.	1.00
Jennie Ellis, Seattle, Wash.	1.00
Geo. F. Carter, Seattle, Wash.	1.00
Nannie R. Webb, Seattle, Wash.	.50
Maude Keizer, Seattle, Wash.	1.10
Joseph Keizer, Seattle, Wash.	1.00
Thomas McPherson, Seattle, Wash.	.25
Mary Costello Moore, Seattle, Wash.	.50
Rachel Famber, Seattle, Wash.	.50
Wm. Famber, Seattle, Wash.	.50
Victoria Bean, Summit, N.J.	25.00
Will Ford, Detroit, Mich.	25.00
Geo. Brothers, South Bend, Ark.	2.00
Walter Estes, N. Edmonton, Canada	15.00
Mr. and Mrs. Manfield Sterkes, Farrell, Pa.	5.00
C. W. Davis, South Bend, Ark.	2.00
Chas. Carter, Carbon, W. Va.	10.00

Mrs. P. S. Waterhouse, New Orleans, La.	15.00
Milwaukee Division, Milwaukee, Wis.	93.10
Danville Division, Danville, Ill.	15.00
Lucy Johnson, Cincinnati, Ohio	4.00
Laura Palmer, Gary, Ind.	12.23
Victoria de Lastunan Div., Prov. de Cuba	25.65
Jean Gillman, Dover, N.J.	10.00
Boyd Timmons, Dover, N.J.	10.00
Leola Darden, Columbus, Ohio	5.00
Mary McDonald, Gary, Ind.	5.00
Embry Darden, Gary, Ind.	5.00
William Patterson, Colp, Ill.	10.00
Frances Frederick, Hartford, Conn.	2.10
Francisco Division, Camaguey, Cuba	100.00
Morales Division, Morales, Guatemala	100.00
George Smith, Brooklyn, N.Y.	5.00
J. S. Patterson, Portland, Oregon	20.00
Total	$4,086.20

Signed:

Universal Negro Improvement Association
Marcus Garvey, President
William Sherrill, 2nd Vice-President
Rudolph Smith, 3rd Vice-President
Henrietta Vinton Davis, 4th Vice-President
G. Emoni Carter, Secretary

Clifford Bourne, Treasurer
Levi F. Lord, Auditor
G. O. Marke
Thomas W. Anderson
Percival L. Burrows
James O'Meally
Norton G. Thomas

Full-page advertisement in the *New York World*, June 25, 1924, p. 15.

87

THE RECONSTRUCTION ERA:
A RECONSIDERATION
as offered by John R. Lynch

John R. Lynch served two terms in the U.S. Congress representing Missis-sippi in the post–Civil War period; he also served in the state legislature and in 1872 was the first—so far the only—Black Speaker of the Mississippi House. With this first-hand and expert experience he was well qualified to pioneer in exposing the racist historiography that made a travesty of Reconstruction's reality. The document that follows is taken from a book by John R. Lynch, published in 1923.

In 1916, in glancing over one of the volumes of Rhodes's history of the United States, I came across the chapters giving information about what took place in the State of Mississippi during the period of Reconstruction. I detected so many statements and representations which, to my knowledge, were absolutely groundless that I decided to read carefully the entire work, which I have done; and I regret to say that, so far as the Reconstruction period is concerned, the history is not only inaccurate and unreliable, but is the most one-sided, biased, partisan and prejudiced historical work I have ever read. In his preface to volume six, the author was frank enough to make the following observation: "Nineteen years' almost exclusive devotion to the study of one period of American history has had the tendency to narrow my field of vision." Without doing violence to the truth he could have appropriately added these words: "And since the sources of my information touching the Reconstruction period were partial, partisan and prejudiced, my field of vision has not only been narrowed, but my mind has been poisoned, my judgment has been warped, my deductions have been biased, and my opinions so influenced that any alleged facts have not only been exaggerated, but my comments, arguments, inferences and deductions based upon them can have very little, if any, value for historical purposes."

Many of his alleged facts were so magnified and others so minimized as to make them harmonize with what the author thought the facts *should* be, rather than what they actually were. In the first place, the very name of his work is a misnomer: "History of the United States from the Compromise of 1850 *to the Final Restoration of Home Rule at the South in 1877.*" I have emphasized the words, "to the final restoration of home rule at the South in 1877" because those are the words that constitute the misnomer. If home rule were finally restored to the South in 1877, the natural and necessary inference is that prior to that time those states were subjected to some other kind of rule, presumably that of foreigners and strangers,—an inference which is wholly at variance with the truth. Another inference to be drawn is that those states had enjoyed home rule until the same was disrupted and set aside by the Reconstruction Acts of Congress, but that it was finally restored in 1877. If this is the inference which the writer intended the reader to draw, it is conclusive evidence that he was unpardonably and inexcusably ignorant of the subject matter about which he wrote. As the term home rule is generally understood, there never was a time when those states did not have it, unless we except the brief period when they were under military control, and even then the military commanders utilized home material in making appointments to office. But since the officers were not elected by the people, it may be plausibly claimed that they did not for that period have home rule. But the state governments organized and brought into existence under the Reconstruction Acts of Congress were the first and only governments in that section which were genuinely Republican in form. The form of government which existed in the ante-bellum days was that of an aristocracy. The government which has existed since what Mr. Rhodes is pleased to term the restoration of home rule is simply that of a local despotic oligarchy. The former *was* not, and the present *is* not, based upon the will and choice of the masses, but the former was by far the better of the two, for whatever may be truthfully said in condemnation and in derogation of the Southern aristocracy of ante-bellum days, it cannot be denied that they represented the wealth, the intelligence, the decency and the respectability of their respective states. While the state governments that were dominated by the aristocrats were not based upon the will of the people as a whole, yet from an administrative point of view they were not necessarily bad. Such cannot be said of those who are now the representatives of what Mr. Rhodes is pleased to term home rule.

John R. Lynch, *Some Historical Errors of James Ford Rhodes* (Boston: Cornhill Pub. Co., 1923), pp. xvii–xx.

88

THE AFRICAN BLOOD BROTHERHOOD

A radical organization of young Black people, the African Blood Brotherhood, appeared in 1919; its orientation was Marxist and its political affinities were Communist. Unlike the Pan-African movement, led by Dr. Du Bois, this Brotherhood emphasized working-class leadership and consciousness; this also distinguished it from Marcus Garvey's movement. As to the latter, it was further differentiated because it felt that a successful struggle for liberation by the Black millions *inside* the United States was possible and necessary and would itself be a decisive contribution to the liberation of Africa. In that regard the Brotherhood's outlook and that of Du Bois were very close.

Publications of the A.B.B. are quite scarce. Published below is one issued probably in 1923. It refers to and quotes from "Governor Dorsey's Statement." This has reference to the quite remarkable *A Statement from*

Governor Hugh M. Dorsey As to the Negro in Georgia, a pamphlet issued in 1921, probably in Atlanta and without pagination; the quotations are accurately extracted from that statement which in its section "The Remedy" represented the first efforts aimed against peonage and lynching to come from a white governor in a southern state.

TALKING POINTS

on the Great Negro Exodus from the South; the reasons for the Exodus; Its Effect on Northern Labor; the Relationship between Colored and White Workers, Etc.

With an Appeal to the Self-Interest of All Workers
Labor Unions and the Negro
(A Statement by a White Labor Leader)

"Among the many short-sighted policies of conservative union leaders few are more harmful than the unfair attitude adopted in many cases toward the admission of colored workers into labor organizations. The Negroes are becoming an ever greater factor in industry. In order that this progress should be accomplished in an orderly fashion, and so that the colored workers should not be used against the white workers, the intelligent thing to do is for the organized white workers to go to great lengths to teach them the necessity for united action of both races as against the exploitation set up by the employers. Unfortunately, however, too often this has not been done. The result is that in many cases the Negro workers, feeling themselves discriminated against, have allowed themselves to be used by the employers to break down union conditions. Many a strike has thus been lost, and many more will be lost if the situation is not remedied. An intelligent policy toward the colored workers is one of the prime needs of the present-day labor movement. Unless it is worked out, organized white labor will pay bitterly enough for its folly by having the employers use the Negroes in industry as an army of strike-breakers. Labor already has more enemies than it can handle. To force the colored workers on to the employers' side, through a stupid union policy, is to invite disaster. The doors of the trade union movement must be thrown wide open to the Negro workers."—Wm. Z. Foster in "The World To-morrow," May, 1923.

And in the Meantime—

the Great Migration of Negro workers from the South continues. Negro workers are pouring North to escape the hellish conditions described in another part of this folder and in search of higher wages and better living conditions. Shall they be tools for the employers' Open Shop plot against Labor or will Organized Labor move to win these workers to its ranks by (1) opening the doors of the labor unions to them on terms of full equality with white workers, not in theory only but in practise; (2) eliminating all discriminatory practices, non-promotable and "dead-line" clauses, unfair legislative enactments, etc., and (3) acquainting the Negro workers with the benefits of unionism and actively bidding for their membership.

A Workers' Organization
What the A.B.B. Is
What It Stands For
What It Is Doing

The African Blood Brotherhood is an organization of Negro workers pledged by its Constitution and Program:

To gain for Negro labor a higher rate of compensation and to prevent capitalist exploitation and oppression of the workers of the Race—Sec. 7, Art. 2, of its Constitution.

To establish a true rapprochement and fellowship within the darker races and with the truly class-conscious white workers—Sec. 9, Art. 3, of its Constitution.

Under the caption of "Higher Wages for Negro Labor, Shorter Hours and Better Living Conditions," the program of the A.B.B. declares:

To gain for Negro Labor a higher rate of compensation and to prevent exploitation because of lack of protective organization we must encourage industrial unionism among our people and at the same time fight to break down the prejudice in the unions which is stimulated and encouraged by the employers. This prejudice is already meeting the attack of the radical and progressive element among white labor union men and must eventually give way before the united onslaught of Colored and White Workers. Wherever it is found impossible to enter the existing labor unions, independent unions should be formed, that Negro Labor be enabled to protect its interests.

The A.B.B. Seeks

To bring about co-operation between colored and white workers on the basis of their identity of interests as workers;

To educate the Negro in the benefits of unionism and to gain admission for him on terms of full equality to the unions;

To bring home to the Negro worker his class interests as a worker and to show him the real source of his exploitation and oppression;

To organize the Negro's labor power into labor and farm organizations;

To foster the principles of consumers' co-operatives as an aid against the high cost of living;

To oppose with counter propaganda the vicious capitalist propaganda against the Negro as a race, which is aimed to keep the workers of both races apart and thus facilitate their exploitation;

To realize a United front of Negro workers and organizations as the first step in an effective fight against oppression and exploitation;

To acquaint the civilized world with the facts about lynchings, peonage, jim-crowism, disfranchisement and other manifestations of race prejudice and mob rule.

Towards These Ends the A.B.B.

Supports a press service—the Crusader Service—for the dissemination to the Negro Press of the facts about conditions and events in the sphere of organized labor; reports of labor's changing and increasingly enlightened attitude towards the colored workers; and sends out news of general race interest, interpreted from the working class point of view. The Service is mailed twice each week and is used regularly by over a hundred Negro papers.

Sends organizers and lecturers into industrial sections to propagate the doctrines of unionism and enlist Negro workers into the ranks of the most militant organization of Negro workers in the country.

Operates forums and classes with the aim of arousing (1) the race consciousness of the Negro workers and (2) their class consciousness. (This is the natural process.)

Guards against the use of the Negro migrants as tools for the Open Shop advocates and other unscrupulous employers who seek to break the power of Organized Labor and to destroy all those gains won for the working class during the last twenty years by those workers who had the good sense to organize for their protection.

Exposes the existence of mob-law, peonage, and other barbarisms in the South and wages relentless war against these evil conditions which force the Southern Negro to flee the South and seek employment in the industrial sections.

The Message to You—

Class-conscious white worker or race-conscious Negro (and the A.B.B. has only one message for both!)—shocked by the conditions under which the Negro is forced to live in the South; the conditions which are driving him northward to create new alignments and strange problems in the industrial sections of the North—you cannot fail to realize the potentialities evoked by this steady stream of unorganized workers from the South. If you are a thinking, rational being you cannot fail to recognize THAT THIS IS YOUR FIGHT and you must help us wage it! The A.B.B. is a workers' organization. It has no source of income other than its membership and the masses. It is upon the workers it must depend. *You* must help us in the work of reaching the Negro masses with the message of unionism, the message of organized power, the message of united action by the workers of both races against the capitalist combinations; against the Wall Streets, the Chambers of Commerce, the Rotarian gang, the Ku Klux Klan, (the American Fascisti) and against all the tools of the interests who would keep the workers apart in order the more effectively to exploit them.

This Is Your Fight! So Help Wage It!

Race-conscious Negro, show that you recognize the source of your oppression!

Class-conscious White Worker, show that you realize the fact of the identity of the interests of the workers of all races!

Reasons for the Negro Exodus from the South

A glimpse of hell was given newspaper readers a few weeks ago in connection with the conditions of peonage in the State of Florida under which young Martin Talbert, a white lad of North Dakota, was wantonly murdered under the lash of a boss-driver's whip. Here's some more of hell!

Mob Law

"In some counties the Negro is being driven out as though he were a wild beast. In others he is being held as a slave. In others, no Negroes remain.

". . . If the condition indicated by these charges should continue, both God and man would justly condemn Georgia more severely than man and God have condemned Belgium and Leopold for the Congo atrocities.

"In only two of the 135 cases cited is the 'usual crime' against white women involved."—Extracts from Governor Dorsey's Statements As to the Negro in Georgia.

Peonage

Case No. 135—"March 30, a Negro, said to have been held in peonage, appealed to a justice of the peace. In the presence of the justice, a Marshal is reported to have beaten the Negro with an axe handle. Nothing has been done to the Marshal.

Case No. 134.—"December, 1920, a white man is reported to have killed a Negro for trying to leave his place. The white man has not been arrested."—Extracts from Governor Dorsey's Statements As to the Negro in Georgia.

The Negro and the Courts

Southern courts are justly notorious for the brand of justice they hand out to the Negro worker. This brand ranges from a fine of $25 for "keeping late hours," with a convict farm and a boss-driver in the offing if the "offender" cannot raise the money, to sentences to death and long term imprisonments for Negroes accused of resisting exploitation. For example, when in Phillips County, Ark., colored farm hands got together to protest and secure legal action against vicious exploitation and downright robbery under the share-cropping system of the South, those colored farm hands were attacked and shot down by their employers and their gangsters. Those who escaped the massacre were locked up charged with inciting to an insurrection against the white people of the county. In an atmosphere charged with race prejudice and the most virulent hatred, twelve of these men were sentenced to death and sixty-seven to long prison terms.

And this horrible frame-up, with its death sentences for 12 and long prison terms for 67, is only one of many such incidents that occur throughout the Southland and, with night-riding, whipping and lynching, contribute to keep the Negro population in a constant state of terrorism and have led to the present Great Migration, coupled with long hours of toil, low wages, unhealthy living conditions, and other forms of savage exploitation.

A Free Africa:—The A.B.B. stands for the waging of a determined and unceasing fight for the liberation of Africa without, however, making any surrenders or compromises on other fronts. We have no patience, therefore, with those Negroes who would distract the attention of the Negro workers from the fight for better conditions in the United States to an illusory empire or republic on the continent of Africa. We believe that the Negro workers of America can best help their blood-brothers in Africa by first making of their own group a power in America. The position of 12,000,000 Negroes at the heart of an imperialist power could not long be ignored were those Negroes intelligently organized, courageously led, and co-operating with the organized white workers on the basis of identity of interests of the entire working-class of the world.

"To Be a Negro in a Day Like This"

THE NEGRO IS

reduced to peonage in the Southern States;
shut out from labor unions in the North;
forced to an inferior status before the courts of the land;
made a subject of public contempt everywhere;
lynched and mobbed with impunity;
deprived of the ballot in the South;
segregated in vile, unsanitary districts in cities, both North and South;
degraded economically, politically and socially;
often persecuted by reason of his very thrift and ambition;
denied (and in this he is not unlike most workers) the security of life guaranteed by the Constitution.

The A.B.B. believes in inter-racial co-operation—not the sham co-operation of the oppressed Negro workers and their oppressors, but the honest co-operation of colored and white workers based upon mutual appreciation of the fact of the identity of their interests as members of the working class. This is the only inter-racial co-operation the A.B.B. believes in!

The Negro's Rock of Gibraltar!

That to a large extent is what the A.B.B. is today. That is what it must be to a much greater degree tomorrow. And that is the task before every member of the A.B.B. And the way to successfully achieve our task is to organize every Negro into the A.B.B. that we possibly can. Get the intelligent and aggressive. Get the race-conscious. Get those who know the source of their oppression and are accordingly class-conscious as well as race-conscious. Get them all! Organize every Negro into the Brotherhood. Once in, it will be our duty to educate them to become effective units for the waging of the Negro Liberation

Struggle. Our educational machinery is functioning perfectly. It has yet to be taxed to capacity. Get them in!

Undated leaflet, probably 1923, in editor's possession. The "Program of the African Blood Brotherhood"—adopted in 1921 or early 1922—is printed in *The Communist Review* (London), April 1922; II: 448–54.

89

THE DEFEAT OF ARKANSAS LYNCH LAW
by Walter F. White

A significant beginning in cracking the open and brutal racism of southern "justice" was the majority decision of the U.S. Supreme Court, rendered by Mr. Justice Holmes, in *Moore* v. *Dempsey,* 261 U.S. 86 (1923). This grew out of the Elaine, Arkansas, outbreak of 1919, dealt with earlier in this volume. To the quotation from Holmes, offered by Walter White in what follows, may be added the Justice's statement that in the instant case "the whole proceding is a mask" and that, therefore, the Court had to assure "to the petitioners their constitutional rights."

On Monday, February 19, the Supreme Court of the United States handed down its decision in the now famous Arkansas Cases, reversing the convictions of the five men in whose behalf appeal was being made, and ordered the *Federal District Court* to inquire into and ascertain if the men received a fair trial in the state courts of Arkansas. This great decision marks the beginning of the end of the cases which have constituted one of the most notable and most difficult struggles ever undertaken by the N.A.A.C.P. in its twelve years of existence.

For three and a half years, at a cost of more than $14,000, and in the face of relentless and bitter opposition on the part of the Arkansas authorities and the whites of the state, the N.A.A.C.P. has fought to save the lives of the twelve men who were condemned to death, and to release from prison the sixty-seven others who were sentenced to long prison terms for alleged connection with the so-called Phillips County, Arkansas, "massacre" of October, 1919. Never has there been a more determined effort to slaughter innocent men than that shown by the whites of Phillips County and of that entire state. Every effort, fair and foul, was used to intimidate the courts that the men should be killed, and the courts themselves seemed peculiarly sensitive to the mob spirit that has dominated these cases from their inception. Only by the carrying of these cases to the highest tribunal in the land could justice or, rather, the prevention of gross injustice, be secured.

The importance of the decision just gained is so immense that it will be interesting to the reader to trace these cases from their inception.

As told in the March *Crisis,* following the rioting in Phillips County, Ark., twelve men were sentenced by the Phillips County Circuit Court to die in December, 1919. Lawyers employed by the N.A.A.C.P. appealed to the Arkansas State Supreme Court in their behalf and that court reversed the conviction of seven of the men and remanded them for retrial in the Phillips County Circuit Court. In the cases of the other five men the convictions were approved. It is this group of cases on which the United States Supreme Court has just rendered its verdict and of which the story is told below.

After the Arkansas State Supreme Court had refused to reverse the verdict of the lower court, Charles H. Brough, then governor of Arkansas, set a new date for their execution. To avoid their execution, the lawyers defending the men applied to the Pulaski Chancery Court for a writ restraining the State of Arkansas from executing the men. Pursuing its vindictive course, the State of Arkansas filed a demurrer to the writ, which demurrer, in effect, said, "Suppose all that you say about these men being unfairly convicted be true, you have no remedy at law." The demurrer was sustained by the court, thus dissolving the writ which was preventing the execution of the men.

Again a new date of execution was set. But the defenders of the men were not beaten. An appeal to the United States Supreme Court on a writ of error was made. The Supreme Court ruled that it could not legally inquire into the cases nor take any action of any sort upon them by means of such a writ. Then a petition was filed in the Federal Court of the Eastern District of Arkansas, setting forth that the men had been deprived of their liberty without due process of law, and stated fully the grounds on which this claim was made. The State demurred to their petition, which demurrer was sustained by Judge Cotteral who presides over that branch of the Federal Court in Arkansas. Judge Cotteral declined to hear the facts but ruled that, since there was probable cause for an appeal, such an appeal be allowed to the United States Supreme Court.

It was on this appeal that Moorfield Storey so ably and so successfully argued in the Supreme Court on January 9 and brought about the favorable decision on February 19.

The majority opinion of the court was delivered by Mr. Justice Oliver Wendell Holmes. Five other justices as follows concurred: Chief Justice Taft, and Associate Justices Brandeis, Butler, Van Devanter and McKenna. A dissenting opinion was rendered by Mr.

Justice McReynolds in which Associate Justice Sutherland concurred. The decision was thus six to two.

After reciting the facts admitted by the demurrer, the majority opinion goes on as follows to outline the facts and the law:

According to the affidavits of two white men and the colored witnesses on whose testimony the petitioners were convicted, produced by the petitioners since the last decision of the (Arkansas State) Supreme Court hereafter mentioned, the Committee (of Seven) made good their promise by calling colored witnesses and having them whipped and tortured until they would say what they wanted, among them being the two relied on to prove the petitioners' guilt. However that may be, a grand jury of white men was organized on October 27th, with one of the Committee of Seven, and it is alleged, with many of those organized to fight the blacks, upon it, and on the morning of the 29th the indictment was returned. On November 3rd, the petitioners were brought into Court, informed that a certain lawyer was appointed their counsel and were placed on trial before a white jury—blacks being systematically excluded from both grand and petit juries. The Court was crowded with a throng that threatened the most dangerous consequences to anyone interfering with the desired result. The counsel did not venture to demand delay or a change of venue, to challenge a juryman or to ask for separate trials. He had had no preliminary consultation with the accused, called no witnesses for the defense although they could have been produced, and did not put the defendants on the stand. The trial lasted about three-quarters of an hour and in less than five minutes the jury brought in a verdict of guilty of murder in the first degree. According to the allegations and affidavits there never was a chance for the petitioners to be acquitted; no juryman could have voted for an acquittal and continued to live in Phillips County and if any prisoner by any chance had been acquitted by a jury he could not have escaped the mob. . . .

We shall not say more concerning the corrective process afforded to the petitioners than that it does not seem to us sufficient to allow a Judge of the United States to escape the duty of examining the facts for himself when if true as alleged they make the trial absolutely void. We have confined the statement to facts admitted by the demurrer. We will not say that they cannot be met, but it appears to us unavoidable that the District Judge should find whether the facts alleged are true and whether they can be explained so far as to leave the state proceedings undisturbed.

Order reversed. The case to stand for hearing before the District Court.

This is what the decision means. The Federal District Judge in Arkansas, in sustaining the demurrer of the State of Arkansas, ruled that the five defendants had no legal remedy. The United States Supreme Court decision reverses that decree and the case is sent back to him to hear the facts. If he finds that the facts are as alleged in the petition, he will grant the writ of *habeas corpus,* and that will mean the defendants are improperly held by the keeper of the penitentiary, must be brought before the court, and there discharged on the ground that they are not held by any legal process. Under the constitution no man can be deprived of life or property without due process of law, and the Supreme Court has held that upon the facts alleged in the petition, if they are true, (in filing a demurrer to these facts, the State of Arkansas does not deny they are true) these defendants are deprived of their liberty without due process of law. It is therefore highly probable that these men who have been under sentence of death since November 3, 1919, will soon be free.

For a minute, let us go back to the cases of Ed Ware and the other five men whose cases were appealed to the Arkansas State Supreme Court after they too were sentenced to death by the Phillips County Circuit Court on November 3, 1919. It will be remembered that the State Supreme Court reversed the lower court and ordered the men to be retried. They were again placed on trial in the Phillips County Court and again convicted and sentenced to death. Again an appeal was made by the N.A.A.C.P. lawyers to the State Supreme Court, and a second time their conviction was reversed by the higher court, this time on the ground that Negroes had been deliberately excluded from the jury in contravention of the Fourteenth Amendment and the Civil Rights Act of 1875. The men were ordered tried a third time by the Phillips County Court.

This second reversal took place on December 6, 1920. Although the attorneys for the men have been ready for trial each time the cases were set, on every occasion the State of Arkansas asked post-ponement. It has been evident that the State was disinclined to risk further discredit through a third reversal, and was waiting until the United States Supreme Court has rendered its decision in the other block of cases. Now that the decision has been rendered, it is quite possible that the State of Arkansas will allow the cases of Ed Ware and the five men to go by default under the statute of limitations which requires release of men who have been awaiting retrial for two years and who have not been tried through unreadiness on the part of the State.

In similar fashion will the cases of the sixty-seven men sentenced to long prison terms be affected. Writs of *habeas corpus* are now being prepared to obtain their release. When this is done, all of the seventy-nine men will be freed, and the biggest case of its kind ever known will have been completed.

Why are these cases so important? Is it simply that twelve innocent men might be saved from death and sixty-seven other men might be released from unjust confinement in prison? By no means. It is, of course, humane and necessary that such struggles to prevent legal murder be waged. But there are two reasons far more important why these cases and their successful conclusion affect the lives and destinies of every colored man and woman in the United States and particularly those who live in the farming sections of the South. It affects with equal force white tenant farmers of that same region.

The first of these reasons is this. If the deliberately manufactured charge which was spread by news despatches throughout the country that these colored men had formed an organization "to massacre white people" had gone unchallenged, Negroes could have been butchered and murdered like wild beasts in all parts of the South and the slaughter justified by the tale that they "had formed an organization to kill white folks just like those Negroes did in Phillips County, Arkansas, in 1919." *That lie has been exploded for all time!*

The second reason is even more important. This decision opens up the entire question of economic exploitation of colored and white farmers alike under the share-cropping and tenant-farming systems of the South. According to Dr. Albert Bushnell Hart of Harvard University, the Negro forms two-fifths of the population of the South but *produces three-fifths of the wealth*. Negro farmers enter into contracts with landowners in all the cotton states through which an equitable division of the crops produced is guaranteed. Under the terrorization which rules the South through mob-law, these Negro farmers are seldom given itemized accountings, are seldom allowed to know the price at which the crops they raised are sold by the landlords, are forced to accept the landlord's figures for supplies received, and dare not question the honesty of the accounting. Bills for supplies are padded, prices received through the sale of crops are whatever the landlord chooses to tell his tenants. In such manner the Negro usually finds himself deeper and deeper in debt every year regardless of how little he used in supplies or how high the price of cotton or corn.

Under the system no Negro is allowed to leave a plantation as long as he remains in debt. Thus, the landlord cannot only take by force and intimidation all of the crop but he can assure his labor supply for the coming year. It was against such a system as this that the colored men in Phillips County, Ark., organized. They knew that any individual Negro who dared dispute the figures given him by his landlord was liable to be classed as a "bad" Negro and lynched if he became too insistent in his demands for an honest settlement. They had learned through bitter experience and through conditions unbelievable to men and women who live in more enlightened sections of the United States, a lesson of organization which many colored people in other parts of the country have not yet learned.

In the final analysis, lynching and mob violence, disfranchisement, unequal distribution of school funds, the Ku Klux Klan and all other forms of racial prejudice are for one great purpose—that of keeping the Negro in the position where he is economically exploitable. A blow so powerful at the fundamental form of exploitation—the share-cropping system through which Negroes are robbed annually of millions of dollars—is the most effective attack on the whole system of race prejudice that could be struck. The Supreme Court decision in these notable cases thus becomes one of the milestones in the Negro's fight for justice—an achievement that is as important as any event since the signing of the Emancipation Proclamation.

The Crisis, April, 1923; XXV, 259–61.

90

THE NATIONAL ASSOCIATION
OF NEGRO MUSICIANS
by Carl Diton

In the period just before, during, and after World War I, when vast stirrings among the Afro-American people occurred, one reflection was the effort to organize nationally the Black musicians. The story of this effort and the nature of the resulting organization, together with an indication of its hopes for the future, are in an essay that follows from the pen of a distinguished Black musician, who at this time was the national organizer of the association he describes.

When a score or more of prominent musicians and artists hailing from different parts of the United States met at the national capital during the latter part of the spring of 1919, little did they surmise that they were taking an initial step toward a national association that would, in less than four years, grow to a membership of over one thousand with 34 branches.

To the association's first presiding officer, Henry Grant, an unusually well-schooled musician and educator, should go the honor of having made the launching of such an invaluable association possible, for it was he who called the first conference and who laid before it a solid, constructive working plan which subsequently became the structural foundation of the present national organization.

In connection with the idea of forming a national association, however, it is fair to record that there were two other prominent men who were ambitious to perform a similar service for the race. In 1914, Clarence Cameron White, violinist-composer and educator, issued a call from Boston for a national meeting, but was compelled to call it off because of the excitement attending the outbreak of the World War. In 1918, Nathaniel Dett, well-known composer, issued a similar summons, only to be frustrated by the memorable influenza epidemic. It is interesting to note though, that the association, young as it is, has shown fine political wisdom in choosing for its second president the former of these two men in recognition of his pioneer effort to bring about closer union among Negro-American musicians.

At present, the most brilliant achievement of the National Association of Negro Musicians is its conventions. This fact should not be under-estimated, for in point of constructive thought, to say nothing of the vast crowds of people attendant upon its evening concert sessions when the standing room of the largest procurable auditoriums is at a premium, these conventions go far towards rivaling those of older and more experienced national associations. Every year brings forth an amazing wealth of the noblest kind of talent which is, even to the older and more seasoned members, vividly startling.

The 1919 convention was held in Chicago. In 1920, the association convened at New York City, the guest of St. Philip's Protestant Episcopal Parish. Nashville received the convention in 1921, the Baptist group and Fisk University co-operating in the entertainment and comfort of the delegates. It is, however, the consensus of opinion that the Columbus, Ohio, convention of 1922, characterized by the absolute satisfaction of the delegates as to their personal comfort, the total absence of anything that savored of graft, and the absolute punctuality of the sessions, was the masterpiece of them all. The character of this year's convention, which will be held at Chicago, July 24 to 26 inclusive, remains to be seen.

The present usefulness of the association then, is assured through its annual meetings. No young Negro musician could possibly make this annual pilgrimage without getting sufficient inspiration to last a twelvemonth. As to its future usefulness, much more must be anticipated. To be fully effective, it must link itself with other large important groups, the School and the Church, for the reasons that it must not suffer for want of intellectual appreciation nor for economic assurance.

Every school devoted to the education of Negro youth including the subject of music in its curriculum, should have a branch of the National Association of Negro Musicians, provided there is not already a branch organization in the respective municipality, for the association will need for its future constituent membership educated musicians to carry on the work of skilled, scientific organization, which is becoming more and more complex every day. Its members must have vision, capacity for creative thought, even more so than now, and appreciation for aggressive propaganda for the future.

With the co-operation of the Church, the National Association of Negro Musicians might well do wonders. It should work toward the improvement of church music by urging the clergy to procure always the best trained organists and to do all in their power to keep them under the instruction of good teachers; to encourage their choir members to follow the Azalia Hackley doctrine of cultivating the voice no matter how beautiful it may be in its natural state; to invite artists of national prominence to their churches for recitals, thus affording the community moments of musical inspiration; and last, but by no means least, to incorporate the spiritual in the order of worship. These are only a few of the myriad possibilities which might well be attempted with some degree of success. Let us hope that the members of the National Association of Negro Musicians will start this movement by assuming a friendly attitude toward some of these reforms.

The Crisis, May, 1923; XXVI, 21–22.

91

FROM JOB TO JOB: A PERSONAL NARRATIVE
by *George S. Schuyler*

From the nineteen-twenties through World War II, Mr. Schuyler was a rather militant and very prolific journalist and author, with articles and columns and books pouring from his pen. Following the war, he moved steadily toward the Right; in the recent past he has been one of the very rare Black people appearing under the auspices of the Birch Society. Below is an autobiographical essay by the young George Schuyler, telling of the vicissitudes of obtaining work.

New York is the Mecca of America. The steps of plutocrat and proletarian alike turn toward this great metropolis. Like some huge magnet it attracts young and old, male and female, clever and stupid, black and white. It is not strange, therefore, that I, too, sought my fortune among its caves and canyons of steel and stone.

Like most strangers who enter this great city, I was not over-burdened with a supply of this world's goods. Hence, I was on a still hunt for work a very short time after I arrived. Having had con-siderable experience as a clerk in the government service, both civil and military, and armed with excellent references, it was only natural that I should seek that sort of work.

Day after day I tramped the streets answering advertisements out of the newspapers. Day after day I was met with refusal. Sometimes I was frankly told that no colored help was wanted. More often I was met with evasions, excuses or profuse apologies. On two or three occasions I *almost* succeeded in getting excellent positions by mail, but the inevitable interviews were sufficient to kill my chances for those jobs. I was soon forced to seek for other work.

Although I was reluctant to leave the city, I was finally forced to take a shipment to a railroad camp from a Bowery agency. I went out as a waiter. The wages offered were sufficiently large to arouse suspicion. When I asked pertinent questions concerning the conditions obtaining at the place I was gruffly told to take the job or leave it. Hungry men seldom ask many questions, so I accepted.

That afternoon we left, ten of us, for the camp in Pennsylvania, where we arrived late that night. The "camp" was a railroad yard with repair shops, roundhouses, etc., in a narrow valley alongside a river, with steep bluffs on each side. There is a large town overlooking the yards. On the edge of the bluff was a barb-wire fence about ten feet high with sentry boxes at intervals in which reclined the heavily armed "guards" of the railroad. The shops were built against the bluff. Near the river was a large shed where the commissary and dining coaches were situated. Between these and the river were the long lines of coaches converted into sleeping cars; three for the Negro workers and about eight cars for the whites. These sleeping cars were steam-heated, unventilated and unsanitary. Fourteen double-deck iron beds were in each car, used alternately by the day and night shifts. A little observation and questioning confirmed my earlier view that it was a scab job. Next morning, despite the threats of gunmen of the company and the refusal of transportation back to the city, I left on foot.

My one night's stay afforded me an opportunity to obtain the views of the Negro strikebreakers. Nearly all of them were dissatisfied and were only staying long enough to "make a stake." Many considered it an excellent opportunity to learn a trade, saying, "If there wasn't a strike we couldn't get a job at this shop work." There were English-, Spanish- and French-West Indian Negroes there, but the majority of the Negroes were from the South. They were not surprised to learn that I was leaving in the morning. I learned that many Negroes had left as soon as they discovered what sort of job it was.

Three days later I was back in New York. This time I sought only restaurant and hotel jobs. Even here I found my color against me in many instances. Some establishments hired no colored help. No Negroes were wanted as counter-men or cashiers. Here and there I found a place that hired Negro waiters. But one must have a certain uniform to wait on tables. After a night or two at the Municipal Lodging House, with its pedigree-taking and other prison-like humilities, I finally succeeded in getting a $14-a-week dishwashing position.

Ten or twelve hours a day, standing over a tub of steaming, soapy water in an oven-like kitchen is not calculated to endear one to the profession of "pearl diver." So, after a few weeks of that sort of thing I sought other fields of employment. On several occasions, however, I have had to return to it.

I have found that more and more factories, plants, and industries cater to Negro labor, but generally for Negro unskilled labor. With the exception of the civil service, there is little opportunity for the Negro clerk, stenographer, accountant or executive; his greatest opportunity is with Negro business concerns. It is seldom that one finds him employed in any other establishments.

Even in the civil service some subtle methods are at times used to keep the successful Negro applicant out of the higher positions. For instance, in 1919 I successfully completed an examination at the Customs House in New York City for first grade clerk in the field service. A month later I got an appointment as timekeeper at the Port of Embarkation at Hoboken. I called at the latter place for interview, as directed, and was sent across the river to the main offices on Broadway. After some questioning by an official at that office, I was told that I would not "do" for the position and that the district secretary of the civil service would be notified accordingly. A day or two later I received a letter from the latter announcing that "In view of the fact that you *refused* the position offered your name has been taken from the eligible list"! Of course, there are many Negroes in the civil service, and this may only be an exceptional case. Still, I have been told of similar experiences.

I have also experienced the inconveniences of carrying a hod. As a member of the union I generally received a square deal. Once a contractor refused to rehire me when a strike was settled. Immediately my white fellow-workers refused to return to work unless I also was allowed to return. Needless to say, the boss was forced to give in. I have worked as a straw boss over white laborers without any difficulty whatever, although a great deal of tact is required in such cases.

As the supply of foreign labor diminishes and the migration of Negro labor to the North continues, both white employes and their employers are being forced to change their traditional attitude toward their black brothers. But there is still room for vast improvement.

The World Tomorrow, May, 1923; VI, 147–48.

92

THE THIRD PAN-AFRICAN CONGRESS

The Third Pan-African Congress held two meetings; the first in London November 7–8, 1923, and the second in Lisbon, December 1–2. Du Bois faced difficulties from the French officials of the congress—Gratien Candace and Isaac Béton—who, in Du Bois' view, were more French than African. Nevertheless, after postponements, the meetings were held and were well attended and attracted considerable international attention. At the London meeting, Du Bois delivered four major papers; in addition, Kamba Simango discussed Portuguese Angola and Mrs. Ida Gibbs Hunt of the United States offered a paper on "The Colored Races and the League of Nations." Remarks were forthcoming at the London meeting from Sir Sidney Olivier, former governor of Jamaica, and from Harold Laski, H. G. Wells, J. H. Tawney, Rayford W. Logan, Chief Amoah III of the Gold Coast Colony in West Africa (presently Ghana), and Bishop Vernon of the A.M.E. Church in the United States. The Resolutions adopted at the London session follow.

The Executive Committee of the Third Pan-African Congress, meeting in London and Lisbon in November, 1923, regards the following matters as those which seem to them to embody the legitimate and immediate needs of the peoples of African descent.

1. A voice in their own government.
2. The right of access to the land and its resources.
3. Trial by juries of their peers under established forms of law.

4. Free elementary education for all; broad training in modern industrial technique; and higher training of selected talent.
5. The development of Africa for the benefit of Africans, and not merely for the profit of Europeans.
6. The abolition of the slave trade and of the liquor traffic.
7. World disarmament and the abolition of war; but failing this, and as long as white folk bear arms against black folk, the right of blacks to bear arm in their own defence.
8. The organization of commerce and industry so as to make the main objects of capital and labour the welfare of the many, rather than the enriching of the few.

These seem to us the eight general and irreducible needs of our people.

Specifically and in particular we ask for the civilized British subjects in *West Africa* and in the *West Indies* the institution of home rule and responsible government, without discrimination as to race and color.

We ask for such areas as *Northern Nigeria, Uganda* and *Basutoland,* a development of native law, industry and education with the specific object of training them in home rule and economic independence, and for eventual participation in the general government of the land.

We ask for *French Africa* the extension of the citizenship rights of voting and of representation in Parliament from Senegal and the West Indies to other parts of the colonies as rapidly as the present comprehensive plans of education can be realized.

We demand for *Kenya, Rhodesia* and the *Union of South Africa* the restoration of rights to the land to the natives, a recognition of their right to a voice in their own government and the abolition of the pretension of a white minority to dominate a black majority, and even to prevent their appeal to the civilized world.

In the *Belgian Congo* we fail yet to see any decisive change from a regime of profit making and exploitation to an attempt to build modern civilization among human beings for their own good and the good of the world. We demand a system of state education, the recognition of native law, a voice in government and the curbing of commercial exploitation in that great land.

For the independent nations of *Abyssinia, Haiti* and *Liberia* we ask not merely political integrity but their emancipation from the grip of economic monopoly and usury at the hands of the money-masters of the world.

For the Negroes of the *United States of America* we ask the suppression of lynching and mob-law, the end of caste and the recognition of full citizenship despite race and color.

We demand the restoration of the *Egyptian Sudan* to an independent Egypt.

We demand for *Portuguese Africa* release from the slave-trading industrial monopolies financed in England and France which today nullify the liberal Portuguese Code in Mozambique.

We urge in *Brazil* and *Central America* that peoples of African descent be no longer satisfied with a solution of the Negro problem which involves their absorption into another race without allowing Negroes as such full recognition of their manhood and right to be.

We ask the *League of Nations* to appoint direct diplomatic representatives in the Mandated territories with duties to investigate and report conditions.

We ask the appointment of representatives of the *Negro* race on the Mandates Commission and in the International Labor Bureau.

In fine, we ask in all the world that black folk be treated as men. We can see no other road to Peace and Progress. What more paradoxical figure today fronts the world than the official head of a great South African State striving blindly to build peace and Good Will in Europe by standing on the necks and hearts of millions of black Africans.

For the Third Pan-Africa Congress,
(Mrs.) Ida Gibbs Hunt, Rayford Logan,
W. E. B. Du Bois, Committee

The Crisis, January, 1924; XXVII, 120–22; there is a brief account of the Lisbon sessions by Du Bois in *The Crisis,* February, 1924; XXVII, 170.

93

SOVIET RUSSIA AND THE NEGRO

by Claude McKay

Claude McKay (1890–1948) began writing poetry as a youngster in his home, Jamaica. Two books of verse appeared by 1912 when he came to the United States and studied briefly at Tuskegee and Kansas State. He moved to New York, took odd jobs, and wrote poetry (sometimes using a pseudonym) in *Seven Arts* and other periodicals. He was in London for much of the time from 1915 to about 1921 and there he wrote for radical workers' magazines. Briefly returning to New York, he was an editor of *The Liberator,* predecessor of *New Masses.* Commencing in 1921, he traveled about Europe and North Africa; his novels—*Home to Harlem* (1928), *Banjo* (1929) and others—were written while he lived in France. He returned to the United States in 1944. Philosophically, he moved rather erratically from warm sympathy for Marxism and the U.S.S.R. to the fervent embracing, at the end of his life, of Roman Catholicism. An account of his experiences in Europe and especially the Soviet Union follows.

The label of propaganda will be affixed to what I say here. I shall not mind; propaganda has now come into its respectable rights and I am proud of being a propagandist. The difference between propaganda and art was impressed on my boyhood mind by a literary mentor, Milton's poetry and his political prose set side by side as the supreme examples. So too, my teacher,—splendid and broadminded though he was, yet unconsciously biased against what he felt was propaganda—thought that that gilt-washed artificiality, *The Picture of Dorian Gray,* would outlive *Arms and the Man* and *John Bull's Other Island.* But inevitably as I grew older I had perforce to revise and change my mind about propaganda. I lighted on one of Milton's greatest sonnets that was pure propaganda and a widening horizon revealed that some of the finest spirits of modern literature—Voltaire, Hugo, Heine, Swift, Shelley, Byron, Tolstoy, Ibsen—had carried the taint of propaganda. The broader view did not merely include propaganda literature in my literary outlook; it also swung me away from the childish age of the enjoyment of creative work for pleasurable curiosity to another extreme where I have always sought for the motivating force or propaganda intent that underlies all literature of interest. My birthright, and the historical background of the race that gave it to me, made me very respectful and receptive of propaganda and world events since the year 1914 have proved that it is no mean science of convincing information.

American Negroes are not as yet deeply permeated with the mass movement spirit and so fail to realize the importance of organized propaganda. It was Marcus Garvey's greatest contribution to the Negro movement; his pioneer work in that field is a feat that the men of broader understanding and sounder ideas who will follow him must continue. It was not until I first came to Europe in 1919 that I came to a full realization and understanding of the effectiveness of the insidious propaganda in general that is maintained against the Negro race. And it was not by the occasional affront of the minority of civilized fiends—mainly those Europeans who had been abroad, engaged in the business of robbing colored peoples in their native land —that I gained my knowledge, but rather through the questions about the Negro that were put to me by genuinely sympathetic and cultured persons.

The average Europeans who read the newspapers, the popular books and journals, and go to see the average play and a Mary Pickford movie, are very dense about the problem of the Negro; and they are the most important section of the general public that the Negro propagandists would reach. For them the tragedy of the American Negro ended with *Uncle Tom's Cabin* and Emancipation. And since then they have been aware only of the comedy—the Negro minstrel and vaudevillian, the boxer, the black mammy and butler of the cinematograph, the caricatures of the romances and the lynched savage who has violated a beautiful white girl.

A very few ask if Booker T. Washington is doing well or if the "Black Star Line" is running; perhaps some one less discreet than sagacious will wonder how colored men can hanker so much after white women in face of the lynching penalty. Misinformation, indifference and levity sum up the attitude of western Europe towards the Negro. There is the superior but very fractional intellectual minority that knows better, but whose influence on public opinion is infinitesimal, and so it may be comparatively easy for white American propagandists —whose interests behoove them to misrepresent the Negro—to turn the general indifference into hostile antagonism if American Negroes who have the intellectual guardianship of racial interests do not organize effectively, and on a world scale, to combat their white exploiters and traducers.

The world war has fundamentally altered the status of Negroes in Europe. It brought thousands of them from America and the British and French colonies to participate in the struggle against the Central Powers. Since then serious clashes have come about in England between the blacks that later settled down in the seaport towns and the natives. France has brought in her black troops to do police duty in the occupied districts of Germany. The color of these troops, and their customs too, are different and strange and the nature of their work would naturally make their presence irritating and unbearable to the inhabitants whose previous knowledge of Negroes has been based, perhaps, on their prowess as cannibals. And besides, the presence of these troops provides rare food for the chauvinists of a once proud and overbearing race, now beaten down and drinking the dirtiest dregs of humiliation under the bayonets of the victor.

However splendid the gesture of Republican France towards colored people, her use of black troops in Germany to further her imperial purpose should meet with nothing less than condemnation from the advanced section of Negroes. The propaganda that Negroes need to put over in Germany is not black troops with bayonets in that unhappy country. As conscript-slave soldiers of Imperial France they can in no wise help the movement of Negroes nor gain the sympathy of the broad-visioned international white groups whose international opponents are also intransigent enemies of Negro progress. In considering the situation of the black troops in Germany, intelligent Negroes should compare it with that of the white troops in India, San Domingo and Haiti. What might not the Haitian propagandists have done with the marines if they had been black instead of white Americans! The world upheaval having brought the three greatest European nations —England, France and Germany—into closer relationship with Negroes, colored Americans should seize the opportunity to promote finer inter-racial understanding. As white Americans in Europe are taking advantage of the situation to intensify their propaganda against the blacks, so must Negroes meet that with a strong counter-movement. Negroes should realize that the supremacy of American capital today proportionately increases American influence in the politics and social life of the world. Every American official abroad, every smug tourist, is a protagonist of dollar culture and a propagandist against the Negro. Besides brandishing the Rooseveltian stick in the face of the lesser new world natives, America holds an economic club over the heads of all the great European nations, excepting Russia, and so those bold individuals in Western Europe who formerly sneered at dollar culture may yet find it necessary and worth while to be discreetly silent. As American influence increases in the world, and especially in Europe, through the extension of American capital, the more necessary it becomes for all struggling minorities of the United States to organize extensively for the world wide propagation of their grievances. Such propaganda efforts, besides strengthening the cause at home, will certainly enlist the sympathy and help of those foreign groups that are carrying on a life and death struggle to escape the octuple arms of American business interests. And the Negro, as the most suppressed and persecuted minority, should use this period of ferment in international affairs to lift his cause out of his national obscurity and force it forward as a prime international issue.

Though Western Europe can be reported as being quite ignorant and apathetic of the Negro in world affairs, there is one great nation with an arm in Europe that is thinking intelligently on the Negro as it does about all international problems. When the Russian workers overturned their infamous government in 1917, one of the first acts of the new Premier, Lenin, was a proclamation greeting all the oppressed peoples throughout the world, exhorting them to organize and unite against the common international oppressor—Private Capitalism. Later on in Moscow, Lenin himself grappled with the question of the American Negroes and spoke on the subject before the Second Congress of the Third International. He consulted with John Reed, the American journalist, and dwelt on the urgent necessity of propaganda and organizational work among the Negroes of the South. The subject was not allowed to drop. When Sen Katayama of Japan, the veteran revolutionist, went from the United States to Russia in 1921 he placed the American Negro problem first upon his full agenda. And ever since he has been working unceasingly and unselfishly to promote the cause of the exploited American Negro among the Soviet councils of Russia.

With the mammoth country securely under their control, and despite the great energy and thought that are being poured into the revival of the national industry, the vanguard of the Russian workers and the national minorities, now set free from imperial oppression are thinking seriously about the fate of the oppressed classes, the suppressed national and racial minorities in the rest of Europe, Asia, Africa and America. They feel themselves kin in spirit to these people. They want to help make them free. And not the least of the oppressed that fill the thoughts of the new Russia are the Negroes of America and Africa. If we look back two decades to recall how the Czarist persecution of the Russian Jews agitated Democratic America, we will get some idea of the mind of Liberated Russia towards the Negroes of America. The Russian people are reading the terrible history of their own recent past in the tragic position of the American Negro to-day. Indeed, the Southern States can well serve the purpose of showing what has happened in Russia. For if the exploited poor whites of the South could ever transform themselves into making common cause with the persecuted and plundered Negroes, overcome the oppressive oligarchy —the political crackers and robber landlords—and deprive it of all political privileges, the situation would be very similar to that of Soviet Russia to-day.

In Moscow I met an old Jewish revolutionist who had done time in Siberia, now young again and filled with the spirit of the triumphant Revolution. We talked about American affairs and touched naturally on the subject of the Negro. I told him of the difficulties of the problem, that the best of the liberal white elements were also working for a better status for the Negro, and he remarked: "When the democratic bourgeoisie of the United States were execrating Czardom for the

Jewish pogroms they were meting out to your people a treatment more savage and barbarous than the Jews ever experienced in the old Russia. America," he said religiously, "had to make some sort of expiatory gesture for her sins. There is no surfeited bourgeoisie here in Russia to make a hobby of ugly social problems, but the Russian workers, who have won through the ordeal of persecution and revolution, extend the hand of international brotherhood to all the suppressed Negro millions of America."

I met with this spirit of sympathetic appreciation and response prevailing in all circles in Moscow and Petrograd. I never guessed what was awaiting me in Russia. I had left America in September of 1922 determined to get there, to see into the new revolutionary life of the people and report on it. I was not a little dismayed when, congenitally averse to notoriety as I am, I found that on stepping upon Russian soil I forthwith became a notorious character. And strangely enough there was nothing unpleasant about my being swept into the surge of revolutionary Russia. For better or for worse every person in Russia is vitally affected by the revolution. No one but a soulless body can live there without being stirred to the depths by it.

I reached Russia in November—the month of the Fourth Congress of the Communist International and the Fifth Anniversary of the Russian Revolution. The whole revolutionary nation was mobilized to honor the occasion, Petrograd was magnificent in red flags and streamers. Red flags fluttered against the snow from all the great granite buildings. Railroad trains, street cars, factories, stores, hotels, schools —all wore decorations. It was a festive month of celebration in which I, as a member of the Negro race, was a very active participant. I was received as though the people had been apprised of, and were prepared for, my coming. When Max Eastman and I tried to bore our way through the dense crowds, that jammed the Tverskaya Street in Moscow on the 7th of November, I was caught, tossed up into the air, and passed along by dozens of stalwart youths.

"How warmly excited they get over a strange face!" said Eastman. A young Russian Communist remarked: "But where is the difference? Some of the Indians are as dark as you." To which another replied: "The lines of the face are different, the Indians have been with us long. The people instinctively see the difference." And so always the conversation revolved around me until my face flamed. The Moscow press printed long articles about the Negroes in America, a poet was inspired to rhyme about the Africans looking to Soviet Russia and soon I was in demand everywhere—at the lectures of poets and journalists, the meetings of soldiers and factory workers. Slowly I began losing self-consciousness with the realization that I was welcomed thus as a symbol as a member of the great American Negro group—kin to the unhappy black slaves of European Imperialism in Africa—that the workers of Soviet Russia, rejoicing in their feedom, were greeting through me.

Russia, in broad terms, is a country where all the races of Europe and of Asia meet and mix. The fact is that under the repressive power of the Czarist bureaucracy the different races preserved a degree of kindly tolerance towards each other. The fierce racial hatreds that flame in the Balkans never existed in Russia. Where in the South no Negro might approach a *"cracker"* as a man for friendly offices, a Jewish pilgrim in old Russia could find rest and sustenance in the home of an orthodox peasant. It is a problem to define the Russian type by features. The Hindu, the Mongolian, the Persian, the Arab, the West European—all these types may be traced woven into the distinctive polyglot population of Moscow. And so, to the Russian, I was merely another type, but stranger, with which they were not yet familiar. They were curious with me, all and sundry, young and old, in a friendly, refreshing manner. Their curiosity had none of the intolerable impertinence and often downright affront that any very dark colored man, be he Negro, Indian or Arab, would experience in Germany and England.

In 1920, while I was trying to get out a volume of my poems in London, I had a visit with Bernard Shaw who remarked that it must be tragic for a sensitive Negro to be an artist. Shaw was right. Some of the English reviews of my book touched the very bottom of journalistic muck. The English reviewer outdid his American cousin (except the South, of course, which could not surprise any white person much less a black) in sprinkling criticism with racial prejudice. The sedate, copperhead "Spectator" as much as said: no "cultured" white man could read a Negro's poetry without prejudice, that instinctively he must search for that "something" that must make him antagonistic to it. But fortunately Mr. McKay did not offend our susceptibilities! The English people from the lowest to the highest, cannot think of a black man as being anything but an entertainer, boxer, a Baptist preacher or a menial. The Germans are just a little worse. Any healthy looking black coon of an adventurous streak can have a wonderful time palming himself off as another Siki or a buck dancer. When an American writer introduced me as a poet to a very cultured German, a lover of all the arts, he could not believe it, and I don't think he does yet. An American student tells his middle class landlady that he is having a black friend to lunch: "But are you sure that he is not a cannibal?" she asks without a flicker of a humorous smile!

But in Petrograd and Moscow, I could not detect a trace of this ignorant snobbishness among the educated classes, and the attitude of the common workers, the soldiers and sailors was still more remarkable. It was so beautifully naïve; for them I was only a black member of the world of humanity. It may be urged that the fine feelings of the Russians towards a Negro was the effect of Bolshevist pressure and propaganda. The fact is that I spent most of my leisure time in non-partisan and anti-bolshevist circles. In Moscow I found the Luxe Hotel where I put up extremely depressing, the dining room was anathema to me and I grew tired to death of meeting the proletarian ambassadors from foreign lands, some of whom bore themselves as if they were the holy messengers of Jesus, Prince of Heaven, instead of working class representatives. And so I spent many of my free evenings at the Domino Café, a notorious den of the dilettante poets and writers. There came the young anarchists and menshevists and all the young aspiring fry to read and discuss their poetry and prose. Sometimes a group of the older men came too. One evening I noticed Pilnyak the novelist, Okonoff the critic, Feodor the translator of Poe, an editor, a theatre manager and their young disciples, beer-drinking through a very interesting literary discussion. There was always music, good folk-singing and bad fiddling, the place was more like a second rate cabaret than a poets' club, but nevertheless much to be enjoyed, with amiable chats and light banter through which the evening wore pleasantly away. This was the meeting place of the frivolous set with whom I eased my mind after writing all day.

The evenings of the proletarian poets held in the Arbot were much more serious affairs. The leadership was communist, the audience working class and attentive like diligent, elementary school children. To these meetings also came some of the keener intellects from the Domino Café. One of these young women told me that she wanted to keep in touch with all the phases of the new culture. In Petrograd the meetings of the intelligentsia seemed more formal and inclusive. There were such notable men there as Chukovsky the critic, Eugene Zamiatan the celebrated novelist and Marshack the poet and translator of Kipling. The artist and theatre world were also represented. There was no communist spirit in evidence at these intelligentsia gatherings. Frankly there was an undercurrent of hostility to the bolshevists. But I was invited to speak and read my poems whenever I appeared at any of them and treated with every courtesy and consideration as a writer. Among those sophisticated and cultured Russians, many of them speaking from two to four languages, there was no overdoing of the correct thing, no vulgar wonderment and bounderish superiority over a Negro's being a poet. I was a poet, that was all, and their keen questions showed that they were much more interested in the technique of my poetry, my views on and my position regarding the modern literary movements than in the difference of my color. Although I will not presume that there was no attraction at all in that little difference!

On my last visit to Petrograd I stayed in the Palace of the Grand Duke Vladimir Alexander, the brother of Czàr Nicholas the Second. His old, kindly steward who looked after my comfort wanders round like a ghost through the great rooms. The house is now the headquarters of the Petrograd intellectuals. A fine painting of the Duke stands curtained in the dining room. I was told that he was liberal minded, a patron of the arts, and much liked by the Russian intelligentsia. The atmosphere of the house was theoretically non-political, but I quickly scented a strong hostility to bolshevist authority. But even here I had only pleasant encounters and illuminating conversations with the inmates and visitors, who freely expressed their views against the Soviet Government, although they knew me to be very sympathetic to it.

During the first days of my visit I felt that the great demonstration of friendliness was somehow expressive of the enthusiastic spirit of the glad anniversary days, that after the month was ended I could calmly settle down to finish the book about the American Negro that the State Publishing Department of Moscow had commissioned me to write, and in the meantime quietly go about making interesting contacts. But my days in Russia were a progression of affectionate enthusiasm of the people towards me. Among the factory workers, the red-starred and chevroned soldiers and sailors, the proletarian students and children, I could not get off as lightly as I did with the intelligentsia. At every meeting I was received with boisterous acclaim, mobbed with friendly demonstration. The women workers of the great bank in Moscow insisted on hearing about the working conditions of the colored women of America and after a brief outline I was asked the most exacting questions concerning the positions that were most available to colored women, their wages and general relationship with the white women workers. The details I could not give; but when I got through, the Russian women passed a resolution sending greetings to the colored women workers of America, exhorting them to organize their forces and send a woman representative to Russia. I received a similar message from the Propaganda Department of the Petrograd Soviet which is managed by Nicoleva, a very energetic woman. There I was shown the new status of the Russian women gained through the revolution of 1917. Capable women can fit themselves for any position; equal pay with men for equal work; full pay during the period of pregnancy and no work for the mother two months before and two months after the confinement. Getting a divorce is comparatively easy and not influenced by money power, detective chicanery and wire pulling. A special department looks into the problems of joint personal property and the guardianship and support of the children. There is no penalty for legal abortion and no legal stigma of illegitimacy attaching to children born out of wedlock.

There were no problems of the submerged lower classes and the suppressed national minorities of the old Russia that could not bear comparison with the grievous position of the millions of Negroes in the United States to-day. Just as Negroes are barred from the American Navy and the higher ranks of the Army, so were the Jews and the sons of the peasantry and proletariat discriminated against in the Russian Empire. It is needless repetition of the obvious to say that Soviet Russia does not tolerate such discriminations, for the actual government of the country is now in the hands of the combined national minorities, the peasantry and the proletariat. By the permission of Leon Trotsky, Commissar-in-chief of the military and naval forces of Soviet Russia, I visited the highest military schools in the Kremlin and environs of Moscow. And there I saw the new material, the sons of the working people in training as cadets by the old officers of the upper classes. For two weeks I was a guest of the Red navy in Petrograd with the same eager proletarian youth of new Russia, who conducted me through the intricate machinery of submarines, took me over aeroplanes captured from the British during the counter-revolutionary war around Petrograd and showed me the making of a warship ready for action. And even of greater interest was the life of the men and the officers, the simplified discipline that was strictly enforced, the food that was served for each and all alike, the extra political educational classes and the extreme tactfulness and elasticity of the political commissars, all communists, who act as advisers and arbitrators between the men and students and the officers. Twice or thrice I was given some of the *kasha* which is sometimes served with the meals. In Moscow I grew to like this food very much, but it was always difficult to get. I had always imagined that it was quite unwholesome and unpalatable and eaten by the Russian peasant only on account of extreme poverty. But on the contrary I found it very rare and sustaining when cooked right with a bit of meat and served with butter—a grain food very much like the common but very delicious West Indian rice-and-peas.

The red cadets are seen in the best light at their gymnasium exercises and at the political assemblies when discipline is set aside. Especially at the latter where a visitor feels that he is in the midst of the early revolutionary days, so hortatory are the speeches, so intense the enthusiasm of the men. At all these meetings I had to speak and the students asked me general questions about the Negro in the American Army and Navy, and when I gave them the common information, known to all American Negroes, students, officers and commissars were unanimous in wishing that a group of young American Negroes would take up training to become officers in the Army and Navy of Soviet Russia.

The proletarian students of Moscow were eager to learn of the life and work of Negro students. They sent messages of encouragement and good will to the Negro students of America and, with a fine gesture of fellowship, elected the Negro delegate of the American Communist Party and myself to honorary membership in the Moscow Soviet.

Those Russian days remain the most memorable of my life. The intellectual Communists and the intelligentsia were interested to know that America had produced a formidable body of Negro intelligentsia and professionals, possessing a distinctive literature and cultural and business interests alien to the white man's. And they think naturally, that the militant leaders of the intelligentsia must feel and express the spirit of revolt that is slumbering in the inarticulate Negro masses, precisely as the emancipation movement of the Russian masses had passed through similar phases.

Russia is prepared and waiting to receive couriers and heralds of good will and interracial understanding from the Negro race. Her demonstration of friendliness and equality for Negroes may not conduce to promote healthy relations between Soviet Russia and democratic America, the anthropologists of 100 per cent pure white Americanism may soon invoke Science to prove that the Russians are not at all God's white people. I even caught a little of American anti-Negro propaganda in Russia. A friend of mine, a member of the Moscow intelligentsia repeated to me the remarks of the lady correspondent of a Danish newspaper: that I should not be taken as a representative

Negro for she had lived in America and found all Negroes lazy, bad and vicious, a terror to white women. In Petrograd I got a like story from Chukovsky, the critic, who was on intimate terms with a high worker of the American Relief Administration and his southern wife. Chukovsky is himself an intellectual "westerner," the term applied to those Russians who put Western-European civilization before Russian culture and believe that Russia's salvation lies in becoming completely westernized. He had spent an impressionable part of his youth in London and adores all things English, and during the world war was very pro-English. For the American democracy, also, he expresses unfeigned admiration. He has more Anglo-American books than Russian in his fine library and considers the literary section of *The New York Times* a journal of a very high standard. He is really a maniac of Anglo-Saxon American culture. Chukovsky was quite incredulous when I gave him the facts of the Negro's status in American civilization.

"The Americans are a people of such great energy and ability," he said, "how could they act so petty towards a racial minority?" And then he related an experience of his in London that bore a strong smell of *cracker* breath. However, I record it here in the belief that it is authentic for Chukovsky is a man of integrity: About the beginning of the century, he was sent to England as correspondent of a newspaper in Odessa, but in London he was more given to poetic dreaming and studying English literature in the British Museum and rarely sent any news home. So he lost his job and had to find cheap, furnished rooms. A few weeks later, after he had taken up his residence in new quarters, a black guest arrived, an American gentleman of the cloth. The preacher procured a room on the top floor and used the dining and sitting room with the other guests, among whom was a white American family. The latter protested the presence of the Negro in the house and especially in the guest room. The landlady was in a dilemma, she could not lose her American boarders and the clergyman's money was not to be despised. At last she compromised by getting the white Americans to agree to the Negro's staying without being allowed the privilege of the guest room, and Chukovsky was asked to tell the Negro the truth. Chukovsky strode upstairs to give the unpleasant facts to the preacher and to offer a litlte consolation, but the black man was not unduly offended:

"The white guests have the right to object to me," he explained, anticipating Garvey, "they belong to a superior race."

"But," said Chukovsky, "*I* do not object to you, *I* don't feel any difference; we don't understand color prejudice in Russia."

"Well," philosophized the preacher, "you are very kind, but taking the scriptures as authority, I don't consider the Russians to be white people."

The Crisis, December, 1923, and January, 1924; XXVII, 61–65, 114–18.

94

THE MASSIVE PETITION
FOR THE HOUSTON PRISONERS

Few events in U.S. history so outraged Afro-American public opinion as the savagery with which the men of the 24th Infantry had been punished after the Houston outbreak of 1917, to which reference was made earlier in this volume. In February, 1924, a delegation of Black men and women representing a united and determined people brought to President Coolidge a petition for pardon signed by over one hundred twenty thousand persons. The leading Republican newspaper, the *New York Tribune,* in reporting the event on February 8 headlined it: EARLY CLEMENCY FORECAST FOR 54 NEGRO SOLDIERS; in fact, the last of the Houston prisoners were released in 1938. Leading the petition effort was the N.A.A.C.P.; this is the report its organ published.

On Thursday, February 7th at noon, President Coolidge received at the White House a delegation of representative colored citizens of the United States who presented to him a petition signed by more than 120,000 people of both races, asking for pardon for the fifty-four men of the Twenty-fourth Infantry who have been confined in Leavenworth Prison since 1917 for alleged participation in the Houston Riots of that year.

The delegation consisted of fourteen persons headed by James Weldon Johnson, Secretary of the N.A.A.C.P., who acted as spokesman. The members of the delegation were:

S. S. Booker, of the Alpha Phi Alpha Fraternity, representing 3,000 college graduates.

Rev. L. K. Williams, of the National Baptist Convention, representing 2,938,579 Baptists.

Nahum D. Brascher, of the Associated Negro Press.

A. Phillip Randolph, Editor of *The Messenger* and representing The Friends of Negro Freedom.

Archibald H. Grimké, of Washington, D.C., distinguished American, former U.S. Minister to Santo Domingo and Spingarn Medallist.

Mrs. Gabrielle Pelham, of the National Race Congress.

Mrs. Daisy Lampkin, of the National Association of Colored Women.

J. E. Mitchell, Editor St. Louis *Argus,* representing National Negro Press Association.

Robert S. Abbott, Editor *Chicago Defender.*

Bishop J. S. Caldwell, of Philadelphia, representing the A.M.E.Z. Church.

Channing H. Tobias, New York City, of the Y.M.C.A.

Robert L. Vann, Editor *Pittsburgh Courier.*

Carl Murphy, Editor Baltimore *Afro-American.*

Cyril V. Briggs, Head of Crusader News Service, representing African Blood Brotherhood.

Bishop John Hurst, of the A.M.E. Church who was also invited to serve as a member of the delegation, could not be in Washington to attend the ceremony but he authorized the use of his name and that of his church with its 548,355 members in connection with the delegation, as did also Mr. B. J. Davis, Editor of the *Atlanta Independent,* who was invited as a representative of the Grand United Order of Odd Fellows. There was also attached to the petition a memorial signed by a committee of fifty composed of coöperating organizations and individuals.

The National Equal Rights League, through William Monroe Trotter, its Secretary, was represented by its own delegation of four members which, according to a telegram from Mr. Trotter to the N.A.A.C.P., came to endorse the petition gathered and presented under the auspices of the N.A.A.C.P.

In presenting the petition, Mr. Johnson said:

Mr. President:

We come as a delegation representing the 120,000 signers of a Petition asking you to exercise the power of executive clemency and pardon the former members of the United States Twenty-fourth Infantry now confined in Leavenworth Prison convicted on charges of rioting at Houston, Texas, in August, 1917. And we come as the representatives not only of those who sign this Petition, but we are the spokesmen of the sentiments, the hopes, the sorrows, too, of the more than ten million colored citizens of the United States.

The Petition asks for the pardon of these men on four grounds:

1. The excellent previous record for discipline, service and soldierly conduct of the Twenty-fourth Infantry.
2. The provocation of local animosity against these men because of their

race and color, which was manifested in insults, threats and acts of violence against these colored soldiers wearing the uniform of the United States Army and waiting to be sent to France to fight.

3. The heavy punishment meted out to members of the Twenty-fourth Infantry, of whom nineteen were hanged, thirteen of them summarily and without right of appeal to the Secretary of War or to the President, their Commander-in-Chief.

4. The exemplary conduct of the men as prisoners.

The record for bravery and loyalty of colored soldiers in every crisis of the nation is too well known to be called to your attention here, and the long history of the Twenty-fourth Infantry is a part of that record. But we do wish to call your attention to the conditions which immediately preceded the riots of August, 1917, in Houston, Texas.

Contrary to all precedent, the provost guard of this colored regiment had been disarmed in a state and in a city where insult was the daily experience of the colored man wearing the uniform of the United States Army. Following a long series of humiliating and harassing incidents, one soldier was brutally beaten and a well beloved non-commissioned officer of the regiment also brutally beaten and fired upon because they had intervened in the mistreatment of a colored woman by local policemen. The report spread among the regiment that their non-commissioned officer, Corporal Baltimore, had been killed. Whatever acts may have been committed by men of the regiment were not the result of any premeditated design. The men were goaded to sudden and frenzied action. This is borne out by the long record of orderly and soldierly conduct on the part of this regiment throughout its whole history up to that time.

The punishment meted out to the members of this regiment was the most drastic and unusual in the history of the Army. Nineteen of the men were hanged, the first thirteen of them summarily and without right of appeal. This wholesale, unprecedented and almost clandestine execution shocked the entire country and appeared to the colored people to savor of vengeance rather than justice. It bore the aspects of a visitation upon color rather than upon crime. This state of mind was intensified by the significant fact that although white persons were involved in the Houston affair and the regiment to which these colored men belonged was officered entirely by white men, none but colored men have ever been prosecuted or condemned. Fifty-four of the men are still in prison serving life and long term sentences.

It is not within the province of this delegation, nor is this the occasion, to argue these cases. But we wish to call your attention to the fact that the men were tried and convicted under a blanket indictment.

The conduct of these men as prisoners at Leavenworth has been more than exemplary. This much has been openly stated by Warden Biddle of the Penitentiary. And it is in behalf of these remaining men of the regiment who have now served nearly six years in prison that we lay before you this Petition signed by more than 120,000 American citizens, white as well as black, asking that by the exercise of executive clemency you pardon these men and restore them to citizenship.

This Petition of 120,000 names represents the earnest efforts through the past four months of every active element among the colored people of the country. It is the result of the united and consecrated work of civic, fraternal, educational and religious organizations, and of that comparatively new but mighty force, the colored press. All of those elements in the race are represented in this delegation.

We have the honor, Mr. President, respectfully to present this Petition in the name of the signers and in the name of the colored people throughout the United States whose attention will be focused upon the action it may please you to take. We present it in the name of the people whose hearts have long carried the harsh fate of these men as a heavy burden and with the feeling that, whatever acts they may have committed, they have already been more than punished; and whose hope for their early pardon has been raised by your recent magnanimous action in the cases of war-time offenders.

President Coolidge received the delegation cordially and listened with attention to Mr. Johnson's presentation of the petition. The President assured the delegation that he was well disposed towards the imprisoned members of the 24th Infantry and that he would do what he could in their behalf. President Coolidge stated that he would order an investigation of the case of each man by the War Department and that if he was empowered to do so he would move to have the men released.

Following President Coolidge's statement, Mr. William Monroe Trotter, Secretary of the National Equal Rights League, made an eloquent plea for the imprisoned men and presented resolutions and letters from congressmen and others, urging pardons.

Following the meeting with President Coolidge at the White House, Mr. Johnson called upon Senator Arthur Capper, of Kansas, and Representative Martin Madden, Chairman of the Committee on Appropriations of the House of Representatives, and both these gentlemen promised to speak to the President and to second the petition presented through the National Association for the Advancement of Colored People.

The full committee, in whose behalf the delegation to the White House presented the petition to President Coolidge, is as follows:

E. W. Abner
  Supreme Commander, American Woodmen.
Sadie Mossell Alexander
  Grand President, Delta Sigma Theta.
J. W. Alstork
  National Grand Commander, Ancient York Masons.
C. R. Blake, Jr.
  Order of Nobles of the Mystic Shrine.

Eva D. Bowles
  Young Women's Christian Association.
Nannie H. Burroughs
  President, National Training School for Women and Girls
C. E. Bush
  National Order of Mosaic Templars of America.
W. S. Cannon
  Supreme Grand Master, Independent Benevolent Order.
R. R. Church
  Lincoln League of America.
James A. Cobb
  Special Assistant U.S. Attorney, 1907–1915. Dean Howard University Law
  School.
George W. Cook
  Professor, Howard University.
B. J. Davis
  Grand United Order of Odd Fellows.
Dorothy Hendrickson
  Secretary, Kappa Gamma Kappa.
John Hurst
  Bishop, A.M.E. Church.
Henry Lincoln Johnson
  Lincoln League of America.
Robert E. Jones
  Bishop, M.E. Church.
Isaac Lane
  Bishop, C.M.E. Church.
J. A. G. Lu Valle
  Editor, *The Washington Tribune.*
Kelly Miller
  Dean Junior College, Howard University
Fred R. Moore
  Editor, *The New York Age.*
Edward H. Morris
  Grand United Order of Odd Fellows.
W. H. Miller
  Grand Secretary, Scottish Rite Masons.
Ruth Logan Roberts
  Alpha Kappa Alpha.
Emmett J. Scott
  Secretary-Treasurer, Howard University.
C. R. Taylor
  Secretary, Phi Beta Sigma.
Maggie L. Walker
  Secretary-Treasurer, Independent Order of St. Luke.
Sadie Warren
  Owner, *New York Amsterdam News.*
J. Finley Wilson

Grand Exalted Ruler, Independent Benevolent & Protective Order of Elks of the World.
J. C. Woods
President, National Baptist Convention, Uninc.

The Crisis, March, 1924; XXVII, 210–12.

95

THE NEGRO AND NON-RESISTANCE
by E. Franklin Frazier

At the beginning of a career that was to make of him one of the most distinguished sociologists in the United States, E. Franklin Frazier (1895–1962) produced an essay that provoked much thought and discussion on a subject that still induces both. After its appearance, Du Bois sent to Frazier copies of some of the letters objecting to his essay. "His answer," wrote Dr. Du Bois, "seems to us so eminently clear and sound that we are publishing it here [*The Crisis,* June, 1924; XIX, 58] as an editorial." Below are published both the original essay and Frazier's reply to his critics.

There is a growing number of colored people who arrogate to themselves the possession of such Christian humility that they must condemn the activities of the so-called agitators and others who insist that the Negro shall enjoy the same rights as other Americans. They even go so far as to repudiate the use of force on the part of their brethren in defending their firesides, on the ground that it is contrary to the example of non-resistance set by Jesus. They go about saying that Southern white people love us when they lynch us and deny us an opportunity for education and even primitive justice; and that we, on our part, entertain in our bosoms the tenderest sentiments toward our oppressors. As spokesmen of the race, they assert that we are satisfied with an inferior status in American society. All of this is done in the name of Christian humility. We cite here one of many cases of this sort of self-abasement. Some months ago in a Southern city at a gathering of colored people where the mayor spoke, one of the leading business men, in describing our attitude toward the treatment we receive, compared us to the boy in the story who brought sweets to the fellow who continued to blacken his eye; and this same gentleman asserted, without qualification, that the more white people kicked us the more sweets we were going to bring them, and that we loved them just the same.

The motives underlying such a strange attitude are not found upon investigation to be very spiritual. They are admitted to be a method of carrying on war with the enemy. They are strategic and not a choice of moral values and moral weapons. But they are the lowest forms of strategy, involving lying, deceit, fawning and hypocrisy. And while they accuse the agitators of not being "spiritual" and "resisting evil," they themselves are guilty of the worst form of immorality. They say Right is Wrong and confess themselves to be moral cowards. While they pretend to emulate the meekness of the Nazarene, they conveniently forget to follow his example of unrestrained denunciation of the injustice and hypocrisy of His day and His refusal to make any truce with wrong-doers. These peace-makers either overlook or are ignorant of the fact that Jesus and His followers taught that human personality was of greater value than race or any of the other vanities of men. Yet they refuse to protest against the greatest crime of the age —the denial of personality to the Negro. While they pretend outwardly to love their oppressors, they admit inwardly that their purpose is to fool white people.

Their deploring of hatred and praise of love is as superficial as despicable. Hatred may have a positive moral value. A few choice souls may rise to a moral elevation where they can love those who oppress them. But the mass of mankind either become accommodated to an enforced inferior status with sentiments consonant with their situation, or save themselves by hating the oppression and the oppressors. In the latter case, hatred is a positive moral force. So if hatred is necessary to prevent the Negro from becoming accommodated to his present state, how can anyone preach love?

But the question of love is irrelevant. It is foolish to go about asserting in the face of facts to the contrary that white people love us, unless perchance some think that by a sort of suggestion white people will be hypnotized into loving us. The Negro does not want love. He wants justice. Modern political communities are not based upon the principles of love but upon certain principles of justice. It is true that sentiment in the final analysis holds a political group together for any length of time; but it is sentiment towards certain fundamental principles of justice, defining the relationship that shall exist between members of the group. The Negro is asking that those who administer justice shall administer it in accordance with the principles of democratic justice which are embodied in the organic law of the United

States. Justice is impersonal. The main difficulty in the South today is that white people have not attained a conception of impersonal justice. In the South a Negro who is the favorite of an influential white man can kill another Negro with impunity. On the other hand, a white man can kill any Negro without any fear of punishment, except where he kills out of pure blood-thirstiness a "good nigger." The killing of a white man is always the signal for a kind of criminal justice resembling primitive tribal revenge. We hold that if a Negro is treated in any situation different from other citizens because he is a Negro, there is a denial of democratic justice and no amount of love will compensate for it. Colored people who talk glibly of the white man's love forget that a man may love his dog. Love may make a man behave very unjustly towards those he loves. Perhaps, in the distant future, men may love each other so that they will not need to define their rights and duties in society; but in the present stage of social evolution, we prefer to fight for the observance of the established principles of democratic political society. Where love has appeared of such dubious value, as in the South, we take our stand under the banner, *Fiat Justitia, ruat Amor.*

The Crisis, March, 1924; XXVIII, 213–14.

FRAZIER'S REPLY TO CRITICS

Let me just make it clear that I could not, in the face of patent facts, believe that wholesale violence on the part of Negroes would win for them the status they desire in this country. Yet, I am convinced that violent defense in local and specific instances has made white men hesitate to make wanton attacks upon Negroes.

I too have beheld the harvest of disease, poverty, famine and bitterness reaped by those who trusted in war to achieve democracy and make an end of wars. And, living in the South as I do, I must breathe in daily the stench of race prejudice. Yet, however much we may lament war, it appears that a disillusioned, but stupid world must undergo another war before white men will learn to respect the darker races. A Britisher remarked to me in England a couple of years ago that once in the Far East you could kick a Japanese with impunity, but since the Russo-Japanese War, the Japanese had become so arrogant that they would take you into court for such an offense! Whether making white people respect Japanese was worth a war I will leave for my critics to decide. How are we to meet the attitude of those supposedly civilized intellectuals of the South, who, according to Frank Tannenbaum, would resort to a general slaughter of Negroes rather than give them justice, but show a greater reluctance in face of the growing disposition on the part of Negroes to retaliate? *

I am primarily interested in saving the Negro's self-respect. If the masses of Negroes can save their self-respect and remain free from hate, so much the better for their moral development. One's refusal to strike back is not always motivated by a belief in the superiority of moral force any more than retaliation is always inspired by courage. In the first case it is often pure cowardice while in the latter, the fear of the censure of the herd. I believe it would be better for the Negro's soul to be seared with hate than dwarfed by self-abasement. Therefore my essay was directed against those Negro leaders who through cowardice and for favors deny that the Negro desires the same treatment as other men. Moreover they are silent in the face of barbarous treatment of their people and would make us believe this is the Christian humility.

I do not oppose the efforts of those who endeavor to instill into the Negro a genuine belief in the brotherhood of man and the superiority of moral force. But suppose there should arise a Gandhi to lead Negroes without hate in their hearts to stop tilling the fields of the South under the peonage system; to cease paying taxes to States that keep their children in ignorance; and to ignore the iniquitous disfranchisement and Jim-Crow laws. I fear we would witness an unprecedented massacre of defenseless black men and women in the name of Law and Order and there would scarcely be enough Christian sentiment in America to stay the flood of blood.

96

INTELLIGENCE TESTS AND PROPAGANDA
by Horace Mann Bond

The misuse of the so-called Intelligence Test to affirm "scientifically" the innate mental inferiority of Black children became a veritable rage in the United States, commencing soon after World War I; this continued into the nineteen-forties and still retains great influence. An early and incisive cri-

* The Sweet case in Detroit, in 1925, soon tested the right of self-defense. See "Has the Negro the Right of Self-Defense?" by the to-be-famous David E. Lilienthal, in *The Nation*, December 23, 1925; CXXI, 724–25.

tique of this shoddiness came from the pen of the then quite young Horace Mann Bond (born in Nashville, Tenn., in 1904) at the beginning of his since distinguished career as a scholar and teacher. Mr. Bond at this time was pursuing graduate studies at the University of Chicago and was teaching at Langston University in Oklahoma.

It has ever been the bane of any development in science that its results, in the hands of partial and biased observers, may be twisted and interpreted in such a manner as to provide traps for the unwary and weapons for the prejudiced. Such was the status, not so long ago, of certain anthropometric investigations which were eagerly seized upon by a little group and made the basis for the establishment of conclusions proving the inferiority of the Negro physique; and, in fact, we have only to revert to the last generation to see the young evolution theory used by a perfervid fanatic in an attempt to show for the final incontrovertible time that Negroes represented the last existing remnant of the anthropoid ape stock.

All such endeavors, born of an unscientific attack, and ending in most undignified controversy and fallacious applications, have eventually been discredited by the sane and fair thought of those in a position to know. But, appealing, as they do, to the mind of the unbalanced multitude, and savoring of those sensational elements which attract the public like so many flies to a dead carcass, they possess in them the capacity for untold harm. That "man came from monkey" was far from the idea which Darwin intended to convey; yet it is the watchword by which the fanatics have hindered the progress of an established natural law for almost a century.

In the same manner, after the school of such perverted thinkers as Madison Grant, Ripley, and Gobineau, who have advocated long and fatuously the predominance of the super-man of Nordic blood, and who in these latter days have gradually lost even the vestiges of the authority they first claimed, there is arising today a school of Educational Psychologists which presents symptoms and features indicating kinship with the former if not actual identity. Intelligence Tests, devised to discover the native capacities, or intellect, of the individual to whom they are given, are in point of time but in their teens; yet, their applications today amount to a furor, and in American Universities, and training schools for teachers, a large part of the curriculum today is devoted to the discussion and revision of these proposed means for calibrating the human brain.

The manner in which these tests and their results are being regarded should cause serious concern on the part of the Negro Intellectual, for in many cases they have ceased to be scientific attempts to gain accurate information and have degenerated into funds for propaganda and encouragements for prejudice. It should therefore be the aim of every Negro student to be in possession of every detail of the operation, use and origin of these tests, in order that he might better equip himself as an active agent against the insidious propaganda which like its prototypes, seeks to demonstrate that the Negro is intellectually and physically incapable of assuming the dignities, rights and duties which devolve upon him as a member of modern society.

Perhaps the greatest proponent of psychometric investigation in the United States has been Professor Terman of California. He it was who took the French version of the Binet tests, in turn devised by a professor at the Sorbonne as a means of differentiating between the grades of feebleminded with which French jurisprudence had to deal, and revised and extended their application throughout all the ranges of intelligence from infancy to an approximation which has generally been accepted by the descriptive, if vague, term of "Genius" as constituting the upper limit of the scale.

That Terman has been influenced by the tendency to evaluate racial differences by the application of these tests is shown by a footnote in his book *The Measurement of Intelligence,* which is used universally by all institutions of learning as a text-book in the study of this field. The footnote follows: "I found that the children along the lower slopes of the intelligence curve were usually Mexican or Negro children."

Is it not interesting that this California investigator should find such a deviation in the case of the two races to which the average South-western white holds an active prejudice?

But Terman's results are not the ones which have been most widely circulated in the form of propaganda as to the inferiority of the Negroid stock. At the beginning of the war several psychologists were retained by the government in order that they should devise some simple and easily applied means for a comparative estimation of the mental abilities of the drafted soldiers. The result of their labor was included in the now famous Alpha Army Tests, so called because they were the first or Alpha of a proposed series. These tests were administered to a large percentage of the drafted soldiers and their indications were depended upon to a certain extent in the promotion of men for the minor ranks of non-commissioned leadership.

It is in the post-war period, however, that these tests have received greatest publicity; and far from their original purpose, they now serve as reservoirs of information, accurate or not, for the use of showing the intellectual inferiority of some of the races who gave without stint of their lives for the maintenance of this country!

Mr. Carl Brigham, of Princeton University, in his recent book, *A Study of American Intelligence,* seeks to demonstrate with incontrovertible assurance the righteousness of his cause. His use of the results is very interesting, and plausible to a degree, save in certain instances connected with the clinching of his main point, concerned with the inherent inferiority of the Negro stock, and other racial elements which just at this time are arousing the ire of the 100 per cent American white. Some of his conclusions, representing as they do the fundamental position take by all the proponents of this particular school, are interesting and deserve attention:

(1) Negroes, of all racial groups, possess the least intelligence.
(2) Negroes from Northern states possess larger increments of intelligence than Negroes from Southern states!
(3) Northern Europeans possess greater intelligence than whites from Southern Europe.

Here we may distinguish two distinctive weapons for the use of the propagandist. There is material (and it has been widely utilized) for the use of the individual attempting to show the undesirability of certain immigrant groups; and the typical "Nordic" conclusion as to the inferiority of the Negro has been used, and is today a means of affirming an old fallacy.

These conclusions are gaining casual and total credence in the scholastic world, as well as in other circles where they are a matter of discussion. Only the other day in a Chicago high school a teacher made the statement that the Alpha Army Tests showed that Negroes and foreigners were inferior to native born whites. A race conscious Negro girl, one of the leaders of the class, objected to this remark, with the result that the teacher obtained the figures and tabulations of Brigham and others and displayed them to the girl. She said to me afterwards with a brave look in her eyes, "I told her that I did not believe that the figures were accurate; but, in the absence of any proof, what could I say?"

And others are wondering what it is possible for them to say in contravention to this dangerous mode of thought. To the list of inferiorities to which the Negro is assigned, is to be added one of helpless and unsurmountable natural mental deficiency; a barrier indeed difficult to hurdle.

The remedy is not far distant. We remember the case of the anthropologist who examined so many *Negro* and so many *white* brains, and from a total of less than a hundred deduced the fact that, since the Negro brains weighed several grams less than the white brains, he had stumbled upon a conclusive evidence testifying to the intellectual inferiority of the Negro. We also remember the sequel to this pseudo-scientific investigation; when an observer, taking the same brains and re-weighing them, this time without knowledge of their racial identity, discovered that the results of his predecessor had been at marked variance with the facts.*

But luckily enough, we are not forced to resort to the subconscious influence of prejudice to explain these results, although when it is considered that all of the investigators, examiners and tabulators saw in every Negro a moron and in every South European an undesirable variation from the Nordic type, we might be excused in ascribing some such effect to pre-conceived and pre-convinced judges. There is a very concrete and solid base upon which we may rest our objections to any conclusion postulating racial inferiority as its theorem; and this basis of fact which can well wreck the pretty fabric of the psychologists is to be found in the explanation of the second conclusion which we have ascribed to Mr. Brigham.

Why should Negroes from Northern states possess larger increments of intelligence than Negroes from Southern states? Mr. Brigham says that this is because the more intelligent have immigrated northward; a very pretty explanation, but not one which can be taken to justify the fact. There is only one obvious explanation; the Negro from the North, because of infinitely superior home, civil and above all school conditions, has been favored by environment in just as great degree as his Southern brother has been deprived of the same.

This admittedly is a rather hard point for Mr. Brigham to overcome; but, true to the ingenuity which prompted him to posit his first theory, he falls back upon that which he hopes to oppose to his critics as a final poser. "I have taken," says Mr. Brigham, "Negroes having the same schooling, from these two sections, and found the same superiority to exist."

As a reviewer noted in passing judgment upon Mr. Brigham's book, by what yardstick does he evaluate the identity of the training to be received in a Southern school and in a Northern school? The recent table printed in *The Crisis,* showing the wide variance of school period and the great deficiency of school funds for Negro education in Southern states, is an answer which no one can dispute. With children

* This has reference to the work of R. B. Bean and F. P. Mall prior to World War I; for details see the editor's book, *Afro-American History: The Modern Era* (N.Y., 1971, Citadel Press), p. 107.

receiving but $3.46 per capita, while those with whom they are to be compared receive from ten to twenty times this sum for educational purposes, it is little wonder that the Negro of the South should not compare with anyone given even the semblance of a chance.

Thus with the list of other "inferiorities" so confidently affirmed by Mr. Brigham and others of his school. Invariably a perusal of those nationalities whom he classes as inferior will be found to have a close correlation existing between the sums of money expended for education and their relatively low standing.

Garth has stated a law which possesses unusual and increasing validity as it is considered in the light of these facts. He says, "Intelligence tests have no value for racial comparison unless care is taken to isolate individuals, as representatives of diverse races, from approximately the same environmental strata as those with whom they are to be compared." This is a law which has been disregarded in the discussion of this question; but it is one that should be considered before we attempt to assign, arbitrarily and without reason, any race to a position of inferiority in the mental scale.

The present writer has examined hundreds of college Freshmen and correlated the marks of many more at Lincoln University. This is an institution located in such a manner that approximately the distribution between the number of students from the two sections—North and South—is equal. The results of this test also disclose the fact that the men from the Northern high schools made higher marks than those from Southern schools; and when the curriculum, the teaching staff, the supervision and the financing of these schools are compared, there are hardly any grounds on which one would agree that the two were equal from the standpoint of preparation.

Yet, when placed in the same environment, given the same treatment, taught by the same staff, it is found that these men from the poorer Southern schools are just as quick in grasping and making the best of the new college surroundings. There is no such marked disproportion existing between the honor list and the sectional location as does exist in the results of the intelligence tests.

The same general results have been found to exist wherever an intelligent effort has been made to make allowance for the environmental factor. In New York City an investigator working among the slum children compared them with the children of those who might be classed as "the respectable middle class." Her findings were a substantial recommendation for adherence to Garth's law, especially when such a delicate question as the racial hypothesis is at issue.

Only recently an investigator working from the University of Texas proclaimed the fact that he found that Negro children possessed but 75 per cent of the average intelligence native to the whites. Further investigation revealed the following facts: In that special locality, the whites, with a school population of 10,000, were expending on an average of $87 per capita for the education of their children. The Negro children received a per capita of $16; and yet this Texas psychologist believes that he has unearthed a brief for Negro inferiority!

The name and the race of the great man who said "No generalization is absolutely right; not even this one," has long since been lost; but we can rest assured that he was not a Nordic. Had he been, and his particular generalization had been one showing the mental inferiority of every other racial stock save that of God's self-elected elect, he would doubtless have said, "This investigation only adds to the cumulative mass of information assuring us of this same fact."

Thus the Educational Psychologist of today forgetting that the work of Frobenius, and of other continental ethnologists and anthropometrists, has long since refuted the contention of those who successively rested their bias of Negroid inferiority upon cranial measurements, or upon any other fanciful figment of pseudo-scientific inquiry.

Yet, what shall we consider as the true value of the Intelligence Tests? It must be admitted that they have proven of inestimable efficiency when used to secure a quantitative idea of the progress, or achievement, of school children who have been exposed to the same curricular and pedagogical conditions. Besides, the standardization effected is of untold value in making the work of American schools more uniform and synthetic.

No, it is not with Intelligence Tests that we have any quarrel; in many ways they do represent a fundamental advance in the methodology of the century. It is solely with certain methods of interpreting the results of these tests that we, as scientific investigators, must differ. So long as intelligence tests are administered, correlated, and tabulated solely with the subjective urge subdued, and with a certain degree of common sense as to their interpretation, we can never criticize them.

But so long as any group of men attempts to use these tests as funds of information for the approximation of crude and inaccurate generalizations, so long must we continue to cry "Hold!" To compare the crowded millions of New York's East Side with the children of some professorial family on Morningside Heights indeed involves a great contradiction; and to claim that the results of the tests given to such diverse groups, drawn from such varying strata of the social complex, are in any wise accurate, is to expose a fatuous sense of unfairness and lack of appreciation of the great environmental factors of modern urban life.

Yet this is the new propaganda which is gradually gaining credence throughout the university world of today. This is the common belief which, in distorted form, reaches the masses; and these 100 per cent masses are always eager to seize upon such facts and to bruit them abroad. There is a danger; and the danger threatens the infant, newly-born race consciousness of our group especially. The time has passed for opposing these false ideas with silence; every university student of Negro blood ought to comprise himself into an agent whose sole purpose is the contravention of such half-truths. We have long been an inert part of this corporate intellectual life, and in many cases, through ignorance of the facts, have chosen to be silent rather than expose our naiveté. But that time has passed. There is no longer any justification for the silence of the educated Negro, when confronted with these assertions; and only through his activity and investigation will the truth be disclosed and the ghosts of racial inferiority, mental or physical, set at rest forever.

The Crisis, June, 1924; XXVIII, 61–64.

97

BLACK WORKERS AND THE A.F.L.:
A PROPOSAL
by the N.A.A.C.P.

The N.A.A.C.P. consistently took a pro-union position and did this despite the racism often manifested by many trade unions and especially by the leadership of the American Federation of Labor. No real dent was made in this attitude and practice until the challenge represented by the creation of the Committee on Industrial Organization in the nineteen-thirties. One of the most significant reflections of this effort to break down jim crow in the A.F.L. was the following resolution (written by Du Bois) adopted at the 15th Annual Convention of the N.A.A.C.P. held in Philadelphia, June 25–July 1, 1924.

For many years the American Negro has been demanding admittance to the ranks of union labor.

For many years your organization has made public profession of your interest in Negro labor, of your desire to have it unionized, and of your hatred of the black "scab." Notwithstanding this apparent surface agreement, Negro labor in the main is outside of the ranks of organized labor, and the reason is, first, that white union labor does not want black labor, and secondly, black labor has ceased to beg admittance to union ranks because of its increasing value and efficiency outside the unions.

We thus face a crisis in inter-racial labor conditions; the continued and determined race prejudices of white labor, together with the limitation of immigration is giving black labor tremendous advantages. The Negro is entering the ranks of semi-skilled and skilled labor and he is entering mainly and necessarily as a "scab." He broke the great steel strike. He will soon be in a position to break any strike when he can gain economic advantage of himself.

On the other hand, intelligent Negroes know full well that a blow at organized labor is a blow at all labor; that black labor profits today by the blood and sweat of labor leaders in the past who have fought oppression and monopoly by organization: If there is built up in America a great black block of non-union laborers who have a right to hate unions, all laborers, black and white, must eventually suffer.

Is it not time, then, that black and white labor get together: Is it not time for white unions to stop bluffing and for black laborers to stop cutting off their noses to spite their faces?

We, therefore, propose that there be formed by the N.A.A.C.P., the A. F. of L., the Railway Brotherhoods and any other bodies agreed upon, an Inter-Racial Commission.

We propose that this Commission undertake:

1. To find out the exact attitude and practice of national labor bodies and local unions toward Negroes and of Negro labor toward unions.
2. To organize systematic propaganda against racial discrimination on the basis of these facts at the great labor meetings, in local assemblies and in local unions.

The N.A.A.C.P. stands ready to take part in such a movement and hereby invites the co-operation of all organized labor. The Association hereby solemnly warns American laborers that unless some such step as this is taken and taken soon the position gained by organized labor in this country is threatened with *irreparable loss.*

98

THE GENTLEMEN'S AGREEMENT
AND THE NEGRO VOTE
by W. E. B. Du Bois

In an unsigned article, Dr. Du Bois in the election year of 1924 made a plea for a full break by the Afro-American voter from the Republican ticket and toward independent voting. The essay notes that in Harlem this had been largely accomplished. It mentions the election of a Black man from Harlem to the state legislature; this was Henri W. Shields (D.) who in 1922 beat the Republican candidate by one thousand votes. The Black man nominated for Congress from Harlem by the Republicans—also mentioned below—was a dentist, Dr. Charles D. Roberts, a former alderman; he was, however, defeated—in part, because the National Colored Coalition Political Association and the National Negro Non-Partisan League (associated with the La Follette candidacy) opposed Roberts as politically reactionary.

There are twelve million Negroes in the United States, born American citizens, yet they constitute the least influential and least effective political unit in the whole country. The Negro demands less by his ballot, not only in actual results but even in mere respect for himself as a voter than any of all the groups that go to make up the American citizenry; although some of these groups are far smaller in numbers and even weaker economically. For all his mass of numbers and his increase in education and wealth, the Negro remains as near being a political nonentity as is possible for a group of citizens in a country with anything that resembles a democratic form of government.

This is a condition that demands analysis and study. This is emphatically true, since the Negro, more than any other group, needs whatever benefits the ballot is able to gain. There are, of course, reasons why this condition exists, and these reasons ought to be found and the facts faced. It is only by such a process that the situation can be changed and remedied.

Why is it that twelve million colored Americans are, in a positive sense, a political nonentity? I say in a positive sense because, negatively, the Negro has been for a hundred years a dominant factor in politics. In the twelve states of the real South the whole structure of politics and all political activities are based on the Negro. In these states the Negro constitutes the prime and, often, the only political issue; indeed, he is the reason for politics. From each of these states men have been elected to the governorship and to Congress solely because in "damning the nigger" they out-did their rivals.

In answering the question raised, it is, first of all, necessary to take into account the practical disfranchisement of the majority of Negro citizens. According to the census of 1920 there were 5,522,475 Negroes of voting age in the United States. Of this number, approximately, 4,500,000 were in the disfranchising states, leaving an approximate 1,000,000 in the states where Negroes vote under the same conditions as other citizens. Here, at once, we have the major reason for the political weakness of the Negro as a group, in comparison with his total number. But even this phase of the question will bear investigation, for colored Americans are too prone to excuse the political impotency of the race on the ground of "disfranchisement," without knowing why or how Negroes are disfranchised in the South.

The average citizen, black or white, when asked how Negroes are disfranchised in the South, will reply that the Southern States have laws prohibiting Negroes the right to vote in the general elections that did not apply to all citizens. How then is the Negro disfranchised in the South? It is done through a combination of processes. There is, to begin with, the *white primary*. The states cannot make laws limiting the right of Negroes to vote in general elections, without violating the Fifteenth Amendment as interpreted by the Supreme Court, but neither the Constitution nor the Supreme Court touches primary elections; so the state can make such laws as they please regarding them. As a result, the Southern states have passed laws providing for white democratic primaries, and that no party that does not poll a certain number of votes in the general election shall hold any primaries at all. In these states the primary elections have been made to supersede the general elections, and the candidates nominated in the primaries are as good as elected. So, colored citizens, denied the right to vote in the primaries, have no incentive for voting in the general elections.

The question might be asked, "Why do not Negroes in the South vote in the Republican primaries?" They do not because in most of the states of the real South there are no Republican primaries; the law providing that no party not polling a certain number of votes shall hold primaries. But there is a still more important reason why there are no Republican primaries, and it is that *those who control the Republican party in those states do not want primaries.* We now begin to get at the heart of the situation. To understand the situation it is necessary to realize this underlying fact—the Republican party in the South is not a political party, it is an office-holding oligarchy. The bosses are not interested in building up a party, they are interested solely in taking a hand-picked delegation every four years to the national convention, and landing on the bandwagon. The only political activity in the so-called Republican party in the South is that involved in contesting delegations going to the national convention. If a Republican president is elected, these bosses have all the federal jobs in the whole empire of the South to parcel out among themselves and their friends. These are fat pickings and are exclusively reserved to, relatively, a very few persons; for the mass of white Southerners are barred by being Democrats. It is here we have the reason for the rise and growth of Lilywhiteism; the white men in the game simply wanted all the jobs.

Indeed, not only do the Republican bosses in the South neglect to build up a strong party—they could make a fair beginning with nearly five million Negro voters to draw from—but a strong Republican party is precisely what they do not want; such a party would develop too much competition for the federal jobs. These bosses, without protest, allow the white South to control the local situation and reduce the Negro to a political zero in exchange for full control of federal patronage. This arrangement suits the white South. It is not considered too great a price to pay for the elimination of the Negro.

Other factors in the process by which the Negro in the South is disfranchised are the registration tests, which are wholly in the hands of the white registration officials, who can apply them so unfairly as to disqualify as many Negroes as they wish; the poll tax, which the bulk of Negroes either neglect to pay or see no use in paying; and the state of apathy on the entire matter into which the great majority of Negroes themselves have fallen. Among all these factors, the importance of the part played by the Republican bosses and the attitude of hopelessness on the part of the Negroes themselves must not be underestimated.

That disposes of the masses disfranchised in the South. But what about the colored citizens in the Northern states, where they vote under the same conditions as other citizens, where their votes are counted and count, and where they could, in many instances, wield the balance of power? They are at the present time well over a million in number. Why are they not able to act politically so as to compel respect for themselves as voters, to secure benefits, and serve as a lever to raise their brothers in the South to a higher citizenship status?

They are not able to do so because they are the victims of a tacit, if not expressed, "Gentlemen's Agreement" between the two major parties, by which they are almost completely eliminated as a political force. This agreement provides that the Republican party will hold the Negro and do as little for him as possible, and that the Democrats will have none of him at all. The pathetic thing is that it is the Negro voters themselves who make possible this annulment of the power they hold in their hands. It is possible because practically every Negro vote is labeled, sealed, delivered and packed away long before election. How can the Negro expect any worthwhile consideration for his vote as long as the politicians are always reasonably sure as to how it will be cast? The Republicans feel sure of it and the Democrats don't expect it.

As a race, we are still in the Fourth of July stage of politics. With us politics is still a matter concerning which we are sentimental. Now, mere sentiment in politics is nothing but sheer bunk. It is the stuff the politicans ladle out for the consumption of the "booboise." For those on the inside, politics is a hard, matter of fact business; indeed, a cold, calculating game. The intelligent voter is one who throws aside at once all the sentimental bunk and tries to get down to brass tacks. Any group of voters who hope to be considered politically because of sentimental reasons are displaying a trait compared with which the trust of a little child is as the cunning of a wolf.

The only way for the Negro to begin to gain political importance and power is by smashing this "Gentlemen's Agreement." He must absolutely destroy the idea that because a man's face is dark he has the word "Republican" indelibly written across his forehead and that it is a badge of villenage from which he will never seek to escape, no matter what his lords may do or may not do. He must keep politicians uncertain as to how he will vote; serving notice that the way his vote will be cast depends upon certain pledges and performances. In a word, he must put a higher price on his vote; the price of recognition as a full-fledged citizen, the price of recognition as a participator in the administration of the affairs of his government. This "agreement," which is the crux of the situation, can be smashed if the Negro uses a modicum of political common sense. Politicians are excessively human, and where contests are close agreements mean little. As an example of what can be done, take New York City. The Negro in Harlem has in a very large degree emancipated himself, and become an intelligent voter. The politicans cannot foretell to a dead certainty how much of that vote will be Republican or Democratic or Socialist or for the Third party. Colored Harlem is now represented in the

Legislature of New York State by a Negro Democrat and in the Aldermanic Board of New York City by a Negro Democrat. Has this made the Republican party less solicitous about Negro votes? Indeed, it has not. On the contrary, the hard-boiled Republican machine has just designated for that district a colored man as the Republican candidate for Congress. Politicians and parties in New York are anxious as to how colored citizens will vote, and that puts the higher price on their votes.

Colored voters in the North tremble and hesitate before the dilemma of voting for apathetic or hypocritical Republicans or voting for Democrats, and thereby strengthening our traditional and avowed enemies in the South; and they settle it by choosing "the lesser of the two evils." There are other ways out; there are other parties besides the two major parties. But suppose we yield on the question of supporting "a party too weak to do us any good," and face the dilemma. Boring from within has always been considered effective strategy for weakening the enemy. Suppose, now, that in some of the Northern states where the vote is close, a number of fairminded Democrats were put in Congress by the colored vote. Would not these men go farther to curb the anti-Negro activities of their Southern colleagues than weak-kneed, sycophantic Republican leaders now go? Would they not be compelled in self-interest to say to the Southern members of their party, "We are here because of colored votes; such and such things you cannot do, or you endanger our seats"? As it is, the Republicans actually gain by Democratic antagonism to the Negro. This is just what they sought to do in the Democratic filibuster in the Senate on the Dyer Anti-Lynching Bill.

This "Gentlemen's Agreement" and its effects are, as I said, the crux of the whole situation. When it is smashed we shall be at the beginning of achieving political power; we can do absolutely nothing until it is. It can be smashed in two ways: in the gradual assertion of political independence on the part of the Negro, or it can be done at one blow. The Negro can serve notice that he is no longer a part of the agreement by voting in the coming elections in each state against Republicans who have betrayed him, who are in league with the Ku Klux Klan, who are found to be hypocrites and liars on the question of the Negro's essential rights, and by letting them know he has done it. I am in favor of doing the job at once. There are timid souls who falter at action of this sort; they have such a keen sense about unknown calamities. There were, probably, some Negroes who were dismayed at the Emancipation Proclamation. They thought that slavery was bad and wanted to escape it, but they thought also, when faced with the unknown, that in slavery, at least, their food and clothing and shelter were secure.

But there is an awakening. The Negro is thinking, thinking political thoughts that would have been considered apostasy a generation ago. He is on his way to complete political emancipation, and will reach it sooner or later. When the Negro in the North does this he will have acquired a power which he can use not only for his own betterment but which he can apply to change conditions in the South.

The Crisis, October, 1924; XXVIII, 260–64.

99

RESTRICTED WEST INDIAN IMMIGRATION AND THE AMERICAN NEGRO
by W. A. Domingo

William A. Domingo (1889–1968) was a Jamaican who early migrated to New York and for some time after World War I was a prominent disciple of Marcus Garvey. What he felt to be Garvey's increasingly excessive extremism led Domingo to break away from the U.N.I.A. He remained an influential figure, especially among West Indians in the New York area; when in 1937 the Jamaican Progressive League of America was founded, Mr. Domingo was its vice-president. The essay below deals with the anti-Black content of the generally racist and anti-Semitic immigration legislation of 1924; it was related to the fact that, beginning in 1910 and starting up again in 1920, the migration of Black West Indians to the United States was fairly considerable.

The Immigration Act of 1924, "to limit the immigration of aliens into the United States, and *for other purposes,*" which came into force July 1, has achieved the object of its framers and sponsors who were mainly concerned about excluding undesirable racial strains. Not only was this accomplished by securing a reduction of non-Nordic Europeans in favor of Nordics, but what is of vital importance to American Negroes, by a palpable discrimination which singled out for quota restriction only those sections of the New World from which an appreciable number of Negroes have come and was likely to come in the future. That this latter achievement is among the "other purposes" of the Act seems of little doubt when the facts are studied and a comparison is made between the present Act and its predecessor of 1921.

The Act of 1921, entitled "An Act to limit the immigration of aliens into the United States," made a perpendicular distinction between immigrants who were eligible to enter the country without special treaty regulations. Those from the Old World were restricted to 3 per cent of their number in the United States in 1910, while those from the New World were admitted on a non-quota basis. In neither case were the immigrants affected by the political status of the country or colony from which they came.

Section 2 of the 1921 Act, dealing with "excepted classes" or non-quota immigrants, included aliens from "the Dominion of Canada, Newfoundland, the Republic of Cuba, the Republic of Mexico, countries of Central and South America, or *adjacent islands*." Under this provision immigrants from all parts of the Americas were on an equal non-quota basis.

The Act of 1924, section 4 (c), defines the term "non-quota immigrant" as "an immigrant who was born in the Dominion of Canada, Newfoundland, the Republic of Haiti, the Republic of Mexico, the Republic of Cuba, the Dominican Republic, the Canal Zone, or an independent country of Central and South America." By specifically naming Canada and Newfoundland for exemption from quota, placing the word "independent" before countries, and omitting the words "adjacent islands," the framers of the Act very adroitly excluded from the non-quota classes those European colonies in the Caribbean Sea from which American Negroes had been receiving any numerical increase. Conclusive proof that the Act, which was passed by the present Republican Administration, was intended to erect a barrier against the comparatively slight immigration of people of African descent from the West Indies is found in President Coolidge's Proclamation of June 30. Subdivision 6 of the Proclamation states: "*In contrast with the law of* 1921 the Immigration Act of 1924 provides that persons born in the colonies or dependencies of European countries sitiuated in Central America and South America or *the islands adjacent* to the American continents . . . will be charged to the quota of the country to which such colony or dependency belongs." The language is clear and unmistakable. It makes a horizontal distinction between British North America and other European colonial possessions in the New World. The distinction is significant in view of the reason that inspired the Act and the racial stock of immigrants from both groups of colonies.

The law to limit immigration into the United States was agitated for and defended on two main grounds: race and culture of recent immigrants and inability of the country to absorb the huge number seeking admission from Europe. The grounds were qualitative and quantitative. To achieve both ends the Census of 1890 was used as the basis to determine the 2 per cent to be admitted yearly until 1927, after which the maximum will be 150,000 annually. Whether or not a colony is self-governing does not affect the issue. In Europe, England, the Mother Country, the Irish Free State, whose status is similar to that of Canada, Malta, having a form of government like that of Jamaica or Barbados, and Gibraltar, a Crown Colony like Antigua and St. Kitts, are subject to a 2 per cent quota, regardless of their varying degrees of autonomy. The same equality of quota exists between truly independent and powerful countries like England and France and vassal states like Hungary and Poland. In the Western World the law makes no distinction between independent countries like Brazil and Argentina and nominally independent countries like Cuba and Costa Rica. It is only when colonial possessions are dealt with that a distinction is made. All British North American possessions are on a non-quota basis, while other European possessions are subject to restriction. In practice this means that only those places in the Western World from which any noticeable number of Negro immigrants had been coming are singled out for quota restrictions! With the uniform treatment accorded to British subjects in Europe it cannot be successfully contended that "self-government" inspired the inequality of treatment given to British subjects in the New World. Nor can it be seriously claimed that the number of immigrants coming from the restricted colonies, compared with the number from Canada and Newfoundland, justified restricting the former and not the latter. The contrary is the truth.

According to the *World Almanac* (1924) the principal sources of immigrants from the New World in 1923 were British North America, 117,011; Mexico, 63,768; and the West Indies, 13,181 (mostly Negroes). If number constitutes a reason for restriction then Canada, rather than the West Indies, furnished the justification. Stating it differently, of the 199,972 immigrants from the American continents who entered the United States in 1923, only 13,181 or less than 7 per cent were from countries with Negro majorities. And as not an inconsiderable portion of the 13,181 were Caucasians, it is clear that the proportion of Negro immigrants who remain in America is less than the proportion that American Negroes bear to the total population. More white immigrants came from Canada and Newfoundland in 1923 than the total number of foreign-born Negroes in the United States that year! Despite this fact and the further fact that while 4,183 West Indians left the United States that year only 2,775 British North Americans and 2,660 Mexicans departed, the former are restricted while the latter are not.

It is nowhere claimed that language or culture constituted the reason for exempting all other American peoples while restricting West Indians. With the exception of English-speaking Canadians, there are no people in the Western World more culturally and linguistically akin to Americans than British West Indians. The great difference between the West Indies and the favored British possessions of North America is that a majority of the inhabitants of the former colonies are of African descent. And this difference explains why the comparatively slight stream of immigration from these islands called for restriction.

Allied by blood to the 12,000,000 Negroes of this country, who have a deep interest in keeping the door of Negro immigration open in these days of discussion of the population question; when everything is being done to make America approximate the Ku Klux ideal of a white man's country by keeping Negroes in a hopeless minority, West Indians can only look to their brothers of the mainland to emulate the late Booker T. Washington who, in 1914, succeeded with the cooperation of other far-sighted leaders in defeating the attempt made at the time to exclude from entry people of African descent. The present law, less frank than the one of ten years ago, has nevertheless achieved the same end, for it means in effect that while the number of immigrants coming from countries that formerly sent a few Negroes will be limited to a couple of hundred yearly, white immigrants will come from Europe to the extent of half a million annually until 1927, and 150,000 after then, while those from Canada and other parts of the American continent will be unlimited. In such a situation, if Negroes are not by their silence to acquiesce in racial discrimination by the Federal government, they will use their influence to see that all immigrants in the Western World are placed upon a quota or none; that the principle of equality among colonies in Europe be applied to colonies in the Americas.

Regardless of explanations and apologies, the bald fact stands out that the present Immigration Act, which is designed to be selective racially, by deliberate discrimination against those countries in the New World from which Negroes had been coming to any extent, while exempting those from which Caucasians are still coming without limit, places Negro blood in despite and serves notice upon American Negroes that they cannot hope to increase their number by immigration. In so many words, they are told that against their natural increase will be pitted not only the natural increase of white America but a constant entry of European immigrants. Such an outlook should engage the serious consideration of the best minds of the Negro race in America.

Opportunity, October, 1924; II, 298–99.

100

LA FOLLETTE AND THE BLACK VOTERS

Attempts were made by such groups as the N.A.A.C.P. and the forces represented by A. Philip Randolph to extract from La Follette's Progressive party some recognition of the particular needs and terrible grievances of the Afro-American people. These were in vain. Nevertheless, because of the relatively enlightened outlook of the La Follette movement, it did get the support of the N.A.A.C.P. (the only time that organization, as such, endorsed a presidential candidate) and of Randolph's *Messenger* group, as well as the endorsement of Bishop John Hurst of the A.M.E. Church. Documents [a], an editorial from *The Crisis;* [b], an essay by Randolph; and [c], the text of the bishop's endorsement, follow.

[a]

THE CRISIS EDITORIAL: LA FOLLETTE

Let Negroes read with thoughtful care and deep understanding the manifesto of the Third Party. It makes no direct reference to our problems. But what are our problems? They are the world's problems and something more. That something more is color prejudice and that is our immediate problem. But back of that and even with that solved are problems as pressing, as imperative, as tremendous for us as for any working people. These we cannot neglect. Simultaneously with our peculiar problems, these others call for solution. They cannot be postponed.

What are they? They rise according to La Follette's Cleveland program from the effort of organized force and greed to destroy liberty; and that program therefore proposes

1. The crushing of private monopoly by Federal power.
2. Freedom of speech.
3. Public ownership of natural resources.
4. Taxation of wealth.
5. Public control of credit.
6. Collective bargaining for farmers and laborers.
7. Public marketing of farm products.
8. Legislation to aid industrial co-öperation.
9. International action to help the world.
10. Public ownership of railroads.
11. Abolition of the tyranny of the courts.
12. Abolition of child labor.
13. A deep waterway from the lakes to the sea.
14. The outlawing of war.

For the uplift of the world this is one of the best programs ever laid down by a political party in America. It can be carried out and still leave black folk and brown and yellow disinherited from many of its benefits. It can triumph and by its very triumph bring new tyrannies upon hated minorities. And yet despite this it will be far better than the present America.

This program then is so good in fact that it is most disheartening to find Mr. La Follette deliberately dodging two tremendous issues—the Ku Klux Klan and the Negro. This is inexcusable. These matters were forced on his attention by this Association and by others. He and his platform are silent. Wherefore we must conclude that Robert La Follette has no opinion so far as the Secret Mob to Foster Race and Religious Hate is concerned and no convictions as to the rights of Black Folk.

Editorial, *The Crisis,* August, 1924; XXVIII, 154.

[b]

THE POLITICAL SITUATION AND THE NEGRO: COOLIDGE, DAVIS OR LA FOLLETTE
by A. Philip Randolph

Politics is the art of government. Through it the social forces or human desires find expression politically in forms of legislation. Legislation is a political device so adjusted as to direct human wants and emotions to certain definite ends in the nature of social improvement or the increase in the satisfaction of human desires. The institution through which this process goes on is government. Government, generally speaking, is an instrument of accommodation. Usually it is accommodation by repression of the weak by the strong, of the workers by the capitalists, of the black by the white race. Its genesis was in the desire of the crafty, cunning, few to be protected in living without working off the labor of the ignorant, credulous, many. It accommodates those who control it. The group controls it which is the dominant economic force in the community or country. That force may be the industrial workers or agrarian farmers or capitalists. Or it may be a compromise coalition of all of these interests. But even here, one of these interests is dominant, expressing the relative economic inequality, politically. When there is a relative economic equality of these several interests in the government, a stalemate or deadlock in its functioning, ensues.

Now ever since the passing of the Witenagemot and the unwieldy town-meeting, government has been manipulated by party organizations. In fact, modern governments may truly be said to be *party-governments*. It must be observed, however, in this connection that a party may be in *office* and still not in *power*. The fact of the British Labor Party being in office but not in power, is an instance in point. But parties are the controlling and manipulating machinery. Their platforms, principles, policies and personnel are dictated by powerful economic combinations of business, labor or farmer interests. Political parties, being in their nature parasitic, respond to the economic interests that supply the funds for their maintenance. It is clear from this fact that mere party name is no indication of the basic class interests the party represents.

This is more evident today than ever before. This is largely based upon the fact that the Great World War wrought a profound change in the economic structure of our modern capitalist society. It was a matter of international practice that individualistic competitive enterprises were transformed into collective agencies in obedience to the unprecedented pressure which the tremendous war demands for increased production made upon them. Nationalistic units, too, such as Austria-Hungary, Russia of the Czar, Germany of the Kaiser, and Turkey of the Porte, with all of their economic ramifications such as debts, etc., have completely collapsed and passed away only to be supplanted by national state units with a larger measure of collective obligations in the production and distribution of goods and services, in the form of railroads, coal mining, housing and farming. And the United States passing rapidly from a peace to a war footing back to a peace status witnessed profound alterations in her economic life, also.

These periods of transition from peace to war and from war to peace were accompanied by an inevitable measure of confusion, the vestiges of which still beset the country, and, willy-nilly, reflect themselves in the political, religious, educational, racial and social life of America. We have only to mention the strife between the Fundamentalists and the Modernists in the domain of religion; the contests between the Presidents, Students' bodies, Alumni and Trustee Boards, in the field of education; and the racial, class, national and social hatreds, antagonisms and wars engendered by that ubiquitous, persistent and sinister organization known as the Ku Klux Klan. And upon close examination, it will be discovered that not even in the groups that are at war with each other is there any unity upon their purposes and aims. For who has not heard of the factional wars among the leadership and rank and file of the Garvey Movement, the Ku Klux Klan, the Communists, Socialists, Fundamentalists, Modernists, Republicans, Democrats, labor unions and even the capitalists. It is well nigh an axiomatic truism that as the economic foundation of a community or country is, so will be the social, political, religious, ethical, educational and aesthetical structures that rest upon it. A slave economy will give birth to a slave religion, moral code and system of education; the same thing will largely be true of a Feudalistic, capitalistic or socialistic-labor, co-operative economy. It should not be strange then that the existing political party organizations are in such an unspeakably chaotic and amorphous state. They are the political mirrors of the economic life of America in particular and the world in general. Out of this amazing muddle will, doubtless, grow, pari-passu, larger and more powerful, and, perhaps, more enlightened combinations of capital and labor that will either engage in violent revolutionary class wars or evolutionary compromises for changes in the present social order.

Meanwhile a brief consideration of the state of the present political parties may reveal tendencies that will be enlightening to the average electorate in the present campaign.

The present political confusion which manifests itself in widespread fusion of formerly exclusive, antagonistic political groups renders it utterly impossible for the voter, Republican, Democrat, Socialist, Farmer-Labor or Communist, to vote in obedience to principle. For no party is standing definitely and squarely on its principles. No party is supporting only members of its proclaimed political faith. Socialists and Farmer-Laborites are supporting Republicans and Democrats and Republicans and Democrats are supporting Socialists and Farmer-

Laborites. Even the reddest of the red, the Communists, plead piteously for the right to support a Republican, La Follette, and only began vilifying him upon his rejection of their plea, and a definite repudiation of their cult.

The regnant law of the life of political parties like all other organisms, is self-preservation. They behave in obedience to the principle of the *greatest gain for the least effort.* "To be or not to be is the paramount question" of organisms in the social as in the animal sphere.

Now just as an individual standing upon a platform finds it difficult to maintain his equilibrium and grabs for any kind of support when that platform is shaken, so a political party whose platform is the economic forms of a community, such as labor or business or farming, or a coalition of all, seeking naturally to maintain its life, will give up any of its principles and frantically seize upon any makeshift such as compromising with its former enemies. Such is the behavior of social, political, religious and ethical groups. The present political shake-up is the direct outgrowth of the social-economic debacle precipitated by the World War. Note the Socialists are not pressing Socialism. Communists are ever ready to "bore from within" without mentioning their creed until they are detected and ejected. Republicans and Democrats are in a catch-as-catch-can contest on matters of principles, offering any fly-paper platform which is calculated to lure the unsuspecting voter. In very truth, parties threatened with complete extinction, are giving up some, and, if necessary, all of their principles in order to continue their existence. The stark realism of the political situation is that when life and principles come into conflict, life always triumphs; for life, in the minds of humans as well as animals, is more important than principles. It is prior to and independent of principles. In fact it is the basis and condition of principles.

Combinations of individuals like single individuals cling desperately to life, not principles. Thus it ought not to be strange that not one of the political parties in the country is presenting a clean cut platform of principles. This is a pragmatic materialistic interpretation of the matter.

Parties are now engaging in deception. It is the method employed by organisms that lack power to achieve their objective. But none of the parties can afford to admit that they have compromised their principles. Each one religiously keeps up the pretense that it is standing steadfastly by the traditions of the party. This is necessary in order to retain the confidence of their followers. For the people love to be fooled. Almost anything under the same old name may be palmed off on them. They seemingly take great pride in being consistent on the question of a name only, utterly regardless of the substance. Note how the Socialists endorse La Follette who opposes, in his platform, the class war, and how La Follette allies himself with the Socialists who support, or rather recognize the fact and welcome the class war. What a confusion of principles! Even "Silent Cal," rock-ribbed reactionary that he is, would not spurn, in these times of political uncertainty, the support of Senators Shipstead and Magnus Johnson of Minnesota, elected on the Farmer-Labor ticket, second-cousin to Socialists. Neither Democrats or Republicans give a rap about the conflict in principles between themselves and organizations that are willing to support them. Being politicians, they want only votes, whether liberals or radicals. For a voter to a politician is like a rat to a cat. He is a subject to be trapped. Even the revolutionary Communists abandoned their rigid Marxian formulas in order to get a hearing from the political "respectables"; thereby securing the color of increased political power. But still the faithful believe that the Communist Party represents the idea that *there is no God but Marx and Lenin is his prophet.* Such is a type of the woeful legacy of disorder bequeathed to American politics in particular and the world in general, by the World War. In England, France, Germany and Italy, this phenomenon of political instability also prevails. To cite only one European instance. The British Labor Party and the Liberal Party who have been at each other's throats for years now lie down in harmony and peace compelled by the brutal realities of the situation, to profess one thing and practice another. Even the hard-boiled reactionary Unionists composed mainly of lords, dukes and earls, the social patricians of the country, are hesitant to drive Ramsay MacDonald, the Labor premier, upon a serious vote of confidence. On the other hand, the Socialist-Labor premier has installed lords in the Labor Cabinet, and, with his comrades, fraternizes with the King and royal society—to the chagrin of the left wing in the party, shakes the mailed fist at little Egypt and bows to the Dawes plan of mortgaging the workers of Europe to the bankers of America and London. But the logical question arises: was there any other alternative? Hardly, except to refuse office. For once in office or power, radical, liberal or conservative must carry on largely in the same old way. It is notorious that Snowden with left tendencies, who introduced the famous, sensational resolution in Parliament for the supersession of Capitalism by Socialism, followed it with a budget which is distinguished and praised as an instrument for entrenching British Capitalism. Such is the political mix-up in English politics. Is it good or bad? That is not the question. The fact is it is. The cause and the effect are the burden of this thesis, not the moral significance. The political instability in England is a reflex of the economic instability wrought by the world conflict.

An examination of the times will reveal that the interests of various economic groups are overflowing into each other's spheres of influence. Sharp lines of economic demarkation are blurred, and it is not always certain which is which. The workers are in capitalist's parties and capitalists are entering the labor parties. The Shop Stewards Movement represents a measure of workers control in industry, and the Company Union is an attempt on the part of capitalists to control labor. In America it will be noted that unions such as the Locomotive Engineers, is even reported to operate an open-shop coal mine in West Virginia. In very truth, it is not always possible to determine when organized labor is functioning in the interest of labor or when capitalists are adopting a strictly capitalist program.

Such is the sociology and philosophy underlying the bigger political aberrations of the present period. Let us note the applications of this analysis to some of the specific perplexing political entanglements of this campaign.

There is no better evidence of the passing of political parties' control and unity, and the approach of bankruptcy than their attitude on the Ku Klux Klan, an organization whose policy of racial and religious intolerance have well-nigh torn the American public in twain. But despite the fact that its sinister, inflammatory tactics tend to incite groups to insurrectionary civil strife and bloodshed, to pit white against black, Jew against Gentile, Protestant against Catholic, which has made a mockery of law and order and constitutional government, no big national political party would dare challenge its power, fearing lest it would cost it votes and ultimate victory. Still none had the moral courage to openly endorse it or invite and accept its endorsement for the very same cowardly reason. Here again is evidence of political parties fighting for life instead of principles.

In the National Convention of the Republican Party, the leaders even frowned upon the raising of the Klan by name as an issue, which was not only the wish but the open and brazen demand of the Hooded Order. And the G.O.P., weak, wicked, corrupt and reactionary, abandoned its traditions and historic policy of opposition to this national peril and surrendered to the threat. Today it is generally conceded that the Ku Kluxers dominate the Republican Party nationally and in the various states. Witness that in Indiana, the Republican candidate for Governor, and the Republican Senator Jim Watson are the Klan's candidates. Then there is the Ku Klux–Republican victory in Maine, followed by the nomination, by 9,000 votes majority of a Ku Klux candidate for Governor in Colorado. Thus it is apparent that the Republican Party, venal and decadent, is no refuge for the Negro from the hateful persecutions of these midnight assassins.

What about the Democrats? The situation is more confused but no less hopeless. For it is a notorious fact that the Klan won its point in the National Convention in New York City to keep its name out of the platform. A survey of the country, however, shows that the Klan is less in control in the Democratic Party than it is in the Republican. For since the June convention, in Kansas the Democratic Party has denounced the Klan by name. In Texas the Democratic Party has denounced the Klan by name and Mrs. Ferguson won an anti-Klan victory by 80,000 votes. In Ohio and Idaho the Democratic Party has denounced the Klan by name, and in Arizona, Governor Hurt won against a Klan candidate in the primaries. Thus the facts would seem to indicate that while the Klan won its point in the National Democratic Convention by a narrow margin, it has been steadily losing ground in the Democratic party in the various states where primaries have been held. This may be assignable to the fact that there is a large number of Irish Catholics, Italian Catholics, French Catholics and Jews in the Democratic party in the North, East and Northwest, whereas, the Republican Party is largely composed of Protestants. Indeed, it is a sort of anomaly that the Democratic Party, the historic bulwark of the Klan, should be assailing it even in its cradle, the South, and some parts of the North, East and West, and the Republican Party, its former nemesis should now connive and wink at its wanton depredations and afford it an asylum of security and moral sanction. But such are some of the paradoxes of history. The Democratic Party then, in spots, is anti-Klan. This is at least more promising to the Negro than the Republican Party.

What has the Progressive Party done about this archfoe of civil peace? In the Cleveland Conference for Progressive Political Action the issue of the Klan was dodged as a policy of political expediency. Though proclaiming the gospel of revolt against the moral degeneration of the two old parties, the Progressives, who were the logical party to take the war-path against this symbol of anarchy and reaction, failed miserably to realize the high, moral mission which confronted it and ignominiously capitulated in obedience to the mandate of political opportunism. But the Progressives too are out for votes and Klansmen votes. The controlling political reason of all parties was whether or not the naming of the Klan would cause them to lose more votes than not naming it. Since a party will not consciously commit political suicide, it is natural and logical that it will always adopt a policy of advantage or what it regards as an advantage, regardless of the question of principle involved, though, at that very time, it may be advertising itself as a party of worthy principles. Therefore, neither in the La Follette Progressive Party may the Negro expect a refuge of protection against this pernicious evil.

Only the Socialist Party in its National Convention had the moral courage to condemn the Klan by name. And if my memory serves me right, the Workers Party too condemned it by name. But as a part of the Cleveland Conference for Progressive Political Action, the Socialists too were silent on the Klan, and even the Workers Party invited La Follette to become their political Messiah without knowing his position on the Order. Thus it is obvious that no party, either radical, liberal or conservative has been unremitting in its opposition to the Klan. From the point of view then of seeking a party which is committed unequivocally to a policy of opposition to the Ku Kluxers, the Negro is a man without a party. Klansmen infest all parties and all parties fear their determined, dogged and aggressive propaganda. The behavior of the parties toward the Klan is simply indicative of the fact that no party will voluntarily assume a liability if it can avoid it, and politicians regard the opposition of as formidable a movement as the Ku Klux Klan as a political liability to a party. The theory that an open and persistent fight on the Klan will win a party more votes than it will lose, is too speculative for the practical politician. So much for the parties and the Klan. Now about the Negro and the parties.

The historical association of the Republican Party with the emancipation of the Negro, the destruction of the old Ku Klux Klan, the enactment of the Thirteenth, Fourteenth and Fifteenth Amendments to the Constitution, and the Summer Civil Rights Bill, the election of Negro Congressmen and Senators and the appointment of Negroes as ministers to Liberia, Haiti, Santo Domingo, Nicaragua, the Registrar of the Treasury and other federal offices, though done by Republican politicians like Lincoln solely for the benefit of the Republican Party, the political mouthpiece of the growing and rising manufacturing, railroad, mining and banking classes, it has had the effect of affording ignorant, venal and designing white and Negro politicians with a convenient pretext and some color of justification for claiming that so far as the Negro is concerned, the "Republican Party is the ship and all else the Sea." While immediately after Slavery the pro-Republican position of Frederick Douglass might have been sound, the conditions that gave birth to that position have passed, and the Negro has become the victim instead of the beneficiary of the great power he was instrumental in helping his erstwhile alleged friend, the Republican Party in securing. For today, though the Republican Party has control of the Presidency, Congress and the Supreme Court, the Thirteenth, Fourteenth and Fifteenth Amendments have been flagrantly violated by the Southern States; the cruel and vicious Black Code and Vagrancy Laws revived; Grandfather clauses disfranchising Negro citizens enacted by Southern state legislatures countenanced; the foul Jim-Crow car permitted to flourish; and, peonage, segregation and lynching unmolested and condoned. Here and there, it must be admitted, however, it has given a federal job to a big Negro Republican politician in order to palliate the growing discontent of the masses. On matters of economic policy, of course, the Republican Party is the faithful spokesman of the big predatory business interests that have opposed the steady march of progressive legislation in the interest of millions of working men, women and children of which the large majority of Negroes are a part.

And still the Republican Party is a name which does not represent the same economic, political and social program in every section or state in the country. For it is not necessary to run the gamut of a protracted argument to show that Senator Brookhart of Iowa, a Republican, where the farmers are clamoring for higher prices for their products and are revolting against the extortionate robber interest and freight rates of bankers and railroads, has little in common with Senator Lodge of Massachusetts, a Republican, where the Eastern bankers, railroad and textile magnates are ever ready to bleed white the industrial workers and naïve farmers. In fact, the Republicans of Wisconsin, North and South Dakotas are more anti-Coolidge and Dawes than are the Democrats of New York and Illinois. This merely illustrates how difficult, in these times of economic and political maladjustment, it is accurately to describe the composition of a party by its label. This is a clear and basic reaffirmation of the materialistic conception of history, or the explanation of political and social phenomena in terms of their economic and environmental situations. It is elementary that the political representatives of the farmers who want to sell their products at high prices and buy clothing and farm machinery at low prices, also to pay farm laborers low wages, have everything in opposition to the political representatives of the Eastern capitalists whose interests are to buy cheap from and sell dear to, the farmers, as well as, to cater to the factory, railroad and mining proletariat who want to buy the products of the farmer cheap, and receive high wages for the production of the agricultural machinery which the farmers buy. So that the Negro cannot logically adopt a policy of blanket repudiation of all Republicans; for that would include La Follette who still regards himself as a Republican. But he is on sound grounds when he repudiates the National Republican Administration, from Mr. Coolidge down, and the National Republican Party machine which is gagged hand and foot by privileged monopolies and the Ku Klux Klan. What about the Democratic Party?

In the mind of the Negro the very name of the Democratic Party connotes and represents a frightful orgy of persecutions, wanton denial of rights and a systematic perpetration of wrongs upon his race. An examination of history will reveal that the Democratic Party was the political head and front of the Old Ku Klux Klan, the Dred Scott decision, the resuscitation of a quasi-slavery in the form of peonage, share-crop and tenant, farming, the iniquitous convict lease system, the Jim-Crow car, segregation and mob law and the systematic nullification of the Thirteenth, Fourteenth and Fifteenth Amendments. As a national organization, the Democratic Party is the voice of the feudo-capitalistic interest in the South and Southwest, and the middle class manufacturing groups in the East, together with some of the aristocratic trade unions.

A break-up, however, has beset the Democratic Party just as it has the Republican Party, in consequence of the revolt of the small business, farmer, professional, soldier and trade union classes, against tyrannical oppression of the super-trusts, entrenched, enriched and fortified out of the World War at the expense of the aforementioned groups. Thus all Democrats are not united on any political policy. For instance Senator Burton K. Wheeler, a Democrat, has less in agreement with John W. Davis, the Democratic candidate for president, than he has in common with Senator Linn Frazier, a Republican of North Dakota. Also Governor Al Smith, a Democrat, of New York, is the implacable foe of Cole Blease, Democratic Senator-elect, of South Carolina. Though both are Democrats they represent varying economic political groups, conditioned by local state situations. There is more in common between a Democrat and a Republican in Mississippi than there is in common between a Democrat in New York and a Democrat in Mississippi. Each corresponds to his local economic, political and social complexes. In other words a political organism is just as much the product of his economic and social environment as a physical organism is the product of his environment. And the same inexorable law of adaption prevails, namely, that when once the correspondence of an organism with his environment is interrupted, death ensues. For organisms must subsist upon something. And political parties, being parasites, do not produce anything which directly sustains life and hence are dependent for life upon groups that do produce, such as labor, business, farmers, etc. And it is obvious that the Democratic farmers of Mississippi have not the same economic and social interests of the Democratic shop keepers or farmers of New York. Hence they will or ought to vote differently. As to the Negro, no one will claim that the Negro can expect the same consideration from a Democrat in Georgia that he will get from a Democrat in Chicago. Here now is the effect of the pressure of the social environment. For Banton, the District Attorney of New York, though a native of Texas, will behave differently in New York toward the Negro than he will in Texas because of environmental differences which compel adaption if he hopes politically to survive. The analysis indicates then that the Democrats like Republicans, are Democrats only in name in the different states. As a National party the Democrats are making no pretense of being a friend of the Negro owing to the South. Now as to the Progressives.

In the Cleveland Conference for Progressive Political Action nothing was said or done to give encouragement to the Negro. In fact, the attempt made to get a mention of the Negro in the platform or resolutions failed to carry. Probably this was due to the fact that the Machinists' and Railroad Unions that have clauses in their constitutions, preventing Negro workers from joining, and who dominated the Conference, would not countenance the adoption of anything dealing with the race question because of their Southern constituency. Being a conference which is supposed to be for the benefit of labor it could not very well adopt any resolution on the Negro without raising the labor aspect, and since the controlling labor groups in the Conference were opposed to Negro labor being taken into their unions, nothing could be said about the rights of Negro workers, setting forth the necessity of organizing them on a basis of equality. The economic program of the Conference was chiefly liberal from the railroad workers' point of view. It was they who called the Conference in order to change or abolish the Esch-Cummins Act and the Railroad Labor Board, legislative measures which regulate railroad labor. It is upon this group of labor, together with the discontented farmers of the Northwest and the Needle Trades, that the La Follette Progressive Movement, rests.

In reality, as a race, the Negro can expect to receive no more consideration from this group than he can from the Republicans or Democrats. Nor is the labor trust as represented by the Machinists and the Big Four Railroad Brotherhood any more liberal than any other trust, either on labor generally or the Negro.

What is the significance of the La Follette Progressive Movement to the Negro? The paramount value lies in the fact that it puts another political party in the field to compete for Negroes' votes. This enables the Negro to bargain more effectively. For the party politicians business is the buying and selling of votes. Parties buy the votes of the people for their backers, the corporations or labor unions. Here, as in any other business, the object is to buy cheap and sell dear. Now in the domain of politics as in economics, the law of supply and demand is operative. As the number of political parties increase which can make an effective demand for the suffrage of the people, the opportunities of the people to secure more substantial concessions in the form of constructive legislation, increase. By the same token, as the parties decrease in number an increasing power of political monopoly is established with the remaining parties. For instance when there are only Democrats and Republicans, the politicians know that the voters must take one or the other. And their (the politicians') fortunes seesawed, according as each one could trump up the best trick to ensnare the voters.

But the rise of a strong third party makes both old parties less secure and sure of themselves. Hence they begin to make bids to any and every group of citizens that have votes in order to retain those followers they have and to get back those that have left. Such is the situation today with the Negro and the Third Party movement. A Third Party would improve the general political position of the Negro even granting that it were not a liberal party. The chief value does not lie so much in the character of the party as it does in its mere existence. Of course, its value to the Negro or any other group, increases when it is liberal, since it forces the other two parties to become more liberal, too. We should welcome a Third Party however even though it were more reactionary than the Republican Party, if that is possible. But new parties usually voice more progressive policies than the old ones, this is their main reason for being.

The Negro should view the La Follette Progressive Party as another party, nothing more, nothing less. I regard it far more important that the Negro realizes that political parties are run for the benefit of certain economic groups than that he should vote for any particular party. As a general proposition, it is a sound policy for the Negro to split his votes. All Negroes should no more vote alike than all white people should vote alike. The platforms of the three parties are not radically different in economic philosophy. Coolidge, Davis and La Follette are all splendid men, with the record of La Follette being the most liberal, constructive and praiseworthy.

As an immediate political policy, however, the national situation would seem to warrant and justify the Negroes' voting in large numbers for the La Follette–Wheeler ticket, not because they love La Follette or the Progressives, but because it is the effective indication to the Republican and Democratic Parties that the Negro is awakening and that he is intelligently bent upon exacting his logical and just share of political, economic and social responsibility and reward in the government and country. Besides it will enhance the Negroes' position in all of the parties in particular and the country in general in definitely impressing the mind of the nation with the fact that the Negro is no longer a *sure thing,* politically. It will also indicate that the Negro is beginning to think in terms of economic, political and social reforms for the benefit of not only himself as a race but for the nation as a whole, especially the non-propertied element of which he is so largely a part. For in American politics today, the La Follette Movement embodies the most liberal and constructive elements in the country, besides constituting a wholesome criticism of the two old parties.

The Messenger, October, 1924; VI, 325–28, 330.

[c]

BISHOP JOHN HURST ENDORSES LA FOLLETTE

Bishop John Hurst, of the African Methodist Episcopal Church, one of the outstanding clergymen among colored people, says of Senator La Follette and the Independent-Progressive movement:

"I am unreservedly for the Progressive candidacy of Senator La Follette and Senator Wheeler for President and Vice President of the United States.

"It must be unmistakably plain to every colored American that there can be no hope for him politically, economically or spiritually under either the Republican or Democratic party.

"The Democratic party has long been the party of the Ku Klux Klan, the party of Jim Crow, disfranchisement and lynching. The Klan was founded in the South half a century ago and was revived in the South ten years ago. Whatever Mr. Davis, the Democratic candidate, may state as to his personal position on the Klan, no colored man will imagine for a moment that he can in any sense wipe out or offset his party's record.

"As for the Republican party, sixty years ago the party of Abraham Lincoln, it has now been taken over bodily by the Klan in the North. It is openly the Klan party in at least a dozen Northern states. Alone among the three candidates Mr. Coolidge has refused to open his lips on the subject of the Klan. The best that we have been able to get from the White House, despite repeated requests, not only by colored men of prominence but by other Americans who rightly object to the Klan on the ground of its fundamental un-Americanism, is a brief statement from the lily-white Mr. C. Bascom Slemp, Mr. Coolidge's secretary, to the effect that Mr. Coolidge is not a Klansman. How gratifying to learn that Mr. Coolidge does not put on a nightshirt and a pillowcase and join the night riders after supper!

"La Follette, on the other hand, is the only candidate who has come out vigorously against the Klan in words that no one can mistake. His entire career shows that he regards all Americans as equal, without regard for race or color. But even had he been totally silent, it would be folly at this time for colored Americans not to take advantage of the glorious opportunity furnished by the birth of this new party, not to ally themselves with it and show the Republican party that there is a limit to the endurance and to the patience of the colored American citizens.

"The colored people of America have been loyal and faithful to the Republican party for half a century. In return, they have received nothing but broken promises. The Republican party has deliberately taken advantage of the existing situation by which it knew that the Negro could not turn to the Democratic party to get justice.

"With the largest majority in Congress since the days of reconstruction, the Republicans allowed a handful of Southerners to filibuster the anti-lynching bill to death, and yet the Republican platform has the impudence and hypocrisy again to come out and urge an anti-lynching bill.

"The Democrats under Woodrow Wilson overthrew by force of arms the independent Republic of Haiti, the Negro republic in the Caribbean, which, under Toussaint L'Ouverture, achieved its independence in 1804, thus making it next to our own the second oldest republic in this hemisphere. In the course of this infamous conquest three thousand Haitians, innocent of any crime but that of being colored, and including women and children, were killed. Mr. Harding made a solemn pre-election promise to right this wrong, but the Republicans have only fastened the shackles more tightly upon that inoffensive little country.

"The progressives are pledged to the withdrawal of our occupation from Haiti.* Mr. La Follette fought vigorously against this infamous crime.

"In every way and from every standpoint, the Progressive movement opens the door of hope to the colored American as at no time in a generation."

La Follette and the Negro: A Consistent Record of 35 Years from 1889 to 1924, pp. 6–8 (n.p., n.d.); pamphlet in editor's possession.

* In his public address in Cincinnati, October 10, and again in Chicago October 11 last, Senator La Follette specifically pledged the immediate restoration of full autonomy to Haiti.

101

ART IS HELPING IN OBLITERATING
THE COLOR LINE
by Lester A. Walton

One of the earliest Afro-American journalists to write with some regularity, under his own byline, for a major commercial metropolitan newspaper was Lester A. Walton, like James Weldon Johnson, a former consular officer for the United States. An article, headlined as above, was published in the *New York World,* May 17, 1925. That the paper featured the story reflects the great interest in the so-called Harlem Renaissance, then at the height of its influence. Note that Mr. Walton tells of the founding of the now world-famous Schomburg Collection of African and Afro-American literature in New York City.

Art is slowly but surely knitting a closer kinship between white and colored Americans. Roland Hayes, Harry Burleigh, Paul Robeson and colored musical shows have been doing their share toward softening race prejudice. Outside of the concert hall and the theatre significant incidents are taking place in the daily life of New York City with art officiating as ambassador for the promotion of mutual understanding, appreciation and respect.

At a recent dinner in honor of aspiring Negro writers, of the 300 persons present nearly one-third were white. College professors, writers of note, book publishers and patrons of the *arts* made up the personnel of the white contingent. Both sexes were represented. One of the most impressive talks was made by Clement Wood * born in the South, who was profuse in his praise of poems written by Negroes and whose predictions as to the future in store for Negro poets were most optimistic.

It was no synthetic interest displayed by Mr. Wood and other white guests. They did not attend the dinner from morbid curiosity, nor were they impelled by maudlin sentiment, or a desire to patronize. They were profoundly concerned in the literary contributions whose evaluation was chiefly based on merit. Because written by Negroes and dealing with Negro life, there was no lugging in of charitable considerations, no belittling of true worth.

On the evening of May 7 the Department of Negro Literature and History was opened at the 135th Street Branch of the New York Public Library. The movement was fostered by A. A. Schomburg, the Rev. Charles Martin, Hubert Harrison and George Young, Negroes, who for years have been interested in the collection of books on race subjects and Miss Ernestine Rose, branch librarian.

A special program was presented with representatives of both races taking part. Franklin F. Hooper, chief of the Circulation Department of the New York Public Library, Paul Kellogg, publisher of the *Survey-Graphic* Magazine and Miss Rose were among the white citizens to commend the establishment of a department in the 135th Street Branch for the purpose of preserving Negro culture. A number of the library's books have been transferred to the new department and others will be added from time to time.

White and colored men attended the testimonial dinner given by the Egelloc Club to Paul Robeson and Walter F. White at the Café Savarin on the evening of May 8. The most appreciative expressions of Robeson's work as a versatile artist were made by N. William Welling and other white admirers. During the evening Robeson announced that arrangements had been made by Eugene O'Neill to star him in *The Emperor Jones* in London.

Invited guests introduced at the dinner were Carl Van Vechten, Dr. W. E. B. Du Bois, Konrad Bercovici, James Weldon Johnson, James Light, Flournoy Miller, Gordon Whyte, Lawrence Brown and the writer. The Egelloc Club is composed of Negro business, professional and literary men of New York City. The officers are: Francis E. Rivers, Presi-

* Clement Wood (1888–1950) was born and educated in Alabama and briefly practiced law there before coming to New York and commencing a remarkable literary career.

dent; James A. Jackson, Vice President; Dr. Peter M. Murray, treasurer, and Harry S. Keelan, Secretary. Executive Council, Elmer S. Imes, Dr. Allen S. Graves and Dr. George C. Booth.

Art is also acting as liaison between white employer and colored employee. The Pullman Company, which employs the largest group of Negro men of any corporation in the country, believes that during recreation hours men's inclinations can best be utilized for mental and physical improvement. With a view to instilling the desired esprit de corps the company provides helpful forms of amusement. The Pullman Porters' Band and Orchestra, organized in December, 1922, at the New York Central and Pennsylvania Railroad Stations, is the pride of local officials as well as the porters.

On the evening of May 7, the musical organization gave its first concert and dance at New Manhattan Casino, 155th Street and Eighth Avenue. Prominent Pullman officials and their families occupied boxes and led in applauding the fifty musicians under Lieut. J. W. Porter, bandmaster of the 369th Infantry. The selections included "Mignonette," "Admiration," "Algonquin," "Princess of India" and "Bridal Rose." The playing of "The Pullman Porters" closed the program. The words to the chorus are:

> *We are the Pullman Porters, we want you all to know us;*
> *When this world seems all gone wrong,*
> *We come strong with our song.*
> *We try to give you service, no matter where you are—*
> *So all good folks will understand the Pullman Porter man.*

When the Pullman Porter Orchestra began to play dance numbers, Pullman officials and their women guests wended their way to the ballroom floor and tripped the light fantastic to their hearts' content. A. Totten, R. H. Petway, E. F. Effoot, W. A. Gaither and E. Davis, in charge of the affair, were in smiles, as was S. J Freeman, welfare agent and investigator for the company; while "Nick" Jefferson and "Bill" Desverney, for many years social lights among Pullman porters and bearing reputations of being very hard to please, looked on approvingly.

Negro hotel bellmen gave their twenty-ninth annual ball at New Star Casino, 107th Street and Lexington Avenue, the last Wednesday in April, which was attended by proprietors and managers of some of the leading hotels of the city, their families and friends. Dance music was not furnished by the bellmen, but many of the white guests found the music played by a Negro orchestra irresistible.

In some quarters art is likely to be called some pretty hard names, accused of treachery and of turning up its nose at tradition. Its path is not always strewn with roses. Art, for instance, found itself in a pretty howdydo at the opening session of the International Council of Women. In the capital of the United States it is the custom either to segregate Negro citizens in places of public accommodation or deny them admittance. Arrangements had been made for Negro singers to take part in the "All-American Festival of Music" at the Washington Auditorium.

When Negro singers learned members of their group were huddled together in one section of the theatre on this "all-American occasion," they promptly left the stage and refused to participate. Here was a clash between art, which knows no color line, and tradition which, on racial matters, knows nothing else.

New York World, May 17, 1925.

102

AMERICAN NEGRO LABOR CONGRESS

The swift growth of an industrial working class among the Afro-American people, during and after World War I, the Bolshevik Revolution and the failure of the intervention against it, the experiences of the mass of Black people at home and abroad, and the fearful repression especially after U.S. entry into the war induced considerable radicalization. One reflection of this was the appearance in 1925 of a Marxist-oriented American Negro Labor Congress. Published below is the original manifesto of that congress, "A Call to Action," issued in the Spring of 1925. The founding meeting was held in October in Chicago; present were thirty-two Black delegates (men and women) and one Mexican-American, identified as A. Rodriguez, representing "Unorganized Mexican Workers, in Brownsville, Texas."

The national organizer of the A.N.L.C. was Lovett Fort-Whiteman of Chicago; delegates represented the African Blood Brotherhood, the Workers Party of America (Communist party), Negro Women's Household League based in Chicago, the Ethiopian Students Alliance of New York, several union locals in the Improved Janitors Union (Chicago), the Hod Carriers and Building Laborers (Topeka, Kans.), Housewives Union (San Jose, Cal.), Amalgamated Clothing Workers (Chicago), United Mine Workers (Primrose, Pa.), and Freight and Express Handlers (Lake Charles, La.).

A CALL TO ACTION

Today, during the closing year of the first quarter of the twentieth century, we note with pride the world-wide stirring of the darker races against European imperialism. The Riff people of Morocco, in Northern

Africa, have signally defeated the Spanish Army and driven the invaders from their soil. The natives of the Sudan are in armed revolt against England's policy of hypocritically pretending to give Egypt her independence and at the same time retaining the richest part, the Sudan, as an organic part of the British empire. In South Africa, the Negro is daily asserting himself, and is throwing the full force of his organizational strength against the unjust measures for his oppression.

During recent years, France has endeavored to institute in her Congo possessions in Africa the barbarous "Red Rubber system" of King Leopold of Belgium, but each day increases the rising tide of revolt on the part of the native people. The present conflict in China arises from the organized opposition of the Chinese working class to the bold aggressions of the European imperialists. The workers and peasants of India are determined to drive every vestige of British authority from the soil of India.

We might go on giving example after example of the growing political self-consciousness of the darker races in other parts of the world and their pronounced determination to free themselves from the yoke of their oppressors.

Yet if we stop to think, there is no racial group in the world more borne down by handicaps of social restraint than the twelve million Negroes of North America. And yet the American Negro is not helpless, for today he holds a large place in the industrial life of the country and his chief weapon is his mass organizational strength. And by virtue of this, the Negro working class alone has the power with which to bring the new emancipation to the race in general. More and more we are coming to recognize this fact. But it means that this particular social force latent in the life of the race must first be mobilized, co-ordinated and shaped into a great national medium expressing the social, political and cultural aspirations of the race.

The idea of the American Negro Labor Congress is to bring together the most potent elements of the Negro race for deliberation and action upon those most irritating and oppressive social problems affecting the life of the race in general and the Negro working class in particular.

The Negro race of America was freed from the bonds of chattel slavery sixty-two years ago. Yet if we examine our present condition, we are obliged to recognize that much of the condition of chattel slavery still clings to us.

The American Negro Labor Congress will consider such problems as the payment of equal wages for equal work, regardless of race and sex. It is a common condition throughout America to find a white worker and a Negro worker employed side by side, and often the white worker receiving fifty per cent more than the Negro worker. It is the same in respect to women doing the same work as men, yet receiving much less pay.

The American Labor Congress will fight for the abolition of industrial discrimination in factories, mills, mines, on the railroads, and in all places where labor is employed. This is a condition that is responsible for there being so few avenues of occupation open to the Negro man and woman of America, resulting in a constant and extraordinary element of unemployment in the race.

This condition reflects itself in our moral life, giving rise to prostitution and too often to an imperfect home life among our people.

The American Negro Labor Congress proposes to stir the working masses to take some organized action against the unjust conditions of residential segregation imposed upon the Negro in our larger cities, which results in our being compelled to pay exorbitantly high rents. Today the matter of paying house rents has become a supreme factor in our daily life, and we note with chagrin an increasing parasitical class within our own race that grows fat on the transfer of apartment houses from whites to Negroes at increased rents.

The white and black workers must be made to see that they have a common cause in the proposal of the American Negro Labor Congress to make plans for the waging of war against the policy of the officialdom of the trade unions which bar Negroes from membership, our aim being, to break down this racial discrimination.

We shall assume an attitude of helpfulness towards the many groups in every part of the country which are at present agitating a nation-wide campaign for shorter hours of the working day for both men and women.

In view of the many futile appeals to our national congress to make lynching a federal crime, the American Negro Labor Congress shall propose that the seat of action be changed to the masses themselves, and shall endeavor to stimulate and promote the organization of inter-racial committees throughout the nation with the aim of bringing about a better feeling between white and black workers as a remedy against lynching and race riots. Racial antagonisms arise from class exploitation. Racial antagonism is not an inherent thing in the mental make-up of the individual. The child, it may be noted in the most remote sections of the Southern states, does not affect racial arrogance until brought in touch with public institutions—the school, the church, the press, etc.

Racial antagonism springs from the present order of society—a society in which less than ten per cent of the people own and control everything, including the agencies of public opinion, and through these agencies of public opinion they carefully cultivate the spirit of hostility between the workers on the basis of racial and religious differences. By so doing, they make it easier for the rulers to exploit, rob and plunder white and black worker alike. Not only must the American Negro and white worker be made to see that they have a common aim, but they must learn that both have a common cause with the working class of the world.

The American Negro Labor Congress shall demand the abolition of Jim Crowism, not only in the Southern states, but throughout the nation.

The American Negro Labor Congress shall bring to bear the full force of its organized strength against any measures on the part of any section of the nation to curtail the right of the ballot of any section of the working class.

We shall demand the right of Negro pupils to attend all schools anywhere within the nation and the right of Negro teachers to teach in any school.

We shall endeavor to arouse the agricultural workers, tenant- and share-farmers of the South to the necessity of organizing among themselves, supported by the industrial workers of the cities, for the purpose of uprooting the hated peonage system and landlordism practiced in the backward agricultural districts of the South.

We shall demand the right of the Negro to equal accommodations with whites in all theaters, restaurants, hotels, etc., better working conditions for Negro men and women everywhere, and the full abolition of child labor. These, as well as many other social abuses weighing heavily upon the life of the Negro, shall be treated by the American Negro Labor Congress.

The American Negro Labor Congress will mark a new epoch in the life of the American Negro and set him upon a new road of thinking. Although this Congress will treat primarily the problems attending the life of the American Negro, yet at the same time we as a race must take on something of an international view-point and come to see that the Negro question is a part of a great and important world question.

The Congress shall be composed of delegates from the various independent Negro labor unions, from mixed unions (white and black), from unorganized factory groups of Negro workers, of representatives of Negro agricultural workers and of individual advocates, both Negro and white, who are well known for their championship of the cause of the Negro working class in particular.

It is planned that the Congress shall take place in Chicago some time during the summer, the exact date of its opening to be decided later. Every Negro working class organization, every Negro leader who is genuinely interested in the uplift of the Negro working class, is being asked to co-operate to make this Congress not a mere passing affair in our daily life but a great and historical event that shall ever remain influential and far-reaching in the national life of the American Negro.

The American Negro may well look with sympathy upon any plans to free Africa from the grip of French and British imperialism. But we cannot escape from the conditions here at home, and we must devote our best energies toward abolishing the social evils that daily affect the life of the Negro here.

The strength of the race rests in its working class, and it alone has the power to lift the race out of the mire and break the shackles of the oppressor!

STAND BEHIND THE NEGRO WORKING CLASS!

RALLY TO THE AMERICAN NEGRO LABOR CONGRESS!

PROMOTE UNITY AND HARMONY BETWEEN THE WORKERS OF ALL RACES!

Signed:

William Bryant, Business Manager of Asphalt Workers Union, Milwaukee, Wis.

Edward L. Doty, Organizer of Negro Plumbers, Chicago.

H. V. Phillips, Organizer of Negro Working-Class Youth, Chicago.

Elizabeth Griffin, President of Chicago Negro Women's Household League.

Everett Greene, Chicago Correspondent of *Afro-American*. Baltimore, Md.

William Scarville, of the *Pittsburgh-American*.

Charles Henry, Representative of Unorganized Negro Steel Workers, Chicago.

Otto Hall, Waiters and Cooks Association, Chicago.

Louis Hunter, Longshoremen's Protective and Benevolent Union, New Orleans, La.

Otto Huiswood, African Blood Brotherhood, New York City.

Lovett Fort-Whiteman, Organizer of Congress.

Aaron Davis, Neighborhood Protective Association, Toomsuba, Miss.

John Owens, Organizer of Negro Agricultural Workers, Ripley, Cal.

Rosina Davis, Secretary of Chicago Negro Women's Household League.

E. A. Lynch, Fraternal Delegate from West African Seamen's Union, Liverpool.

Jack Edwards, Representative Negro Pullman Car Workers, Chicago.

Sahir Karimji, Fraternal Delegate from Natal Agricultural Workers, South Africa.

A four-page pamphlet, published in Chicago by the Daily Worker Publishing Co. (n.d.); in editor's possession. In the Schomburg Collection of the New York Public Library will be found papers and news releases dealing with the A.N.L.C.

103

THE FISK STUDENT STRIKE OF 1925

Elsewhere, the editor has described and analyzed the background to the strikes of Black students in several colleges during the nineteen-twenties.* The first of these rocked the Fisk University campus in February, 1925. Published below is a four-page leaflet issued at the time by the protesting students.

Is It Fair?

Fisk students did not *riot,* nor *shoot up* the campus, nor *threaten* Dr. [F. A.] McKenzie's life or the lives of the faculty. Why then, these unjust persecutions? The men suspended were not even accused of being in the demonstration. They were "undesirable" because they had the courage to tell Dr. McKenzie that he was not *playing fair.* The students elected leaders in their movement. Dr. McKenzie and his intimates opposed this movement. The opportunity came for him to avenge himself upon these defenseless youths. He did so, under the false colors of law and order.

Is It Fair?

Many endorsements of Dr. McKenzie's administration at Fisk University come from people who admire particularly his alleged stand for law and order. In this respect Dr. McKenzie has taken unto himself undeserved laurels. Calling for police to quell a small sized disturbance which did not "terrorize" nor "unusually disturb" the neighborhood (we have signed statements supporting this assertion), and ar-

* H. Aptheker, *Afro-American History: The Modern Era* (New York: Citadel Press, 1971), pp. 173–90.

resting five men and expelling five whose greatest offense was their testimony against his methods at the Trustee meeting, do not justify this great parading of virtue.

We ask you to investigate the student side of the question. The students did not precipitate the crisis. The fault lies at the door of this self-styled peacemaker between the races, who did more to break the peace than to preserve it.

This brief is prepared with the hope and expectation that you will investigate thoroughly and without prejudice the claims which we have set forth here. The public generally has received the wrong impression about the situation at Fisk and the character and number of students involved. Unfortunately, the daily press was prejudiced when the "demonstration" of some of the Fisk men took place. The truth from the standpoint of the students is not generally known. What we state here, we can prove, however.

We submit the following excerpt from Court testimony:

Officer: "Professor McKenzie, why did you give me the names of these boys?"

Dr. McKenzie: "It's a long story, your honor. These men have spoken against my administration and my policies all during the year. While I had no actual proof that they were in the disturbance, I felt that they might be behind this or anything of its nature."

Geo. W. Streator, Nashville, Tenn.
Chas. S. Lewis, Chattanooga, Tenn.

Brief History of Fisk Trouble

I. Eight years of discontent growing in intensity each year.

A. General reaction against the McKenzie administration which destroyed student activities already in existence on campus.

1. Student paper suppressed in 1916.

2. Student Council abandoned 1918.

3. Athletic Association discouraged and finally suppressed in 1920.

4. Y.M.C.A. crippled and practically let die in 1920.

5. Independence of literary clubs threatened by Dr. McKenzie's ambition in 1921, to select membership of each club and to supervise each meeting.

6. Baseball stricken from sport calendar in 1921.

7. Track meets forbidden in 1924.

8. Reluctance to allow a student to represent students in International student conference in 1924.

9. Discouragement of dramatics and self-expression in general by minute supervision, to the point that all student orations, debates, etc., were practically written by faculty and approved by President.

10. Breach driven between student bodies of Fisk and Meharry by Dean of Women and two members of faculty in letter which insulted Meharry men.

11. President even rendered ineffective efforts made to beautify campus by discouraging attempts made to pull weeds and plant flowers.

B. Individual students penalized for efforts to bring adjustment between President and student.

II. November "demonstration," before Trustee meeting.

A. An outbreak "typical" not only "of Negro colleges" but of all schools, colleges and universities from time immemorial.

1. Staged in protest to "tyrannical" attitude of President McKenzie toward student body.

2. "Grievances" of student body posted on door-posts and on bulletin boards. Promptly torn down by hostile members of faculty.

B. Students successfully organized and a committee of fourteen to represent students before Trustees appointed.

III. A. Students heard by Trustees. "Grievances" called "Constructive Criticism" by Mr. Cravath and various other members of board.

B. Students asked for a "greater freedom."

1. "Remove the spirit of oppression."

2. "Remove the spirit of distrust."

3. "Relieve us of the spy-system."

4. Allow us student activities.

5. Sympathetic teachers and instructors.

6. Encouragement of student endeavor.

(a) "Allow us some originality."

(b) "If we make mistakes, help us up; don't crush us down."

C. Definite Requests:

1. Student Council.

2. Reorganization of athletics.

3. Student publication.

4. Fraternities and sororities.

IV. After meeting with Trustees, Dr. McKenzie made weak promises to cooperate with students in re-making the Athletic Association and Student Council on January 2, 1925.

A. Students willing to cooperate, and Dr. McKenzie was notified on several occasions, and made further promises which he did not carry out.

B. Efforts made to disorganize and discourage students by insidious propaganda carried on by various members of faculty and staff. (We hold proof of this.)

V. Things that gave rise to demonstration of February 4, 1925:

A. Failure of administration to cooperate with student's committee in working upon student's request.

B. Dr. Jefferson's unnecessary interference with the play of the sophomores and freshmen.

C. General feeling of being suppressed.

   1. Lack of student activities which other colleges have.

     (a) Student council.

     (b) Athletic association.

     (c) Student publication.

     (d) Permission to join fraternities and sororities.

   2. Poor football team due to twenty-five-hour rule, which was temporarily suspended near the end of the season on condition that the request would not be made again.

   3. Ignoring of Y.M.C.A. letter by the President, which letter offered to aid President in effecting adjustment between students and faculty.

   4. Making petty rules without explanation.

   5. Favoring white people in preference to colored in everything.

D. Attempts at coercion and absolute domination of Fisk students.

VI. Causes of student walkout February 6, 1925:

A. Indictment of five boys and suspension of five from school which appeared unjustifiable from student point of view.

   1. Lack of evidence that these men were responsible for the demonstration.

     (a) Crawford and Streator were not on the campus during the time of the demonstration.

     (b) Perry took no active part in the student movement.

     (c) Failure of the President to prosecute the boys at court.

     (d) Failure of the President to appear at chapel Friday morning, which action seemed cowardly to the students.

B. Substitution of civil authority for school authority in stopping demonstration Wednesday night, February 4.

   1. No effort was made to use school authority.

     (a) President came with police.

2. Practice of duress by forcing students to sign incriminating paper by threat of being sent home or sent to jail.

(a) "Start chamber" procedure.

(b) President refused to hear Lewis, Anderson, Goodwin, Taylor and Perry, whom he had arrested.

3. Inhuman treatment of boys by police.

(a) Eaton and Harrison were clubbed.

(b) Boys cursed and kicked.

(c) President saw this and said nothing.

(This outline was drawn up by D. T. McElroy, J. Mathes, E. Anderson, A. Davis, C. Boatwright, F. Williams, J. D. Brackeen, Floyd L. Buck.)

Summary

A. Unrest among students for at least seven years.

1. Students kept disorganized by faculty's "spy-system." With few exceptions a student's confidence was a thing not to be respected.

2. "Reign of terror" kept down effective protest.

3. Intimidation; low marks; "hounding" of former students who entered other schools.

B. Students expelled were duly elected and supported by representatives of student body. No attempt was made to prove that they were in demonstration.

C. No one act provoked the series of outbreaks. The President's attitude through a period of several years finally provoked them.

D. In connection with the "demonstration," there was *no shooting,* neither were there *threats* against the life of anybody. Nobody made any attempt to go to Jubilee Hall.

E. And, above all, Fisk students did not raise the race issue. Definite proof points to the fact that the race issue was injected by Dr. McKenzie and by men and women more or less intimately connected with the administration.

F. Some parents have sent their children back to school. True. The students have had no organized agency for propaganda. The parents do not know what their children undergo at Fisk.

G. Students returning to school are not satisfied nor contented, and are not returning because they are satisfied with Fisk and the conduct of the administration.

From original pamphlet (n.d., n.p.) in editor's possession.

104

NEGROES IN NEW ABOLITION MOVEMENT
by Robert W. Bagnall

For several years in its earlier period Robert W. Bagnall, a Black man whose name is all-but-forgotten, was the Director of Branches of the N.A. A.C.P. There follows a description from Mr. Bagnall's pen of the work of the association, published in the widely circulated and influential monthly, *Current History*, then owned by the *New York Times* Company.

The old Negro has passed away—a new Negro is here. He is restless, discontented, eager, ambitious. He wears the mask and smiles when he feels it to be wisdom, but he hates the mask. He loves to look his white neighbor in the eye and to talk to him in the plainest speech. He is found in every part of the land and in every degree of culture. Plantation and city, North and South, all know him. He feels that America has cheated him. He has given her loyalty and devotion. He has given his blood, his all for her. No group here holds America's ideals more sincerely; no group here is more American. There are no cords of other lands that bind him; for the most part he knows only America. Africa is to him a dim and far off tradition. He has done his full part to develop the wealth of America—hewn down her forests, dredged her rivers, tilled her fields, worked her mines. Today it is said that he furnishes one-tenth of the transportation workers, one-third of the organized coal miners, a large portion of the workers in iron and steel and in prepared foodstuffs. Some of the most useful inventions in this country are his—the flange of the car wheel, automatic lubrication, the modern shoe-making machine among others. Yet in turn for this fealty America has lynched 4,000 of her black sons and daughters, practically disfranchised 8,000,000, robbed them of their hand-earned wages, denied them economic or cultural opportunities except in a most limited way, refused them even-handed justice in courts of law, ghettoed them and shunted them apart like lepers in places of public service, or denied them admittance as if they were outcasts. It has given them the stones of insults and contempt when they asked for bread.

The American Negro, it is true, has refused to be crushed under the heavy load laid on him. In spite of calumny and misrepresentation, the world has been forced to acknowledge that he has made and is making most remarkable progress, the story of which is too well known to need repetition. But America has stood with the two edged fiery sword of prejudice barring the way to full freedom and opportunity. Is it any wonder then that the Negro is restless and discontented?

Yet, because of his wonderful gift of mysticism, his resentment is not against America, for she, he will tell you, is his country, and some day will do him full justice. His resentment is against the whites within her bounds who hold that all her rights should not be his, and who, in his mind, he differentiates from that mystical thing, his country. The Negro, it should be remembered, constitutes one-tenth of our population, and therefore his restlessness, his discontent and his growing hatred may, in some crisis of this land, assume great importance, and are things not to be disregarded.

It is this which gives added significance to the new abolition movement in America known as the National Association for the Advancement of Colored People. This organization believes that its work is patriotic in the best sense, for it makes for full democracy—a thing which cannot exist so long as one-tenth of our citizens are denied their rights. It offers what it believes must prove the only solution of the vexing so-called race problem, which increases steadily in intensity under the present conditions. It points out that deportation and colonization are impossible; that the steady economic and cultural progress of the Negro must make him increasingly unwilling to accept anything less than the same treatment accorded all other citizens; and it believes that its work serves the best interest of both races.

The old abolition movement sought to free the Negro from chattel slavery; the new abolition movement seeks to free him from caste slavery. Its aim is to secure for the Negro the same treatment accorded whites in this country. Like the old abolition movement, this new one is composed of both races and contains some of the most distinguished persons in America: Moorfield Storey, Mary White Ovington, Jane Addams, Florence Kelley, Joel and Arthur Spingarn, Oswald Garrison Villard, Senator Capper, Bishop Hurst, Charles Edward Russell, William English Walling, W. E. B. Du Bois, Archibald Grimké are among its officers. Congressmen, Governors, Senators, Judges, college Presidents, journalists and authors, Mayors of many cities and citizens in every walk of life are among its members. Of its executive staff Horace M. Bond writes:

The National Association for the Advancement of Colored People requires for its operation the services of the most able and best trained of the Negro race. There can be but little hesitation in regarding this group, composed of Du Bois protégés and intimates, as the most influential and policy determining in the race today. The able group of speakers who compose the staff of the above-named organization are forceful, polished, convincing, as any one who has heard Pickens, Bagnall or James Weldon Johnson can testify. And they are reaching the Negro not only of the upper strata but of the lower levels in a manner almost as effective as that with which Washington enshrined himself in the hearts of his people. Covering the country with a blanket of information and publicity as to their endeavors, appearing before large audiences in points of strategic importance, these men have accomplished a work of great significance in the light of the present conditions.

The same writer, speaking of Dr. Du Bois, states: "He is the most vital and interest-compelling figure in the Negro world today." The article further declares that Dr. Du Bois has influenced ideals, politics, the Church, the press and culture among Negroes as has no other man; and, further, that he is an international force in his work of securing rapprochement of black intellectuals in Africa and other lands with those of America.

Dr. Du Bois is editor of *The Crisis,* official organ of the association, and its Director of Research. Its Executive Secretary, James Weldon Johnson, is nationally known as a poet, journalist and novelist. He is also an able executive and a gifted lobbyist who has had many years' experience in the diplomatic service of this country. The Assistant Secretary, Walter White, is the investigator of over thirty-eight lynchings and three race riots and the author of one of the most warmly discussed novels of the year—*The Fire in the Flint.* The association's 400 branches, covering 44 States, with a membership running into five ciphers, are directed by the author of this article. Its Field Secretary is William Pickens, one of the foremost orators of America. The publicity of the association is managed by Herbert J. Seligmann, and its press releases appear in over 200 colored newspapers and many white journals. Its official organ, *The Crisis,* has the distinction of being the only self-supporting propaganda organ in America.

The National Association for the Advancement of Colored People is generally looked upon by Negroes all over this land as their one hope for full opportunity and freedom, and has their full confidence. It is not without enemies, however. The Ku Klux Klan regards it as anathema; the solid white South is afraid and suspicious of it, many Southern communities refusing to allow *The Crisis* to be circulated within their borders; Negro politicians do not love it, and Negro tools of whites term it "radical." On the other hand, Presidents of the United States have commended its good work and the leading agencies of the country have acknowledged its worth.

The new abolitionist movement holds John Brown in high regard, but unlike this old fighter it does not believe in physical violence, although it asserts the rights of citizens to protect themselves against mobs. Its methods are peaceful and within the law. These are: (1) the education of public opinion; (2) the use of the courts—especially the higher courts; (3) legislation; (4) the intelligent use of the ballot; (5) cultural and economic stimulus.

The Association knows that its cause is unpopular, that its fight must be long and difficult—but it also knows that every reform that has been won is the result of the education of public opinion. It remembers how men said chattel slavery would never end; how Calhoun boasted that he would count his slaves at the foot of Bunker Hill; how Northerner and Southerner were against the hated abolitionist. It also has not forgotten the ribald jests made against woman suffrage and what a forlorn hope it seemed to many. It remembers that a hundred years ago books were written essaying to prove that the Negro was a beast in human form, without a soul, and realizes that it is a long road to the present when books are being written attempting to prove that he is inherently inferior to the white man. It has full confidence in the power of the right sort of propaganda.

How efficiently it does this work is seen in its fight on lynching. It has been generally reported—and was commonly believed—that lynching was usually the result of crimes on the part of Negroes against white women. There was a time when Southern editors commended lynching; when preachers led the mob of lynchers, and when the North regarded it with indifference. The work of the National Association for the Advancement of Colored People has largely changed this.

It made the first scientific investigation of the 3,000 recorded lynchings that had occurred in thirty years in this country and found that only two-fifths of the lynched persons were charged with rape. It revealed that according to the statistics of the United States Senatorial Commission on Emigration, the Negro, instead of being peculiarly addicted to crimes against women, was less given to this offense than any other group in America. The Association held the first anti-lynching conference, the call being signed by Governors, Mayors, Congressmen and eminent men in many walks of life, many of whom appeared on the program. Among these were Senators Root and Borah and Charles Evans Hughes. It organized thousands of anti-lynching mass meetings all over the country, held parlor and forum meetings, conferences and college groups, disseminated millions of pieces of literature. It held anti-lynching demonstrations in England and on the Continent, investigated every new lynching, demanding the punishment of lynchers. It sent all over the world the accounts of lynchings, so that Europe became stirred over the lawlessness of America, and Americans visiting the Continent began to have European friends inquire whether it was true that in America they burned human beings alive. In fact, it made America's lawlessness so well known that G. Bernard Shaw, when invited to visit America, declined "lest they whip his wife in Texas or lynch him," and G. K. Chesterton, when Americans criticized England's policy in India, replied that before America criticized England she had best mend her own treatment of her Negroes. It was the Association that pointed out the inconsistency of the claim that the better citizens of the South disapproved of lynching when there was no attempt to punish lynchers, although often the members of the mob were known and photo-cards showing the lynching and lynchers were hawked about the street. It introduced the Dyer Anti-Lynching bill, which would make lynching a Federal offense, and aroused its followers to send thousands of letters and telegrams to Congress demanding its passage. It succeeded in forcing the Republican Party to put the passage of an anti-lynching bill into its platform and secured resolutions against lynching from all sorts of organizations. It aroused the press of America—North and South—to condemn lynching as the shame of America. It stirred Southern women to organize to fight lynchings, and as the result of the stir the N.A.A.C.P. created, Southern inter-racial commissions came into being and took up the fight, as did also the Federation of Churches.

The N.A.A.C.P. published a full-page advertisement telling the horrors of lynching in five great metropolitan papers, and thus reached millions. It presented to Congress what one Senator termed the most remarkable memorial he had even seen—a petition asking Congress to take action to remove the blot of shame in America produced by lynching, signed by Governors of over half the States, Mayors of twenty-four cities, clergymen of eminence in many faiths, educators, jurists, journalists and other prominent citizens.

It succeeded in having the Dyer Anti-Lynching bill passed in the lower house of Congress by a vote of two to one and so frightened the Southern Senators that they organized a filibuster to prevent it from coming to a vote in the Senate. As a result of its fight, Southern Sheriffs began to resist mobs, Southern States passed anti-lynching bills, and lynching diminished from 68 in 1922 to 28 in 1923 and 16 in 1924. In the present year only 10 lynchings occurred to the middle of August. An organization that fights so ably is bound to be a power.

This new abolition society has been no less efficient in the use of its second method—the courts of law. It has a long list of victories in the courts to its credit. Its two most outstanding cases have been those of the Arkansas peons and the Louisville segregation ordinance. Its victory in the first of these cases served notice on the South that no Negro, however humble, could be railroaded to death while this organization existed, and the second case put an end to the rapidly growing practice of legislating the Negro into ghettoes.

The Arkansas cases resulted from Negro tenant farmers in Elaine County daring to organize to take the landlord into the courts to force a proper payment of their share of the crop. The whites started wild rumors, shot into the Negroes in a meeting, drove them into a swamp and killed more than one hundred. The militia came, responding to the wild rumors that Negroes were rising to kill whites, and killed more Negroes. Seventy-nine Negroes were then arrested and in a ten-minute trial twelve were condemned to death and the remainder to long imprisonment. After five trials the association got the cases into the United States Supreme Court on a writ of certiorari and won their victory. The cases were again remanded to the State Supreme Court of Arkansas, where those sentenced to death were acquitted, the remaining cases being dropped shortly afterward. In this victory the United States Supreme Court reversed itself and determined an important point in the interest of justice. In the Leo Frank case the United States Supreme Court had decided that when all the forms of law had been complied with, the trial was valid; in the Arkansas cases when it was acknowledged that the witnesses had been tortured, though proved that all forms of law had been complied with, the United States Supreme Court declared that there had been no trial.

In the Louisville segregation case the unconstitutionality of segregation by ordinance on account of color or race was clearly made manifest by the decision of the United States Supreme Court.* The association is now conducting two important cases—the first, to test the right of a group in a block who have entered into an agreement to debar Negroes from that block to use the courts to enforce the agreement, and

* Reference is to the 1917 decision—*Buchanan* v. *Warley,* 245 U.S. 60; the case was argued by Moorfield Storey.

the other, to decide the constitutionality of the white primary in the South.

The success of the association in legislation has been equally remarkable. It has had many civil rights bills passed and assisted in the passage of a number of anti–Ku Klux Klan laws. It has also defeated many bills which would have restricted the rights of the Negro.

It is the work of teaching the Negro to use the ballot intelligently that has aroused the opposition of the corrupt Negro politician and the dyed-in-the-wool partisan. The National Association points out to Negroes that the way to power is to emancipate themselves from all party slavery and to vote for the friends of the race and its interests and against its enemies, regardless of party. This may eventuate in a Negro bloc—but seems demanded as a protective measure because of the treatment the Negro receives.

An illustration of the spread of this idea of political independence is seen in the defeat of Patrick Kelly of Michigan. Kelly was backed by Henry Ford, but he had opposed the anti-lynching bill and the Negro vote defeated him. A more striking example is the defeat of Congressman Caleb Layton of Delaware as the result of the adverse vote of Negroes, although he was backed by Senator Du Pont and was a Republican. In the last election many Negroes voted for the Democratic and third party. In Indianapolis it is said that over 80 per cent of the Negro voters cast other than Republican ballots as the result of the K.K.K. affiliation of Republican candidates. The new political independence is destined to become far-reaching, and with the addition of the two and a half million Negroes who have come North since the World War is fraught with importance.

The association cooperates with other agencies in stimulating Negroes to organize and to enter the unions when they are received on a plane of equality. It advises Negroes, however, when white unions will not receive them, to use their power to break down such opposition. It encourages business and economic cooperation and cultural attainments. It has conducted fights for better public schools in the South and has won fights against segregated schools in the North, and it seeks to stimulate the arts among Negroes.

To emancipate America from caste prejudice, to set the Negro free from the barriers which now confront him, to open to America the large gifts of this great group of her population—this is the ambitious task of this new abolition movement.

Pamphlet issued by the N.A.A.C.P., reprinted from *Current History*, December, 1925, pp. 378–82.

105

ON BEING YOUNG—A WOMAN—AND COLORED
by Marita O. Bonner

Among the different kinds of contests conducted by *The Crisis*, when edited by Du Bois, was one devoted to the essay form. In 1925 the prize essay was the one published below; its author was a recent graduate from Radcliffe College and at this time taught English in the Armstrong High School in Washington, D.C.

You start out after you have gone from kindergarten to sheepskin covered with sundry Latin phrases.

At least you know what you want life to give you. A career as fixed and as calmly brilliant as the North Star. The one real thing that money buys. Time. Time to do things. A house that can be as delectably out of order and as easily put in order as the doll-house of "playing-house" days. And of course, a husband you can look up to without looking down on yourself.

Somehow you feel like a kitten in a sunny catnip field that sees sleek, plump brown field mice and yellow baby chicks sitting coyly, side by side, under each leaf. A desire to dash three or four ways seizes you.

That's Youth.

But you know that things learned need testing—acid testing—to see if they are really after all, an interwoven part of you. All your life you have heard of the debt you owe "Your People" because you have managed to have the things they have not largely had.

So you find a spot where there are hordes of them—of course below the Line—to be your catnip field while you close your eyes to mice and chickens alike.

If you have never lived among your own, you feel prodigal. Some warm untouched current flows through them—through you—and drags you out into the deep waters of a new sea of human foibles and mannerisms; of a peculiar psychology and prejudices. And one day you find yourself entangled—enmeshed—pinioned in the seaweed of a Black Ghetto.

Not a Ghetto, placid like the Strasse that flows, outwardly unperturbed and calm in a stream of religious belief, but a peculiar group.

Cut off, flung together, shoved aside in a bundle because of color and with no more in common.

Unless color is, after all, the real bond.

Milling around like live fish in a basket. Those at the bottom crushed into a sort of stupid apathy by the weight of those on top. Those on top leaping, leaping; leaping to scale the sides; to get out.

There are two "colored" movies, innumerable parties—and cards. Cards played so intensely that it fascinates and repulses at once.

Movies.

Movies worthy and worthless—but not even a low-caste spoken stage.

Parties, plentiful. Music and dancing and much that is wit and color and gaiety. But they are like the richest chocolate; stuffed costly chocolates that make the taste go stale if you have too many of them. That make plain whole bread taste like ashes.

There are all the earmarks of a group within a group. Cut off all around from ingress from or egress to other groups. A sameness of type. The smug self-satisfaction of an inner measurement; a measurement by standards known within a limited group and not those of an unlimited, seeing, world. . . . Like the blind, blind mice. Mice whose eyes have been blinded.

Strange longing seizes hold of you. You wish yourself back where you can lay your dollar down and sit in a dollar seat to hear voices, strings, reeds that have lifted the World out, up, beyond things that have bodies 'and walls. Where you can marvel at new marbles and bronzes and flat colors that will make men forget that things exist in a flesh more often than in spirit. Where you can sink your body in a cushioned seat and sink your soul at the same time into a section of life set before you on the boards for a few hours.

You hear that up at New York this is to be seen; that, to be heard.

You decide the next train will take you there.

You decide the next second that that train will not take you, nor the next—nor the next for some time to come.

For you know that—being a woman—you cannot twice a month or twice a year, for that matter, break away to see or hear anything in a city that is supposed to see and hear too much.

That's being a woman. A woman of any color.

You decide that something is wrong with a world that stifles and chokes; that cuts off and stunts; hedging in, pressing down on eyes, ears and throat. Somehow all wrong.

You wonder how it happens there that—say five hundred miles from the Bay State—Anglo Saxon intelligence is so warped and stunted.

How judgment and discernment are bred out of the race. And what has become of discrimination? Discrimination of the right sort. Discrimination that the best minds have told you weighs shadows and nuances and spiritual differences before it catalogues. The kind they have taught you all of your life was best: that looks clearly past generalization and past appearance to dissect, to dig down to the real heart of matters. That casts aside rapid summary conclusions, drawn from primary inference, as Daniel did the spiced meats.

Why can't they then perceive that there is a difference in the glance from a pair of eyes that look, mildly docile, at "white ladies" and those that, impersonally and perceptively—aware of distinctions—see only women who happen to be white?

Why do they see a colored woman only as a gross collection of desires, all uncontrolled, reaching out for their Apollos and the Quasimodos with avid indiscrimination?

Why unless you talk in staccato squawks—brittle as sea-shells—unless you "champ" gum—unless you cover two yards square when you laugh—unless your taste runs to violent colors—impossible perfumes and more impossible clothes—are you a feminine Caliban craving to pass for Ariel?

An empty imitation of an empty invitation. A mime; a sham; a copy-cat. A hollow re-echo. A froth, a foam. A fleck of the ashes of superficiality?

Everything you touch or taste now is like the flesh of an unripe persimmon.

. . . Do you need to be told what that is being. . . ?

Old ideas, old fundamentals seem worm-eaten, out-grown, worthless, bitter; fit for the scrap-heap of Wisdom.

What you had thought tangible and practical has turned out to be a collection of "blue-flower" theories.

If they have not discovered how to use their accumulation of facts, they are useless to you in Their world.

Every part of you becomes bitter.

But—"In Heaven's name, do not grow bitter. Be bigger than they are",—exhort white friends who have never had to draw breath in a Jim-Crow train. Who have never had petty putrid insult dragged over them—drawing blood—like pebbled sand on your body where the skin is tenderest. On your body where the skin is thinnest and tenderest.

You long to explode and hurt everything white; friendly; unfriendly. But you know that you cannot live with a chip on your shoulder even if you can manage a smile around your eyes—without getting steely and brittle and losing the softness that makes you a woman.

For chips make you bend your body to balance them. And once you bend, you lose your poise, your balance, and the chip gets into you. The real you. You get hard.

. . . And many things in you can ossify. . . .

And you know, being a woman, you have to go about it gently and quietly, to find out and to discover just what is wrong. Just what can be done.

You see clearly that they have acquired things.

Money; money. Money to build with, money to destroy. Money to swim in. Money to drown in. Money.

An ascendancy of wisdom. An incalculable hoard of wisdom in all fields, in all things collected from all quarters of humanity.

A stupendous mass of things.

Things.

So, too, the Greeks. . . . Things.

And the Romans. . . .

And you wonder and wonder why they have not discovered how to handle deftly and skillfully, Wisdom, stored up for them—like the honey for the Gods on Olympus—since time unknown.

You wonder and you wonder until you wander out into Infinity, where—if it is to be found anywhere—Truth really exists.

The Greeks had possessions, culture. They were lost because they did not understand.

The Romans owned more than anyone else. Trampled under the heel of Vandals and Civilization, because they would not understand.

Greeks. Did not understand.

Romans. Would not understand.

"They." Will not understand.

So you find, they have shut Wisdom up and have forgotten to find the key that will let her out. They have trapped, trammeled, lashed her to sea and earth and air to bring every treasure to her. But she sulks themselves with thews and thongs and theories. They have ransacked and will not work for a world with a whitish hue because it has snubbed her twin sister, Understanding.

You see clearly—off there is Infinity—Understanding. Standing alone, waiting for someone to really want her.

But she is so far out there is no way to snatch at her and drag her in.

So—being a woman—you can wait.

You must sit quietly without a chip. Not sodden—and weighted as if your feet were cast in the iron of your soul. Not wasting strength in enervating gestures as if two hundred years of bonds and whips had really tricked you into nervous uncertainty.

But quiet; quiet. Like Buddha—who brown like I am—sat entirely at ease, entirely sure of himself; motionless and knowing, a thousand years before the white man knew there was so very much difference between feet and hands.

Motionless on the outside. But inside?

Silent.

Still . . . "Perhaps Buddha is a woman."

So you too. Still; quiet; with a smile, ever so slight, at the eyes so that Life will flow into and not by you. And you can gather, as it passes, the essences, the overtones, the tints, the shadows; draw understanding to your self.

And then you can, when Time is ripe, swoop to your feet—at your full height—at a single gesture.

Ready to go where?

Why . . . Wherever God motions.

The Crisis, December, 1925; XXXI, 63–65.

106

GO TO HIGH SCHOOL—
GO TO COLLEGE CAMPAIGN

The actual beginnings of education for significant numbers of Black young men and women date from the post–World War I period. This development induced and was further stimulated by a campaign backed by sororities and fraternities of Black people; its director was Raymond W. Cannon, who was general president of Alpha Phi Alpha Fraternity. The basic document used in this nationwide effort is published below; it is undated but was issued in 1925.

The following outline is suggested for the consideration of speakers assigned by the State Campaign Managers as well as the chapters:

  I. Alpha Phi Alpha Fraternity

    a. Origin.

1. Date of establishment.
2. Purpose (Service—Uplift—etc.).
3. A few words about our ideals, standards, scholarship, etc.
4. Mention some of our prominent Brothers and their fields of endeavor, i.e., Brothers Du Bois, Roberts, Scott, Malone, Vann, Cook, Moreland, Tobias, Hall, George E. Cannon, E. K. Jones and others.

    b. Size of the organization, number of chapters, located at leading institutions of learning, etc.

II. The Go To High School, Go To College Campaign. Explanation of.

    a. Describe.
    b. Origin.
        1. Cause of its establishment.
        2. Purposes.

The idea to convey here is that Alpha Phi Alpha had been in existence for twelve years at the time it created within itself this institution—our educational campaign. In the twelfth convention the delegates came to the conclusion that it was not enough for them to continue along merely for their own mutual uplift, betterment, and to have the Fraternity merely insist upon the personal progress of its members. They began to cast about. Some statistics were presented. The Brothers desired to enter upon something more valuable and constructive in rendition of service. So they established the Go To High School, Go to College Campaign which has commanded the attention of the nation.

III. Education

    a. The ability to do.
    b. Ability to know and understand surrounding conditions and environment.
    c. Initiative.
    d. Conception of Nature and laws of Nature.
    e. Preparation.

IV. The Purpose of an Education

    a. To develop the individual.
        1. Morally.
        2. Mentally.
        3. Physically.
    b. To develop self respect.
        1. For and of the individual.
        2. For and of the Race.

   c. To better social conditions.

   d. To eradicate all misunderstanding.

   e. To develop the mind.

   f. Elevation of moral standards.

   g. Elevation of living conditions.

   h. To develop appreciation for the higher and the finer things of life.

V. History of Education among Negroes in America

   a. Show the progress of the individual.

   b. Show that the whole group has made not enough progress.

   c. Give statistics bearing on illiteracy among Negroes.

   d. Statistics showing what progress has been made.

   e. Show what is necessary for greater progress in the fields of learning and education.

References: *College Bred Negro* by W. E. B. Du Bois, Year Book compiled by Tuskegee Institute; Statistics available at National Urban League.

Aim to show in a measure that as a Race we could have made greater progress if we had stimulated the ambition of the individual to make the most of his opportunities, etc.

VI. Values of Education

   a. To the State.

     1. Better citizenship.

     2. Better Laws, intelligent living, less suffering.

   b. To the Race.

     1. Indispensable factor to progress.

     2. Ability to uplift and aid.

     3. Ability to defend and protect.

     4. An example for others to follow.

     5. Arouse the ambitions of the group to higher things.

     6. Ability to help promote co-operation and understanding.

   c. To the individual.

     1. Satisfaction derived.

     2. Enjoyment obtained.

     3. Better associations.

     4. Greater earning capacity.

     5. Less competition.

     6. Opportunity for useful service to fellow men.

     7. Enables conception and appreciation to be had of the higher and finer things of life.

8. Enables one to give his or her contribution to the world.

9. Enables one to contribute to the social, political, civic and industrial development of his community in an intelligent manner and with effect.

10. Creates self respect, confidence, ambition, initiative.

11. More regard for fellow men, etc.

VII. Appeal and Plea to Boys and Girls

a. Those out of school to enter if possible.

b. Those out for financial reasons, tell them some of the ways in which to work their way through school.

c. Those in school, exhort to continue and remain until they have accomplished something definite.

d. Their duty to be learned and efficient.

VIII. Appeal and Plea to Parents

a. Arouse their ambition, that they may stimulate the ambition of their boys and girls for education.

b. Show the danger of neglect in this matter.

c. Impress them with the fact that they owe this duty to the world, the nation, our group, themselves, their children.

d. Make them know the progress of our group, and its future, is dependent upon the education of our youth.

IX. The Appeal to All Alumni of Our Race

X. The Appeal to All our Social and Welfare Agencies, etc.

XI. The Appeal for the Co-operation of Our Ministers and Churches

XII. Our Duty and Debt to Our Youth

XIII. The General Appeal

From original leaflet, in editor's possession.

107

THE AIKEN, S.C., LYNCHINGS

Three young Black people—a youngster of fifteen years, a woman of twenty-seven, and a man of twenty-two—were shot to death near Aiken, South Carolina, in October, 1926. The documents that follow are: [a] an account of the case in the Report for November by Secretary James W. Johnson to the N.A.A.C.P. board; [b] an editorial devoted to the case from the New York *Amsterdam News* (November 3, 1926); and [c] an account of the case's impact in South Carolina as carried in the mimeographed press release of the N.A.A.C.P., dated January 28, 1926. To these documents may be added the fact that on January 28, 1926, the Aiken County Grand Jury failed to return any indictments, though leaders of the lynch mob were publicly known; this stimulated efforts to obtain federal anti-lynching legislation.

[a]

THE SECRETARY'S REPORT:
THE AIKEN (S.C.) LYNCHING

At 3:00 A.M. on October 8th, a mob took from the Aiken, S.C. jail two colored boys and a colored woman, Demon Lowman, age 22, Clarence Lowman, age 15, and Bertha Lowman, age 27, carried them a mile and a half from Aiken and shot them to death. The Assistant Secretary [Walter White], going as a Special Correspondent of the New York *World*, went to South Carolina, visiting in Spartanburg, Columbia, Aiken, Warrenville, Graniteville and other towns, and made a full investigation of the lynching. The complete story of the case is given in a press story sent to the colored press on October 29th, copy of which was sent to the members of the Board.

The Aiken lynchings offer undoubtedly the most convincing testimony we have ever secured of the inability of the States to prevent lynching. The Assistant Secretary was able to get in touch with certain responsible white and colored people of South Carolina who were in possession of definite facts. These facts were carefully investigated and on his return to New York City, the Assistant Secretary wrote a seven-page letter to Governor McLeod giving him the names of twenty-two members of the mob and of eight spectators which included the sheriff, his two deputies, policemen of the city of Aiken, three cousins of Governor McLeod, two members of the Grand Jury which is investigating the lynching, and other persons equally prominent; gave the Governor the name of the lawyer in whose office the Klansmen met and planned the lynching, and furnished him with detailed information regarding each one of the participants in the murder.

It will be remembered that the victims were charged with the murder of Sheriff H. H. Howard who, on receipt of an anonymous letter, had gone with three deputies all dressed in civilian clothes and not wearing badges, to arrest the Lowmans on a charge of selling liquor. Demon Lowman having been called from his home at night two weeks before by a group of Klansmen and severely beaten, the Lowmans were apprehensive and rushed into the house. The four white men ran towards the house drawing guns and in the melee, Mrs. Annie Lowman, 55, was killed by Deputy Sheriff (later sheriff) Nolle Robinson. Bertha and Clarence Lowman were very dangerously wounded and Demon Lowman was shot. They were tried and convicted in a farcical trial and their cases appealed to the State Supreme Court which reversed the convictions and remanded the case for retrial.

On retrial, the State's case fell down so completely that the presiding judge granted a motion for a directed verdict in the case of one of the three defendants and it seemed probable that the other two would go free also. It was at this point that the mob stepped in and lynched the three.

At the time of the writing of this report, Governor [Thomas G.] McLeod has not replied to the Assistant Secretary's letter.

[b]

LYNCHERS UNMASKED

Thanks to Walter White, Assistant Secretary of the National Association for the Advancement of Colored People, South Carolina will be unable to claim that the mob that lynched three persons, including a woman, are unknown to her and for that reason cannot be brought to justice, for Mr. White has just furnished Governor Thomas G. McLeod with a six-page communication in which are listed the names of the murderers, and the part each played in the cowardly and disgraceful deed.

When the Governor peruses this list, he will find on it the names of the sheriff and his deputies of the County in which the lynching took place, the names of prominent business men and three of his own relatives. According to the information given Mr. White, the sheriff and his deputies, far from attempting to frustrate the plans of the lynchers, actually dragged the three defendants from their cells and turned them over to the mob—a common occurrence, though not always stressed.

Nor is it surprising that the scroll contains the names of the Governor's own relatives and prominent business men, for it is by fostering such outrages against civilization that the average politician in the South convinces his fellowmen that he is a one hundred per cent American.

[c]

SOUTH CAROLINA ROUSED AS GRAND JURY GETS EVIDENCE ON AIKEN LYNCHING

New Governor John G. Richards, Presiding Judge Johnson, and Newspapers Demand Indictments

The entire State of South Carolina is aroused over the Aiken lynchings now that the Aiken County Grand Jury has met and is hearing the testimony of twenty-eight witnesses, according to reports received by the National Association for the Advancement of Colored People. The outstanding developments in the situation are as follows:

1. Governor John G. Richards on January 24 issued a statement saying that the case was "one of the most important matters inherited by my administration" and that he was "deeply concerned in the outcome of the State's efforts to bring to justice those who participated in the murder of the Lowmans."

2. The leading newspapers of South Carolina are making strong editorial demands for action by the Grand Jury. The Columbia *Record,* edited by Charlton Wright, in a front-page editorial, unmercifully condemns the previous Grand Jury which failed to act and says that the present case "is the most important case, in all probability, that any Grand Jury in South Carolina had had to consider within the past twenty years. Upon its actions and decisions in that case depends the honor, not alone of Aiken County, but of the whole people of South Carolina."

3. A charge to the Grand Jury by Judge J. Henry Johnson, calls the lynchings "deliberate, wilful, cowardly murder," and continues: "The time for words is past. It is time for action. Say you propose to bring them to justice or say you don't propose to do anything. And God help Aiken County and South Carolina if you fail to do something."

4. Governor Richards has reappointed Detective W. W. Rogers who had been in charge of the lynching investigation under the preceding administration.

5. A front-page news story in the Charleston *News & Courier* explicitly credits Walter White, Assistant Secretary of the N.A.A.C.P., with bringing about the exposé of the lynching, as follows: "Walter White (after the Coroner's jury had failed to indict) then appeared on

the scene as an investigator for the Association for the Advancement
of the Colored Race (meaning N.A.A.C.P.) and also with a commission from a New York newspaper. After a day or two in Aiken County
he compiled a report that led the newspaper to send one of its staff men
to investigate the circumstances. White's report, it became known, gave
a long list of alleged participants and spectators at the lynching. . . ."

On January 26, the first day the Grand Jury heard testimony, nine
witnesses were called, including eight who were prisoners in the Aiken
jail at the time of the lynching when, it is charged, the Sheriff and
other officers delivered the Lowmans to the mob. Nineteen more witnesses are being called by the State and it is not expected that they
will have concluded their testimony today.

The present investigation by the Grand Jury of Aiken County is
the third time the Grand Jury has met for this purpose. At each of the
other two sessions, the Grand Jurors, of whom two were members
of the lynching mob according to evidence gathered by Mr. White,
reported inability to reach definite results and were discharged at their
own request. The present Grand Jury, of 18 members, contains six
hold-overs from the Grand Jury which previously admitted failure.

108

DETROIT
by James Weldon Johnson

In the fifteen years preceding 1925, the Afro-American population of
Detroit rose from about ten thousand to about eighty thousand. With it grew
the ghetto, police brutality, and intense housing shortages. Racism was
deliberately fanned—in particular, by the powerful K.K.K. Early in 1925
several mob assaults were made upon Black families seeking homes in areas
previously lily-white. This culminated in September, 1925, with an attack by
hundreds of crazed racists upon the home and family of a Black physician,
Dr. Ossian Sweet. The doctor, with his wife, two brothers, and seven
friends—having ten guns amongst them—fired upon the mob after rocks,
bottles and other missiles had been hurled for hours. One white man, Leon
Breiner, was killed. Immediately, police arrested all within the Sweet home
and all—with the exception of Mrs. Sweet—were held without bail on the
charge of murder.

The first trial was held late in 1925; the defense attorneys were Clarence
Darrow, Arthur Garfield Hays and Walter Nelson, Julian Perry, Cecil
Rowlette, and Charles Mahoney. That trial—with an all-white jury—ended

in disagreement and no verdict. In the second trial the defense insisted successfully on individual defendants. Henry Sweet, brother of the physician,
was the defendant; Clarence Darrow, Thomas Chawke, and Julian Perry
were the defense attorneys. Again, the jury was all white. In May, 1926,
Judge Frank Murphy (later a governor of Michigan and a Justice of the U.S.
Supreme Court) presiding, the jury brought in a verdict of "Not Guilty,"
thus supporting the defense's argument for the right of self-defense.

An account of the second trial forms the document that follows.

For eight months the National Office has been steeped in the Sweet
case. It has whipped up every energy and drawn upon every resource
to carry the fight through to victory. All of us at the office realized the
responsibility involved, and carried the whole matter on our hearts.

But when I entered the Recorder's Court of Detroit on Monday
morning, May 3, in the midst of the second trial, I felt myself thrust
suddenly, as an individual, into an arena of vital conflict and personally
engaged in the struggle. I was at once so gripped by the tense drama
being enacted before my eyes that I became a part of the tragedy. And
tragedy it was. The atmosphere was tragic. The serried rows of colored
faces that packed the courtroom from the rail to the back wall, watching
and waiting, were like so many tragic masks. The mild, soft-spoken
boy being tried for murder in the first degree and, for the time, carrying
the onus of the other ten defendants, and upon whose fate hung the
right of the black man to defend himself in his home, was an extremely
tragic figure. The twelve white men sitting over against him, under
oath to disregard prejudice and to render a true and just verdict between black and white in a land where race prejudice is far more
vital than religion, also became tragic figures. The rugged face of
Clarence Darrow, more haggard and lined by the anxious days, with
the deep, brooding eyes, heightened the intense effect of the whole.

For a week I listened to testimony and the examination of witnesses.
Each day the courtroom on the other side of the rail was packed as
tightly as the space would permit. First, the witnesses for the prosecution, most of them members of the police force, evading the truth,
distorting the truth, actually lying. And why? Because they were opposed to a Negro moving into a white neighborhood? Not primarily. The
policemen who testified felt, even though a man's liberty was at stake,
that they had to justify the course which the police had followed in the
case. And so policeman after policeman, under oath, testified that on
the night of the shooting, the streets around the Sweet house were almost
deserted. From their description of the scene the vicinity was like Gold-
smith's "Deserted Village." And thus they showed themselves willing

to swear away a man's liberty for life in order to save the face of the Police Department. For if it was shown that there was a mob around the Sweet home on that fateful night the Police Department would become responsible for all the consequences, because it allowed that mob to assemble. But it was proven that there was a mob of five hundred persons or more. This was proven by disinterested witnesses for the defense; and the police did nothing to prevent the gathering of that mob. From their own testimony they did not ask a single person what he was doing there or to move away.

The witnesses for the prosecution who were not policemen were admittedly prejudiced against colored people and opposed to their living in white neighborhoods. They were for the most part members of the Waterworks Improvement Association, organized for the purpose of keeping colored people out of white neighborhoods, and home owners in the vicinity in which Dr. Sweet had purchased. And so, like the policemen, they were interested witnesses. They did not have their faces to save but they felt that they had their property to save. One of these witnesses with a Germanic name and the face of a moron, on Mr. Darrow's cross-examination, stated that he and his neighbors were organized to keep "undesirables" out of the neighborhood. He, of course, listed Negroes at the head of the "undesirables." When further pressed by Mr. Darrow he added "Italians." When still further pressed he stated that they did not want anybody but Americans. When Mr. Darrow asked him if he knew that Negroes had been in America for more than three hundred years, longer than any of his ancestors, and that America was discovered by a great Italian, he had no words for answer.

Witnesses for the defense restored my faith in human nature—and not because they were for the defense but because they showed they were telling the truth. The white witnesses for the defense were absolutely without interest. It was plain that they could have no motive for testifying that there was a mob around the Sweet house on that eventful night, except in behalf of truth. And although racial interest might have been imputed to the colored witnesses, nevertheless, because they were speaking the truth they carried conviction. And perhaps more impressive still was the fact that the colored witnesses who testified showed themselves far superior intellectually, culturally and socially, to the white witnesses who were among those opposed to the Sweets moving into their neighborhood.

During all the days of the testimony the court and the crowd listened intently to every word that fell from the lips of the witnesses. The crowd was sensitive, like a barometer, to the ups and downs of the testimony. Whenever Darrow or Chawke scored in their cross-examination a ray of light lit the sea of dark faces, and when the prosecutors won a point sombre tragedy would again settle down.

On Saturday night, May 8, both sides rested.

On Monday morning the attorneys for the defense made the motions for dismissal or a directed verdict and, as was expected, the motions were denied. The argument for the State was then opened by the Assistant Prosecuting Attorney who made a fierce attack upon the Sweets and their motives. He closed by drawing for the jury a picture of the cold, stark body of Leon Breiner, the white man who had been killed. He stressed the words, "I hold a brief for Leon Breiner." He was followed in the afternoon by Mr. Chawke for the Defense. Mr. Chawke spoke with all of the skill and power of the great criminal lawyer that he is.

On Tuesday morning every available space in the courtroom was taken up. Even within the railing spectators were closely packed together. There were hundreds of colored people and a large number of interested whites. There were prominent lawyers and jurists of Detroit. When the court opened not another person could be squeezed into the courtroom. Clarence Darrow was to speak.

For nearly seven hours he talked to the jury. I sat where I could catch every word and every expression of his face. It was the most wonderful flow of words I ever heard from a man's lips. Clarence Darrow, the veteran criminal lawyer, the psychologist, the philosopher, the great humanist, the great apostle of liberty, was bringing into play every bit of skill, drawing upon all the knowledge, and using every power that he possessed. Court and jury and spectators had unrolled before them a complete panorama of the experiences, physical and spiritual, of the American Negro, beginning with his African background, down to the present—a panorama of his sufferings, his struggles, his achievements, his aspirations. Mr. Darrow's argument was at once an appeal for the Negro because of the injustice he has suffered, a tribute to him for what he has achieved in spite of handicaps and obstacles, and an indictment of the morality and civilization of America because of the hypocrisies and brutalities of race prejudice. At times his voice was as low as though he were coaxing a reluctant child. At such times the strain upon the listeners to catch his words made them appear almost rigid. At other times his words came like flashes of lightning and crashes of thunder. He closed his argument with an appeal that did not leave a dry eye in the courtroom. When he finished I walked over to him to express in behalf of the National Association for the Advancement of Colored People my appreciation and thanks. His eyes were shining and wet. He placed his hands on my shoulders. I stammered out a few words but broke down and wept, and I was not ashamed of my tears.

On the following morning the Prosecutor closed the argument for the State. He began as though he intended to rival Mr. Darrow in paying a tribute to the Negro race, but his beginning was only a background to set off what he really meant to say. Some of the things he said brought quick and firm objections from our lawyers. He spoke in rather high terms of the National Association for the Advancement of Colored People and then added that if he had a mind like some people he would say it was an organization for the purpose of foisting colored people into white neighborhoods, for the purpose of promoting social equality, and for the purpose of bringing about an amalgamation of the races. The defense attorneys objected and the Judge admonished, but this appeal to prejudice the jury had already heard. At another time he virtually asked the jury what would they as twelve white men, if they brought in a verdict of not guilty, answer to white men who asked them about their verdict. Here again the defense lawyers objected, but the jury again had heard. In his zeal to convict, the Prosecutor overstepped legal lines and called the jury's attention to the fact that the defendant had not taken the stand and testified in his own behalf to contradict certain statements which had been made. Mr. Chawke was immediately on his feet and objected. The objection was sustained and the grounds were laid for a reversible error. The point was one which has been several times sustained by the Supreme Court of Michigan and the courts of various other states. When the Prosecutor finished the court adjourned for the day.

The next morning, Thursday, the courtroom was again crowded, to hear the charge of the Judge. For two and a half hours Judge Murphy charged the jury. The charge contemplated the law involved from every point and yet it was not the dry dust of the law books. It was eloquent and moving. In his charge, as in presiding over the case, Judge Murphy showed himself absolutely fair and impartial. Indeed, he was in the highest degree the just judge. The jury went into deliberation immediately after lunch. We were hopeful but not sanguine. We counted that the worst we could get would be another mistrial. It was commonly expressed that a mistrial was the probable verdict. We were heartened by the fact that, in case of a verdict of guilty in any degree, we held in our hands the ace of a reversible error.

I left the courtroom after the charge to the jury and sent a telegram to the National Office. I walked over to Judge Jayne's court and talked with him for a while. Then, feeling not at all like eating, I went back to the courtroom to wait. The crowd that had waited patiently for days was still waiting. Suddenly there was a pounding on the jury room door. The officer in charge of the jury answered and found that the jury wanted further instructions. Neither the Judge nor the attorneys had yet returned from lunch. There was nothing to indicate the need of hurry. Everybody expected the jury would ask for further instructions and be locked up for the night. A little later the Judge and the attorneys returned to the court. The attorneys began to draft instructions that would be acceptable to both sides on the point raised by the jury. I sat in the Judge's ante-chamber and watched them while they worked. Mr. Chawke made the first draft on a yellow pad. The Prosecuting Attorney revised and amended. Mr. Darrow and the Assistant Prosecuting Attorney expressed their views. The draft was at last agreed upon by the four attorneys. The Prosecutor had just torn from the pad the sheets that contained the written words to pass them in to the Judge when the officer in charge of the jury entered the room and announced that a verdict had been reached. Everybody in the room was amazed. We for the defense, in spite of ourselves, were seized with apprehension. The probabilities were that a verdict so quickly reached was a compromise verdict. There was even the possibility of a verdict of guilty as charged. These thoughts ran through all our minds. They showed themselves in the quickly changing expressions of the Prosecutors. Both attorneys for the prosecution, perhaps unconsciously, assumed a magnanimous air. It was as much as to say, "We are sorry; it is too bad; but we had to do our official duty." These thoughts were quickly transmitted to the waiting crowd in the courtroom and with the crowd the fears and apprehensions were magnified.

The court re-convened. The Judge ascended to the bench. Mr. Chawke came over and whispered a word of encouragement to Henry Sweet. I sat next to Henry Sweet. I put my hand on his arm and said, "No matter what happens the National Association will stand by you to the end."

The jury was called in. They filed in solemnly and took their places facing the bench. The clerk asked, "Gentlemen, have you arrived at a verdict?" The answer was, "We have." I then began to live the most intense thirty seconds of my whole life. The verdict was pronounced by the foreman in a strong, clear voice which filled the courtroom, "Not Guilty."

The effect is electrical. We are transported in a flash from the depths to the heights. Someone starts to applaud but brings his hands together only once. A simultaneous sign of relief goes up from the hundreds outside the rail. I look around. Women are sobbing convulsively, and tears are running down the cheeks of men. I get a confused vision of Henry Sweet, Dr. Sweet and his wife shaking hands with the jury and thanking them, shaking hands with Mr. Darrow and Mr. Chawke and thanking them. They are followed by others. It seems that everybody is shaking hands and giving thanks.

The verdict was recorded upon the oath of the jury and thus was reached what we believe to be the end of the most dramatic court trial involving the fundamental rights of the Negro in his whole history in this country.

The Crisis, July, 1926; XXXII, 117–20. There is a full account of the first trial in *The Crisis,* January, 1926; XXXI, 125–29. A good recent account is Kenneth G. Weinberg, *A Man's Home A Man's Castle* (New York: McCall Publishing Co., 1971).

109

KRIGWA PLAYERS
LITTLE NEGRO THEATRE

Theatres run by and for Black people and producing works by Black artists appeared in the nineteen-twenties in several cities. One of the most important began its history in 1926 with a series of one-act plays given in the basement of the 135th Street Branch of the New York Public Library.

A four-page leaflet, illustrated by Aaron Douglas with text by Dr. Du Bois, describing the project and offering a program for the first three plays, is published below.

An attempt to establish in High Harlem, New York City, a Little Theatre which shall be primarily a center where Negro actors before Negro audiences interpret Negro life as depicted by Negro artists; but which shall also always have a welcome for all artists of all races and for all sympathetic comers and for all beautiful ideas.

Season of 1926
MONDAYS, MAY 3, 10 and 17, at 8:30 P.M.

COMPROMISE

A Play in One Act, from "The New Negro,"
by Willis Richardson

Characters

Jane Lee	Eulalie Spence
Aleck Lee	William G. Holly
Annie Lee	{ Mrs. Philitus Joyce { Doralyne Spence
Ruth Lee	{ Catherine Johnson { Helen Lankford
Ben Carter	Joseph Steber

THE CHURCH FIGHT
A *Crisis* Prize Play in One Act
by Mrs. Ruth Ada Gaines-Shelton

Characters

Brother Ananias	Richard J. Huey
Sister Sapphira	Laura Smith
Sister Instigator	Ethel Bennett
Brother Investigator	Harlan A. Carter
Sister Meddler	Andrades Lindsay
Sister Experience	Ardelle Dabney
Brother Judas	John S. Brown
Sister Take-It-Back	Mrs. Marian King
Sister Two-Face	Mrs. Estelle Anderson
Parson Procrastinator	Ira DeA. Reid

THE BROKEN BANJO
A *Crisis* Prize Play in One Act
by Willis Richardson

Characters

Emma	Lilla Hawkins
Matt	Charles Burroughs
Sam	William Trent Andrews, Jr.
Adam	{ Frank L. Horne { R. Oscar Flanner
Police Officer	Myles A. Paige

THE KRIGWA PLAYERS

THE CABINET

W. E. B. Du Bois, Chairman, 69 Fifth Avenue, New York

Charles Burroughs	Frank L. Horne
Zora Neale Hurston	Louise Latimer

MEMBERS

Laura Smith
Zora Neale Hurston
Harlan A. Carter
Aaron Douglas
Frank L. Horne
Margaret C. Welmon
Eulalie Spence
William G. Holly
James P. Holbrook
Louise Reba Latimer
Mrs. Estelle Anderson
R. Oscar Flanner
Mrs. Philitus W. Joyce
Ira DeA. Reid
John S. Brown, Jr.
Ernestine Rose
Myles A. Paige
Minnie Brown
Mrs. Daisy Reed

Dorothy Peterson
Harold Jackman
Mr. and Mrs. William Andrews
Gladys Hirst
Mr. and Mrs. George Cuffee
Charles Burroughs
Andrades Lindsay
Richard J. Huey
Catherine Johnson
W. E. B. Du Bois
Lilla Hawkins
Dr. Ardelle Dabney
Ethel Bennett
Joseph Steber
Thomas Moseley
Helen Lankford
Mrs. Marian King
Augustus Granville Dill

Anyone wishing to join the Krigwa Players can do so by complying with certain simple conditions. Please write the cabinet.

A LITTLE NEGRO THEATRE

Today, as the renaissance of art comes among American Negroes, the theatre calls for new birth. But most people do not realize just where the novelty must come in. The Negro is already in the theatre and has been there for a long time; but his presence there is not yet thoroughly normal. His audience is mainly a white audience and the Negro actor has, for a long time, been asked to entertain this more or less alien group. The demands and ideals of the white group, and their conception of Negroes, have set the norm of the black actor. He has been a minstrel, comedian, singer and lay figure of all sorts. Only recently has he begun tentatively to emerge as an ordinary human being with everyday reactions. And here he is still handicapped and put forth with much hesitation, as in the case of *The Nigger, Lulu Belle* and the *Emperor Jones.*

In all this development naturally then the best of the Negro actor and the most poignant Negro drama have not been called for. This could be evoked only by a Negro audience desiring to see its own life depicted by its own writers and actors.

For this reason, a new Negro theatre is demanded and it is slowly coming. It needs, however, guiding lights. For instance, some excellent groups of colored amateurs are entertaining colored audiences in Cleveland, in Philadelphia and elsewhere. Almost invariably, however, they miss the real path. They play Shakespeare or Synge or reset a successful Broadway play with colored principals.

The movement which has begun this year in Harlem, New York City, lays down four fundamental principles. The plays of a real Negro theatre must be: *One: About us.* That is, they must have plots which reveal Negro life as it is. *Two: By us.* That is, they must be written by Negro authors who understand from birth and continual association just what it means to be a Negro today. *Three: For us.* That is, the theatre must cater primarily to Negro audiences and be supported and sustained by their entertainment and approval. *Four: Near Us.* The theatre must be in a Negro neighborhood near the mass of ordinary Negro people.

Only in this way can a real folk play movement of American Negroes be built up.

Our Playhouse

The Krigwa Players Little Negro Theatre is a free stage. It has been equipped by the joint effort of the Public Library and the Players. It will be further decorated by colored artists. Any one who has a play or any group which wishes to give a play is invited to use the playhouse, under certain easy conditions which the Library and the Players will formulate. We hope by plays, lectures and informal social gatherings to make this room a place of wide inspiration for all dark people everywhere and for all their friends.

110

THE NEGRO ARTIST AND
THE RACIAL MOUNTAIN
by Langston Hughes

The Harlem Renaissance was expressive, aesthetically, of the leap forward of the Black liberation movement that followed World War I. One of the most seminal essays and deepest analyses of that Renaissance was the following by a leading figure in it—Langston Hughes—whose productivity was to endure until his death in 1970. In the essay itself Hughes mentions several of the key figures in this Renaissance, but the two individuals most influential as inspirers and organizers of it were Alain Locke and W. E. B. Du Bois. The artist, Winold Reiss (1887–1953), mentioned by Hughes, was a white man born in Germany who was a professor of mural painting at New York University. He devoted his art to depicting Indian peoples from Canada to Central America and the Afro-American. Reiss did the layout, cover design, and decorative features of the influential book, *The New Negro,* edited by Locke and first published in 1925.

One of the most promising of young Negro poets said to me once, "I want to be a poet—not a Negro poet," meaning, I believe, "I want to write like a white poet"; meaning subconsciously, "I would like to be a white poet"; meaning behind that, "I would like to be white." And I was sorry the young man said that, for no great poet has ever been afraid of being himself. And I doubted then that, with his desire to run away spiritually from his race, this boy would ever be a great poet. But this is the mountain standing in the way of any true Negro art in America—this urge within the race toward whiteness, the desire to pour racial individuality into the mold of American standardization, and to be as little Negro and as much American as possible.

But let us look at the immediate background of this young poet. His family is of what I suppose one would call the Negro middle class: people who are by no means rich yet never uncomfortable nor hungry —smug, contented, respectable folk, members of the Baptist church. The father goes to work every morning. He is a chief steward at a large white club. The mother sometimes does fancy sewing or supervises parties for the rich families of the town. The children go to a mixed school. In the home they read white papers and magazines. And the mother often says "Don't be like niggers" when the children are bad. A frequent phrase from the father is, "Look how well a white man does things." And so the word white comes to be unconsciously a symbol of all the virtues. It holds for the children beauty, morality, and money. The whisper "I want to be white" runs silently through their minds. This young poet's home is, I believe, a fairly typical home of the colored middle class. One sees immediately how difficult it would be for an artist born in such a home to interest himself in interpreting the beauty of his own people. He is never taught to see that beauty. He is taught rather not to see it, or if he does, to be ashamed of it when it is not according to Caucasian patterns.

For racial culture that home of a self-styled "high-class" Negro has nothing better to offer. Instead there will perhaps be more aping of things white than in a less cultured or less wealthy home. The father is perhaps a doctor, lawyer, landowner, or politician. The mother may be a social worker, or a teacher, or she may do nothing and have a maid. Father is often dark but he has usually married the lightest woman he could find. The family attend a fashionable church where few really colored faces are to be found. And they themselves draw a color line. In the North they go to white theaters and white movies. And in the South they have at least two cars and a house "like white folks." Nordic manners, Nordic faces, Nordic hair, Nordic art (if any), and an Episcopal heaven. A very high mountain indeed for the would-be racial artist to climb in order to discover himself and his people.

But then there are the low-down folks, the so-called common element, and they are the majority—may the Lord be praised! The people who have their nip of gin on Saturday nights and are not too important to themselves or the community, or too well fed, or too learned to watch the lazy world go round. They live on Seventh Street in Washington or State Street in Chicago and they do not particularly care whether they are like white folks or anybody else. Their joy runs, bang! into ecstasy. Their religion soars to a shout. Work maybe a little today, rest a little tomorrow. Play awhile. Sing awhile. O, let's dance! These common people are not afraid of spirituals, as for a long time their more intellectual brethren were, and jazz is their child. They furnish a wealth of colorful, distinctive material for any artist because they still hold their own individuality in the face of American standardizations. And perhaps these common people will give to the world its truly great Negro artist, the one who is not afraid to be himself. Whereas the better-class Negro would tell the artist what to do, the people at least let him alone when he does appear. And they are not ashamed of him—if they know he exists at all. And they accept what beauty is their own without question.

Certainly there is, for the American Negro artist who can escape the restrictions the more advanced among his own group would put upon him, a great field of unused material ready for his art. Without going outside his race, and even among the better classes with their "white" culture and conscious American manners, but still Negro enough to be different, there is sufficient matter to furnish a black artist with a lifetime of creative work. And when he chooses to touch on the relations between Negroes and whites in this country with their innumerable overtones and undertones, surely, and especially for literature and the drama, there is an inexhaustible supply of themes at hand. To these the Negro artist can give his racial individuality, his heritage of rhythm and warmth, and his incongruous humor that so often, as in the Blues, becomes ironic laughter mixed with tears. But let us look again at the mountain.

A prominent Negro clubwoman in Philadelphia paid eleven dollars to hear Raquel Meller sing Andalusian popular songs. But she told me a few weeks before she would not think of going to hear "that woman," Clara Smith, a great black artist, sing Negro folksongs. And many an upper-class Negro church, even now, would not dream of employing a spiritual in its services. The drab melodies in white folks' hymnbooks are much to be preferred. "We want to worship the Lord correctly and quietly. We don't believe in 'shouting.' Let's be dull like the Nordics," they say, in effect.

The road for the serious black artist, then, who would produce a racial art is most certainly rocky and the mountain is high. Until recently he received almost no encouragement for his work from either white or colored people. The fine novels of Chestnut go out of print with neither race noticing their passing. The quaint charm and humor of Dunbar's dialect verse brought to him, in his day, largely the same kind of encouragement one would give a side-show freak (A colored man writing poetry! How odd!) A clown (How amusing!).

The present vogue in things Negro, although it may do as much harm as good for the budding colored artist, has at least done this: it has brought him forcibly to the attention of his own people among whom for so long, unless the other race had noticed him beforehand, he was a prophet with little honor. I understand that Charles Gilpin acted for years in Negro theaters without any special acclaim from his own, but when Broadway gave him eight curtain calls, Negroes, too, began to beat a tin pan in his honor. I know a young colored writer, a manual worker by day, who had been writing well for the colored magazines for some years, but it was not until he recently broke into the white publications and his first book was accepted by a prominent New York publisher that the "best" Negroes in his city took the trouble to discover that he lived there. Then almost immediately they decided to give a grand dinner for him. But the society ladies were careful to whisper to his mother that perhaps she'd better not come. They were not sure she would have an evening gown.

The Negro artist works against an undertow of sharp criticism and misunderstanding from his own group and unintentional bribes from the whites. "O, be respectable, write about nice people, show how good we are," say the Negroes. "Be stereotyped, don't go too far, don't shatter our illusions about you, don't amuse us too seriously. We will pay you," say the whites. Both would have told Jean Toomer not to write *Cane*. The colored people did not praise it. The white people did not buy it. Most of the colored people who did read *Cane* hate it. They are afraid of it. Although the critics gave it good reviews, the public remained indifferent. Yet (excepting the work of Du Bois) *Cane* contains the finest prose written by a Negro in America. And like the singing of Robeson, it is truly racial.

But in spite of the Nordicized Negro intelligentsia and the desires of some white editors we have an honest American Negro literature already with us. Now I await the rise of the Negro theater. Our folk music, having achieved world-wide fame, offers itself to the genius of the great individual American Negro composer who is to come. And within the next decade I expect to see the work of a growing school of colored artists who paint and model the beauty of dark faces and create with new technique the expressions of their own soul-world. And the Negro dancers who will dance like flame and the singers who will continue to carry our songs to all who listen—they will be with us in even greater numbers tomorrow.

Most of my own poems are racial in theme and treatment, derived from the life I know. In many of them I try to grasp and hold some of the meanings and rhythms of jazz. I am sincere as I know how to be in these poems and yet after every reading I answer questions like these from my own people: Do you think Negroes should always write about Negroes? I wish you wouldn't read some of your poems to white folks. How do you find anything interesting in a place like a cabaret? Why do you write about black people? You aren't black. What makes you do so many jazz poems?

But jazz to me is one of the inherent expressions of Negro life in America: the eternal tom-tom beating in the Negro soul—the tom-tom of revolt against weariness in a white world, a world of subway trains, and work, work, work; the tom-tom of joy and laughter, and pain swallowed in a smile. Yet the Philadelphia clubwoman is ashamed to say that her race created it and she does not like me to write about it. The old subconscious "white is best" runs through her mind. Years of study under white teachers, a lifetime of white books, pictures, and papers, and white manners, morals, and Puritan standards made her dislike the spirituals. And now she turns up her nose at jazz and all its manifestations—likewise almost everything else distinctly racial. She doesn't care for the Winold Reiss portraits of Negroes because they are "too Negro." She does not want a true picture of herself from anybody. She wants the artist to flatter her, to make the white world believe that all Negroes are as smug and as near white in soul as she wants to be. But, to my mind, it is the duty of the younger Negro artist, if he accepts any duties at all from outsiders, to change through the force of his art that old whispering "I want to be white," hidden in the aspirations of his people, to "Why should I want to be white? I am a Negro—and beautiful!"

So I am ashamed for the black poet who says, "I want to be a poet, not a Negro poet," as though his own racial world were not as interesting as any other world. I am ashamed, too, for the colored artist who runs from the painting of Negro faces to the painting of sunsets after the manner of the academicians because he fears the strange unwhiteness of his own features. An artist must be free to choose what he does, certainly, but he must also never be afraid to do what he might choose.

Let the blare of Negro jazz bands and the bellowing voice of Bessie Smith singing Blues penetrate the closed ears of the colored near-intellectuals until they listen and perhaps understand. Let Paul Robeson singing "Water Boy," and Rudolph Fisher writing about the streets of Harlem, and Jean Toomer holding the heart of Georgia in his hands, and Aaron Douglas drawing strange black fantasies cause the smug Negro middle class to turn from their white, respectable, ordinary books and papers to catch a glimmer of their own beauty. We younger Negro artists who create now intend to express our individual dark-skinned selves without fear or shame. If white people are pleased we are glad. If they are not, it doesn't matter. We know we are beautiful. And ugly too. The tom-tom cries and the tom-tom laughs. If colored people are pleased we are glad. If they are not, their displeasure doesn't matter either. We build our temples for tomorrow, strong as we know how, and we stand on top of the mountain, free within ourselves.

The Nation, June 23, 1926; CXXII, 692–94. An important recent study on the subject is *Harlem Renaissance,* by Nathan I. Huggins (N.Y., Oxford University Press, 1971).

111

THE NATIONAL NEGRO
BANKERS' ASSOCIATION

Still another expression of the development of the Afro-American people was the appearance of a significant bourgeoisie. The roots of this class among Black people in the United States go back to the eighteenth century, but in fairly considerable numbers and in organized form the first reflections come at the close of the nineteenth century. Prior to World War I, the National Negro Business Men's League was formed* (Booker T. Washington was a leading force); but in the nineteen-twenties growth had reached the point not only of several banks under the control of Black people, but a consciousness among them of the usefulness of national organization. The result is detailed in the following document.

MINUTES OF MEETING OF NEGRO BANKERS' ASSOCIATION

A meeting of the National Negro Bankers' Association was held in the Knights of Pythias Hall, Philadelphia, Pa., Wednesday, September 15, 1926.

The meeting was called to order at 10:30 A.M. by Major R. R. Wright, Sr., President of the Citizens & Southern Bank and Trust Company of Philadelphia, Pa., acting as Temporary Chairman. By common consent Wilson Lovett, President First Standard Bank, of Louisville, Ky., was called upon to act as Temporary Secretary. The following delegates were present:

C. C. Spaulding, Mechanics & Farmers Bank, Durham, N.C.

J. C. Asbury, Keystone Cooperative Banking Association, Philadelphia, Pa.

Walter S. Carter, Industrial Savings Bank, Washington, D.C.

Wilson Lovett, First Standard Bank, Louisville, Ky.

Henry Allen Boyd, Citizens Savings & Trust Co., Nashville, Tenn.

C. H. Douglas, Middle Georgia Savings & Investment Co., Macon, Ga.

W. H. Harvey, Victory Savings Bank, Columbia, S.C.

Jacob L. Phillips, Modern State Bank, Pittsburgh, Pa.

T. K. Gibson, First Standard Bank, Louisville, Ky.

C. L. McKissack, Peoples Bank & Trust Co., Nashville, Tenn.

L. M. Pollard, Savannah Savings and Real Estate Corporation, Savannah, Ga.

Major R. R. Wright, Citizens & Southern Bank & Trust Company, Philadelphia, Pa.

R. R. Wright, Jr., Citizens & Southern Bank & Trust Co., Philadelphia, Pa.

Session opened with prayer and singing, led by Bishop J. S. Caldwell of the Zion A.M.E. Church.

Then by common consent the following program was adopted and carried out:

* See the present work (1951), 845–47.

WEDNESDAY.

10:30 o'clock Sharp, Daylight-Saving Time.
Knights of Pythias Hall.

Address—Mr. O. Howard Wolfe—Philadelphia-Girard National Bank, "Bank Loans and Investments."

Address—Mr. Wilson Lovett ...... First Standard Bank, Louisville, Ky "Loans and Discounts."

General Discussion.

WEDNESDAY.

3:30 o'clock Sharp, Daylight-Saving Time.
Knights of Pythias Hall.

Address—Mr. R. S. McKinley, Bank of North America & Trust Co.

Address—Mrs. W. H. Harvey, Victory Savings Bank, Columbia, S.C.

WEDNESDAY.

8:30 o'clock Sharp, Daylight-Saving Time.
Union Baptist Church
(Rev. J. E. Kirkland, D.D., Pastor.)

Call to Order—Major R. R. Wright, Sr., Presiding Officer.

Instrumental Music—Joseph Lockett, pianist (graduate pupil of Carl Diton) "Scherzo in B minor" .... By Chopin

Invocation .... Bishop J. S. Caldwell of the A.M.E. Zion Church

Remarks .... Presiding Officer

Welcome Address .... Dr. Davis, representing the Mayor

Address ...... Dr. R. R. Wright, Jr., Citizens and Southern Bank and Trust Co., Philadelphia.

Response . Mr. Anthony Overton, Douglass National Bank, Chicago, Ill.

Music .... Miss Viola Hill, coloratura soprano (pupil of Pearly Dunn Aldrich) .... (Russell Johnson at the piano)

Solo (a) Will O' The Wisp .... By Spross
(b) Mad Scene (from *Lucia Di Lammermoor*) ...... By Donizetti

Address—Mr. C. C. Spaulding, Mechanics and Farmers Bank, Durham, N.C., "Life Insurance Trusts."

Solo—(a) Trees .... By Rasboch
(b) .... Song of the Toreador (from *Carmen*) .... Mr. Carl Diton (pupil of Pearly Dunn Aldridge) Russell Johnson at the piano (graduate of Carl Diton).

Address .... Mr. Henry Allen Boyd

THURSDAY.

10:30 o'clock Sharp, Daylight Saving Time.
Knights of Pythias Hall.

Address. . Mr. W. S. Carter, Industrial Savings Bank, Washington D.C. "Advertising and its Special Reference to Banking and Other Financial Institutions."

Address. . . . Mr. Calvin L. McKissack, People's Bank & Trust Co., Nashville, Tenn., "The Necessity for a Close Corporation Among Colored Banks."

THURSDAY.

3:30 o'clock Sharp, Daylight Saving Time.
Knights of Pythias Hall.

Address. . Adolph Sixto, St. Thomas, Virgin Islands, "Banking in the Virgin Islands."

Address—C. C. Spaulding, Mechanics & Farmers Bank, Durham, N.C. "Life Insurance Trusts."

General Discussion . . . . "The Organization of a National Bankers' Association."

THURSDAY.

8:30 o'clock Sharp, Daylight Saving Time.
Knights of Pythias Hall.

BANKERS' BANQUET.

After a short address by the Temporary Chairman, Major R. R. Wright, Sr., giving an outline of the purposes, Mr. O. Howard Wolfe, Cashier of the Philadelphia-Girard National Bank, spoke on "Bank Loans and Investments." A discussion followed covering points brought out in the address of Mr. Wolfe.

Following this an address was delivered by Wilson Lovett, President of the First Standard Bank, Louisville, Ky., on "Loans and Discounts." A general discussion followed this address led by Mr. C. C. Spaulding. Various delegates were then called on to make remarks, including Mr. Phillips, Mr. Asbury, Mr. Carter and others.

On proper motion it was passed that a committee on permanent organization be named; said committee to bring in its report at the afternoon session. On motion duly authorized the chairman appointed the following as members on the Committee on Permanent Organization:

Walter S. Carter, C. H. Douglas, R. R. Wright, Jr., C. C. Spalding, Wilson Lovett.

After remarks by various visitors the morning session was adjourned: the delegates being requested to reconvene at 3:30 o'clock in the afternoon.

Major R. R. Wright had previously arranged for a mid-day meal at a local tea room. The delegates were greatly pleased.

The afternoon session of the National Negro Bankers' Association was called to order by Major R. R. Wright as temporary chairman promptly at 3:30 P.M. Major Wright then introduced Mr. R. S. McKinley of the Bank of North America & Trust Company who addressed the Association on the "Needs of Colored Banks."

Mr. T. K. Gibson, president of the Supreme Life & Casualty Company, took part in the discussion which followed, using for his subject, "Banking Problems from the Standpoint of a Layman." A general discussion then followed, participated in by Messrs. Boyd, Harvey, McKissack, Carter, Spaulding, R. R. Wright, Jr., and others.

The Secretary then read a communication from Mr. Harry H. Pace, President Northeastern Life Insurance Company of Newark, New Jersey, outlining a proposed program for an association to be composed of executives of banks and life insurance companies, and giving certain very definite suggestions as to the purposes of such an association and benefits to be derived from same. After an extended discussion of Mr. Pace's memorandum on proper motion it was passed that Mr. Pace be thanked for the communication and that the Secretary be instructed to write him the sense of the meeting as follows: That it was deemed wise to form a separate organization of executives of banks at the present meeting with the idea in mind that the various life insurance executives might also form a separate organization at an early date— and that each year thereafter the annual meeting of each organization be held on the same day in the same city. In other words, that each association hold its executive session simultaneously in the same city on the same date, the first day to thrash out problems having reference particularly to either banks or insurance companies as the case may be, and that on the second day of the meeting that the executives of both the banks and insurance companies hold a joint meeting for the discussion and action upon problems common to both institutions. At the request of Mr. Spaulding the Secretary was instructed to notify Mr. Pace also of an invitation extended by Mr. Spaulding for the insurance executives to meet at Durham, N.C., in 1927.

The Committee on Permanent Organization thereupon made its report as follows: (1) "That a permanent organization be formed at this meeting under the name of the National Negro Bankers' Association, and (2) That the subjoined Constitution and By-Laws be adopted. We further (3) recommend that the present temporary officers be elected as permanent for a period of one year from date as follows:

Major R. R. Wright, Sr., President; Wilson Lovett, Secretary.

That the following additional officers be elected to serve for one year from date:

Henry Allen Boyd, First Vice President.

C. H. Douglas, Second Vice President.

Walter S. Carter, Third Vice President.

C. C. Spaulding, Treasurer.

That the following compose the Executive Committee to serve for one year from date:

W. H. Harvey, J. L. Phillips, L. M. Pollard, J. C. Asbury, C. L. McKissack, T. K. Gibson, R. R. Wright, Jr.

We further recommend that in order to promote the general welfare and usefulness of Banks and Banking Institutions, and to secure uniformity of action, together with the practical benefits to be derived from personal acquaintance and from the discussion of subjects of importance to the banking and commercial interests of the country, and especially in order to secure the proper consideration of questions regarding the financial and commercial usages, customs and laws which affect the banking interests of the country, and for protection against loss by crime or otherwise, the following Constitution and By-Laws for the "National Negro Bankers' Association" are recommended:

Article I.

Section 1. The name of the Association shall be the "National Negro Bankers' Association."

Sec. 2. Any National or State Bank, Trust Company, Savings Bank, Bank Clearing House, Building & Loan Association and other organizations having banking as a feature of its business, in the country may become a member of this Association upon the payment of such annual dues as shall be provided for by the Association's bylaws.

All members in good standing may send a delegate to the meetings of the Association and of the Executive Committee in the absence of the questions coming before the Association.

It shall be the duty of the First Vice President to preside at meetings of the Association and of the Executive Committee in the absence of the President and of the Second and Third Vice Presidents to act in the same capacity in the absence of either the President or the other Vice Presidents.

Sec. 3. A delegate must be an officer, director, or trustee of the institution he represents, or a member of a Banking Firm, or an individual doing business as a Banker.

Sec. 4. Delegates shall vote in person; no voting by proxy shall be allowed, nor shall a delegate vote in more than one capacity.

Sec. 5. All votes shall be viva voce, unless otherwise ordered; any delegate may demand a division upon any question.

Sec. 6. Delegates and alternates to represent this Association in the conventions of the National Negro Business League shall be elected at the annual conventions.

Article II.

Section 1. The officers of this Association shall be a President, First, Second and Third Vice Presidents and a Treasurer, who shall be elected annually, and a Secretary, who shall be appointed by the Executive Committee, and shall receive such compensation as the Executive Committee may determine. The officers shall be ex-officio members of the Executive Committee. An Executive Committee composed of seven members shall be elected for one year.

Sec. 2. Any five members of the Executive Committee shall constitute a quorum.

Sec. 3. Annual conventions of the Association shall be held at such times and places as shall be determined by the Association, which may be changed by the Executive Committee for good reasons. The Executive Committee shall submit at each annual convention a report of their official acts, and recommend to the Association such action as they may deem proper. A majority of the Executive Committee shall have power to call a special meeting of the Association whenever they deem it necessary.

Article III.

Section 1. It shall be the duty of the President to preside at the meetings of the Association, and he shall be Chairman of the Executive Committee.

Sec. 2. The Secretary shall make and have charge of the records of the Association, shall collect the annual dues and turn receipts over to the Treasurer, and shall attend to the correspondence and other clerical work incident to the general conduct of the Association.

Sec. 3. The Treasurer shall have custody of the money and property of the Association, and pay the liabilities of the Association on vouchers approved by the President; but no liabilities shall be incurred beyond the annual dues or money specially collected. He shall give to the National Bankers' Association a bond satisfactory in amount and form to the Executive Committee.

Article IV.

Section 1. By-Laws may be adopted not inconsistent with the Constitution or contrary to the various State Laws; and this Constitution may be amended, altered or suspended at any regular meeting of the Association by a vote of two-thirds of the members present.

BY-LAWS.

Annual dues shall be $25.00 per year for each member of the Association and shall be payable on the first day of December of each year, in advance, at which time the fiscal year of the Association shall begin.

It shall be the duty of each member of the Association to notify the President of any fraud or crime attempted or committed against any banking institution or firm that will be of general interest, and if the President shall deem it advisable he shall immediately notify each member of the Association thereof.

Any member desiring to withdraw from the Association must give notice in writing to the Chairman of the Executive Committee at least three months in advance.

The Executive Committee shall meet at such time and place as may be selected by the Executive Committee, on the first Saturday in December and the day previous to the annual convention, and at such other times as may be determined by the President or a majority of the members of the Executive Committee.

Order of business at Association meetings:

1. Call of roll.
2. Reading of Minutes.
3. Address of the President.
4. Report of the Secretary.
5. Report of the Treasurer.
6. Report of the Executive Committee.
7. Report of Special Committees.

8. Unfinished business.

9. New business.

10. Election of delegates and alternates to National Negro Business League on last day of meeting.

11. Selecting time and place for next Annual Convention, on last day of meeting.

12. Installation of President-elect.

13. Adjournment.

> Signed: Committee on Permanent Organization,
> Wilson Lovett, Chairman
> W. S. Carter
> C. H. Douglas
> C. C. Spaulding
> R. R. Wright, Jr.

On proper motion it was passed that the recommendations of the Committee on Permanent Organization be adopted and that a full and complete record of same be made.

After general discussion on proper motion it was passed that the Secretary, together with the advice and assistance of the President and Treasurer be instructed to get into communication as promptly as possible with all the banks and all other financial institutions (as named in the constitution) in the United States managed and operated by Negroes, and that such banks and other financial institutions be invited and urged to become members of the National Negro Bankers' Association.

On proper motion it was also passed that the Secretary together with the advice and assistance of the President and Treasurer, assign to each member of this Association a certain section of the country, and that such individual as delegated be asked to become personally responsible to secure the membership of the various banking institutions in his particular community and that such invitation, where necessary, be extended in person, the cost of such visits as may be necessary in this connection, to be borne by the National Negro Bankers' Association.

THURSDAY.

A very interesting paper, "Live Insurance Trusts," was thereupon read by a Mr. C. C. Spaulding, and after considerable discussion it was passed that this paper be referred to a Committee on Advertising and Publicity, which was thereupon appointed by the Chairman as follows:

T. K. Gibson, C. C. Spaulding, Wilson Lovett, C. L. McKissack.

With instructions to have printed extracts from this paper so that the various members of the Association might in turn make reprints for individual distribution on the part of the member banks.

Mr. C. C. Spaulding also brought to the attention of the National Negro Bankers' Association, the purposes and accomplishments of National Negro Finance Corporation, and after some discussion, on proper motion it was passed that the matter of participation on the part of members' banks in the program of the National Negro Finance Corporation be referred to the Executive Committee for appropriate recommendations.

An invitation was extended to the National Negro Bankers' Association to hold its 1927 Session in the following cities:

Columbus, Ohio, Durham, N.C., Louisville, Ky.

Said invitations being extended by Messrs. T. K. Gibson, C. C. Spaulding and Wilson Lovett on behalf of their respective institutions. Upon the matter being put to a vote it was finally and unanimously passed that the invitation of Mr. Spaulding be accepted and that the 1927 Session of the National Negro Bankers' Association be held in Durham, N.C., the date and time to be determined by the Executive Committee.

Upon motion by Mr. Spaulding it was passed that the National Negro Bankers' Association express their appreciation and thanks to Major R. R. Wright, Sr. and to the Citizens of Philadelphia for making the meetings of the Association so successful and for the extension of the many courtesies received.

There being no further business before the Association the meeting was adjourned.

R. R. Wright, Sr., President
Wilson Lovett, Secretary

Minutes of Meeting of National Negro Bankers' Association, September 15, 1926, Philadelphia, Pa. (Louisville, Ky., 1926), eight-page pamphlet in editor's possession.

112

RESOLUTION ON THE NEGRO QUESTION: ANTI-IMPERIALIST CONGRESS

Early in 1927 an International Congress Against Colonial Oppression and Imperialism convened in Brussels. This congress, on February 13, adopted a

"Common Resolution on the Negro Question," largely the work of Richard B. Moore, at this time representing both the American Negro Labor Congress and Garvey's Universal Negro Improvement Association. The text of this Resolution follows.

For five hundred years the Negro Peoples of the World have been victims of a most terrible and ruthless oppression. The institution of the slave trade, as a consequence of the commercial revolution and expansion of Europe, was the beginning of a regime of terror and robbery that is one of the most horrible in the history of mankind. As a result of this traffic, Africa lost over one hundred million of her people. Four out of every five of these were killed in the bloody business of capture and transport, the survivors being consigned to a most cruel slavery in the New World.

The immense wealth derived from this gruesome trade was the foundation of the wealth and development of European merchants and states. But the development of the African peoples was thereby abruptly arrested, and their civilization which in many areas had reached a high state of advancement was almost completely destroyed. These peoples hence-forward were declared to be heathen and savage, an inferior race, ordained by the Christian God to be slaves of the superior Europeans, without any rights that a white man is bound to respect. And a bitter and hostile prejudice arose against the Negro race which has dominated the feeling of almost all Europeans toward them, causing them to be subjected to numerous unequal, degrading, and pernicious prescriptions.

The abolition of chattel slavery freed the Negro peoples only from the thralldom of being legally held as personal property; the enslavement, exploitation, and extermination of these peoples continue until the present moment. The process of subjugation was greatly accelerated by the mad scramble of European powers for African territory between 1880 and 1890. By force and fraud the independent African states were subjected, their lands and possessions almost all forcibly expropriated and distributed among European corporations and persons, and their peoples driven by a most brutal and inhuman system to produce immense wealth for their oppressors. Virulent diseases were introduced among the people, and communicated to their cattle. The appalling toll of death and devastation can be realized from the fact that despite the great virility and fecundity of the African peoples, Africa is now the least populous of the continents of the world.

Thus were the blessings of Christianity and civilization brought to the Africans. So that today in that vast continent of 11,500,000 square miles only two small states, Abyssinia and Liberia, are accounted independent. The former is now menaced by the Anglo-Italian pact, and the latter with its customs and constabulary in the hands of American officials, and a great concession granted to a Wall Street Corporation, can no longer be considered free. The expropriation of the lands and extermination of the people proceeds grimly in Kenya and the Sudan, the reward of the imperialists to the Africans whom they sacrificed in the great World War which was heralded as a war "to make the world safe for democracy and for the rights of weaker peoples."

Similarly in the Union of South Africa, there has recently been enacted a Color Bar Bill which prohibits the natives from working with machinery and from employment in the civil services. This adds new burdens to these people already suppressed by Pass Laws, Hut Taxes and the like, and who are herded into miserable reservations and compounds and terribly exploited on the farms and in the mines. Everywhere also in Africa, excepting a small area on the West Coast where the lands and customs of the natives have been maintained by them, there exists a rigorous repression of the people under the yoke of foreign imperialists. The productivity of this area which is 8 times greater than that of neighboring areas of European owned plantations, is an irrefutable proof of the utterly wanton and vicious nature of this system of modern slavery.

In the United States, the 12 million Negroes, though guaranteed equal rights under the Constitution, are denied full and equal participation in the life of the nation. This oppression is greater in the Southern states where the spirit of chattel slavery still predominates. Segregation, disfranchisement, legal injustice, debt and convict slavery, and lynching and mob violence degrade and crush these peoples. This vicious system of suppression operates to reduce this race to an inferior servile caste, exploited and abused by all other classes of society.

Haiti, established by Toussaint l'Ouverture and his fellow-slaves by the first successful slave revolution in history, is now crushed and subjugated by the marines of that very power which proclaimed "the war for democracy." More than 3,000 Haitians have been murdered and large numbers are enslaved for the building of military roads under corvée systems. They have been despoiled of their lands and liberties, and imprisonment and torture is the lot of all who dare to speak for their freedom. In the Caribbean colonies, the Negro peoples are subjected under varying forms of imperialist rule. Limited franchise and oppressive plantation systems reduce these masses to a permanent condition of serfdom and penury. In Latin America, Negroes suffer no special suppression except where alien imperialists dominate. The cordial relations resulting from the social and political equality of the races in these countries prove that there is no inherent antagonism between them.

For the Republic of Haiti, Cuba, Santo Domingo and for the peoples of Porto Rico and the Virgin Islands, we must demand complete political and economic independence, and the immediate withdrawal of all imperialist troops. For the other Caribbean colonies, we must likewise demand and obtain self-government. The Confederation of the British West Indies should be achieved and the Union of all these peoples accomplished.

For the emancipation of the Negro peoples of the world, we must wage a resolute and unyielding struggle to achieve:

1. Complete freedom of the peoples of Africa and African origin.
2. Complete equality between the Negro race and all other races.
3. Control of the land and governments of Africa by the Africans.
4. Immediate abolition of all compulsory labor and unjust taxation.
5. Immediate abolition of all racial restrictions, social, political and economic.
6. Immediate abolition of military conscription and recruiting.
7. Freedom of movement within Africa and elsewhere.
8. Freedom of speech, press and assembly.
9. The right of education in all branches.
10. The right to organize trade unions.

To accomplish these ends we must prosecute the following measures:

1. The organization of the economic and political power of the people.
   (a) Unionization of Negro workers.
   (b) Organization of co-operatives.
2. Organization and co-ordination of the Negro liberation movements.
3. Prosecution of the fight against imperialist ideology: Chauvinism, fascism, ku kluxism, and race prejudice.
4. Admission of the workers of all races into all unions on the basis of equality.
5. Unity with all other suppressed peoples and classes for the fight against world imperialism.

HAIL THE HEROIC AND EPOCHAL STRUGGLE OF THE CHINESE PEOPLE AGAINST IMPERIALISM!

HAIL THE SUCCESS OF THE FIGHT OF THE SUPPRESSED PEOPLES AND CLASSES AGAINST WORLD IMPERIALISM!

Richard B. Moore, American Negro Labor Congress, Universal Negro Improvement Association, Incorporated, U.S.A.

Lamine Senghor, and

Jamille St. Jacques, Committee for the Defense of the Negro Race, Paris, France

Josiah T. Gumede, African National Congress, South Africa

James A. Laguma, Native Workers of South Africa

H. Bloncourt, League Against Imperialism, Martinique, French West Indies

Ibrahim Youssef, Egyptian National Radical Party

From mimeographed copy in editor's possession.

113

AMERICAN INTER-RACIAL PEACE COMMITTEE

An early attempt to bring Afro-American people as a group within the organized peace movement—and to make that movement aware of the presence of Black people—resulted, in 1927, in the appearance of the American Inter-Racial Peace Committee, with headquarters in Philadelphia. The nature of this committee is conveyed in the text of one of its leaflets, reproduced below. The officers of this committee were: Leslie Pinckney Hill chairman; Wilbur K. Thomas, treasurer; Alice Dunbar-Nelson, executive secretary. Among its members were Mary McLeod Bethune, Crystal Bird, Charlotte Hawkins Brown, Addie W. Dickerson, Addie W. Hunton, J. Finley Wilson, William Pickens, Chandler Owen, Channing Tobias, and Dr. Du Bois.

The American Inter-Racial Peace Committee is the joint effort of representative American Negroes working in close co-operation with the American Friends' Service Committee, to develop and enlist the active support of the Negroes of America in the cause of Peace.

It aims to promote the spirit of understanding, good-will and co-operation between the races in America, as the basic principle of the Christ-way of life.

It will present to the Nation and to the world those talents and accomplishments of Negroes that may serve the cause of peace.

It will make known and provide facilities for the expression of that increasing body of white citizens who are united in spirit with this cause.

It will seek for the Negro the open door of fraternal co-operation with all those agencies—industrial, social, religious and political— devoted to the cause of peace.

It will stimulate a public peace opinion in the press and on the platform.

It will stress loyalty to the fundamental ideals of the Declaration of Independence and the Constitution of the United States.

It will teach the fundamental equality of all races.

It will join hands with all those organizations that are aiming to make war impossible.

Any American citizen who may be interested in furthering the cause of peace, by the development of those right human relations which are the basis of peace, is eligible for membership.

From four-page leaflet, entitled *American Inter-Racial Peace Committee* (Philadelphia, n.d.); in editor's possession.

114

THE FOURTH PAN-AFRICAN CONGRESS

Following the 1923 Pan-African Congress, attempts were made to hold the Fourth Congress in 1925 in Africa (Tunis was the choice) or in the West Indies, but France and Great Britain prevented this. As a result the Fourth Congress was not held until the summer of 1927 when it met in New York City. The conveners were Black women who belonged to the Circle for Peace and Foreign Relations, whose members were prominent in the N.A.A.C.P. and in the Inter-Racial Peace Committee, noted earlier. The Executive Committee of the Circle consisted of ten women whose names will be found at the conclusion of document [a] below announcing the congress. Document [b] was a four-page folder compiled by the Publicity Committee (headed by Mrs. A. W. Hunton) entitled *About the Fourth Pan-African Congress*. Document [c] is the press release issued on August 26 by the N.A.A.C.P. briefly indicating the actions of the congress. Very active participants in this congress were Charles H. Wesley, Rayford W. Logan, and Otto Huiswoud.

[a]

The Circle for Peace and Foreign Relations of New York City, with the co-operation of many persons and organizations throughout the United States, is hereby calling a Fourth Pan-African Congress to meet in the City of New York, United States of America, August 21, 22, 23 and 24, 1927. The Circle and those who are united in this call believe:

1. That conference is the beginning of wisdom.
2. That the three Pan-African Congresses of 1919, 1921, 1923, held in London, Paris, Brussels and Lisbon, were valuable steps in bringing together widely separated groups of men and women of Negro blood and their friends to consult on the present condition and the future of the black race and to achieve mutual understanding and acquaintanceship.
3. That such conferences—undertaken in no spirit of racial exclusiveness and with no thought of aggression upon the rights of others, but only with the earnest desire for light, freedom and self-expression for all men— are real steps for the social uplift of black folk; and that the day is far past when any man or group can speak for a people who are able and willing to speak for themselves.

Therefore the Circle for Peace and Foreign Relations invites you and your friends to be present at this Congress and to take part in it; and to induce as many others to attend as you may be able.

Signed for the Circle for Peace and Foreign Relations:

THE EXECUTIVE COMMITTEE

Addie Waite Hunton	Lillian A. Alexander
Dorothy R. Peterson	Sadie E. Stockton
Minta B. Trotman	Eunice Hunton Carter
Nina G. Du Bois	Minnie McA. Pickens
Lottie Cooper	Annie M. Dingle

Room 688 Bible House, Astor Place, New York, N.Y., U.S.A.

[b]

1. When is the Fourth Pan-African Congress to be held?
   The Fourth Pan-African Congress will be held August 21–24, 1927.
2. Where is the Fourth Pan-African Congress to be held?
   In New York City, United States of America.
3. Who is sponsoring the Fourth Pan-African Congress?
   The Circle for Peace and Foreign Relations with offices at Room 688, Bible House, Astor Place, New York City.
4. What is the reason for calling a Congress in 1927?
   Various problems of Africa at the present time make all of our national and local problems international and world wide.
5. Why is it expedient to have the Fourth Pan-African Congress in the United States?
   We shall never be able to settle the question of race equality and

full citizenship in the United States as long as there are a continent and 150 million people whose rights and status are questioned.

6. What is the object of the Fourth Pan-African Congress?

We come to the Fourth Pan-African Congress with no settled procedure or reform, but we come demanding and spreading information and working toward a wider acquaintance of the leaders among people of the colored race and of the oppressed classes throughout the world.

7. What will be the method of procedure at the Fourth Pan-African Congress?

The Congress will be primarily a sort of Chautauqua where definite information concerning Africa will be discussed. As far as possible the present conditions will be explained by representative Africans, by inhabitants of various areas and by representatives of groups and classes of every race and locality.

8. What topics will be discussed during the Fourth Pan-African Congress?

The proposed tentative program is as follows:

(A) The morning sessions will be given over to personal expositions of conditions by natives of different countries. There will be given also time for questions and debate.

(B) The four afternoon sessions will include discussions of the topics:

(1.) African Missions.

(2.) Education in Africa.

(3.) Art and Literature in Africa.

(4.) The Political Partition of Africa.

(C) During the four main evening sessions there will be discussions of:

(1.) The History of Africa.

(2.) The Slave Trade and the Dispersed Children of Africa.

(3.) The Economical Development of Africa and its Importance in the World.

(4.) The Future of Africa.

9. Who will be present at the Fourth Pan-African Congress?

As well as many prominent American Negroes, there will be present representatives from Europe, Africa and the Caribbean Islands.

10. Will persons of non-African descent be permitted to participate in the Congress?

Requests have come from many prominent white Americans and organizations of white Americans, asking that they be permitted to be represented at the Congress. They have been assured a cordial welcome.

11. How may one become eligible to participate in the Congress?

The payment of Five ($5.00) Dollars entitles any person or organization to one vote. Organizations that have contributed to the support of the Congress are entitled to as many votes as their contribution divided by five indicates.

12. What living arrangement will be made for delegates to the Fourth Pan-African Congress?

Upon the application to the entertainment committee, through the office of the Circle for Peace and Foreign Relations, delegates will be given sleeping quarters at a reasonable rate. Luncheons will be served at the place of meeting at a nominal charge.

13. Where will the sessions of the Fourth Pan-African Congress be held?

With the possible exception of one evening meeting these sessions will be held in the churches of uptown New York. The exact location will be announced later from convention headquarters.

14. Where will persons attending the Fourth Pan-African Congress go to register and secure information on August 20–21?

Members of the Reception Committee will be found at Grace Congregational Church, 139th St., West of Eighth Avenue, New York City.

15. Who is helping the Circle for Peace and Foreign Relations carry out the project of the Fourth Pan-African Congress?

The following are lending their valuable assistance in the work:

(A) The ladies of the New York Pan-African Congress Committee.

(B) A Committee of about thirty (30) Hostesses from various cities of the United States.

(C) Prominent American Negro business and professional men organized into the American Reception Committee.

(D) Editors and owners of the American Negro Press organized into an honorary publicity committee.

16. How is the Fourth Pan-African Congress being supported?

By contributions from individuals and organizations.

17. How may I assist in furthering the Fourth Pan-African Congress?

By spreading information and urging persons with whom I come in contact to give their moral and financial support to the effort of the Circle for Peace and Foreign Relations, which is sponsoring the Fourth Pan-African Congress.

18. What is the Circle for Peace and Foreign Relations?

The Circle for Peace and Foreign Relations is an organization of American women who believe in the universality of the race problem. This year they have appointed a special committee to assemble the Fourth Pan-African Congress. This committee has its headquarters in Room 688, Bible House, 45 Astor Place, New York City, U.S.A., and will be glad to answer all inquiries sent them.

[c]

PRESS SERVICE OF THE N.A.A.C.P.

The Fourth Pan-African Congress, ending its sessions here Wednesday night [Aug. 24] published a manifesto in the name of its delegates "from 20 American states, from nearly all the West Indies Islands, from Germany, Japan, India, South America, Sierra Leone, Gold Coast, Nigeria, Liberia and South Africa." The manifesto states the following main demands of Negroes throughout the world:

1. A voice in their own government.
2. Native rights to the land and its natural resources.
3. Modern education for all children.
4. The development of Africa for the Africans and not merely for the profit of Europeans.
5. The re-organization of commerce and industry so as to make the main object of capital and labor the welfare of the many rather than the enriching of the few.
6. The treatment of civilized men as civilized despite differences of birth, race or color.

The manifesto further demands the withdrawal of American armed forces from the black Republic of Haiti and the restoration of self-government there; condemns the attempt of white South Africans to monopolize the land belonging to the black natives; and after touching on African conditions says of conditions in America:

We believe that the Negroes of the United States should begin the effective use of their political power and that instead of working for a few minor offices or for merely local favors and concessions, they should vote with their eyes fixed upon the international problems of the color line and the national problems which affect the Negro race in the United States.

The manifesto urges the entrance of Negroes into trade unions in this country and says:

We urge the white workers of the world to realize that no program of labor uplift can be successfully carried through in Europe or America so long as colored labor is exploited and enslaved and deprived of all political powers.

On International affairs the Pan-African Congress expresses itself as desiring freedom and national independence in Egypt, China, and India and the cessation of interference by the United States in Central and South American countries.

Two members of the staff of the National Association for the Advancement of Colored People, Robert Bagnall, Director of Branches, and William Pickens, Field Secretary, served as regular delegates to the Congress. An international committee has been chosen to plan the next session of the Congress two years hence.

Commenting upon the sessions just ended Dr. W. E. B. Du Bois, founder of the movement, said: "The Fourth Congress with its upwards of 200 delegates was the largest in the series and that it had received the largest amount of carefully catalogued information concerning the peoples of African descent presented to any such session." The international committee chosen to plan the Fifth Pan-African Congress was also going to work out a permanent international organization, said Dr. Du Bois.

The New York Times, August 14, 1927, carried a fairly full story about the coming congress; the Brooklyn *Daily Eagle,* August 28, 1927, gave the congress a ful' page. A detailed unsigned account is in *The Crisis,* October, 1927; XXXIII, 263-64.

115

BATTLING SEGREGATION AND DISCRIMINATION

The *18th Annual Report, for 1927, of the N.A.A.C.P.,* contains details concerning struggles against segregation and discrimination. The first selection from this Report discussed segregation efforts in public schools in several northern cities; the second treats of the discrimination manifested by state and federal authorities after the disastrous Mississippi flood, and efforts to eliminate segregation in government agencies in Washington, D.C.

School Segregation: Sweeping court decisions against the practice of segregating colored school children in northern states were won in two important test cases. The first of these arose at *Toms River, New Jersey,* where Edward M. Fink, Supervising Principal, ordered the colored pupils of the public school to be transferred to a small church building. The colored parents declined to send their children to the segregated school and were thereupon called into court on complaint of the truant officer. Judge Harry E. Newman, at the hearing, found the parents not guilty of the offense charged.

The National Office and the New Jersey branches then took up the children's case, Eugene R. Hayne of Asbury Park, being retained as attorney. On March 28 a delegation headed by the Association's Secretary and composed of representatives of the New Jersey branches of the Association, and of other organizations, called upon Governor A. Harry Moore to protest against the segregation. The Governor stated he was powerless and that redress must be sought in the State Supreme Court.

Mr. Hayne summoned the school board of Toms River to appear before that Court on a writ of mandamus, hearing being held on April 6. On June 15, Justice Parker overruled the demurrer which had been filed by the Board of Education and on June 29, the thirty colored children who had been excluded from the Toms River public school were ordered by State Education Commissioner John H. Logan to be reinstated.

The National Office contributed $500 toward the expenses of the case.

The second dramatic school segregation case occurred in *Gary, Indiana,* where several hundred white students went on "strike," September 26, against the continued presence in the Emerson High School of twenty-four colored students. The School Board of Gary bowed to the demands of the white students and the City Council, on September 29, acquiesced to the extent of appropriating $15,000 for a temporary high school to house the colored students.

The Gary Branch of the Association, backed by the National Office, fought this attempt from the outset. Suit was brought on October 3, in the names of A. J. Terry and the Rev. Charles Hawkins, pastor of the First Baptist Church of Gary, for an injunction against the School Board, the Mayor, the City Clerk and the City Comptroller, to restrain the appropriation of taxpayers' money to erect a segregated school. The National Office appropriated $500.00 for the fight, sending Attorney R. L. Bailey of Indianapolis to assist the attorneys retained by the Gary Branch: Messrs. F. Lawrence Anderson, Charles H. Mason, Edward McKinley Bacoyn, and Lewis Spurling.

On October 24, Judge Grant Crumpacker temporarily restrained the City from paying, and the Board of Education from receiving the $15,000 appropriation; and on November 7 this order was continued as a temporary injunction, with the final hearing set for December 13.

Mayor Floyd E. Williams was quoted in the Gary *Post-Tribune* as saying he was convinced that the action of the City Council appropriating the $15,000 was illegal and that it was a useless waste of money to try to defeat the injunction.

In Judge Crumpacker's court, on December 12, the N.A.A.C.P. attorneys and those employed by the City agreed to dismiss the case with the understanding that the injunction be made permanent and that the court costs be paid by the City of Gary. It is now a matter of record in the courts that a Negro high school cannot be built in Gary with the money voted out by the City Council.

On December 23, just before the Christmas recess, all the colored students in the Emerson High School but three were called into the office of Superintendent William Wirt and were told that on January 2, 1928, they were to report to a segregated institution. The Association at once took steps to contest this during 1928.

A third school segregation case, originating in *Atlantic City* where two segregated schools had been established for colored children, was taken to the courts at the end of the year, Mr. Eugene R. Hayne being retained as attorney. This fight will extend into 1928.

Discrimination: Two forms of discrimination were met by special activity on the part of the Association in 1927. The first of these was brought to light during the Mississippi floods, when it was made known not only that relief agencies were being used to help perpetuate the peonage practiced on the delta plantations, but that Negroes were being grossly discriminated against in the administration of supplies and relief.

The Assistant Secretary, sent to investigate, found that Negroes were being prevented from leaving concentration camps without the consent of their landlords; that attempts were being made to charge Negroes for relief administered; and that some Negroes preferred to escape from refugee camps and go without shelter, food and clothing rather than be returned to the plantations from which the flood had driven them.

The Assistant Secretary's findings were made the basis of a report to the authorities in charge of flood relief.

A second investigation made in October by Miss —— substantiated the findings of the first investigation and brought to light many details which were published in *The Crisis.**

During the height of the flood emergency, in response to requests from outside persons for a distributing agency, the New Orleans Branch

* January, February, March, 1928; the investigator was Helen Boardman, a white woman.

of the Association, under the leadership of Dr. George W. Lucas, volunteered to receive and did receive through the National Office and distribute donations for the Negro sufferers from the flood in the sum of $741.48.

Another form of discrimination fought during the year with conspicuous success in several instances was the long standing segregation in the Government Bureaus in Washington.

So early as 1913, in its annual report, the Association had said:

> The recent effort of the present administration to segregate its colored employees gave this Association a great opportunity to put its program on record, an opportunity it was not slow to seize. . . . The campaign opened by our releasing on August 15 . . . an Open Letter to Woodrow Wilson. . . . This was followed by a series of meetings held by our branches all over the country. The Secretary was then sent to Washington to make an investigation and her report was printed and sent to the news services, 600 dailies, the colored press, secret societies, fifty magazines, to members of Congress, etc.

Since that time the N.A.A.C.P. has protested against segregation in the government departments, through letters to the President of the United States, through publicity, and otherwise. It was realized, however, that mere protest, to the President or in any other form, would have slight effect if the victims of this segregation were unwilling to give definite and specific information upon which a case could be built.

In 1923 the National Office tried to get at the facts of segregation in the departments through the District of Columbia Branch, and Mr. Shelby J. Davidson, then Secretary of the Branch, did, over a period of several months, gather considerable evidence. Mr. Davidson again found that one of the main difficulties was to obtain definite proof which could be freely used. He found that a number of government employees would talk about the matter but would not be responsible for statements concerning rulings and practices in the departments which would make tangible evidence on which to proceed.

During 1927 the matter was taken up by the District of Columbia Branch, under the leadership of Mr. Neval H. Thomas, President of the Branch. Mr. Thomas launched a vigorous campaign and offered to take full responsibility for the fight, but the clerks involved insisted on sharing the responsibility and readily gave information and data on which the Branch might proceed. Mr. Thomas and the colored clerks were backed up by a country-wide press campaign released from the National Office.

The first breach in the segregation policy was made in the Department of the Interior when two Negro clerks were ordered to report as pension examiners. Soon after this 42 colored employees in the same department were ordered back to their old and unsegregated posts. This ended segregation in the Pension Bureau, Department of the Interior, Secretary Hubert Work's memorandum directing "that all the employees in the Pension Bureau, both white and colored, affected by the new organization of the Division of Files be restored to the location and work assignments they formerly occupied."

The Branch next attacked discrimination against colored clerks in the General Land Office. Fifteen out of the twenty-one clerks affected signed a letter addressed to Secretary Work, protesting against the enforced segregation. Following this, segregation of clerks in the Treasury Department was protested, not only in the Department bureaus, restaurants, rest rooms, etc., but also the complete Negro department in the office of the Register of the Treasury.

The breaches in the segregation policy made during 1927 were the consequence of the well-planned policy waged by the Branch and engineered by its President, with the cooperation of other bodies. In the course of the campaign Mr. Thomas several times headed delegations which called upon department officials. In several of the delegations were Mr. A. S. Pinkett, Secretary of the Branch; Mr. Robert J. Nelson, Editor of the *Washington Eagle;* Mr. Thomas A. Johnson of the Equal Rights League. Mr. Nelson also represented the Elks.

The colored press of the country rallied almost as a unit in this campaign and the Branch was able to present to department officials copies of newspapers from every part of the United States showing that sentiment was united against the practice which had been inaugurated in government departments.

The above selections appear on pp. 9–11 and 20–23 of cited printed Report. On discrimination in Washington's government buildings at this time, see the editor's article in *Science and Society,* Winter, 1964; XXVIII, 86–91.

116

THE HIGH COST OF PREJUDICE

by Alain Locke

Alain Locke (1886–1954) was born in Philadelphia, graduated from Harvard, was the first Black Rhodes Scholar in Oxford, and earned his doctorate at the University of Berlin. In 1925 he began a long teaching career at Howard University (in the Philosophy Department); he edited the very significant book, *The New Negro* (the first edition appeared December, 1925), and remained a decisive figure in Afro-American cultural affairs until his death. The essay that follows was written in reply to the question: "Should the Negro Be Encouraged to Cultural Equality?"; the negative was argued by Lothrop Stoddard, then a leading ideologist of white supremacy. Published also is Alain Locke's brief rebuttal to the Stoddard essay.

The Negro question is too often put forward merely as the Negro question. It is just as much, and even more seriously, the question of democracy. The position of the Negro in American society is its one great outstanding anomaly. Instead of being solely the plight of an oppressed minority facing prejudice and proscription, it is the predicament of an obsessed majority confronted with increasing social dilemma and self-contradiction. No reasonable person expects a society to reform itself for the sake of abstract consistency; but nevertheless I believe there would be a profound change of social attitude toward the Negro if we were more generally aware of the high cost of prejudice. Enlightened self-interest would then operate to forestall the inevitable consequences of social short-sightedness. And if, instead of pleading by sentiment and Fourth of July rhetoric at the bar of democratic theory, the intelligent Negro would put his case in terms of the common-sense practicalities of the concrete situation; if instead of being the great suppliant at the feet of the nation, he would become the great critic and challenging analyst of our institutions, he would then confront America with this dilemma of its own making and balance for self-interested judgment the alternatives of recognition and non-recognition.

Indeed, just as in the matter of the Negro's physical freedom the delay of gradual manumission forced the issue of summary emancipation, so in the matter of his larger freedom the denial of cultural recognition where it has been earned will sooner or later precipitate the more embarrassing issue of mass recognition on demand. There is a compound interest in such matters that an enlightened society ought not force subsequent generations to pay. Prejudice, moreover, as a wholesale generalization of social inferiority and cultural incapacity,— even granting that it was ever true or warrantable,—becomes, as a matter of course, more contrary to fact with every decade,—yes, with every day. The dilemmas of non-recognition become correspondingly deeper. Apart from the injustice and reactionary unwisdom, there is tragic irony and imminent social farce in the acceptance by "White America" of the Negro's cultural gifts while at the same time withholding cultural recognition,—the reward that all genius merits and even requires.

The orthodox social mind on this race issue suffers from the pathetic delusion that it can negate what it denies. It can, I admit, retard, but only at general social or net loss. In most cases it is putting itself in a more and more untenable position. Indeed, in the sweeping generalizations about the Negro's "place in society," by predicating wholesale the incapacity of the Negro group for higher cultural development, the issues of recognition have been sharpened and the ultimate dilemma brought closer. If, for instance, the general question had never been raised, Negro genius and talent could have been explained away as the exception (which it probably is for all groups) and expropriated without question by the dominant group. As it is, the Negro has been publicly dared, in prejudice so to speak, to produce the exceptional. Ethnic arrogance has blatantly called the world to referee the question. Negro genius has thus been made the champion of a staked issue and when it wins recognition (and who doubts the eventual recognition of genius?) it must have it not merely in its own right, but in the full force of its group representativeness and as the vindication of the controversy.

Mass proof of the Negro's capacities will slowly and eventually come, but by the circumstances of this general challenge, American opinion must meet the issue and recant its position much in advance of any such general solution. That is why, I believe, the question of cultural recognition must be met and conceded by this present generation. In advance of the patiently plodding millions, the question raised can and must be settled in terms of the representative vindication of the exceptional few. For the asserted inferiority of the Negro does not pivot on the average man,—black or white,—and can not be settled by mass comparisons; as a challenge it must be fought out in terms of the exceptional man and the highest values of civilization. It is the price of prejudice and it should be.

This explains why, with only a little more than two generations of physical freedom,—as far as the masses go,—with his political freedom temporarily checked and frustrated, with educational and economic self-emancipation just beginning to gather mass headway and momentum, the Negro's talent and energy are turning with such force to the field of cultural competition. As his ambition, blocked or thwarted elsewhere, comes to this relatively free and unblockable avenue, it becomes apparent that what normally comes last in a people's development may very likely come first with the American Negro. Instead of being the by-product of his leisure and the fruit of his material success, his cultural development seems about to become a special channel of test and proof, an accepted vehicle of recognition.

In fact, the denial of equality, through the hard discipline it inflicts, has just this tendency to spur on and build up a moral and spiritual superiority. With the rush of long suppressed ambition and the urge of special motives, Negro talent to-day is pouring into its one free outlet in an endeavor to compete and qualify in terms of the highest acknowledged values of the White man's civilization,—in art and science, in creative and inventive contribution,—and through making such contributions, to demonstrate cultural capacity more effectively than it could be demonstrated by a high general average in the mere assimilation of American ways and standards. Cultural recognition, we may be sure, will not be prematurely conceded; it will be granted only when it is demonstrably inevitable; but to my way of thinking, by virtue of these peculiar conditions, it is less remote than political or economic equality, because less dependent upon the condition of the masses. In the light of the present attainment of the Negro of the younger generation, in cultural and artistic expression especially, and in the prospective social enlightment of our talented tenth, I should say that cultural recognition of the Negro was imminent.

The continuance of the present attitude toward the Negro is in fact possible only as long as it is possible to take as most representative of the Negro his worst rather than his best. His greatest disadvantage is not that of inequality of condition but inequality of comparison. For successful peoples are rated, and rate themselves, in terms of their best. Racial and national prestige is, after all, the product of the exceptional few. So when Negro life begins to produce poets, artists, thinkers and to make creative contributions that must be recognized not only as outstanding but as nationally representative, the old attitudes become untenable. In American music and poetry and drama it is impossible to name the foremost talents without including some Negroes; and the promise of the rapid developments of this aspect of Negro achievement, especially as centered in the younger New York group, make the same very probable in the next few years for fiction and the fine arts generally. A Roland Hayes, a Paul Robeson, a Countee Cullen, a Langston Hughes or a Weldon Johnson shift the burden of proof from 'Rastus Jones and the general average; and the crux of the matter becomes the question of what position and recognition must be accorded the cultured and culture producing Negro in American society.

The greatest ground for hope in the situation is that by these developments on the upper levels of Negro life, the representative classes are appealed to, not so much in terms of something for the Negro,—something to be granted for his special interest,—but in terms of common interest and mutual gain. As has been repeatedly said recently,—and as is now being gradually realized in the current developments of cultural expression,—the Negro comes bearing gifts, and assumes for the first time the rôle of a contributor to joint and universal interests. It becomes then not solely a matter of recognizing the Negro, but more the question whether America can afford not to recognize in him those qualities upon which we must increasingly put a premium. Representative Negro opinion prefers to have the question put and settled upon that basis, prefers to point out that the typical contemporary demands of Negro life are, as it is aptly stated, "not for alms, but for opportunity." The Negro of to-day would rather have the competitive and rigidly selective democracy of the square deal and equal opportunity than the unearned philanthropic democracy of paper rights and class legislation.

The force of this sane and inevitable position may at first affect only a few,—indeed, only the most enlightened and liberal sectors of our society,—but fortunately in such matters the few are yet the arbiters, and already the most enlightened and liberal elements are reaching out toward these exponents of Negro culture in warm and unreserved recognition not only of the product but of the individuals who are producing it. They, at least, may be expected to appreciate that mass recognition is not immediately in question, that it is a case of putting the premium upon the capable few, and thus of accelerating the "leveling up" processes in American society. In a recent discussion of this subject, John Haynes Holmes very aptly says: "The logic of social equality is a social system absolutely fluid, in which each man rises or falls according to his own specific gravity of character or merit. This will give you not all men of a certain type at a fixed level, but some men of every type at all levels." It is this sort of social and cultural equality which contemporary Negro life merits and is demanding. It is this which in the light of the most recent trends of social attitude, Negro life seems in a fair way to gain. And it is this which is necessary if we are to maintain in American life that most essential of all democratic conditions,—an open career for talent.

The cultural recognition of the Negro, I admit, has its costs. But so also has non-recognition, and the situation should be pragmatically balanced in terms of these two costs. It merely fogs the issue when the creed of the slavocracy is sentimentally extended to classes and sections and situations that have no practical reason for holding to it, beyond the fact that it is the traditional way to think and feel. Even in circles that are so representative and stable that they should have no hysteria on the subject of race amalgamation, "no social equality,"—in short,

"White Supremacy,"—is held to be the one reservation every typical White man is supposed to make and every typical Negro is expected to concede.

Cultural recognition, on the other hand, means the removal of wholesale social proscription and, therefore, the conscious scrapping of the mood and creed of "White Supremacy." It means an open society instead of a closed ethnic shop. For what? For making possible free and unbiased contacts between the races on the selective basis of common interests and mutual consent, in contrast with what prevails at present,—dictated relations of inequality based on caste psychology and class exploitation. It is predicated on new sorts of social contact,—less intimate in fact, however, than those it means to supplant. Indeed, instead of leaving society open at the bottom, as it now is, for the economic and sex exploitation of the weaker and less desirable elements of Negro life, it means the opening of society at the top for equal and self-respecting intercourse as warranted by mutual gain and common interests.

Before rejecting this new scheme of interracial contacts, let us take stock of the actual situation and the cost of the old traditional scheme of the relationship of black and white. The traditional opponent of social equality for the Negro,—the typical Negrophobe,—claims that race prejudice is primarily the instinct of race-preservation and its chief arm of maintenance. The logic of his attitude is just this: that person to person relations are the danger of White society. It is the very same man, however, whose social régime and life most depend upon close personal relations with Negroes,—in familiar and household relations at that,—and whose chief delight is to be instantly and widely familiar with Negroes provided he can protect sentimentally his caste pride and personal egotism, to which, as a matter of fact, such relations are the chief sustaining foil. It is this type of man who in open or clandestine relations, by the sex exploitation of the socially and economically unprotected Negro woman, has bred a social dilution which threatens at its weakest point the race integrity he boasts of maintaining and upholding.

In the light of this active contradiction of its own social creed by its own social practice, White orthodoxy on the race question becomes not a consistent creed of race superiority and inner conviction, but the social self-defense of a bad conscience, the hysterical ruse of a self-defeatist vice. It fumes about keeping society closed at the top and insists on keeping it viciously open at the bottom. It claims to eliminate social contact between the races, but actually promotes race mixing. Under conditions and habits such as these contradictions have bred, a rabidly "White America" can not refuse to recognize the Negro and long remain White. For it is pride rather than prejudice that keeps social groups intact; and normally with the Negro there would be more sentimental and practical motives for group cohesion under conditions of social recognition than under those of social proscription, and less intermarriage under free association than miscegenation under forced social subserviency. The enlightened New South may be expected to see this. They already do. For these reasons as well as in the interest of general community reform and progress, they are gradually seeing the necessity for helping re-establish the group morale of the Negro.

Since we started out to be pragmatists rather than sentimentalists in the matter, let us see frankly if enlightened self-interest dictates the social recognition of the culturally advancing type of Negro. Let us remember that this is a complete reversal of the yet very prevalent the-Negro-is-all-right-in-his-place philosophy. Let us remember also that there is no way of putting a social premium upon a product and at the same time putting a social discount upon its active producers. Either they must be recognized in their particular persons as the accredited exponents of culture, or their output and its quality will be below par. The man who contributes to culture must fully participate in its best and most stimulating aspects. Negro genius to-day isn't to be expected to come in from the kitchen to entertain. Negro genius of the new generation consciously confronts only two alternatives,—front door recognition or voluntary expatriation. But let us admit, except, in a few most enlightened quarters, the existence of the old reactionary attitudes. Let us concede the dominant majority the power they temporarily have to withhold this sort of recognition and, by so doing, to retard considerably the development of the better elements of Negro life.

Black effort has gone forward and will still go forward almost as fast under the spur of non-recognition as under the wand of encouragement, —with a different course and temper, to be sure. Some genius will continue to be snuffed out, as in the past; considerably more will again be diverted to controversy and agitation and wastefully consumed in social friction. But some, in spite of everything, will break through to recognition. Genius is the most fluid social capital. Ideas are not subject to embargoes. Negro genius,—as witness Roland Hayes and Henry Tanner,—will bid for recognition abroad and will receive it. And in the self-involved dilemma of having repudiated at home, even as racially representative, what in the universal eye will stand as nationally representative, American public opinion can eventually do only one thing,—

gracefully capitulate. Whitman and Poe underwent the same experience, —so it isn't at bottom a race question.

But contemporary America does not wish to leave it to Europe to recognize American genius. And consequently the instant recognition of genius at home is to-day a very vital question for an America that realizes her cultural poverty in the midst of her material richness. For American self-esteem can not successfully subsist another generation upon the glitter of purely materialistic developments, upon the vaingloriousness of a gigantic civilization of utilities. With the quest for culture rapidly succeeding the quest for the dollar, America is not in a position to be restrictive or discriminatory in the field of cultural productiveness; and a group bearing cultural gifts can not be denied recognition,—even a Negro group. The cultural flowering of Negro talent, the attempt of the present generation to capitalize the race's spiritual creativeness, therefore comes most opportunely and takes a strategic position in the front alignments of contemporary American endeavor.

Apart, however, from this broad question that creative genius is the hardest and costliest thing to refuse to recognize, in a suppressed minority group it is the most dangerous thing to deny it free play and recognition. The balked intelligence of such a group, thrown back upon the repressed masses, invariably comes forward within another generation's time in the uglier form of radical leadership. Behind it rally the aroused masses and their harsh demands. As with the Jewish intellectuals of Russia, subverted social light may readily become revolutionary fire. I am not an alarmist; but I can see danger ahead in this persistent American lumping of the best with the worst in Negro life. Race war? Not exactly. Class war, more likely,—with the Negro group temper profoundly changed from its present patient amiability to social desperation, having in its ultimate disillusionment discovered that it has so little to lose.

Both as an American and as a Negro, I would so much prefer to see the black masses going gradually forward under the leadership of a recognized and representative and responsible élite than see a frustrated group of malcontents later hurl these masses at society in doubtful but desperate strife. The only way out of mob psychology and mass hysteria,—and they threaten now not from one side but from both,— is through the building up of the representative elements of Negro life; and this involves not merely the Negro effort to improve and qualify, but the Caucasian will and vision to reward and recognize by putting at social premium not the worst, but the best.

For the present it seems that the interest in the cultural expression of Negro life is genuine, and that it heralds an almost revolutionary revaluation of the Negro. But that still remains to be seen definitely. Certainly this interest is rapidly spreading from the first accepted point of vital human contact in music and folk-lore to poetry, drama, fiction, and art very generally. Moreover, in enlightened circles the interest in the Negro's art is stimulating interest in the artist personally. Roland Hayes, Paul Robeson, several of the younger poets have achieved, in addition to reputation, distinct personal popularity and success. Especially among the younger liberal and radical groups, and also to an extent in serious collegiate and youth movement groups, the work of the younger Negro artists is being taken as the new basis of approach for the sympathetic study and understanding of the Negro; and the dour, abstract-problem approach of the older generation is being laid aside. Occasionally direct efforts are made by such groups to cultivate person to person acquaintanceship with members of the more representative classes of the race.

Culturally significant beyond all this comes the eager adoption of Negro themes and material as a serious problem of artistic interpretation, even in the literature of the New South: Du Bose Heyward's *Porgy*, Julia Peterkin's *Green Thursday*, Sherwood Anderson's *Dark Laughter*, —to mention some outstanding examples. This moving out of Negro currents into the main stream of contemporary art is a cultural recognition more significant even than the acceptance of the Negro artist, for it occurs as a reciprocal effect of the enlargement of vision which he has brought about. Moreover, it is achieved upon the basis of universality, a basis that must ultimately be achieved in all things; but one that may yet be, except in art, several generations' dip below our present horizons. So within the last few years this question has become something more than academic; we are actually confronted with a liberal array of Negro talent in active cultural expression and an almost parallel emergence of the disposition to recognize it.

It is to be hoped that general American opinion can be persuaded to follow its most enlightened segment in this direction of progressive recognition of the Negro. Beyond the fact that it is not in the interests of democracy itself to allow an illiterate, unprogressive White man the conviction that he is better than the best Negro, it ought to be apparent that the most effective leverage upon the undesirable in the race situation is through the moral pressure that will come by recognizing the desirable. Otherwise even the sincerest criticism and the best of advice is spurned as unwarrantable persecution. If public opinion does change in this regard, and we hope it may, it will have discovered a new philosophy for pivoting a rapid and favorable shift in the social adjustment of the two races. By recognizing the talent and the representative types among Negroes, an easing and vindicating satisfaction can be carried down into the Negro masses, as well as the most quickening and stimulating sort of inspiration that could be given them. Their élite would then become symbols in advance of expected justice and of a peaceful eventual solution. They would be literally an investment in democracy.

The cutting edge of prejudice will thus have been safely blunted if American public opinion begins to scrap its unfair wholesale generalizations, and gives recognition where it is due. Besides affording a stimulus to Negro genius and increasing the general fund of common culture, much that is socially threatening for the future may be forestalled. For no prejudice is more fraught with social danger than that which outlives its causes and adds social insult to social injury. Negro effort, beginning to move under its own momentum, has reached a point where the vital question is not how much progress the Negro has made or is capable of making, but rather, how much of it will achieve recognition and be socially accredited. A pivotal adjustment of social attitudes is called for; and American society will have no more tactful and advantageous opportunity offered it than comes by way of the present generation's overture of a possible cultural recognition of Negro talent in its own intrinsic rights of accomplishment. Not only great satisfaction, but great social incentive can be created for the masses in the recognition of the outstanding few,—as group representative, however, and not with the reservations to which Negro talent of a previous generation had to submit, namely, of being regarded quite as a prodigy, a biological sport.

For the younger Negro artists and leaders of to-day are proudly race-conscious, and their work is in many cases frankly based on a conscious interpretation of their race life. They have, so to speak, two audiences, and are in many cases strained to know upon which to concentrate. As artists, it would be best for them to face America and humanity at large. Otherwise, two alternatives, each entailing heavy and general social loss, would confront the talented Negro: either to march off to foreign fields and repeat for the whole American situation what has already tragically happened in the South, where the best and sturdiest have moved off and left an inert and almost leaderless mass to constitute a still heavier social drag and danger; or else to turn in narrowed and vindictive vision to the only course that will give him a chance and swing the hammer of mass action behind the cutting edge of genius.

The Forum, October, 1927; LXXVIII, 500–10.

Editor of *The Forum:*

M. André Siegfried, looking at the same situation with none of Mr. Stoddard's Freudian obsessions, sees in the Young Negro point of view just the opposite attitude on the question of race relations. Describing "advanced Negro thought" in his book *America Comes of Age,* he credits "this American élite" with "strengthening the unity of the darker races all over the world." "Among these people," he continues, "a Negro who 'passes' is a traitor, a woman who marries white is criticized, and if she becomes a white man's mistress loses caste entirely." This reading is far nearer the truth than Mr. Stoddard's. Race fusion is in our minds too tainted with the assumptions of White dominance and aggression, too associated with the stigma of inferiority rather than equality, for race amalgamation to be the social ideal and objective of an intelligent and self-respecting race consciousness such as we are now developing. In brief, the progressive Negro of to-day wants cultural opportunity and cultural recognition, and wants it as a Negro.

It is Mr. Stoddard and the position he defends that are illogical. He says, "Let there be no mistake: White America will not abolish the color-line, will not admit the Negro to social equality, will not open the door to racial amalgamation." Since when has the color-line become blood-tight? It is notoriously not a blood barrier but a culture barrier. It is a sign of the Negro's lapsing sense of inferiority that he recognizes this clearly, and that, to put it bluntly, he says to the America of Mr. Stoddard's persuasion, "Spare your blood, and share your civilization." I suspect that the real cause for frenzy and alarm among the advocates of White Supremacy is based upon this real threat of economic and cultural competition, unless it be the inner panic of having contradicted themselves biologically.

Like a modern Canute, with imperial condescension, Mr. Stoddard moves back the throne of White Supremacy a few paces before the "rising tide of color." He offers a "biracial" régime based not on caste discrimination and economic subordination but on fair and equitable separation,—"a vertical line drawn through society from top to bottom, permitting individuals to rise as high as their talents will take them, on their side of the line." To the extent that it is possible, American prejudice is already building this expensive sort of social structure. The Negro has everything to gain and little to lose by it. But I predict one or the other of two things: either the general costs will be so great that subsequent generations not afflicted with colorphobia will refuse to continue to pay them, or that the general relation of the white and the colored peoples in the world at large will have so altered that it will be actually dangerous for America thus to maintain a socially solid black minority. Of all persons, the author of *The Rising Tide of Color* and *The Revolt Against Civilization* ought to appreciate the latter alternative.

Alain Locke

The Forum, December, 1927; LXXVIII, 542–43.

117

THE HAMPTON STRIKE
by W. E. B. Du Bois

Earlier notice was taken of the fact that strikes and demonstrations by Black college students occurred frequently in the nineteen-twenties. One occurred in 1927 at the Hampton Institute in Virginia, then identified—as was Tuskegee—with the concept of vocational education where ideas of student protest and manifestations of student unrest were supposed to be unthinkable. All the greater, therefore, was the effect of the Hampton strike; Du Bois' comment on it, reprinted below, was characteristically profound and made a significant impact.

The most sinister thing about the Hampton strike, is not the attitude of the authorities of Hampton. It has long been known, and the knowledge discounted among American Negroes, that Hampton trustees and teachers did not all have feelings, opinions or ideals toward American Negroes, which were acceptable to self-respecting black men. There has always been at Hampton a degree of race discrimination and of repression that has been hateful and exasperating. It has long been endured, just as beggars often endure the insult of impudent alms-giving. The time for an end to that endurance is surely at hand, unless we Negroes are willing to bring up our children in the same attitude of subserviency and uncomplaining submission to caste which our fathers inherited from slavery. The Hampton attitude must be distinctly and firmly repudiated.

But the most disconcerting thing in the Hampton strike is the way in which graduates and parents repudiated their own children. The best of schools is imperfect. The worst is intolerable. The students present upon the grounds are in the long run the best and only judges of the efficiency of the education offered. They are far better judges than parents or alumni. If mature college students believe that a school is going wrong, what are they going to do but openly protest? In any white northern college that protest would immediately be heeded, even if accompanied by violence, and there would not be any silly insistence upon dumb, unthinking obedience. Students are not sent to school to learn to obey. They are sent there to learn to do, to think, to execute, to be men and women. Self-reliance, self-expression, honesty and decision are to be learned in school if anywhere. We complain bitterly of the lack of these qualities in our young people, but do we encourage their development? At Fisk and at Hampton there were parents and alumni who turned upon their own children like wild beasts, ready to beat them into submission; insisting that even if the school authorities were wrong, it was the business of black boys and girls to submit. At Hampton, the Alumni actually published to the world a statement; declaring, first, that they gave complete approval and consent to what the Hampton authorities had done, including the wholesale suspensions, and then, finally, promising that they would investigate.

Negro colleges with few exceptions are standing together to punish and penalize for life and exclude from all chances of education the brave, orderly and clear-headed young men and women who led the Hampton strike, just because Hampton tells them to.

At this rate, what will the next generation be? What kind of crawling cowards are we seeking to spawn? It is possible, indeed, it is probable, that striking students at Hampton, Fisk, Shaw, Howard and elsewhere, have made their mistakes, but there is absolutely no question or shadow of doubt but that when 400 students, well-trained, orderly, with excellent records, are willing to take their future in their hands and jeopardize their whole lives in an appeal to the world for justice, that something must be absolutely and radically wrong, and the business of parents and Alumni is to investigate before they condemn, to encourage and uphold their protesting children, instead of cowing and disgracing them. It is the Principal and Faculty of Hampton that are really at the bar of Justice and not the students who refused to sing for the entertainment of a white Englishman.

In "Postscript" department, by W. E. B. Du Bois, *The Crisis,* December, 1927; XXXIV, 347–48.

118

CONDITIONS IN MARYLAND
by Jesse L. Nicholas

In the nineteen-twenties, as a result of the mounting strength of the resistance of Black people and a gathering sense of horror at the persistence of gruesome lynchings, various so-called interracial private bodies and organizations made their appearance in both North and South. There also came into being official, governmental interracial commissions in order to gather data and offer recommendations. Characteristic of the latter was the Interracial Commission of Maryland, established in 1925, by the legislature; on its Executive Committee in 1927–1928, were six people, of whom four (including chairman, vice-chairman, and treasurer) were white. The secretary, a Black man, was Jesse L. Nicholas of Govans, Maryland. From the 1928 Report of this commission, drafted by Mr. Nicholas, are reprinted sections detailing salient features of the life of Afro-Americans in a border state in the late nineteen-twenties.

Health, Housing and Sanitation

Conditions in 1929* are practically the same as in 1927. The acquisition of Provident Hospital, while an outstanding achievement in the medical history of the State, still does not meet the need for general hospital treatment and there should be larger provision for hospital beds for both City and State in the care of the colored population.

Statistics of 1927 have shown Baltimore has the highest infant mortality of the largest ten cities of the United States. It is obvious that any effort to reduce this rating must be primarily directed at Negro mortality in Baltimore City and in the counties. There is decided need for pre-natal instruction for mothers, together with attendance at birth of a physician if possible, or at least a licensed mid-wife. Supervision during pre-school age is also of great importance.

The Bureau of Child Hygiene of the State Department of Health conducts monthly child health conferences for colored children in those counties where there is a large Negro population. At these conferences children are examined and mothers advised as to the feeding and care of children, they are strongly urged to consult their own physicians for treatment and subsequent care.

The infant mortality rate among colored infants is double that among white, due largely to lack of satisfactory care. Colored mothers are almost entirely without the benefit of pre-natal advice. A campaign of information and instruction is needed among colored people to show the importance of extending pre-natal care.

The undermining of general health and a consequent decreased earning capacity through the prevalence of social diseases, calls for an extended state program of education through the distribution of litera-

* The Report was dated January 4, 1929; presumably, this should read 1928.

ture, following the plan of the United States Public Health Service during and following the war.

The first effort on the part of the State to care for Negro tubercular children has been initiated at Henryton. Space has been set aside for from thirty to thirty-five children. The dire need at present is for an appropriation at the per capita rate of $1.79 per day, with salary and maintenance for two additional nurses. The support of this project would be a vital contribution to the already fine standard which Henryton has given to the State in its fight against tuberculosis.

Dr. W. S. Baer, noted specialist, says there is far from sufficient hospital provision made for colored crippled children, for in the City of Baltimore there are now only eight beds available for them. We urge support for his well defined plan for increased facilities for this class of patients.

Negroes would be greatly benefited through the enactment of a general State Housing Code, as health and living conditions are closely allied. Successful experiments in modern housing for colored people have been made in Washington, Philadelphia and New York, the last by Mr. John D. Rockefeller, Jr. By lending financial aid and his business experience Mr. Rockefeller has made possible the erection of a series of beautiful, modern apartments, and is working out plans to aid Negroes to own these apartments and at the same time lead better, more sanitary and happier lives. It is to be regretted that similar efforts have not been attempted in Maryland.

The high death rate of the Negro is admittedly alarming, but when one takes into consideration the fact that he is forced by economic necessity to perform the most hazardous, the most unwholesome, the most unhealthy and the most arduous tasks, and at the same time live in unimproved houses in the least sanitary districts, this high death rate is not to be wondered at.

If the State of Maryland, every city and town, every nook and corner in the cities and towns, be made a fit place for human habitation, the death rate of all the people will decrease.

The Commission acknowledges the assistance of Mrs. Sarah Fernandis in preparing this part of the report.

Recommendation

This Commission recommends the establishment of a preventorium for Negro children exposed to a tubercular environment, in some part of the State where climatic conditions are favorable.

Public Service

In 1904 the Legislature of Maryland enacted a law to require railroads to provide separate cars for white and colored passengers upon all lines of traffic in the State. However, the Court of Appeals subsequently held that the law could not be enforced as to interstate passengers, thus leaving the terms of the Act to apply only to those passengers traveling from point to point within the State.

As from 80 to 90 per cent of the colored passengers either begin or end their journey beyond the limits of the State, and as the Act has been construed as not applying to local city lines, it would seem that the time has come for the repeal of this discriminatory law. It serves no good purpose and is obnoxious to peaceful, law-abiding citizens.

Recommendation

This Commission recommends that the Act of 1904, and any other Acts relative thereto, prescribing regulations for the separation of white and Negro passengers on public carriers be repealed.

Industry and Economic Life

Where the work is heavy, as in the steel mills and on construction jobs, or where the work is disagreeable, as in the fertilizer plants and tanneries, or where the hours are long, as in domestic service—in these places Negroes are to be found employed in large numbers. Of the Negroes gainfully employed in the State approximately one-half are in domestic service pursuits. Large numbers are employed in the building trades, as longshoremen, and as helpers on the truck farms.

Negro women form a large percentage of these colored workers and in the recent industrial depression, when Negro men were forced to idleness, the women workers, in many instances, shouldered the burden of supporting the family.

In the trades and industries of Maryland the thousands of gainfully employed Negroes face certain obstacles that should be removed. Most important of these industrial handicaps are:—

Limited Opportunities.—There are certain occupations and jobs in which Negroes are seldom, if ever, used no matter what the capacity or talent of the individual colored worker. Moreover, the level above which the Negro worker may not advance is strictly drawn. This tends to slay ambition and to destroy the incentive to do a better grade of work.

The public utilities and public service jobs are largely closed to Negroes. There are no colored employees on the street railway lines as motormen or conductors; no colored policemen or firemen; no colored meter readers. These are occupations to which each citizen must contribute in one way or another and all citizens should have an opportunity for a livelihood from these resources.

Low Wages.—While Negro wage earners are to be found in a wide variety of plants, the jobs held by them are largely of the types that require little or no preparation. As a consequence, the wage for the work they perform is low. Poor food, poor housing, poor health and low moral standards all may emanate from low pay, now or later.

Seasonal Work.—Not only are Negroes in the lowest paid occupations, but thousands of them are in those jobs which are most affected by seasons. Common labor and construction workers suffer greatly through loss of employment—even in normal times—due to seasonal changes in the amount of work. Families must be supported even when work is slack.

There are few suitable openings for the boys and girls who are finishing our high schools and other institutions of higher learning. If Maryland fails to make provision for these young people on whom the State is spending its money, they have no alternative save that of seeking openings elsewhere. This State can ill afford to have its educated and trained Negro youth desert it while the less ambitious remain.

Legislative action can do little to alleviate the conditions mentioned above. But the State might well set the proper example by the employment of Negroes in positions other than that of teaching. It cannot be too strongly emphasized that the circumscription of industrial opportunities is the basic evil from which spring poor housing, poor health, disease and crime.

Rehabilitation of workers.—The rehabilitation of persons incapacitated by accident or disease is attracting the attention of social experts and benevolent persons. Much loss to society may be averted by proper methods of restoration.

The Commission acknowledges the help of Mr. R. Maurice Moss, secretary of the Urban League, in preparing this section. The Commission makes no recommendation at this time.

Report with Recommendations of the Interracial Commission of Maryland to the Governor and General Assembly of Maryland (Baltimore, 1928), pp. 15–19.

119

MARCUS GARVEY AND THE N.A.A.C.P.
by W. E. B. Du Bois

A brief but illuminating summary of Du Bois' relationship with and attitude toward Garvey and his movement was published in *The Crisis* soon after President Coolidge (whose election Garvey had favored) released him from prison in 1927 and ordered his deportation.

Many persons are under the impression that the N.A.A.C.P. has been the persistent enemy of Marcus Garvey. This is due to repeated accusations published in the *Negro World* without the slightest basis of fact. For the sake of the truth, it may be well to recall certain matters of clear record.

The Crisis has published five articles on Marcus Garvey. The first two articles, March 1920 and January 1921 ended with this summary:

To sum up: Garvey is a sincere, hard-working idealist; he is also a stubborn, domineering leader of the mass; he has worthy industrial and commercial schemes but he is an inexperienced business man. His dreams of Negro industry, commerce and the ultimate freedom of Africa are feasible; but his methods are bombastic, wasteful, illogical and ineffective, and almost illegal. If he learns by experience, attracts strong and capable friends and helpers instead of making needless enemies; if he gives up secrecy and suspicion and substitutes open and frank reports as to his income and expenses, and above all if he is willing to be a co-worker and not a czar, he may yet in time succeed in at least starting some of his schemes toward accomplishment. But unless he does these things and does them quickly he cannot escape failure.

No more prophetic word was ever written about Marcus Garvey!

The third and fourth articles dealt with the Black Star Line and the Universal Negro Improvement Association and were based on published documents with little comment.

It was not until September, 1922, that *The Crisis* had a sharp word of criticism. This was based on Garvey's threats against his critics, his connection with the Ku Klux Klan and his distribution of pamphlet propaganda against American Negroes. We quoted, among other things, this:

"The white race can best help the Negro by telling him the truth, and not by flattering him into believing that he is as good as any white man."

Concerning this we said:

"Not even Tom Dixon or Ben Tillman or the hatefullest enemies of the Negro have ever stooped to a more vicious campaign than Marcus Garvey, sane or insane, is carrying on. He is not attacking white prejudice, he is grovelling before it and applauding it; his only attack is on men of his own race who are striving for freedom; his only contempt is for Negroes; his only threats are for black blood."

On the other hand Garvey's attacks on the N.A.A.C.P. have been continuous, preposterous and false. He has claimed:

1. That we kept his representative from activity in Paris in 1919.

2. That Moorfield Storey came from Boston to secure his conviction in 1924.

3. That the collapse of the Black Star Line came about "because men were paid to make this trouble by certain organizations calling themselves Negro Advancement Associations. They paid men to dismantle our machinery and otherwise damage it so as to bring about the downfall of the movement."

4. That the N.A.A.C.P. was responsible for his incarceration and deportation.

Every single statement in these and dozens of similar charges are absolutely false and without any basis of fact whatsoever. As *The Crisis* said in May, 1924:

No Negro in America ever had a fairer and more patient trial than Marcus Garvey. He convicted himself by his own admissions, his swaggering monkey-shines in the court room with monocle and long tailed coat and his insults to the judge and prosecuting attorney.

Marcus Garvey was long refused bail, not because of his color, but because of the repeated threats and cold blooded assaults charged against his organization. He himself openly threatened to "get" the District Attorney. His followers had repeatedly to be warned from intimidating witnesses and one was sent to jail therefor. One of his former trusted officials after being put out of the Garvey organization brought the long concealed cash account of the organization to this office and we published it. Within two weeks the man was shot in the back in New Orleans and killed.

Everybody, including the writer, who has dared to make the slightest criticism of Garvey has been intimidated by threats and threatened with libel suits. Over fifty court cases have been brought by Garvey in ten years.

We are reminding our readers of all this not to revive forgotten rancor but for the sake of historical accuracy. When Garvey was sent to Atlanta, no word or action of ours accomplished the result. His release and deportation was a matter of law which no deed or wish of ours influenced in the slightest degree. We have today, no enmity against Marcus Garvey. He has a great and worthy dream. We wish him well. He is free; he has a following; he still has a chance to carry on his work in his own home and among his own people and to accomplish some of his ideals. Let him do it. We will be the first to applaud any success that he may have.

Unsigned, but written by W. E. B. Du Bois, in *The Crisis*, February, 1928; XXXV, 51.

120

A NEW RELIGION FOR THE NEGRO
by *Eugene Gordon*

Eugene Gordon, born in Florida in 1901, was educated at Howard University and Boston University and lived for many years as a newspaperman and essayist in Boston. His writings were published in Mencken's *American Mercury*, as well as in *Scribner's* and other widely circulated magazines. The essay that follows appeared in the short-lived Boston monthly, *The Lantern*, an explicitly anti-fascist journal (it ran from October, 1927, through August, 1929), whose editorial board included Powers Hapgood and Gardner Jackson and whose covers were done, from time to time, by Rockwell Kent and Boardman Robinson. At the time this essay was published, Eugene Gordon was the assistant feature editor of the *Boston Post*.

"You may have the world but give *me* Jesus," sang the Uncle Toms and Mammy Cloes of the pre-Lincoln era. And their masters, always generous with nebulous and intangible gifts, lavished upon the serfs more and ever more Jesus. And their gift remains, despite efforts of many Aframericans of this generation to exchange some of Jesus for a bit of the world.

Today, thanks to the generosity of master and prodigality of slave, the Aframerican is rich in Jesus even if poor in the world. Today's American colored man is the most thoroughly Christianized of all God's chillun. In exercising the Christian virtues he surpasses even the hundred-percent Nordic American, a most remarkable feat. For the Aframerican of the Twentieth century often defends the faith against the very Nordics who forced it upon him. White men may have conceived Christianity and, later, shared it with their black brethren, but these latter behave as though *they* designed it and for their especial salvation.

Consider for a moment the case of Clarence Darrow. A year or so ago he virtually *gave* his services in defense of a Negro family charged with murder. It seems that in Detroit some colored folks, naïvely believing in the Bill of Rights and certain guarantees of the Constitution, moved into a so-called white neighborhood. Nordic followers of the cross (whether of Jesus or of the Klan is unimportant) rose in wrath and assailed the foolish intruders, demolishing windows and destroying household goods. Thereupon, the black head of the family, being exceeding quick of temper, did shoot a firearm into the Christian assemblage, killing a Nordic.

In a court of law, Mr. Darrow prevailed against the intense passion of those who sought the black man's life, and lo! the prisoner was freed. Nevertheless, despite Mr. Darrow's act of benevolence, an act for which unsullied Christians might lift their heads in pride, he is, alas, agnostic. It becomes the duty, therefore, of black Christians to defend the faith against him. Hence, according to the *Baltimore Afro-American,* "the doors of Washington churches were barred" not long since when he was invited thither to address some colored people. And although the weather was raw with a cold mist, Darrow had to speak in an open pavilion, where his scant audience "sat on wooden benches without backs." Commenting editorially on the speech, the *Washington Tribune* in justification of the church's action, said:

"That Mr. Darrow is an able lawyer, a humanitarian and a courageous thinker brooks no denial, but when he attempts, even with the best possible motive to advise the Negro to pay less attention to prayer and the church, he is wrong."

Thus do the Aframerican pulpit and press combine in defense of something which, years ago, was administered to blacks as an effective opiate. For Darrow was urging his hearers to relinquish some of the intangible and to grasp some of the tangible. He was advising the colored folk to experiment for a while with actual and personal effort toward securing what they desired, after their having experimented for centuries with prayer. "If there be a God," he told his listeners, "He saw the first slave ship come across the waters, and every other one." Going on, Darrow assured the colored brethren that "if preaching and praying would help you, you would have had your rights long years ago." He added:

"Talk about the preachers' telling God something, I do not think there is any of them, black or white, intelligent enough to tell him anything. Talk about their having any influence with Him, if they have, it is only the white preachers. It is pretty plain, or ought to be by this time, that if there is a God He is white, isn't it? If He had been black He would have done something for you. It is pretty plain if there is any God He has used such strength as He has against you instead of for you. Everybody who thinks *knows* it."

Perhaps; but what Mr. Darrow does not know is that the average Aframerican Christian prefers and, when he gets there, expects to meet in heaven, a white God, not a black one. Who told Mr. Darrow that the colored man suspected God of being black? Most emphatically, he does not! If he did have such suspicion he would quite likely be wholly indifferent about the fate of his soul.

II

At this point I must disgress for a moment. It is necessary to point out here the cause of this amazing preference for a white God. In doing so I shall have to show what Christian influence did for the slave. The digression taken as a whole, however, will tend toward proving my thesis: The Negro in America should have his own religion.

Christianity was an excellent opiate, in the hands of the masters, to induce sluggish content. So effectively were the blacks narcotized that recorded instances of slave rebellion make dull and wearisome reading. And why? Because such rebellions were only half-formed, sissified gestures. They lacked vigor and snap and fire. Had it not been for Christianity's mollycoddling there would doubtless have been numerous and lively insurrections.

"Of course," my honored revilers will argue, "you realize, I suppose, that *you* would not be here today if that had happened."

I *do* realize. The blacks undoubtedly would have been exterminated, but what of that? Historians would have written of them, "God, what men!" But the old-time religion, having rotted the very fabric of their moral stamina, circumvented any such display of manly bellicosity. Thus the Negro survived. And at what a shameful cost!

I may as well add here that, anyway, Christianity is not a virile man's religion, and that is why virile men are seldom if ever *true* Christians. They wear the Christian mask for business or social or political or other reasons, but that is all. The black American, because of his innate guilelessness and his genuine naïveté, approaches nearer the Christian ideal. (What I should say is the Nazarene ideal. For if Jesus came through Ellis Island tomorrow [provided the Palestinian quota was not already filled] He would not recognize *this* religion as His. It is not. The doctrine of Jesus could not fit into modern society without destroying the present civilization. If Morgan, Ford, the Consolidated Gas Company, Wanamaker's, the United States Treasury, the Pennsylvania coal barons, and the movie moguls, not to mention Dr. Cadman and many another famous disciples all began simultaneously to conduct their affairs strictly in accordance with the teachings of Jesus, they would cause economic, social, and political chaos. And when the smoke cleared away the whole structure of our civilization would be found insecure.)

The Aframerican, I repeat, comes nearer to following the original precepts of the Lowly One. As a result, observe him! Slavery in its very essence forbade the serf's participation in earthly joys. Christianity was slavery's ally in that it taught the blacks that earthly pleasures were a delusion and a snare, and that the only joy worth while would be found in a Golden City beyond the stars. It is significant that this garish city could be reached only by way of the grave. So the blacks thought less and less about release *on earth* from their miserable degradation and lived solely for the final release. Thus they were meek. They were content. And they sang of heaven at their wretched tasks. They were Christians!

And white became the acme of desirability. "Marster," "Missus," and the overseer with the whip, were all white. The Big House was painted dazzlingly white. On Sunday "Marster's" white minister assured the slaves that although the Great White God had made them black as punishment for errors of Ham, yet, if they were good slaves,—meek, submissive, hard-laboring, honest, truthful, angelic,—then that same Great White God would reward them when they died by changing them into beautiful white angels.

Could there be a consummation more devoutly to be wished? There could *not* be! The limited range of a slave imagination could encompass nothing that approached nearer perfection. Shivering in the paroxysm of his ecstasy the serf cried aloud: "Wash me, and I shall be whiter than snow! Wash me in the blood of the lamb!"

And that is why those Aframericans who will get into Beulah Land will be chagrined—nay, outraged, if they are welcomed by a black God. On this point they and the Ku Klux Klan are in brotherly accord.

III

So long as the Negro remains a devout Christian he will remain at least psychologically a slave. And if one doubts the Christ-like virtue of the masses of Aframericans let one study the Southern race problem. In that vast and spiritually flowering section there is more actual love of God and communion with the Holy Ghost than may be found in all the rest of North America. It may not be, as I already pointed out, the Nazarene doctrine that pervades, but it passes for that. It is there that men by bearing witness to their immaculate Christianity defend their women, their personal honor, and the integrity of their great and superior race. The noble and worthy Ku Klux Klan was reorganized in the South to meet a Christian need. In the name of Jesus it selected the cross for its emblem, and although, strangely enough, it conceals its face behind a mask when it goes a-crusading on dark nights, yet it does all in the name of the Father, the Son, and the Holy Ghost.

It is patent that to live at peace in such a section one must observe the same religious tenets as the greater and lesser cyclops. In fact, it is imperative for the preservation of one's good health that one be Christian. The colored folk there, then, *are* Christian. To show how thoroughly Christian they are, I shall cite a few instances of their exhibiting Christly fortitude.

Between 1885 and 1926 there were lynched in the United States 3205 Negroes, almost all of them in the South. This unique American sport was followed mostly by gentlemen and ladies who, fired by Christian zeal, were determined to keep the Negro in his place and to preserve, thereby, a tottering white supremacy. Each of the blacks killed went to his death in the presence sometimes of thousands of sanctified followers of the cross. They were all Protestant, one-hundred-percent Nordic Americans. And the men and women lynched were also devout Christians. Do not lose sight of that fact. True, they may not have been actually practising their religion at the precise moment the rope was tauted or the lighted match applied, but reports have been brought back describing the fortitude and Christian forbearance of the victims.

There are other little practises of the Christian Southern whites against their black Christian brethren; little practices that emphasize especially the genuineness of the latter's religion. The whites forbid the blacks' exercising the right of franchise, although the Constitution of the United States declares that such rights shall not be abridged. In Congress noble-browed gentlemen like Carter Glass, Cole Blease and Tom Heflin successfully defend their Christian attitude. White Christians insist that black Christians must have separate and inferior churches, schools, railway carriages, amusement houses, parks, residential sections, Y.M.C.A. and Y.W.C.A. organizations, and graveyards. White Christians tell black brethren that God is just (though white), and that because of the blacks' docile suffering He will reward them. The reward, of course, will be white exteriors and a harp.

And throughout it all the blacks remain staunch, unwavering in their faith and loyalty, and prayerful. They obligingly turn the other cheek whenever demand is made for it, nor question why. They pray at night, "Father, forgive. them, for they know not what they do." It takes, almost, a Christ Himself to utter that historic platitude with convincing sincerity. And the Negro does it!

The foregoing paragraphs, I submit, contain evidence aplenty to prove the Southern Negro's genuine Christianity. He is the chief sufferer. The masses of Negroes in the North are spiritually similar to the masses of the cottonfield. These too want golden slippers, white wings, flowing white robes, a golden harp (although I have never seen a Negro playing on a harp), and a chance to jazz all over a white God's heaven. But they feel less acutely the perpetual need of religion. As a consequence, they have more time to think about their earthly existence. But even they are in need of emancipation. When troubles assail them, they fly to the consolation of the good old-time religion with all the passionate haste of a frightened child to its mother. In both North and South Negroes, as do people elsewhere, recognize the *need* of religion.

IV

Without the stimulation of religious hashish the masses of mankind could not stand up. That is true because the *masses* of mankind are the wretchedest. Various and countless factors, important among which are poverty and its attendants, combine to make them wretched. Therefore, religion is, for these people, indubitably the most important thing in life. Living for the sheer joy of living is unknown to them; *they* live for the sake of dying. To them the grave is the entrance-way to a kingdom in which all the deficiencies of earthly life will be supplied a thousand times a thousand fold.

The general belief that the American Negro is the happiest of God's creatures is not wholly erroneous. What is erroneous is the belief that this happiness is derived from earthly joys. The Aframerican's fictitious happiness is due to his belief that he holds a one-way ticket to Glory. In the contemplation of such good fortune, all present ills become as nothing: the eyes are fastened immovable on eternity.

Now that, I hold, is immorally unfortunate. Men have no right to enslave the minds of other men, religiously or otherwise. Religiously enslaved, the mind neglects the very real and very present *now* for the delirious pleasure of wandering in a vague, remote, and uncertain hereafter. Religion's true function is to help men to live on earth, not to prepare them to leave the earth. The average Aframerican's time is more than ninety percent occupied with preparations for the long sleep.

That the true function of religion is to help men live on earth, is proved by a study of the origin of most existing beliefs. For example, when Moses invented Yahveh the Hebrews needed just such a smoke-belching, fire-eating deity. The gods they had been worshipping were no longer adequate. So Yahveh filled all particulars perfectly—for a while. As changes occurred in the Jews' social status their God gradually altered his mein and manners accordingly. And what was true of the Hebrews' religion has been true with respect to others—Mohammedanism, Confucianism, Buddhism, and Christianity. Each was subtly changed, in time, to meet the changed status of those for whom it was originated.

The original doctrine of Jesus, as I have previously indicated, could not possibly fit into our scheme of living. Therefore, it has been changed. No one, of course, called a council of ministers or priests together and said, "Now, Christianity does not work, so let's change it." Changes in religions do not come about in that way. They occur, instead, like fashions in clothes or automobiles. And "good" Christians do not like to admit that there has been a change, despite the over-whelming evidence. Instead of admitting it, they say: "Oh, but Christianity would be all right *if we practiced it!*" But it would not, of course, be all right. The very fact that the whole idea of Jesus's teachings has subtly changed proves that it would not and could not be all right today.

It being true that Christianity ill becomes the white man, who admittedly has everything, how much more ludicrously must it sit upon the black man, who admittedly has nothing—but his soul and his faith. The logical inference then is that the Negro in America needs a religion by which he can get the most profit out of his business of living. Christianity has made of him a workable tool for others; he needs a religion that will make a man of him for himself.

Objections are immediately raised. The loudest comes from the Negro minister, who speaks for that strange Christian anomaly, the Negro *church*. He maintains that the church has played a most important part in Negro life. I agree. It *has* played a most important part, unfortunately. And so has the Negro minister. But it happens that I am not discussing either the *Negro* church or the Negro minister. I am discussing religion. Had I the inclination, I could easily prove that both the Negro minister and his church are much overrated: That as an ally of Christianity, the church through its greedy exactions of time and money, has held the Aframerican in moral, intellectual, spiritual, and economic thrall; that the over-praised church-supported "college" inflicts upon the race and America graduates who are generally well read in holy literature, but who face the world fit only for priest-craft or Y.M.C.A. secretaryship; that most Negro preachers are half illiterates who, having swallowed the Bible whole, have been unable to digest it; that in all this broad land there are not more than two dozen well-educated, unsuperstitious Negro preachers who are, at the same time, leaders of men. I could, I repeat, easily prove all that if I chose, but it happens that this paper deals with something else.

It is distasteful to me to contemplate segregation of so-called race groups in America. I believe that the salvation of the country lies in these groups getting as close together and living as close together as possible. Yet I do propose for the Aframerican group a religion distinctly and peculiarly its own. Having developed himself by means of this new religion, the Negro will be the better able to fit himself into the larger scheme. He needs a religion by which he can live *here* and *now;* one which will aid him to give a minimum of his attention to some vague celestial city after death and more to the city in which he now moves and has his being.

Christianity makes the Negro meek when he should be proud. It makes him humble when he should be arrogant. It teaches him to turn the other cheek when he should retaliate in kind. It lays emphasis upon future life to the neglect and detriment of present life in a hard-fisted, uncompromising, cunning, and militant world. My proposal is that the existing religions of the world—Judaism, Mohammedanism, Hinduism, Buddhism, Christianity—be studied by a commission designated for that purpose, and that those principles of each of those religions that most suitably fit the Aframerican's situation be combined to form a new religion.

To illustrate. From Islam take the spirit of militancy which the Southern Negroes, especially need; from Confucianism the abolishment of fear of the hereafter and renunciation of the idea of heaven; from Judaism the righteousness of retaliation; and so on.

The manner of propagating the new religion would be left to the commission. I have made no effort to work out a program.

The Lantern (Boston), October, 1928; II, 3–6. The editor is indebted to Mr. L. C. Cartwright of New York City, who owns a complete file of this fascinating magazine.

121

AN APPEAL TO AMERICA
[The 1928 Elections]

In October, 1928, an open letter—as it were—was issued on behalf of large segments of organized Afro-American life in protest against the virulent racism that characterized the campaigns of both the Republican, Herbert Hoover, and the Democrat, Alfred E. Smith of New York. While very widely reproduced in the Black press, it was otherwise largely ignored. In publishing it in *The Crisis,* Dr. Du Bois commented: "It deserves to be re-read and preserved"; with such an opinion from such a source, it is published herewith.

The persons whose names are signed beneath are alike in the fact that we all have Negro slaves among our ancestors. In other respects, we differ widely; in descent, in dwelling place, in age and occupation, and, to some extent, in our approach to what is known as the Negro problem.

More especially we differ in political thought and allegiance: some of us are Republicans by inheritance and long custom; others are Democrats, by affiliation and party membership; still others are Socialists.

But all of us are at this moment united in the solemn conviction that in the presidential campaign of 1928, more than in previous campaigns since the Civil War, the American Negro was treated in a manner which is unfair and discouraging.

We accuse the political leaders of this campaign of permitting without protest, public and repeated assertions on the platform, in the press, and by word of mouth, that color and race constitute in themselves an imputation of guilt and crime.

It has been said, North and South, East and West, and by partisans of the leading candidates:

1. That Negro voters should not be appealed to, or their support welcomed by the advocates of just causes.

2. That colored persons should not hold public office, no matter what their character may be nor how well they do their work nor how competently they satisfy their constituents.

3. That the contact of white people and black people in govern-

ment, in business, and in daily life, in common effort and co-operation, calls for explanation and apology.

4. That the honesty and integrity of party organization depend on the complete removal of all Negroes from voice and authority.

5. That the appointment of a public official is an act which concerns only white citizens, and that colored citizens should have neither voice nor consideration in such appointments.

These assertions, which sound bald and almost unbelievable when stated without embellishment, have appeared as full-page advertisements in the public press, as the subject of leading editorials, and as displayed news stories; they have been repeated on the public platform in open debate and over the radio by both Republican and Democratic speakers, and they have been received by the nation and by the adherents of these and other parties in almost complete silence. A few persons have deprecated this gratuitous lugging in of the race problem, but for the most part, this astonishing campaign of public insult toward one-tenth of the nation has evoked no word of protest from the leading party candidates or from their official spokesmen; and from few religious ministers, Protestant or Catholic, or Jewish, and from almost no leading social reformer.

Much has been said and rightly of the danger in a republic like ours of making sincere religious belief a matter of political controversy and of diverting public attention from great questions of public policy to petty matters of private life. But, Citizens of America, bad as religious hatred and evil personal gossip are, they have not the seeds of evil and disaster that lie in continued, unlimited and unrestrained appeal to race prejudice. The emphasis on racial contempt and hatred which was made in this campaign is an appeal to the lowest and most primitive of human motives, and as long as this appeal can successfully be made, there is for this land no real peace, no sincere religion, no national unity, no social progress, even in matters far removed from racial controversy.

Do not misunderstand us: we are not asking equality where there is no equality. We are not demanding or even discussing purely social intermingling. We have not the slightest desire for intermarriage between the races. We frankly recognize that the aftermath of slavery must involve long years of poverty, crime and contempt; for all of this that the past has brought and the present gives we have paid in good temper, quiet work and unfaltering faith. But we do solemnly affirm that in a civilized land and in a Christian culture and among increasingly intelligent people, somewhere and sometime, limits must be put to race disparagement and separation and to campaigns of racial calumny which seek to set twelve million human beings outside the pale of ordinary humanity.

We believe that this nation and every part of it must come to admit that the gradual disappearance of inequalities between racial groups and the gradual softening of prejudice and hatred, is a sign of advance and not of retrogression and should be hailed as such by all decent folk and we think it monstrous to wage a political campaign in which the fading and softening of racial animosity and the increase of co-operation can be held up to the nation as a fault and not as a virtue. We do not believe that the majority of the white people whether North or South believe in the necessity or the truth of the assertions current in this campaign; but we are astonished to see the number of persons who are whipped to silence in the presence of such obvious and ancient political trickery.

You cannot set the requirements of political honesty and intelligence too high to gain our consent. We have absolutely no quarrel with standards of ability and character which will bring to public office in America the very highest type of public servant. We are more troubled over political dishonesty among black folk than you are among white. We are not seeking political domination. But, on the other hand, it is too late for us to submit to political slavery and we most earnestly protest against the unchallenged assumption that every American Negro is dishonest and incompetent and that color in itself is a crime.

It is not so much the virulence of the attack in this case. It is its subtle and complacent character and the assenting silence in which it is received. Gravely and openly these assertions are made and few care, few protest, few answer. Has not the time come when as a nation, North and South, black and white, we can stop this tragic fooling and demand, not to be sure, everything that all Negroes might wish, nor all that some white people might prefer, but a certain balance of decency and logic in the discussion of race? Can we not as a nation assert that the Constitution is the law of the land and that the 13th, 14th, 15th and 19th Amendments as well as the 18th are still valid; that it is no crime for a colored man to vote if he meets the legal requirements; that it is not a crime to appoint a colored man to office unless he is incompetent; and if he is incompetent, the crime lies in his incompetency and not in his color; that in this modern world of necessarily increasing human contact it is inevitable that persons of different race work together in private and public service; that this contact is not wrong unless the persons are unable to do their work properly or unless their helpful co-operation is proven impossible?

We are asking, therefore, in this appeal, for a public repudiation of this campaign of racial hatred. Silence and whispering in this case are worse than in matters of personal character and religion. Will white America make no protest? Will the candidates continue to remain silent? Will the Church say nothing? Is there in truth any issue in this campaign, either religious tolerance, liquor, water-power, tariff or farm relief, that touches in weight the transcendent and fundamental question of the open, loyal and unchallenged recognition of the essential humanity of twelve million Americans who happen to be dark-skinned?

R. R. Moton, Principal of Tuskegee Institute, Tuskegee, Alabama.

W. E. B. Du Bois, Editor, *Crisis* Magazine, New York.

John Hope, President of Morehouse College, Atlanta, Ga.

Mordecai W. Johnson, President, Howard University, Washington, D.C.

Harry E. Davis, Civil Service Commissioner, City of Cleveland, Ohio.

George C. Clement, Bishop, A.M.E. Zion Church, Louisville, Kentucky.

Sallie W. Stewart, President, National Association of Colored Women, Evanston, Indiana.

C. C. Spaulding, President, North Carolina Mutual Insurance Company, Durham, North Carolina.

James Weldon Johnson, Secretary, The National Association for the Advancement of Colored People, New York.

Fred R. Moore, Alderman of the City of New York, Editor of the *New York Age,* New York.

Eugene K. Jones, Secretary of the National Urban League, New York.

W. T. B. Williams, Field Agent of Jeanes and Slater Funds, Tuskegee Institute, Tuskegee, Alabama.

Walter White, Assistant Secretary, The National Association for the Advancement of Colored People, New York.

C. A. Barnett, Director, Associated Negro Press, Chicago, Illinois.

R. Nathaniel Dett, Head of the Department of Music, Hampton Institute, Hampton, Virginia.

Ferdinand Q. Morton, Municipal Civil Service Commissioner, New York City.

Mary McLeod Bethune, President Bethune-Cookman College, Daytona, Florida.

William H. Lewis, former Assistant Attorney General of the United States, Attorney-at-Law, Boston, Massachusetts.

George W. Harris, former Alderman of the City of New York, Editor, *The New York News,* New York.

E. P. Roberts, Physician, New York City.

George E. Haynes, Secretary of the Federal Council of the Churches of Christ in America, New York.

Monroe N. Work, Director of Research, Tuskegee Institute, Tuskegee, Alabama.

John R. Hawkins, Financial Secretary of the African Methodist Episcopal Church, Chairman of the Colored Republican Voters Division, Washington, D.C.

Reverdy C. Ransom, Bishop, African Methodist Episcopal Church, Nashville, Tennessee.

Archibald J. Carey, Bishop, African M.E. Church, Chicago, Illinois, Civil Service Commissioner, Chicago.

The Crisis, December, 1928; XXXV, 416, 428.

122

FOR THE RECOGNITION OF THE SOVIET UNION
by William Pickens

For the eleventh anniversary of the Bolshevik Revolution, William Pickens, then field secretary of the N.A.A.C.P., wrote the following appeal for U.S. diplomatic recognition of the U.S.S.R. This essay was published in the organ of the left-wing International Labor Defense, a journal edited by Carl Reeve.

When the Czar and the Grand Dukes were overthrown in Russia, there was some justification in the refusal of other governments to recognize the "revolution." One cannot extend "credit" until there is some accumulated "capital" as security. But eleven years after the revolutionary government has established itself, the situation is vastly different. A government that could stay for a decade and control the lives of nearly two hundred million people, certainly has become a *fact* and ought to be recognized in practice if not in theory and formality. The failure of formal recognition under such circumstances becomes almost an act of hostility.

We have at least friendship and normal relations to gain by recognizing Russia. What is there to gain by refusing recognition?

Russian delegates at Geneva [in 1928] stood alone among the great nations in proposing complete and actual disarmament.

We used to object to recognizing Russia because of their "propaganda," but that has proven to be a ghost. They are certainly entitled to have whatever sort of government they will accept or tolerate. Recognition does not mean detailed and unqualified endorsement. Recognition means recognition.

Labor Defender (New York), November, 1928, p. 241.

123

RACE PREJUDICE AND THE NEGRO ARTIST

by James Weldon Johnson

Among the most significant essays dealing with the Harlem Renaissance period was that by the executive secretary of the N.A.A.C.P. himself, of course, a person of extraordinary cultural achievement. This appeared in *Harper's,* then perhaps an even more influential magazine than it is in the final period of the present century.

What Americans call the Negro problem is almost as old as America itself. For three centuries the Negro in this country has been tagged with an interrogation point; the question propounded, however, has not always been the same. Indeed, the question has run all the way from whether or not the Negro was a human being, down—or up—to whether or not the Negro shall be accorded full and unlimited American citizenship. Therefore, the Negro problem is not a problem in the sense of being a fixed proposition involving certain invariable factors and waiting to be worked out according to certain defined rules. It is not a static condition; rather, it is and always has been a series of shifting interracial situations, never precisely the same in any two generations. As these situations have shifted, the methods and manners of dealing with them have constantly changed. And never has there been such a swift and vital shift as the one which is taking place at the present moment; and never was there a more revolutionary change in attitudes than the one which is now going on.

The question of the races—white and black—has occupied much of America's time and thought. Many methods for a solution of the problem have been tried—most of them tried *on* the Negro, for one of the mistakes commonly made in dealing with this matter has been the failure of white America to take into account the Negro himself and the forces he was generating and sending out. The question repeated generation after generation has been: what shall we do with the Negro? —ignoring completely the power of the Negro to do something for himself, and even something to America. It is a new thought that the Negro has helped to shape and mold and make America. It is, perhaps, a startling thought that America would not be precisely the America it is to-day except for the powerful, if silent, influence the Negro has exerted upon it—both positively and negatively. It is a certainty that the nation would be shocked by a contemplation of the effects which have been wrought upon its inherent character by the negative power which the Negro has involuntarily and unwittingly wielded.

A number of approaches to the heart of the race problem have been tried: religious, educational, political, industrial, ethical, economic, sociological. Along several of these approaches considerable progress has been made. To-day a newer approach is being tried, an approach which discards most of the older methods. It requires a minimum of pleas, or propaganda, or philanthropy. It depends more upon what the Negro himself does than upon what someone does for him. It is the approach along the line of intellectual and artistic achievement by Ne-groes, and may be called the art approach to the Negro problem. This method of approaching a solution of the race question has the advan-tage of affording great and rapid progress with least friction and of pro-viding a common platform upon which most people are willing to stand. The results of this method seem to carry a high degree of finality, to be the thing itself that was to be demonstrated.

I have said that this is a newer approach to the race problem; that is only in a sense true. The Negro has been using this method for a very long time; for a longer time than he has used any other method, and, perhaps, with farther-reaching effectiveness. For more than a cen-tury his great folk-art contributions have been exerting an ameliorating effect, slight and perhaps, in any one period, imperceptible, neverthe-less, cumulative. In countless and diverse situations song and dance have been both a sword and a shield for the Negro. Take the Spirituals: for sixty years, beginning with their introduction to the world by the Fisk Jubilee Singers, these songs have touched and stirred the hearts of people and brought about a smoothing down of the rougher edges of prejudice against the Negro. Indeed, nobody can hear Negroes sing this wonderful music in its primitive beauty without a softening of feel-ing toward them.

What is there, then, that is new? What is new consists largely in the changing attitude of the American people. There is a coming to light and notice of efforts that have been going on for a long while, and a public appreciation of their results. Note, for example, the change in the reaction to the Spirituals. Fifty years ago white people who heard the Spirituals were touched and moved with sympathy and pity for the "poor Negro." To-day the effect is not one of pity for the Negro's condition, but admiration for the creative genius of the race.

All of the Negro's folk-art creations have undergone a new evaluation. His sacred music—the Spirituals; his secular music—Ragtime, Blues, Jazz, and the work songs; his folk lore—the Uncle Remus plantation tales; and his dances have received a new and higher appreciation. Indeed, I dare to say that it is now more or less generally acknowledged that the only things artistic that have sprung from American soil and out of American life, and been universally recognized as distinctively American products, are the folk creations of the Negro. The one thing that may be termed artistic, but for which the United States is known the world over, is its Negro-derived popular music. The folk creations of the Negro have not only received a new appreciation; they have—the Spirituals excepted—been taken over and assimilated. They are no longer racial, they are national; they have become a part of our common cultural fund. Negro secular music has been developed into American popular music; Negro dances have been made into our national art of dancing; even the plantation tales have been transformed and have come out as popular bedtime stories. The Spirituals are still distinct Negro folk songs, but sooner or later our serious composers will take them as material to go into the making of the "great American music" that has so long been looked for.

But the story does not halt at this point. The Negro has done a great deal through his folk-art creations to change the national attitudes toward him; and now the efforts of the race have been reinforced and magnified by the individual Negro artist, the conscious artist. It is fortunate that the individual Negro artist has emerged; for it is more than probable that with the ending of the creative period of Blues, which seems to be at hand, the whole folk creative effort of the Negro in the United States will come to a close. All the psychological and environmental forces are working to that end. At any rate, it is the individual Negro artist that is now doing most to effect a crumbling of the inner walls of race prejudice; there are outer and inner walls. The emergence of the individual artist is the result of the same phenomenon that brought about the new evaluation and appreciation of the folk-art creations. But it should be borne in mind that the conscious Aframerican artist is not an entirely new thing. What is new about him is chiefly the evaluation and public recognition of his work.

II

When and how did this happen? The entire change, which is marked by the shedding of a new light on the artistic and intellectual achievements of the Negro, the whole period which has become ineptly known as "the Negro renaissance," is the matter of a decade; it has all taken place within the last ten years. More forces than anyone can name have been at work to create the existing state; however, several of them may be pointed out. What took place had no appearance of a development; it seemed more like a sudden awakening, an almost instantaneous change. There was nothing that immediately preceded it which foreshadowed what was to follow. Those who were in the midst of the movement were as much astonished as anyone else to see the transformation. Overnight, as it were, America became aware that there were Negro artists and that they had something worth while to offer. This awareness first manifested itself in black America, for, strange as it may seem, Negroes themselves, as a mass, had had little or no consciousness of their own individual artists. Black America awoke first to the fact that it possessed poets. This awakening followed the entry of the United States into the Great War. Before this country had been in the war very long there was bitter disillusionment on the part of American Negroes—on the part both of those working at home and those fighting in France to make the world safe for democracy. The disappointment and bitterness were taken up and voiced by a group of seven or eight Negro poets. They expressed what the race felt, what the race wanted to hear. They made the group at large articulate. Some of this poetry was the poetry of despair, but most of it was the poetry of protest and rebellion. Fenton Johnson wrote of civilization:

I am tired of work; I am tired of building up somebody else's civilization.
Let us take a rest, M'lissy Jane.

You will let the old shanty go to rot, the white people's clothes turn to dust, and the Calvary Baptist Church sink to the bottomless pit.

Throw the children into the river; civilization has given too many. It is better to die than it is to grow up and find out that you are colored.
Pluck the stars out of the heavens. The stars mark our destiny. The stars marked my destiny.

I am tired of civilization.

Joseph Cotter, a youth of twenty, inquired plaintively from the invalid's bed to which he was confined:

Brother, come!
And let us go unto our God.
And when we stand before Him
I shall say,
"Lord, I do not hate
I am hated.
I scourge no one,
I am scourged.
I covet no lands,
My lands are coveted.
I mock no peoples,
My people are mocked."
And, brother, what shall you say?

But among this whole group the voice that was most powerful was that of Claude McKay. Here was a true poet of great skill and wide range, who turned from creating the mood of poetic beauty in the absolute, as he had so fully done in such poems as "Spring in New Hampshire," "The Harlem Dancer," and "Flame Heart," for example, and began pouring out cynicism, bitterness, and invective. For this purpose, incongruous as it may seem, he took the sonnet form as his medium. There is nothing in American literature that strikes a more portentous note than these sonnet-tragedies of McKay. Here is the sestet of his sonnet, "The Lynching":

Day dawned, and soon the mixed crowds came to view
The ghastly body swaying in the sun:
The women thronged to look, but never a one Showed sorrow in her eyes of
    steely blue; And little lads, lynchers that were to be, Danced round the
    dreadful thing in fiendish glee.

The summer of 1919 was a terrifying period for the American Negro. There were race riots in Chicago and in Washington and in Omaha and in Phillips County, Arkansas; and in Longview, Texas; and in Knoxville, Tennessee; and in Norfolk, Virginia; and in other communities. Colored men and women, by dozens and by scores, were chased and beaten and killed in the streets. And from Claude McKay came this cry of defiant despair, sounded from the last ditch:

If we must die—let it not be like hogs
Hunted and penned in an inglorious spot,

Oh, Kinsmen! We must meet the common foe;
Though far outnumbered, let us still be brave,
And for their thousand blows deal one death-blow!
What though before us lies the open grave?
Like men we'll face the murderous, cowardly pack,
Pressed to the wall, dying, but—fighting back!

But not all the terror of the time could smother the poet of beauty and universality in McKay. In "America," which opens with these lines:

Although she feeds me bread of bitterness,
And sinks into my throat her tiger's tooth,
Stealing my breath of life, I will confess
I love this cultured hell that tests my youth

he fused these elements of fear and bitterness and hate into verse which by every test is true poetry and a fine sonnet.

The poems of the Negro poets of the immediate post-war period were widely printed in Negro periodicals; they were committed to memory; they were recited at school exercises and public meetings; and were discussed at private gatherings. Now, Negro poets were not new; their line goes back a long way in Aframerican history. Between Phillis Wheatley, who as a girl of eight or nine was landed in Boston from an African slave ship, in 1761, and who published a volume of poems in 1773, and Paul Laurence Dunbar, who died in 1906, there were more than thirty Negroes who published volumes of verse—some of it good, most of it mediocre, and much of it bad. The new thing was the effect produced by these poets who sprang up out of the war period. Negro poets had sounded similar notes before, but now for the first time they succeeded in setting up a reverberating response, even in their own group. But the effect was not limited to black America; several of these later poets in some subtle way affected white America. In any event, at just this time white America began to become aware and to awaken. In the correlation of forces that brought about this result it might be pointed out that the culminating effect of the folk-art creations had gone far toward inducing a favorable state of mind. Doubtless it is also true that the new knowledge and opinions about the Negro in Africa—that he was not just a howling savage, that he had a culture, that he had produced a vital art—had directly affected opinion about the Negro in America. However it may have been, the Negro poets growing out of the war period were the fore-runners of the individuals whose work is now being assayed and is receiving recognition in accordance with its worth.

III

And yet, contemporaneously with the work of these poets a significant effort was made in another field of art—an effort which might have
gone much farther at the time had it not been cut off by our entry into
the War, but which, nevertheless, had its effect. Early in 1917, in fact
on the very day we entered the War, Mrs. Emily Hapgood produced at
the Madison Square Garden Theater three plays of Negro life by Ridgley
Torrence, staged by Robert Edmond Jones, and played by an all-
Negro cast. This was the first time that Negro actors in drama commanded the serious attention of the critics and the general public. Two
of the players, Opal Cooper and Inez Clough, were listed by George
Jean Nathan among the ten actors giving the most distinguished performances of the year. No one who heard Opal Cooper chant the dream
in the *Rider of Dreams* can ever forget the thrill of it. A sensational
feature of the production was the singing orchestra of Negro performers
under the direction of J. Rosamond Johnson—singing orchestras in
theaters have since become common. The plays moved from the Garden
Theater to the Garrick, but the stress of war crushed them out. In
1920, Charles Gilpin was enthusiastically and universally acclaimed
for his acting in *The Emperor Jones*. The American stage has seldom
seen such an outburst of acclamation. Mr. Gilpin was one of the ten
persons voted by the Drama League as having done most for the American theater during the year. Most of the readers of these pages will
remember the almost national crisis caused by his invitation to the
Drama League Dinner. And along came *Shuffle Along;* and all of New
York flocked to an out of the way theater in West Sixty-third Street
to hear the most joyous singing and see the most exhilarating dancing
to be found on any stage in the city. The dancing steps originally
used by the "policeman" in *Shuffle Along* furnished new material for
hundreds of dancing men. *Shuffle Along* was actually an epoch-making
musical comedy. Out of *Shuffle Along* came Florence Mills, who,
unfortunately, died so young but lived long enough to be acknowledged here and in Europe as one of the finest singing comediennes the
stage had ever seen and an artist of positive genius. In 1923 Roland
Hayes stepped out on the American stage in a blaze of glory, making his
first appearances as soloist with the Boston Symphony Orchestra and
later with the Philharmonic. Few single artists have packed such
crowds into Carnegie Hall and the finest concert halls throughout
the country as has Roland Hayes; and, notwithstanding the éclat with
which America first received him, his reputation has continued to in-

crease and, besides, he is rated as one of the best box-office attractions in the whole concert field. Miss Marian Anderson appeared as soloist with the Philadelphia Symphony Orchestra and in concert at the Lewisohn Stadium at New York City College. Paul Robeson and J. Rosamond Johnson and Taylor Gordon sang Spirituals to large and appreciative audiences in New York and over the country, giving to those songs a fresh interpretation and a new vogue.

Paul Robeson—that most versatile of men, who has made a national reputation as athlete, singer, and actor—played in Eugene O'Neill's *All God's Chillun* and added to his reputation on the stage, and, moreover, put to the test an ancient taboo; he played the principal role opposite a white woman. This feature of the play gave rise to a more acute crisis than did Gilpin's invitation to the Drama League Dinner. Some sensational newspapers predicted race riots and other dire disasters, but nothing of the sort happened; the play went over without a boo. Robeson played the title role in a revival of *The Emperor Jones* and almost duplicated the sensation produced by Gilpin in the original presentation. There followed on the stage Julius Bledsoe, Rose McClendon, Frank Wilson, and Abbie Mitchell, all of whom gained recognition. At the time of this writing each of these four is playing in a Broadway production. Paradoxical it may seem, but no Negro comedian gained recognition in this decade. Negro comedians have long been a recognized American institution and there are several now before the public who are well known, but their reputations were made before this period. The only new reputations made on the comedy stage were made by women, Florence Mills and Ethel Waters. In addition there are the two famous Smiths, Bessie and Clara, singers of Blues and favorites of vaudeville, phonograph, and radio audiences. Of course there is Josephine Baker, but her reputation was made entirely in Europe. Nevertheless, these magical ten years have worked a change upon Negro comedy. Before Miller and Lyles brought *Shuffle Along* to New York, managers here could hardly conceive of a Negro musical comedy playing a Broadway house. When Williams and Walker, Cole and Johnson, and Ernest Hogan were in their heyday, people who wanted to see them had to go to theaters outside the great white-light zone. George Walker died before the "new day," and up to his retirement from the stage he kept up a constant fight for a chance for his company to play a strictly Broadway theater. Since *Shuffle Along,* hardly a season has passed without seeing one or more Negro musical comedies playing in the finest theaters in New York. In fact, Negro plays and Negro performers in white plays on Broadway had become usual occurrences.

Odd has been the fate of the younger poets who were instrumental in bringing about the present state of affairs. It is a fact that none of them, with the exception of Claude McKay, quite succeeded in bridging over into it. Three of them, Roscoe Jamison, Lucian Watkins, and Joseph Cotter, are dead, all dying in their youth. Fenton Johnson is almost silent. And Claude McKay has for the past four or five years lived practically in exile. However, several of the older writers are busily at work, and there has sprung up in the last three or four years a group of newer creative writers. Countee Cullen and Langston Hughes have achieved recognition as poets. Jean Toomer, Walter White, Eric Walrond, and Rudolph Fisher have made a place among writers of fiction. And Claude McKay, after a period of silence as a poet, has published his *Home to Harlem,* a generally acclaimed novel. These are names that carry literary significance, and they take their places according to individual merit in the list of the makers of contemporary American literature. In addition, there are more than a score of younger writers who are not yet quite in the public eye, but will soon be more widely known. Writers such as these are bound to be known and in larger numbers, because their work now has the chance to gain whatever appreciation it merits. To-day the reagents that will discover what of it is good are at work, the arbiters of our national letters are disposed to regard their good work as a part of American literature, and the public is prepared to accept it as such. This has not always been the case. Until this recent period, the several achievements in writing that have come to light have been regarded as more or less sporadic and isolated efforts, and not in any sense as having a direct relation to the national literature. Had the existing forces been at work at the time, the remarkable decade from 1895 to 1905, which brought forth Booker T. Washington's *Up from Slavery,* W. E. Burghardt Du Bois's *The Souls of Black Folk,* Charles Chesnutt's stories of Negro life, and Paul Laurence Dunbar's poetry, might have signalled the beginning of the "Negro literary renaissance."

During the present decade the individual Negro artist has definitely emerged in three fields, in literature, in the theater, and on the concert stage; in other fields he has not won marked distinction. To point to any achievement of distinction in painting the Negro must go back of this decade, back to H. O. Tanner, who has lived in Europe for the past thirty-five years; or farther back to E. M. Bannister, who gained considerable recognition a half century ago. Nevertheless, there is the work of W. E. Scott, a mural painter, who lives in Chicago and has done a number of public buildings in the Middle West, and of Archibald J.

Motley, who recently held a one-man exhibit in New York which attracted very favorable attention. The drawings of Aaron Douglas have won for him a place among American illustrators. To point to any work of acknowledged excellence in sculpture the Negro must go back of this decade to the work of two women, Edmonia Lewis and Meta Warrick Fuller, both of whom received chiefly in Europe such recognition as they gained. There are several young painters and sculptors who are winning recognition. But the strangest lack is that with all the great native musical endowment he is conceded to possess, the Negro has not in this most propitious time produced a single outstanding composer. There are competent musicians and talented composers of songs and detached bits of music, but no original composer who, in amount and standard of work and in recognition achieved, is at all comparable with S. Coleridge-Taylor, the English Negro composer. Nor can the Negro in the United States point back of this decade to even one such artist. It is a curious fact that the American Negro through his whole history has done more highly sustained and more fully recognized work in the composition of letters than in the composition of music. It is the more curious when we consider that music is so innately a characteristic method of expression for the Negro.

IV

What, now, is the significance of this artistic activity on the part of the Negro and of its reactions on the American people? I think it is twofold. In the first place, the Negro is making some distinctive contributions to our common cultural store. I do not claim it is possible for these individual artists to produce anything comparable to the folk-art in distinctive values, but I do believe they are bringing something fresh and vital into American art, something from the store of their own racial genius: warmth, color, movement, rhythm, and abandon; depth and swiftness of emotion and the beauty of sensuousness. I believe American art will be richer because of these elements in fuller quantity.

But what is of deeper significance to the Negro himself is the effect that this artistic activity is producing upon his condition and status as a man and citizen. I do not believe it an overstatement to say that the "race problem" is fast reaching the stage of being more a question of national mental attitudes toward the Negro than a question of his actual condition. That is to say, it is not at all the problem of a moribund people sinking into a slough of ignorance, poverty, and decay in the very midst of our civilization and despite all our efforts to save them;

that would indeed be a problem. Rather is the problem coming to consist in the hesitation and refusal to open new doors of opportunity at which these people are constantly knocking. In other words, the problem for the Negro is reaching the plane where it is becoming less a matter of dealing with what he is and more a matter of dealing with what America thinks he is.

Now, the truth is that the great majority of Americans have not thought about the Negro at all, except in a vague sort of way and in the form of traditional and erroneous stereotypes. Some of these stereotyped forms of thought are quite absurd, yet they have had serious effects. Millions of Americans have had their opinions and attitudes regarding their fellow colored citizens determined by such a phrase as, "A nigger will steal," or "Niggers are lazy," or "Niggers are dirty." But there is a common, widespread, and persistent stereotyped idea regarding the Negro, and it is that he is here only to receive; to be shaped into something new and unquestionably better. The common idea is that the Negro reached America intellectually, culturally, and morally empty, and that he is here to be filled—filled with education, filled with religion, filled with morality, filled with culture. In a word, the stereotype is that the Negro is nothing more than a beggar at the gate of the nation, waiting to be thrown the crumbs of civilization. Through his artistic efforts the Negro is smashing this immemorial stereotype faster than he has ever done through any other method he has been able to use. He is making it realized that he is the possessor of a wealth of natural endowments and that he has long been a generous giver to America. He is impressing upon the national mind the conviction that he is an active and important force in American life; that he is a creator as well as a creature; that he has given as well as received; that he is the potential giver of larger and richer contributions.

In this way the Negro is bringing about an entirely new national conception of himself; he has placed himself in an entirely new light before the American people. I do not think it too much to say that through artistic achievement the Negro has found a means of getting at the very core of the prejudice against him, by challenging the Nordic superiority complex. A great deal has been accomplished in this decade of "renaissance." Enough has been accomplished to make it seem almost amazing when we realize that there are less than twenty-five Negro artists who have more or less of national recognition; and that it is they who have chiefly done the work. A great part of what they have accomplished has been done through the sort of publicity they have secured for the race. A generation ago the Negro was receiving lots of publicity, but nearly all of it was bad. There were front page stories with such headings as, "Negro Criminal," "Negro Brute." To-day one may see undesirable stories, but one may also read stories about Negro singers, Negro actors, Negro authors, Negro poets. The connotations of the very word "Negro" have been changed. A generation ago many Negroes were half or wholly ashamed of the term. To-day they have every reason to be proud of it.

For many years and by many methods the Negro has been overcoming the coarser prejudices against him; and when we consider how many of the subtler prejudices have crumbled, and crumbled rapidly under the process of art creation by the Negro, we are justified in taking a hopeful outlook toward the effect that the increase of recognized individual artists fivefold, tenfold, twentyfold, will have on this most perplexing and vital question before the American people.

Harper's Magazine, November, 1928; CLVII, 769–76.

124

SOCIAL WORK AMONG NEGROES
by *Eugene K. Jones*

The nineteen-twenties was one of several periods in U.S. history when the white world "discovered" Black people; each time this has occurred the one discovered has been called "the new Negro." Reflecting this discovery was the appearance of entire issues of magazines—as the *Survey Graphic* and *The World Tomorrow*—devoted to "The Negro Question." In 1928 the organ of the prestigious American Academy of Political and Social Science fell into line and under the editorship of a white man—Donald Strong—brought out an issue devoted to "The American Negro." Among the essays were those by Horace Mann Bond on "Self-Respect as a Factor in Racial Advancement," Kelly Miller on "Government and the Negro," as well as that by Eugene Kinckle Jones, which is published below. At this time, Mr. Jones was executive secretary of the National Urban League. The Mrs. Baldwin to whom Mr. Jones refers early in his essay was the wife of an executive officer of the Long Island Railroad and of the Southern Railway and a trustee of Tuskegee Institute.

The modern idea of social work among Negroes is less than twenty years old. The first Negro to set forth in a comprehensive manner an organized social work plan was George E. Haynes who, in 1910, appeared before the Committee on the Improvement of Industrial Conditions of Negroes in New York, an organization founded in 1906, to present at its request a program for investigating social conditions as a basis for practical social service in New York City.

Practical Social Service

From this plan was developed the Committee on Urban Conditions among Negroes which during the same year, 1910, was organized in the home of Mrs. William H. Baldwin, Jr., in New York City for the following purposes:

1. To bring about coordination and cooperation among existing agencies and organizations for improving the industrial, economic and social conditions of Negroes and to develop other agencies and organizations, where necessary.
2. To secure and train Negro social workers.
3. To make studies of the industrial, economic and social conditions among Negroes.
4. To promote, encourage, assist and engage in any and all kinds of work for improving the industrial, economic and social conditions among Negroes.

Also, in 1906, there was organized the National League for the Protection of Colored Women, which sought to do Travelers' Aid Work among the colored girls and women who were arriving in New York City principally by coastwise steamers seeking employment and better living conditions. The National League for the Protection of Colored Women had branches in Philadelphia under the leadership of Mrs. S. W. Layten and in Baltimore and in Norfolk where travelers' aid was the principal function.

The White Rose Home for Colored Working Girls, organized in 1900 by Mrs. Victoria Earle Matthews, antedated this movement by six years. Prior to the opening of this institution, Mrs. Matthews had with great sacrifice and unselfish devotion conducted volunteer travelers' aid activities in conjunction with colored women's club work.

The first colored woman to be employed as a professional family case worker was Miss Jessie Sleet (now Mrs. J. R. Scales), a trained nurse who was taken on as a case worker in the New York Charity Organization Society in 1902 by Dr. E. T. Devine, then Secretary of the Charity Organization Society. Thus it seems that Dr. Devine was the first white social work executive to realize the value of using competent, trained Negro social workers for work among their own people, whose problems they could understand and whose needs they could well interpret.

Of course, social work, as commonly understood, has been done among Negroes throughout most of the period of the Negro's life in America. As early as 1793, Catherine (Katy) Ferguson, a Negro woman, organized in New York City the first Sunday School in America. During her life she reared or placed in suitable private homes forty-eight children, twenty of whom were white. Possibly "Katy" Ferguson had no institution to which she could send these helpless little ones, but at least she saw the advantages of the "placing out" system over that of institutional care. During the pre–Civil War anti-slavery agitation period, Isabella, a Negro woman better known as "Sojourner Truth," because of the fact that she was an itinerant lecturer, famed for her frank utterances, was a great woman's suffrage and temperance worker. In 1851, she delivered a most impressive address on woman's suffrage at the Woman's Suffrage Convention in Akron, Ohio. In 1861, she was found to be working among the wounded soldiers in Washington. The colored orphan home in New York now know as the Riverdale Colored Orphan Asylum and Association for the Benefit of Colored Children, was organized in 1838; the Old Folks' Home attached to the Lincoln Hospital was organized in 1839. Anthony Bowen, who was employed in the office of Colonel Chauncey Langdon, founder of the National Convention of the Y.M.C.A. in Boston in 1851, first presented the idea of a Young Men's Christian Association for colored people, the first formal branch of which was organized in 1888 in Norfolk, Va., with W. A. Hunton, a young colored Canadian, as the first secretary. The first colored Young Women's Christian Association was organized in 1876.

Purpose of Social Work

One usually thinks of social work as an organized community effort to change social forces so as to reduce the likelihood of individuals becoming handicapped through mental defectiveness, moral delinquency or economic dependency. It comprises not only work of prevention which consumes the major portion of the time of the social worker of today, but also the great volume of social effort prosecuted in connection with family case work organizations, hospital social service and visiting nursing, instruction of the deaf, dumb and blind, training of the feebleminded, psychoanalysis, and other work with abnormal and subnormal persons—the purpose being to restore as nearly as possible to the normal, persons who have congenitally or through accident, become handicapped. The Negro social worker is enlisted in this service, but he has as his added responsibility the task of bringing the whole Negro group as a separate social entity up to a higher level of social status. In order to satisfy the critical Negro public he must show from time to time his success in securing larger opportunity for the Negro as a separate racial group.

The Negro attitude seems paradoxical. The whole idea of racial segregation is obnoxious to him, yet he demands that the Negro social worker specialize in the Negro's peculiar social problems, treat the problems of the Negro as special group problems. He wants the Negro social worker so to handle his cases that he can report on some Negro industrial worker who has a better job than any Negro has before held in a certain industry; some Negro child who is admitted to some institution for training in a field hitherto denied to Negro youth; some hospital to which a Negro patient has been admitted for the first time or to which a young Negro physician is admitted for interneship, though barred hitherto; some recreational opportunities provided for Negro youth in a playground or camp or community center not before opened to them.

The most important force at work in interest of the Negro today from the point of view of the social worker is that movement which is active in making communities feel that the Negro is part and parcel of society as a whole, and that general social agencies should always consider the Negro's social needs as proportionate parts of the total social service needs of all of the People.

This would mean that whenever the Boy Scout Movement, the family welfare organization, the health agency and the prison association should begin their activities within any community, there should be a conscious and definite effort on the part of those activities to include in their programs operations within the Negro group that would vouchsafe to the Negro population steady improvement in their boy life, in their family standards, in their health status or in their moral codes. Coincidentally, there should be an extension of the facilities for the training of Negro social workers for these activities and the placing of them in strategic positions with these organizations so that the most effective work may be done.

Complementary to all of this is the demand for accurate and adequate social research and investigations among Negroes so that the actual facts of social conditions among Negroes might be ascertained as bases for intelligent and effective social work. There is hardly a large city today in America with a large Negro population in which the social work movement among Negroes has not become a vital factor in the life of the people. Southern Negro communities still suffer greatly because of the slow growth of social work among the white population, the custom being to postpone the establishment of a social agency among Negroes until a similar activity has gained a foothold among the white population of the community.

Social Worker Activities

The national organizations which are most widely established among Negroes are the Young Women's Christian Association with about seventy branches for Negroes; the Young Men's Christian Association with about seventy-five city and industrial branches; the National Urban League with forty-two branches; the Boy Scouts of America with 5,923 colored scouts in 305 troops in 176 cities, and the Playground and Recreation Association with 103 locals doing work among colored people. The American Social Hygiene Association employs a Negro field worker whose health lectures have proved most helpful. (The work of the Young Women's Christian Association is similar to that of the Young Men's Christian Association—an account of whose program is given in another article in this series. I shall therefore confine my statement to the social work activities of other types of agencies.)

The National Urban League makes a speciality of seeking to improve the living and working conditions of Negroes in cities. Its Boards of Control, both national and local, are made up of white and colored citizens. Through its national office, located in New York City, with a southern field office at Atlanta, Georgia, it publishes a monthly magazine, *Opportunity, Journal of Negro Life,* which presents results of social investigations and the products of the writings of white and colored persons on the problems relating to interracial contacts or to the Negro. It conducts a Department of Research and Investigations which assembles facts on Negro life which it furnishes to writers, lecturers, and students of race problems. This Department makes surveys of the social conditions among Negroes in cities, usually under the auspices of local community chests or interracial committees, the findings of which are used by these local committees as bases for inaugurating social service programs in interest of Negro welfare. The Chicago Urban League and the University of Chicago have just completed a cooperative arrangement for maintaining a similar department for local service.

The National Urban League also maintains in New York its National Industrial Relations Department which through publicity of various kinds seeks to bring to the attention of employers of labor the availability and the dependability of Negro labor. In like manner it seems to bring to the front competent Negro workers who may be available for the jobs that are opened up through this publicity method. This Department conducts intensive industrial campaigns in selected cities to bring Negro workers and employers together, and to bring into helpful cooperation Negro and white workers.

In working with the forty-two local Urban Leagues, this Department of Industrial Relations aims toward standardizing at least the mechanics of the locals' employment service so that there may be uniform records for exchange of information helpful to the workers.

The national office sends out monthly bulletins on the changing employment conditions so that the Negro public may know where there is a shortage of workers and in what communities there is an oversupply of workers. The purpose is to aid in the solution of the unemployment problem.

The National Urban League also maintains fellowships for the training of Negro social workers at leading schools of social work such as the New York School of Social Work, the University of Pittsburgh and the Graduate School of Social Administration of the University of Chicago. The Philadelphia Armstrong Association (the Philadelphia "Urban League") has annual scholarships at the Pennsylvania School of Social and Health Work, and this year for the first time the Columbus Urban League has a Fellow at the Ohio State University.

During the past seventeen years there have been about sixty different Fellows to receive this training through the national organizations—their field work experience being gained in connection with the local Urban Leagues, social service positions being secured for most of them by the Urban League at the conclusion of their training. Many of them are holding most important positions such as social worker executives, psychiatric social workers, family case workers, teachers of social sciences, social investigator and recreation supervisors.

The local Leagues have programs to meet the peculiar needs of the communities in which they are located. Practically all of them maintain employment finding facilities for opening up new lines of occupations to Negroes and placing skilled and semi-skilled workers in these positions. They usually become the clearing houses for social service activities among Negroes. They seek to encourage the spirit of cooperation in social work for Negroes. Frequently, their programs include community houses where there are clubs and classes of various kinds for the young and for the old. They conduct health education campaigns and arrange for public interracial meetings. Emphasis is placed on securing publicity in the form of newspaper and magazine articles on Negro life to enlighten the public and to add recruits to the work of furthering interracial good will and understanding.

Community Activities

In the family case work field, Negro workers are increasingly being employed where the Negro case load is high. Boston, Cleveland, Chicago, Atlanta, Detroit, Baltimore, Memphis, Richmond, Tampa, New York, Philadelphia, Columbus, Ohio, St. Louis, Indianapolis, Louisville, Pittsburgh, Minneapolis, Cincinnati, and Washington are among the cities which thus far have begun to use from one to six case workers each. Visiting nurses are used in most of the larger cities, and some southern states such as Arkansas, North Carolina, Alabama, Georgia and Virginia have definitely committed themselves to the use of Negro nurses in connection with their state-wide work.

Some cities in connection with their health work are using Negro city physicians, and one experiment in community health deserves special mention: that is, the North Carolina Health and Hospital Association, Inc., which is seeking through the organization of the Negro families of Halifax County, North Carolina, to assure to all member-families on the payment of a small monthly fee of less than fifty cents per member free hospital service and medical advice and attention.

The Playground and Recreation Association of America since the World War, when it began its work as the War Camp Community Service, has conducted a special program for the organization of community activities for Negroes. It maintains a summer school for the training of its workers and seeks to provide leisure-time activities in the form of play, choral and pageant work and community house activities.

The work of the visiting teacher is being extended somewhat among Negroes, so that the colored children in many public schools are receiving the benefit of professional advice to parents on the causes of retardation. New York City and Philadelphia are outstanding cases of success in this direction, and the Jeannes and Slater Funds' teachers are being instructed to carry out these ideas in connection with their work.

The outstanding health center among Negroes is probably the Shoemaker Center in Cincinnati, sponsored by the Public Health Federation and financed by the Cincinnati Community Chest. During the fiscal year closing April 1, 1928, there were 5,248 patients who visited the clinic. The activities consisted of the Family Service Department, Dental Clinic, Baby Clinic and General Health Clinic. The General Health Clinic includes gynecological examinations and venereal disease treatments. The staff of this Center is made up of white and colored physicians, nurses and case workers.

The Settlement House movement among colored people has never gained very great headway, although there are reputable settlement houses in Boston, Minneapolis, and in Cleveland.

The probation work movement has gained considerable headway, most of the larger cities having Negro probation officers for work with juveniles, and in some cities probation officers are at work in connection with the courts for adults. Birmingham, Atlanta, Savannah, Richmond, Baltimore, New York, Cleveland, Chicago, Louisville are among the cities which have this work.

Child welfare in the form of day nurseries and kindergarten independent public school systems has been quite widely extended. This year, the first child welfare center, specializing in children between the kindergarten and high school ages, is being inaugurated in New York by the Utopia Neighborhood House developed by a group of Negro club women.

Outstanding social housing experiments are the Schmidlapp houses in Cincinnati, a group of five- and six-room duplex homes in a detached section of Walnut Hills; the Dunbar Garden Apartments in New York City, comprising 2,000 families and occupying a whole city block, erected by Mr. John D. Rockefeller, Jr., and sold to the tenants on the cooperative plan; the City and Suburban Homes Company's group of houses in the Columbus Hill section on the west side of New York City, and a Philadelphia Housing Association. With the exception of the Dunbar Garden Apartments, the policy is to rent the houses at a low rental but sufficient to bear a legal rate of interest on the invested funds to allow for amortization.

The cost of social work among Negroes is not nearly as much in proportion as that for whites. Reports from Community Chests in sixteen cities which have member organizations doing specific work for Negroes indicated that last year a total of $367,919.51 was expended through these agencies, and that possibly about $750,000 was expended altogether by these same sixteen agencies for all of their Negro work, including the cost of social service done by white agencies for colored persons.

There are probably as many as 1,500 Negroes in America who are doing some form of social work, although possibly not more than 500 have received any special training in this field. The majority of the social work agencies today, however, are demanding not only that their workers be possessed of a college training, or its equivalent, but that some special training also be secured in the profession.

Twenty family service societies return a total of 9,060 Negro cases during 1927. This is not a full indication of the relief needs of colored families, as these agencies quite uniformly report that the Negro families are the last to apply for relief and the first to become independent again.

Many church organizations are establishing institutional features, although most of these institutional churches confine their social service activities to young people's meetings. Several churches have inaugurated very elaborate social service programs. For instance, the Abyssinian Baptist Church of New York City has a $325,000 building including a gymnasium, employment service, Red Cross nurse training center, adult classes and domestic science courses. The St. John's Congregational Church of Springfield, Mass., has a public library, a working girls' home, a boys' club house and a number of apartment houses, and two-family and single-family houses which it lets out at low rentals to its parishioners.

Negro Workers

Negro students in social work are accepted at all of the social service training schools in the North. In the South there are two training centers, especially designed for Negro workers,—the Atlanta School of Social Work and the Bishop Tuttle Training School for Social Workers connected with the St. Augustine College, at Raleigh, N.C. This latter institution specializes in religious workers. The Atlanta School of Social Work is especially designed to train the students for general social service.

There is probably no profession in which Negro members are on as cordial relationships with white members as is that of the social worker. In practically all of the state conferences of social work, whether north or south, there are Negro members. The National Conference of Social Work makes no discrimination in the status of its members as to race or religion. On two occasions, a colored member has been elected to the Executive Board at its annual conferences in the general elections when five members were elected from a slate of fifteen candidates, and on two other occasions Negroes have been nominated for the Board by the Executive Committee to fill out an unexpired term. Negroes have served on five or six of the twelve division committees for the past eight or ten years, and from five to twelve Negro social workers have been speakers on the annual division programs during recent years and frequently on the evening general programs of the Conference.

There is a very close connection between social work among Negroes and the whole problem of race relations in America. Effective social work among Negroes will tend to raise the level of intelligence, of physical vigor and industrial status of the group. It will give them a stronger economic foundation and a better appreciation of social values. It will develop competent and dependable leadership within the racial group. It will bring into closer cooperation white and colored leaders who are concerned about community welfare and will have the effect of making of Negroes an articulate group in the community. It will destroy all arguments against giving the Negro his rights on the ground tht he cannot use these rights properly. It will remove from the Negro masses the feeling of insufficiency or inferiority which might cause Negroes to hesitate in their yearnings for larger opportunities and their demands for the chance to occupy their rightful place in the life of the nation. It will help to produce a hearty race, a self-contained group, a resourceful people from whom will emerge outstanding characters whose special contributions to the welfare of man will tend to bring more respect for and more confidence in the Negro as a people. And this is the essential element in the solution of what has been described as "America's greatest problem."

The Annals, November, 1928; CXXX, 287–93.

125

THE NATIONAL INTER-RACIAL CONFERENCE

Stimulated by the situation described in the preceding documents, professors and organizational leaders—white and Black—met in Washington, D.C., December 16–19, 1928, in a National Interracial Conference. Using the facilities of Howard University and—for public meetings—the auditorium of the Department of Interior building, participants discussed subjects that included health, education, industry and agriculture, recreation, housing, law, citizenship, and race relations. Papers were presented by Louis L. Dublin,

Herbert A. Miller, W. E. B. Du Bois, Monroe N. Work, Niles Carpenter, T. J. Woofter; participants included James Weldon Johnson, Walter White, Clark Foreman, Alain Locke, Ira Reid, and Charles H. Wesley.

The conference was chaired by Mary Van Kleeck of the Russell Sage Foundation; George E. Haynes was the executive secretary; and Charles S. Johnson, then head of the Social Science Department at Fisk, served as research secretary. At the conference's conclusion, summaries of each of the panels were prepared; that "On Agriculture and Industry," done by Charles H. Wesley, is published below.

ON AGRICULTURE AND INDUSTRY
by Charles H. Wesley

One of the most important periods of the morning session was devoted to study of the Negro in agriculture and in industry, Monroe N. Work of Tuskegee presenting the facts on agriculture, and Dr. Niles Carpenter of the University of Buffalo the facts on industry. Such a discussion is of special value when it is recognized that 60 per cent of the Negro population, ten years and over, are workers. It has been estimated that this group performs one-seventh of all the labor in the United States. Over two million Negroes are engaged in agriculture, and about one million are in domestic and personal service. Sixty-seven per cent of the gainfully employed are in these two fields.

A.—Agriculture

Ownership of Farms—The census of 1920 showed a decrease in the ownership of farms by Negroes, as compared with the census of 1910, and a corresponding increase in tenancy. By 1925, the number of Negro farms showed an increase. Similar trends are noted for the white population of the South. In this connection, it was noted that white farm tenants move more than colored farm tenants.

Size of Farms—The conclusion was drawn that the greatest increase in number of farms between 1880 and 1925 had occurred in farms of from 10 to 49 acres, thereby disproving the popular belief that a combination of small farms into large ones is a marked feature of southern agriculture.

Farm Population—Negro farm population has decreased by over 700,000, which is in agreement with the general loss of farm population throughout the South. Two southern states, South Carolina and Georgia, have lost over 100,000. It was pointed out that Negro males outnumber Negro females in the farm population, and that the largest age group in the South is between five and fourteen years.

Crop Production and Raising of Livestock—There has been no great increase in production of crops per acre, but the total amount of agricultural products has increased as has also the acreage under cultivation.

The problems which the Negro farmer faces were listed under three headings:

(1) How to increase production with greater profit to the farmer.
(2) How to buy and sell by co-operative marketing methods.
(3) The problem of credit.

These problems have not been solved by either the Smith-Lever Act or the Smith-Hughes Act, because the workers among Negro farmers are too few and the allocations of funds from these sources are about as faulty as are the allocations of other funds in the southern states.

In answer to the question, "Are Negro farmers making progress?", Mr. Work replied that "visiting their fairs and their farms, one must come to the conclusion that, in spite of handicaps, they are making some progress."

B.—Industry

The session on the Negro in industry was begun with a presentation of facts concerning Negro women and children. Negro women were found to be still engaged, as in the past, in domestic and personal service, and in the so-called borderline occupations. Throughout the history of Negro labor in the United States during the nineteenth century, it was found that certain industries like the tobacco, the peanut, and canning factories have attracted Negro women because it was possible to locate such factories near the place of production. In the North, Negro women are found in the textile industries. Garment workers in the factories and in the homes have increased. One fact is outstanding in this connection: Negro women show a higher percentage of those engaged in these gainful occupations than any other group in the population. In West Virginia there was found a higher percentage of males gainfully employed and the lowest percentage of women gainfully employed. This was attributed to the mining industry.

The effect of this large employment of women was regarded as having deep significance for the Negro home. Dr. Carpenter ventured the suggestion that we might infer that in proportion as Negro women and children leave these gainful occupations, Negro men are rising in the economic sphere. In this way, women would be relieved for the duties of home-making and children would be relieved for education. This suggestion did not take into consideration the new ʼwoman, of whom we hear so much, who does not desire to confine her interests entirely to the home circle.

The major part of the presentation was devoted to the Negro male in industry. It was noted that 67 per cent of the Negroes were engaged in domestic and personal service, as against 35 per cent for all groups in the country as a whole. A second group of occupations was called the "semi-domestic," including porters, janitors, et cetera, in southern mills. A third group was termed "bottom structure" occupations, such as the unskilled labor in the iron and steel industries. A fourth group included the semi-skilled occupations, which were termed the "pushing-up" in which Negroes were pushing their way to more skilled work, and the "vacuum" occupations, which were being entered by workers for the first time. The fifth group covered the skilled occupations. In New York City on certain derrick and crane work, the Negro has excellent opportunity for skilled labor, and in Cleveland a recent survey showed that 11 out of 12 foundries had promoted Negroes to skilled work.

The Negro is finding his place in American industry not only by reason of the World War and migration, but by his own efforts in pushing his way up toward more skilled labor. The problem of efficiency was difficult to solve. Various and contradictory opinions were given. Nevertheless, the majority of employers say that Negroes are about as good as whites and in some cases better. The Negro turnover was said to be large, but Dr. Carpenter stated that in at least one center—Cleveland —the figures showed that the turnover depended upon management, wages, and working conditions more than upon racial temperament.

In regard to the prospect for Negro labor, a division was made of positive and negative factors. The positive factors were:

(1) American industry will continue to demand a large amount of unskilled labor.

(2) The greatest success will come where Negro labor is carrying on a mass invasion.

(3) There is less resistance in the "vacuum" industries.

(4) The Negro possesses certain advantages over some other groups such as the English language, good nature, the co-operative spirit, and adaptability.

The negative factors were:

(1) Unskilled labor may be replaced by machinery.

(2) In periods of high turnover, the workers in unskilled occupations are the first to go without work.

(3) Opposition on account of color.

Report of the Committee on Findings, National Interracial Conference (Washington, 1928) (mimeographed), pp. 18–22; in editor's possession. Alain Locke described this conference in *The Survey,* January 15, 1929; LXI, 469–72. On its basis Charles S. Johnson produced the book, *The Negro in American Civilization* (New York: Holt, 1930); this contains the text of Du Bois' speech at the conference but the Reports of the committees are not reproduced.

126

16-YEAR OLD YOUTH BATTLES 200 POLICE
CHICAGO POLICE KILL 16-YEAR OLD BOY
IN OWN HOME

The above headline appeared in a radical Black newspaper in December, 1928; it and the story which follows might well have been published at any moment in the generations that have followed.

For 5 hours 200 policemen, barricaded behind furniture seized in nearby apartments, fired into one poor alley apartment on the rear Northside here, with a steady stream of bullets and other projectiles from machine guns, revolvers, automatics, shotguns, and rifles; tear gas bombs were hurled, and hand grenades of high explosives were flung into the alley window.

Finally an entry was effected and a volley of bullets shot into the enemy.

The enemy was sixteen year old Ernest Wickhurst, a Negro boy who became frightened early in the day because he knew of horrible brutalities visited upon Negro workers arrested by the Chicago police, and who had heard he was to be arrested, having been accused of breaking a plate glass window. So he barricaded himself in his apartment with a gun, and sold his life as dearly as he could, wounding nine of the army of 200 or more police gunmen sent against him, before he fell, riddled with more than 30 bullets.

When the police broke into the apartment they had been so industriously bombing and showering with bullets, it was seen that Ernest had given the best and safest places, the closet and behind the barricade made in one corner with a bed, to his older sister and three small brothers. An infant sister was wrapped in the blankets of the bed.

Deputy Commissioner of Police Martin Mullen and Commissioner of Police William Russell, personally directed the five hour bombardment.

Mary, one of the youth's frightened sisters, a cripple, in the end admitted the police through the door they had vainly tried to batter down. The sisters and brothers had crouched beneath their beds while bullets were pouring in through the windows. As the girl opened the door slightly, a squad, led by Deputy Commissioner John Stege of the Detective Bureau, Deputy Commissioner Mullen, Detective Chief John E. Gan and Lieutenant William Cussak, all carrying steel shields, made a rush for it. Acting Sergeant Thomas Connelly stepped from behind his shield and fired a shot into the Negro's head. A volley from the others followed and he fell with thirty bullets in his body.

The Negro Champion (New York City), December 29, 1928, p. 2.

127

A STATEMENT OF FACT [ON LYNCHING]
by *Walter White*

As earlier documents have shown, Walter White of the N.A.A.C.P. was indefatigable in his battle against lynching. In 1929 Alfred A. Knopf published a full-length study by Mr. White of the atrocious practice. From its appendix is taken the factual summary.

There have been lynched in the United States 4951 persons in the forty-six years beginning in 1882 and extending through 1927. Of the victims 3513 were Negroes and 1438 whites. Ninety-two were women—sixteen of them white and seventy-six colored. Mississippi leads in this exhibition of masculine chivalry, with sixteen women victims; Texas is second with twelve; Alabama and Arkansas are tied for third place with nine each; Georgia follows with eight; Tennessee and South Carolina mobs have bravely murdered seven women each; Kentucky and Louisiana five each, Florida and Oklahoma three each; Missouri and North Carolina two each; and Nebraska, Virginia, and Wyoming one each. Three of the twelve Texas victims were a mother and her two young daughters killed by a mob, in 1918, when they "threatened a white man." Thus was white civilization maintained!

Lynchings were not considered sufficiently important for recording prior to 1882, when the *Chicago Tribune* included in its summary of the year's crimes, disasters, and other phenomena the mob murders of that year. The first scientific and exhaustive study of lynching was that made by Professor James Elbert Cutler of Yale University and Wellesley College. *Lynch-Law* was published in 1905 and covered the years from 1882 through 1903. Unfortunately the book has long been out of print and is practically unobtainable.

Cutler sought "as a student of society and social phenomena" to determine "from the history the causes for the prevalence of the practice, to determine what the social conditions are under which lynch-law operates, and to test the validity of the arguments which have been advanced in justification of lynching." He took the figures as compiled by the *Chicago Tribune* as a basis for his study. With great care he verified and corrected the *Tribune* data through correspondence, and by comparison with the files of other newspapers, such as *The New York Times* and the New York *Tribune,* and through study of all available magazine articles which had been written upon the subject. Because of the care and thoroughness with which he sifted the facts Cutler's study stands as the most thorough examination yet made of the years 1882–1903.

In 1919 the National Association for the Advancement of Colored People published its exceedingly valuable statistical study, *Thirty Years of Lynching in the United States, 1889–1918.* Competent research-workers employed by the Association spent more than six months in the Congressional Library at Washington searching newspaper files; a vast amount of material gathered over a period of ten years by the Association was examined; and, in brief, every source where authoritative evidence could be gained was consulted. Personal investigations of a number of lynchings had been made by members of the Association's staff, and of others by detectives.

Relying upon under- instead of over-statement, the foreword to *Thirty Years* states that "it is believed that more persons have been lynched than those whose names are given. . . . Only such cases have been included as were authenticated by such evidence as was given credence by a recognized newspaper or confirmed by a responsible investigator."

This great caution causes discrepancies between the figures of Cutler and those of the Association. Cutler for the years beginning in 1889 and extending through 1903 gives a higher total in eleven of the fifteen years, and in three others his figures are the same as those of the Association. As Cutler's study was made twenty years nearer to the

TABLE I

Number of Persons Lynched, by Years and by Race, 1882–1927

Year	Total	Whites	Negroes
1882	114		
1883	134		
1884	211		
1885	184		
1886	138		
1887	122		
1888	142		
1889	176		
1890	128		
1891	195		
1892	235		
1893	200		
1894	197		
1895	180		
1896	131		
1897	165		
1898	127		
1899	107		
1900	115		
1901	135		
1902	97		
1903	104 (3337) *	(1277) *	(2060) *
1904	86	7	79
1905	65	5	60
1906	68	4	64
1907	62	3	59
1908	100	8	92
1909	89	14	75
1910	90	10	80
1911	80	8	72
1912	89	3	86
1913	86	1	85
1914	74	5	69
1915	145	46	99
1916	72	7	65
1917	54	2	52
1918	67	4	63
1919	83	4	79
1920	65	8	57
1921	64	6	58
1922	61	7	54
1923	28	2	26
1924	16	0	16
1925	18	0	18
1926	34	5	29
1927	18	2	16
	4951	1438	3513

* Totals by race for years 1882–1903 given by Cutler.

TABLE II

Number of Persons Lynched, by States and by Race, 1882–1927

State	Total	Whites	Negroes
Alabama	356	52	304
Arizona	31	31	0
Arkansas	313	69	244
California	50	48	2
Colorado	68	64	4
Connecticut	1	1	0
Delaware	1	0	1
Florida	275	28	247
Georgia	549	39	510
Idaho	21	21	0
Illinois	32	13	19
Indiana	52	41	11
Iowa	18	17	1
Kansas	55	36	19
Kentucky	233	79	154
Louisiana	409	62	347
Maine	1	1	0
Maryland	27	2	25
Michigan	8	7	1
Minnesota	9	5	4
Mississippi	561	44	517
Missouri	117	51	66
Montana	89	87	2
Nebraska	58	55	3
Nevada	6	6	0
New Jersey	1	0	1
New Mexico	38	35	3
New York	3	2	1
North Carolina	100	20	80
North and South Dakota	35	34	1
Ohio	26	11	15
Oklahoma (Indian Territory)	141	97	44
Oregon	20	19	1
Pennsylvania	8	2	6
South Carolina	174	9	165
Tennessee	268	55	213
Texas	534	164	370
Utah	8	6	2
Virginia	109	24	85
Washington	28	27	1
West Virginia	54	21	33
Wisconsin	6	6	0
Wyoming	41	37	4
Alaska and Places Unknown	16	15	1
Totals	4950	1437	3513

Walter F. White, *Rope and Faggot: A Biography of Judge Lynch* (New York: Knopf, 1929), pp. 229–32.

period, 1889–1903, and because of the care he exercised, his figures for that period are accepted in the present study. This is especially safe inasmuch as the Association's figures are the *minimum* ones.

As further means of checking the above figures, they were compared with the figures of lynchings in the *World Almanac* (1927), prepared by Monroe N. Work of Tuskegee Institute. These figures, covering the period 1885–1925, are in several instances considerably higher than those of Cutler or the Association, especially during the earlier years. For very recent years they are generally slightly lower than those of the Association.

The tables which precede have been prepared, therefore, by combining Cutler's and the Association's figures and carefully checking them with the *World Almanac* figures to insure maximum accuracy.

Table I gives totals of lynchings by years and by race for the years beginning with 1882 and extending through 1927. The figures for the years up to and including 1903 are taken from Cutler. Unfortunately, he indicated the division by race only on a graph, but he gave the totals by years and by race for the fifteen years he studied. For 1904 and the years following, the figures are taken from *Thirty Years*.

Table II lists the lynchings by states and by race. Only four states of the Union have never been stained by a lynching—Massachusetts, Rhode Island, New Hampshire, and Vermont.

128

THE MENACE OF CAPITALIST "FRIENDSHIP"

In the Spring of 1928, the Afro-American people who had been associated with the African Blood Brotherhood, the Workers (Communist) party, and the American Negro Labor Congress launched a weekly newspaper, *The Negro Champion*, in New York City. The editor was Cyril Briggs; contributing editors were W. C. Francis, Pittsburgh; James W. Ford, Chicago; C. W. Fulp, Primrose, Pa.; John H. Owens, Ripley, Cal.; W. J. Burroughs, Jamaica, N.Y.; Otto Huiswoud, New York; L. Fort-Whiteman, New York; Henry Rosemond, Brooklyn, N.Y.; Richard B. Moore, New York; Irving Durjee, New York; and a West African named J. G. Lumon.

Reflective of the particular class approach that characterized this paper was the following editorial from its issue dated March 23, 1929.

Living in a world in which Negro workers are often discriminated against by white workers under the leadership of the reactionary A. F.

or L. bureaucracy, and in which white capitalists pose as "friends" of Negro labor on the grounds of their condescension to exploit us (at lower pay and longer hours!), Negro workers are apt to become confused on important issues of the Class Struggle. Such confusion is deliberately sought and fostered by the agents and beneficiaries of the capitalist system.

That race hatreds and antagonisms are propagated by the capitalist class and for the definite purpose of facilitating and making more profitable the exploitation of the workers of all races, will be at once apparent to anyone who will investigate the role played by the press, the church, the cinema, the schools, the stage and other social forces operative in modern life, and further investigates the *controlling and directing power behind these forces*. What group is it that controls the press, the church, the cinema, etc.? The white members of the working-class, the white workers, or the big employers and capitalists? The answer is self-evident. If then, the capitalist press engages in a campaign of vicious slander, or of as vicious silence, against the Negro, who is responsible? Is this a sign of capitalist "friendship" for the Negro?

When the capitalists-controlled church helps to maintain the present social system in the South and condones, or at least maintains an acquiescent silence toward lynching and other forms of white terrorism, is this another sign of capitalist-christian "love" for the lowly Negro? And the cinema and stage? When these lend themselves, as they very often do, to the campaign of slander and race hatred, is this still another indication of capitalist friendship for us?

And the Red Cross, controlled by northern white capitalists—when the Red Cross goes south to give aid and comfort to the victims of natural catastrophes, and lends itself to maintaining the Southern system, actually acting as slave-catchers for white Southern planters, is this another evidence of capitalist affection?

And the New York Telephone Company, which refuses to employ a single colored girl as operator, in spite of the fact that thousands of its subscribers are Negroes? The Western Union, which in the North, finds it inconvenient to employ a Negro even as messenger boy, but in the South, where this work is considered menial, employs only Negro messenger boys? Is that helping to perpetuate race inferiority notions, or not?

The Childs Restaurant Company and countless other big capitalist enterprises, where the most open discrimination is practised against the Negro, both in the way of employment and of service—are these "friends" of the Negro?

The Metropolitan Life Insurance Company which employs not a single known Negro as an agent, in spite of the fact that thousands of its customers are Negroes? This same company a few months ago tried to introduce in New Jersey southern jim-crowism by opening a separate office for Negroes—is this another sign of capitalist friendship for the Negro?

The facts are, of course, that the capitalists are responsible for the keeping alive and the intensification of race prejudice—they dose the working-class with it through the press, the schools, the cinema, etc. Having isolated the Negro, they deal him a double dose of exploitation, in the form of longer hours, lower pay, segregation in houses they would otherwise have to tear down and higher rents for these dumps than white workers have to pay for homes, which while not ideal, are nevertheless incomparably better. And when the Negro kicks the whole force of the capitalist system is directed against him, including the courts, the police, the militia, army and navy—for these are also controlled by the capitalists. And this is the "friendship" the Negro workers are offered as against their class-interests with the workers of every race and clime, as against their natural and destined alliance with the revolutionary workers of all countries! This mess of pottage!

That Negro workers are beginning to see these facts clearly and to recognize that collaboration with their exploiters is against their own interests, is being daily demonstrated by their increasing participation in the struggles of the revolutionary wing of the working-class—the left-wing workers who practise no discrimination and who for several years past have sternly led the fight in and out of the A. F. of L. against discrimination and race hatred.

129

INTERNATIONAL COUNCIL OF WOMEN OF THE DARKER RACES

Previous documents have reflected efforts—particularly on the part of Afro-American women—to create movements combining an awareness of the integral connection between the efforts to eliminate racism and war. In 1929, with Mrs. Booker T. Washington as founder, there appeared another such effort, fated to be short lived, especially in view of the onset late in 1929 of the economic crash.

Purpose

1. Study the needs, conditions and problems of the women of the darker races.

2. Enlist the women of those races in a program of education, social and economic welfare.

3. Publish and disseminate information for the enlightenment of all races on the problem affecting the peoples of the darker races.

4. Stimulate and develop appreciation for the contribution of all races toward our present civilization.

5. Emphasize world unity and peace as the necessities of modern civilization and denounce the inconsistency between ideals and acts of governments and religions in this respect.

6. Unite with other agencies, national and international, that are working for world peace and world fellowship.

7. Work against class legislation and discrimination of all kinds on account of race or color.

Membership

Any woman who is actively and officially connected with a national organization whose ideals and purposes are in harmony with the ideals and purposes of this organization is eligible to membership in the International Council of Women of the Darker Races. Applications are presented thru members of the council.

Fees

The joining fee is $25.00 and $10.00 per year.

Funds

The funds from memberships, gifts, benefits, and bequests shall be devoted entirely to the work of propaganda and publicity approved in advance by the Council on its Executive Commission.

1929–30 Program

1. Issue or sponsor one Study dealing with a vital problem affecting the interest of the darker races.

2. Hold a conclave of the women of the darker races in the city of New York.

3. Have a representative at Geneva.

Officers

Addie W. Hunton, Honorary President
Addie W. Dickerson, President 4800 Chester Ave., Phila., **Pa.**
Marian B. Williams, Vice Pres. Orangeburg, S.C.
Emily H. Williams, Cor. Sec. Tuskegee Inst., Alabama
Elizabeth C. Carter, Rec. Sec. 211 Park St., New Bedford, Mass.
Mary Isenberger, Treas.
Nannie H. Burroughs, Ch'm. Ex. Board

Printed leaflet, in editor's possession.

130

THE THOMPSON-NEGRO ALLIANCE
by Ralph J. Bunche

The potential of Afro-American political power—especially within urban centers with ghettoes—was first demonstrated in Chicago politics, commencing during the years of World War I. This was symbolized in the heavy dependence upon William Hale Thompson, the city's "boss" for many years, upon the Black vote and the fact that the "boss" responded by providing some among his Black constituents with important positions. (This forms, incidentally, a main feature of Du Bois' novel *Dark Princess* (1928) in which he correctly prophesied the election to Congress of the first Black person from the North.) The development of this alliance is traced and analyzed by a young graduate from the University of California (Berkeley) who was to receive his doctorate from Harvard, become a professor at Howard, and then, of course, as assistant secretary-general of the United Nations, was to be the first Afro-American to win the Nobel Peace Prize.

Chicago, America's most sensational municipality, with its "pineapple"* politics and racketeers, has become the "seventh heaven" of Negro political activity.

The state of Illinois, Cook County (of which the midwestern metrop-

* The name given to the bombs hurled by Chicago gangsters.

olis comprises the major part), and Chicago boast a greater degree of Negro political participation and influence than any city, county or state in the nation. The toga of Negro political leadership adorns the Illinois Negro. His influence is vitally felt at every election. His vote is often the conclusive determinant in hot races for political office. His reward for support of the successful candidate is the usual consideration condoned by contemporary American political practice.

Any analysis of the political development of the Negro in Chicago must concern itself with, first, the very nature of the characteristically American system of "machine" government and "bossism," and, second, the political carer of William Hale Thompson,—"Big Bill the Builder," "Friend of the Plain People," "Democracy's Child," as he is variously and significantly called.

Before relating the interesting history of the Thompson-Negro alliance, it is appropriate to indicate the essential features of American boss rule as it exists in our larger urban centers.

To begin with, town hall democracy is a thing of the dim past. The political machine steps in when democracy becomes impersonal and institutionalized, as it inevitably must when city life becomes complex and involved. The gang then develops as the antithesis of local democracy. Congested living explains the gang in any great city. Chicago's not unusual problem is particularly aggravated by its peculiar situation and the many nationalities within its confines. Altogether it houses more or less sizeable homogeneous groups representing thirty-two nationalities.

The machine, and the political boss at its helm, appreciate the inescapable fact that honesty and efficiency will not of themselves suffice to make an administration successful in our local government. The successful administration must establish itself on terms of intimacy with the whole body of the people, whether that administration is honest or corrupt. It is here that the boss asserts himself. Personality counts for much in politics. The successful boss, as Plunkitt of Tammany Hall put it, "must study human nature and act accordin'." His power is to be found in his individual personality, the extent to which the local political system is complicated, and the amount of patronage at his disposal. Ex-president Roosevelt once remarked that the political boss was just like any other boss, i.e., his object was to "get the job done." Existing local government philosophy seems to interpret this in a strictly *Machiavellian* sense.

"Big Bill" Thompson is the political "boss" of Chicago. The Negro political leaders have, by and large, been cogs in his well-oiled machine. Thompson apparently has the customary politician's affection for the plain people. Seemingly humane, tolerant, the "angel of the under-dog" and a "good fellow," he has won to power because he has won the good will of hundreds of minor ward and precinct "bosses"—many of them Negroes.

"He is the wholesaler, they the retailers in a government built on friendship and this friendship thrives on trades in patronage and favor."

Chicago, the second black city, the sixth German city in the world, with a large Polish element, an Italian city comparable to Naples, is an ideal place in which to assemble unrelated minorities. Organization here counts tremendously in election results. "Big Bill" proceeded to build up a powerful organization, and the Negro minority plays a vital role in it. Patronage and favor are "swapped" for black ballots.

Chicago today has a Negro population of approximately 200,000. When Mayor Thompson was first elected in the spring of 1915, approximately 55,000 Negroes were residents of the city. These were concentrated chiefly in the district just south of the "loop," politically designated as the second ward. Many years before, Thompson had been elected alderman from this same ward on the strength of the Negro vote. In the municipal election of 1915 he was solidly supported by the same electorate—gaining a majority of more than 10,000 votes over his opponent in the Negro district. He was elected, and served two terms (until 1923), during which time the political influence of the Negro population of the city began to assume important proportions. Indeed, in 1919, when Mayor Thompson was reelected by a plurality of 21,622 votes in a total city vote of 698,920, his poll in the Negro wards was 15,569 to his nearest opponent's 3,313. The Negro support was consequently sufficiently strong to control the result.

It was during Thompson's first two administrations that the first Negro alderman was returned to the city council, and the mayor promptly appointed him floor leader. At the same time there were three Negroes appointed as assistant corporation counsels; another to a comparatively lucrative position as attorney for the traction commission; and a number of minor appointments in other city offices were made. This representation in the government of the city served to stimulate the political interest of the Negro groups. The ballot was seen as an effective instrument whereby they might to no little extent select those who were to govern them and at the same time win moderate prestige for their race. Negro political leaders with actual political experience were being developed, and the war placed new power in their hands. They found welcome places in the "machine." The exodus from the south greatly augmented their population and the number of Negro inhabitants in Chicago jumped startlingly from 44,103 in 1910 to 109,595 in 1920, an increase of 148 per cent, most of which occurred between 1916 and 1919. This increase virtually trebled the number of Negro voters, many of whom were of the ignorant, peasant class—fine raw material for machine digestion.

Mayor Thompson did not run in the 1923 election but was a candidate for a third term in the spring of 1927. Never since the fire of 1871, was Chicago so aroused over a local affair. It is no small matter that stirs 3,000,000 people with anxious interest and sends over 1,000,000 to the polls. The Negro was destined to play a stellar role in this mighty political melodrama. Unfortunately, the racial issue early became predominant. This was due in part to the size of the potential Negro vote, which was known to be strongly in support of Thompson; and in part to the fact that some of the supporters of Mayor Dever's candidacy viciously attacked Thompson as the "Negro candidate." The inevitable result was to stampede the Negro vote to the Thompson banner more solidly than ever. "Big Bill" won the Negro leaders behind him almost to a man. What with kissing dark-hued babies and abusing Irish police who raided the Negro clubs and sometimes made mistakes and raided Negro homes, he held the Negro vote practically unanimously.

A good deal of vilification and scurrilous propaganda was circulated during the hectic campaign. Hoaxes were perpetrated, calliopes paraded the streets piping the strains of "Bye, Bye, Blackbird"; a typical circular displayed a trainload of Negroes headed from Georgia with Thompson as pilot of the train, and the significant legend inscribed below: "This train will start for Chicago, April 6, if Thompson is elected."

Election day brought out a record vote. Thompson surprised political prophets by winning over Dever by a plurality of 82,938 votes. A total of 1,010,582 ballots was cast, of which 10,739 were disqualified. By far the major portion of this plurality was gained in the "south side" or Negro wards, where Thompson's majorities ran from eight to one to as high as sixteen to one. The second, third and fourth wards, with a Negro population respectively of about 98, 95 and 60 per cent,—the "strongholds of the Negro vote,"—gave 59,215 votes of the Thompson plurality of 82,938.

With the Thompson victory and the campaign excitement abated, the color issue was flatly dropped, and but scant mention was made of it by the local press, which had featured it so prominently in the pre-election ballyhoo. Interest now centered on the prospective po-

litical "house-cleaning" by the new administration. In the new city
appointments Negro political leaders shared generously. In general
the men appointed have been from among the higher levels of the
Negro race, well trained and capable. One of the first to be designated
was Bishop A. J. Carey, presiding bishop of the fourth district of the
A.M.E. Church, as a member of the Chicago civil service commission,
—a cabinet office. This commission is composed of three members,
two Republicans and one Democrat, who supervise the recruiting of
more than 30,000 city employees, including the members of the police
and fire departments. Another Negro has been appointed as legal adviser to the city in matters pertaining to state legislation of vital interest
to Chicago. Six of the best trained young lawyers of the group hold
appointments as assistant corporation counsels. In the city attorney's
office the race is represented by an assistant city attorney. Two representatives are also found as assistant attorneys for the board of local
improvements. In the office of the city prosecutors are five more as
assistant city prosecutors. Another, appointed as a member of the
library board, with no salary, has jurisdiction over approximately 3,000
employees.

These men are all entrusted with responsible positions. In illustration, in the office of the corporation counsel, a Negro, as assistant
corporation counsel and trial lawyer in property damage litigation,
represents the city in suits mounting to millions of dollars yearly. There
are approximately twenty Negro investigators in the various legal departments. Additional appointments in the many city departments, as
teachers, clerks, police, et cetera, run into the hundreds.

It is of especial significance to note that many of these appointees
are from other than dominantly Negro wards. One of the Negro assis-
tants in the corporation counsel's office has residence in a ward of which
the Negro voters number approximately 1,500 out of a total registered
vote of 30,000. Another, attorney to the board of local improvements, is
likewise from a district in which the Negro voters represent only about
one-seventh of the resident vote; a third, in the city prosecutor's office,
hails from the aristocratic "silk-stocking" sixth ward. Many similar
appointments have been made.

All of the Negro political representation in Chicago is not, however,
by appointment. In the two strong Negro wards, the second and third,
the majority group has elected two of its own members as aldermen. A
Negro municipal court judge with a salary of $10,000 has also been
nominated and elected.*

The natural result of this stimulated political activity found its ex-

* Albert B. George.

pression in an increased interest by Negroes in state political affairs. Four Negroes have been elected to the lower house of the Illinois state legislature and one state senator. State appointments have been numerous. A Negro serves as the governor's appointee on the powerful Illinois industrial board, which controls the workmen's compensation awards. Another serves as state commerce commissioner, one of a commission of seven members, controlling all public utilities and state commercial enterprises. A Negro is serving as an assistant attorney-general of Illinois on the special commission whose object is the purging of Chicago politics of vice and corruption. Mr. Oscar De Priest, of course, has been elected to the National Congress as Representative from the first congressional district, with a plurality of about 4,000 votes over his white opponent.

Since the 1928 cataclysm in the Republican primary the political situation has taken on a much less roseate hue for "Big Bill" and his machine. The primary last April was a much more grim and sinister and a much less circus-like affair than the 1927 election on the crest of which the "big boss" rode to supremacy. The excitement was there— open violence, sluggings, shootings, kidnappings and murder all graced election day. But the Small-Crowe-Thompson combine was unmercifully repudiated by the voters both in the city of Chicago and the state of Illinois. The tables were turned and the public planted a "pineapple" under the "machine." Thompson himself, of course, has three years remaining of his term. It apparently goes without saying that he will have done his last turn at the helm of Chicago politics when 1931 rolls around.

What then, is the future of the Negro in Chicago politics, whose political development has been so intimately related to the Thompson organization? There was a perceptible defection of the Negro vote from the Thompson banner in the April primary. The Negro, along with the rest of the Chicago electorate, had lost much of its faith in "Big Bill." His favorite ballyhoo, his "crack-King-George-on-the-snoot" buffoonery had evidently lost its potency. And perhaps the black belt like other sections of the city, had become surfeited with the vice, thuggery, murder and shamefully flagrant lawlessness which were the inevitable concomitants of his avowed policy of a "wide-open town". At any rate it scarcely seems probable that the Thompson machine could again feel assured of anything approaching a solid black vote.

Thompson has helped the Negro to develop and assert his potential political power in Chicago politics. The Negro electorate must certainly be taken into serious account henceforth by the machines which succeed the present administration. The Negro is established politically in

Illinois today and can be relied upon to shift for himself from now on. He has capable leaders, well-trained for their tasks. The earlier leaders were often of a rather low type, but those of the newer generations are of much higher caliber. The Negro has acquired a new confidence in his political ability. It can probably be safely predicted that the Chicago Negro in future years will continue to wield as much influence and to hold as many (if not more) offices, as he now does under the Thompson regime.

Even the most casual survey of the contemporary situation in Chicago must convey the impression that its Negro electorate is much more intelligent and much more capably represented than ever before in the city's history.

The affiliation of the Negro vote with a machine so nationally notorious for its rottenness is indeed regrettable. Out of this association the Negro has gotten no little patronage and favor, a significant increase in recognition and influence, and a whole lot of bad government. Yet the Negro vote was only a small, albeit a vital part of the half-million votes which so enthusiastically and boisterously endorsed the Thompson regime in 1927. The indictment lies not against the Negro, but against Chicago; or perhaps it is simply another back-hand slap at democracy's ridiculous fetish—*vox populi, vox Dei.*

Opportunity, March, 1929; VII, 78–80.

131

A BLACK MAN ENTERS CONGRESS

The preceding document noted the election of Oscar De Priest of Chicago to the House of Representatives in 1928. When Mr. De Priest took his seat he was the first Afro-American representative since George H. White of North Carolina left in 1901. There follow two documents marking this event: [a] the commentary by Francis J. Grimké, undated but clearly written soon after the event; [b] an article by Lester A. Walton, who had been managing editor of the *New York Age.*

[a]

F. J. GRIMKÉ'S COMMENTS

The appearance of a Negro in Congress, after the lapse of more than two decades, is an event of more than passing interest.

1. To the colored people it means much in the way of encouragement politically. It means that things are beginning to take on a brighter hue, that the outlook is brightening. It presents the Negro as an office-holder, not by appointment but by election of the duly qualified voters. It is a certification of his right to hold office and to be voted for just as any other citizen. As a member of Congress, the highest legislative body of the country, there he stands, side by side with other representatives from every state in the union. It means a great deal to the ten million Negroes in this country to see in Congress a member of their race. It has been rather humiliating, during these latter years, to see not even one representative of the race included in that law-making group. But since Mr. De Priest has entered Congress, it has seemed entirely different. It gives us a new interest in that body of law-makers. We feel now as if we have a part in it, as we ought to have, and would long since have had had our citizenship rights been respected.

2. This reappearance of a colored man in Congress should have still another effect upon us: we should never again be satisfied not to be represented in that body. There is no reason why from other sections of the North, with proper organization, other representatives should not be sent. It is not merely to have a colored man in Congress, but his presence there will be one of the most effective ways of keeping the citizenship of the Negro before the country, and thus hasten the time when the South will not be allowed to suppress the Negro vote to the detriment of the Negro and to the whole country. Several Negroes in Congress will call the Nation's attention to the oppressive conditions in the South and will lead to some action to remove those oppressive conditions.

3. This appearance of a colored man in Congress has also in it a lesson for the white people of the country. It should remind them very forcibly that the Negro is an American citizen, otherwise this representative would not be where he is: and should lead them, as an act of justice and true patriotism, to see that his citizenship is respected as is the citizenship of other elements of the Nation. His presence in Congress gives the lie to the sentiment that is so largely prevalent in the South, that the Negro has no right to vote or be voted for. That he has a right to vote and to be voted for is proclaimed by his presence as a member of Congress before the whole country and the world, Southern sentiment to the contrary notwithstanding. And that is a great deal. It is a great object lesson.

4. Still another thing, connected with this reappearance of the Negro in Congress, that is worthy of note. It has opened the doors of both

of our great military and naval schools at West Point and Annapolis again to colored men. For years they have been shut out, as no white Congressman ever thinks of naming a member of the race for either. Now, however, since the election of Congressman De Priest, colored men have been named for both.

Not that I care anything about either of these schools. The sooner they are both discarded and all similar schools throughout the world, the better it will be. There is no good reason why in the twentieth century with the principles and ideals of the Christian religion in operation, that we should be training men to fight each other. It is a shame that such should be the case. As long as such schools exist, however, the Negro as a part of the population, and, who, in the hour of danger must come to the defence of the country, even to the laying down of his life, should not be excluded from them on the ground of his color. It is an invidious distinction in citizenship that should be steadily and persistently resisted. This is one, among other reasons, why, however it is possible, we should see that some representative of the race is in Congress, and is kept there. In this and in many other ways, it will mean much to us in vindicating our citizenship.

Woodson, ed., *Francis J. Grimké, op. cit.*, III, pp. 323–25.

[b]

THE NEGRO COMES BACK TO THE
UNITED STATES CONGRESS
by Lester A. Walton

When Representative Oscar De Priest of Chicago took his seat as a member from the First Illinois Congressional District at the opening of the seventy-first session on April 15, 1929, it signalled the return of the Negro to the halls of Congress after an interlude of twenty-eight years.

The first Negro Congressman from the North was elected on Nov. 6, to succeed the late Martin B. Madden, Chairman of the Appropriations Committee. He defeated his white opponent on the Democratic ticket by more than 3,000 votes and ran far ahead of the colored independent candidate. The First Illinois Congressional District is the wealthiest in the State, having within its boundaries Chicago's greatest business section, the Loop. At the death of Representative Madden his successor was selected as the Republican nominee by the five ward committeemen in the First Illinois Congressional District. Representative De Priest was the choice of Mayor Thompson, an old friend and political colleague.

Before Representative De Priest, the twenty-second of his race to sit in the Lower House at the Capitol, this distinction was enjoyed by Representative George H. White of North Carolina, who in an impassioned speech on the floor of the House near the close of the fifty-sixth session concluded his valedictory by saying: "This, Mr. Chairman, is perhaps the Negro's temporary farewell to the American Congress; but let me say, Phoenix-like he will rise up some day and come again. These parting words are in behalf of an outraged, heart-broken, bruised and bleeding, but God-fearing people, faithful, industrious, loyal people, rising full of potential force. The only apology I have to make for the earnestness with which I have spoken is that I am pleading for the life, the liberty, the future happiness and manhood suffrage of one-eighth of the entire population of the United States." * Colored Americans throughout the country are interpreting Oscar De Priest's election to Congress as a fulfillment of George H. White's prophecy. They are referring to the Chicago Representative as "a star of hope in a midnight sky" and "a symbol of the race's political aspirations."

To become a national legislator Oscar De Priest had to overcome many obstacles. Immediately after his selection as Republican nominee for Congress, an element of his people voiced unalterable opposition, advancing the argument that in such unprecedented circumstances a more representative type ought to be sent to Washington. However, by November much of the hostility had disappeared and the disgruntled decided to heed the importunities of leaders who urged the race to present a united front at the polls for De Priest lest the golden opportunity to make history by sending the first Negro to Congress from a northern State be lost. Last October, an indictment was brought against De Priest by a special grand jury in connection with the disorders at the primary in April, 1928. The accused promptly issued a statement declaring that his indictment was part of a plot hatched by a political faction opposed to Mayor Thompson. Not until a few days before the extra session convened at Washington was the case called and dismissed by Chicago officials, much to the elation of Negroes in all sections of the country.

Fifty-seven years of age, Oscar De Priest was born at Florence, Ala. When a child his parents moved to Salina, Kan., where he spent

* The text of a speech by Congressman White, in 1900, denouncing the disfranchisement of Black people is in I, 816–17, of this work.

his boyhood. Thirty years ago he settled in Chicago, working as a painter and decorator. He was the first Negro member of the Chicago City Council, and for two terms County Commissioner of Cook County. When elected to Congress he was Assistant Illinois Commerce Commissioner by appointment and Republican Committeeman from the Third Ward. "It will be my aim to represent the whole district without regard to race or color," he said, after his election. "I am mindful of the service required for the great financial interests in the district; for in the territory there are located some of the largest banks and financial institutions in the United States. I should like to have the people think of me first as an American citizen. I have no race consciousness of the kind that is consumed in the vain notions of social equality. I appreciate also that over 12,000,000 loyal American citizens of a certain group will look to the Congressman from the First Illinois Congressional District as their Congressman-at-large. I realize fully the weight of the duties and responsibilities, and I appreciate the congratulations that are coming to me from my district and throughout the country."

For a decade there have been sporadic and unsuccessful efforts to elect Negroes to Congress. These activities have been confined solely to the North, where the numerical strength and influence of the race have been steadily on the increase. And in this agitation Chicago has led. Thousands of migrants, seeking to improve their economic, political and social status and to provide better school facilities for their children, have since the war settled with their families on Chicago's South Side, appreciably swelling the city's population. Those of voting age have availed themselves of the long-desired privilege of enjoying the right of franchise. Hence, 80 per cent of the voters casting their ballots in the First Illinois Congressional District are Negroes. For years Representative Madden, when seeking renomination and reelection, was opposed by colored aspirants. But the majority of Negro voters reasoned that as chairman of the all-powerful Committee on Appropriations, Representative Madden could serve them more advantageously than any other, and so the opposition to him was negligible.

Because of the movement of the Negro farmhand from the South to large industrial communities in the East and Middle West, the prediction was made in 1924 by political observers that the next Negro Congressmen would come from Chicago, New York and St. Louis, in the order named. Chicago has fulfilled its part of the prediction, and now we turn to New York. There, in what is known as North Harlem, the colored population is estimated at between 250,000 and 300,000.

Included in this number are West Indians, Cubans, Porto Ricans and others who are not naturalized, though some have taken out their first papers. Political leaders of both races and of the dominant parties in the district frankly confess that, if one-half of those eligible were to register and vote, the likelihood of one member of the New York Congressional delegation being a Negro would not be remote. If a Negro were sent to the House of Representatives from Harlem he might be either a Democrat or a Republican. For ten years the race has displayed marked independence at the polls, especially in local elections, when the majority of districts have gone Democratic more often than Republican. The spectacle of a colored Democrat from the North and a white Democrat from the South expressing agreement on political issues is within the realm of possibility.

In 1924, the Republican nominee for Congress in the Twenty-first New York District was Dr. Charles Roberts, who was defeated by Royal H. Weller, Democrat. Last November Mr. Weller defeated his Republican opponent, a Negro, E. A. Johnson, receiving 56,518 votes to the latter's 41,691. The colored candidate on the Socialist ticket pulled nearly 4,000 votes. The sudden death of Representative Weller on March 1 precipitated an unexpected and complicated situation, but no special election was held before the convening of the special session. It remains to be seen whether the Negroes can use the opportunity to secure the election of another Congressman.

In St. Louis during the last Presidential campaign the unusual spectacle was presented of a Negro running for Congress on the Democratic ticket. The contest was between Representative Dyer, author of the anti-lynching bill bearing his name, who for years has represented the Twelfth Missouri District, and Joseph L. McLemore, a young lawyer. The result was: Dyer, 24,686; McLemore, 17,720. The Democratic nominee is said to have polled almost twice as many votes as Representative Dyer two years before.

One of the anomalies of this situation was that in Dyer's home precinct, which is white, he lost to McLemore; while in McLemore's precinct, which is colored, Dyer was given the larger vote. The support accorded the colored candidate by white voters in St. Louis was unprecedented.

Besides the twenty-one Negroes to hold seats in the House of Representatives at Washington between the fortieth and fifty-sixth sessions of Congress, all from Southern constituencies, two Negroes have also served as United States Senators. Hiram R. Revels was the first. He was born free and held office in 1870 and 1871, representing the State of Mississippi. Blanche K. Bruce, born a slave, was Senator from Mississippi from 1875 to 1881. Of the Negroes who sat in the House of Representatives some held important committee assignments and creditably acquitted themselves. Joseph H. Rainey was at one time chairman of a subcommittee of the Committee on Appropriations. Two Negro Congressmen of the Reconstruction period are alive today. John R. Lynch, who served three terms as a Representative from Mississippi, lives in Chicago. Despite his 80 years he is practicing law. Thomas H. Miller, formerly of South Carolina, resides in Philadelphia. He strongly advocated the election of Alfred E. Smith as President.

Shortly after the Civil War, when the Negro became a lawmaker at the Capitol, the race was 95 per cent illiterate; today it is less than 20 per cent illiterate. Then its property holdings were small; now, exclusive of educational and church property, it owns $1,700,000,000 in realty. Having grown in importance, standing and influence as a citizen, the Negro feels justified in declaring, as did the colonist in Revolutionary days, "Taxation without representation is tyranny." Eliminated as a national legislator because of disfranchisement laws passed in the South, the Negro harbors the hope of regaining his lost political prestige by reaching the national capital from the North.

Current History, June, 1929; XXX, 461–63.

132

NEGRO LABOR AND THE CHURCH
by A. Philip Randolph

In 1929 Mr. Randolph, as a Socialist, Black trade union leader, participated in a symposium dealing with the working class and religion, organized by Jerome Davis, then a professor at Yale University. This essay may well be compared with that written by Eugene Gordon the previous year and published earlier in this work.

The African Negro Church, like most primitive tribal forms of religious worship, was built around taboos, totems and fetiches. The slave trade tore asunder the socio-religious-political institutional arrangements and transplanted, with the African slave, in the Western world, all of the religious mechanisms the African possessed in his native land.

The early slave religious worship in the Americas, a distinctly New-world environment, was a virtual replica of the African tribal forms. But, naturally, this outward manifestation of religious similarity could not persist. The dominant religion of the New World, Christianity, decreed the doom of African animism.

In the Americas, religious worship in the alleged civilized form, among the slaves, began in the established white churches. This was the mandate of the slave owners, so as to prevent and render unnecessary clandestine religious gatherings of the slaves, that might have, incidentally, served as convenient occasions for fomenting insurrections against the whites, and plots for escape in the Underground Railroad.

Doubtless, the slave owners' fear of rebellion among the slaves rested on sound grounds; for there had already been twenty-five recorded slave insurrections in the Colonies before the Revolution. The slave régime had been deeply stirred and shaken into a hectic feverish fear of slave uprisings, led by General Gabriel, in 1800; Denmark Vesey, in 1822; and Nat Turner, in 1831. As a precaution against recurrent slave revolts, rigorous and oppressive laws were enacted against the assemblies of slaves, following these efforts of black bondmen to secure their freedom.

Although the entrance of a Negro into a wealthy and beautiful temple of religion of white Americans today may severely test and strain their profession of belief in the Christ's ethic, because of the tribal Nordic outcry of superiority against all Alpines, Mediterraneans, Mongoloids and Negroids, the African slave enjoyed the blessings of the Christian doctrine, beside their white masters, in order that they (the slaves) might not engage in mischievous and sinister conspiracy against the holy order of Southern slavery. Thus, the black and white Church were practically one under the slave power.

The formal Negro Church was born as a protest against discrimination in the white church, as was the case with the African Methodist Episcopal Church; or it had been set up by white missionaries, or it was the result of too large a congregation in the white church, which divided invariably into black and white groups or into separate religious bodies by, for and of Negroes.

The foregoing brief historical account of the Negro Church shows that its background is both proletarian and revolutionary. In the North, it was composed of Negroes escaped from slavery through the Underground Railroad, Negroes who bought their freedom, and Negroes who had been freed by the passage of laws for the abolition of slavery in the Northern colonies. The Black Church was led by former slave preachers, such as Lott Carey, who organized the African Missionary Society, and Richard Allen, who founded the African Methodist Episcopal Church as a protest against persecution by the whites in their churches. The Negro Church in the North prayed and struggled and fought for freedom of the slaves in the South.

It may not be amiss to observe here, also, that before the Civil War, there were probably not a half dozen Negro churches, if any, in the South. They were banned on the grounds of being places of gatherings of slaves which constituted a menace, unless supervised by whites, to the safety and security of slavery.

The early Negro Church then championed the cause of freedom for the black bondmen. During the Reconstruction period, Negro churches served as centers of agitation for the validation and enforcement of civil and political rights of the freed men, and black religious leaders rang the changes for the political and civil liberty of the black proletariat who constituted practically ninety-nine percent of the Negro population.

But with the coming of freedom, the Negro lost the security of his maintenance in terms of food, clothing and shelter, which was assured under the slave régime. He must now find employment in which to make wages, with which to purchase food, clothing and shelter, upon which his life depended. His first thought, then, was the getting of a job. The economic reward of the job was a secondary consideration. Next to the question of getting a job, was the matter of preparation for the new demands which were manifesting themselves as a result of the march of the industrialization of the South. That the Negro might not be the flotsam and jetsam of a new industrial era which was rapidly assuming ascendancy in America, as a result of the American industrial revolution, Booker T. Washington, great American educator, conceived the Tuskegee Idea, and sought, with the aid of white philanthropists, to create black artisans, to take their places in the building of industrial America. His was the vision of a prophet. He wrought more nobly and wisely than he knew. But under the stress of the industrial and commercial profit system, which was more and more functioning through gigantic trusts and mergers as a result of the increasing concentration of productive capital into fewer and fewer hands, the Negro, like the white worker, began to realize that in order to sell his labor at a favorable wage level, besides industrial training, he needed economic power, which came only from organization.

Thus, the Negro worker, as a result of economic necessity, began thinking in terms of collective bargaining. During the Reconstruction period, Negro workers had organized a National Negro Labor Union, which unfortunately fell under the leadership of Negroes whose political philosophy took precedence over the economic, and resulted in sacrificing the economic movement to political expediency. Negro workers had also entered the Knights of labor, and began joining international unions of the American Federation of Labor, as soon as that body was formed.

While the Negro Church comprehended the struggle of the black workers for jobs and the industrial educational preparation for jobs, it did not readily grasp the nature, scope and meaning of the Negro workers' economic efforts to raise their wages, shorten hours of work, and improve working conditions. Only the job-getting and the industrial training efforts met with no resolute resistance, for white Northern philanthropists had shown themselves greatly favorable to Negro industrial education. Probably one cogent reason for the Negro preachers' indifference and opposition to the organization of Negro workers for economic advantage, in many cases, was that the powerful white capitalists who had sometimes appeared as friendly philanthropists, themselves opposed black wage earners organizing as they opposed the organizing of white wage earners. Moreover, organized labor had become anathema in the eyes of the Negro generally, because of the feeling that Negro workers were discriminated against by white labor unions, both with respect to securing jobs under the control of unions and union cards in order to get union jobs. This feeling among Negroes was not without foundation, for there are several international unions that still prevent Negro workers from joining them. It is well to note in this connection, however, that the American Federation of Labor as a National Body, in convention after convention, has gone on record as opposed to all forms of discrimination among workers because of color, race, creed or nationality. But, of course, international unions are autonomous and usually determine their own constitutional policies, which may or may not be favorable to the inclusion of certain race groups in their bodies. This short-sighted policy of some international trade unions will be corrected by the organization of Negro workers, despite discrimination; and the forces of industrial necessity and education will develop in the white workers a recognition of the fact that their interests are common with the black workers and that the salvation of the workers of both races are bound irretrievably together.

The attitude of the Negro Church toward labor may be best viewed concretely in relation to the movement to organize the Pullman porters. Fundamentally, one cannot accurately aver that the Negro Church is either for or against organized labor. Although it is fair to add that it is rare to find a Negro preacher who is committed to the philosophy of labor unionism. Of course, white preachers are not numerous either who can be counted upon to champion the cause of the trade union, although many may express general sympathy with the principle of collective bargaining, which they regard as having sufficient latitude to include company unions, variously known as employee representation plans, works councils, shop committees, industrial democracy parliaments, and congresses. Upon discussing a company union, in contrast to a trade union, with the average preacher, white or colored, one readily discovers, among the large majority, a very definite misunderstanding of the difference between these two economic structures. Negro ministers, as a rule, take it for granted that a company union in which Negro workers are forced to be members, is a form of a beneficent economic philanthropy, which is to be accepted with gratitude instead of rejected with condemnation.

Because the Negro preachers regarded the industrial paternalism of the Pullman Company, manifested in its Employee Representation Plan and the Pullman Porters Benefit Association, as a generous concession to the race, they viewed the rise of the Brotherhood of Sleeping Car Porters in August, 1925, with mingled suspicion, distrust and fear. What is true of the attitude of Negro preachers was characteristic of most Negro leaders toward the porters' union.[1]

One of the outstanding instances of a Negro preacher resisting the corrupting influences of the Pullman Company was the flat refusal of Dr. W. D. Cook, of the Community Church of Chicago, to accept a consideration of five hundred dollars in order to keep the Brotherhood from holding a meeting in its church which had been extensively advertised throughout the city. Dr. Cook attested to the fact that the offer

[1] The outstanding, independent, progressive, intellectual Negro preachers, however, such as Dr. Mordecai Johnson, President, Howard University; the Reverends A. Clayton Powell, of the Abyssinian Baptist Church; W. P. Hayes, of the Mount Olivet Baptist Church; John G. Robinson, of St. Marks Methodist Episcopal Church; A. C. Garner, of the Grace Congregational Church; William Lloyd Imes, of the St. James Presbyterian Church; George Frazier Miller, of St. Augustine Episcopal Church; Shelton Hale Bishop, St. Philips Episcopal Church, of New York; Dr. Prince of Denver; Dr. W. D. Cook, of the Community Church; Dr. Burton, of Chicago; Dr. Griffith of St. Louis; Dr. Cassius A. Ward, of Ebenezer Baptist Church of Boston, Mass.; and Dr. Francis Grimké, of Washington, have consistently supported the Porters' Union.

was made him by a prominent Negro business man, who doubtlessly served as a mediator for the Pullman Company.

In Denver, Colorado, Dr. Prince, pastor of one of the large Baptist churches, refused an offer of three hundred dollars to prevent the meeting of the Brotherhood from being held in his church. He publicly expressed, in a church meeting, his sympathy with the Brotherhood and condemned those who attempted to corrupt him against the porters' cause. In the beginning of the movement, every effort was made to close the doors of churches throughout the country to the porters' fight. In every city, however, the organization was able to secure a large prominent church for its meetings, though sometimes it was necessary to pay fifty dollars therefor. In some instances, the use of the churches was given the union without any cost.

Probably the most notorious instance of Negro preachers taking the side of the Pullman Company against the porters' organization, was the occasion of a conference in Washington which was called ostensibly in the interest of fighting race segregation in the Federal Departments at Washington, by Melvin Chisum, self-styled as an efficiency engineer. This conference was presided over by Bishop A. J. Carey, of the African Methodist Episcopal Church; many of the ministers in his diocese were mobilized by him to attend the conference, the expenses of which, including the cost of transportation to and from the conference, together with hotel bills while at the conference, were defrayed by the Pullman Company through its agent Mr. Chisum. A large number of prominent Negro leaders had been lured into this conference without a complete knowledge of its purpose. The main object was to adopt a resolution endorsing the Pullman Employee Representation Plan, as an expression of the sentiment of the Negro leaders of the country. The assumption was that such a resolution would serve as a condemnation of the Brotherhood of Sleeping Car Porters and cause a stampede of the porters out of the Union. Of course, it did not have the desired effect, because most of the prominent men who attended, upon receiving an explanation of the purpose and significance of the conference by the writer, expressed their disavowal of the conference and their lack of sympathy with its program.

Bishop Reverdy C. Ransom, of the African Methodist Episcopal Church, when approached to lend his name and influence to the above-named conference, definitely refused and sharply condemned its purpose. The Brotherhood counts him among its most powerful champions in the ministry.

In several cities Negro ministerial groups have endorsed the union. An effort was made to secure the endorsement of the General Conference of the African Methodist Episcopal Church which convened in Chicago, in June, 1928, but to no avail, because of the influence of Bishop A. J. Carey, who dominated the conference.

The Baptist Ministers' Alliance in Chicago, which met in the church of Rev. L. K. Williams, President of the National Baptist Convention, in the Summer of 1926, was reported to have endorsed the Brotherhood through a resolution which, however, could never be secured. No minister who was a part of the meeting in which the resolution was supposed to have been adopted, was ever able to give an explanation of the reason why the said resolution could not be secured, or the fact that the Alliance would not permit the Brotherhood to announce that the Union had been indorsed. One reason advanced for the refusal of the Baptist Alliance to come out for the Brotherhood is that the railroads who are interlocked with the Pullman Company give passes, through the President of the Baptist Convention, to the preachers, which enable them to travel throughout the country at half-fare rates.

Since the Negro Church is largely composed of Negro workers there is no good reason why it should not express and champion a proletarian philosophy. There are few men of wealth in the Negro race. Those who possess considerable property do not employ large numbers of Negro workers, and hence could have no economic reason for opposing Negro labor organizations that are concerned with increasing the wage income of its members. Such is not the case with the white ministers. They must preach a Christian doctrine which will not offend their rich communicants.

As to the Negro workers' attitude toward the Church, most of them are members of some Church, although they feel that Negro preachers are not so militant for their cause as they should be.

Negro labor leaders are not anti-Church, though they may not be Church members. All of them feel that the Church can be of constructive social, educational and spiritual service to the Negro workers.

If the Church, white or black, is to express the true philosophy of Jesus Christ, Himself a worker, it will not lend itself to the creed of oppressive capitalism which would deny to the servant his just hire.

Jerome Davis, ed., *Labor Speaks For Itself on Religion: A Symposium of Labor Leaders Throughout the World* (New York: Macmillan, 1929), pp. 74–83.

133

THE NEGRO WORKER: A PROBLEM OF VITAL CONCERN TO THE ENTIRE LABOR MOVEMENT
by Abram L. Harris

The Conference for Progressive Labor Action came into being in 1929; its official organ was the monthly *Labor Age* which had commenced publication in November, 1921, taking over the subscription list of the *Intercollegiate Socialist* (itself begun in 1913). The chairman of the C.P.L.A. was A. J. Muste, at the time dean of Brookwood Labor College and vice-president of the American Federation of Teachers. Others associated with this effort, in the earlier period, were Francis J. Gorman of the Textile Workers and Professors Paul F. Brissenden and Rexford G. Tugwell.

From one of the pamphlets issued by the C.P.L.A. is taken material on the Black workers. Its author at this time was an instructor in economics at Howard and studying at Columbia on a Rosenwald Fellowship. In 1932 he, with Sterling D. Spero, published through Columbia University the influential and still useful book, *The Black Worker*.

The Problem

The known Negro union membership is about 56,000. The total number of Negro workers employed in transportation, extraction of minerals and manufacturing is around 1,300,000. So Negro workers are only about 4.3 per cent organized.

About twenty-one per cent (20.8%) of all American wage earners, excluding agricultural workers, are trade union members. Therefore the Negro is only about a third as well organized as all workers.

The problem doesn't stop there, however. There are three hundred and forty-eight thousand Negro workers employed in iron and steel, meat packing, textiles, lumber and furniture, and tobacco—industries of unskilled and semi-skilled workers which are hardly touched by unionization. The organization of the Negro, therefore, involves the greater problem of organizing the unskilled and semi-skilled in the basic industries which lies at the root of militant unionism.

An Outline of Progressive Labor Action

1. Intelligent appraisal of concrete situations where Negro and white workers are brought together, to determine the best way to bring about efficient co-operation between them.
2. Recognition of the right of Negro workers to union membership and to participation in labor political, co-operative and educational activities on equal terms with white workers.
3. Vigorous efforts to organize Negroes as well as white workers in all trades and industries, especially in the basic industries employing large masses of semi-skilled and unskilled workers.
4. Building a Labor Party which will connect the Negroes' special racial demands with the broader economic and social reforms of the movement.
5. Special study of the problems of Negro workers by local branches of the C.P.L.A., and the establishment wherever it seems advisable of special committees or conferences including both Negro and white workers and labor sympathizers.
6. Educational activities among both white and Negro workers to show how race prejudice is fatal to their economic interests and social welfare.
7. Especial attention to thorough-going and persistent workers' education movements among Negro workers. Such a movement would explain to them our modern industrial system, and the history, aims, achievements and possibilities of organized labor. It would also seek to break down the influence of opportunistic, middle-class leaders among the Negroes who are trying to build up a Negro petit-capitalism, and who teach Negro workers that their economic interest lies on the side of the employer rather than that of their fellow workers, and that their national interest is best protected by the Republican Party.

The Delusion of Building a Negro Capitalism

On the economic side, the Negro masses have been taught that their welfare is best promoted by adopting a conciliatory attitude to those who control industrial and economic opportunity, through subservience to the wealthy, and through the establishment of a sort of self-sufficient Negro petit-capitalism. Here the progressive laborites must demonstrate to the Negro workers that their problems, like that of the white workers, is inevitably that of work and wages. For even if the Negro leaders who look upon the creation of Negro financial and business enterprise as the economic salvation of the Negro masses, are successful in realizing their ideal, the institutions that they hope to establish are to be run on the basis of economic individualism and private profit, despite the tendency of these leaders to confuse "racial cooperation in business" with genuine consumer cooperation.

The success of a Negro petit-capitalism will give economic reality merely to our contemporary Negro middle class which is temperamentally detached from the realities of the working class life. But however successful Negro business enterprises may be, and whether it proceeds on a quasi-self-sufficient racial basis or takes its chances for survival in the general competitive arena, it must in the nature of things remain a diminutive force in modern industrialism, which is to say, that its heralded power for meeting the problem of Negro unemployment will be of small importance. The great masses of Negro workers will continue to find their employment with those who now control finance and industry. And the few Negroes who will obtain work at the hands of the black capitalists of tomorrow will not thereby cease to be wage earners. Their problem will merely be shifted from the center of modern economic life where white capitalists dominate to the margin where small Negro enterprisers earn the wages of management.

The Immediate Task

The Negro working masses ought to be made to understand the causes of unemployment, low wages, and the need for labor unionism and co-operation, in general. They must be made to see the reasons that explain the specific severity of industrial disadvantage upon them as a racial group, in particular. But none of these lessons will take root if they are presented in any but a realistic, clear-cut and progressive way, and, above all, if the white workers are unwilling to accept Negroes into working class fellowship. The difficulties ahead are great, to be sure, but a policy of letting well enough alone or one of delay will not overcome them.

It is the duty of advanced, thinking laborites to begin to grapple with the problems and difficulties now. Thus they will take an important step in the accomplishment of their general tasks, *viz.*, the organization of those workers who have been neglected by traditional trade unionism;

The re-establishment of unionism in those industries where it has petered out or failed to establish control because of lethargic and self-satisfied leadership which refuses to recognize the inadequacy of craft unionism in such highly integrated and mechanized industries as packing, steel, rubber and automobiles;

The stimulation of an offensive against the open shop, company union, employee welfare, capitalism of the trustified industries; and

Weaning labor from subservience to the two major political parties in order to create independent working-class political action.

Abram L. Harris, *The Negro Worker: A Problem of Vital Concern to the Entire Labor Movement,* Progressive Labor Library, pamphlet No. 3, Conference for Progressive Labor Action (New York, 1930), pp. 10–11, 16–17. In the March, 1930 issue of *Labor Age* and also of *The Crisis* was published an article similar to the pamphlet by Mr. Harris, entitled, "The Negro Worker: A Problem of Progressive Labor Action."

134

THE AUTUMN LEAF CLUB
by Everett W. Grimes

Rare are the descriptions of everyday life in the rural Midwest as experienced within the Black community and as reported by one of its members. What follows is a graphic example of one such rarity.

Twenty-four years ago a few friends and relatives gathered at the home of Mr. and Mrs. Walter Grimes for the purpose of finding a way to band themselves closer together and improve the coming generation by giving them the opportunities they were deprived of. Out of this meeting resulted the club that now meets every three weeks. It has to be something real big to cause a meeting to be postponed.

These people gathered on the night of September the twenty-ninth, right in the heart of the beautiful Wisconsin fall season. Mrs. Oliver Davis of Madison suggested the name, "Autumn Leaf," and that name has been carried ever since. The regular procedure of starting a club was followed, a constitution drawn and officers elected. A committee was appointed to appeal to the state for a charter which was granted in October of 1906.

The club meets every three weeks in rotation at the various member's homes. After the meeting a short period is usually devoted to the great all-American pastime, "gossip." Also during this period the hostess is busy preparing a lunch which has played an important part in the existence of the club. The first meeting in the month is purely a business meeting in which problems of interest to improving of general conditions of the club and its members are discussed. If there is any sickness or sorrow in the community, provision is always made to see about it. When more than one meeting occurs in a month this is a pleasure one. The program committee always has a varied program to offer and topics of the present day are talked over.

Lancaster is located eighty-five miles southwest of Madison, Wisconsin, and thirty miles from Dubuque, Iowa. There were at one time around two hundred colored people living in this immediate part of the State. Today there are only twenty-four residents in Lancaster and vicinity. The youngest is six, and the oldest is at the grand old age of ninety. Adventure, opportunity, matrimony, and death have told very hard on our group.

This club has formed itself so firmly in our hearts that we use it as our official organ here. The citizens of Lancaster respect its members and the club is also quite widely known throughout the southwestern part of the state. The big reason for this is that every year they stage a big "Barbeque and Bowery," on the Thomas Greene farm, six miles southwest of the town, in what used to be the center of the colored population here. There are no colored people living closer than the above mentioned two cities, and they rally to help us put over what we call the biggest day in the year. This is usually held on or near August the fourth, and always draws a big crowd. Sometimes there are over three thousand people.

A family dinner is held at noon, a program of the best talent is put on in the afternoon, and at night is the big bowery dance. A lively orchestra furnishes the music and everybody forgets the cares of life for a period of four hours. This past year the Club scored another triumph. Mr. George Abernathy and his "Royal Knights" of Milwaukee, furnished the music, and thus for the first time a colored orchestra played in Lancaster. Throughout the afternoon and evening the crowd may have their choice of barbequed pork, beef, or chicken, cooked by Joseph Grimes. He and another also put on several barbeques throughout the country at various times during the summer season. A refreshment stand is erected, and Dick Lewis and his helpers are kept real busy dispensing candy, cigars, soft drinks and ice-cream. In the years that this picnic has been held there has never been any disorder, which we feel is quite a record.

The present residents of Lancaster are living a typical home life as one would expect in a country town. There are no factories or industries to offer employment. Farm labor, odd jobs about town are all a man can get. Some men however, have good records of service. C. E. Shepard has been with a hardware firm for over twenty-five years. Joseph M. Grimes has been with a family doing housework for over eighteen years, and S. C. Craig has a good record for janitor service in the various churches and schools. Some of the women are employed in private homes, some do catering for parties among the best people here, and their ability is greatly respected in that line.

There at one time was a colored church here but it was a log structure and was taken down in 1923, after most of the people had joined churches in town. A very nice building was erected on the church site and is used only to house tools or in case of bad weather during a funeral. This building and cemetery are kept up from the fund collected at the picnics and club treasury.

In most clubs finance plays an important part, but in ours the dues are small and yet they cover all of our desires. If there is any need for funds, a supper, basket social or bazaar is held and we try to give our kind helpers full value for their money.

The Autumn Leaf Club boasts of the following records:

Ten graduates of the Lancaster High School, and twenty-four graduates of grade schools. In high school, the boys all made good records in athletics.

Four active service men in the World War.

Six active service men in previous wars, one of whom is still living, Mr. Thomas Greene, who is now ninety years of age.

In the business world we can count dentists, garage owners, restaurant proprietors and owners, four school teachers, tailors, club stewards, and two of our group have enviable records and positions on the Rock Island and Northwestern Railroads.

Sunday is quite a big day here, as it is usually a get-together day. There are sometimes out-of-town friends calling on some one, and everybody has to see them before they make their departure. Every home has a telephone or automobile so it is no trouble to get all at one home in a very short time.

The present charter members have so instilled the spirit in the younger members that all are anxious to stick until the twenty-five years are over. Whether it will continue is up to the group entirely, but at present we do not see how we can drop such an important thing. A big celebration is being planned and we want to make it the biggest reunion ever held here in Lancaster.

We are always willing to do what we can for the benefit of our race and take an active interest in the happenings of the outside world, and if called upon we will not fail in our part. There is no through transportation here, but some family is always willing to accommodate any strangers.

135

SPECIAL REPORT OF THE PRINCIPAL TO THE BOARD OF TRUSTEES, THE TUSKEGEE NORMAL AND INDUSTRIAL INSTITUTE

by Robert R. Moton

A report to the Tuskegee Board of Trustees, dated April 1, 1930, by the institute's principal, offers insights and estimates of its program and accomplishments. At this time the Board of Trustees consisted of three members of the institute's staff (Warren Logan, William H. Carter, and Dr. Moton) and sixteen white people, six of them southern. Among the white persons were William J. Schieffelin, Charles E. Mason, Julius Rosenwald, William M. Scott, Irving S. Merrell, Paul M. Warburg, and Winthrop W. Aldrich.

Finances

The work of Tuskegee Institute was begun with an appropriation of $2,000 from the Alabama State Legislature, to be used for paying teachers' salaries. No buildings were provided nor any land. It was necessary for the first Principal to provide both housing and equipment from outside sources. The Institute has been faced with this same necessity ever since. In the last ten years, the annual appropriation from the State Legislature has been increased to $5,000 while the needs of the school have increased to nearly $700,000 annually. The raising of the necessary funds has always been a heavy responsibility upon the Principal of the Institute, but never more so than in the early years of its history when the struggle was ofttimes truly heartbreaking. Few persons now living can ever know the difficulties, the discouragements, the hardships, and the sacrifices faced and endured by the Founder and his associates in the establishment of this institution. They are a part of our imponderable heritage, a legacy of inspiration whose value it is impossible to estimate.

But as the work itself began to grow, the approval and support of the public were not long withheld, and though the task of financing the work has all along been arduous, it has not been fraught with the discouragements and hardships characteristic of the earlier days. This is particularly true since the Twenty-fifth Anniversary Celebration, an event that attracted widespread and most favorable notice to the accomplishments of the institution in the way of education and the progress of the Negro. The following table indicates at a glance the expansion in the Institute's resources, by five year periods, since that time:

	Permanent Endowment	Current Expenditure	Value of Plant
1906	$1,299,727	$236,216	$ 695,342
1911	1,918,665	277,090	1,310,225
1916	2,312,149	291,602	1,482,716
1921	2,617,058	490,266	1,993,866
1926	6,681,838	508,203	2,188,271
1929	7,772,106	584,687	2,143,606

The figures given above are for the close of the fiscal year of the date indicated. The figures covering the endowment represent productive resources: they are to be increased by sums representing annuities, legacies, and other funds which were not at the time yielding an income, but which nevertheless were part of the capital of the Institute. The figures for current expenses do not represent the complete expenditures for a year, and are to be supplemented by various items for repairs and improvements for which special appropriations were made. The value of the plant is a conservative estimate which does not at all represent the cost of replacement. The chief significance of these figures is in the continuous growth which they indicate.

There is every reason to believe that this progress will continue. The Principal has confidential knowledge of large sums of money assigned to the school in the wills of friends who are not yet deceased. In some instances we have been definitely advised to this effect by quotations from these instruments. Outstanding legacies from wills already probated will amount to more than $800,000; the Eastman gift to the Campaign Fund will release the income from another million dollars in the near future. In addition to this a recent reorganization in our Campaign Department has already produced a gratifying increase in the volume of our current donations.

In view of the existing margin between our operating expenses and our assured income, we are continually concerned to investigate every possible outlook for increasing our income. On the immediate horizon the following sources appear with reasonably certain prospects: Increases in tuition fees for the regular term and the summer school should yield about $8,000; increased charges for board both for the regular term and the summer school should yield about $23,000. (The latter sum will not, however, mean a wholly net increase in income.)

There is hopeful prospect also of an increase of $20,000 from the State of Alabama when the next Legislature assembles. A group of our local citizens on their own initiative have indicated their intention to see that such a recommendation is placed before the Legislature and we have good reason to believe that it will have the approval of the Governor.

Altogether the outlook for the next few years gives promise that by possible and probable increases our income should in the near future reach something like $100,000 more than at present, with the prospect of its continuing permanently.

In response to the wise insistence of the Board, we have so managed the affairs of the institution as to live within the budget as adopted at the annual meeting. This does not mean, of course, that we have anticipated all the needs of the Institute in the course of the year, nor that emergencies have not arisen which have required us to depart from the original specifications of the budget; but it does mean that we have maintained such careful oversight of the expenditures of the Institute as to avoid embarrassments in our financing and any charge of recklessness in our disbursements. The present indications are that we will come well within the budget allowance for the current year.

It is my judgment that the Institute should continue the policy of gradually increasing the tuition fee of students as well as the charge for board as authorized by the Trustees. In view of the generally increased facilities that are being placed within reach of those who seek the advantages of training at Tuskegee Institute there need be no apology for asking the parents to share in an increasing degree the expense incident to those improvements. Our experience has been that this has produced no appreciable hardship upon the parents of the youth who come to us, save in the few cases which have thus far been taken care of through our funds for student aid. Neither is there any indication of any material falling off in the number of our students. In fact, it serves in some degree as a selective measure to retain within the Institute only those students who are most worthy of the opportunities which are provided here.

It would seem desirable in this connection also to make some systematic regulations for extending aid to deserving students, in such a way that the students themselves may know exactly what assistance may be expected and under what conditions it may be received. The past three years have been hard ones for the farmers of this section, and the effect is seen in the increasing difficulty among some of the students in meeting their bills. In some cases where the accumulated indebtedness has been large and the students' outlook not very promising we have found it desirable to drop them from the roll. But we have striven diligently to avoid dropping any worthy student for financial reasons alone.

The indications are that the period of stress and struggle is past. This does not mean, however, that we can at any time in the near future abandon the persistent, systematic effort to balance our yearly budget, and to add to the resources of the institution; but I am satisfied that the institution is so well established in the confidence of the public that, if it continues to do its work in the spirit of its Founder, there will always be a response to its appeal sufficient to meet its needs, both of operation and expansion. As one of our own Trustees has said, "We may trust future generations to be as generous and as thoughtful as our own."

Aims and Policies

In view of the widespread public interest in all that goes on at Tuskegee and particularly because of the recent developments in Tuskegee's own educational program, it is desirable for the sake of clarification to restate the aims of the institution as projected by its Founder, and maintained consistently throughout its nearly half-century of existence. It is not likely that these were the definitely conceived ends of the Institute when Dr. Washington began his work, but it is certain that clear-sighted, practical, common sense formulated these policies with the definite purpose of making the institution serve its largest and most productive function in the advancement of an impoverished, restricted and undeveloped people.

The name Tuskegee, more than other perhaps, is associated throughout the world with the idea of industrial education, now called vocational education; not that the idea originated at Tuskegee, but that the Founder of the institution advocated it both as a policy of social advancement and as an educational method with such persistence and effectiveness as ultimately to win its practical and universal acceptance in both fields. Reduced to its simplest terms, the vocational method in education is the adaptation of the standards of the so-called professions to the manual arts. The traditional school room practice is combined with the program of trade apprenticeship, to the consequent enrichment and vitalizing of both.

Time was when at Tuskegee the work of the shops was begun on the lower academic levels because of the fact that the majority of students for one reason and another did not remain at the Institute to complete the prescribed courses of both academic and trade work. Gradually, however, there has been an extension upward of the academic requirements for those receiving systematic instruction in the trades, until we finally adopted and enforced the rule that no student should be graduated from the institution who had not completed some definite trade or vocation.

Within the last half dozen years a further step has been taken and that is in the direction of raising the vocational work itself to higher academic levels, involving an extension of technical knowledge to supplement manual skill. The net result of this plan is that industrial education at Tuskegee Institute extends with systematic and progressive instruction through a period of eight years, embracing both the high school and the college. In this process, Tuskegee has not departed one iota from the principles or policies of its Founder. It continues to exemplify the philosophy enunciated by its first Principal, "We shall prosper in proportion as we learn to dignify and glorify labor and put brains and skill into the common occupations of life."

Such is Tuskegee as a school; but Tuskegee Institute is more than a school; it is a community. It exists not alone for the students who register in its classes, but from the very beginning it has consistently maintained within its purview the needs of that vastly larger body of the Negro race to whom the opportunities and privileges of a school were denied. In addition to inviting the children to the school, its Founder was equally zealous in carrying the school to their parents. Beside this, he was conscious of the significance which the work that he was doing had for the race as a whole in stimulating the general desire for progress and in developing an attitude of sympathy and cooperation on the part of white Americans by whom, in the last analysis, the progress of the Negro is so largely conditioned.

This outlook for the institution has made of Tuskegee Institute something more than the conventional school. It is a community constituting in itself a veritable social laboratory where the measures and activities calculated most effectively to advance the interests of the Negro race are set in operation with a view to their adoption in other places and by other organizations through which they may be enlarged and extended.

As these measures prove effective in the advancement of the race, there must of necessity be some modification and re-adaptation of the form which these activities will take; but Tuskegee Institute in perpetuating the policies of the Founder, will continue to promote certain of these activities which must have increasing value, not only for the Negro race, but for all peoples who face similar problems of social advancement. In the main these activities present themselves in four distinct types of service.

Tuskegee: A Demonstration

Tuskegee Institute is a demonstration of Negro capacity in maintaining a self-sufficient community; that is to say, a community in which Negroes are responsible for all of the activities incident to the maintenance of community life. Not that the community is in every instance the original source of supply for all of its needs, but that, whatever its needs, Negroes are the agents for supplying these needs whether from internal or external sources. So long as Negroes are skeptical or wanting in initiative in the development of their own social life, and so long as any considerable body of the public remains skeptical of the Negro's capacity for functioning in these directions, it is desirable to have at least one spot in the world where a continuous demonstration of this character goes on. The world looks to Tuskegee Institute more than to any other place for this sort of demonstration. It may be that the cost of certain activities may thus be greater than would be the case if our community availed itself of services contributed from the outside, but so long as the need continues for impressing the popular mind with the latent capacities to be found within retarded groups, such a demonstration is abundantly worth the cost of its maintenance.

The popular mind still persists in associating the Negro with a limited field of activity. It remains an indispensable service to convince the nation that there are within the race capacities for functioning in all fields, whether of economic, industrial, commercial, financial, professional, artistic or social endeavor.

Tuskegee: A Social Laboratory

Beyond our local campus, in the course of its history, Tuskegee has projected a number of movements looking to the advancement of the Negro race as a whole, which have been of incalculable service, some of which are still included in the school's program, others of which have been taken over by other organizations and given an application and expansion not possible to the limited resources of the Institute.

Among the first of these was the Farmers' Conference which, though held on the Institute grounds, carried its message of land ownership, improved agricultural methods and rural life in general to the farthest reaches of Negro population. After this came the Farm Demonstration Service inaugurated at Tuskegee with the Jesup Wagon, now taken over by the United States Department of Agriculture. After that came the National Negro Business League, still functioning under the leadership of Tuskegee Institute, with an increasing program for the stimulation of enterprise and efficiency in Negro business.

This was followed in time by National Negro Health Week, focusing the attention of the race and the nation upon the problems of Negro mortality and morbidity, to which has come the support and coopera- tion of more than a dozen national agencies interested in the improve- ment of public health, including the United States Public Health Serv- ice. Then came the Rosenwald schools, the prototypes of which were a half dozen rural schools for Negroes in Macon County, the first of which cost only $900, but which have grown into a vast system of nearly five thousand school buildings, providing facilities for approximately 40 per cent of the Negro school children of the rural districts of the South, involving an expenditure of more than twenty millions of dollars. Fol- lowing the war came the Inter-racial Commission with headquarters in Atlanta, Georgia, inaugurated with simultaneous meetings in Atlanta and Tuskegee, and functioning today in the closest cooperation with the Institute.

It will be enlightening to some to know that the first plans for the organization of the General Education Board were laid in Thrasher Hall at Tuskegee, while the Jeanes Fund owes its establishment to the active cooperation of Hampton and Tuskegee in encouraging the interest of Miss Anna T. Jeanes in the problems of Negro education; and only recently the Institute has had a large share in effecting the organization of Negro farmers to profit by the provision of the Agricultural Market- ing Act, administered by the Federal Farm Board.

This is only a partial list of the varied services which Tuskegee Institute renders the race and the nation outside its classroom walls; these have contributed to giving to the Institute its present prestige and leadership in the life of the race, as they have also encouraged the generosity of the public in the maintenance and expansion of an institution which is making so signal a contribution to national welfare. It is certain that were Tuskegee Institute nothing more than the traditional school, and were its activities confined to the operations of the classroom and the shop, it would not have received the generous, continuing and expanding support which has made it unique among educational institutions in this country and in the world. To remain true to her heritage and traditions, Tuskegee must continue to be such a center for experiment and initiative in social policies, having the Negro race as a whole as its objective.

Tuskegee: A Research Center

For those outside the Institute, both of the Negro race and of other races of our own country and of other countries, Tuskegee has become a center for the study of the problems of racial development and interracial contact. Very early in the course of his public activities, the Founder of the institution began to present to the world accurate data on Negro life and progress to replace the generalizations that were often the cause of misunderstanding and of real, though unintentional, misrepresentation. This matter was eventually published in the form of the *Negro Year Book,* which has become an authoritative source-book throughout the world on the facts of Negro life. This has recently been supplemented by Monroe N. Work's *Bibliography on the Negro* which was instantly accepted as the authoritative work in its field.

The books by the Founder of the Institute, including his world-renowned autobiography, *Up From Slavery* and his *History of the American Negro,* are all a part of this accumulation of data about the Negro. Recently another book from the Institute, *What The Negro Thinks,* has attracted public attention anew to the problems of the Negro, and has brought a veritable flood of testimonials concerning its usefulness to the whole cause of Negro advancement. Besides this, we have in our library a large collection of publications by Negro authors and about Negroes by authors of both races, which are invaluable to the student of racial and interracial matters.

In the personnel of our faculty, we have a group of men and women possessed of as large and intimate an acquaintance with Negro life in America as may be found in any institution in the world, and perhaps larger. There is scarcely any line of activity on behalf of the race concerning which accurate, complete, and authentic data cannot be secured at Tuskegee. With the awakened interest in Negro life, Tuskegee is at the point of rendering its largest service in supplying dependable information for the guiding of public interest and the shaping of public opinion. As this interest increases, and more intelligent effort is applied to the solution of the difficulties occasioned by the presence of the Negro in America, investigation and research to these ends must be expanded. The history and service of Tuskegee Institute in the years past make it the logical point to prosecuting these endeavors.

Tuskegee: A Point of Interracial Contact

But equally conspicuous has been the service of Tuskegee Institute as a point of contact between the two races in America in their efforts toward understanding and cooperation in the promotion of good-will. The platform laid down by the Founder of the Institute in his famous Atlanta address was eagerly accepted by white America as the point of approach toward an equitable adjustment of interracial misunderstandings and the basis for constructive achievement in the progress of the race. This program, so broad in its Christian charity, though taken advantage of in some quarters to increase the disabilities and disadvantages of the Negro in our national life, was also accepted by others, whose number constantly increases, as the basis for the ultimate removal of all such disabilities and disadvantages, and the establishment of the race in the way of progress and full participation in the benefits of our national existence. The institution has made it possible for many a friend in the white race to manifest his interest in the welfare of the Negro without defense or apology.

Tuskegee has been the spearhead of the Negro's peaceful penetration into the areas of hostility and discrimination in which the Negro's lot has been cast. Tuskegee in any other role would be unthinkable; without it the race would be without one of its major instruments in the effort to secure justice and equality before the law, as well as to promote self-respect and mutual good-will between the races.

Amid the foregoing facts, certain conclusions stand out sharply: To begin with, Tuskegee Institute is as it always has been, a growing institution that dare not contemplate the time when its needs will not be in excess of its immediate resources. On the other hand, we need not fear that any legitimate need of the institution will not be supplied by a generous, interested, and sympathetic public. I am reminded of an expression attributed to the late President Eliot to the effect that "any educational institution that lives within its income should be investigated." All our great educational institutions have continued to grow in response to the needs of a growing nation.

Tuskegee Institute serves a steadily advancing people. The continued progress of the race will call for a corresponding expansion in the program of the institution that heretofore has stood in the vanguard of its progress. It is an interesting and compelling fact that the budget of Tuskegee Institute today is more than three times as large as the entire educational budget for the State of Alabama in the year in which Tuskegee was established. The public will demand of us efficient service and progressive methods, along with a continuous and practical interpretation of the needs of the time. If we meet this demand, I have faith to believe that succeeding generations will supply the institution with the resources necessary for its successful functioning.

Because of its past, as well as its prospects for the future, I am anxious that whatever we do at Tuskegee shall be done as well as it can possibly be done by anybody under the circumstances. I am anxious that our equipment shall be of the best, consistent with rational economy and intelligent efficiency. I am anxious, too, that our teachers and workers should be representative of the best in character, culture, training, and spirit that are to be found anywhere. In our methods of service, changes are unavoidable to meet the changing times and conditions; but always the institution must be faithful to the heritage of unselfishness, service, and good-will left us by the Founder. It is a proud privilege to work at Tuskegee Institute. My own conviction is that nowhere else in the world is a larger opportunity presented to be of direct, helpful, and lasting service, not only to the Negro race, but to all mankind. It is our constant desire to measure up to this opportunity and its responsibilities.

Special Report of the Principal to the Board of Trustees, The Tuskegee Normal and Industrial Institute (Tuskegee, Ala., 1930), pp. 23–33.

136

CATHOLIC JUSTICE

Forms of Protestantism constituted the overwhelming organizational structure for Afro-American churchgoers from the eighteenth century on. With, however, increasing urbanization—especially in northern cities where the

Roman Catholic Church was quite strong—interest in Catholicism grew among Black people with some rather slight return of that interest, in the beginning, from the Church authorities. In 1925 there was formed the Federated Colored Catholics whose object was to break the color line that made mock of the name Catholic. The battle has been long and hard—and still continues. The Sixth Annual Convention of the Federated Colored Catholics met in Detroit September, 1930, and issued a call for Catholic justice in these words.

We wish to earn a decent livelihood; free from interference based upon merely racial attitudes.

We desire to educate all our boys and girls in Catholic schools, from the primary school to the university, according to each one's native ability.

We desire admission to Catholic institutions, where the denial of such admission involves the loss of tangible goods, to which, as Catholics and human beings, we may legitimately lay claim.

We wish as Catholics to insist on the sacredness of human life. We condemn every violation of law in the taking of life, no matter what the crime.

We wish to enjoy the full rights of citizenship, in direct proportion to the duties and sacrifices expected of our group, and cheerfully rendered by us to our country in peace and in war.

We wish all our fellow citizens, without exception, to be freed from the obsession that Negroes' progress is harmful to American civilization; and to recognize in word and deed that ours is a common cause; that the good of one group is the good of all.

We do not wish to be treated as "a problem," but as a multitude of human beings, sharing a common destiny and the common privilege of the Redemption with all mankind.

Published as a boxed filler accompanying an article by John M. Cooper, M.D., "Negro and Nordic," in *Interracial Review,* May, 1934; VII, 59. See John La Farge, S.J., *The Catholic Viewpoint on Race Relations* (Garden City, N.Y., 1956), pp. 62–63.

137

WHITE MEN AND A COLORED WOMAN

Anonymous

In introducing this article, reflective of a recurrent pattern of racist behavior, the editor of *The Crisis* (Dr. Du Bois) remarked: "This article is from a large Western city, and we have the name and address of the writer. She says, naturally, 'In case you use it, it must be anonymous. My name must not be appended.' "

The scene opens in a room in the Chamber of Commerce building an afternoon in April. A group of representative citizens, nine white and three colored, are gathered in their second meeting to improve educational conditions in our city by electing a Non-Partisan ticket for the school board. There are five men and four women in the white group, each one a person of some importance or prominence in a certain field. Their names are well and favorably known in community affairs as well as in the business world. An insurance agent is the sole male member in the colored group. The wife of a prominent physician and I are the Negro women present.

There is much shaking of hands and cordial greetings are exchanged before the business is entered upon. Not a shade of unpleasantness, not a suggestion of race discrimination is evinced. Mention is made and stressed that the support of the colored population is needed and that much is expected from the three delegates present in helping arouse interest in the program.

The well-known attorney seated next to me makes interesting comments from time to time on various points under discussion. They are made in undertones to me, yet are loud enough to be heard by those nearby. He asks me a question about our schools; my reply is received with doubt, evidenced by a surprised look and a lift of the eyebrows. The meeting closes and we gather in two's and three's before leaving the room. The attorney follows up his query to me by trying to disprove my answer. I like his interest in my race. I am serious and emphatic in my views and am certain I know whereof I speak. I try to marshal facts that will be convincing to him, but before I have spoken a moment he glances quickly around, lowers his voice and interrupts "I'm perfectly crazy about you, I want you to come to my office. Here is my telephone number." A card is offered me. Another glance around, a brisk handshake and he walks over to one of the other groups before leaving the room.

I am too dazed for words. Surprise, resentment, hot anger each struggle within me, all the fiercer because I know I have in no wise brought upon myself this affront. I am positive there is nothing in my appearance or actions that would lead any man to feel I would respond favorably to his advances. I am considered attractive—I admit the visage that greets me in my mirror is an agreeable one. But my manner is serious and conservative, often to the point of sternness, as those who know me most intimately will testify. Why then, does this man misjudge me?

Yet I realize I can not afford even to look conscious. For the benefit of any observers I place the card carefully in my pocketbook, nod to a white woman close by, chat for a moment with a group near the door while I wait for the other colored woman present. As we ride home together I do not mention the experience to her.

In like manner the Board of Directors of the local branch of a well-known Negro charitable organization is made up of representative persons from both races. For two years I am an active member, interested in all the phases of the work.

A new white member is elected. His subtle advances to me can not be misunderstood even though I try to ignore them. Then come telephone calls at my home. As soon as I recognize the speaker, I hang up the receiver. A dozen roses come anonymously delivered by an A.D.T. boy. I am morally certain I know the sender; yet to return them to him would be making myself ridiculous since I have no proof.

Several days later a Negro chauffeur stops at my door and hands me a note soliciting an appointment and assuring me of safety in the arrangement. It is unsigned but too well I know the writer. I ask who sent it. The chauffeur's suggestive smile and knowing look as he confirms my belief, infuriate me. The primitive in me rushes to the surface. I tear the note into pieces and fling them in the Negro's face. I vent all my rage toward his employer on him because he and I are of one blood and his insult in my opinion is the greater. He slinks away from my door, enters his car and drives rapidly away.

The Civic Betterment Group in my city is a whole souled body. Such splendid white men and women, I have never before met. In fact they often put us, the colored members, to shame as they show such broad mindedness, such fairness, such open candor in their efforts to bring about a better understanding between the races. Our deep sense of injustice rankles and makes us bitter, but they accept our partisan views good naturedly and try to show us the better, brighter side.

A minister has been the outstanding one among them. I serve on a committee with him and two others and we make an important survey. The contact is pleasant. We exchange books twice.

He invites my husband and me to a lecture at his church. We meet his wife, a woman of decidedly superior attainments. I find her charming. Sometimes he brings to a meeting a clipping for me along a line we have discussed; again, he calls my attention to a magazine article that is worth while. I frankly enjoy knowing him.

When the group meets at my home he arrives early. Casual remarks pass, a current topic is mentioned, and then before I realize it he is telling me in rapid impassioned words how he has come to admire me and how much more he wants me to mean in his life. A flood of horror rushes over me. Disgust and disappointment struggle for utterance. The deference and respect he had shown me were but masks for this dreadful thing. I want to scream, tear my hair, and yet I sit dumb as if paralyzed. The bell rings and one by one the other members arrive. I am afterwards told that my meeting was one of the best ever held. I can not remember one word that was uttered during the evening.

My husband has always been exceedingly proud of my activities in the civic and community affairs. Now, he regrets keenly my indifference and lack of interest, especially when cooperation between the races is desired. What would he think if he knew the reasons for it?

The Crisis, December, 1930; XXXVII, 416.

138

THE AMERICAN NEGRO LABOR CONGRESS

As documented earlier, the Marxist American Negro Labor Congress was formed in 1925. Though its actual members were not numerous, its contacts were wide and its impact considerable. The latter intensified as economic conditions deteriorated, commencing in the South in 1927 and devastating the entire nation by 1930. While conditions for the white working people were hard, for the Black millions they were appalling.

Commencing in 1928–1929 this congress, and the Communist Party itself, turned its attention increasingly southward and organizers, taking their lives in their hands, worked in the South. Early in 1930 the American Negro Labor Congress published a four-page folder descriptive of its purposes and work and calling attention to its forthcoming 1930 convention, to meet in St. Louis in May; the text of that folder forms document [a] below. After the convention, the congress issued a six-page program; the text of that pamphlet constitutes document [b].

[a]

What It Is:

The American Negro Labor Congress is an organization uniting Negro workers and class-conscious white workers in a common struggle against racial, social and economic oppression.

What It Stands For:

The American Negro Labor Congress stands for a militant and uncompromising struggle against all forms of white ruling-class terrorism: lynchings, etc.; against the attempts of the employers to set one group of workers against the other in order to continue more easily their exploitation of both black and white workers. The American Negro Labor Congress stands for the right of workers to organize for self-defense.

The American Negro Labor Congress fights relentlessly the fakers in the American Federation of Labor who deliberately aid the employers by refusal to organize the unorganized, by barring Negroes from membership in existing unions and discriminating against the few who have fought their way into these unions in spite of every attempt to keep them out. The American Negro Labor Congress not only fights against the oppressors and exploiters of black and white labor, and their tools and allies in the reactionary American Federation of Labor, but against the treacherous middle-class Negro leaders who have consistently betrayed and fooled the Negro masses and whose leadership of the race, heretofore unchallenged, has been one long record of cowardly wavering and out and out treachery to the interests of the masses. The American Negro Labor Congress stands for a stern struggle against all enemies of the working class and for the linking up of the struggles of the American Negro workers with the struggles of the enslaved colonial masses and of the class-conscious white workers in all countries.

In order successfully to resist the attacks of the employers, the workers must be organized into industrial unions on a basis of complete equality and full participation by the Negro workers in the leadership of the unions.

In order successfully to resist white ruling class terrorism in the South and fight for the right to determine their own form of government in those sections where Negroes form the majority of the population, the Negro masses of the South must have the active support of the Negro workers in the North and of the white workers, North and South. Negro and white workers must make this fight together! There must be more instances of working-class solidarity as at Gastonia, N.C., where Southern white and Negro workers stood shoulder to shoulder, under the leadership of the National Textile Workers Union (affiliated with the T.U.U.L.), against the mill owners ònd their racial hostility propaganda.

What It H ıs Done:

The American Negro Labor Congress during the four years of its existence has led many struggles of the Negro workers against exploitation on the job, oppressive landlordism and bad housing conditions, discrimination in public places, white ruling class terrorism: lynching, police brutality, savage sentences, extradition of Negro workers to the South to face harsh prison conditions and possible lynching.

The American Negro Labor Congress led the Fig and Date workers strike in Chicago, Ill., the laundry workers' strike in Carteret, N.J.; the Moving Picture Operators' strike in New York City, and gave active support to many other struggles of Negro and white workers, including the recent Subway workers' strike in New York City. It has supported all efforts to organize the industries in which Negroes work.

The American Negro Labor Congress has helped the harassed Negro tenants to organize to fight the landlords, their rent raises and evictions. It has led the way in organizing several tenant leagues throughout the country.

The American Negro Labor Congress has organized and led demonstrations of black and white workers against restaurants and theatres which discriminate against Negroes.

The American Negro Labor Congress, in cooperation with other militant working-class organizations (such as the International Labor Defense, the Workers International Relief, the Trade Union Unity League and its affiliated unions, the All-America Anti-Imperialist League, etc.) has carried on an extensive agitation against the influence of the imperialist ideology of racial separation and hostility among the working class, and has been able, in many instances, to get Negro and white workers to co-operate in their common struggle.

The American Negro Labor Congress sent delegates to both the first and second congresses of the League Against Imperialism and aided materially in organizing the world-wide front of the workers and colonial masses against world imperialism.

What It Is Doing:

In its task of organizing the Negro workers and farmers, North and South, to resist the growing attacks of the bosses, the American Negro Labor Congress is calling its national convention in May, 1930. In its determination to carry the fight into the South, St. Louis, Mo., has been selected for the convention.

The American Negro Labor Congress is also one of the chief sponsors for the international conference of Negro workers called for July, 1930, in London, England.

The Congress is holding mass meetings throughout the country protesting the conditions under which Negroes are forced to live in this country, protesting the American occupation of Haiti, and mobilizing the masses, black and white, for the struggle for Negro liberation.

Conclusion:

The Negro masses throughout the world are the victims of one of the most monstrous systems of exploitation the world has known. In Africa, the West Indies, the United States, etc., our lot is that of an oppressed and exploited subject race. Mob violence, lynching, peonage, segregation, debt imprisonment, convict lease labor laws, jim-crowism, denial of education, are some of the methods used by the landowners and employers, in collusion with the banks, courts and police, to enslave the Negro masses.

These terrible conditions, which face the Negro not only in the South but throughout the imperialist world, call for effective organization and militant methods of struggle on the part of the Negro workers and farmers, in alliance with the class-conscious white workers.

It is futile to expect the wavering, treacherous middle-class Negro leaders to give militant leadership to the struggles of the masses. Such leadership can only come from the workers in the factories and shops who constitute the membership of the American Negro Labor Congress. Only through trained, intelligent and courageous working-class leadership can the masses resist oppression and achieve real emancipation.

Every Negro worker and farmer should join the American Negro Labor Congress. Every class-conscious white worker should give it his support.

Join the American Negro Labor Congress!
Build Working-Class Leadership!
Help Organize the Unorganized Into Militant Industrial Unions!
Fight the A. F. of L. Fakers!
Expose the Negro Reformist Leaders!
Protest the Murder of Haitian Workers and Peasants By United States Imperialists!
Demand Immediate Withdrawal of Marines from Haiti, Nicaragua and China!
Fight Against Imperialist Wars!
Down With U.S. Imperialism!
Down With World Imperialism!
Long Live the Heroic Workers and Peasants of Haiti!

[b]

PROGRAM OF THE AMERICAN NEGRO LABOR CONGRESS
Preamble

The condition of the twelve million Negroes in the United States is that of an oppressed and exploited subject race overwhelmingly composed of workers and poor farmers.

The abolition of chattel slavery changed only the form of oppression by the wealthy white ruling class. The brutal system of torture and intimidation by means of which the Negro was held in subjection under chattel slavery has been maintained to keep the "freed" Negro masses as a slave caste at the bottom of American society. Lynchings and mob violence, jim-crowism, discrimination, disfranchisement, segregation, are some of the forms by which white domination is perpetuated. Every instrument of capitalism and its government (the legislatures, the courts, army, police, etc.) is used to further Negro oppression.

It is a fundamental error to assume that our oppression arises from racial differences. Racial differences simply serve to make more brutal this oppression by making possible a more intensive exploitation of Negro workers than of white workers, who are also exploited by the ruling class. Negroes thus suffer a double exploitation, being exploited both as Negroes and as workers.

To appreciate the true nature of our oppression it is necessary that we understand the class structure of the society in which we live. In capitalist society we distinguish two classes: one class, the workers or proletariat, possessing only its labor power and compelled to sell it in order to exist; and another class possessing all means of production and known as the capitalist or bourgeoisie. To the first class belong the vast bulk of the Negroes in this country.

Between these two main classes are various intermediate classes (intermediate because they do not belong completely to the working class—the proletariat—nor to the big bourgeoisie—the capitalists). These intermediate classes are called the petty bourgeoisie. To them belong the small landowners, the small tradesmen, and also the intelligentsia (the intellectuals) who are in the service of the bourgeoisie (big capitalists).

These intermediate classes take a vacillating position in the struggle between the two main classes, inclining more particularly to the side of the big capitalists (the bourgeoisie) and only under certain conditions to the side of the working class (the proletariat). Between the two main classes an everlasting struggle goes on. The history of present day society is the history of class struggle. On one side the workers struggling for the right to exist decently, the right to higher wages and shorter work day, the right to organize to fight for their demands (as the workers advance politically these demands take on the form of a struggle to possess the wealth created by their labor power, which develops into a struggle for the conquest of power—the capture of the State—as the only means through which this can be achieved). On the other side we see the capitalists, the employing class, themselves wallowing in luxury, fighting to force ever lower standards of living upon the working class, lower wages, longer hours, the employment of children in the mines and factories, rationalization (the installing of machinery and the forcing of one worker to do work which formerly took three and four workers to perform). At the same time, the capitalists attempt to increase the price of necessities to the workers, by raising rents, food prices, etc. To maintain this evil system, the capitalists promote strong nationalist sentiments, race hatreds, prejudices against the Negro, the Japanese, the Chinese, and the white foreign-born workers, religious superstitions, etc., in the attempt to divide the workers along lines of nationalism, race and religion and to get cannon-fodder for their imperialist wars through which they accomplish the murder of the workers of other countries and the subjugation of the peoples of Asia and Africa.

Slavery, officially abolished, still exists in the south. Negro workers and working farmers are arrested for slight offenses and farmed out to white planters. Negroes are forced to work for starvation wages on the plantations and find it necessary to borrow from their employers in order to live. They are charged robbery prices for supplies which they must buy from the landlord or employer. They go into debt and are then required by the law to remain on the plantation until they work out their debt. In the meantime their condition forces them deeper and deeper into the debt of the landlord and employer, who may sell or transfer his claim against the Negro share cropper—which really amounts to selling the Negro workers.

Three-quarters of the Negro population of the United States still remain in the South, toiling on the land, creating wealth for the white master class. Few of them own the land they work on. The victims of a gigantic and brutal conspiracy on the part of the landowners, the banks, the courts, religious bodies and fascist organizations like the Ku Klux Klan, the American Legion, the state militia, they are forced into a position of economic helplessness and dependence. The most bold-faced robbery is perpetrated upon them by the landlords and employers. They are kept continuously on the border of starvation. Forced to live in flimsy shacks, in unsanitary, low-lying sections not fit for human habitation, the Negro workers are the worst sufferers from the storms and floods which frequently devastate the south.

With the rapid industrialization of the south, and the mass migration of recent years, over two and a half million Negroes have deserted the land for industry. In industry they find every obstacle which the white worker has to overcome tremendously multiplied. Because of their color they are easily set apart by employers for an especially brutal exploitation. They are paid less for the same work and forced to toil at the most menial and tiring tasks, at longer hours than their white fellow workers and under intolerable working conditions. In addition to the struggle against economic oppression and exploitation they must wage as workers, they are faced with the necessity of waging a struggle against race prejudice and white domination.

Race prejudice, fostered by the employers, is also utilized by the reactionary trade union leaders to deprive Negro workers of the benefits of unionization. Only a handful of labor unions admit Negroes to their ranks, and of these only the left wing unions concede them full equality and participation in leadership. Thus of two million and a half Negroes in the industries, scarcely 200,000 are organized into unions.

The majority of Negro workers who are in the industries are not organized and are a part of the great bulk of unorganized labor whom the reactionary officials of the American Federation of Labor refuse to organize. The organization of these Negro workers together with their white fellow workers into powerful industrial unions is absolutely essential for the improvement of their conditions.

There is urgent need for a militant mass Negro organization to lead the struggle of the Negro workers and working farmers. To be effective such a mass organization must be under the leadership of the Negro proletariat, as the only class capable of waging the struggle. There already exist organizations of workers under the leadership and control of the Negro middle class (petty bourgeoisie). These organizations have failed to prosecute the struggle for emancipation of the Negro masses for the very reason that they are controlled by the Negro middle-class. The leaders of these organizations are not concerned with the demands of the working-class except in so far as the formulation of these demands can be used to force concessions for their own set or class. These leaders (property owners, landlords, real estate agents, preachers, prostitute college professors, editors of middle-class magazines and newspapers, heads of various "advancement" and "improvement" associations) have a stake in the system under which the masses of Negroes are oppressed and exploited. They are therefore not in favor of its abolition, but merely seek a fuller share in the exploitation of their own people and a higher social status for their own class. Moreover, they are incapable of leading the struggle because they have neither a clear understanding of the nature of the struggle (which is essentially a class struggle, and not, as they pretend, a purely racial struggle) nor the courage to prosecute it militantly enough to insure success.

To carry out the purpose stated in the preamble and to fill the need for a Negro mass organization under the leadership of the Negro proletariat, the American Negro Labor Congress was organized with the program which follows.

The American Negro Labor Congress calls upon all Negro and white workers who agree with its program and purposes and are ready to obey its constitution to join the ranks of the American Negro Labor Congress.

The Organization of All Negro and White Workers into Industrial Unions

No less than two million Negroes are employed in American industry. This number is constantly increasing, due to intolerable conditions on the farms, the rapid industrialization of the South, and the mass migrations of Negroes away from Southern white ruling class terrorism.

These Negro workers are largely unorganized as a result of the refusal of the American Federation of Labor to organize the unorganized workers. Most of the A. F. of L. craft unions either bar Negroes from membership or practise gross discriminations against them. Thus does reactionary trade union leadership play the game of the employers, which is to set one group of workers against another and prevent the unity of the working class.

Because Negroes are unorganized, they are paid less than white workers doing the same work, they are worked longer hours under intolerable conditions, and at the most menial jobs.

The organization of the large mass of Negro and white workers in the same industrial unions is imperative to the emancipation of the working class.

The AMERICAN NEGRO LABOR CONGRESS fights for:

The removal of all restrictions against the admittance of Negro workers into existing trade unions and their full participation in all offices and affairs of the union.

The immediate organization of all Negro and white workers into industrial unions in industries where no union now exists.

The calling of Inter-Racial Labor Conferences as a step toward the organization of Negro workers and for the promotion of the solidarity of all workers regardless of race or color.

The Emancipation of Negro Farmers and Agricultural Laborers

Three-quarters of the Negroes in the United States still remain in the South, toiling on the land. Few of them own their own farms. Where they do, the farm is heavily mortgaged, including live stock and implements. The crop, too, is often mortgaged and the Negro farmer is usually forced to sell at a price set by the white banker or plantation owner. The Negro tenant farmer is constantly in fear of eviction and is at the mercy of the landlord, the banks, and the courts which operate in favor of the white ruling class.

The Negro farm laborer is a virtual slave on the land, frequently held against his will, paid any wage that the white plantation owner chooses to give, subject to arbitrary dismissal if he refuses to accept the most outrageous deductions for board, lodging and supplies.

Once in debt, Negroes are compelled by the law of the white ruling class to remain on the farms as peons, until the debt is worked out. Claims for debt can be sold or transferred, which really amounts to selling the Negro.

A vicious system of vagrancy laws, debt imprisonment, convict lease labor, is used by the white ruling class of the South for the actual re-enslavement of large masses of Negro workers. Whippings, shootings and deliberate murder of Negroes seeking to escape are of frequent occurrence.

The only effective method of combating this vicious system is the organization of all poor farmers and farm laborers, Negro and white.

The AMERICAN NEGRO LABOR CONGRESS fights for:

The organization of Negro agricultural workers and farmers to put a stop to existing conditions of landlord domination; to abolish oppressive conditions of work on the farms, and to establish on all farms the eight-hour day and the five-day week.

The building of farmers' co-operatives of Negro and white farmers, to get cheap credit, purchase seed, machinery and live stock and to market crops.

The abolition of imprisonment for debt and the convict lease system under which Negroes and workers of other oppressed races are framed up, put in jail and farmed out to private corporations under conditions of unspeakable brutality for the personal profit of the business interests and state officials.

The drawing of all oppressed farmers, black and white, into a united nationwide movement for their liberation and the establishment of the closest ties between the industrial workers and the farmers.

Against "Jim-Crowism" and Social Restrictions

In the South, the Negro is restricted by law to separate sections in street cars, waiting rooms and all places of assemblage and amusement. Negro and white workers may not meet together, under penalty of lynching.

In the North, the Negro finds himself barred from many restaurants, theatres, hotels, and is often forcibly ejected when he attempts to enter these places. Fear of race riots, lynchings, police brutality, injustice in the courts, has operated to "keep the Negro in his place"—the place set for him by the white ruling class. This attitude of surrender must be changed to one of active resistance to "Jim-Crowism," whether it shows itself in legal or semi-legal restrictions or merely as social intolerance.

The AMERICAN NEGRO LABOR CONGRESS will organize groups of white workers to join with Negro workers in exercising their right to enter all public places on the same basis as white workers.

The AMERICAN NEGRO LABOR CONGRESS fights for:

The right of freedom of press, speech and assemblage.

The removal of all legal and extra-legal hindrances to the full exercise of these rights, including the abolition of restrictions against intermarriage between individuals of different races or color.

Removal of All Restrictions Against Negroes in the Military Service

The "caste" system operates against Negroes in the military arm of the government just as it does in the economic, industrial and social spheres, and it must be just as uncompromisingly fought.

While the AMERICAN NEGRO LABOR CONGRESS brands as mass murder every form of imperialist aggression and warfare, it insists that Negroes be given the same status in the army, navy and air forces as whites.

The system in operation under which workers, both Negro and white, are placed under the arbitrary control of officers who are set apart from the "privates" through a cunningly contrived system of selection and training must be uncompromisingly fought. Soldiers and sailors must demand the selection of their own officers from their own ranks. Opportunities for training must be equally available to all drafted and enlisted men, black or white, and all branches of the service must be open to all, regardless of race or color. Obstacles thrown in the way of Negroes receiving training as officers, of being promoted to high ranks or serving as officers, in white forces, must be wiped out.

The AMERICAN NEGRO LABOR CONGRESS fights for:

The removal of all color restrictions in all branches of the military service, both in war and peace.

Removal of all "Jim-Crow" practices in military and officers' training schools and camps.

For the right of Negroes to fill office of any rank.

Discontinuance of the present practice of using Negro troops as "labor battalions."

For the right of all service men to organize and elect their own officers

Against Segregation and High Rents

Negroes are forced to live in segregated districts, notorious for their unsanitary and unhealthy condition. This is true in northern as well as in southern communities. Real estate agents and landlords, black and white, deliberately foster this caste system in order to squeeze the last drop of profit out of the extortionate rents charged Negro tenants. Negro districts are the object of wanton neglect by both the landlords and the city authorities.

High rents on low incomes mean overcrowding, lodgers; mothers and children forced into industry. The result is sickness and death out of all proportion to the number of the Negro population. Deaths from tuberculosis are from three to six times the rate among whites. The death rate of Negro children is terrific.

Negroes must be organized into tenants' leagues to resist segregation and the accompanying evils of landlordism.

The AMERICAN NEGRO LABOR CONGRESS fights for:

The removal of all legal restrictions which force Negroes to live in segregated districts.

The enforcement of penalties against all landlords who discriminate against Negroes in renting, in charging them higher rents than they charge white tenants, or in refusing to make adequate repairs or maintain houses in sanitary condition.

The abolition of the right to evict unemployed workers and the widow or unemployed children of deceased workers.

Expenditure of public funds for paving streets, for parks, water supply, sewage, lighting and other city improvements in proportion to the population of a particular district regardless of race or color.

Organization of Negro and white workers into tenants' leagues to attain these demands.

Equal School Facilities for Negro and White Children

The educational system of the United States is deliberately designed to perpetuate capitalist control of the lives of the workers of the country. The schools are used as a weapon of white oppression to keep Negroes as a degraded caste at the bottom of capitalist society. Negro children are segregated into "Jim-Crow" schools, which are overcrowded, dilapidated and unsanitary; the teaching force is inadequate, untrained, and under-paid; the courses of study are below the standards set for white children. In the South appropriations for Negro schools are less than half the amount spent on white schools. The school term is so short that it is impossible for a child to complete even an elementary course of study before reaching adulthood. In the entire country only a little over one per cent of Negro children ever reach high school.

Text books and courses of study are designed to instill into the minds of both Negro and white children the inferiority of the Negro. The Negro is sent out into the world with a hopeless, servile attitude of mind, which is an excellent preparation for the exploitation practised on him throughout his working life by the white ruling class; the white child leaves school with prejudice and contempt for his Negro brother and thus becomes a ready accomplice in perpetuating racial separation, hatred and oppression.

The AMERICAN NEGRO LABOR CONGRESS fights for:

The right of every Negro child to a free, adequate education fitting him for any occupation or calling he desires.

The immediate abolition of "Jim-Crow" schools.

Equal school facilities for communities where Negroes are in majority.

Uniform expenditures for all schools in proportion to population regardless of race or color.

Equal pay for Negro and white teachers.

Selection and promotion of all teachers on a merit basis regardless of race or color.

Unionization of all school teachers in the same organization regardless of race or color.

Inclusion in the school curriculum of the contribution of Negroes to the revolutionary struggles throughout the world; their outstanding contributions to art and science and a true picture of the outrages practised on them by the white ruling classes of the world in transporting them into slavery from their native homes in Africa, with the subsequent stealing of their countries by the imperialists.

Against Political Disfranchisement

Even the delusion fostered among the white workers that they control the government by their ballot is denied the Negro in the South. Negroes are threatened with violence if they attempt to vote. They are denied the slightest pretense to a voice in the affairs of their communities.

Only organized resistance will overcome this attitude of the white ruling class. The AMERICAN NEGRO LABOR CONGRESS knows that it is futile to expect justice for either Negro or white workers under the present system of government, run as it is in the interests of landlords, financiers and manufacturers. At the same time, we must organize to exercise our rights at the polls regardless of threats and violence.

The AMERICAN NEGRO LABOR CONGRESS fights for:

The removal of all restrictions, actual or implied, which operate to prevent Negroes from voting, and will organize Negro and white workers to resist the terrorist tactics of the fascist American Legion, Ku Klux Klan, Vigilante Committees and other agents of white ruling class government against Negro voters.

Against Discrimination in the Courts

All branches of government are made use of against the workers, and particularly the Negro workers. Barbarous jail sentences, extortionate fines, are the legal weapons by which the white master class keeps the Negro in subjection.

The AMERICAN NEGRO LABOR CONGRESS fights for:

The abolition of all discriminatory practices in the courts.

To resist mob violence, police brutality and the attacks of the Ku Klux Klan and similar terrorist groups.

The immediate enactment of a Federal law against lynching as a capital crime, with severe penalties against all states and counties where lynchings occur.

For the Organization of the Negro Masses Against Imperialism

Millions of Negroes in Africa, Central America and the West Indies suffer under imperialist aggression and domination.

These colonials are victims of one of the most monstrous systems of exploitation the world has known.

Following the World War, the pauperization of the colonials has assumed unprecedented dimensions as the imperialist plunderers proceed to distill the blood of the colonial workers and peasants into huge profits for the payment of their war debts and the renewed preparations for another world slaughter in which they are now brazenly engaged.

Robbed of their lands, their village communes deliberately destroyed, the once independent and happy peasantry of Africa and Asia is being forced into the mines and the huge privately-owned plantations of white imperialists. In Trinidad, in Jamaica and the other West Indian islands, imperialism shows the same manifestations, a large strata of pauperized workers forced to begging on the streets and their women to open prostitution.

African and Indian workers and peasants are being murdered by the thousands for daring to protest against the atrocious conditions which imperialism inflicts upon the masses. The blood of thousands of natives of Ruanda, East Africa, has been spilled by British and Belgian imperialists acting in collusion. In Central America, in Haiti, in the Virgin Islands many thousands of workers and peasants have been sacrificed to the bloody greed of American imperialism. In the seat of Toussaint L'Ouverture, in the seat of Dessalines and Christophe, there now sits a middle-class traitor, who as puppet president aids in the foreign exploitation of the Haitian masses. The free republic of Haiti, established by the unparalleled heroism of her former black slaves, who won for the Negro race the distinction of being the only race in history that, weakened and degraded by chattel slavery, succeeded in the face of the hostility of the entire imperialist world in winning its liberty on the battle-field, lies raped and bleeding, a victim to rising Yankee imperialism. In Santo Domingo, the same middle class which furnished traitors against the interests of the masses, both in Haiti and the United States (in fact, throughout the world) has further helped to shackle the country with the chains of a new Dawes Plan.

The World War, the Russian Revolution and the great movements of revolt against imperialism on the part of the Asiatic and Mussulman nationalities brought inspiration to and helped arouse the consciousness of millions of Negroes in Africa and the West Indies, as well as in the United States.

The history of the Negro in the United States fits him for an important rôle in the liberation struggle of the entire African race. The U.S. is today the center of modern Negro culture and the crystallization of Negro protest.

It is the task of the AMERICAN NEGRO LABOR CONGRESS to point out to the Negro masses that they are not the only people suffering from oppression of capitalism and imperialism; that the workers and peasants of Europe and Asia and of America also are the victims of imperialism; that the struggle against imperialism is not the struggle of any one people, but of all the peoples of the world; that in India and China, in Persia and Turkey, as in Egypt, Morocco and the Congo, the oppressed colored colonial peoples are struggling heroically against their imperialist exploiters.

It is the task of the AMERICAN NEGRO LABOR CONGRESS to rally the Negro masses of America to the international struggle against imperialism, and to courageously point out what is of great moment to the Liberation Struggle of the Negro peoples of the world: that that portion of the white workers and peasants which is in struggle against imperialism and capitalism, and which has repeatedly shown its willingness and desire to establish a common front of struggle with the colored masses against imperialism (i.e., the active opposition of the French Communists to the imperialist war against the Moroccans which took the form of sabotaging the French Army, delaying mobilization, blowing up transports, etc., the material help extended by the workers and peasants of the Soviet Union and the Communist Parties of the world, to the Chinese Revolution and the Turkish, Indian and Egyptian Nationalist movements, to the demand for a Black South African Republic, etc.) is led by the Communist International, whose membership numbers many millions of black, white, brown and yellow workers throughout the world.

The AMERICAN NEGRO LABOR CONGRESS fights:

Against imperialist oppression.

Against the American occupation of Haiti and the presence of United States marines in Nicaragua and other Central American countries.

Against American imperialist aggression in Mexico.

For the freedom of Africa, of Haiti, of Santo Domingo, of Central America, and for a free Federated West Indian Republic.

Pamphlet, without pagination, issued in New York City in 1930. Reprinted in full; original in editor's possession.

139

NEGRO AUTHORS WEEK: AN EXPERIMENT
by C. Ruth Wright

The effort to encourage Afro-American authorship and readership is quite old. One such organized attempt, occurring late in 1930, is described in the following article.

To have an entire week devoted to the study and promotion of Negro literature and Negro writers seemed an excellent idea to Dr. R. R. Wright, Jr., editor of *The Christian Recorder* and pastor of Jones Tabernacle A.M.E. Church in Philadelphia. He communicated this idea to some of the younger members of his congregation and they seized upon it enthusiastically.

The idea was to have an entire week devoted to a series of lectures with a distinguished Negro author speaking each night and a comprehensive exhibit of books by and about Negroes. The members and committee decided that the lecture and exhibit should be held at the church and a nominal admission fee charged to cover expenses. The purpose of the week should be "to encourage the young Negro to greater aspiration in the field of literature; to acquaint the citizens of Philadelphia with the achievements of the Negroes in literature; and to increase interest in the same."

That such an idea could be successfully put over caused a little doubt in the minds of the promoters, as lectures are not exactly popular among Philadelphia colored people. Concerts, dramas, and the purely social affairs, as dances, etc., are often successes, financially and otherwise. But to have five lectures in nightly succession and *charge* for them seemed, in advance, indicative of failure.

Preparations for a big Negro Authors' Week were started, however, and eight prominent authors were invited to appear during the week of December 7. A committee of young people was formed in the church, and a patrons' committee composed of Philadelphia citizens was organized. Each member of the latter committee sent to the secretary a list of from ten to twenty names of persons who would probably be interested in Negro Authors Week to the extent of becoming a patron by purchasing two season tickets. A mailing list was compiled in this way, which, though not very extensive (numbering hardly five hundred names in all) was nevertheless valuable. A high percentage of persons responded with checks to the letters sent them. Through the contributions of patrons there was enough money to meet expenses the week before the first lecture was given.

Advertisement took the form largely of correspondence although the press provided advance notices. Announcements were sent through the churches and the public schools, and free admission tickets for the children were given to those schools whose principals asked for them. Some teachers had exhibits of colored authors' pictures in their classrooms.

The Week opened Monday night, December 7, with Mr. James Weldon Johnson as the speaker on "The Negro in Art and Literature", and Mr. Arthur Huff Fauset, a public school principal and author, presiding. A large and enthusiastic audience of white and colored people met Mr. Johnson, whose delightful manner, "charmingly nonchalant" as it was described by one enthusiastic youngster, completely won over his listeners.

Tuesday night, Dr. Kelly Miller of Howard University, spoke on the subject of "The Negro Writing in His Own Defense." Dr. Miller gave an informing talk of the development of journalism among Negroes.

Wednesday night brought the largest audience of the week. Dr. W. E. B. Du Bois of *The Crisis* was the speaker on "The Opportunities for the Negro in the Field of Fiction." The speaker defended the failure of the Negro writer to measure up fully to standards of genuine artistry. "Publishers now refuse to publish books of Negro writers unless they are the type he feels will appeal to the white reader. The Negro writer, therefore, must produce a book in which the picture drawn of the Negro dovetails with the mental picture the whites have of the Negro." Mrs. Alice Dunbar-Nelson presided.

On Thursday night the subject of "Negro History" was capably handled by Dr. Carter G. Woodson, the historian and director of the Associated Publishers of Washington, D.C. Dr. Woodson reviewed for his hearers the various problems of Negro research.

Friday night was Poets' Night. A number of local poets read their compositions. The audience was disappointed at the absence of Langston Hughes, who was ill, but again became enthusiastic under the spell of Dr. Leslie P. Hill's introduction to the subject of Negro poetry. Mrs. Georgia Douglass Johnson, of Washington, charmed the audience with a delightfully intimate and personal sketch of various present day poets of her own acquaintance.

In addition to the lectures, a large exhibit of books was offered. About two dozen publishers cooperated by sending their publications by and about Negroes. The Library of Congress sent a collection of books for exhibit and the local colored newspapers lent files and old editions of their papers for exhibition.

These books were put on exhibit in the small lecture rooms surrounding the main auditorium and were classified as follows: Fiction, Poetry, Biography, History and Sociology, Religion, Music, Drama, Journalism, Philadelphia Authors, Government Exhibit, and Rare books, including Ph.D. theses and old books, some of the latter over 100 years old.

The sale of books, however, did not come up to the rather large expectation of the committee, and many had to be returned to the publishers. This may have been due, partly of course, to the general economic depression, but it was also indicative of what almost every speaker during the week had stated—that Negroes have not yet reached the stage where they will buy books in anything like large numbers.

Nevertheless there is no reason to doubt that a very real and perhaps far-reaching interest was stimulated by this exhibit which gave hundreds of Negroes the chance to see the literary productions of their race.

The most popular authors as far as sales went, were James Weldon Johnson, Carter G. Woodson, Arthur Fauset, and W. E. B. Du Bois. The publisher whose books proved most salable was the Associated Publishers, Inc., of Washington, D.C., a Negro concern. Sales in fiction were surprisingly low. Poetry was most popular, and history and sociology ranked next. This was probably due to the fact that many persons buying were making their first contacts with Negro literature and when they asked the sales people for recommendations of good books, they were usually directed to some anthology, or history of literature.

The attendance at the meetings averaged about 300 people a night. Of the total attendance of 1500, the committee estimated that about 1200 of the number attended at least one lecture. Quite a few patrons, incidentally, attended three or four lectures and some were present every night.

We do not hesitate to say that if such a Negro Authors Week under efficient management should be held every year in a hundred American cities, the outlook for Negro literature would be entirely revolutionized.

The Crisis, April, 1931; XXXVIII, 124.

140

THE YOKINEN TRIAL

On February 27, 1931, the Communist Party of the United States announced that a public trial would be held of August Yokinen, a member, on the charge of white chauvinism. The trial was held before two thousand people at the Harlem Casino the afternoon of February 28. Fraternal orders and organizations sent delegates; the audience selected fourteen people—seven white, seven Black (one of the latter a woman)—as the jury. Presiding at the trial was Alfred Wagenknecht; prosecuting was Clarence A. Hathaway; defending was Richard B. Moore. The trial was part of the process of growing concern in the Party about the Afro-American and the South; in 1928 the position of the Party emphasized what it saw as the class, race, and national elements combining in the special oppression of Black people and in 1929 the Party became fully involved in organizational efforts in the South with the Gastonia, N.C., strike as a highlight. Soon after this trial, the Party devoted itself in particular to the defense of the Scottsboro Boys.

Shortly after this trial, Yokinen was arrested by the U.S. Immigration

Service and held for deportation. He was defended by the International Labor Defense, but did suffer deportation late in 1932. The trial captured headlines in the Black press and in *The New York Times*. From one of the former follows an account of the trial itself.

August Yokinen, white, a member and janitor of the Finnish Workers' Club, 15 W. 126th Street, facing a workers jury at the Harlem Casino, 116th Street and Lenox Avenue, on charges of showing race prejudice against Negroes, was indefinitely expelled from the party.

A mixed crowd of about 2,000 crowded the hall until police turned them away because of lack of space. It was the first public Communist trial held in the United States, but according to a member of the party's secretariat, more will take place if its members fail to carry out the program laid down.

Thousands of leaflets were distributed, especially in Harlem, and letters were sent to many working class organizations to send delegates. One hundred thirteen organizations responded with 211 delegates.

Alfred Wagenknecht, white, presided as judge, while C. A. Hathaway, also white, a leading member of the Communist party and editor of the *Daily Worker,* was prosecutor.

The offense with which Yokinen was charged, occurred about two months ago when Harold Williams, and other workers attended a dance at the Finnish Hall and were pushed into a corner, shunned and even threatened with being ejected.

Hathaway branded Yokinen's actions as being detrimental to the working class struggle achieved by working class solidarity and greatly in discord with the party program. Yokinen, according to the prosecutor, showed a chauvinistic tendency by not coming to the rescue of these workers and by saying: "If Negroes come into the dance hall and poolroom they will want to use our baths ("for which they are justly proud," said Hathaway) and I for one do not want to bathe with a Negro."

Hathaway recalled the case of discrimination against Lewis, a Negro worker at Stalingrad, by a white engineer from the U.S., who was tried for the act, and deported from the Soviet Union; he also recalled the Gastonia strike where the white workers saved Otto Hall from a lynching mob by rushing him to another town.

Richard B. Moore, national Negro director of the International Labor Defense, who was the Communist candidate for state attorney-general, was counsel for the defense. He asked the jury not to be severe with Yokinen after admitting that his client was guilty of a grievous crime, but to place the blame where it rightfully belongs. "The vicious bourgeois system, the damnable capitalist system, which preaches corruption and discrimination, is the real criminal," he said.

Moore pointed out that Yokinen was not as schooled as were some of our comrades, who practiced these same tendencies and were never brought to trial and that he spoke and understood very little English and was therefore not able to read the documents and instructions from the party organs that the prosecutor offered as exhibits.

"Let us not yell for the blood of Yokinen, but examine ourselves to see how far we have contributed to this thing with which the defendant is charged.

"I would rather have my head severed from my body by the lynchers than be expelled from the Communist Internationale," shouted Moore. At this the crowd broke into tremendous applause and cheering.

The jury, composed of seven Negro workers, including a woman, and seven white workers, selected by the workers present, retired after the attorneys had summarized, and remained out for about thirty minutes, and after quite a bit of deliberation returned with a verdict of guilty. Eleven voted for expulsion.

The verdict proclaimed that he be expelled with one condition: that he might be re-admitted to the party after he had demonstrated in deeds his solidarity with the Negro workers and proved his worthiness by performing among other tasks (1) the selling of an adequate number of *The Liberator,* organ of the League of Struggle for Negro Rights, and (2) also to join this organization; (3) to lead demonstrations against certain restaurants that discriminate against Negroes in Harlem; (4) to immediately go to the Finnish Club, call a mass meeting and give them the report of the trial, couched in such terms as to destroy white chauvinistic tendencies in the club, and (5) to carry on in the club a persistent struggle for the admittance of Negro workers and the granting of all privileges, including use of the poolroom, bathroom and restaurant.

All during the procedure Yokinen sat with bowed head.

Never before in the history of his membership in the party had Moore met defeat from another speaker, regardless of the nature of the discussion or debate, and it is the general opinion of the masses that he more than credited himself against Hathaway.

The Afro-American (Baltimore), March 7, 1931, p. 7. See *The New York Times,* February 28, 1931, p. 22; March 2, 1931, pp. 1–2.

141

EQUAL OPPORTUNITY: NO MORE, NO LESS!

by the Manhattan Medical Society

In May, 1930, Afro-American physicians, facing the racism characteristic of the general organized medical profession, formed the Manhattan Medical Society. The original Executive Committee was chaired by Dr. Ernest R. Alexander; remaining members of the committee were doctors: Aaron L. MacGhee, Harold L. Ellis, W. A. Freeman, L. C. Wormley, R. S. Wilkinson, J. L. Wilson, Louis T. Wright, and R. H. Young. Its first publication was a pamphlet, issued January 28, 1931, and addressed to Edwin R. Embree, president of the Julius Rosenwald Fund. It follows in full.

Dear Sir:

In the *Pittsburgh Courier* under date of December 31, 1930, there is a statement released through the Associated Negro Press of your remarks at the dedicatory exercises of the Nurses' Home of the Mercy Hospital in Philadelphia. In these remarks there are many issues of vital interest to the Negro members of the medical profession, and, since we disagree with you on so many points, we feel it incumbent upon us to formally answer your statements and to ask you a few pertinent questions.

Your remarks have been interpreted by us, and we think not incorrectly, as justifying the acceptance of the so-called Negro hospitals in Northern states. We are led to believe that you and the Julius Rosenwald Fund feel that such hospitals should increase in number. From the study of the 1930 Julius Rosenwald Fund Report we find that the Julius Rosenwald Fund has a national hospital program for Negroes that we disapprove of thoroughly. In *The New York Times* of January 14, there is an editorial dealing with the subject matter of your 1930 Fund Report, and making reference to the fact that a Negro was burned at stake. The editorial quotes from your report as follows: "All is quiet on the Negro front—the race question is being solved. Negro progress is satisfactory." All is not quiet on the Negro front as long as human beings are being barbarously burned alive; Negro progress is anything but satisfactory in the educational and professional fields.

It is unsatisfactory because the Negro college graduate and professional man is denied simple justice. They have been blinded by charity.

All methods and movements that are practiced by the Julius Rosenwald Fund fix for the Negro citizen a definite status less than that of an American citizen. Set-ups are arranged for him that are different from those employed by other racial groups in America. This we submit is wrong. The Negro citizen, for his own advancement and progress along professional lines, needs no separate institutions. What the Negro physician needs is equal opportunity for training and practice—no more, no less.

In your Philadelphia speech referred to above, you stated that: "A few men in a Northern city have recently criticized the Julius Rosenwald Fund on the ground that we are advocating segregated hospitalization for Negroes, but we do not advocate segregation of any group; but we are keenly aware of the need for training and experience for physicians and nurses."

Our answer to this, Mr. Embree, is that as far as the public knowledge is concerned, the activity of the Julius Rosenwald Fund has been essentially to establish and to aid in the establishment of Negro institutions and hospitals. You deny segregation theoretically, but in fact the Julius Rosenwald Fund has stimulated and advanced tremendously the separation of the Negro race from all other races. We further feel that in the North the Julius Rosenwald Fund has stimulated the segregation of the Negro particularly with respect to health and education. As an evidence of this, we quote from an article by Dr. B. C. H. Harvey, Dean, Medical Students, University of Chicago, in the Journal of the National Medical Association, October-December, 1930, on page 187, where Dr. Harvey states: "The conditions show plainly that the United States needs medical care of the sick Negroes and more sanitary education of Negroes. This need of the country imposes certain obligations definitely on the medical school and hospital." Further on he states, in discussing the Negro students at the University of Chicago, of whom there were fourteen in 1928, that: "These few colored students should be trained as well as possible, for there will be a great need for their services as colored doctors. But the facilities are lacking. We have long been able to carry them through the first two pre-clinical years without difficulty. But difficulties that are almost insuperable appear at once when they begin the work of the third year and the difficulties continue through the fourth and fifth or interne year. It is not practicable to assign colored students to clerkships in white hospitals in a routine way. We have tried it in the Billings Hospital in a small experimental way with one or two tactful students. It can be done, perhaps, to a small extent, but it creates an embarrassing situation and cannot be a real solution of the problem."

Dr. Harvey further states. "Interneships for colored students can be served only in colored hospitals or general hospitals with many colored patients." And under a heading of "What We Are Doing in Chicago," Dr. Harvey states: "The Trustees of the Provident Hospital in co-operation with the University of Chicago have established such a hospital in this city. The Rosenwald Fund and the General Education Board have helped them. Many others have helped through the campaign just conducted under the leadership of Mr. Rosenwald, Dr. Frank Billings and Mr. A. A. Sprague," and Dr. Harvey has the effrontery to say: "The devoted efforts of these three men have conferred on the Negro doctors a great and lasting benefit." So it seems that the proposed enlargement of the Provident Hospital is to save the University of Chicago embarrassment and to relieve it of responsibility as regards the colored student and interne.

Dean Harvey declares that the Negro medical student becomes a problem after his pre-clinical years in medical college. This is not true generally speaking, and whenever true it is entirely due to either first, a definite inclination on the part of the properly constituted authority for such to exist, to later justify whatever unfair and partisan attitude they may care to adopt; or secondly, lack of courage and firmness in demanding and giving to the colored student simple justice and equality of opportunity, the latter in itself the most cherished democratic ideal. After all, when a colored man enters a university he becomes a ward of that university and as long as he maintains the educational and moral standards prescribed by the institution he is entitled to all of the opportunities for development given to all of the other wards. In failing to assure him justice after accepting him the university is akin to the sheriff who tacitly turns his Negro prisoner over to the mob for the exercise of lynch law. In not accepting Negro students an institution brands itself as un-American and lacking in the fundamental concept of its creed. In England and France there is no discrimination against colored medical students who may come from any of their colonies.

Offhand, we should say that Dr. Harvey should be removed at once as Dean of Medical Students, University of Chicago. He is un-American in his sentiments, attitude and written word. Such a man should not hold a position in the teaching of medicine, which is one of the humanities.

Quoting again from your 1930 Julius Rosenwald Fund Report on page 24, you state: "In Chicago the Provident Hospital, which has a record of service under great difficulties covering forty years, arranged an affiliation with the University of Chicago whereby the University agreed to use the hospital for the teaching of Negro medical students for 'refresher courses' for Negro doctors and for training of internes and nurses." Further on in the same paragraph you state: "Of even more significance is the fact that now for the first time a great American university has taken direct responsibility for the education of the Negro undergraduate and postgraduate medical student and for the conduct of the Negro teaching hospital." At this point we would like to interject that Mr. Rosenwald is a trustee of Chicago University and it seems pertinent to inquire if he thus endorsed the segregation of Negro doctors in the medical school of this University. Such segregation is wrong. It is an admission of the fact that the University of Chicago is not a great American university for if it were great in the true sense of the word there would be no occasion for any separate arrangement for the Negro undergraduate or postgraduate medical student. They should be accepted in the University and trained as all other American students and citizens under a democratic form of government. To do otherwise is to create a menace to the training of the Negro in medicine. It sets him apart from all other citizens as being a different kind of citizen, and a different kind of medical student and physician, which you know and we know is not the case.

The high mortality and morbidity rate of Negroes, about which you talk so much, cannot be cut down in this way. Death rates can be cut down among colored people in exactly the same way they are cut down among all other racial groups. The Negro medical student needs exactly the same fine institutions, contacts, opportunities and inspirations that other students need. The formation of Negro hospitals in Negro communities by persons other than Negroes is in violation of the fundamental right of citizenship that is guaranteed by the Constitution of the United States. But you did not mention the fact, Mr. Embree, that Mr. Rosenwald has not, as far as we know, advocated the segregation of Jewish students at the University of Chicago and the sending of Jewish students to Jewish hospitals for their clinical clerkships and interneships.

The issues are much larger than those of hospital facilities alone. Your hospital program represents a further step which would justify the denial on the part of the properly constituted authorities of our inalienable rights as citizens. If there are to be hospitals in the North exclusively for the Negroes, then such hospitals must be established, maintained and directed by Negroes. Of course, groups of Negro physicians in the North have the undoubted right to establish and maintain sanitariums or hospitals for their own race. As to Negro hospitals of any character in the South, that is a matter which we will not discuss here.

If we are not citizens we feel that we should be honest with ourselves and say so. If we are not entitled to the rights of citizenship as guaranteed by the Constitution of the United States we feel that we should be honest with ourselves and with you. On the other hand, we feel that sound progress, as far as the colored physician goes, is to work and struggle as members of all other racial groups have done to improve ourselves, our contacts, and to establish our rights. No other position, in our minds, can be compatible with self-respect or intellectual growth.

The beginning of a so-called Negro hospital may be briefly sketched as follows: The colored people of the community decide to erect and maintain a colored hospital. They conduct a campaign for funds. As the amount obtained is generally insufficient to build a decent building with, therefore a worn-out hospital building formerly used by whites is purchased and by this time there are no funds available for adequate equipment or maintenance. The aid of "white friends" is then sought and in time this proves usually insufficient. Then the aid of the municipality is sought and obtained and the result is that a second-rate institution maintained by private and public funds is permanently established. Conditions existing in institutions of this character everywhere are most deplorable. An investigation and report made by Dr. Haven Emerson, of a certain colored hospital in a midwestern city typical of this class, discloses the alarming state of affairs existing in such hospitals.

The nursing and interne staffs are poorly trained. The medical and surgical staffs are invariably mediocre in type. Medical research is unknown. Inspiration is lacking and the mortality is unwarrantably high. It is needless, Mr. Embree, to point out that needy sick Negroes require exactly the same excellent hospital facilities, the same fine equipment, the same skillful care for recovery as do the needy sick of other racial groups, and they should not be subjected to makeshift medical methods of second-rate institutions. Many "white friends" contribute to such "Jim-Crow" projects under a misguided sense of philanthropy, but when they do so they do not benefit the race but in fact unwittingly aid in doing it irreparable harm. Segregated hospitals represent a duality of citizenship in a democratic government that is wrong. They are invariably neglected. At times the names of notable medical characters are to be found on the staff of these hospitals, but such men are usually lacking entirely in interest and devote but little time to the project. Their names are, to a large extent, camouflage to cover the hopelessness of the underlying situation. And in other instances where they give sincerely and earnestly of their time and learning they cannot raise the institutions to a satisfactory standard because the human mind cannot work at its best under such circumstances. Colored men have made no inconsiderable contributions to medical science, but none of these men were trained or developed in institutions of this character.

We maintain that a "Jim-Crow" set-up *per se* produces a sense of servility, suppresses inspiration, and creates artificial and dishonest standards. We submit also that the Julius Rosenwald Fund has contributed in no small way to this unsatisfactory state of affairs. Colored medical students going to the same school as medical students of any other racial group have rated in their school work on the average as the equal of any other medical mind, and on the State Board examinations they average the same as members of any other racial group. We reiterate that what the Negro doctor needs is simple justice—no more, no less. He has no peculiar needs and therefore requires no special or unique arrangements. In proof of this we would submit the names of men like Solomon C. Fuller, William A. Hinton, Julian E. Lewis, and Ernest E. Just. None of these men is a product of a "Jim-Crow" set-up.

You state, Mr. Embree, that the same consideration affects another special group, namely, women; that it was difficult for women internes to get posts in general hospitals and for this reason women's hospitals have been organized. We agree with you in this, but at the same time we must point out that where women physicians have segregated themselves in a separate institution, that institution does not rank with the best institutions and that such organizations have to be rated as second-rate, and that the same psychological factor works in these institutions to render the work unsatisfactory, as in the case of segregated Negro hospitals.

You state also that there are special Jewish hospitals; that Jewish men and internes found great difficulty in getting posts in general hospitals. We submit, Mr. Embree, in answer to this, that there are several reasons for the establishment of Jewish hospitals which you doubtless unintentionally overlooked or did not consider. Namely: 1. Religion. Strict orthodox Jews insist on eating Kosher meat, which is unavailable in general American hospitals; 2. Many Jews do not speak the English language and for that reason it is desirable that they be in a separate institution.

In the case of surveys, we submit that in all surveys made of Jews, they were not surveyed by Gentiles but by Jews and that in the case of all Jewish hospitals, they were not financed and their policies dictated by members of other races but by members of the Hebrew race. We submit that Jews resent such dictation and direction of their racial affairs by Gentiles. Many Jewish students are refused admission to medical schools in this country because of race and only a certain number can enter. May we ask, why has not Mr. Rosenwald established a Jewish medical school for these Jewish candidates for the study of medicine?

We resent the statement that, "The association of the Negro doctor and the white doctor exploits the white doctor," and, although we do not doubt your sincerity when you state that, "This does not mean the submerging of the Negro doctor in the white profession," we know that such is not the case.

The Negro race and the Negro doctor can never advance this way. Whenever colored hospitals are established, other hospitals in the community which have been admitting Negroes immediately begin to refuse admission to them, referring them to the colored hospital, which in many cases is rather small. In this way the mortality and morbidity rate of colored people in the North will be immeasurably increased. We have seen the process work in other cities and as regards other things. Many white institutions are only too glad to rid themselves of their responsibility as regards the health of the Negro.

In spite of your slogan to the contrary, Mr. Embree, the Rosenwald hospitals are "Jim-Crow" in spirit and "Jim-Crow" in fact, and they establish in the minds of the white doctor and citizen a superiority complex and they also establish in the minds of the colored doctor and colored citizen an inferiority complex. These two complexes obstruct clear thinking and militate against mutual understanding, and mutual self-respect. The Negro doctor trained as you propose, Mr. Embree, would not be a physician to minister to the needs of all mankind irrespective of color, but he would be trained and taught that he is a Negro doctor—one who can treat only Negroes. It is this that has undermined the confidence of the colored and the white citizen in the Negro physician, irrespective of his ability or qualifications. And the acceptance of such a false proposition by the Negro physician condemns him to hopeless mediocrity and a lack of self-respect. But little protection is afforded the nation by poorly trained physicians of any race.

We object also to having the destiny of the Negro physician and the health of 12,000,000 colored people left in the hands of the Julius Rosenwald Fund. We feel that the Fund has essentially failed to establish the necessary groundwork for the sound advancement of the Negro physician and for the proper remedy in handling the question of Negro health. We do, however, view your program with grave concern and we believe that unless it is defeated the Negro doctor will occupy an inferior status. We feel that the Negro patient should have the free and unrestricted use of established hospitals and the Negro doctors should have equal opportunity for training in these institutions. We believe that the establishment of this principle of equality of opportunity for all, regardless of race, in hospitals throughout the North is not too much to hope for. This, however, will never come to pass if your program based as it is upon a false and vicious principle should prevail.

The death rate of the Negro has not been and is not dependent alone or to any great extent upon the establishment of Negro hospitals or the training of Negro doctors in separate institutions. The high Negro death rate is dependent upon factors that are much more fundamental, namely, poor economic conditions, discrimination—which increases the economic obstacles of the colored citizen—and illiteracy.

Now, Mr. Embree, since you have essayed to speak as one well qualified and authoritatively as regards the needs of the Negro doctor, it is pertinent to inquire at this juncture into your qualifications. A few weeks ago we read in the public press of a controversy between Mr. William Pickens and yourself over a statement purporting to have been made by you, namely, that the Southern white man was the Negro's best friend. This interested us and we learned upon inquiry that you are a Southerner. We submit that this fact alone renders you incompetent to pass dispassionate judgment upon such a grave social question. You state that the Southern white man is the Negro's "best friend." Yes, he is the Negro's "best friend" so long as the Negro is willing to accept the status of inferiority.

We would like to point out a fact relative to the so-called Negro hospital that is of interest and illustrates the lack of confidence on the part of white and colored citizens generally. A few weeks ago Dr. Robert Russa Moton, President of Tuskegee Institute, where he has established a Negro hospital, traveled over a thousand miles from his colored hospital to a Northern city to be operated upon not by a Negro but by a white surgeon. This, Mr. Embree, is a daily occurrence as regards colored people. Now, why is it that, if these colored hospitals are the equal of all other hospitals, the men who contribute most to the formation and maintenance of these institutions fear to go therein to have their diseases treated? How can you or Dr. Moton expect Negroes to have confidence in Negro hospitals under such circumstances? You know and we know that they are not up to standard because if they were, intelligent Negroes and even intelligent whites for that matter would not hesitate to go to them for medical service in serious cases.

We, therefore, hope, Mr. Embree, that in future public addresses you will not attempt to justify an un-American approach to a problem that is of equal importance to the citizens of all racial groups in this country. Truth and simple justice, we feel, will of themselves have sufficient strength to win over the most seemingly hopeless battle. But you know, as far as the health of the American Negro goes, all of the money contributed by the Julius Rosenwald Fund, and all of the other Funds, does not even scratch the surface. We feel that in writing you this open letter we are sincerely interested in doing a service to the Julius Rosenwald Fund by pointing out its inadequacies as they seem to us. This we would have done through private correspondence had you not so arbitrarily disposed in one address of the needs of the Negro doctor, nurse and patient. We do not mean for anything in this letter to be taken personally. We are interested only in the facts and in the general program. We do not charge you or the Julius Rosenwald Fund with insincerity, but we do charge the Julius Rosenwald Fund with establishing and attempting to maintain a health program and a hospital program that contravenes the Constitution of the United States, bows its head low before race prejudice, and offers a minimum of health protection to the American people.

We submit in conclusion that it is infinitely better for the Negro doctor to struggle, study, work, sacrifice, and advance slowly but soundly without philanthropic aid that emasculates and prostitutes his mind rather than have him stumbling along the scientifically unsafe and apparently peaceful blind alley into which you are leading him.

Submitted by Executive Committee,
Manhattan Medical Society

An eight-page pamphlet, in editor's possession. There is a mimeographed account of this society, written in 1935 by Dr. Ernest R. Alexander, in the file on "Medical Societies," in the Schomburg Collection of the N.Y. Public Library. *The New York Times,* January 30, 1931, carried a lengthy report concerning this matter.

142

"WITH TEARS IN MY EYES"

by Eugene Brown

John L. Spivak, a well-known newspaperman and author of *Georgia Nigger* (1931), the novelized exposure of peonage and chain gangs, published a pamphlet in 1932 complete with photographs of Black prisoners undergoing various forms of torture. A letter from one such prisoner in Gwinnett

County, Georgia, dated May 2, 1931, and addressed to a Prison Commission official named E. L. Reany is reprinted from that pamphlet.

Mr. E L Reany lissen here Mr Reiny This is Eugene Brown talking Mr. Reiney I am begging you with tears in my eyies for a trancefor Becais I cannot make my time here Becais this worden and country C B M is beating us over the head with pick handle and they draw their guns on us and make us stand and let these trustes Beat us up and Let the hare gun to Mr Reiny I dont Belive that you know how they is treating us prizners you auto come and see Mr Reiney I want you to do all you can I am willing to go anywhere and make my Time Becais my hand is all messed up and every time I ask the doctor for anything they is ready to punish me my hand is so bad till i cant hardely hold a shurvle and I am asking you now for help I am looking for your awancer wright away Yors

Eugene Brown

John L. Spivak, *On The Chain Gang* (New York: International Publishers, 1932), pp. 11–12.

143

THE MISEDUCATION OF THE NEGRO
by *Carter G. Woodson*

Carter G. Woodson is known, quite properly, as a chief founder of the scientific study of African and Afro-American history. He also was, however, a very effective journalist and speaker and as such played an important and militant role not only in recording history but also in making it. Illustrative of this latter relatively unknown side of Dr. Woodson is the following essay.

In their own as well as in mixed schools, Negroes are taught to admire the Hebrew, the Greek, the Latin and the Teuton and to despise the African. The thought of the inferiority of the Negro is drilled into him in almost every class he enters. If he happens to leave school after he has mastered the fundamentals, before he has finished high school or reached college, he will naturally escape from some of this bias and may recover in time to be of service to his people.

Practically all of the successful Negroes in this country are those who never learned this prejudice "scientifically" because they entered upon their life's work without formal education. The large majority of the Negroes who have put on the finishing touches of our best colleges, however, are all but worthless in the uplift of their people. If, after leaving school, they have the opportunity to give out to Negroes what traducers of the race have taught them, such persons may earn a living by teaching or preaching to Negroes what someone would like to have them know, but they never become a constructive force in the elevation of those far down. They become estranged from the masses and the gap between them widens as the years go by.

The explanation of this is a simple problem. The schools and colleges of this country are so conducted as to produce this result. For example, an officer of a Negro university, thinking that an additional course on the Negro should be given there, called upon a Negro Doctor of Philosophy of the faculty to offer such work. He promptly informed the officer that he knew nothing about the Negro. He did not go to school to waste his time that way. He went to be educated.

Last year at one of the Negro summer schools, a white instructor gave a course on the Negro, using for his text a work of Jerome Dowd, who teaches that whites are superior to blacks. When asked by one of the students why he used such a textbook, the instructor replied that he wanted them to get Dowd's point of view. If schools for Negroes are places where they must be convinced of their inferiority, they cannot escape from their tormentors and rise to recognition and usefulness.

As another has well said, to handicap a student for life by teaching him that his black face is a curse and that his struggle to change his condition is hopeless is the worst kind of lynching. It kills one's aspirations and dooms him to vagabondage and crime.

In most cases, moreover, when the teachers of Negroes are persons of good intentions, the result is the same. In the school of business administration, for example, Negroes are trained exclusively in the economics and psychology of Wall Street, and are thereby made to despise the opportunities to conduct laundries, repair shoes, run ice wagons, push banana carts, and sell peanuts among their own people. Foreigners, who have not studied economics and psychology but have studied Negroes, take up this business and grow rich while the "highly educated" Negroes are complaining because the native American whites do not permit the blacks to share what others have developed.

In schools of journalism Negroes are being taught how to edit such metropolitan dailies as the *Chicago Tribune* and *The New York Times,* which would hardly hire a Negro as a janitor; and when such graduates come to the Negro weeklies for employment they are not prepared to function in such establishments, which to be successful must be built upon accurate knowledge of the psychology and philosophy of the Negro.

In the schools of religion Negro ministers devote their time to dead languages and dead issues, to the dogma of other races, the schism produced by unnecessary disputes, and the conflicts by which fanatics have moistened the soil of Asia and Europe with the blood of unoffending people. These "highly educated" Negro ministers, then, know practically nothing of the religious background of their parishioners, do not appreciate their philosophy of life, and do not understand their spiritual development as influenced by African survivals in America and the peculiar development of the Negro church. The result, therefore, is that while the illiterate minister who has given attention to these things preaches to the masses, the "highly educated" Negro minister talks to benches.

The Negroes who have been trained the most serve the least. Our physicians and lawyers who have undergone training in the leading universities of the land often have difficulty in making a living. Teachers of "ripe scholarship" influence the youth less than those of limited training. Such maladjusted workers complain that, since Negroes are ignorant, they prefer ignorant leaders; but the trouble is not that the people are ignorant, but that these misfits are ignorant of the people.

Unfortunately these conditions have continued because schools for Negroes have always been established in mushroom fashion, without giving sufficient thought to the needs of the people to be thus served, and most of those now promoting Negro education are proceeding in the same way. Talking the other day with one of the men now giving millions to establish four Negro universities in the South, I find that he is of the opinion that you can go almost anywhere and build a three million dollar plant, place in charge a man to do what you want accomplished, and in a short while he can secure or have trained to order the men necessary to make a university.

Such a thing cannot be done because there are not sufficient Negroes or whites in this country qualified to conduct for Negroes such a university as they need. Most of the whites who are now serving Negroes as educators come to them as persons bearing gifts from a foreign shore, and the Negroes gather around them in childlike fashion, gazing with astonishment and excitement to find out what these things mean.

All things being equal, however, there should be no different method of approach or appeal to Negro students that cannot be made just as well by a white teacher to Negro students or a Negro teacher to white students, if such teachers are properly informed and have the human attitude; but tradition, race hate, and terrorism have made such a thing impossible. However, I am not an advocate of segregation. I do not believe in separate schools. I am merely emphasizing the necessity for common-sense schools and teachers who understand and continue in sympathy with those whom they instruct.

Those who take the position to the contrary have the idea that education is merely a process of imparting information. One who can give out these things or devise an easy plan for so doing, then, is an educator. In a sense this is true, this machine method accounts for most of the troubles of the Negro. For me, education means to inspire people to live more abundantly, to learn to begin with life as they find it and make it better.

The instruction so far given in Negro Colleges and universities has worked to the contrary. In most cases such graduates have merely increased the number of mal-contents who offer no program for changing the undesirable conditions about which they complain.

The seat of the trouble is in what Negroes are now being taught. Their education does not bring their minds into harmony with life as they must face it. When a Negro student works his way through college by shining shoes he does not think of making a special study of the science underlying the production and distribution of leather and its products, that he may some day figure in this sphere. The Negro boy sent to college by a mechanic seldom dreams of learning mechanical engineering to build upon the foundation his father has laid, that in years to come he may figure as a contractor or a consulting engineer. The Negro girl who goes to college hardly wants to return to her mother if she is a washerwoman, but this girl should come back with sufficient knowledge of physics and chemistry and business administration to use her mother's work as a nucleus for a modern steam laundry.

A white professor of a Southern university recently resigned his position to get rich by running a laundry for Negroes. A Negro college instructor would have considered such a suggestion an insult. The so-called education of Negro college graduates leads them to throw away opportunities which they have and go in quest of those which they do not find. A school system which thus handicaps people for life by setting them adrift is not worthy of public support.

In the case of the white youth in this country, they can choose their courses more at random and still succeed because of numerous opportunities offered by their people, but even they show so much more wisdom than do Negroes. For example, a year or two after I left Harvard I found out West a schoolmate who was studying wool. "How did you happen to get into this sort of thing," I enquired. His people, he replied, had had some experience in wool and in college he prepared himself for this work by studying its economic foundation. When I was at Harvard I studied Aristotle, Plato, Marsiglio of Padua, and Pascasius Rathbertus. My friend who studied wool, however, is now independently rich and has sufficient leisure to enjoy the cultural side of life which his knowledge of the science underlying his business developed, but I have to make my living by begging for a struggling cause.

From this indictment of our schools, then, one may conclude that it would serve the public better to keep Negroes away from them. Such an unwise course, however, is not herein suggested. The thing needed is reform. Negro institutions of learning and those of whites, too, especially those white institutions which are training teachers who have to deal with large numbers of Negroes, should reconstruct their curricula. These institutions should abandon a large portion of the traditional courses which have been retained throughout the years because they are supposedly cultural, and they should offer instead training in things which are also cultural and at the same time have a bearing on the life of the people thus taught. Certainly the Negro should learn something about the history and culture of the white man with whom he has to deal daily, and the white man should likewise learn the same about the Negro; but if the education of either is made a one-sided effort neither one will understand or appreciate the other, and interracial cooperation will be impossible.

Looking over the recent catalogues of the leading Negro colleges, I find their courses drawn up without much thought about the Negro. Invariably these institutions give courses in ancient, mediaeval, and modern Europe, but they do not offer courses in ancient, mediaeval, and modern Africa. Yet Africa, according to recent discoveries, has contributed about as much to the progress of mankind as Europe has, and the early civilization of the Mediterranean world was decidely influenced by the so-called Dark Continent.

Negro colleges offer courses bearing on the European colonists prior to their coming to America, their settlement on these shores, and their development here toward independence. Why not be equally as generous with the Negroes in treating their status in Africa prior to enslavement, their first transplantation to the West Indies, the Latinization of certain Negroes in contradistinction to the development of others under the influence of the Teuton, and the effort of the race toward self expression in America?

A further examination of the curricula of Negro colleges shows, too, that as a rule they offer courses in Greek philosophy and in modern European thought, but direct no attention to the philosophy of the Negro. Negroes have and always have had their own ideas about purpose, chance, time, and space, about appearance and reality, and about freedom and necessity. The effort of the Negro to interpret man's relation to the universe shows just as much intelligence as we find in the philosophy of the Greeks. There were many Africans who were just as wise as Socrates.

Again I find in some of these catalogues numerous courses in art, but no well defined course in Negro or African art. The art of Africa, however, influenced the art of the Greeks to the extent that thinkers are now saying that the most ancient culture of the Mediterranean was chiefly African. Most of these colleges, too, do not even direct special attention to Negro music in which the race has made an outstanding contribution in America.

The unreasonable attitude is that because the whites do not have these things in their schools the Negroes must not have them in theirs. The Catholics and Jews, therefore, are wrong in establishing special schools to teach the principles of their religion, and the Germans in the United States are unwise in having their children taught their mother tongue.

The higher education of the Negro, then, has been largely meaningless imitation. When the Negro finishes his course in one of our schools, he knows what others have done, but he has not been inspired to do much for himself. If he makes a success in life it comes largely by accident.

The Crisis, August, 1931; XXXVIII, 266–67.

144

COMMUNISM AND THE NEGRO TENANT FARMER
by Elmer A. Carter

In the midst of the murderous conditions created by the Depression, especially for the Black people in the rural South, efforts at self-organization went forward to create either kinds of trade unions and/or producer and consumer cooperatives. An important and heroic role was played in this effort by radicals, Black and white, and very often Communists. Slaughter and mayhem was the frequent reply of the plantation owners and their political servants; an outstanding example of this occurred in Camp Hill, Alabama, in 1931. The following editorial, from the organ of the rather conservative National Urban League, treats of that event.

That open racial conflict would be precipitated in Alabama sooner or later was to be expected. The fall in the price of cotton, the cultivation of which in the South is still dependent on black tenant farmers; the industrial depression which has intensified the competition for jobs between blacks and whites; the sentence of death imposed on eight young Negroes at Scottsboro under circumstances which obviously precluded a fair and impartial trial; the constant agitation of Communist organizers whose work among Negroes is unquestionably bearing fruit; these were the factors which constitute the major causes of the recent clash at Camp Hill, Alabama, in which at least two men, one white and one black, were killed, a score or more wounded and a Negro church burned to the ground. For the present, there is a cessation of hostilities, but the danger of their recurrence on a far wider front in the South may not be remote and the fundamental issues involved transcend sectional and racial boundaries and affect the rights of all minority groups in America.

The immediate cause of the outbreak was the organization of Negro Share Croppers—the tenant farmers of the Camp Hill District who attempted to establish the principle of collective bargaining in their relationship to the plantation owners. They had made certain demands which certainly do not appear to be exorbitant. They were: (1) Food advances until crop settlement time. (2) Full cash settlement. (3) The right to sell their crop where and when they saw fit. (4) The right to cultivate a garden for home use, etc. They asked for a minimum wage of two dollars per day. There can be no doubt but that this organized effort of the share croppers has been stimulated by Communists. But all of the propaganda and all of the effort which the Communists might employ in a century of agitation, would not have impelled the Negro tenant farmers to even so much as protest, if the conditions under which they have been forced to exist had not become so intolerable that a promise of deliverance from any source seemed to be a blessing.

Communism?

And what do the black tenant farmers of Alabama know of economic determinism and the Marxian philosophy?

Nothing.

But these things they do know.

They know of grinding toil at miserably inadequate wages.

They know of endless years of debt.

They know of two and three months school.

They know of forced labor and peonage.

When the sheriff and his deputies invaded the Negro church and broke up the meeting of the Share Croppers Union, they were guilty of a flagrant violation of one of the basic guarantees of American Democracy. The right of peaceful assembly for the purpose of discussing grievances is so fundamental that its abrogation anywhere must be abhorrent to every right thinking individual. The threat of Communism among black tenant farmers in the South will not disappear through repression and force for on these it feeds and grows. Rather, it will diminish in proportion to the efforts which the enlightened South puts forth to end the deplorable conditions which prevail to such a large extent in its rural areas.

Editorial, *Opportunity*, August, 1931; IX, 234–35. Elmer A. Carter was the editor.

145

ON RACIST TEXTBOOKS
by Walter White

On September 16, 1931, Walter White prepared the following memorandum for the consideration of the semimonthly meeting of the Committee on Administration of the N.A.A.C.P. to take place twelve days later. It marks the beginnings of a campaign against racist textbooks in public school systems which in the ensuing forty years has achieved notable but still partial successes.

The semi-monthly meetings of the Committee on Administration will be resumed on Monday, September 28.

Among other matters which should be considered at that time is one which has recently been brought to the attention of the National Office by Miss Josephine Wooten, a teacher in the New York Public School. After reading the following memorandum on this and my proposal of steps to be taken, will you not be good enough to communicate with me at once regarding it.

Miss Wooten has loaned the Secretary one of the text books now being used in the New York Public Schools, the volume in question being *How the United States Became a World Power,* in the City History Series, by Helen F. Giles, published by the Charles E. Merrill Company, New York. This volume is used in the second half of the sixth year.

In discussion of the Reconstruction Era, such statements as the following are made:

When they (Negroes) realized that they were free, many thought they must get away from the plantations where they had lived as slaves, though they had little idea of where to go or what to do. They had no homes and no money. They began to wander about, stealing and plundering. In one week in a Georgia town, one hundred fifty Negroes were arrested for thieving.

Many ignorant Negroes thought that the property owned by their former masters was theirs now and some even took possession of land and began building houses and planting their farms. Often they were insulting to the white people. In some localities conditions were so bad that the white women were afraid to go outside their homes even in the day-time. Many of the white people slept with a gun within reach so that they could protect themselves in case they might be attacked by a Negro. (Page 6)

By 1871 Congress had pardoned most of the white leaders of the War, and they were again allowed to vote and hold office. But it was almost impossible for white men to be elected in four of the states, because there were many more Negroes than white men in these states. So the white men decided to take other means to get the power back into their own hands. A secret society, known as the Ku Klux Klan, was organized, and its members set out to spread terror among the ignorant Negroes. Knowing that the Negroes were very much afraid of spirits, or ghosts, the members would dress in long white robes with hoods over their heads and grinning masks hiding their faces. Disguised in this way, they would visit the home of a Negro in the dead of night. When they had roused the trembling Negro from sleep, they would make all sorts of threats of horrible things that would happen to him if he dared vote in the next election. The Negroes were quite terrified and nothing could make them go to the polls after such a visit. (Page 12)

It is the Secretary's feeling that something should be done immediately regarding such statements being taught to the several million pupils in the New York City Public Schools.

Effort was made some months ago to get the New York Women's Auxiliary to appoint a committee to go over all the text books, especially history and civic text books, to compile material such as the above and to prepare therefrom an authoritative document as the basis for a protest to the Board of Education and to the Mayor.

No city in the country offers a more likely chance of successful elimination of such paragraphs than New York, and especially in view of the coming elections. The example set by New York would undoubtedly be followed by branches in other cities.

Aside from the good done, such a protest would be especially helpful right now when the N.A.A.C.P. Drive for Membership is on. Such action on our part would more directly touch the colored people in Harlem than even the Scottsboro Cases, for there are no people there who do not have children or friends with children in the public schools.

The Secretary has been asked by Mr. Edgar N. Parks, who has been a most faithful worker for many years for the Association, to help find employment for his niece, Mrs. Eloise Walker Percival. Mrs. Percival is an honor graduate of New York University.

Miss Wooten is securing for us a list of text books approved by the New York Board of Education. She informs me that all these books are on file at the Board of Education Building at Fifty-ninth Street and Park Avenue.

The Secretary would like to recommend that Mrs. Percival, or someone equally competent and who could be engaged for not more than $25.00 a week, be engaged to go to the Board of Education Building and go carefully through the textbooks on history, civics, etc., and make exact copies of all passages which may be objectionable. Such work ought not take more than two weeks. If this work were started immediately we could make public this study during the course of the Membership Drive which Mrs. [Daisy] Lampkin is preparing for in Harlem, the actual drive to occur during the first two weeks in October.

We could commence this work at once if the Committee thinks well of it.

From carbon copy of the typed original, in editor's possession.

146

RIGHTS AND PRIVILEGES AS CITIZENS
by Oscar De Priest

A rather typical speech coming from successful Black politicians in the period between the two world wars is the following address made by the only Afro-American Member of Congress at the time—a Republican from

Chicago. Mr. De Priest delivered this speech at Howard University on February 8, 1932.

Mr. Chairman and my fellow Americans, I say fellow Americans to remind you of the fact that you are American citizens and entitled to all the rights and privileges that every other citizen enjoys—the right to vote and be voted for as a candidate for any office in the gift of the people.

We will never enjoy our constitutional rights in this country until we combine our forces and support those men for public office who are willing to enact such laws as will enforce the Constitution and all amendments thereto.

By our loyalty and devotion we are entitled to our rights under the Constitution. This comes to us as a sacred heritage, bought through loyalty and sacrifice beginning with the heroic Crispus Attucks, who fell on Boston Common, and continuing through to Flanders Field to an European battle ground, all of which participation, through the ages, has demonstrated that we are willing and brave enough to lay down our lives for our country.

Crispus Attucks was among the first to sacrifice his life in the interest of the American Colonies. Before we were a United States of America he fertilized the soil of this land with his lifeblood dedicated to liberty and freedom.

During the activities of the Continental Army, Negroes to the number of about 3,000 enlisted to fight to preserve the Colonies and to make it possible to form these United States, when the motto was "All for one and one for all."

During the War of 1812, our second engagement with England, with Jackson at New Orleans and with Perry at Lake Erie, Negro soldiers made the great contribution to the war strength of our Army.

The war drums sounded long and loud in '61 as we pushed our way into the Civil War. Negroes, 200,000 strong, joined the irrepressible conflict and took part in some of the most notable battles of that war. They are remembered well at Fort Wagner and at Pillow; they marched with Sherman from Atlanta to the sea; they participated in other engagements too numerous to mention.

Again the people are called to arms. Spectacular and exciting were the days of President McKinley and the Spanish-American War, which brought out the soldier, Theodore Roosevelt, with his celebrated Rough Riders, and who met strong resistance by the soldiery in the Spanish blockhouses. It remained for the Negro troops to save the day, not only for the United States but for the intrepid Roosevelt himself. These colored soldiers marched on the Spanish blockhouses singing "There'll be a hot time in the old town to-night."

The famous Tenth Cavalry, along with the Ninth and the Twenty-fourth and Twenty-fifth Infantry, became a part of the fighting forces of our country by act of Congress in 1866. The Tenth Cavalry was one of the regiments that took part in the assault upon the Spanish blockhouses at San Juan Hill.

During the great World War the men of my race enlisted, 380,000 strong, to fight for world democracy, and we are now praying, longing, and hoping for the day to come when of a truth we will have democracy in every State of the Union and whereby every American citizen 21 years of age can cast his ballot any place in America and that ballot be counted as cast. Until that time comes, this will not be the true democracy about which we so much proclaim.

We have earned our rights in this country, under the Stars and Stripes, by the loyal support and devotion we have given, and while we are not satisfied with present conditions in and around our country; where we are denied our constitutional rights and the use of the ballot, free and untrammeled, nevertheless America is our home; our parents were born in this country, and here we must fight out our destiny. We of this generation were born here, and our children were born here. It is the only country we know; the only home we have. We shall continue to contend for both our civil and political rights—the full privilege of the ballot.

With all the wrongs imposed upon us and all the injustice visited upon us, we are still American citizens and propose always to be loyal to the Government which is ours, and we will maintain, unsullied, the reputation and fact that none of our group has ever conspired against this Government or joined any movement calculated to attempt the destruction of our institutions or aid any alien propaganda in this land of the free and home of the brave.

But with all that we have done we wonder if we are properly appreciated. When we see orders issued by the War Department modifying the regular soldierly routine of the Tenth Cavalry, relieving them of all commanding officers, taking away their side arms and assigning them around to different Army posts to do orderly work, which is nothing but servant work, we wonder if the department has the proper respect and appreciation of the valor of these Negro troops and their importance at this particular time.

From a communication I received from the War Department it is claimed this is necessary under the plan to reduce certain branches of the services in favor of an increase of the Air Corps of the country. That may all be correct, but if we are going to numerically reduce the Infantry and Cavalry services, why not give us an opportunity to join the Air Corps service and let black soldiers learn to fly and be of extended service like all other American fighting units so we will be able to render our Government better service in the future and be equal to any other American soldier.

It seems to be the policy of the Government to demote the Negro troops in the fighting units and establish and make of them labor battalions. That is most discouraging, un-American, and not giving us that square deal every American is entitled to receive.

I want to read for you a table showing you the enlisted strength of the Army of the United States, the reduced numerical strength of Negro troops, their utter absence from the Air Corps service, and see if we have had fair treatment:

Enlisted strength of the United States Army, June 30, 1931

Quartermaster Corps	7,444
Medical Department	6,612
Finance Department	369
Corps of Engineers	4,326
Ordnance Department	2,179
Signal Corps	2,575
Chemical Warfare Service	451
Cavalry	7,692
Field Artillery	14,815
Coast Artillery Corps	12,711
Infantry	40,569
Air Corps	13,194
Detached list	6,073
Retired (on active duty)	24
Total	119,034

Colored units

Ninth Cavalry	528
Tenth Cavalry	475
Second Squadron	307
Machine-gun Troop	128
Twenty-fourth Infantry	722
Twenty-fifth Infantry	437
First Battalion	237
Third Battalion	244
Total	3,078

Though 10 per cent of the population, Negro troops are only 2.5 plus per cent of the Army. They are 18 plus per cent of the Cavalry and 4 plus per cent of the Infantry, with none in the Air Corps.

Since our people not only from a military standpoint but during the long 250 years of slavery hewed the wood and tilled the soil to make America what it is, I plead with all Americans to help my racial group to secure their rights under the Constitution.

The enactment of laws will not secure our rights without a healthy public sentiment back of it. I am appealing to those of the religious world, interested interracial groups in America, Representatives in Congress and in the Senate, men of the press, magazine editors, and all to help create such a public sentiment that America will be what it claims to be—the melting pot of the world, where each man shall have his full rights under an orderly government of free men and women.

I am also appealing to the lawmakers of the country, municipal, State, and national, to enact such laws as will benefit all Americans, thereby creating such a healthy respect for law and order that no community will feel it necessary to try to take the law in their own hands and commit the crime of joining a mob and resort to lynching and burning, for such lynchings and burnings create a disrespect of law and order and break down the morale of the community where such things occur.

I am going to prophesy the time will come in America when every law-abiding citizen and every God-fearing man will stand up and support America, for we are going to save America for Americans.

There are forces at work in our communities now trying to spread a doctrine of disrespect of law and order and teaching insurrection, which is un-American, unsuited to our form of government. They are preaching and agitating the people to a degree bordering on revolution and trying to convince the people with their unbelief in the Almighty. They are organizing against the religious forces of the world. I contend that no force can stand on this earth, in these days of enlightenment, that is set against the teachings of Jesus Christ.

As the only Negro Representative in Congress, I especially appeal to you to so shape and guide yourselves that by your conduct and education you will understand our rights in America; that this may be brought about under the guidance of the best American citizens, white and black, so that right and not might shall prevail.

Congressional Record, February 9, 1932; 72nd Cong., 1st sess., LXXV, 3625-26.

147

NEGRO EDITORS ON COMMUNISM

With the Depression, growth of the Left in general, of radical thinking among increasing numbers of Black people—especially youth—and with the activity of the Communist Party, particularly around Scottsboro, commanding nationwide attention, Du Bois wrote to sixteen editors of leading Afro-American newspapers "asking their opinion of Communism." Fourteen replied, and these are published in full.

Carl Murphy, The Afro-American, Maryland

The Communists appear to be the only party going our way. They are as radical as the N.A.A.C.P. were twenty years ago.

Since the abolitionists passed off the scene, no white group of national prominence has openly advocated the economic, political and social equality of black folks.

Mr. Clarence Darrow speaking in Washington recently declared that we should not care what political candidates think of prohibition, the League of Nations, the tariff or any other general issue. What we should demand, Mr. Darrow said, is candidates who are right on all questions affecting the colored people. I agree with him.

Communism would appeal to Mr. Darrow if he were in my place.

Communists in Maryland saved Orphan Jones from a legal lynching. They secured a change of venue from the mob-ridden Easton Shore.

They fought the exclusion of colored men from the jury, and on that ground financed an appeal of the case to Maryland's highest court. They compelled estimable Judge Duncan of Towson, Maryland, to testify that he had never considered colored people in picking jurors in his court for twenty-six years.

The Communists are going our way, for which Allah be praised.

P. B. Young, Norfolk Journal and Guide, Virginia

Because we recognize that throughout all ages new voices and new movements for the creation of a better social order have always been anathema to the "old guards" and the "stand-patters" of the period, it has been the policy of The Journal and Guide not to view Communism as a thoroughgoing, death-dealing evil but to regard it as just one of the factors in a growing world-wide ideal to improve the conditions of the under-privileged, to make government more the servant of all the people, to give the rank and file of those who labor a larger share of the fruits of production, and to afford to all men equality before the law, and equal opportunity to work and live.

The Communists in America have commendably contended for and have practiced equality of all races, and in their many activities, have accepted Negroes into their ranks in both high and lowly positions; more, they have dramatized the disadvantages of the Negro by walking in a body out of a jim-crow Pittsburgh hospital, by aiding ejected tenement dwellers, and in industrial strikes directed by them fighting against the practice of excluding Negroes from labor unions. All these accomplishments go to the credit side for the Communists.

To the debit side must go, however, the fact that they in their efforts to "sell" Communism, have not taken into full consideration the economic dependence of the Negro race, its minority position, and the traditional aversion of the rank and file of Americans to the "blood and thunder" appeals of "revolution" and "mass action." Forgetful, they have aroused such charged feelings in many sections which make it difficult for the best of both races to get together and study and correct problems in an orderly way. Besides, because the Negro is marked racially, he becomes a ready target for anti-Communist venom whenever that develops as at Camp Hill and in Chicago.

The Negro is patriotic and loyal, if he is anything, and Communism has gained adherents, and will continue to do so, only because traditional American conditions with their race prejudice, economic semi-enslavement, lack of equal opportunity, and discrimination of all sorts have made the Negro susceptible to any doctrine which promises a brighter future, where race and color will not be a penalty.

These barriers to the more abundant growth of the Negro must be removed, but despite the theories behind Communism, we do not think it offers the way out for the Negro which shall be most beneficial and lasting in the long run.

If the Negro masses are to be made Communism-proof, the disadvantages which have been raised against them by the white majority in power, must be voided by the union of the whites and Negroes of vision working together—fighting by all legal and sane means the proscriptions which are neither Christian, humane, or in the spirit of the fundamental laws of the land.

William M. Kelley, Amsterdam News, *New York*

"Neither was there any among them that lacked: for as many as were possessors of lands or houses, sold them, and brought the prices of the things that were sold,

"And laid them down at the apostles' feet, and distribution was made unto every man according as he had need."—Acts IV; 34, 35.

This Communistic pronouncement, written about two thousand years before Karl Marx and Frederick Engels issued their famous Communistic Manifesto, proves conclusively that the idea back of the middle-class Socialistic movement and the working-class Communistic movement is by no means a new one. However, it is only in comparatively recent years that the Negro in America has given any thought whatever to the subject.

Since America's twelve million Negro population is so largely identified with the working class, the wonder is not that the Negro is beginning, at least, to think along Communistic lines, but that he did not embrace that doctrine enmasse long ago. Oppressed on every hand, denied equal educational facilities, discriminated against in public places and in employment, Jim-Crowed on street cars and railroad trains, imprisoned for long terms without due process of law and even lynched, it would seem that any program—Communistic or Socialistic, inaugurated by force or brought about by pacifistic means—should readily find converts among American Negroes.

The one question for the Negro to decide is whether it is better to continue to remain loyal to a republican form of government under a Federal Constitution that is being grossly violated where he is concerned, or, to throw his support to a communistic form of government and help bring about a dictatorship under a propertyless white proletariat.

We have no quarrel with Communism in theory for, like Christianity, its doctrine is applicable to any race or nationality; but similarly like the latter, which was cited to justify human slavery, and which at the present time exerts but little influence against racial prejudice, Communism in America can also be made to function in a manner contrary to its principles and detrimental to the Negro.

The treatment given the few thousand Negroes in Russia under the Soviet form of government is not, necessarily, the same treatment that would be accorded the twelve million Negroes in America should this propertyless white proletariat come into power; for it is this same ignorant white class in the North and South which now fails to respond to just and intelligent appeals for racial and religious tolerance—the same ignorant white working class which forms the backbone of every lynching mob.

Communism in Russia has brought about revolutionary reforms affecting the welfare of that nation's hitherto subjugated masses; but these are for the most part white. And, white members of the party here have, almost without exception, revealed themselves as being without bias as to race or creed—we need have no fear so long as they are in control—but it is such a far cry from Ku Klux Klanism to Communism, and from the narrow-minded, unwieldy white working-class in America to the unlettered, but wieldy, masses in Russia, the Negro can well afford to wait until he has more definite information as to how Communism in America would be practiced by those poor whites upon whose shoulders would ultimately fall the responsibilities of government.

E. Washington Rhodes, Philadelphia Tribune, Pennsylvania

Whether for better or for worse, thousands of Negroes are playing with the Communists. They approach Communism, the glittering symbol of absolute equality, carefully and almost fearfully—as a child takes up a strange toy. But the evidence shows that Negroes *are* flirting with Communism. Many of them, perhaps, without understanding the deeper significance of its principles, are preaching the gospel of the "Reds."

Thousands of converts have sought solace and comfort within the folds of the deep-pink banner of the party of Lenin and Stalin. Is it not paradoxical that Negroes must seek protection under some flag other than the Stars and Stripes, the flag for which they have fought to keep flying in the cause of justice and human liberty?

The ideals of the Soviet Union, of Russia have a fascinating appeal to American Negroes because they hold out a ray of hope for equality of opportunity which the present American system denies to them.

Thoughtful Negroes may reason that the philosophy and economic theories of Communism are unsound and will not obtain for them a more equitable distribution of the products of their labor, or a larger degree of justice—but a drowning man will grab at a straw.

When it is considered that equality is the theory of Communism, and that inequality is the result of the present system, it is amazing that millions of Negroes have not joined the followers of the Red flag, instead of a few thousands.

The Communists have been conducting a special drive for Negro adherents. They believe that racial prejudice makes the Negro a fertile field for the sowing of revolutionary propaganda. It will be difficult for the seeds to sprout and bring forth much fruit because of the peculiar love which Negroes have for America and American institutions—a love which transcends all human understanding.

I am told that there are more dark-skinned than white Communists in Philadelphia. If numbers mean success, then the drive for Negro members succeeded. In fact, the leaders of the movement are anxious now to prevent it from becoming a black party. This is undesirable because it is the purpose of the organizers to make the Communist party inter-racial. It is difficult to ascertain just how seriously Negroes are considering the Red movement. I doubt that many of those who are members of the "party" would participate in a revolution requiring physical violence. However, the Reds are masters of propaganda. They are painting vivid pictures of justice and equality for all men under a Communistic form of government. They went into Scottsboro and Salisbury with banners flying, condemning the persecution of Negroes. That these expressions of goodwill have had their effect in swaying Negroes is indisputable. Were not Negroes affected thereby, they would not be human.

Whether it is better for the Negro to endure his present ills or fly to others he knows not of, I am unable to say. But this one thing I know —Negroes are flirting with Communism; and if it develops into something more serious, the white American must blame himself.

J. Alston Atkins, Houston Informer and Texas Freeman, *Texas*

I believe that any people who put their trust in a name will sooner or later be disappointed. A mere shibboleth has never been adequate for the solution of personal or group problems. The more complex and intricate the problem, the less adequate mere words become. It is my understanding that in Soviet Russia, Communism represents the "Plan" by which the Communist Party is undertaking to construct a new social order. In the life of the American Negro, Communism does not represent any plan for the solution of his problems: it is but a name. So far as I can discover it represents a planned urge to rebel against the oppression and injustices from which Negroes suffer. It gives me the impression of an emotional, desperate effort to break away, rather than a scientific and experimental program, evolved out of a careful and objective study of the facts and forces which make the problems of American Negroes as a minority peculiarly different from the problems of the homogeneous majority in Soviet Russia, or even the oppressed of the majority in the United States.

Furthermore, in Russia, Communism is planned, continually improved upon, and assiduously worked by the Russians, themselves from within. In the life of the American Negro every expression which is labeled "Communism" is for the most part both planned and worked from without. In my opinion we can not solve the problems which Negroes face in America except as we develop our own plan suited to our own needs, and as we ourselves continually improve upon and sacrificially and unselfishly work that plan from within. It can not be done by having some person from the outside pin a badge upon our lapels.

On the other hand, American Negroes have no program of their own for the solution of their peculiar problems; and they have as yet no Lenin who is wise enough and unselfish enough to formulate such a plan, and who is in a position to start a tendency toward its realization. When such a new leader arises, he will no doubt learn something from Communism, something from the philosophy and program of Booker Washington, something from the continually developing ideas of Du Bois, something from his own creative genius, working upon the facts and forces in operation in his own day and generation.

Until that time arrives, Negroes may be expected, like other drowning people grabbing at straws, to be lured by Communism and every other name that holds out to them bright hopes for relief from their burdens. The influence of so-called Communistic propaganda in the Scottsboro incident is the most natural thing in the world for a people who must always wait for typical emergencies to arise, before they decide what to do about them. Nor will Negro leaders who themselves have no plan,—nothing but a hue and cry against the dark dangers of Communism,—be able to stem this tide.

Frank M. Davis, The Atlanta World, *Georgia*

If, when the United States awoke some morning, it were suddenly discovered that everybody classed as a Negro had gone Red, it would cause an immediate change in race relations. There might be trouble for a day or so, but it would not long last. Whites, thoroughly aroused and afraid, would attempt to remove those injustices heaped upon Afro-

America which cradled black Communists; for 12,000,000 souls, backed by the U.S.S.R. and possibly other jealous nations wishing secretly to wreck the United States, would be too big a group to deal with by force.

This is too remote and improbable, however, to merit serious consideration.

It is a fact that the Negro, getting the dirty end of the economic social and political stick, finds in Communistic ideals those panacea he seeks. Yet I believe that were our government adjusted according to Red Standards, few members of this kaleidoscopic race would have sense enough to take advantage of it.

Actually, the Negro as a whole fears Communism—probably because white America has not accepted it. Some frankly believe Red promises would be forgotten were they in power, for aren't they white men too? Further: would the average, every-day white man be willing to forget his prejudices even if ruled by and imbued with Communistic ideals?

Small groups of Negroes in the South going Red have harmed themselves and others in the community. Violence and bloodshed have resulted. The defense that black Reds "started it" has been an A-1 excuse for police officials killing and wounding Negroes. Camp Hill bears this out and last year's sentiment in Alabama is proof of the damage done to race relations.

I have known personally of some racial brethren going Red purely because of the chance to mingle freely with white women in the movement. Then they need no longer ogle secretly or with their personal safety threatened. Talks with a few Atlanta relatives of the Scottsboro boys showed me that Communistic friendliness, pronouncements of social equality, the use of "Mr." and "Mrs." and their treatment in Dixie as men and women instead of Negroes was what got 'em.

But I have no fear of the rainbow brotherhood going Red in wholesale numbers—at least not until white America takes long steps in that direction. This race is slow to change. It would prefer keeping its present status, no matter how long, than fly to a system, no matter what its worth, that is constantly lambasted by press and radio. Too, the Negro considers himself too dependent upon white America to take any chance at losing the crusts now thrown him. Nor is the Communistic policy of crude and noisy militancy liked by this race, for every Negro knows that what he has obtained from white men has been through diplomacy or basically intellectual campaigning.

The past two years has been a mating season for Reds with blacks, yet few of the 12,000,000 have wed. If the Communists cannot make headway amid the disgust of Negroes with our economic order by which they lose their jobs in times of industrial illness, there is hardly any chance of success when the nation rides high.

If enough of us would go Red, Okeh; when we get that way in little bunches it breathes nothing but new trouble for an already over-burdened race.

` C. F. Richardson, Houston Defender, Texas

For several decades following his liberation from the thralldom of human bondage, the American Negro was rather reluctant to pay attention to strange and peculiar political panaceas and governmental doctrines. However, after observing that the existing political parties, governmental agencies and public officials had either left or counted him out of the equation, many modern-day Negroes, both literate and illiterate, educated and uneducated, are at least willing to lend a listening ear to any school of political thought and economy which promises to improve the race's political, economic, industrial and civic status in this country.

Most new cults and "isms" seek to appeal to the weaknesses and prejudices of the desired converts and prospective adherents, just as the klan movement did in its sweep of the country immediately after the World War. Today the majority of its duped followers are sadder but wiser men.

Communism is trying to capitalize the injustices and inequalities meted out to American Negroes and is making a bold bid for racial support and members through the assurance that their organization will change these unsavory and unwholesome conditions and make the Negro a free and full-grown American citizen, exercising and enjoying the same constitutional rights and warranties as other racial groups in our polyglot population.

While the end is certainly worthy of attainment, the means employed are destined to defeat the Communistic program and objective. Negroes are being impressed, however, by the doctrines and activities of the Communists, since the black race has been held literally between the Republican Scylla and Democratic Charybdis, with the capitalistic and ruling class holding the masses in virtual serfdom in several sections of the country.

Communism is a form of socialistic government which advocates the doctrine of having or possessing all property in common, or popular ownership and control of all property. Fundamentally, Communism is opposed to violence and does not seek nor advocate revolutionary methods to change existing conditions and governments, but essays to accomplish political reformation and economic equality through orderly and evolutionary processes.

Being an exploited, maltreated and disadvantaged minority group, there is grave danger that Negroes will embrace any doctrine which offers them relief from certain oppressive, repressive and depressive conditions under which they live and eke out an existence in various parts of the United States.

If Communism is a menace to American ideals and institutions, the only panacea or solution appears to be *real democracy*—"government of *the people,* for *the people* and by *the people,* rather than government of *a people,* for *a people* and by *a people.*

Robert L. Vann, Pittsburgh Courier, *Penna.*

Communism is defined as any theory or system of social organization embracing common ownership of the agents of production as well as equality in the distribution of the products of industry; a sort of socialism unformulated.

We have our serious doubts that the average American Negro understands communism. Communistic leaders are confused also. They think the radicalism of the present-day Negro fits him precisely for Communism. This is error. The radical Negro is nevertheless intelligent; he knows what he wants. He also knows he does not want Communism. It is significant to note that few intelligent Negroes are to be found in the Communistic movement. Almost all Negroes following Communism are being used chiefly to lend a semblance of democracy to the cause. The few intellectuals espousing the cause are no closer to the movement than the average ballyhoo man is to the circus he advertises. Communism will never make the Negro white, blue or green. In fact, as long as the Negro retains his present identity his absorption is next to impossible. If the cause of Communism ever rises in power to the point of assuming governmental control, the Negro will be treated by his Communistic leaders then just as the Negro is treated by the Republicans and Democrats now. The Negro's hope of escape lies in a concentrated production to balance the ledger of his present consumption. To teach him to do this simple thing, the Negro perhaps needs a club more than he needs Communism.

We have no criticism of Negroes who desire to become Communists provided always they are thoroughly prepared to accept the ultimate consequences, whatever they may be.

J. E. Mitchel, St. Louis Argus, Missouri

As we view the situation, we take the position that this so-called Communism is a spirit of unrest among the oppressed people of the world. It has among its adherents many persons of wealth and affluence. There are many, many more white people who are affiliated with this organization than there are colored. In fact, as far as we are able to know, colored people were not thought of in the beginning of such a movement; but the leaders have been wise enough to see a fruitful field among the Negroes for the growth of their propaganda, and they are cultivating it.

The colored man is suffering from the many inequalities that are imposed upon him in this country. The yoke under which he labors is galling at times. He has patiently hoped and waited for something to come along which offered a relief, and, quite naturally, he is willing to join with those who hold out a promise of relief. The Communists say that they are for the equal protection of the law for all citizens alike, and many of their followers have gone to jail and suffered to demonstrate their belief.

This sort of thing has had a very marked influence upon the Negro and, as time goes on and the Communists continue their devotion to the cause they represent, there will be no use to talk to the Negro about the danger of Communism.

C. A. Franklin, Kansas City Call, Missouri

Communism is bound to make a strong appeal to the Negro in the United States, because he has had his appetite whetted for change. The double burden of class and color which he has borne makes him have little to lose whatever happens. Looking backward, he has a bitter memory of small reward for his patience and long suffering. His present efforts in politics and business make him realize that power is sweet. He is ripe for change.

Communism, so far as the Negro is concerned, comes at the strategic moment. Being himself more imbued with the idea of helping himself than of hurting others—even those who have been responsible for the limitations he has borne—he sees no harm in working for a change. Mark how our support has turned from our own men who bid us be patient, to those who tell us we have the power to work out our own salvation. It is only a step farther to believe we can carry out a racial program the easier and quicker under an entire new system.

The present day Americanism, "A place for the Negro and the Negro in his place," cannot withstand the determined advance we are making, now that education has given us knowledge of what the world offers other men. I look for a more tolerant age to let the door of opportunity respond to our thrust. If not, then some change, possibly Communism.

Fred R. Moore, New York Age, *New York*

Through Communistic philosophy it may be possible for the Negro to see Utopian dreams come true in Russia or in some other foreign land, but not in the United States.

Eliminating for the moment the question of race and its attendant vexatious problems, the probability or possibility of many million Americans joining the ranks of Communism is extremely remote. If Russian autocracy was first overthrown by Socialist Revolutionists led by Kerensky, and then the Bolshevists came into power on the heels of another bloody uprising, there is little or no prospect of the United States becoming dominated by communists through revolution or otherwise. The system of government on which our great American nation was founded and has prospered is the very antithesis of Communism.

At heart the American Negro is of the bourgeoisie, and Soviet Russia's system of mass action and the suppression of individual initiative and accomplishment would have no appeal. Those of the race affiliated with the Communist Party in the United States have been appealed to through their emotions and moved to righteous indignation in protest of lynching, disfranchisement, segregation, color prejudice in the courts and other forms of injustice.

A study of Russia's five-year plan deals fundamentally with economics and not human or political rights. As a matter of fact, the program contemplates the abridgement of what the Negro considers his privileges and prerogatives.

Everything must have its good points. When Communists attack labor unions for keeping the Negro from earning his bread and butter I find no reason to disagree. When in speech and on large banners Communists advocate fair play for the Negro and launch a movement to secure the freedom of eight lads illegally convicted of rape, I do not accuse them of being wholly prompted by selfish motives. I find all political parties more or less selfish as are most organizations.

The status of the Negro in the United States—numerically, economically and politically—is well known. If voting en masse for more than fifty years he failed to win social and political considerations to which he is justly entitled, what should be expected of the handful of colored Communists, aided by their white comrades, whose policy seems to be one of agitation and iconoclasm?

Whatever the American Negro has gained has been through loyalty to his government, respect for law and order and by appealing to the better nature and hearts of the dominant race. Capital, the Communist's bugaboo, has been far more friendly and sympathetic to the Negro than either organized or unorganized labor.

It is the bounden duty of the Negro to intelligently and consistently fight for his rights at all times. But he should keep in mind that his problems are going to be solved in the United States—not in Russia; and not by Russia.

W. P. Dabney, The Union, *Ohio*

It is as hard for people who are prosperous to visualize the great growth of Communism among American Citizens, as it is for them to realize the suffering that drives folk into its folds.

The Negro has, for many reasons, been considered immune to participation in such movement. His good humor and adaptability to vicissitudes of fortune are proverbial. His vast faith in the beatitudes of Eternity that gave birth to this song, "You may have all the world but give me Jesus." Last but not least, the class or caste of white Communists. From the earliest days of slavery, the Negro was taught by his owners to hate the "Po white man," for they knew the value of keeping the enemy divided.

That hatred, almost venomous in its intensity, was so sincerely reciprocated, that though sixty-six years have fled since Lee bowed his head in defeat, caste in the South has lost neither spite nor opportunity for its indulgence. But, "the age of miracles" has not passed! "The unexpected has happened!" Thousands of Colored Citizens have joined the Communists, and far more thousands leniently look in that directions. Poor Negroes now gather in parks and halls. They have lost their humoı and theiı God. "If One exists," they say, "He is the friend of the rich, a patron of preachers, those fatted parasites who should be exterminated."

They argue that they have all to gain, nothing to lose. That better to die fighting like men than starve or fall victims to lynchers, as have thousands of their innocent brethren. *"Equal rights,"* the goal for which they strive. *They are sick,* of the U.S. Constitution with its impotent laws, political parties reeking with hypocrisy, philanthropists whose gold-fed institutions emasculate our intelligentsia and blind the pathetically small number of white friends to "Color" Segregation, that most cruel of all castes.

The Communists came, not bringing charity but brotherhood, not bringing words but deeds! What matters motive? When a man is drowning does he demand reasons for the helping hand? "'Tis an ill wind that blows nobody good." The world is beginning to see the tragedy that rocks and shocks "The Souls of Black Folk." Driven to desperation, they are thinking! Why should they be barred, segregated, deprived of opportunity because of circumstances beyond their control? Is it any wonder that thousands are yielding to Communism's appeal?

There will be no Black Communists in America when fair play rules, merit is recognized, race prejudice ostracised. Will Pharaoh Heed?

Roscoe Dunjee, Black Dispatch, *Oklahoma*

By far, the most perplexing problem I have faced during my adult years, rests in the determination of the attitude I should assume towards Communism. For the past seven years, I am frank to say, my mind has been in virtual chaos on this important subject. Today my orientation is not complete.

I always have argued that sooner or later the poor white man here in America must come to the realization that his economic problems are wrapt up with the interests of the Negro; that the ruling class whites have subtly kept the masses of the two races apart. During the past twenty years, I have stood on many platforms and proclaimed this doctrine to mixed audiences. The mental picture I have carried of the day when the two races would sit down side by side on a basis of equality and brotherhood, has always been my rainbow.

My consternation today, however, develops out of the fact that I have at my door a poor white man who talks, acts and preaches the kind and sort of equality about which across the years I have given sanction. He wants to fight about it; he calls meetings and stages parades. Boldly he carries banners through the streets of Dixie, with inscriptions which fairly scream and say all my previous demoted citizenship must vanish. Jim Crow, segregation and anti-marriage laws, yes, everything which has hitherto separated the white and the black here in America, is denounced by this poor white, who brings along with him his woman, and she joins him in the demand for racial equality amidst the confusion which swirls about my head.

This same white man, who preaches brotherhood and equality, has, however, his faults as well as his virtues. With one mighty arm he draws me into his embrace, while with the other he casts bombs at our existing governmental system. His economic nostrums are anti-individualistic. Fear grips me and says: Alliance with him may cause the seldom used Negro labor unit to be boycotted; alliance with him may destroy the black man's traditional record of loyalty towards the Stars and Stripes.

What the black man's attitude should be towards this complex situation is the burning issue. Here, standing at our door is the poor white, who heretofore has constituted the major portion of the mob; who hitherto has joined with the ruling class in denying us equality and opportunity. Shall we turn our back upon the Communist entirely, because of his political notions and economic theories, or, shall we join with him in wrecking the vicious social barriers, which he voluntarily expresses a desire to destroy?

Communism, as a political and economic theory, does not meet and join fully with my ideal notion of government. The Indian in his tribal life represents Communism flourescent. To my way of seeing things, individualism, with its street addresses and titles to property, is the proven pavement to all sound, economic progress.

Regardless of the foregoing viewpoint, I believe some definite course should be charted by Negro leadership with reference to Communism. I believe we are today standing on the brink of revolutionary changes in our social and racial attitudes. Perhaps the wrath of the Nordic, generated during the period of Reconstruction, has spent its force; perhaps we are now about to enter a new era, similar to the ideal approach of the Brazilians to the Negro problem. Whatever the trend, Negro leadership should not overlook the chance to make the most of this moment.

The radical of today is the conservative of tomorrow. Ten years ago the N.A.A.C.P. was classified by many as dangerous to American institutions; so also were the Abolitionists, prior to the Civil War. In those days, motives and objectives were imputed to these two liberty loving organizations which were far from just and fair. The world has long since learned to accept and respect the brotherhood and justice in these two militant organizations. It is entirely possible that history may repeat itself. The Negro who fears the radicalism of Communism today may be classified by black leadership of another and future generation as traitors to the cause of liberty.

The important question for the Negro to decide is the method by which he may cement into lasting bonds of friendship this new relationship between the whites and the blacks of America. We cannot afford to make a mistake.

Yonder stands the poor white with a bomb under his arm—yet love in his heart for me. What shall I do about it? Does that unsanitary looking human being hold within his grasp my rainbow of promise, and the power which I so sorely need? Is Communism the instrumentality through which I am to secure the racial opportunity which for years I have longed for and prayed?

J. Willis Cole, Louisville Leader, *Ky.*

In seeking numerical strength the Communists could hardly overlook the Negro because Communistic seed finds fertile soil in distressing economic conditions.

Equal industrial opportunities and equality before the law naturally have a strong appeal for the Negro, and Communistic propaganda always emphasize these points. But the hatred of God and all forms of religion; abolition of representative or democratic government, freedom of speech, of the press, of assembly, of trial by jury; world revolution and dictatorship of the proletariat and ultimately a world-wide Communistic state with its capital at Moscow, are certain of their principles which the Communists keep in the background.

To be a real Communist one must subscribe to all of its principles and tenets, even those that are not generally known by the masses. Can the Negro, with his unchangeable religious nature, his predilection for democratic government, and his reputation for loyalty to constituted authority, subscribe to the whole category of Communistic teachings?

Certainly the Scottsboro case, the mixed parties in New Jersey and the rent-eviction disturbances would advertise Communism, recommend it highly, and make a strong appeal to a certain number of a much abused race. But in serious meditation upon Communism, the Negro will be disposed to ask himself whether the Communists can go through with their program; whether Communism is really a cure for the ills of the race, whether it points the way out of our social, economic and political forest; whether in working out their scheme and enjoying its benefits the Communist will be absolutely fair with the Negro. The Negro will also keep in mind that Communism is now simply an experiment on a larger scale than heretofore; but that previous trials on a much smaller scale and under favorable conditions were failures.

The Negro will not forget that among those who must make up the back bone of Communism in America are those who have contributed most to his economic ills, those who gave life to the Ku Klux Klan and give strength to the mob whose victim is usually a fellow Negro laborer. And the Negro will be careful not to line himself up with a project that bucks capitalism, which has helped him to the strength he has, and given him what protection and pursuit of happiness he enjoys.

In the last September *Crisis,* Dr. W. E. B. Du Bois well said: "American courts from the Supreme Court down are dominated by wealth and Big Business, yet they are today the Negroes' only protection against complete disfranchisement, segregation and the abolition of his schools. Higher education for Negroes is the gift of the Standard Oil, the Power Trust, the Steel Trust together with the aristocratic Christian Church; but these have given Negroes 40,000 black leaders to fight white folks on their own level and in their own language. Big industry in the last ten years has opened occupation for a million Negro workmen, without which we would have starved in jails and gutters." *

The Crisis, April and May, 1932; XXXIX, 117–19, 154–56, 170.

* The quotation from Du Bois' essay in *The Crisis* for September, 1931, is accurate, but so removed from context as to amount to distortion. Thus that essay commences with praise for the U.S.S.R., affirms regard for the purposes of Communists, but questions their wisdom and knowledge of realities in the South and adds that they seek too much too soon. The essay concludes with these two paragraphs, the first one italicized in the original: *"Present organization of industry for private profit and control of government by concentrated wealth is doomed to disaster. It must change and fall if civilization survives. The foundation of its present worldwide power is the slavery and semi-slavery of the colored world including the American Negroes. Until the colored man, yellow, red, brown and black, becomes free, articulate, intelligent and the receiver of a decent income, white capital will use the profit derived from his degradation to keep white labor in chains.*

"There is no doubt, then, as to the future, or as to where the interests of American Negroes lie. There is no doubt, too, that the first step toward the emancipation of colored labor must come from white labor" (p. 318 of cited *Crisis*).

148

THE NEGRO SOCIAL WORKER
EVALUATES BIRTH CONTROL
by Constance Fisher

With the Depression there appeared a rising interest in limiting family size; while there was present in the Afro-American communities the fear that birth control was a form of genocide fostered by racists, there was also a mounting call for such practices from Black people, especially women. An expression of the latter feeling came from a Black social worker, a district supervisor in the Associated Charities organization in Cleveland, Ohio.

With the general tendency today of more tolerance of birth control clinics and information, and with the increasing freedom in asking for direction in matters concerning birth control, attention is drawn to cross sections of people as well as to the general group. We are naturally interested to know what this new trend means in terms of social conditions or solutions of problems.

The Negro has been emerging from an agricultural to an industrial state of existence in the past fifteen years, more or less. Just before and after the World War the transition seemed to take place speedily. In earlier years, in the more predominantly agricultural state, each child born to a family became an economic asset; all life was a struggle with nature and the more children there were to fight, the easier and better it was. Moreover, the large family was supposed to be the happy family and the more children a man had the more he won the respect and regard of his community. Then, too, there was the sense of security in old age, which parents felt because of the children who would always take them in and care for them. But when the pendulum began to swing in the direction of an industrial existence, it seemed that a wage Utopia had come and it was no longer necessary to have such large families to insure the bare necessities of life; still every additional person was of value in bringing in extra money and security to the home.

With the present period of economic depression the story has begun to change. When a plant closes down for lack of work or when Negro labor or help is being replaced by others, the larger family does not help matters. When landlords refuse to accept a family because of too many children, and force it to go from house to house hunting a place to stay, the children become liabilities rather than assets. Despite the fact that many say "the Lord will provide," each new baby seems, inevitably, more of a burden than the last. Negroes are usually the first to feel any cuts in jobs or wages or any general lay-off. What their future in industry is no one knows. Suffice to say that in the present situation the smaller family is an asset.

Family case workers frequently hear what might be called the song of regret from their clients who are finding their other problems intensified because of the narrow economic margin on which they are forced to exist; they want no more children now and they ask often where they may obtain *bona fide* and scientific information concerning this. Not only is the question coming from those concerned chiefly over their economic situation, but also from those homes in which the social worker finds domestic incompatibility, alcoholism, and many other social ailments. In many instances the case worker sees the need for birth control where and when the couple involved do not. Where there is low mentality, a serious health impairment, or other very obvious complications, it is very easy to see the need for information of this sort.

In making a study of desertion a few years ago, the writer was impressed with the fact that in even the small sample studied at the time, the factor at the bottom of the difficulties in well over half the situations was sex maladjustment. This frequently bred feelings of inadequacy, insecurities of every sort, alcoholism, infidelity, desertion, and generally broken homes. And in most of the families the objections to constant pregnancy came from the mother, though the father was often greatly discouraged over the situation too.

Obviously the family case worker must play some role in this new trend in public opinion, whether it is active or passive. When her clients come to her with their questions and problems, she must make some effort to help them find solutions, and when she goes into their homes she needs to be alert for causative factors as well as symptoms of difficulties. Her job is not to proselytize, but to administer her treatment of the case on as sound and thoughtful a basis as possible. If the family recognizes the need for birth control as either one of or the chief factor in working out its problems, and asks the worker for advice on the matter, she must meet her responsibility adequately. In instances where she sees a definite need for advice of this sort, the writer feels that she owes it to the community, as well as to the family, to use the birth control clinic as a tool for preventive social therapy as well as remedial or palliative treatment.

The trend toward greater use of birth control clinics is one which must be recognized and reckoned with. Not every worker is qualified to suggest or advise procedures to families on this level of treatment, any more than every medical doctor is capable of diagnosing a psychosis or neurosis, but in the hands of an alert and capable worker, there is little danger. The Negro client is feeling less and less guilty about asking for and receiving information on birth control and is expressing himself freely as having wanted such guidance for a long time without knowing where to get it. There are still a great many who have not lost their sense of sinning in seeking such help, or who have superstitions concerning it, or who fear that it will only breed greater difficulties in the home. Yet, there are increasing numbers who seek birth control information because they feel that if they go on resenting themselves and their mates for physical, economic, and emotional reasons, greater problems are certain to arise, and the existing tensions in their family life are bound to be stretched to their logical ends—the breaking point.

Birth Control Review, June, 1932; XVI, 174–75.

149

WAR IN THE EAST
by Cyril Briggs

A leading Black Communist of the nineteen-twenties and nineteen-thirties was Cyril Briggs, noted in earlier documents. Quite early in the course of the invasion of China by Japan, Briggs called upon the Afro-American to be alert to its meaning in a magazine then issued by the Communist Party, under extremely difficult conditions, in Alabama.

The monstrous counter-revolutionary plans of Japanese imperialism for armed intervention against the successful building of Socialism in the Soviet Union are openly stated in the pamphlet *Presenting Japan's Side of the Case,* published by the Japanese Association in China.

No longer daring to pretend contempt for the Soviet Five-Year-Plan, world imperialism, with the Japanese imperialists in the role of spearhead, are now preparing to start the most reactionary of wars—war against the proletarian dictatorship, war against the rising, flourishing world of Socialism, of working-class emancipation, of liberation of the former oppressed nationalities and national minorities

The pamphlet admits a tremendous improvement in the material and cultural conditions of the Soviet masses as a result of the overthrow of Tsarist-capitalism and the establishment of the proletarian dictatorship. The people of Russia have the satisfaction of knowing that the profits from their toil are being expended for the betterment of their living and working conditions and for national defense. The billions that roll into the state treasury from official enterprises and co-operative farms are used to purchase all manner of railway, textile, electrical, mining and other industrial machinery; to erect houses, lay out new cities; to build roads, waterworks, sewers, public utilities, schools, social and amusement centers and other betterments designed for public welfare.

And for this reason it is necessary to wage a war of annihilation against the workers' fatherland because the success of the Soviet Five-Year-Plan "will bring a revolution in world economy," "a new and better outlook will be created for the other workers of the world," and this will result in "disaster to other industrial nations, and overturn the existing social order" (p. 11).

"Japan sees the handwriting on the wall and her military leaders have appealed to the right of self-defense" (p. 34).

Already the triumphant advance of Socialism in the Soviet Union is stirring the oppressed masses of Asia to throw off their chains, to overthrow their native and imperialist oppressors.

"The Soviet Philosophy has permeated all of Central Asia" (p. 12).

Dying capitalism must defend its loot, its "right" to rob and oppress the toiling masses. Revolutionary China must be destroyed, China dismembered, victorious Socialist construction in the Soviet Union interrupted, the hopes of the toiling masses of the whole world, based on the glorious achievements in the building of Socialism in the Soviet Union, destroyed, the lives of tens of millions of workers sacrificed. All in order to postpone the inevitable destruction of the insane, accursed capitalist system.

That which was secretly stated in the notorious Tanaka Document of 1927, in which was laid down the program now being faithfully carried out in the present robber war of Japanese imperialism against China and the fast maturing plans for an armed attack against the proletarian state, is now openly stated in the present pamphlet, *Presenting Japan's Side of the Case.*

But it is no longer a question of words. Japanese troops are already mobilized on the Soviet border. Tsarist White Guard elements in Manchuria are being organized and armed by the Japanese. Japanese War Minister Araki has openly stated in the Japanese Diet that Japan is to send more troops into Manchuria, that Manchuria is to be converted into a military base against the Soviet Union, and moreover, that the situation arising out of Japan's robber aims in Manchuria is "more serious than the Russo-Japanese War" of 1905. And the American imperialist press has hailed Japan's decision to send more troops into Manchuria, towards the Soviet frontier, as a "return to the big objective"—armed intervention against the Soviet Union.

Defense of the Soviet Union is defense of the interests of the whole world working class! Negro Workers! Rally to the fight against the Japanese robber war! Against the imperialist war inciters and war criminals! For the immediate withdrawal of all imperialist troops and gunboats from China! Against the partition of China and for the defense of the Chinese Soviet districts! For the defense of the Soviet Union and socialist construction! For brotherly solidarity with the Soviet Union and for socialist emancipation of all exploited masses and oppressed colonies!

Remember that we are among the most oppressed of all colonial peoples. That the only way in which we can win our freedom is by uniting together with the working class of all races and the exploited peoples of all lands against the imperialist class, whether it be British, American, French or Japanese.

The Negro Worker, May, 1932; II, No. 5, 6–8.

150

SCOTTSBORO BOYS APPEAL FROM DEATH CELLS TO THE TOILERS OF THE WORLD

One of the most notorious instances of racist frame-up in U.S. history was the attempt to legally lynch the Scottsboro Boys. On April 1, 1932, from their prison in Montgomery, Alabama, they sent the following jointly signed letter. Due basically to the Left and the Communist movement in particular —finally achieving unity in action from the entire Afro-American people—

and also arousing worldwide public opinion, none of the intended victims was executed and all were (after years of struggle) freed.

From the death cells in Kilby Prison, where they have been held under conditions of the most ghastly torture ever since the mock trials in the lower court at Scottsboro, Ala., the eight Scottsboro boys send the following appeal to the workers of the whole world to rally to the mass fight to smash the hideous frame-up and lynch murder verdicts:

From the death cell here in Kilby Prison, eight of us Scottsboro boys is writing this to you.

We have been sentenced to die for something we ain't never done. Us poor boys been sentenced to burn up on the electric chair for the reason that we is workers—and the color of our skin is black. We like any one of you workers is none of us older than 20. Two of us is 14 and one is 13 years old.

What we guilty of? Nothing but being out of a job. Nothing but looking for work. Our kinfolk was starving for food. We wanted to help them out. So we hopped a freight—just like any one of you workers might a done—to go down to Mobile to hunt work. We was taken off the train by a mob and framed up on rape charges.

At the trial they give us in Scottsboro we could hear the crowds yelling, "Lynch the Niggers." We could see them toting those big shotguns. Call 'at a fair trial?

And while we lay here in jail, the boss-man make us watch 'em burning up other Negroes on the electric chair. "This is what you'll get," they say to us.

What for? We ain't done nothing to be in here at all. All we done was to look for a job. Anyone of you might have done the same thing—and got framed up on the same charge just like we did.

Only ones helped us down here been the International Labor Defense and the League of Struggle for Negro Rights. We don't put no faith in the National Association for the Advancement of Colored People. They give some of us boys eats to go against the other boys who talked for the I.L.D. But we wouldn't split. Nohow. We know our friends and our enemies.

Working class boys, we asks you to save us from being burnt on the electric chair. We's only poor working class boys whose skin is black. We shouldn't die for that.

We hear about working people holding meetings for us all over the world. We asks for more big meetings. It'll take a lot of big meetings to help the I.L.D. and the L.S.N.R to save us from the boss-man down here.

Help us boys. We ain't done nothing wrong. We are only workers like you are. Only our skin is black.

(Signed) Andy Wright, Olen Montgomery, Ozie Powell, Charlie Weems, Clarence Norris, Haywood Patterson, Eugene Williams, Willie Robertson.

Text as originally printed in *The Negro Worker,* May, 1932; II, No. 5, 8-9.

151

DISCRIMINATION IN FEDERAL FLOOD
CONTROL CONSTRUCTION

by Walter White

Towards the latter half of 1932, shortly before the presidential elections of November, the N.A.A.C.P. effectively exposed the racist and near-slave conditions imposed upon Black men performing flood control work directly for the federal government itself. The account that follows is taken from Mr. White's (mimeographed) report, on September 12, 1932, to the Board of Directors of the association.

As reported to the Board of Directors at the June meeting, the National Office took advantage of the offer of Miss Helen Boardman, who was to be in the West on other business, to make a investigation of discrimination against Negroes in the construction of federal flood control along the Mississippi River.

Miss Boardman completed her investigation in July and made her report to the National Office. The report disclosed that:

1. Colored American citizens are being employed with the funds of the United States government at an average wage of ten cents an hour, and that they are being worked almost without exception on a twelve-hour day, with a seven-day week and no holidays and no pay for overtime; that those long hours are in force despite the fact that all the projects are from six weeks to six months ahead of schedule.

2. The wages for colored labor range from one dollar to three dollars for a twelve-hour day, with very few cases of a three-dollar wage. The average wage is ten cents an hour.

3. A commissary system is in effect in most camps, which insures that the contractor will not have to pay more than maintenance for his labor. In many instances Negro laborers pay out from fifty to seventy-five per cent of their wages in commissary charges or other items imposed by the contractors.

4. The attitude of many contractors toward their labor is reminiscent of slavery at its worst. Men are beaten on the slightest pretext and fired without pay on the slightest provocation.

5. Colored men work under most unsanitary living conditions, in crowded, floorless tents. No provision is made for the disposal of garbage; and disease is rampant.

A copy of Miss Boardman's detailed report was sent, on August 22, to President Hoover with the request that the machinery of the federal government be set in motion to correct the conditions cited. The report was sent also to Secretary of War, Patrick J. Hurley and to Attorney General William DeWitt Mitchell; also to twenty-six United States senators. President Hoover referred the report to the War Department, and under date of August 25, a letter was received from Major General Brown, which showed that he evidently was angered because of the revelations of this investigation made under the auspices of the N.A.A.C.P. General Brown did not deny the facts as set forth in the report but instead excused the low wages paid by stating that the government made it a policy to pay the wage customary in the region in which its projects are being worked. He excused the long hours by saying the flood control work was of an emergency nature but did not explain why the twelve-hour double shifts were necessary when all the work is from six weeks to six months ahead of schedule. Also, General Brown attempted to belittle the reports of brutality by saying that no names and addresses of men beaten were given, and he made the preposterous suggestion that the men complaining take their cases to court. General Brown, a native of Tennessee, cannot help but know that it is worth any Negro's life to let it be known that he has told of conditions in these camps.

The National Office replied to General Brown's letter pointing out that "the tone of your reference to this report distinctly indicates an attitude of hostility which, to say the least, is most astounding in an employe of the United States government," and that the proper procedure was for the government "vigorously, swiftly, courageously and without bias" to make a thorough investigation of the alleged conditions, to correct them and to follow up the correction by strict, periodic inspections to see that such conditions are not re-established.

Copy of General Brown's letter together with copy of the reply was sent to President Hoover, the National Office stating that "this Association takes very definite exception to the attitude of Major General Brown in his reception of this report." The request was made of the President that he instruct the War Department to investigate and correct the conditions reported, without bias.

Under date of August 31 the National Office received the following letter from Secretary of War Hurley, who had not up to this time acknowledged the report which had been sent directly to him:

My dear Mr. White:

Your letter of August 29th to the President has been handed to me by him personally.

General Brown's letter to you and yours to him have been carefully noted. I have no reason to be partial to General Brown, but must be just to him in that efforts to get fair and humane treatment to labor under this Department on the projects for river and harbor improvement under my direction and in his charge have been initiated and carried into execution by him.

I regret that General Brown did not assure you of a thorough, unbiased and fair investigation of your complaints. I will do so now. Accordingly, the President of the Mississippi River Commission has been directed to institute such an investigation. Should the results show that wrong in any way is being inflicted on the labor engaged on the Mississippi River project, appropriate action will be taken by me to apply the necessary remedies.

(Signed) Patrick J. Hurley
Secretary of War

In acknowledging Secretary Hurley's letter the National Office made the suggestion that since the contract system on the flood control work has necessitated two investigations of alleged abuses in less than a year, the system be abolished and the work taken over by army engineers.

Closely following the communication from the Secretary of War came a letter from Major General Brown, under date of September 1, asking for the name and address of the investigator for the N.A.A.C.P. so that arrangements might be made for this agent to testify at an inquiry being instituted by Secretary Hurley. The National Office promptly offered to produce the investigator at the time and place of the hearing. Under date of September 6 Major General Brown wrote that the investigation is being conducted by the President of the Mississippi River Commission at Vicksburg, Mississippi, adding:

Should you desire the testimony of your investigator to be taken, I will transmit his name and address, with the desire, to the President, Mississippi River Commission, and he will make all arrangements for the testimony. If you do not desire that the testimony of your investigator be taken, or if you are indifferent in the matter, kindly consider my request for the necessary information as cancelled.

Upon receipt of this latest communication from Major General Brown, the National Office wrote immediately to the Secretary of War telling him of the correspondence with Major General Brown and stating that the N.A.A.C.P. "will decline to send any investigator or anyone connected with this Association to Vicksburg or to any other city in Mississippi for investigation. We do not believe that in the atmosphere which prevails in the State of Mississippi . . . any person, white or colored, connected with this organization could be heard without intimidation or insult and possible bodily injury." The National Office offered to produce its agent in either Washington or New York and to have the testimony given orally or in the form of a deposition.

All the twenty-six senators to whom copies of Miss Boardman's report were sent were absent from Washington for the summer, but the material was forwarded to some of them at their homes, and from these acknowledgements and comments have been received. Both Senator Arthur Capper and Senator Robert F. Wagner expressed the opinion that such conditions should not be allowed to continue.

On September 6 the Secretary and the Assistant Secretary called on Senator Wagner at his New York office for a conference which lasted about an hour. Senator Wagner was most deeply stirred by the revelations in this whole matter. The Secretary pointed out to him that we were convinced that unless the matter could be kept alive there would be the usual whitewashing with correction, perhaps, of the more patent and notorious evils, at least until after the elections; that the only hope of really correcting conditions was through a senatorial investigation. Senator Wagner agreed to the request that he not only introduce a resolution in the Senate when it reconvenes for such an investigation but that he announce now from his own office that he will introduce such a resolution.

It was pointed out to the Senator also that this was a part of the whole problem of Negroes getting jobs on government-financed projects such as the Hoover Dam, constructing of post offices and highways and other self liquidating projects as provided for in the Wagner Bill. The Assistant Secretary brought to the Senator's attention the situation in Mississippi where the only way in which federal moneys are to be expended is through the state highway projects, upon which no Negroes are employed, according to statements being published in the newspapers of Mississippi.

Senator Wagner promised not only to follow up the Mississippi Flood Control project but all other instances which we might bring to his attention of discrimination against Negroes in employment on projects financed wholly or in part by government funds.

152

THE BANKRUPTCY OF CAPITALISM AND CAPITALIST EDUCATION

by James W. Ford

In 1932 the Communist Party, for the first time in the history of the United States, ran a White and Black presidential ticket, with William Z. Foster for President and James W. Ford for Vice President. A fairly characteristic speech by the latter delivered during that campaign was that from which extracts are published below; it was delivered August 4, 1932, in New York City at the Twelfth Annual Teachers' and Students' Educational Conference.

In the face of capitalist bankruptcy, the capitalists and their agents are making desperate efforts to convince the workers that capitalism is still the best system in the world. In the face of Socialist construction in the Soviet Union they continue to proclaim the superiority of their own declining system of society. They tremble at the prospect of millions of workers taking the Soviet way out of the crisis. Let us take two of the most recent and typical of the assurances of the soundness and superiority of the profit system. On July 11, for example, Dr. Marcus Nadler, director of the Institute of International Finance, assured the Institute of Public Affairs at the University of Virginia that capitalism was doomed. "The capitalistic system," he said, "is still the best economic system which the human brain has devised, but it must be shorn of the excessive greed for profits of the individual or the corporation and must be replaced by a sense of broad social responsibility to the entire community. A democracy which lives on hollow phrases and which permits politically free men to starve has indeed outlived its usefulness."

Former President Calvin Coolidge, in the July 15 issue of *Collier's Weekly,* also tries to convince the impoverished and starving people of the United States that the capitalists' "system has worked better, and is now working better than any other that was ever devised. Under it we have more progress and more comfort than ever came to any other people. Even in our present distress we are better taken care of than we could be under any other system."

Of course, only a person with the imagination and mentality of a

Coolidge could take a social catastrophe of the depth and scope of the present crisis as a basis for an exultant and self-satisfied boasting of the "achievements" of the capitalist system. Actually, however, we are dealing here with a typical example of the shameless lies to which the capitalists resort in order to prevent the workers from resisting starvation, wage cuts and a general lowering of their standard of living. It is a positive proof that the capitalists, rolling in wealth and luxury, are absolutely unable and unwilling to understand or feel what unemployment, hunger and suffering mean to the working class! For the rest, how much stock we can put in the "hollow phrases" of both the Nadlers and Coolidges can be seen from the fact that while the "scientific" Dr. Nadler assures us that capitalism will continue to be the best system, especially if it is "shorn of the excessive greed for profits," silent Mr. Coolidge, who ought to know, insists that "we are wise enough to know that there is no system of property rights that is proof against human folly and greed."

However, no amount of such assurances of the superiority of this system of "human folly and greed" can hide the fundamental fact that the more capitalism produces, the worse are the crises it unleashes. The present crisis is the worst crisis in the history of capitalism. It has come at a time when capitalist technique and capitalist industry have attained their highest development. It has come *after* Hoover proclaimed before the whole world that poverty had practically been abolished and eternal prosperity would reign over the country. The present crisis differs from all previous crises in precisely this, that despite and *because* capitalism has reached the *height* of its development, it has produced the deepest, most far-reaching and protracted crisis in its history. Such a contradiction is possible only in a system which is already in the process of decline and decay. Moreover, the present capitalist crisis has occurred at a time when a hundred and sixty million people, occupying one-sixth of the earth's surface, have overthrown their capitalist rulers and have shown in life itself that the world *can* be run without bloodsucking usurers and profit-mongers; indeed, that only by driving out the capitalists and establishing a workers' and farmers' Socialist system can the world be *freed* from devastating crises, mass unemployment and bloody wars.

After a hundred and fifty years of development, capitalism is bankrupt. All the achievements of modern science, all the conquests over the forces of nature, the whole unprecedented increase in the social forces of production have, *under capitalist control,* only succeeded in piling up fabulous wealth for a handful of parasites while spreading hunger and misery throughout the great majority of the population. Like the charred ruins of a fire that has devastated a whole country, fifteen million unemployed American workers stand as a living indictment of the whole capitalist system. The great majority of people in this country are today faced with a life and death issue: shall we accept mass unemployment, wage cuts, continually falling standards of living, mass poverty and ever-growing menace of a new imperialist war; in short, shall we accept the capitalist way out of the present crisis, or shall we follow the example of the Soviet Union and forge our own working class way out, by freeing the factories from the death grip of a handful of billionaires and producing for the welfare of all instead of the profit of the few. The whole progress of the world, of the forward development of civilization, the future of the working people, depends upon the determination and the ability of the oppressed and exploited to unite in a mighty and irresistable movement to achieve this end. Society has reached such a point that it is possible not only to produce enough for the bounteous consumption of all members of society and for a generous reserve fund, but also to allow each individual sufficient leisure so that the permanent achievements of culture are not only preserved but transformed and further developed from a monopoly of the ruling class into the common property of the whole of society. With the development of the productivity of human labor to a point where the monopoly of its products by a handful of parasites transforms superabundance into immeasurable poverty of the majority, the last pretext has disappeared for the existence of a ruling class. The final argument in defense of class difference has always been: there must always be a class which will not have to struggle producing its daily means of subsistence, so that it can have time to accomplish the intellectual labor of society. This argument which once had its historical justification, has had its very root destroyed once for all not only by the great industrial revolution of the last hundred and fifty years, but by the present crisis of "overpopulation." The existence of a ruling class has become a hindrance to the development of science and art. The capitalist class not only stands in the way of life, but in the way of free education and development of the great majority of people.

Let us examine the state of education at the present time. The decline, the moral and spiritual decay which characterizes capitalism as a whole, is also reflected in the sphere of education. In fact, education reproduces in miniature all the general features of the crisis and in turn supplies a penetrating measure of the decay of a system which blocks and retards all the forces of progress at a time when it is materially best able to advance them. Overproduction, unemployment, wage cuts, lower living standards, and the reduction of educational expenditures, have characterized the educational situation during the last three years, resulting in a worsening of the conditions of instruction and impairing the quality of the teaching.

Charles H. Judd, of the University of Chicago, summarizing the educational situation in the *American Journal of Sociology* for May, 1932, stated:

> Shrinkage in revenues available for the conduct of public schools amounted in some cases to as much as 20 per cent. A canvass of public school systems made in the middle of the year showed that there were practically no cases in which increases in resources could be reported and that in 40 per cent of the school systems school revenues were reduced below the level of the year preceding. Many of the systems which escaped reduction in their budgets during 1931 were quite certain to experience curtailment during 1932.
>
> There is no uniformity in the methods adopted to effect retrenchment. In most centers there is a disposition to maintain, as far as possible, the schedules of the teachers' salaries. In a few cases salaries for the year have been reduced either through the closing of schools for a period or through consent on the part of the teachers to serve for a time without pay. Economies of minor types have been very common. The supervisory force has been reduced. Summer schools have been abandoned. Classes for adults have been closed. More fundamental changes have been introduced in the form of reorganization of classes. Classes have sometimes been increased in size, and periods of instruction in laboratories and shops have been shortened.

• • • • •

Perhaps the most typical example of wage cuts, elimination of social insurance and a general lowering of the standards of living of school teachers at a time when capitalism has reached its greatest material wealth, is the school situation in the middle west, and particularly in Chicago, the second largest city in the richest country in the world. Two days ago, the New York *Times* reported that the thousands of Chicago's school teachers and school employees who have received no pay for more than half a year, *may* receive wages for the last half of *March,* "if the legal requirements can be arranged." Many of the school teachers are actually starving; cases of fainting in the class room from lack of food have become quite common. Most of the teachers have exhausted their credit and many of them have lost their little homes. The usual educational trips abroad during the summer vacation period have become a thing of the past. Naturally, under such circumstances, the quality of teaching is at its lowest ebb.

The picture is equally black, if not worse, as far as the working class school children are concerned. According to a report by Don O. Rogers, director of a building survey for the Chicago Board of Education, "more than 67,000 Chicago school children are being handicapped in their effort to obtain an education by lack of adequate accommodations in elementary, junior and senior high schools."

The schools are dangerously overcrowded and makeshift schemes have been adopted to distribute the children. "Portable" schools similar to the old one-room country school houses, are being used. They cluster like outcast hovels around the main school buildings which have exhausted their seating capacity. A total of 14,000 children are compelled to work in poorly lighted basement rooms, which is ruinous to their eyesight and health. Twenty-five thousand have had their schedules arranged in a most inconvenient manner, having to attend school before and after the regular session of other classes. Concentration for the children in many cases is impossible. They are compelled to attend what is called "double" schools, where one group recites while another group in the same room studies; or they are forced to hold classes in improvised rented quarters. For example, one school of 1,200 children attended classes in a rented factory. The boasted "facilities and equipment" of the modern capitalist school are unknown to many school children in Chicago. Many of them have never been in a school gymnasium or auditorium. According to the report, some classes are held in "old and dilapidated" buildings, endangering the lives of pupils.

Moreover, there are thousands of children who cannot take advantage of even these limited educational facilities because of lack of clothes to wear, actual weakness from hunger or because of the necessity to help support the family in one way or another.

Jim-Crowism and segregation is prevalent in the sphere of education as well as in every other sphere of capitalist society. Throughout the South, separate Jim-Crow schools are maintained for Negro children. All told, school terms are shorter, and equipment is poorer than in the white schools. In South Carolina, for example, the total expenditure per pupil enrolled in 1928 was $60.25 in the white schools and $7.65 in the Negro schools. School property (building, equipment, etc.) was valued at $134 per pupil in the white schools and $17 in the Negro schools. Even in Charleston County which had the higher average salaries for Negro teachers in South Carolina, they were paid less than half as much as white teachers.

Compare these facts with the advance of the cultural revolution in the Soviet Union. Expenditures for popular education in 1930 were over

$1,000,000,000. In 1932 the national budget calls for an expenditure of 9,200,000,000 rubles for social-cultural enterprises. Some 450,000,-000 books were printed last year in the Soviet Union, or about four times the pre-war output. Illiteracy is steadily decreasing and among trade unionists has almost entirely disappeared. Before the November Revolution only about 7,000,000 children attended school; now there are 23,000,000. In the secondary schools there are now eight times as many pupils as in prewar days. Altogether, 46,000,000 people, or one-third of the population, are attending educational institutions. In 1913 only about 25 per cent above the age of ten could read; 90 per cent of women were illiterate. Illiteracy has now been practically eliminated from the industrial centers. And by the end of this year, it is to be liquidated completely.

• • • • •

However, the immediate, and most tangible evidence of the cultural decay of capitalism is the increasing unemployment of scientific workers, technicians and engineers. After spending years in preparatory training, thousands of these professional men are unable to find work. One might imagine that the blessings of science have become so great and widespread that the services of the men of science are no longer necessary. But the fact that increasing numbers of these men themselves are rendered jobless and thrust upon the mercy of capitalist charity reveals the absurd and reactionary contradiction of capitalism today. Here too is revealed the helpless anarchy of a system which not only requires a decreasing number of scientists in the face of mass starvation and misery, but which at the same time permits a "surplus" of these very scientists and technicians to be added to this army of unemployment and hunger.

• • • • •

Capitalist education thus stands bankrupt and in the iron grip of the same process of decline and decay affecting the entire capitalist system. The crisis has demonstrated the utter futility of the conception of education as a self-sufficient force divorced from the fundamental processes of social development. It has demonstrated the falsity of artificially erecting arbitrary barriers between education and the ever-sharpening class struggle in society today.

In spite of the much vaunted superiority of the technical and educational achievements of capitalism, the fact remains that its highly developed educational apparatus has not prevented the chaos of the present economic crisis. On the contrary, less than three years ago its most advanced thinkers and teachers tried to convince the world that crises had been abolished and that poverty had seen its end. The achievements of scientific research have even contributed towards the development of the present economic crisis.

Education has failed to prevent the crisis or even to affect its development, because the capitalist system, which produces crises, is not a rational system of production in which the ultimate actions of society are identical with its original purposes. In a system which is not based upon a planned economy but upon an essential anarchy of social production, education and reason, insofar as it is the education and reason of the ruling class, are utterly helpless. This was clearly grasped and expressed recently by a leading capitalist educator, Dr. Paul Klapper, dean of the School of Education at the College of the City of New York:

"Education in our democracy is a much indicted institution," Dr. Klapper declared. "People ascribe to the failure of the school many of our social ills, forgetting that education has ever been a product of existing social order, charged with the function of rationalizing and perpetuating the society that supports it. However progressive the teacher and however free and unfettered the school, they nevertheless seek to justify what is.

Only in this light can we understand the role education is playing and can play at the present time. To the extent that education remains an adjunct of capitalism, both educators and educated will suffer from the unarrestable decline and decay of capitalism.

• • • • •

The inescapable truth of this should be particularly clear to the Negro people and the Negro intellectuals. The highest achievements of capitalism have trickled down to the Negroes over a blood-stained wall built up out of Jim-Crowism, segregation, peonage, and lynching during the last 150 years. At the height of its material and cultural development American capitalism has lynched over 150 Negro workers and farmers in the last year and a half. The Negro people, constituting one-tenth of the population, are a social outcast. Unemployment among Negroes is from 75 to 100 per cent greater than among whites. The death rate is as much as 200 per cent higher. Unsanitary housing and overcrowding is beyond description, resulting in a terrific disease toil. Every illiterate Negro knows these facts from his own experience. Despite all the hypocritical promise of Republicans, Democrats and Socialists, the Negro people have nothing to gain from the capitalist system. But the Negro people cannot free themselves without waging a determined revolutionary struggle against capitalist oppression and slavery. On the other hand, they cannot free themselves alone, just as labor in the white skin cannot be free as long as labor in the black skin is oppressed and enslaved. But the Negro people will not have to fight alone. The revolutionary white workers, under the leadership of the Communist Party, have shown their determination to fight shoulder to shoulder with the Negro workers and the Negro people in the struggle for emancipation. The struggle to free the nine Scottsboro boys, in which revolutionary white workers have already given their lives, is at the same time a struggle for the freedom of the entire Negro people from the very system that produces lynch frame-ups and holds over nine million people in peonage and bondage.

It is necessary to break through the traditional conception of education if our understanding is to become a practical force in shaping the course of history. The idea that education is confined to educational institutions, that it is merely a study of books, is at best an unreal and poverty-stricken conception. It does not grasp the real relationship of education to social life. If ideas are to become a force they must seize hold of the masses. In this respect, the basic struggle of society today is the struggle between the ideas of capitalism and the ideas of Communism; the struggle between the capitalist way out of the crisis and the revolutionary working class way out of the crisis.

• • • • •

The Communist, September, 1932; XI, 831–42.

153

THE BONUSEERS BAN JIM CROW
by Roy Wilkins

About twenty-five thousand impoverished veterans and their families converged on Washington in the Spring and Summer of 1932 demanding the immediate payment of a bonus—amounting to from fifty to one hundred dollars—rather than in 1945 as provided in the original legislation. Congress adjourned on July 17 without taking any action. On July 28 police attacked several hundred veterans, "sitting-in" at a federal building, and killed two of them. President Hoover then ordered the army—under General MacArthur, Lieutenant Colonel Eisenhower, and Major Patton—to drive out all the veterans. A massive assault upon their shacks and women and children ensued; scores were severely injured and one infant was killed and the army won the Battle of Anacostia Heights. Just before the July violence, Roy

Wilkins visited the Black and white veterans of the Bonus Army. Here is what he saw.

Floating clear on the slight breeze of a hot June night in Washington came a tinkling, mournful melody, a song known by now in every corner of the globe. Lilting piano notes carried the tune that set my foot patting, in spite of myself, on the trampled grass of the little hill. Then, as I was about to start humming the words, a voice took up the cadence and rode over the Anacostia Flats on the off-key notes—

Feelin' tomorrow,
  Lak I feel today—
Feelin' tomorrow,
  Lak I feel today—
I'll pack my trunk and make my get a-way

Never, I thought, was there a more perfect setting for W. C. Handy's famous *St. Louis Blues*. No soft lights and swaying bodies here; no moaning trombone or piercing trumpet; no fantastic stage setting; no white shirt fronts, impeccably tailored band master or waving baton. Instead, a black boy in a pair of ragged trousers and a torn, soiled shirt squatting on a box before a piano perched on a rude platform four or five feet off the ground. A single electric light bulb disclosed him in the surrounding gloom. Skillfully his fingers ran over the keys, bringing out all the Handy secrets of the song. Plaintively he sang the well-known words. A little of the entertainer was here, for there is a little of it hidden in most of us, but the plaintive note was largely the reflection of an actual condition, not the product of an entertainer.

On the ground about and below him were grouped white and colored men listening, smoking and quietly talking. From my elevation I could see camp fires flickering here and there and hear the murmur of talk over the flats. Here was the main camp of the Bonus Army, the Bonus Expeditionary Force, as it chose to call itself, and here, in my musical introduction to it, was struck the note which marked the ill-starred gathering as a significant one for Negro Americans.

For in this army which had gathered literally to "Sing the Blues" with economic phrases, there was one absentee: James Crow. It is not strictly true, as I shall explain a little later, to say that Mr. Crow was not present at all; it is an absolute fact that he was Absent With Leave a great part of the time.

He was brought along and trotted out occasionally by some of the Southern delegations and, strange to say, by some of the colored groups themselves.

The men of the B.E.F. were come together on serious business; they had no time for North, East, South, West, black and white divisions. The main problem was not to prove and maintain the superiority of a group but to secure relief from the ills which beset them, black and white alike. In the season of despair it is foolhardy to expend energy in any direction except that likely to bring life and hope. At Washington, numbers and unity were the important factors, therefore recruits of any color were made welcome and Jim Crow got scant attention.

Here they were, then, the brown and black men who had fought (some with their tongues in their cheeks) to save the world for democracy. They were scattered about in various state delegations or grouped in their own cluster of rude shelters. A lonely brownskin in the delegation from North Platte, Nebr.; one or two encamped with Seattle, Wash.; increasing numbers bivouacked with California and the northern states east of the Mississippi River; and, of course, the larger numbers with the states from below the Mason and Dixon line.

And at Anacostia, the main encampment, there was only one example of Jim Crow among the 10,000 men there and that, oddly enough, was started and maintained by colored bonuseers themselves, who hailed from New Orleans and other towns in Louisiana. They had erected a section of shacks for themselves and they insisted on their own mess kitchen.

A stroll down through the camp was an education in the simplified business of living, living not complicated by a maze of social philosophy and tabus. It is hard for one who has not actually seen the camp to imagine the crudity of the self-constructed accommodations in which these men lived for eight weeks.

Fairly regular company streets stretched across the flats, lined on both sides with shelters of every description. Here was a tent; here a piano box; there a radio packing case; there three doors arranged with the ground as the fourth side; here the smallest of "pup" tents; there a spacious canvas shelter housing eight or ten men; here some tin nailed to a few boards; there some tar paper.

Bedding and flooring consisted of straw, old bed ticks stuffed with straw, magazines and newspapers spread as evenly and as thickly as possible, discarded mattresses and cardboard.

At Anacostia some Negroes had their own shacks and some slept in with white boys. There was no residential segregation. A Negro "house" might be next door to a white "house" or across the street, and no one thought of passing an ordinance to "preserve property values." In the California contingent which arrived shortly before I left there were several Negroes and they shared with their white buddies the large tents which someone secured for them from a government warehouse. The Chicago group had several hundred Negroes in it and they worked, ate, slept and played with their white comrades. The Negroes shared tasks with the whites from kitchen work to camp M.P. duty.

In gadding about I came across white toes and black toes sticking out from tent flaps and boxes as their owners sought to sleep away the day. They were far from the spouters of Nordic nonsense, addressing themselves to the business of living together. They were in another world, although Jim Crow Washington, D.C. was only a stone's throw from their doors.

All about were signs containing homely philosophy and sarcasm on the treatment of veterans by the country, such as: "The Heroes of 1918 Are the Bums of 1932." I believe many of the white campers were bitter and sarcastic. They meant what they said on those signs. But disappointment and disillusionment is an old story to Negroes. They were philosophic about this bonus business. They had wished for so many things to which they were justly entitled in this life and received so little that they could not get fighting mad over what was generally considered among them as the government's ingratitude. They had been told in 1917 that they were fighting for a better world, for true democracy; that a new deal would come for them; that jobs would come to them on merit, that lynching would be stopped; that they would have schools, homes, justice and the franchise. But these Negroes found out as long ago as 1919 that they had been fooled. Some of them could not even wear their uniforms back home. So, while the indifference of the government to the bonus agitation might be a bitter pill to the whites, it was nothing unusual to Negroes. They addressed themselves to humorous take-offs in signs, to cards and to music, the latter two shared by whites.

Thus it was I came across such signs on Negro shacks as "Douglas Hotel, Chicago"; "Euclid Avenue"; "South Parkway"; and "St. Antoine St." A card game had reunited four buddies from San Francisco, Detroit and Indianapolis and they were swapping stories to the swish of the cards.

Over in one corner a white vet was playing a ukulele and singing what could have been the theme song of the camp: "In a Shanty in Old Shanty Town." On a Sunday afternoon the camp piano was played alternately by a brown lad with a New York accent, and a red-necked white boy from Florida, while a few rods away Elder Micheaux's visiting choir was giving voice, in stop-time, to a hymn, "God's Tomorrow Will Be Brighter Than Today." Negroes and whites availed themselves of the free choice of patting their feet either outdoors to the piano or in the gospel tent to the choir.

Outside the main camp (there were four settlements) James Crow made brief and intermittent appearances, chiefly because the largest Southern delegations were not at Anacostia. But even in the Southern and border contingents there was no hard and fast color line. On Pennsylvania avenue, where the men had taken over a number of abandoned buildings in the process of being torn down, were camped the Carolina, Florida, Alabama and Texas delegations as well as a scattering from Virginia, Tennessee and West Virginia.

In a five story building a company of Negroes was assigned the fifth floor, but they all received treatment from the same medical center on the first floor. At first they all ate together, but there was so much confusion and so many men (not necessarily Negroes) were coming in on the tail end of the mess line, that a system whereby each floor took turns being first in the mess line was adopted. This was an equitable arrangement, but even here whites and Negroes lined up together and ate together; no absolute separation was possible, nor was it attempted.

In a mess kitchen which served only Southerners I saw Negroes and whites mixed together in line and grouped together eating. I was told there had been a few personal fights and a few hard words passed, but the attitude of the die-hard, strictly Jim Crow whites had not been adopted officially. Such Southern whites as I met showed the greatest courtesy and mingled freely with the Negroes.

Captain A. B. Simmons, colored, who headed his company, hails from Houston, Tex. He and his men were loud in their declarations of the fair treatment they had received on the march to Washington. They were served meals in Southern towns, by Southern white waitresses, in Main Street Southern restaurants along with their white companions. They rode freights and trucks and hiked together. Never a sign of Jim Crow through Northern Texas, Arkansas, Tennessee, or Virginia. Captain Simmons attended the regular company commanders' councils and helped with the problems of administration. His fellow officers, all white Southerners, accorded him the same consideration given others of his rank.

His story was corroborated by others. A long, hard-boiled Negro from West Virginia who had just stepped out of the mess line behind a white man from Florida said: "Shucks, they ain't got time for that stuff here and those that has, we gets 'em told personally." And said a cook in the North Carolina mess kitchen (helping whites peel potatoes): "No, sir, things is different here than down home."

In general assemblies and in marches there were no special places "for Negroes." The black boys did not have to tag along at the end of the line of march; there was no "special" section reserved for them at assemblies. They were shot all through the B.E.F. In the rallies on the steps of the nation's capitol they were in front, in the middle and in the rear.

One of the many significant aspects of the bonuseers' banishment of Jim Crow is the lie it gives to United States army officials who have been diligently spreading the doctrine that whites and blacks could not function together in the army; that they could not use the same mess tents, mingle in the same companies, council together on military problems. The B.E.F. proved that Negroes and whites can do all these things together, that even Negroes and white Southerners can do them together.

How can the army higher-ups explain that? Why can't the United States army with its equipment and its discipline enlist Negroes and whites together in all branches of the service? It can, but it will not. The army is concerned with refined democracy, with tabus, with the maintenance of poses. The B.E.F. is concerned with raw democracy and with reality. But hereafter the army will have to hide behind its self-erected tradition, for the B.E.F. has demonstrated, right under the august army nose, that the thing can be done.

And right there was the tragedy of it all. I stood again on the little rise above the Anacostia Flats and looked out over the camp on my last night in town. Men and women can live, eat, play and work together be they black or white, just as the B.E.F. demonstrated. Countless thousands of people know it, but they go on pretending, building their paper fences and their cardboard arguments. Back home in Waycross, Miami, Pulaski, Waxahachie, Pine Bluff, Cairo, Petersburg, Des Moines, Cincinnati, Philadelphia, Kansas City and St. Louis they go on pretending, glaring, jabbing, insulting, fighting. In St. Louis, where I first saw daylight, they separate them in everything except street cars.

A dump of a shanty town below the majestic Washington monument and the imperious national capitol. . . . Ragged torch bearers futilely striving to light the path for the blind overlords who will not see. . . . A blue camp, its cheerfulness undershot with tragedy. . . . A blue race problem, its surface gayety undershot with poignant sorrow. . . .

As I turned away, stumbling in the dark over a hose which brought water to the camp from a nearby fire hydrant, a soft Negro voice and the tinkling piano notes came faintly to me:

I got the Saint Louis Blues
Just as Blue as I can be ...

The Crisis, October, 1932; XXXIX, 316-17, 332.

154

HERBERT HOOVER
by W. E. B. Du Bois

In characteristically thorough and devastating fashion, Dr. Du Bois offered the following analysis of the presidency of Herbert Hoover—especially insofar as the Black 10 percent of the United States was concerned—just prior to the elections, which in fact saw an overwhelming move of the Black voters out of the Republican column and into that of the Democratic party and its candidate, Franklin D. Roosevelt.

The indictment which Americans of Negro descent have against Herbert Hoover is long, and to my mind, unanswerable. The chief counts are the following:

Lily-White-ism

Mr. Hoover did not hesitate in 1928 to use the old methods of manipulating Southern delegates in order to secure his nomination. Notwithstanding this, when he was elected to the presidency, he adopted into the program of the "Lily-Whites," and sought to disfranchise Negroes in the councils of the Republican Party. At the same time, he kept in his councils white Southern Republicans like Creager and Slemp. In other words, Mr. Hoover tried to get rid of Negroes and not dishonesty in Southern politics. And the basic cause of dishonesty, illegal disfranchisement, he never mentioned.

Race-Hatred

During the campaign of 1928, when Mr. Hoover was seeking Southern votes it was necessary for the leaders of the Negro race, including nine officials of national Negro organizations, three bishops of Negro churches, four public officials, four college presidents, and two leading editors, to protest bitterly against the methods of Hoover's Southern friends. Never since Emancipation and the bargain of 1876, was a more dangerous attack made on the right of Negroes to vote. The protest said:

We are asking in this appeal, for a public repudiation of this campaign of racial hatred. Silence and whispering in this case are worse than in matters of personal character and religion. Will white America make no protest? Will the candidates continue to remain silent? Will the Church say nothing? Is there in truth any issue in this campaign, either religious tolerance, liquor, water-power, tariff or farm relief, that touches in weight the transcendent and fundamental question of the open, loyal and unchallenged recognition of the essential humanity of twelve million Americans who happen to be dark-skinned?

To this national protest, Herbert Hoover did not answer a single word. On the contrary, his "Lily-White" policy continued the campaign.

Nominations for Office

Mr. Hoover's persistence in this attitude was further proven by his willingness to appoint to public office known enemies of the Negro race. In the face of wide protest and plain facts, he appointed William N. Doak as Secretary of Labor, knowing that Doak was the head of a trade union which specifically excludes Negroes, and that for years he was active in West Virginia in depriving Negroes of the right to work, especially on the railways. The recent systematic campaign against Negro firemen in the South is a movement in the same direction and resulted last year alone in seven Negro firemen killed and fourteen seriously injured by their white fellow workers.

Mr. Hoover nominated as Justice of the United States Supreme Court John J. Parker of North Carolina, in spite of the fact that Parker had opposed the right of Negroes to vote. We have been told that Parker was willing to repudiate this stand but that the White House refused to let him; at any rate, while Mr. Hoover hastened to explain Parker's labor decisions, he treated his anti-Negro attitude with disdainful silence and despite advice and pleading, insisted upon sending this nomination to the Senate. It was finally defeated by a narrow margin by the influence of the Negro and labor vote and despite every effort of the administration to force it through.

Haiti and Liberia

Mr. Hoover nominated as Justice of* Negro governments in Haiti and Liberia has blown both hot and cold, and ended most unfortunately in both cases. He refused to appoint a Negro member to the Haitian Commission, and while his commission made excellent recommendations, Mr. Hoover followed them slowly and with long periods of hesitation, and he still insists, at the dictation of great financial interests, that the United States keep indefinite control of Haitian finance.

In the same way, in Liberia, he is refusing his assent to the excellent plan of reform drawn up by the League of Nations and assented to by Liberia and he is demanding a dictator who will destroy the independence of Liberia. The United States refuses to be represented at Geneva but the Firestone Rubber Company has headquarters there in the same hotel with Mr. Hoover's unofficial adviser; it dictates Mr. Hoover's policy; it demands the right to name the proposed dictator, and refuses to recognize a Negro government which has lived more than a century.

The Color Bar

Mr. Hoover has permitted and ordered outrageous discrimination based on color. He sent colored Gold Star mothers on separate ships with inferior accommodations to visit their son's graves; in officers' training camps, he refused nearly all Negro applicants. He was begged to stop open discrimination against Negroes in Red Cross relief, following the Mississippi flood in 1927; he first denied the facts, and when they were confirmed by his own committee, he suppressed their report, and never applied adequate remedies.

In the same way, he is today allowing the War Department to whitewash the equally unjustifiable discrimination against Negroes and bad treatment of workers in the government contracts in flood control.

Colored Appointments

Herbert Hoover practically promised in his 1928 campaign speech at Elizabethton, Tenn., that he would appoint to office no persons to whom

* By typographical error this line repeats the opening line of the preceding paragraph; presumably, it should read something like, "Mr. Hoover's attitude towards the".

white Southerners objected. He has more than carried out this promise and has made fewer first-class appointments of Negroes to office than any President since Andrew Johnson. His few minor appointments have been mediocre and political. Particularly, in cases like Haiti and Ethiopia, where logic and courtesy gave him unusual opportunity to recognize Negroes, he flatly ignored them. In the Civil Service, he has allowed eligible Negroes systematically to be refused appointment, and colored appointees to be dismissed from their positions; while in the diplomatic and consular service, he has reduced the number of incumbents and made few new appointments.

The Forgotten Black Man

Especially has it been true that President Hoover, knowing as he must, the extraordinary and unprecedented struggle of the American Negro, his handicaps and disadvantages, not to mention his continuing illegal oppression, has in the four years that he has been in the White House, made only the vaguest reference to this race and its needs. He has said absolutely nothing about disfranchisement, peonage nor racial segregation, and next to nothing about lynching and mob law, although fifty-seven Negroes, unconvicted by any court of any crime, have been lynched during his administration. He has done nothing to correct discrimination in the distribution of government educational funds, although he knows that of the more than six million dollars a year, divided by the government among seventeen Southern states for education, only $340,000 goes to black people who form one-fourth of the population.

The Negro and the Nation

It may be said that the above arraignment, even if true, is partial and one-sided, in that it judges the acts of a public official elected to serve 123 million people from the point of view of the special interests and desires of 12 million.

If the demands of 12 million colored Americans were antagonistic to those of their 111 million fellows, there would remain a grave question of duty and sacrifice and a nice dilemma as to how far a nation can ask a tenth of its souls to commit suicide.

But we Negroes contend that our problem is but a microcosm of the nation and that the president who fails us fails all.

Take the great national problems: the Depression of Industry; the International Debts; the Tariff. In all these, President Hoover has been either wrong or helplessly inadequate and each of these failures affects us.

Stubbornly and blindly, the President for three years denied that there was any depression; allowed the figures of unemployment to be falsified, and refused to sanction adequate and thorough-going relief. When he was forced to face relief, he went to the rescue of banks, railroads and corporations. Yet, we Negroes were the first and severest sufferers from depression and the last to be relieved.

The world owes this nation a fantastic sum which it cannot pay and never will. It is arming for war as fast as it can. Here Mr. Hoover's leadership is vacillating and contradictory. He calls for a temporary moratorium and then refuses to discuss the problems it raises. He evolves a formula for peace which makes others disarm and allows us to increase armament. He demands that the League of Nations rule in Manchuria but not in Liberia. He wants treaties observed by Japan in China and not by the United States in Haiti. As a result, Peace, industry, and international good will suffer. America becomes the best-hated nation on earth. No one credits her with either good sense or good intentions, and yet all must dance attendance on her organized and despotic economic power. And this economic power crushes Negro labor at home, just as it retards European recovery abroad.

As a manufacturing nation, we need to sell goods all over the earth. We can only sell to those who can pay. Nations pay for imports with exports. Herbert Hoover signed a bill which taxed imports so highly that nations cannot afford to buy our goods. Hoover knew the rates were too high, yet he signed the bill. Our exports decline, our factories close and we starve. And we Negroes starve first and longest.

Moreover, we cannot as a nation secure control of industry and politics as long as the rotten boroughs of the South, with political power based on disfranchised black and white labor, make a third party movement impossible. No one in our day has helped disfranchisement and race hatred more than Herbert Hoover by his "Lily-White" policy, his appointments to office, and his failure to recognize or appreciate the plight of the Forgotten Black Man.

The Crisis, November, 1932; XXXIX, 362–63.

Index

A

Abbott, Robert S., 22, 374, 445
Abyssinia, 341, 382, 431, 541
Abyssinian Baptist Church, 604
Adams, J. H., Jr., 1, 2
Adams, Lewis, 125, 126
Adams, Samuel B., 178
Addams, Jane, 28, 499
Africa, 25, 26, 179, 248–52, 325, 335, 357, 368, 378, 402, 407, 413, 418–19, 430–31, 492, 540–41, 546 (*see also* Pan-Africa)
African Blood Brotherhood, 347, 413–420, 445, 488, 614
African Methodist Episcopal Church, 286, 483, 635
agitation, need for, 24–25
agriculture, 606–08
Aiken, S. C., 512–16
Alabama, 30, 34, 118, 123, 126, 127, 142, 186, 237, 304, 306, 486, 643, 692, 720
Albuquerque, N.M., 157–58
Aldrich, Winthrop W., 643
Alexander, Ernest R., 677
Alexander, Lillian A., 545
Alpha Phi Alpha, 509–10
Algeo, Sarah, 145
Amenia Conference, 130–35
American Bar Association, 167
American Civil Liberties Union, 317
American Federation of Labor, 212, 244, 246, 266, 459–60, 633, 657
American Friends' Service Committee, 543
American Inter-Racial Peace Committee, 543–49
American Negro Labor Congress, 488–92, 540, 614, 656–71
Americus, Ga., 314–15
Amherst College, 13
Anderson, Charles W., 221
Anderson, Marian, 592
Anderson, Sherwood, 561
Anniston, Ala., 304
Anthony, Susan B., 99
Arkansas, 66, 85, 185, 209, 252, 279–82, 316, 320, 420–24, 503

Armstrong, Samuel C., 4, 124, 128
Arnold, Matthew, 103
Association for the Study of Negro Life and History, 348–54
Athens, Ohio, 20n.
Atkins, J. A., 704–05
Atlanta, Ga., 5, 6, 7, 119, 169, 170–77, 198–99, 604
Atlanta University, 138, 169
Atlantic City, N.J., 22, 271
Austin, Tex., 270
Austria, 225

B

Bagnall, Robert W., 371, 377, 382, 498–504, 549
Bailey v. Alabama, 31n.
Baker, Newton, 207, 213, 293
Baker, Ray S., 131, 298
Baldwin, Maria L., 28, 111–12, 166
Baldwin, William H., Mrs., 596–97
Ballou, Adin, 208, 210
Baltimore, Md., 23–24, 37, 120, 146, 169, 566
Bannister, E. M., 593
Barnett, Claude A., 583
Bass, J. B., 374–75
Belgium, 340, 387, 539
Bell, J. W., 215
Berlin, Germany, 35
Bethune, Mary M., 104, 543, 583
Birch, John, Society, 427
Bird, Crystal, 88, 543
Birmingham, Ala., 119, 239, 270
birth control, 716–18
Birth of a Nation, the film, 87–90, 148, 153, 157, 159, 161, 162, 166
Blascoer, Frances, 27
Blease, Cole, 62, 480, 576
Bledsoe, Jules, 592
Boardman, Helen, 551, 722–23
Boas, Franz, 353
Bogalusa, La., 282–84
Bolshevik Revolution, 195, 197–98, 245, 262, 265, 299, 332, 335, 370, 488
Bond, Horace M., 452–59, 499–500
Bonner, Marita O., 505–09